ROCK
DECADES

THE GREATEST
SONGS OF OUR TIME

TOBY CRESWELL

hardie grant books

This one goes out to
Samantha and Alice

This is an adaptation of a book first
published as *1001 Songs* in 2005
This edition published in 2015
by Hardie Grant Books

Hardie Grant Books (Australia)
Ground Floor, Building 1
658 Church Street
Richmond, Victoria 3121
www.hardiegrant.com.au

Hardie Grant Books (UK)
5th & 6th Floors
52–54 Southwark Street
London SE1 1UN
www.hardiegrant.co.uk

A Cataloguing-in-Publication
entry is available from the
catalogue of the National Library
of Australia at www.nla.gov.au

RocKwiz Decades

ISBN 978 1 74379 067 0

Cover design by Next Episode
Typeset in 9.5/14 Avenir by Pauline Haas
Printed in Australia by Griffin Press

Acknowledgements

This book was commissioned by Julie
Pinkham and Rachel Day has done a
magnificent job of wrestling it into shape.
It is a version of an earlier book, *1001
Songs*. Some songs have been deleted
and others added. Pauline Haas and Kate
Daniel worked tirelessly. Hardie Grant in
general is an author's delight. Love them.

My appreciation goes to Rose Creswell
who was my agent for the first version.
Rose (no relation) is one of the giants
of Australian publishing and I can't find
words to express my love and respect for
her. Jane Cameron, her former partner,
is also wonderful. I owe a great debt to
Jane Burridge at The Other Woman who
brokered this edition – a woman of grace
and sympathy in difficult times.

I am grateful to Ed Kuepper, Brad
Lonard, Murray Power, Chris Moss, Tom
Kristensen, Alice Trenoweth-Creswell and
David Messer for their suggestions on
selections.

For assistance of all kinds I would like
to thank Stuart Rubin, Paul Goldman,
Lisa Anthony, Megan LeMasurier,
Martin Fabinyi, Larry Meltzer, Catherine
Courtenay, Ross Brookes, Anne Briggs,
Bruce Daly, Margaret Merten, Geoffrey
Datson and Annette Hughes, John Bush,
Kate Butchart, Martin Pedersen, Tara
Anderson, Clinton Walker, Lisa Anthony
and Mark Danta. Thanks also to Tony
Smythe and EastsideFM.

This would not have been possible
without Tim Singleton, Anne, James,
Sean and Giovanna Trenoweth and
Glenda Fisher.

I also cannot thank John O'Donnell,
Tara Anderson and Jolyon Burnett enough.

NOTE: The songs in this book have many and varied provenances. The year generally refers to the first recording or publishing of the song. The album cited is the preferred album on which the track can be found.

Remember that up until about 1966 albums were often cobbled together from singles and other tracks. Many of the selections even pre-date the long-playing record. Also, record companies change over time and according to the country, so the record company listed is mostly there as a guide.

The main research source for *RocKwiz Decades* was the All Music Guide (www.allmusic.com). When in doubt, this has been consulted for release dates, songwriting credits and album listings.

The other invaluable resource was the website Rock's Backpages (www.rocksbackpages.com), a repository for some of the world's best writing on popular music.

Foreword

It's all about songs.

Without the songs we have nothing. All those magical moments that make music fans swoon – the singles, the albums, the concerts, the books, the DVDs, the liner notes, the dance-floor fillers, the car tapes and the carefully compiled CD burns, the posters on our bedroom walls – all this joy simply would not exist without songs.

For me, it started with songs. I remember listening to 'White Room' by Cream on a radio built into the bedhead in a motel in Wagga Wagga while my brother shivered with chicken pox and my mum mopped his brow from a Tupperware bowl. I remember hearing 'Pretty Woman' by Roy Orbison on a brown transistor, sitting beside the Goulburn River with my dad, fishing and twiddling that radio dial. I remember my next-door neighbour Merrilee dancing to 'Love Me Do', and I remember singing 'Pamela Pamela' by Wayne Fontana in front of my bemused Grade Six class.

I don't remember much about my HSC biology classes, but I vividly recall huddling around a neglected Bunsen burner in the back of the science lab with Roger and Andy, passionately debating the much maligned 1970 Bob Dylan album, *Self-Portrait*. We didn't care that the critics hated it or that most serious Dylan fans were confused or outraged. We loved it, and we loved it because of the songs.

RocKwiz Decades was first released as *1001 Songs* in 2005, the year that *RocKwiz* began screening on SBS television. I remember buying the book and instantly realising that not only was it a goldmine of eye-opening, essential information but, just as importantly, it was also filled with smart, strong opinions from a writer I'd respected over many years. It has been an incredible resource in the creation of the *RocKwiz* scripts and questions.

There are old favourites in here, songs I wasn't familiar with, plenty of contemporary artists and, of course, songs that you don't really want to hear, but you're happy to read about. I don't need to listen to 'Relax' by Frankie Goes to Hollywood again, but I was fascinated to read that it has the same beat as *Saturday Night Fever*, that the heavy breathing and the stuttering musical passages were a nod to Donna Summer, and that guest musicians included members of Ian Dury's Blockheads and Steve Howe from Yes!

So, on behalf of all the fine folk at *RocKwiz*, I hereby take great pleasure in lending our full support, with true excitement and much gratitude, to this edition of Toby's book *RocKwiz Decades*.

Brian Nankervis

Introduction

I believe it was the American singer/songwriter Beck who observed that music made in 1969 could not have been made in 1960 or that music we listened to in 1979 could not have been imagined in 1970 and so forth. So much of our history is written in song, our lives are traced through the tunes on the hit parade. With each decade comes a particular sensibility and style that befits the times.

The '60s were a time of liberation; of innovation, of new ideas and new ways of life. At the beginning of that decade in music you had the teenage dreams of Carole King and the Beach Boys capturing a time when the guns of world war had stopped, when the world was full of new machines, new technologies.

Then came the Beatles. They were a completely new phenomenon; new sound that came with a fashion code but, more importantly, the Beatles made pop music the most important art form in the world. Bob Dylan chimed in with his Beat-inspired poetry and the Rolling Stones showed up with the sex and the drugs. In 1965 rock & roll stepped up to a whole new level. Songwriting was no longer "Tell your ma/Tell your pa/Our love's gonna grow/Ooh wah ooh wah." It could now be a complex way of telling personal stories or conveying information.

In the mid-1960s drugs, especially LSD, influenced a further subculture, and with those drugs came the creative notion of taking a journey to the centre of your mind. It was the idea of really looking through rose-coloured glasses, of changing what reality actually was. In this psychedelic era, songs went from being 3 minutes in length to upwards of 20 minutes. After two years of psychedelic, Bob Dylan went to Nashville, the Stones made *Beggars' Banquet* and it was all back to the roots; old school rock & roll.

The Vietnam War, which raged through the 1960s, defined much of the music of that era. Straight-up folk songs like 'A Hard Rain's Gonna Fall' gave way to music that was more expressionistic. Jimi Hendrix was a key figure here. His guitar playing, the sound of the feedback and the rough and raw guitar lines expressed, in their novelty, a new world of chaos and danger and anarchy. Hendrix's music – whether the song was specifically about something or simply a love ballad – drenched in this maelstrom, gave context to the times. We were all living through a world that was fuzzy around the edges and likely to explode at any time.

The Rolling Stones' track 'Gimme Shelter' which was released in 1969 is the perfect song of that era. Backup singer Merry Clayton wails about a fire that's sweeping our lives just a shot away, just a kiss away. That same year Brian Jones died and the Rolling Stones played Hyde Park, releasing hundreds of white birds in his memory. A few weeks later half a million kids created Woodstock and the Woodstock nation.

The '60s had started as a time of so much promise but they ended with Charles Manson in the Hollywood Hills, with the tragedy of the Stones' Altamont concert and with the end of the Beatles.

The '70s was a period of decadence, of polymorphously perverse sexuality, of hard drugs instead of acid. It was a time of struggle and the songs reflect that. In the last few years of the Vietnam War a whole new mood descended on the US. Bruce Springsteen later captured that better than anyone with his songs such as 'Racing in the Street' and 'Born in the USA'. Vietnam became not just a military expedition but a state of mind. Its effects were felt in the rush of heroin to American streets ('I'm Waiting for My Man' by the Velvet Underground) and in the collapse of optimism for young people ('The Pretender' by Jackson Browne).

In the middle of the '70s, after the oil shocks caused a global recession and Richard Nixon had fought a war on the hippies, a solution came through. Or rather two solutions: punk rock and disco music. Punk was a throwback to the early 1960s but in England it had a different context. Punk was about the voice of the working class, it was the last ditch attempt to use music for political change.

Obviously the Sex Pistols and the Clash were highly political in everything they did but there were many others: Elvis Costello, the Specials, Midnight Oil, Billy Bragg, X-Ray Spex, Sham 69 and a few years later in the US, Black Flag and Fugazi.

Disco was mostly the hedonistic sound of the clubs but it could also, in the hands of Chic and others later, be an authentic voice of the streets. Machine's 'There But for the Grace Go I', the Isley Brothers' 'Fight the Power', Heaven 17's 'Ball of Confusion' and the Temptations' 'Law of the Land' all express the pressure of oppressive governments and the struggle in the streets against poverty, drug abuse and crime.

In the 1980s, with the recession fading, there was an upsurge of rock & roll. The songs were confident and brash and often could be witty and sexy. This was the new sound of black America and it seemed to get into every place on the planet. Great artistry was the hallmark and it was never less than innovative.

In England you had the Blitz kids in the south enjoying the new prosperity. In the north there were the more depressive types, but nonetheless great music came from the likes of New Order. This group from Manchester in the 1980s profoundly changed music.

The 1980s was a great period for Australian music. So many Australian artists and groups crossed the pond and had success in the American charts or influence on the British underground music scene. INXS, Men at Work and Kylie Minogue were huge stars in the US and the UK, while the Triffids and Nick Cave were critics' favourites.

Generation X came to maturity in the 1990s. The era began with Nirvana's *Smells Like Teen Spirit*, labelled an anthem for the hordes of lonely disaffected kids across the western world. The sound itself was part Beatles and part Black Sabbath but it somehow worked.

Hip hop and rap, which had been bubbling along in the 1980s, really hit its stride in the '90s with artists such as Ice Cube. The music which had started in the 1960s with the poetry and jazz of LeRoi Jones and Gil Scott-Heron was reimagined by DJs at block parties in the Bronx, then kept evolving through the groundbreaking work of Public Enemy and De La Soul in New York, while on the West Coast, crews such as NWA and its main man Dr Dre created their own new flavour which crossed over to a white audience. Dre's work with Eminem was particularly influential.

In the UK in the 1990s there was suddenly a new confidence. Hip hop crews had forged the luxurious Bristol sound while Cool Britannia was on show with bands such as Pulp, Blur and Oasis. England was just nuts in the '90s.

No-one has any real idea what happened in the first decade of the 21st century. The Internet arrived and ripped the guts out of the music industry. Plus the format changed. In the early '60s the main format was the 45 rpm single. After *Sgt. Pepper's* the dominant form became the album, delivered in 12" vinyl, then cassette tapes in the 1970s, CDs and now music is delivered by a computer file.

The album is disappearing and we are going back to singles effectively. The 21st century, then, is all about the big records. We live in an era of Divas and Playas and those massive statement albums that seep into everyone's life have mostly disappeared. People no longer have the time to sit back and listen to *Sgt. Pepper's* from beginning to end or indeed *The Wall* or *Dark Side of the Moon* or the first Velvet Underground album or *Pet Sounds*. Those days are gone. It's now all about the single; the song that is the anthem of the times.

Pop, you can't escape from it.

I'm hoping that these stories will make a patchwork of contemporary music and what it all means. With each chapter I have included a playlist that reflects some of the main issues, influences or movements of that time. I hope that you find some things you were looking for and find some things that you didn't know you wanted to know.

The Sixties

PSYCHEDELIC CLASSICS

**I Had Too Much to Dream
(Last Night)**
The Electric Prunes

You're Gonna Miss Me
13th Floor Elevators

Psychotic Reaction
Count Five

Tomorrow Never Knows
The Beatles

A Day in the Life
The Beatles

Happiness Stan
The Small Faces

**Saturday Afternoon /
Eskimo Blue Day**
Jefferson Airplane

Manic Depression
Jimi Hendrix

Season of the Witch
Donovan

Inna Gadda Da Vida
Iron Butterfly

Interstella Overdrive
Pink Floyd

Mr Guy Fawkes
The Dave Miller Set

The Real Thing
Russell Morris

East West
Butterfield Blues Band

The Soft Parade
The Doors

Purple Haze
Jimi Hendrix

Dark Star
The Grateful Dead

Why Do I Cry
The Remains

The Little Black Egg
The Nightcrawlers

Let It Out (Let It All Hang Out)
The Hombres

**Journey to the Center
of the Mind**
The Amboy Dukes

The Witch
The Sonics

Time Has Come Today
The Chambers Brothers

Magic Carpet Ride
Steppenwolf

Tales of Brave Ulysses
Cream

For Your Love
Yardbirds

Fire
The Crazy World of Arthur Brown

EXP / Up from the Skies
Jimi Hendrix Experience

2000 Light Years From Home
The Rolling Stones

**Just Dropped In (to See What
Condition My Condition Was In)**
The First Edition

True Love Ways Buddy Holly

(Buddy Holly/Norman Petty) ❊ Coral ❊ 1960 ❊
Appears on: *The Complete Buddy Holly*

Although best known for his geeky look and spectacles, Buddy Holly's influence spread profoundly through popular music following his death in January 1959. Holly had a gift for melody whether in R&B or country, rockabilly or pop. He also encouraged the songcraft of others – he helped Waylon Jennings and others get started. Where most '50s rockers were either bland or mad, Holly trod a neat line. He came out of Texas a hayseed country boy. But soon after moving to New York in 1958 he expanded his horizons.

'True Love Ways' is a gorgeous ballad with a touch of western swing in its arrangement, but mostly it's a sophisticated pop song of its era. Holly expanded his backing from the rockabilly trio to include jazzy horns and piano.

'True Love Ways' didn't appear until after Holly's death at age twenty-two. Author Jonathon Cott dug up a high-school essay Holly had written shortly before rock & roll took off. "My life has been what you might call an uneventful one, and it seems there is not much of interest to tell," he wrote. "I have many hobbies. Some of them are hunting, fishing, leatherwork, reading, painting and playing western music. I have thought about making a career out of western music if I am good enough but I will just have to wait and see how that turns out ..."

My Favourite Things John Coltrane

(Richard Rodgers/Oscar Hammerstein II) ❊ Atlantic ❊ 1960 ❊
Appears on: *My Favourite Things*

The Sound of Music opened on Broadway in 1959. By 1965 it would be the biggest movie of its era and its songs – 'Do-re-mi', 'Edelweiss', 'The Sound of Music' and 'My Favourite Things' – part of the fabric of society. Fortunately, by then John Coltrane had been able to interpret 'My Favourite Things'.

The thirty-four-year-old saxophonist had recently left Miles Davis and made his own very impressive statement with his 1959 album *Giant Steps*. He had assembled his classic quartet (McCoy Tyner on piano, Jimmy Garrison on bass, and Elvin Jones on drums). Coltrane's agenda involved the modal style developed with Miles and his own spiritual journey, which included an interest in Asian scales and influences. Coltrane had studied Indian music through his friend Ravi Shankar and that's part of the mix of 'My Favourite Things'.

"I knew it was going to be an experience because John had composed *Giant Steps* and some other great tunes," McCoy Tyner said of joining Coltrane's quartet. "I was aware of it because he did some of the composing in his mother's home in Philadelphia, and it was during that period that I really got close to him. It was an amazing challenge for me. I knew that that's where I belonged, and that was the next step for me. We got along very well. We had a good feeling for each other, similar conceptually as far as music was concerned. I knew that is where I needed to be. I was really anxious and excited about it.

"I think with that band, the form wasn't set. We had a tonality that was set, we had a key we were in, of course, but we had the freedom to do what we wanted. One thing about John, and I think Miles Davis had this as well, is that he knew how to pick people to play with. That is very important. If it didn't work, you don't force it, and I think that happens a lot of times. Communication is very important, and I think the Quartet is a testament to that, because we were able to do things like make up a song around a scale, and that was it! It wasn't in your typical form. It wasn't completely 'out there', it had some form, but it wasn't limiting."

'My Favourite Things' was a popular success. Casual jazz fans easily understood it. It's a piece of rare beauty with exceptional nuances from Coltrane, Jones and Tyner that keep the piece timeless.

I've Got My Mojo Working Muddy Waters

(Preston Foster) ✳ Chess ✳ 1960 ✳ Appears on: *At Newport*

Mojos were common throughout the Mississippi Delta right up until the second world war. "We all believed in mojo hands," Muddy Waters told Robert Palmer. "You get you a mojo, and if you're gamblin', it'll take care of that; you win. If you're after the girls, you can work that on the woman you want and win. Black people really believed in this hoodoo." The culture of West Africa came to America on the slave ships less than a full generation before. Those beliefs and religions relating to curses and potions like black cat bones or the St John the Conqueror root were still very much alive.

Muddy Waters was born in 1915 in the Delta to a poor rural family. He grew up on and around Stovall's plantation where Charlie Patton had set the fire that would become the blues. Muddy was a gifted guitar player who learnt first- and second- hand from the greats. The music of the blues was just another cultural tradition imported from Africa like mojos.

In 1943 Muddy joined the exodus from the Delta north to Chicago where his sister told him, "They don't listen to that kind of old blues you're doin' now, don't nobody listen to that, not in Chicago".

Muddy adapted to the electric blues. He kept the openness and the swing of the Delta but his new sound was tough as steel, his slide playing sharp and piercing. In conjunction with harmonica player Little Walter Jacobs, Muddy Waters drew the blue print for the Chicago blues sound.

'I Got My Mojo Working' was like a reference to how far they had come from the plantations of the Delta to the modern city. Having once spent his hard won money on a worthless piece of superstition, he could now laugh about the quaint country ways.

'I Got My Mojo Working' was written by songwriter Preston Foster and first appeared around 1957. Waters put it into his act. While he no longer believed in the voodoo alchemy, 'I Got My Mojo Working' has its own magic. It's a song of lust and in his performance at the Newport Folk Festival he piles on the power, pounding out the riff and pumping the anticipation to the point where you think its going to explode.

This song put "mojo" into everyday speech providing the name for an estimable music magazine and giving Austin Powers his catchphrase.

Will You Love Me Tomorrow? The Shirelles

(Gerry Goffin/Carole King) ✳ Scepter ✳ 1960 ✳ Appears on: *Girl Group Greats*

Carole King first made the charts as the subject of a song. Her school friend Neil Sedaka had a major hit with his song 'Oh! Carol'. Carole King tried her hand at being a performer with little success. Then she met Gerry Goffin, a pharmacist who aspired to write.

"When I met Gerry he had a play that he had written, complete with lyrics, but he wanted music," she told the journalist known as Miles. "He was interested in the theatre and Broadway and jazz at that time. Didn't think much of rock – rock & roll, that's what it was then. It was just before people in the Village, the intellectuals, the neo-Beats, got turned on to it. And we began to write rock & roll. I wrote music for his play, which never went anywhere, and he wrote lyrics for my rock & roll songs, which did go somewhere! And so we stayed with that because it was financially lucrative, which was, at the beginning, our main concern. We were either about to or were getting married and I was also pregnant so money was definitely an issue."

At first Goffin and King held down day jobs (as a chemist and secretary respectively) and worked for Don Kirshner's Aldon music on the side, until Kirshner heard 'Will You Love Me Tomorrow', at which point he advanced them $10,000 and they never looked back.

Florence Greenberg of Scepter Records gave Goffin/King their first hit, 'Will You Love Me Tomorrow?'

"I remember giving her baby a bottle while Carole was writing the song," said Greenberg.

"I came up with the basic melody one day and Gerry came home from work, he was a chemist at the time ... he came home from work and I played him the melody and he wrote the lyric," said King. "It was as if he'd been thinking of the lyric all day at work and I'd been writing the melody and, you know ... 'Tonight you're mine ...' That's really how it happened."

In the late '60s the lyrics were obviously risqué – the implication being a girl wondering whether she should spend the night with a man clearly not her husband. Shirelles' lead singer Shirley Owens brings a full, woman-like sensuality to the song. Nonetheless, the song was a number one hit in November 1960, heralding the permissive society and the era of girl groups.

As a consequence of this hit Goffin and King were able to get an office in the Brill Building and become the most popular songwriting team of the decade and Carole King the most successful woman songwriter of the century.

Stand by Me Ben E King

(Ben E King) ✻ Atlantic ✻ 1961 ✻ Appears on: *Stand by Me: The Best of Ben E King*

Ben E King joined the Drifters and brought a tougher edge to their R&B sound. Most of their material was supplied by the extraordinary production/songwriting duo of Jerry Leiber and Mike Stoller, but King also penned hits. In the late '50s, R&B was still finding its comfortable blend of gospel, blues and pop music. Most of the singers came from a church background and that sense of the divine opened up their melodies.

"I took 'Stand by Me' from an old gospel song recorded by Sam Cooke and the Soul Stirrers called 'Lord I'm Standing By' or something," King recalled. "The song more or less wrote itself. I rehearsed it with the Drifters and they liked it very much. We went downtown to the Drifters' manager and he liked it but he looked at me and said, 'It's not a bad song but we're not looking for material at the moment.'"

King left the Drifters soon after. When cutting some tracks with Leiber and Stoller they asked if he had anything. He presented 'Stand by Me' and they wrote an arrangement on the spot. Up-ending a snare drum and stroking the springs against the drum skin created the distinctive percussive noise that flows through the song.

'Stand by Me' was a moderate hit on its release. It had a second lease of life in the mid-'70s when John Lennon recorded a particularly moving version for his *Rock & Roll* album. Then in the '80s the song appeared in a Levis ad and its title was used for a Rob Reiner/Stephen King film and it all started again, turning King's version into a classic.

The mixture of a rich deep vocal and a spare gospel arrangement is timeless.

Runaway Del Shannon

(Max Crook/Del Shannon) ❊ Mercury ❊ 1961 ❊ Appears on: *Greatest Hits*

Del Shannon knew about heartbreak. "There was once a girl I really thought was in love with me," he said frequently in interviews. "I mean, my heart would pound when she came around. She gave me her bracelet to wear, or, well, more likely I pestered her till she let me wear it. And the next day I saw her out with this other guy.

"I took that bracelet off and laid it out on a railroad track. I mean – I was that person. I couldn't get songs which expressed that from anybody else, they just didn't write what I felt. So I had to write. Sure I wanted someone to give me hits, but they all just wrote stuff that sounded like the last song I'd written myself."

The song he wrote called 'Runaway' made him a pop star.

He was Charles Westover playing the Hi-Lo Club in Battle Creek Michigan, backed by an ensemble with Max Crook playing an organ called a Musitron.

"I was tired of doing the same old C, A minor, F and G sounds, which was like 'Blue Moon' a hundred times over with different words," Shannon recalled. "One night, Max Crook, at the Hi-Lo Club in Battle Creek, played an A minor and G, and I said, 'I never heard such a great change.' I said, 'Follow me!' So I went right down the scale. Then I remembered a Hank Williams song called 'Kaw-Liga' where it went from minor to major, and I said, 'Kick into A major! I'm a walkin' in ...'"

So began 'Runaway' – one of the most aching songs: "I'm a-walkin' in the rain/Tears are fallin' and I feel the pain". With its galloping tempo and the weird organ, Shannon had one of the most distinctive sounds – the Musitron plus Shannon's lonesome countryish voice – in pop.

"I remember calling up the record company from the Hi-Lo to see how 'Runaway' was doin' and they said, 'The record's sellin' 80,000 a day; you open at the Brooklyn Paramount next week.'"

Runaround Sue Dion and the Belmonts

(Dion DiMucci/Ernie Maresca) ❊ Laurie ❊ 1961 ❊ Appears on: *Runaround Sue*

When Dion DiMucci puts on a rare show in Manhattan, the guest list includes Paul Simon, Billy Joel, Lou Reed and Bruce Springsteen. All these artists were inspired by Dion's late '50s and early '60s hits. With his Italian tough-guy attitude and a magnificently expressive voice, Dion was New York's first white rock & roll star. His background was in street-corner doo-wop, but with 'Runaround Sue' he created a crossover hit that prefigured rock & roll writing. Most of all, though, there are incredible rhythms in the vocal parts. The song bounces around like a pinball, the Belmonts providing support and encouragement. Sue may be running around with other guys, but Dion isn't wasting tears over her.

"It was primitive," Dion told biographer Gene Sculatti. "It had a rhythm, a back beat and nothing else. The problem was in trying to record it. Drummers, I don't know what it is, but they hear a certain tempo and they want to play what they know. I said, 'No, it goes like this', and we simplified it back to what it was when it was created – spontaneously, with people clapping and banging on things."

'Runaround Sue' was one of the last great New York songs before the Beatles came and changed everything three years later.

Town Without Pity Gene Pitney

(Dimitri Tiomkin/Ned Washington) ❊ Musicor ❊ 1961 ❊ Appears on: *The Anthology*

Gene Pitney's voice was the sound of heartbreak itself. He had a jazz tone and a country singer's twang and the whole effect was dramatic, lending itself to narrative songs such as this, which dealt with the difficulty of modern relationships. His songs were also very adult in their lyrics although Pitney appealed to teens as well. 'Town Without Pity' is an epic tale of two young people whose love is thwarted by the town in which they live and its constrictive morals. This is a theme that would run through pop music for the rest of the '60s.

Pitney started playing music in high school with his band the Genials in Connecticut, just outside New York. By the time he had finished high school he was recording his own material and playing all the instruments. He started writing songs and in a brief career wrote 'He's a Rebel' for the Crystals and 'Hello Mary Lou' for Rick Nelson. However, Pitney was best known as a vocalist. 'Town Without Pity' was his first major hit record. Film composer Dimitri Tiomkin wrote the tune for the film of the same name, hence the melodramatic exposition. The song was nominated for an Academy Award and won a Golden Globe. It's a song with portentous strings and female vocals that are more than a little camp as Pitney pines for the freedom to express his love.

Moon River   Henry Mancini & His Orchestra

(Johnny Mercer/Henry Mancini) ✳ RCA ✳ 1961 ✳ Appears on: *Breakfast at Tiffany's*

Written for the film adaptation of Truman Capote's novella, *Breakfast at Tiffany's*, 'Moon River' combines Henry Mancini's Italianate romanticism with Johnny Mercer's southern idyllic reverie. The song is brief – a couple of verses, but it encapsulates a lifetime of experience.

In Blake Edwards' adaptation of Capote's book, Holly Golightly is a girl who has run away from the poverty and narrow horizons of her southern past for the glittering lights of a sophisticated New York. Johnny Mercer left his home in Savannah, Georgia, twenty years earlier. Broke and hoping to find work in New York as an actor, Mercer discovered his real talent was as a songwriter and by the time he teamed up with Mancini for 'Moon River' he was firmly established as one of the great American composers.

Nonetheless, in 'Moon River' you can hear nostalgia for Mercer's childhood on Burnside Island in the Back River, where he spent early summer afternoons picking wild huckleberries with his friends. The song neatly pivots on nostalgia for a lost youth and the romance of the future.

Mancini's music is even more powerful than the lyric. Mancini has said that the tune was inspired by the script and Audrey Hepburn. "I kind of knew what to write, at least what track I should I be on, by reading the script," he told Hepburn's biographer. "And Audrey's big eyes gave me the push to get a little more sentimental than I usually do. Those eyes of hers could carry it. I knew that. 'Moon River' was written for her. No-one else has ever understood it so completely."

Legend has it that a Paramount executive wanted the song taken out of the film and replaced by something more sprightly but Hepburn, in particular, insisted that the song stay. The liner notes to the soundtrack album quote a letter from the star to the composer: "Dear Henry, I have just seen our picture – *Breakfast at Tiffany's* – this time with your score. A movie without music is a little bit like an aeroplane without fuel. However beautifully the job is done, we are still on the ground and in a world of reality. Your music has lifted us all up and sent us soaring. Everything we cannot say with words or show with action you have expressed for us. You have done this with so much imagination, fun and beauty. You are the hippest of cats – and the most sensitive of composers! Thank you, dear Hank. Lots of love, Audrey."

'Moon River' has survived the film for which it was written. It has had thousands of cover versions of all kinds – notably by Frank Sinatra – and its melody has become a part of the fabric of our culture.

Crazy Patsy Cline

(Willie Nelson) ❋ MCA ❋ 1961 ❋ Appears on: *The Patsy Cline Story*

Patsy Cline had bigger hits than 'Crazy'; however, the song has outlasted its time and place. Young songwriter Willie Nelson penned the tune in his first attempts to break into the Nashville scene. 'Crazy' bears the marks of Nelson's idiosyncratic personality – it's pop and jazz and western and not quite pure country.

Perhaps that's why Patsy Cline was reluctant to record the track when producer Owen Bradley introduced her to the song in August of 1961. At the time, Cline was walking with crutches after a car smash.

"Her ribs had been broken, and she couldn't hold the notes out," guitarist Harold Bradley told *Mix* magazine. "When we were doing this, there were no overdubs. She had to do it all live, and we all had to do it all live. By that time, we had progressed to three-track, but they wouldn't put anything in the middle. They put the band and the voice and spread everything left and right. But on this particular session, Patsy couldn't sing with the band."

Owen Bradley ran the sessions in his studio from behind a Hammond organ. The session players laid down the backing track two weeks later. There's an ephemeral quality to the lyric and the vocal line – it's got a pixie kind of feel, as though it may all just disappear in a plume of smoke. Cline came in to do the vocal and got it in one take.

"That was the magic session," said Harold Bradley. "It was the toughness of it – and the magic of it, too – that made it an incredible session. Neither one of them wanted to do anything else with it. They said, 'That's it.'"

Only the Lonely Roy Orbison

(Joe Melson/Roy Orbison) ❊ Monument ❊ 1961 ❊ Appears on: *Sings Lonely and Blue*

Roy Orbison said that he was tagged as "the lonely singer". His Texan, falsetto voice was steeped in country. With a slight quivering he could just embody heartbreak.

Having made his name as a rockabilly artist with Sun in Memphis, Orbison moved to Nashville where he worked with producer Fred Foster. After some success writing 'Claudette' for the Everly Brothers, Orbison was concentrating on perfecting his songwriting. Foster suggested that two half-good songs could be combined and 'Only the Lonely' was born. The Everly Brothers turned it down when first approached so Orbison took his version to number two on the national charts.

The song had the ethereal echo sound of his best work and that stoic vocal that seems to be holding back an ocean of heartbreak. Orbison's best work was filled with paranoia and fear.

"When I wrote, let's say, a sad song, a melancholy song, I was feeling good at the time," he said in his last interview. "I have to feel good and at peace with myself before I can think creatively. I've heard guys say, 'Well, I got my heart ripped out and got wasted for three weeks and wrote this song.' I couldn't do that. I'd be crying, I couldn't eat and all that. Of course, I knew what 'Only the Lonely' was about when I wrote that. I had been alone and lonely. I wasn't at the time, though."

You Better Move On Arthur Alexander

(Arthur Alexander) ❊ Dot ❊ 1962 ❊ Appears on: *The Muscle Shoals Sound*

Paul McCartney is reported to have said, "If the Beatles ever wanted a sound, it was R&B. That was what we listened to, what we wanted to be like – Arthur Alexander." One of the first soul singers, Alexander grew up in Alabama and was an integral part of the group of songwriters and players who founded southern soul in the '60s and established Muscle Shoals as a music capital.

Alexander had seen some minor success when he was working in a Muscle

Shoals hotel and wrote 'You Better Move On', inspired by his future wife, who already had a boyfriend.

"When I met her out of high school, he was still hanging in there," he recalled. "His family was pretty well off. I didn't have no money, but I knew she liked me. It was a small town and people would be talking. That's where I got the idea for the song. I didn't talk to him personally. I said it in song."

The track was recorded in an abandoned tobacco warehouse. It found a home at Dot and was the beginning of a string of hits such as 'Anna', 'Every Day I Have to Cry' and 'Sally Sue Brown', which were covered widely by the Beatles, Dusty Springfield and the Rolling Stones (who cut 'You Better Move On'). Like almost all his colleagues, Alexander saw none of the royalties and his career was dogged by disappointment, although he staged a few comebacks before his death in 1993.

Cry for a Shadow The Beatles

(George Harrison/John Lennon) ✳ Polydor ✳ 1962 ✳ Appears on: *Anthology 1*

The first recorded Beatle song was not credited to John Lennon/Paul McCartney. George Harrison, age eighteen, had written an instrumental spoof based on the sound of the Shadows, then Britain's leading hit-makers. While the Silver Beatles were in Hamburg playing dive bars with third-division British singers like Tony Sheridan, they came to the attention of Bert Kaempfert, a South African bandleader known for cheesy instrumentals.

Kaempfert put Sheridan in the studio with the Beatles to cut 'My Bonnie' and 'When the Saints Go Marchin' In' and he passed over the group's other originals, preferring this Harrison tune for the B-side.

'Cry for a Shadow' shows Harrison's already inventive guitar work – especially in reaction to John Lennon's driving rhythm guitar. The influence of the Sun players is there and also a possibly grudging nod to the Shadows' Hank Marvin who was the closest thing Britain had to a guitar hero until Eric Clapton came along.

According to drummer Pete Best, "'Cry for a Shadow' was born during our first Hamburg tour, the result of trying to take the mickey out of Rory Storm. It was put together by George in a few minutes after Rory had called in on us during a rehearsal at the Kaiserkeller. He was telling us how much he liked the Shadows' song 'Frightened City'. 'Can you play it?', he asked. 'It goes like this', he added, starting to sing the opening bars. George intentionally began to play around with the Shadows' melody in a sort of counterpart –

without Rory having the slightest suspicion that he was being sent up. John joined in and I picked up the beat. What emerged was a catchy little number in unmistakable Shadows' style, which we liked well enough to include in our repertoire."

While this song shows the wit and spirit of the Beatles, it was a request for the vastly less interesting 'My Bonnie' at the record bar in Brian Epstein's store that sent the young furniture salesman down to the Cavern Club and he resolved to make them Fab.

Love Me Do The Beatles

(John Lennon/Paul McCartney) ❋ Parlophone ❋ 1962 ❋

Appears on: *Please Please Me*

EMI's house producer George Martin had liked the Beatles at their audition but was not happy with the drummer. Between the audition and the Beatles' first proper session Ringo Starr replaced Pete Best. The first time they cut 'Love Me Do' Ringo's drumming was judged poor and session player Alan White was behind the kit for the second try. Martin eventually gave Ringo the OK and the song was recut, but the White version appeared on the album.

George Martin recalls, "In about January '62, I met Brian Epstein and he was tryin' to get the Beatles off the ground and get some record label together. Anyways, to cut a long story short, when I heard what Brian had to offer on tape, it wasn't very good. In fact, it was awful. But I said, I really wanted to find out more about them ... there was something about them that I wanted to investigate. So, they came down a couple of months later, and I spent an evening, afternoon, and evening with them in Abbey Roads Studios. I fell in love with them. I thought they were wonderful people. I mean, they showed no signs of being great songwriters. The best they could offer me were pretty ordinary songs. I thought 'Love Me Do' was the best. 'PS I Love You' was another one and 'One after 909'. They weren't great songs, but they had tremendous charisma."

'Love Me Do' has a tough R&B feel with a delicious pop melody and the incredible close harmony singing of Lennon and McCartney. Lennon's harmonica riff, inspired by American Delbert McClinton, with whom the Beatles had toured, lifted the song and added to its blues edge.

If the song seemed slight, it cut through the pop charts of the day with a new sound that would, as you know, change everything.

She Thinks I Still Care George Jones

(Steve Duffy/Dickey Lee Lipscomb) ❋ Musicor ❋ 1962 ❋

Appears on: *The New Favourites of George Jones*

Having started out as a rockabilly singer with 'Why Baby Why', George Jones really found his stride on country ballads. His voice is rich and expressive and he brings to it the baggage of a life lived hard. Sometimes he's dealing with the consequences of his actions and other times he's dealing out tough lessons. This track falls into the latter category.

The song's main writer, Dickey Lee Lipscomb, was like Jones – a journeyman singer doing a bit of rock and bit of country as the market demanded. This song is a small masterpiece. It's been covered extensively by artists including Elvis Presley. Jones, however, has the definitive reading. Spare, with lots of room for the vocal, this song is sung by Jones with an ambiguity that is beguiling.

"I don't think there's anyone in the business that can touch George," said his ex-wife Tammy Wynette. "There never has been, never will be. I've always said that, regardless of marriage, divorce, whatever. He isn't part of country music, he is country music."

Watermelon Man Herbie Hancock

(Herbie Hancock) ❋ Blue Note ❋ 1962 ❋ Appears on: *Takin' Off*

Despite his contribution to Miles Davis' legendary mid-'60s Quintet, the successes of his own projects and a continuing influence on R&B, jazz purists regard Herbie Hancock with suspicion. A child prodigy on the piano, Hancock moved from classical studies to jazz. He came to the attention of Coleman Hawkins and Donald Byrd – the latter bringing him to New York and the attention of the Blue Note label. At twenty-two he recorded this, his first solo album. The opening cut, 'Watermelon Man', is a joyous, bluesy piano riff that drew from R&B, soul-jazz and bebop and put it all into a pop hook. 'Watermelon Man' became a hit for Mongo Santamaria and for Hancock, and was to return when he moved to jazz-fusion a decade later. Hancock's style was to form a bridge in sensitivity to acid jazz in the early '90s.

Here on *Takin' Off* he's joined by horn players Dexter Gordon and Freddie Hubbard and the immensely funky rhythm section of bassist Butch Warren and drummer Billy Higgins. The key here is always the groove. Hancock loved to swing and if his changes were less hard-edged they were audacious and colourful. It was his sense of adventure that led him into Davis' group shortly after this album was recorded and from there onto fusion and beyond.

Ruler of My Heart   Irma Thomas

(Naomi Neville) ❋ Minit ❋ 1962 ❋ Appears on: *Ruler of Hearts*

By the age of seventeen, Irma Thomas had three children and a second husband. She had also made a hit record, the belting '(You Can Have My Husband, But Please) Don't Mess with My Man'. She moved to New Orleans producer Allen Toussaint's care at Minit records and began cutting sides with him. Toussaint wrote 'Ruler of My Heart' under his mother's maiden name (Naomi Neville) and although it didn't make the charts, it remains one of the most elegant and powerful soul tracks of the '60s. Thomas keeps her cool the whole way. Toussaint keeps the backing understated but insistent, slowly drawing closer to climaxes on the chorus but never going right over the top. Thomas' strong and warm voice is sensual and generous. There's something quite hypnotic about 'Ruler of My Heart'.

Although never a big star, Thomas had her fans: Otis Redding's version of 'Ruler' became 'Pain in My Heart' and Keith Richards encouraged the Rolling Stones to cover this tune and another Thomas song, 'Time is on My Side'.

The James Bond Theme   John Barry Orchestra

(Monty Norman) ❋ EMI ❋ 1962 ❋
Appears on: *The Best of James Bond: 30th Anniversary*

The producers of *Dr No*, the second James Bond film (but the first with Sean Connery), engaged London songwriter Monty Norman to score the film. He began the job but, apparently due to time pressure, the producers thought he needed some assistance. John Barry, the leader of John Barry and the Seven, was brought it. Norman and Barry finished the 'Theme' and Barry went on to score the film.

Relying on an inventive horn arrangement and swinging but quite tough percussion, 'The James Bond Theme' evokes danger, exotica and sex appeal. Mostly, though, it is modern in its sound. A touch of R&B rhythm with jazz phrasing makes it swing like the '60s were just about to. Barry's father had operated a cinema and he had run a jazz band for many years and understood the marriage of the two so well.

"John Barry came into our lives when we were making *Dr No*," recalled director Terence Young. "We had someone else doing the music and although the score was all right, we didn't have anything exciting for the title music. I think it was someone at Chappell who said you must listen to him. He had a little band called the John Barry Seven [sic] and he came in and wrote this Bond theme."

The theme, especially when accompanied by the silhouette animation in the original title sequence, says everything you need to know about James Bond. And no character, before or since, has been so tied to a piece of music.

The Loco-Motion Little Eva

(Gerry Goffin/Carole King) ✻ Dimension ✻ 1962 ✻ Appears on: *The Loco-Motion*

The tale behind this song is a true Cinderella story. Eva Narcissus Boyd came up from Bellhaven, North Carolina, to New York where she babysat the two daughters of Gerry Goffin and Carole King.

By day, the husband and wife team worked for Don Kirshner's Aldon Music in an office at 1650 Broadway, described as an annex to the Brill Building. "We were part of the thing that involved Donny Kirshner saying 'So-and-so is *up* and needs a *follow-up!*' and all the writers would go into their cubicles and work away," King told Barry Miles, describing the Brill Building scene. "We would just simply go home because we happened to be married, but it was the same idea. You would come in the next day and everyone would play their song, hoping that *they* would be the one to get the follow-up, *knowing* that the others were also doing the same thing."

Goffin and King came up with a dance-craze song, 'The Loco-Motion', and used their babysitter to do a guide vocal on the demo. Kirshner liked it so much he put the demo out as the first release on his Dimension label and the first Gerry Goffin production, and the song shot to number one. It was also a big hit for Grand Funk Railroad in the '70s and for Kylie Minogue in the '80s.

According to Carole King, "There never was a dance called the loco-motion until after it was a hit. Everyone said, 'How does this dance go?', so Little Eva had to make up a dance."

Blowin' in the Wind Peter, Paul & Mary

(Bob Dylan) ❄ Warner Bros. ❄ 1962 ❄ Appears on: *In the Wind*

Until around 1965 most people knew about Bob Dylan as a songwriter, chiefly for Peter, Paul & Mary. The folk trio was assembled by manager Albert Grossman as an act that could put folk music into the pop charts. And it worked. Peter Yarrow and Paul Stookey looked mildly bohemian but dressed in good suits; the collegiate friends to the lanky Mary Travers, her long blonde hair drifting breezily around her shoulders. Peter, Paul & Mary were vigorous, clean-cut and very good with their own songs and traditional love songs. There was also no danger that they would go all political like Pete Seeger and the Weavers had done.

Grossman, who was the king of the folk scene, took on management of Bob Dylan and so it was natural that he would offer Dylan's songs to Peter, Paul & Mary. He encouraged the trio to have a crack at the bitter love ballad 'Don't Think Twice It's All Right'. When they covered 'Blowin' in the Wind' instead they put protest music into every home in the western world.

"Instinctively, we knew the song carried the moment of its own time," said Yarrow.

According to his friends, Dylan realised early on that 'Blowin' in the Wind' was a powerful song. His friend David Blue claimed that the song was finished on 16 April 1962. He recalled that they had been drinking coffee at the Fat Black Pussycat. Dylan pulled out his guitar and went through the song, inspired by the traditional slave song 'Auction Block'. That evening, Dylan and Blue took the tune to the hoot night at Gerde's Folk City, where Gil Turner debuted the song to unanimous acclaim.

Dylan's fame went up a notch.

Two months later, at the Finjan Club, Montreal, Dylan introduced the song himself as: "Here's one that's called 'How Many Roads Must a Man Walk Down?' Here's a song that's in sort of a set ... set pattern of songs that say ... a little more than 'I love you, and you love me/An' ... let's go over to the banks of Italy/And we'll raise a half a family/You for me, and me for me'."

For a time, Dylan blew apart the market for 'I Love You' folk songs. Once Peter, Paul & Mary topped the charts with 'Blowin' in the Wind' it became possible to have left-wing songs and hits at the same time. The impact was enormous.

"If you could imagine the March on Washington with Martin Luther King, and singing that song in front of a quarter of a million people, black and white, who believed they could make America more generous and compassionate in a nonviolent way, you begin to know how incredible that belief was," said Travers. "And still is. To sing the line, 'How many years can some people exist before they're allowed to be free?' in front of some crummy little building that refuses to admit Jews in 1983, the song elicits the same response now as it did then. It addresses the same questions. 'How many deaths will it take till they know that too many people have died?' Sing that line in a prison yard where political prisoners from El Salvador are being kept. Or sing it with Bishop Tutu. Same response. Same questions."

In Dreams Roy Orbison

(Roy Orbison) ❊ Monument ❊ 1962 ❊ Appears on: *In Dreams*

"I wasn't trying to be weird, you know? I didn't have a manager who told me how to dress or how to present myself or anything," said Orbison twenty-five years later. "But the image developed of a man of mystery and a quiet man in black and somewhat of a recluse, although I never was, really."

'In Dreams' was an extraordinary record. A soulful country ballad with surreal lyrics that fit with the singer drifting off to sleep. He seems liberated from the usual conventions of popular music. The arrangement that starts off simply enough gradually builds through the introduction of the rhythm section and an orchestra. The lonely reality of the day to day is transformed into a dream world where the boy can get the girl.

While Fred Foster's production is masterful, the song depends entirely on the versatility of Roy Orbison's voice.

"Once I started singing, it was sort of a wonder," Orbison said. "I've always been in love with my voice. It was it. It's a gift, and a blessing, just to have a voice. And I'm proud that people do appreciate it, you know? It's a long way from being overwhelmed because you don't know whether you are worthy, to realising that if you have a gift, it should be precious to you and you should look after it and respect it."

A quarter of a century after its first release, David Lynch made 'In Dreams' the centrepiece of his film *Blue Velvet* and the eerie song came alive in that grotesque context. 'In Dreams' is a song outside its time and space.

Bring It on Home to Me Sam Cooke

(Sam Cooke) ❋ RCA ❋ 1962 ❋ Appears on: *The Best of Sam Cooke*

Although not much of a hit at the time, 'Bring It on Home to Me' is one of Sam Cooke's best-known and oft-covered songs. The key to the track is the simple but irresistible groove.

Cooke was one of the original soul stylists. He took the R&B of the '50s and brought a particular smoothness and sophistication to the grooves. Cooke was also a gospel singer, so there was that passion and sweetness together that made his solo records so distinctive.

'Bring It on Home to Me' was cut on 26 April 1962 as the B-side of his next single 'Havin' a Party'.

"Once we got our sounds, Sam pretty much produced himself," engineer Al Schmitt told *Mix* magazine. "He wrote most of the songs; he knew what he wanted. He had a vision in his head of the way these things should be, and that was pretty much it. He worked fast in the studio. We'd do three and sometimes even four songs in three hours, and then we'd usually choose the best take and that was the record.

"There was almost never any overdubbing with Sam, unless he was going to do his own backing vocal or something. And when I did 'Bring It on Home', that was Lou Rawls with Sam and that was live; they sang it together."

The song took off in England when the Animals had a hit with a cover version and it became almost a standard for groups of the era as well as for soul singers in the US.

"Sam was the best. He was the easiest person I ever worked with. Just a fabulous guy. We became really good friends. Everybody loved him. And he was a total professional, too."

I Want to Hold Your Hand The Beatles

(John Lennon/Paul McCartney) ❋ Parlophone ❋ 1963 ❋
Appears on: *The Beatles 1962–1966*

Beatlemania had already started in the UK in 1963 but it wasn't until this single appeared in early 1964 in the US that things went over the top. This was the first British rock hit in the US and it opened up that country to a new style of music. The fact that the Beatles had borrowed most of the tropes from the Americans wasn't an issue. They reinterpreted it – they had their own dynamics of light and shade; loud and soft sections; they had their screams; and they had tense licks from Harrison to complement McCartney's agile bass playing.

The song was begun in the basement of Jane and Peter Asher's parents. Jane Asher was McCartney's girlfriend. Peter Asher was a singer who later became a record producer, first for Apple and then for everybody. McCartney was at the piano and Lennon on the pump organ when the song began and when McCartney hit a discord by mistake, Lennon suggested that was the beginning of the song. The record is deceptively simple. It's the details like the ascending choruses and the syncopated melody that really lift the song out of itself.

The lyrics are typical of the period – all euphemism and innuendo. They're carried by the sheer energy of the Beatles. The key to the Beatles, unlike so many of the bands of the time, was that they had spent many hard years playing live in clubs under often hostile conditions and their sessions have that energy still. The combination of their performances and the fact that they were such great singers and were also writing reasonable material had an enormous impact.

Bob Dylan recalled his reaction to hearing this record as: "They were doing things nobody was doing. Their chords were outrageous, just outrageous, and their harmonies made it all valid."

Please Please Me The Beatles

(John Lennon/Paul McCartney) ✳ EMI ✳ 1963 ✳ Appears on: *Please Please Me*

The Beatles' second single, 'Please Please Me', was written largely by John Lennon, inspired by Bing Crosby's 1932 hit 'Please', which Lennon claimed had been a favourite of his late mother. The other influence was Roy Orbison's 'Only the Lonely', which was then a hit on the radio.

The Beatles cut the track in their second session with Parlophone and needed to rearrange the song significantly to avoid comparisons with Roy Orbison's sound. Indeed, this is the Beatles' trademarked Merseybeat sound – the hyped-up energy from years of playing clubs, the harmony vocals and the neat sharp licks from George Harrison's guitar. 'Please Please Me' confirmed that the Beatles were not a quick fad and also confirmed that their unique ability came from being able to meld rhythm and blues with the traditional popular song.

She Loves You The Beatles

(John Lennon/Paul McCartney) ✻ Parlophone ✻ 1963 ✻ Appears on: *With the Beatles*

Lennon and McCartney wrote 'She Loves You' on 26 June 1963 after the initial success of 'Love Me Do'. The pair were still finding their feet as songwriters. The biggest selling British single of the '60s, 'She Loves You' was a watershed for the Beatles. The chorus with its "yeah, yeah, yeah" refrain sounded very working class and modern to British and some American ears. There was nothing polite about it. The words weren't tightened up from the street vernacular and it grated against the Establishment. Not only were these boys not cutting their hair, they seemed indifferent to polite society. Even McCartney's father was reputedly not happy with the lyric.

That lyric, combined with an impossibly catchy hook in the melody and the Beatles' exuberance, then became a catchphrase. Of course nonsense and gimmicky hooks had been common in rock & roll for some time, but not in white British music and there was an immediate social divide between the kids and the Establishment who thought the whole thing lowbrow and working class. The track also moves. The energy level of the Beatles' recordings and the simplicity of this lyric provided the template for the garage bands that would follow in their wave for the next ten years, at least until the Ramones.

Da Doo Ron Ron (When He Walked Me Home)
The Crystals

(Jeff Barry/Ellie Greenwich/Phil Spector) ✻ Phillies ✻ 1963 ✻ Appears on: *Back to Mono*

The title of this song is one of those perfect pop abstractions, an onomatopoeia for the sound of a crush. "We'd gotten stuck and didn't know what to say there," said songwriter Ellie Greenwich. "So it was like, 'Why don't we just keep "da doo ron ron"? It sounds right, it feels like fun, so let's just leave it.'"

According to Sonny Bono, a Spector protégé, "It took me some time to understand that when Phil asked, 'Is it dumb enough?' what he really meant was, 'Is everybody going to get the simplicity of this?' Will the simplicity of the hook cut through everything and grab them? I was standing beside him as the final playback of 'Da Doo Ron Ron' finished. Phil pointed to the speakers and flashed me a sneaky smile. Trying to impress him, I said, 'Man, that sure is dumb enough.' 'No Sonny', he said. 'That's gold. That's gold coming out of that speaker.'"

"I met him on a Monday and my heart stood still/Somebody told me that his name was Bill" is pretty much "dumb" but Spector turned this commonplace into a masterpiece for the ages. Part of it was the casting – getting the personality of the vocalist to fit the lyric. Much of the rest was orchestration – the loading up of percussion and the arrangements of the parts – a bit of R&B, a touch of Latin and a slice of jazz in the phrasing and then getting the whole thing to sit in a majestic sea of echo.

Although credited to the Crystals, 'Da Doo Ron Ron' was first cut with Darlene Love doing the vocals in Los Angeles. The Crystals were in Washington DC. Unhappy with the results, Spector flew the group to New York to cut the backgrounds. They caught a flight in the morning, did the session and were back in Washington for that night's show. The youngest Crystal, LaLa Brooks, was shuttled to Los Angeles to sing the lead part the next day.

"A Phil Spector session was a party session," said drummer Hal Blaine. "There'd sometimes be more percussionists than orchestra. I used to call it the Phil-harmonic. It was an absolute ball."

"Those records, when I was making them," said Spector, "they were the greatest love of my life."

Surf City Jan & Dean

(Jan Berry/Brian Wilson) ❋ Liberty ❋ 1963 ❋
Appears on: *Surf City and Other Swingin' Cities*

Jan Berry and Dean Torrence were a singing duo who were swept up in the wave of the California surf sound. Berry, the creative force in the pair, befriended the Beach Boys' Brian Wilson to crank out anthems for an idealised Californian summer. 'Surf City' is the greatest teen anthem of the '60s. The song is set in an adventure – young kids going into the new paradise of the beach where there was "Two girls for every boy".

Berry was by all accounts a creditable producer, but nothing compared with Wilson. Jan & Dean were destined to be also rans to the Beach Boys. If Berry, who sings the lead on this track, had been any better the record would lose much of its garage charm.

Berry did most of his recording at Western Recorders on Sunset Boulevard with the same team of A-class players as Phil Spector, the Beach Boys and the Byrds used. Wilson was at this date too and sang the falsetto part, somewhat edging out Torrence. According to Wilson, "Jan asked me. He said, 'Will you sing with me on the lead part?' So I doubled with him, but he was louder than I was. Ya know, he didn't wanna make me louder than him on a Jan & Dean record." Wilson's participation was uncredited, as he was then contracted to a rival label, but the sound was so much of a piece with the early Beach Boys that it was all just part of one long beach party.

The song hit number one in July 1963. California surf music was an extraordinary phenomenon. On the basis of a couple of records, a fantasy world of unblemished teenagers having innocent, wacky hijinks while engaging in water sports was sold to teenagers the world over. It was more popular in the Midwest of the US and in the UK than it was in California. Surf music and 'Surf City', in particular, was the last innocent utopia on the airwaves.

Louie Louie   The Kingsmen

(Richard Berry) ✳ Jerdon ✳ 1963 ✳
Appears on: *The Kingsmen in Person Featuring Louie Louie*

'Louie Louie' became more than a song. It is an anthem that symbolises the phenomenon of garage rock. In the forty years since the Kingsmen's version broke out of the Pacific Northwest to hit number one on the Cashbox charts the song has been covered more than 1500 times, been the subject of a thirty-one-month investigation by the FBI, and inspired millions of would-be rock stars.

The song was written by Richard Berry as an R&B/calypso tune. The lyric was a tale told by a homesick and lovesick sailor to his barman. As such it was a minor West Coast hit in 1959. Oregon band the Wailers adapted it and it became a regional standard in the early '60s. As such it entered the repertoire of Oregon bands such as Paul Revere and the Raiders and the Kingsmen – Jack Ely (guitar and vocals), Mike Mitchell (guitar), Dan Gallucci (piano), Bob Norby (bass) and Lynn Earton (drums). The Kingsmen cut their version as a demo to secure a job working a cruise ship bound for Australia.

The session cost $36 and took less than an hour at Northwest Recorders in Portland, Oregon. The band ran the song down live in the studio with one microphone. This guttural pumping, full of amateurish enthusiasm and little technique, is simply perfect. Even better is that the muddy sound drowns out Jack Ely's vocal, making the lyrics, as the FBI discovered, unintelligible.

Local impresario Jerry Dennon pressed a few hundred copies on his regional label, Jerdon. The disc became a cult favourite in Boston and was re-released by Wand and worked into a minor hit in several cities. Then suddenly rumours began to spread about the real subject of the lyrics – it was believed that hidden meanings could be determined when the 45 was played at 33⅓. Parents were outraged to the extent that the state of Indiana banned the song. The FBI began an investigation (some of the files are now available at www.thesmokinggun.com). The controversy sent the single to the top of the charts.

'Louie Louie' symbolised the subversive nature of rock & roll to the straight world. At the same time its ham-fisted arrangement of the classic one-four-five chord structure was an inspiration to millions of kids. The song could be played just as well after drinking gallons of beer. The combination of stupidity and illicit sex made the song a classic amongst college students. The Kingsmen, too, were famous for a year or so – even appearing in the beach party movie *How to Stuff a Wild Bikini*. But talent will out.

The song has a mojo all its own. Amongst its many permutations, Toots and the Maytals turned it into reggae and the Stooges performed an epic three-minute vamping of the song as Iggy Pop is beaten by Hell's Angels.

As Dave Marsh wrote in his book on the song, "Embrace 'Louie Louie' tightly enough and you may come to know more about yourself than it's easy to contemplate, let alone tolerate."

Surfin' Bird The Trashmen

(Al Frazier/Robert Harris/Carl White/Brian Wilson) ✳ Garrett ✳ 1963 ✳
Appears on: *Surfin' Bird*

The esteemed rock critic R Meltzer claimed in his definitive, if indecipherable, *The Aesthetics of Rock* that 'Surfin' Bird' was the apotheosis of rock & roll songs. Not quite, but close.

The Trashmen (originally Jim Thaxter & the Travelers) were a surf band from the landlocked state of Minnesota who had come to surf music after following the crazes that had preceded it. 'Surfin' Bird' is a medley of the Rivingtons' 'Pa Pa Ooh Mow Mow' and 'The Bird's the Word'. With the lyrics thus pasted together, the Trashmen added a psychotic and generic surf instrumental that rocked into overdrive and pushed the pulsing vocal and ratcheted up the echo on the whole thing so it sounded like it came straight from hell. And the entire song is just three minutes (or less) of glorious insanity. The track was rightly a hit and was resurrected in the '70s by the Ramones and became a classic covered notably by the Cramps and Silverchair. Stanley Kubrick used the Trashmen's single in *Full Metal Jacket* to capture the insanity of the Vietnam War and it worked a treat.

House of the Rising Sun The Animals

(Traditional/arrangement Alan Price) ✳ Track ✳ 1964 ✳

Appears on: *The Animals*

"We had a three-hour session booked, did two takes of 'House of the Rising Sun' in fifteen minutes, completely live, in mono, kept take two and made the rest of the album in the remaining two-and-three quarters hours," recalled producer Mickie Most of the session that gave him a career. "It's one of the greatest keyboard solos of all time – if not the best. Alan wrote it. Beautiful soul/jazz feel on that little Vox organ. I can remember putting 'two minutes sixty-eight seconds' on one single. As long as they saw the two it was OK, a three and they got worried."

The song was a traditional folk song about a brothel and the lyric caused some radio stations to stay away from the track. However, the performance was so strong that most stations turned a blind ear and the track became an international number one hit.

Success was not for everyone. The Animals were known for their internal volatility and keyboard player Alan Price in particular was unhappy with topping the charts.

"Essentially, all of the product was the result of a conflict of interest," he told *Goldmine* magazine. "We had a missionary zeal about blues music, and I felt, particularly, that Mickie Most was attempting to homogenise, sweeten, and make it accessible for the mass market. Which is understandable if you're the producer, but aggravating if you're the artist.

"As I say, the Animals had a particular concept of themselves as a band. There was an anarchic spirit in it, which was being flattened by commercial designs, attitudes, and needs."

Price left the band shortly after.

I Feel Fine The Beatles

(John Lennon/Paul McCartney) ✳ Parlophone ✳ 1964 ✳

Appears on: *The Beatles 1962–1966*

John Lennon proudly claimed the distinction of being the first guitarist to use guitar feedback on a pop record with this single. "That's me, including the guitar lick with the first feedback ever recorded," he said in 1980. "I defy anybody to find an earlier record – unless it is some old blues record from the twenties – with feedback on it."

Lennon started writing the song at the beginning of October 1964 while trying to figure out his part for 'Eight Days a Week'. "Anyway, going into the studio one morning, I said to Ringo, 'I've written this song but it's lousy.' We tried it, complete with riff and it sounded like an A-side, so we decided to release it just like that."

One of Lennon's few optimistic songs, possibly because he didn't think too much about the lyrics, its super-charged riff and sense of abandon took the Beatles one step further into their own. Coming on the back of *A Hard Day's Night*, which was their first all-original long player, the Beatles were further emboldened to find their own style. Backed with 'She's a Woman', the 45 was yet another number one hit. The track wasn't included on *Beatles for Sale*, the album they compiled for Christmas 1964, but the liner notes of that disc from Derek Taylor could easily apply here. He wrote, "There's priceless history between these covers. When, in a generation or so, a radioactive, cigar-smoking child, picnicking on Saturn, asks you what the Beatle affair was all about, don't try to explain all about the long hair and the screams! Just play them a few tracks from this album and he'll probably understand. The kids of AD 2000 will draw from the music much the same sense of well being and warmth as we do today."

The Times They Are a-Changin' Bob Dylan

(Bob Dylan) ✳ Columbia ✳ 1964 ✳ Appears on: *The Times They Are a-Changin'*

Quoting the Bible and referencing Irish and Scottish balladry, Bob Dylan's 'The Times' was a manifesto that implicated his elders in slowing the progress of the world. Although he had a reputation in folk circles, Dylan's name at this point was based on his "protest" songs as popularised by Peter, Paul and Mary. In 1964 the times were indeed a-changin' fast, even though the issues of Vietnam, sexual liberation, women's liberation and the race riots of the '60s were yet to come.

Not only is Dylan anticipating the coming troubles, he lays the blame on the shoulders of the older generation. "Your sons and your daughters are beyond your command," he said somewhat pretentiously and indeed they soon would be.

In December 1963 Dylan had given a speech to the Emergency Civil Liberties Committee where he said, "I only wish that all you people who are sitting out here tonight weren't here and I could see all kinds of faces with hair on their head ... because you people should be at the beach.

"Old people when their hair grows out, they should go out. And I look down to see the people who are governing me and making my rules and they haven't got any hair on their head. I get very uptight about it."

Clearly Dylan's battle wasn't just with conservatives but was more with conservative ways of doing things – whether that be running Civil Rights marches or traditional politics. This is the song of a young man in a hurry. It's full of the arrogance of youth. While it clearly refers to the changes in American society at the time – the civil rights movement, which was gathering apace, the spirit of liberalism that was then ascendant, the changing values in post-war society and the nuclear age – the song also reflects Dylan's personal struggle. It's not just Roosevelt and Goldwater that are in the way but jazz tragics like Mitch Miller and the ossified New York folk scene that were just as conservative.

The effect of 'The Times' was shocking. The song instantly polarised Dylan's audience. The album of that name was a stark, black-and-white affair with an unsmiling, unaccompanied Dylan with verse and polemics coming straight from the cold heart of America. There were none of the love songs to ameliorate the powerful tales of racial violence and political hypocrisy. "I knew exactly what I wanted to say and who I wanted to say it to," he said.

The phrase "the times they are a-changin'" went quickly into the vernacular as one of the catch-phrases of that decade.

Of course, within six months of the album's release, Dylan stopped writing his overtly political songs.

"I wanted to write a big song, some kind of theme song, with short, concise verses that piled up on each other in a hypnotic way. This is definitely a song with a purpose."

Walk on By Dionne Warwick

(Burt Bacharach/Hal David) ❋ Scepter ❋ 1964 ❋ Appears on: *Make Way For*

Burt Bacharach brought the lush romanticism of Debussy, Ellington and Gil Evans to R&B and created some of the most sophisticated pop music of the '60s. In Dionne Warwick, Bacharach and his partner Hal David found their muse. Warwick had a background in gospel that added to the richness of her voice. She had an enormous elegance and restraint. David was a writer of precise and acute lyrics whose often adventurous metre matched Bacharach's languid tempos. In the end, though, it all sounded effortless and in the case of 'Walk on By', heartbreaking.

Bacharach met Warwick in February 1961 on a session for the Drifters. "She had pigtails and dirty white sneakers," Bacharach recalled in 1970, "and she just shone. The group was dynamite but there was something about the way she carried herself that made me want to hear her sing by herself. After I did, she started to do all our demos."

"We've got a tremendous thing going between us," Bacharach said of his relationship with the singer. "There's a great kind of love transmitted, a happiness, she's the thing that makes everything lighter."

Prior to meeting Dionne Warwick, Bacharach and Davis were songwriters for hire – sometimes as a pair and sometimes with others. Together, though, there was a real chemistry that resulted in a series of sublime masterpieces from 1962 to 1973.

'Walk on By' was one of their first collaborations. Bacharach orchestrated the song with woodblock percussion and a halting tempo like the rhythm of deep sobbing, while the flugelhorn played its unearthly tune.

"We had done 'Walk on By' and 'Anyone Who had a Heart' at the same recording session," Davis recalled. "And we couldn't make up our minds which record to go with first. And we went back and forth and back and forth and finally elected to come out with 'Anyone Who had a Heart'". And so 'Walk on By' was always meant to be the next one."

"They're *songs*," Bacharach told Lillian Ross of the *New Yorker*. "The songs are basically sophisticated. I write the music the way I feel. Hal David, my lyricist, writes the words the way *he* feels. No matter how groovy the electronic devices are these days, there's got to be a song. Electronic devices are marvellous. But nobody's going to whistle electronic devices. You've got to have a song."

Twenty-Four Hours from Tulsa Gene Pitney

(Burt Bacharach/Hal David) ❋ Musicor ❋ 1964 ❋ Appears on: *Blue Gene*

Gene Pitney's almost cracking upper register and his histrionic delivery lent itself to narrative songs such as this and Bacharach and David's 'The Man who Shot Liberty Vallence'. 'Tulsa' has since become a classic although a feud with his label Musicor and Bacharach and David meant that the song was never supported in the US.

The origin of the lyric is a mystery to Hal David. It just sounded like it was going to be a good story. From there he constructed a narrative of a travelling man on his way home and "only one day away from your arms" when his heart is taken by another woman. There is so much drama in this song – the sense of motion and the advancing time – as David sketches out the landscape of the interstate and the motels and truck stops. The tempo of Bacharach's tune propels the melody. There's the kind of jittery feeling that comes from driving too long on too little sleep and too much bad food. There's a sense of being in limbo and of the salvation that is offered by the singer's home. A salvation that he will never reach. This is one of the most inventive break-up songs, but really only works because of Gene Pitney's delivery of Bacharach's very complex melody. It's a song of mystery and romance, of a life changed in a moment.

Killing Floor Howlin' Wolf

(Chester Arthur Burnett) ✳ Chess ✳ 1964 ✳ Appears on: *The Chess Box*

"If I had to pick one person who does everything I loved about the blues, it would be Howlin' Wolf," Bonnie Raitt once said. "It would be the size of his voice, or just the size of *him*. When you're a little pre-teenage girl and you imagine what a naked man in full arousal is like, it's Howlin' Wolf. That's how I feel when I hear Howlin' Wolf – and when I met him it was the same thing. He was the scariest, most deliciously frightening bit of male testosterone I've ever experienced in my life."

Chester Burnett was forty-one years old when he made his recording debut for Sam Phillips' Sun label in Memphis in 1951. He had a lifetime of the blues already in his voice. He stood 6' 3" and weighed over 300 pounds. He had a voice to match – strong and versatile and expressive, capable of carrying heavy loads.

Wolf was inspired to become a blues singer after a meeting with Delta legend Charley Patton. His sister married Sonny Boy Williamson and that relationship encouraged his harmonica playing. Through it all Wolf had a sense of a hard driving beat and his growling voice.

Wolf specialised in songs that were at best morally ambiguous. He wasn't a hearts and flowers kind of guy; instead, his songs were mostly about lust and evil. His own guitar style tended towards sharp slide playing and aggressive riffs.

After moving to Chicago, Wolf teamed up with guitarist Hubert Sumlin, who would prove to be his consummate foil. Sumlin didn't play chords so much as little jabs of guitar spiking out of the melody. He was one of the most distinctive electric blues guitarists. The combination of the two made for a series of hits unmatched in the Chess catalogue.

'Killing Floor' is the perfect tag team of Wolf and Sumlin. It was first recorded in August 1964 with the great Sam Lay on drums, Lafayette Leake on piano and Buddy Guy playing acoustic guitar. Sumlin's slide tears off shards and shards of vicious melody. Howlin' Wolf broods and smoulders in his anger and disgust at the relationship he's comparing to the killing floor of an abattoir. 'Killing Floor', especially Sumlin's guitar, inspired the next generation of blues players – Jimi Hendrix, Mike Bloomfield and Jimmy Page all covered the song (the latter retitled it as 'The Lemon Song'). This was perhaps the bridge between the real blues and the blues-rock that dominated the late '60s.

A Love Supreme John Coltrane

(John Coltrane) ❋ Impulse! ❋ 1964 ❋ Appears on: *A Love Supreme*

John Coltrane's masterpiece was comprised of four suites over two sides of an LP. Recorded with his quartet (McCoy Tyner, Elvin Jones and Jimmy Garrison), the piece was a musical interpretation of a spiritual journey. Coltrane's mother was a church pianist and his father played violin. Both his grandfathers were ordained ministers in the African Methodist Episcopal Zion Church. Music and God were entwined for Coltrane. 'A Love Supreme' is a sublime piece of sacred music. The slowly revealing theme and its embellishments culminate in the hypnotic chanting of the title at the climax of the piece. Coltrane composed the song while reading one of his poems, 'A Psalm', on the music stand.

"I remember that Rudy Van Gelder, who was a premier jazz recording engineer at the time, cut the lights down, which made it more like a club atmosphere," pianist McCoy Tyner recalled of the *A Love Supreme* session. "I don't think we even rehearsed that music. Usually John would play the music and then we would record it and see what could happen, because it usually developed. Once we started playing it, new ideas would form ...

"Many of the arrangements were head arrangements. There was only one horn so we were able to do that easily, and he just had things sketched out that he would want – nothing in detail. We had reached a point where we had that kind of high level communication between us."

Esteemed jazz writer Gary Giddins regards *A Love Supreme* as one of the pinnacles of jazz. "Coltrane," he said, "was a great jazz composer who created original and unforgettable melodic ideas, which is something you can say about relatively few jazz musicians. *A Love Supreme* was just filled with them. It had vocals; it had the group chanting 'A love supreme', which was completely novel at the time. Everything about the record lets you know that this was an important event."

Ring of Fire   Johnny Cash

(June Carter Cash/Merle Kilgore) ❋ Columbia ❋ 1964 ❋
Appears on: *The Essential Johnny Cash*

Johnny Cash was so much the Man in Black that even when he fell in love he imagined it would be like hell. One of Johnny Cash's most endearing songs was written by his wife, June Carter Cash, and Merle Kilgore. With Cash's massive bass voice and his weary persona the 'Ring of Fire' of passion becomes the bittersweet fire of hell.

"I connected with June Carter the first time in 1956 backstage at the Grand Ole Opry, but it was about five years before I saw her again," Johnny Cash recalled of the woman who would be his love, saviour and muse for the rest of his life. "She was living in New York, going to dramatic school. But in late '61 we played the Big D in Dallas, Texas, and my manager at that time, Saul Holiff, said, 'We need a girl singer on the show tonight. They want more than just you and your band.' And I said, 'Well, get one.' He said, 'What do you think about June Carter?' and I said, 'I've always been a fan of hers.' So we booked June Carter on the Big D in Dallas and then that night she did such a great job, my manager asked if she would work the next tour with us.

"Merle Kilgore happened to be on that tour, and they were writing songs together and one of them was 'Love's Firey Ring'. And they worked it over until they changed it to 'Ring of Fire' and Anita Carter, June's sister, recorded it. And I said, 'Anita, I'll give you about five or six months, and if you don't hit with it, I'm gonna record it the way I feel it.' She said, 'OK.' Well, one night, not that I can claim any psychic powers or anything, I dreamed I heard 'Ring of Fire' with trumpets which was an outlandish kind of an innovation for country music. I called Don Law who was producing my records and I said, 'I want to record a song with trumpets with a Tex-Mex sound of trumpets.' And he said, 'Are you sure? Let's just bring in the Tennessee Three', and I said, 'No, I want two trumpet players in Nashville for this session for one song and when you hear it, you'll know. I think you'll go along with it.' He didn't really, but he hired the trumpet players, and I went to Nashville and recorded 'Ring of Fire'."

Not only did it help the path of true love, 'Ring of Fire' put Johnny Cash back in the charts. Its adventurous production and forceful arrangement made the song a pop hit and revived his career for the '60s.

My Boy Lollipop Millie

(Johnny Roberts/Morris Levy) ❋ Fontana ❋ 1964 ❋ Appears on: *Tougher than Tough*

Little Millie Small was a popular Jamaican singer. The English producer Chris Blackwell, who spent a lot of time in Jamaica and is largely responsible for introducing Jamaican music to the west, brought her to London to cover this old R&B song.

'My Boy Lollipop' was recorded by Barbie Gaye in 1956 and was a regional hit. Millicent Small had been singing in ska (also then known as blue beat) bands for some time and was generally regarded as one of the few solid female artists in the genre.

Blackwell took her to London and brought in a Birmingham band, the Five Dimensions, who at one point had featured a young Rod Stewart. Contrary to myth, Stewart doesn't play the distinctive harmonica part. Jamaican guitar legend Ernest Raglin, however, does feature on the track.

Recorded at Olympic in London, Blackwell was keen to get close to the reverb and rangy sound of Kingston studios. "On that record, the reverb came from a sort of cupboard in the back of the studio that we used as a live chamber," Blackwell recalled. "It was a mono record, and we fed the sound in, adding a bit more of the reverb on Millie's voice."

It was partly the exotic blue beat sound and Millie's cute demeanour that made the record an instant hit on its release in November 1964. "The record worked well for radio," said Blackwell. "Partly because it was a minute and fifty-one seconds. That was important for people at radio who were putting playlists together. Also, Millie's voice was irresistible – for a certain length of time, anyway. So a short record worked well for her."

The song was the first commercial ska/blue beat record and went on to make number two in the US and sell seven million copies. Later it had a new (and less naïve) lease of life as a track for the Spice Girls.

Mississippi Goddam Nina Simone

(Nina Simone) ❋ Philips ❋ 1964 ❋ Appears on: *Nina Simone in Concert*

Nina Simone intended to be a classical pianist. To put herself through study in the '50s she worked in Atlantic City bars playing jazz. Gradually her eclectic tastes, which ranged from pop hits to Kurt Weill, traditional blues and jazz, extended. Simone was always politically militant and she kept step with the civil rights movement in the '60s.

In June 1963, Byron Beckwith, who was twice acquitted by all-white juries, gunned down civil rights activist Medgar Evers outside his house in Jackson, Mississippi. In September a group of white supremacists bombed a church in Birmingham, Alabama, killing four black children. Simone's response was the searing 'Mississippi Goddam', the most strident song of its era.

"This is a show tune, but the show hasn't been written for it yet," Simone told her Carnegie Hall audience in 1964. She was treading the same territory as Bertolt Brecht and Bob Dylan but with less compromise in her music. Simone was rare amongst protest singers because she underpinned her message with a soulful alto voice and a rare musicality.

Her uncompromising nature and radical politics didn't help her career much. Through the early '70s she became disillusioned with the black struggle and contemptuous of America – eventually moving first to Africa and then to France.

"After Martin Luther King and Malcom X got killed, after Lorraine Hansberry and Langston Hughes and Medgar Evers died, and after Stokley Carmichael and Miriam Makeba went to Africa, yes, I felt the movement died," she said. "I left because I didn't feel that black people were going to get their due, and I still don't.

"There's no other purpose, so far as I am concerned, for us except to reflect the times. The situations around us, and the things we're able to say through our art, the things that millions of people can't say." Very few said it all so well.

You've Lost that Lovin' Feelin' The Righteous Brothers

(Phil Spector/Barry Mann/Cynthia Weill) ❊ Phillies/A&M ❊ 1964 ❊

Appears on: *You've Lost that Lovin' Feelin'*

There is an often-told story that when Phil Spector first laid out the arrangement of this song he gave the lion's share to tenor Bill Medley. Bass singer Bobby Hatfield then sarcastically enquired what was he supposed to do: "What do I do when he's singing the whole first verse." Spector quipped, "You can go directly to the bank."

"That's true," Spector told Mick Brown of the *Saturday Telegraph* in 2003. "It's also true that they didn't want to do 'Lovin' Feelin''. They wanted to do rock & roll, ooh-bop-a-doo stuff.

"I worked six months on that fucking record, overdubbing and re-overdubbing, and finally I had it down right where I thought it was pretty good, but I was worried that nobody would get it. I played it for a few people and nobody had heard anything like it. I didn't know whether we'd changed the world or done something completely catastrophic. So I had to go back to New York.

"I played it for Barry Mann and Cynthia Weill. I put it on, the record goes, 'You never close your eyes', and Barry says, 'Whoah, whoah, wait. Wrong speed.' I said, 'What?' He goes, 'Wrong speed, Phil.' That's the first comment I hear.

"So I immediately called Dr Kaplan, my psychiatrist, and I said, 'Doc, I have to see you right away. I just worked six months on this record; it cost me $35,000 and the fucking co-writer thinks it's on the wrong fucking speed.' I called Larry Levine, my engineer, and said, 'You given me the right pressing?' I'm fucking paranoid. I didn't know what to do. So I called Donnie Kirshner, the co-publisher, and said, 'Donnie, I got to play you this record.' He said, 'I hear it's a monster.' I said, 'You've got the best ears in the business.' So I bring it over and put it on. He goes, 'Boops, it's great, it's great, it's great; what do you call it?' I said, 'You've Lost that Lovin' Feelin''. He said, 'How many you got pressed up?' I said, 'Half a million.' He said, 'Bring Back that Lovin' Feelin'' – that's your title.'

"That's the second opinion. So I call Dr Kaplan again.

"Then I call Murray the K, the biggest DJ in New York City. I said, 'Murray, I have this new Righteous Brothers record. I need you to play it on the show, because it's a four minute and five second record; there's never been a record this long before.' And I'm lying on the label; I put three minutes five seconds – I got in a lot of fucking trouble for that. So he comes over and he listens to the record. This is the last opinion of the day – five o'clock in the afternoon. And he's listening and listening, and it gets to the middle section, and he says, 'That bass line, that 'La Bamba' thing, what's that?' I said, 'That's part of the song.' He said, 'That's fucking sensational.' I said, 'Well, yeah.' He said, 'That's how it should begin.' I said, 'It can't begin that way, Murray.' He said, 'Make that the beginning.'

"And those are my three experts: the co-writer, the co-publisher and the number one disc-jockey in America all killed me. I didn't sleep for a week when that record came out. I was so sick, I got a spastic colon; I had an ulcer."

He needn't have worried. 'You've Lost that Lovin' Feelin'' topped the charts around the world – twice – and has been successfully covered many times. For Spector though it was his most adventurous production to date.

The husband and wife team of Mann and Weill wrote the bulk of the song in their room at the Chateau Marmont; Spector helped them finish the tune and then began assembling the track. Jazz guitar legend Barney Kessel, who played on the song, described Spector's sessions "like he was going to invade Moscow".

Spector discovered the Righteous Brothers at San Francisco's Cow Palace in 1964 and took over their contract from Moonglow Records. They proved to be argumentative, not especially cooperative with each other or Spector and a far cry from the more pliable girl groups he had worked with. Medley and Hatfield were clearly nervous doing a blue-eyed-soul aria that seethed sexuality.

"We knew it was a phenomenal production and a great record," said Medley. "But you have to remember that kind of record was not topping the charts in those days. It was a real adult song. Compared to what was going on."

It's All Over Now The Rolling Stones

(Bobby Womack/Shirley Jean Womack) ❊ Decca ❊ 1964 ❊
Appears on: *The Rolling Stones*

Bobby Womack and his brother Curtis were discovered by soul stirrer Sam Cooke and put to work recording gospel songs as the Valentinos in Los Angeles.

"He said, 'Get on Route 66 and stay on it all the way.' I talked my oldest brother into buying a Cadillac, because that's what I saw all the pimps in the neighbourhood driving," Womack recalled of his invitation to join the music business. "Of course, we get on the freeway and it starts to rain, the wind--shield wipers won't turn on, and the car's running out of gas every fifteen seconds because the tank's got a hole in it. We wound up in the hospital for a week, because we were overcome by gas fumes. And then the headlights came off!

"Two weeks later, we show up in LA, pushin' the car down Hollywood Boulevard, all of us with our do-rags on. We called Sam, and he said, 'Man, where the hell are y'all?' 'We on Sunset. The car ain't got no more gas.'"

They didn't do well with gospel either and switched to R&B, where they had a major hit in 1962 with 'Lookin' for a Love' and a minor hit with 'It's All Over Now'.

"The Stones was over here at Chess Records looking for songs," said Womack. "Our record had just come out and it was very big. The Stones heard it and said, 'Man, we got to cut that song.' Sam came to me and said 'Bobby, I got some good news and bad. The Rolling Stones want to cover your song.' And I said, 'Man, when these Pat Boones gonna stop?'

"Sam said, 'Bobby, they'll do more for your career than you'll ever believe.

This group is gonna be huge and the longer they live, the bigger they're gonna get. It's a new thing happening, man, and I can see it already.' So I just said, 'I don't want them to sing the song. Tell 'em to get their own song.' Sam says, 'Bobby, they sell tons of records. This is gonna be the first record that breaks for them in the States. You know what that means? You introduced 'em.'"

The strong beat in the track and its eclectic melody made the track perfect for a crossover to pop radio – a little blacker than most white pop bands of the time. It was ideal for the Rolling Stones' image and it certainly launched Womack's name as a writer. He has since become firm friends, to the point of writing and producing Ron Wood's brilliant album *Now Look*. At the time, though, the track was an important bridge across the genres.

"They came out with 'It's All Over Now' so quick and I was laughin' because some of the words they thought we said, we didn't say. Mick said something totally different. I said, 'This is how a black person talk, the English sound different.' We were laughing, but I was still furious. They took our song and everybody thinks it's their song, never mind Sam talking about it's gonna make me a legend and all that. But I remember the first cheque I received, it was about $400,000. I been chasing 'em ever since tryin' to get 'em to do one of my songs."

Oh, Pretty Woman Roy Orbison

(Bill Dees/Roy Orbison) ❋ Monument ❋ 1964 ❋ Appears on: *Oh, Pretty Woman*

Even on this sunny return to his rockabilly roots, Roy Orbison sounds a little perverse. The song was written after admiring his wife Claudette and it is a kind of anthem for voyeurs.

No matter. Orbison rocks into this track with a perfect country rock boogie sound. His vocal is uncharacteristically exuberant – especially the little expletive "Mercy!" in the break.

Orbison was pigeonholed as a ballad singer but he had started out in Texas doing western swing country music and then rockabilly. Those influences come together perfectly on 'Oh, Pretty Woman.'

"Even in 'Pretty Woman', it goes through a lot of emotions," he said. "I didn't think of this as we were writing the song, but the guy's observing the girl, and he hits on her, real cool and macho, and then he gets worried and gets to pleading, and then he says, 'OK, forget it, I'm still cool', and then at the end she comes back to him, and he turns into the guy he really is. That range of emotion in a short piece of music I think is very important."

Remember (Walkin' in the Sand) The Shangri-Las

(Shadow Morton) ❋ Redbird ❋ 1964 ❋

Appears on: *Golden Hits of the Shangri-Las*

The Shangri-Las had a sexuality that would steal the breath right out of your body. They were cute and pure but you could tell that they knew what was really going on and that, given the right boy, they would go there. Mary Weiss whispered stories of suburban romance. The most epic of their songs is 'Leader of the Pack' – a song that was revolutionary when it came out and has now entered the vernacular. But the Shangri-Las were never better than on their first disc.

Shadow Morton was a childhood acquaintance of Ellie Greenwich, who, by 1963, had become a very successful songwriter in the Brill Building factory. Greenwich's partner, Jeff Barry, dared Morton to make a record in four days.

Morton rounded up musicians and a local girl group, the Shangri-Las – sisters Mary and Betty Weiss, and twins Mary Ann and Marge Gander. Although there were officially four, generally the twins rotated according to other commitments.

According to his own legend, Shadow Morton was on his way to the studio to cut his first record when he discovered that he didn't have a song so he pulled over to the side of the road and wrote 'Remember', complete with a four-minute spoken introduction. It's the tale of a girl who has just been dumped by her boyfriend and her world has ended.

The song is magnificent in its simplicity. Mary's vocal lags just behind the beat from a vamping piano (played by Billy Joel). Everything is compressed and disciplined as though her chest is barely able to contain the devastation and the tragedy. Then comes the chorus with the girls – release! Reminiscence of the good times. Although even there, the relationship is muted and constrained.

Rock & roll music just doesn't get more passionate than this.

Morton found them nice cinematic pop tunes about the lives of girls who do. The Shangri-Las had other hits – notably 'Out in the Streets' and 'Give Him a Great Big Kiss'. But we always remember the first time.

The Sound of Silence Simon & Garfunkel

(Paul Simon) ❋ Columbia ❋ 1964 ❋ Appears on: *The Sound of Silence*

No-one was more surprised at the success of 'The Sound of Silence' than Paul Simon. He and Art Garfunkel had cut the track with just Simon's acoustic guitar as backing for their album *Wednesday, 3 AM*. That LP was a flop and Simon & Garfunkel disbanded. Garfunkel went back to university to study maths and architecture and Simon went to Europe to be a solo troubadour around the folk clubs. Meanwhile, folk rock took off. Columbia, which represented the Byrds and Bob Dylan, enlisted Dylan's producer Tom Wilson to add an electric backing to the song with the same session players Dylan used. As they didn't bother to inform Simon of this, the first he knew of it was picking up a copy of *Billboard* while in Denmark and seeing his song racing up the charts.

"We were in my kitchen in my apartment on Amsterdam Avenue, uptown in Manhattan, when I was a student at Columbia College," Garfunkel recalled. "Paul would drive in from Queens, showing me these new songs. And that was the sixth song he had written, 'The Sound of Silence'. And he showed it to me in my kitchen and I went crazy for how cool it was."

Simon & Garfunkel began their career as a rock & roll vocal group in the '50s when they were still at school. Things changed quickly for Simon after he heard Bob Dylan and he began to write material that was more personal. The potent opening line, "Hello darkness my old friend," was inspired by his habit of playing his guitar in a darkened bathroom for the echo effect. From there the song ranges across many personal and general themes.

"'The Sound of Silence', which I wrote when I was twenty-one, I never would have wrote it were it not for Bob Dylan," said Simon. "Never. He was the first guy to come along in a serious way that wasn't writing a teen language song. I saw him as a major guy whose work I didn't want to imitate in the least. Not because I didn't admire it but because I didn't see any way out of being in his shadow if I was going to be anything like that. And I looked at him and said that's really fabulous and the Beatles are really fabulous and the Rolling Stones are really fabulous and it's going to be really hard for my little group – me and my friend, Art Garfunkel – to even find a slice of this pie that is original. And it was so hard because those guys were so great at what they did it was like, 'Well, what can you be?'"

His first song released, however, went to number one in the charts. Simon & Garfunkel hastily reformed and cut a folk rock album.

"I had just come back from England, and Art was still living at home," said Simon. "He was still at college and we were sitting in my car ... smoking. And 'The Sound of Silence' came on and they said: 'Number one record 'The Sound of Silence' by Simon & Garfunkel.' We were just sitting there at night, we hadn't anything to do, and Artie turned to me and he said: 'Those guys must be having so much fun!'"

Hanky Panky Tommy James & the Shondells

(Jeff Barry/Elle Greenwich) ✳ Snap ✳ 1964 ✳ Appears on: *Anthology*

Tommy James was only twelve years old when he cut the original version of 'Hanky Panky' at the studios of radio station WNIL in Niles, Michigan. Written by the songwriting duo of Barry and Greenwich and recorded by them as the Raindrops, Tommy James had seen a local band play it in their set, so he included it in his.

Ostensibly, the hanky panky was a dance, but even a twelve-year-old boy knew better than that.

Tommy James and the Shondells rearranged the song, stripping it right back to its elemental three chords and the progression that pulses forward until it climaxes in a "Ohhhhhh!". The guitar solo is a wild freak-out, as orgasmic as the singing. James' vocal is perfect. He has a sweetness to his tone but there's also a part of the song where he gets very guttural and primitive. There's no doubt that it is a song of desire.

'Hanky Panky' was recorded live to two-track and pressed up on local indie Snap, where it gathered dust for two years. Then in 1965, out of the blue, a disc jockey in Pittsburgh started playing the track and it became a regional hit and then, with a label change, a national hit.

'Hanky Panky' is pop music at its most simple and innocent. It's three great chords and a cute lyric conceit cut live and in its moment. There are more sophisticated records, better produced, more intelligent, and there are many moments that equal the pure perfection of 'Hanky Panky', but it never ever gets better than this.

In My Life The Beatles

(John Lennon/Paul McCartney) ✳ Parlophone ✳ 1965 ✳ Appears on: *Rubber Soul*

The *Rubber Soul* album, which this closes, shows the influence that Bob Dylan was having on the Beatles. No longer were they churning out cute love songs. With this record they started writing songs that were clearly based on the experiences of their lives. 'In My Life' was Lennon's attempt to write a direct autobiography. "Before, we were just writing songs à la Everly Brothers, Buddy Holly – pop songs with no more thought to them than that," he said in 1980. The words were irrelevant. "'In My Life' started out as a bus journey from my house at 250 Menlove Avenue to town, mentioning all the places I could recall. I wrote it all down and it was boring. But then I laid back and these lyrics started coming to me about the places I remember ... I'd struggled for days and hours trying to write clever lyrics. Then I gave up and 'In My life' came to me." The song is a very moving reverie on life and death, referring at one point to the fifth Beatle, Stu Sutcliffe.

McCartney came around and offered to help. Lennon claimed that the tune was almost completely his. Musicologists have trawled for clues but it's now generally accepted that the tune has the other Beatle's fingerprints all over it.

"He either forgot or didn't think I wrote the tune," said McCartney. "I remember he had the words, like a poem – sort of faces he remembered ... and I recall going off for half-an-hour and sitting with the Mellotron he had, writing the tune, which was Miracles-inspired, as I remember."

The keyboard solo came from George Martin, while the Beatles were out of the room. "I thought it would be rather nice to have a harpsichord-like solo ... I did it with what I call a 'wound up' piano, which was at double speed – partly because you get a harpsichord sound by shortening the attack of everything, but also because I couldn't play it at real speed anyway," said Martin. "So I played it on piano at exactly half normal speed, and down an octave. And when you bring the tape back to normal speed again, it sounds pretty brilliant. It's a way of tricking everybody into thinking you can do something really well."

I Fought the Law The Bobby Fuller Four

(Sonny Curtis) ❋ Mustang ❋ 1965 ❋ Appears on: *The Best of the Bobby Fuller Four*

Sonny Curtis of Buddy Holly's band the Crickets recorded this song in 1959. It was another Texan, Bobby Fuller, who made the song a major hit.

Fuller was a native of El Paso, Texas, and a devotee of Buddy Holly. In 1964 he and his band moved to Los Angeles. Fuller was making some headway with his own brand of Texas rockabilly. In October 1965, Fuller cut 'I Fought the Law' and in February 1966 the song peaked in the Top 10.

Then, in the morning of 18 July 1966, Fuller's corpse was discovered on the front seat of his mother's 1962 Oldsmobile, which was parked outside his Hollywood apartment. The body was covered in gasoline. The coroner ruled the death a suicide but many of Fuller's friends suggested that he had become involved in the drug scene and that he was murdered by organised crime figures.

The ultimate rebel anthem, 'I Fought the Law' tells the tragic story of a man seduced into a life of crime but who gets his comeuppance. However, the song has become a rebel anthem for groups from the Clash to Green Day. The galloping tempo of the song and the powerful six shots from the drums at the finale just add to the exuberance of the outlaw hymn.

Highway 61 Revisited Bob Dylan

(Bob Dylan) ❄ Columbia ❄ 1965 ❄ Appears on: *Highway 61 Revisited*

Bob Dylan grew up on Highway 61. This interstate highway runs north/south parallel to the Mississippi River. It passes Duluth, Minnesota, just before hitting the Canadian border, near where Dylan spent his early childhood years. Highway 61 was the road travelled by many of the blues artists heading out of the cotton fields of the Mississippi Delta and up to the industrialised cities of Chicago and Detroit. 'Highway 61' was also the title of a blues song by Mississippi Fred McDowell. Dylan's version is therefore revisiting it. His *Highway 61 Revisited* album was a bold beginning to a new chapter in what was essentially a blues tradition.

'Highway 61 Revisited' was recorded on 2 August 1965. Mike Bloomfield, then the pre-eminent white blues guitarist, provided searing guitar lines. Al Kooper backed Dylan with a warm and animated organ sound that glued the music together. Dylan ranted through this song with a series of vignettes satirising the state of the world. In those mid-'60s records Dylan just piled on the imagery, lashing out at the hypocrisy he saw around him in the world of politics and show business.

While the song is full of dark imagery, essentially it's a black comedy. The words are very much in the style of Dylan's talking blues – comic narratives such as 'Talking Bear Mountain Picnic' or 'Motorpsycho Nightmare' rather than being a specific commentary. It's likely also that Dylan loved the way that Bloomfield mimicked the sound of a police siren in his guitar licks. Al Kooper had brought the whistle to the sessions and used to blow it when someone was using drugs. Dylan fixed the toy whistle into his harmonica rack and blew so hard producer Bob Johnston thought his head was coming off.

Like a Rolling Stone Bob Dylan

(Bob Dylan) ❄ Columbia ❄ 1965 ❄ Appears on: *Highway 61 Revisited*

Al Kooper, who played the distinctive organ on the track, recalled that he snuck into Columbia Studios in the hope of playing on a Dylan date. He was a session guitarist and songwriter looking for a chance. As he waited for Dylan to arrive, Michael Bloomfield arrived with his Fender Telecaster. Bloomfield had no case for the instrument so he just brushed the snow off and began tuning up. Kooper realised that he couldn't compete so he stood behind the Hammond organ – an instrument he had not played before. Dylan arrived and ran 'Rolling Stone' down, Kooper busking his part. When it came to the playback, producer Tom Wilson tried to keep Kooper's organ in the background but Dylan told him to turn it up. These few minutes would influence the rest of Al Kooper's life.

'Like a Rolling Stone' was so different, so sophisticated, that it shaped the future of rock & roll.

"My wife and I lived in a little cabin in Woodstock, which we rented from Peter Yarrow's mother," said Dylan. "I wrote the song there in this cabin. We had come up from New York and I had about three days off up there to get some stuff together. It just came you know. It started with that 'La Bamba' riff."

It's likely that at least one character in the song was Edie Sedgwick, an aristocratic waif who had come to New York and fallen in with Andy Warhol's Factory crowd. Dylan spent some time with her and Warhol – whom he seemed not to like much – around this time. Sedgwick was a doomed beauty who may have been romantically involved with Dylan and was certainly involved with his friend Bob Neuwirth.

The last session that Dylan would have with producer Tom Wilson included pianist Paul Griffin, bassist Russ Savakus and Bobby Gregg, whose sharp crack on the snare drum announces the start of the song. While Dylan had taught Bloomfield the chord changes most of the musicians were improvising from beginning to end.

Bob Dylan wrote in *Rolling Stone* magazine, "The song was written on an old upright piano in the key of G sharp, then later at Columbia recording studios transferred to the key of C on the guitar. The chorus part came to me first and I'd sorta hum that over and over, then later figured out that the verses would start low and move on up. The first two lines which rhymed 'kiddin' you' with 'didn't you' just about knocked me out; and later on, when I got to the jugglers and the chrome horse and the princess on the steeple, it all just about got to be too much."

Subterranean Homesick Blues Bob Dylan

(Bob Dylan) ❋ Columbia ❋ 1965 ❋ Appears on: *Bringing It All Back Home*

Dylan notes on the *Biograph* box set, "Probably 'Too Much Monkey Business' is in here somewhere. I don't even think we rehearsed it." It's a flat-out rock & roll song that neatly ties Chuck Berry's rant about the straight world into a new context of middle-class poetics and the hipster world of the mid-'60s.

The lyric was written in one burst in the apartment of his manager's friend shortly before the session in January 1965. Obviously cut live in one take, there is a beautiful, ramshackle energy to the track. Dylan's rhythmic singing seems to recall the chanting of jazz poetry rather than trying to follow the melody.

For Dylan's audience, this was a revolutionary act in itself. He was at the time the king of the protest singers and with this track he donned a leather jacket and joined the ranks of the rockers.

Apart from satirising the Establishment and the police, the theme here is paranoia, partly related to illegal drugs, but it also hints at the chasm that was about to broaden even further with the coming generation gap. As the '60s progressed and resistance to the Vietnam War increased, the level of fear about the authorities also increased.

While not a protest song in the manner of his acoustic ballads, this is a rebel song of which Woody Guthrie would have been proud. Dylan is rejecting the work-day world and suggesting that the worldview as presented by the mass media may in fact be completely crazy and he would have no part in it.

Some radicals took the song too far and named their militant organisation the Weathermen after a line in the song ("you don't need a weatherman to know which way the wind blows"). DA Pennebaker shot a short film of Dylan standing in an alley with flip cards of the lyrics (while poet Allen Ginsberg plays a vandal) which he added to his film *Don't Look Back*, and it's generally regarded as the first music video.

The song was Dylan's first hit single despite having no chorus or mention of the title in the words.

People Get Ready The Impressions

(Curtis Mayfield) ❋ ABC ❋ 1965 ❋ Appears on: *People Get Ready*

The gospel style of this single seemed to be just the salvation ordered in 1965. The civil rights movement, the generation gap and the Vietnam War were starting to reach boiling point. Then this soul song with a big dose of gospel came along like a reality check. The deep soul groove of the song is played off against the gospel vocal parts and the meeting-the-maker tempo.

There is a calm directness in the vocal that is compassionate but doesn't avoid the dark realities – including death. This is basic redemptive preaching. Curtis Mayfield has said that the influence for the song came directly from the pulpit. The song was not a big hit at the time but it has become one of the longest-lasting soul singles of all time. Aretha Franklin's cover version on *Lady Soul* helped; the Vanilla Fudge's version gave it to a rock audience. The song has survived hundreds of readings. Its message has stayed fresh.

"As a youngster and a black, I was quite concerned with what was going on at the time. I wanted to bring a little gospel into the drive for reality with the song," Mayfield said. "And it also lent a pride to those who were oppressed and trying to define themselves on another level."

Papa's Got a Brand New Bag James Brown

(James Brown) ✳ King ✳ 1965 ✳ Appears on: *Papa's Got a Brand New Bag*

"Gospel always had the One," Brown told Barney Hoskyns, "but it became more dominant once I clarified it. You go to church now, you hear more James Brown than you do in the dance halls. Because it's a way of life. We put our foot down, we lead off with the left foot most times – that's what soldiers and everybody do – and go from left to right, left to right, and we try to put it down solid each time."

It was that simple lesson that created funk.

In February 1965 James Brown and the JBs cut this track, placing the emphasis on the first and the third beats. The JBs included Maceo Parker, Jimmy Nolan and Bernard Odum and the track jammed for seven minutes. The key was "the One". The players could do what they liked so long as they returned together to the first beat in the bar. This gave James Brown incredible propulsion, a shunting force supported by the horns and his own alchemical phrasing.

Few songs have changed music as much as the edited version of 'Papa's Got a Brand New Bag'. At this point soul music met funk and was changed forever.

Al Capone Prince Buster

(Cecil Campbell) ✳ Melodisc ✳ 1965 ✳

Appears on: *The Story of Jamaican Music: Tougher Than Tough*

Prince Buster (aka Cecil Campbell) was one of the first Jamaican record producers. He ran a sound system in the early '60s for which he produced his own records. According to writer Steve Barrows, Buster wanted to create a distinctive sound so he had his guitarist Jah Jerry play on the after-beat thus creating the stop start rhythm of reggae music. Prince Buster was popular with mods and his records, especially 'Madness', were seized upon by the Two-Tone movement in the UK in the early '80s – not least by the group Madness.

The Jamaican sound system producers were churning out discs to satisfy their dance club audiences, many of them instrumental. The MCs started talking over the top of the grooves in what was called toasting. Eventually this influenced the start of rap in the US.

Like the rappers, the early reggae and ska musicians identified with outlaws. There was a massive gun culture in Jamaica and a large drug industry.

'Al Capone' was homage to the Chicago gangster. Buster's track is mostly instrumental with some toasting. The sound is huge – courtesy of the Skalights' backing. The track is a classic ska cut with the rhythm section right on top of every beat, the sound effects of police and the attitude. This same blueprint would be followed twenty years later by Ice-T and the gangsta rappers. Buster's song, however, is both lighter and more intense.

(I Can't Get No) Satisfaction The Rolling Stones

(Mick Jagger/Keith Richards) ✳ Decca ✳ 1965 ✳ Appears on: *Out of Our Heads*

The perfect rock & roll record. The riff. The lyric. The delivery. Perfect.

The song began in guitarist Keith Richards' fitful sleep on 9 May 1965 in a Clearwater, Florida, motel. He woke and bashed the blues figure and the title out on an acoustic guitar into his cassette recorder and then fell back asleep. The next morning, as they sat by the motel pool, Jagger added a lyric. "It was my view of the world. My frustration with everything. Simple teenage aggression," said Jagger. "It was about America, its advertising syndrome, the constant barrage."

A few days later they began to record the song in the Chess studios in Chicago. These studios had been the home of Muddy Waters, Howlin' Wolf, Willie Dixon and Chuck Berry. For the Stones to record there was akin to a pilgrimage. However, the song wasn't finished until a marathon session at RCA studios in Los Angeles. As Charlie Watts noted, the same studio in which Duke Ellington cut 'Take the "A" Train'.

The song as Richards imagined it had a soul feel with a horn section carrying the riff, which he had sketched using fuzz tone guitar. "When it was by the pool it was a rather lilting acoustic melody," said Jagger. "It only got to the snarl when we got this fuzz box in the studio, which was the first time we'd used one." Producer/manager Andrew Loog Oldham, however, understood the power of the track.

"To my mind," said Richards, "the fuzz tone was really there to denote what the horns would be doing. But Andrew spotted the spirit of the track and we were already back on the road before we heard that they'd decided that 'Satisfaction' was going to be the single. We had thought we were going to cut a better version."

The song is grounded in Chicago blues; the guitar feel is not a million miles from Hubert Sumlin or Jimmy Reed.

Jagger's lyric pulls it all together – sexual frustration, contempt for consumer culture, alienation. He's witty but he also means it. He sings with the beat, improvising lyrics to match Watts' feel, and the staccato lyrics impress the point of the song. The lyric, no matter how appropriate and witty, is just dressing the anti-social attitude. Everything is in the nuance of Jagger's vocal. He sings the song like he really doesn't care about the nine-to-five world that is being marketed to him. That indifference made this the most revolutionary record of the '60s. Their pop comrades the Beatles were part of the machine, manufacturing Beatles wigs and Beatles cartoon shows and Beatles lunchboxes and adding to extraneous crap. Bob Dylan wasn't really on the mainstream radar. Out in the suburbs he was regarded as a poet who couldn't sing. The Rolling Stones, however, couldn't be denied and they didn't give a fuck. The straight world could deal with rock & roll until the Stones announced with this single that they wouldn't be coming to the negotiation table. While all that has changed, the song remains relevant today.

"We were just saying what anybody would say among their own generation," said Richards. "It was the reaction that was interesting: we were shocked to find out they were shocked."

The Tracks of My Tears Smokey Robinson & the Miracles

(Smokey Robinson/Pete Moore/Marv Tarpin) ❊ Tamie ❊ 1965 ❊

Appears on: *Going to a Go Go*

The creation of the Smokey Robinson and the Miracles classic was a long and complex process in which many people – sometimes unwittingly – played a part. The first artist in the chain was Harry Belafonte, whose calypso hit 'The Banana Boat Song' gave Miracle guitarist Marv Tarplin the inspiration for the melody. "It's basically the same changes," said Tarplin, "but at another tempo with another type of feeling."

"Marvin used to come up with lots of licks and melodies and when Smokey and I heard one we liked, we would write a song to it," recalled Pete Moore. "This was a little more difficult than most. We wanted to make sure that the lyrics were real meaningful."

According to Robinson, he had a flash of inspiration one Friday afternoon. "No-one had ever said 'tracks of my tears'. The whole thought of tears was that you could wipe them away so no-one could tell you'd been crying," he told Motown historian Nelson George. "To say that I can't even wipe them away because they've left these tracks, y'know? I thought that was a good idea."

Most of the lyric came from Robinson with some key couplets from Moore. Then Motown managing director Berry Gordy added his view on extending the refrain at the end to create maximum intensity.

The recording went smoothly once the basic issues had been sorted out. Most of all there is the gossamer sweet vocal from Smokey Robinson that floats above the groove.

"There was just something about it that people loved," said Moore. "It had some underlying feel which really tapped into the depth of their emotions. Every time we sang that song people in the audience would cry."

Strychnine The Sonics

(Gerry Roslie) ❊ Norton ❊ 1965 ❊ Appears on: *Here are the Sonics!!!*

"A lot of groups at that time were more into the love songs and pretty notes and we were more into the energy," said guitarist Larry Parypa. "If our records sound distorted, it's because they are," added bass player Andy Parypa. "My brother [Larry] was always fooling around with the amps. They were always overdriven. Or he was disconnecting the speakers and poking a hole in them with an ice pick. That's how we ended up sounding like a train wreck."

The rock scene around Seattle in the mid-'60s was very vibrant and arguably the Sonics ruled. Gerry Roslie's powerful expressive voice and the wild attitude of the band made them into a more viscious version of the Rolling Stones. They had a couple of Stones classics such as 'The Witch', 'Have Love Will Travel' and 'Strychnine'. The last track, recorded live in the studio, has the perfect balance between psychedelic guitar playing and the hard, driving Rolling Stones feel. 'Strychnine' also swings, and the lyric is agreeably tongue in cheek. "We were nasty," said Larry Parypa. "Everything you've heard people say about us is true."

Uptight (Everything's Alright) Stevie Wonder

(Henry Cosby/Sylvia Moy/Stevie Wonder) ✳ Motown ✳ 1965 ✳
Appears on: *Hitsville US*

At the tender age of fifteen it looked like Stevie Wonder was washed up. The child star's voice had broken and his recent records hadn't cracked the Top 20. It was time for Little Stevie Wonder to grow up. He came up with a hook and his producer Clarence Paul brought in Motown writers Sylvia Moy and Henry Cosby to write a song. Wonder earned his first songwriting credit on the track. His other input came from suggesting a more aggressive push in the rhythm department. He had been touring with the Rolling Stones and was impressed with the jazzy propulsion coming from Charlie Watts' drum kit. Consequently 'Uptight' positively bounces out of the blocks. It's way the most interesting thing that Wonder had done to this point and its tempo and changes were getting towards the blues – much tougher than the usual Motown sound. 'Uptight' put Stevie Wonder at the top of the R&B charts and assured his place in Hitsville.

Stop in the Name of Love The Supremes

(Brian Holland/Lamont Dozier/Eddie Holland) ✳ Motown ✳ 1965 ✳
Appears on: *More Hits by the Supremes*

For three years in the mid-'60s, the Supremes defined the evolving face of American womanhood, from doe-eyed innocent to streetwise sister. They did it with fifteen sweet, sassy soul singles of which ten reached number one.

This song was inspired by a disagreement between one of the songwriters, Lamont Dozier, and his girlfriend. The argument reached fever pitch when one of them shouted, "Stop, in the name of love!," and they both dissolved in laughter at the absurdity of the line.

On first listening, Diana Ross and her soul sisters, Mary Wilson and Florence Ballard, thought the song insufficiently feminine, too forthright. Once in the studio, however, they had a lot of fun with it and later developed the song's trademark choreography with the help of the Temptations on the Motown Revue British tour of 1965.

The record's rich, dynamic sound was created by producers Brian Holland and Lamont Dozier and the incomparable Motown session band. Three guitars (played by Robert White, Eddie Willis and Joe Messina) were layered to fatten the rhythm, whose foundation was laid by James Jamerson on bass and Benny Benjamin on drums. Two keyboardists (Earl Van Dyke and Johnny Griffith) were enlisted, while James Gittens' vibes and Mike Terry's bold baritone sax set the song apart.

When the record was finished, the producers called a bunch of other acts into the studio to hear it. "Motown was like a small community," Mary Wilson told *Rolling Stone*. "You'd have Marvin Gaye, the Temps, the Supremes, the Marvelettes, all in the studio listening. Then we'd take the records home and pass them out around the projects."

I Can't Explain The Who

(Pete Townshend) ✳ Brunswick ✳ 1965 ✳ Appears on: *Meaty, Beaty, Big and Bouncy*

When the Who went into the studio to cut this track in late 1964 they were a mod R&B combo from Shepherd's Bush with one failed single under their belt. There was so little expected from the group that producer Shel Talmy had booked guitarist Jimmy Page for the session to cover for Pete Townshend, and girl group the Ivy League to cover difficulties with the vocals. At the end of the two hours it took to cut two sides, the Who emerged with a unique, explosive sound and a songwriter who would change the course of rock & roll a few times.

Talmy had produced the Kinks, London's other major group, and aspired, as did the Who, to make a record that sounded like the Kinks.

"Well, Shel Talmy didn't think that Pete's lead guitar playing was up to it and he didn't think our backing vocals were up to it," recalled singer Roger Daltrey. "He was right about the backing vocals. And obviously in those days you weren't in overdub facilities. You made the record and that was it. So if you wanted to put a solo on you had to do it when you were doing the record." (Page plays rhythm guitar on the track and lead on the flipside, Talmy's tune 'Bald-Headed Woman'.)

"There is little to say about how I wrote this," Townshend wrote in 1971. "It came out of the top of my head when I was eighteen-and-a-half. It seems to be about the frustrations of a young person who is so incoherent and uneducated that he can't state his case to the bourgeoisie intellectual blah blah blah. Or, of course, it might be about drugs."

My Generation The Who

(Pete Townshend) ✳ Brunswick ✳ 1965 ✳ Appears on: *The Who Sings My Generation*

The demo tape of 'My Generation' sounded like "Jimmy Reed at ten years old suffering from nervous indigestion," according to Pete Townshend, its author.

The song has since become an anthem for several generations. Nothing expresses the urgency and passion of youth better than the line "Hope I die before I get old". Townshend recalls the song's beginnings as being somewhat more prosaic. It was, he has written, a slow blues that appeared when he mucked around with his new tape machines.

In 1971 he wrote, "I had written the lines of 'Generation' without thinking, hurrying them, scribbling on a piece of paper in the back of a car. For years I've had to live by them, waiting for the day someone says, 'I thought you said you hoped you'd die when you got old in that song. Well, you are old. What now?' Of course most people are too polite to say that sort of thing to a dying pop star. I say it often to myself."

The Who's managers Chris Stamp and Kit Lambert immediately recognised the brilliance of this song, which so perfectly captured the generation gap. In the hands of a group with the anarchic mindset of the Who, 'My Generation' was a monster.

Having penned the anthem, Townshend had made himself the spokesman for his generation. He needed to articulate the meaning of the song. It has variously been described as representing the mods in particular and the hippies in general; sometimes he talks about how the song relates to his relationship with Roger Daltrey. The reality is that Townshend tapped into the Zeitgeist and his interpretation of the song (and, indeed, the public's) represents his position at any particular point in time. In 1977 when punk rock was sweeping the Who's generation from history, the song was without irony adopted by the punk rockers. If the '60s generation wish to remember the joys of their youth, 'My Generation' is a touchstone for them.

Like most Who sessions, this one with producer Shel Talmy was quick. "Well, for the *My Generation* album, there was nothing to be nervous about in them days," Daltrey told *Goldmine* magazine. "We used to take every day as it came. Every day was just a gig and I think we did the recording between gigs literally. We did the whole album in two afternoons and by the end of the week we were playing the stuff on stage."

Talmy, who also produced the Kinks, was not averse to keeping some of the Who's rough edges. He cut the song in two takes on 13 October 1965. It was on the street three weeks later. Townshend's guitar feeds back and becomes a feature of the song. Roger Daltrey famously sings with a speech impediment and that too becomes a feature. "Kit Lambert [manager] came up to me and said, 'Stutter the words – it makes it sound like you're pilled.'"

Then there is the group's ensemble playing – Keith Moon ignites the session with a frenetic figure on the drums that the rest of the group race to catch. This is not a groove song; it's like the rush of history and you're swept up in its wake. The feedback, the fumbling for words (which promise they're going to be obscene), the manic rhythm section, the ascending key changes, create an atmosphere of chaos and disorder and that's the revolutionary meaning behind the song.

"It's a fucking great record," said Daltrey. "It really is."

You're Gonna Miss Me The 13th Floor Elevators

(Roky Erickson) ✻ International Artists ✻ 1966 ✻

Appears on: *The Psychedelic Sounds of the 13th Floor Elevators*

Of all the groups of the garage punk era, the Elevators were the most timeless. They matched the Rolling Stones for inventive, hard, guitar-based R&B. Their songs such as 'You're Gonna Miss Me' and 'Fire Engine' prefigured the New Wave by more than a decade. Driving, angry and impassioned, the Elevators had an attitude and a sophistication that put them way ahead of their contemporaries. This wasn't long, meandering improvisation, nor was it filled with the wonder of the universe. The Elevators had a different acid rock trip – it was hypnotic and deranged and dirty. It was the other side of acid – when your mind is blown and the wind whistles through the haunted corridors between your ears. Stacey Sutherland's guitar was nasty and often brutal in its riffs while Tommy Hall's electric jug added a particular weirdness. The key was Roky Erickson's vocals – big and rich and theatrical.

What cut the Elevators' career short was the same thing that lengthened their legend. Roky was known as a man who took the acid in acid rock seriously – at every level. According to the legend he took hundreds of psychedelic trips and eventually fried his brains. When he was arrested for marijuana possession in 1969, he pleaded insanity and spent three years in a mental hospital. Some say that it was the acid, some say it was the incarceration but, whatever the cause, Roky never made much sense again.

Be all that as it may, this debut from the Elevators lives up to its title and may be the definitive garage punk album of all time. 'You're Gonna Miss Me' was the enduring punk pop classic where the three-chord pyramid of rock & roll met the third eye in the centre of Roky's troubled head.

Got to Get You Into My Life The Beatles

(John Lennon/Paul McCartney) ❋ Parlophone ❋ 1966 ❋ Appears on: *Revolver*

The Beatles' studio innovations weren't always about acid rock gimmicks. As the group were getting more spacey, McCartney pulled out this gem – a homage to soul music that was every bit as powerful as anything coming out of Detroit, the home of Motown, at the time.

According to engineer Geoff Emerick, "I was getting frustrated listening to American records like the Motown stuff because the bass content was a lot stronger than we were putting on our records. We were governed by certain rules and regulations at Abbey Road, so I could never get the sound I really wanted. So in desperation one day I figured that we could use a loudspeaker as a microphone – it works the same way in reverse, so it's effectively the same thing. That way the speaker could take the weight of the air vibrations from a bass. There was also a woollen sweater with four necks that they had received from a fan – they wore it on one of their Christmas shows. It was around the studio, so I stuffed it into the bass drum to deaden the sound. And I moved the bass drum microphone very close to the drum itself, which wasn't really considered the thing to do at that time."

McCartney allegedly claimed that the song was inspired by marijuana and referred to it as "an ode to pot, like someone else might write an ode to chocolate or a good claret".

The main thing here is the sheer size of the song. "You listen to early Beatles mixes and the bass and bass drum aren't there at all," said McCartney. "We were starting to take over ourselves and bass was coming to the fore in many ways ... I was listening to a lot of Motown, Marvin Gaye and Stax stuff, who were putting some nice little bass lines in."

Rain The Beatles

(John Lennon/Paul McCartney) ❊ Parlophone ❊ 1966 ❊ Appears on: *Hey Jude*

Decidedly psychedelic, 'Rain' is a gentle, lazy observation of the outside world that is one of John Lennon's most interesting songs. The track has entered history as the first use of backward tape. Lennon claimed that he discovered the technique while fooling around at home, although Beatles' producer George Martin also takes credit. In those days music was recorded onto magnetic tape, which ran through "heads" on the console. Obviously, spooling the tape in reverse gives a completely different sound. It was a popular technique as the Beatles continued to use it up until the *White* album. Ringo was particularly happy with his drum part. Lennon's vocals were recorded slow and then speeded up to give the melody an extra trippy feel. Backward vocals tagged onto the back of tracks eventually became de rigueur with death metal bands.

'Rain' and the *Revolver* album, which followed, were high points for the Beatles' sonic experiments. Twisting sounds soon became pretentious, gimmicky and meaningless. However, here they are at the top of their form.

She Said She Said The Beatles

(John Lennon/Paul McCartney) ❊ Parlophone ❊ 1966 ❊ Appears on: *Revolver*

If ever there was acid rock this is it. The song was inspired by Lennon and Harrison tripping on LSD with actor Peter Fonda and the Byrds in Los Angeles in 1965. "I remember sitting on the deck of the house with George, who was telling me that he thought he was dying," Fonda recalled. "I told him there was nothing to be afraid of and that all he needed to do was to relax. I said that I knew what it was like to be dead because when I was ten years old, I'd accidentally shot myself in the stomach and my heart stopped beating three times because I lost so much blood. John was passing at the time and heard me say 'I know what it's like to be dead.' He looked at me and said, 'You're making me feel like I've never been born. Who put all that shit in your head?'"

Fonda actually reprised the scene and some of the dialogue for the acid sequence in his film *Easy Rider*.

When it came to recording the track, the Beatles, George Martin and engineer Geoff Emerick threw all their ingenuity into it to capture the spacey, brittle and a touch nasty edge of the song.

"John brought it into the studio pretty much finished," McCartney said. "I'm not sure, but I think it's one of the only Beatles records that I never played on. I think we'd had a barney, or something, and I said, 'Oh, fuck you!' and they said, 'We'll do it.' I think George played bass."

One of the earliest takes has the lines: "Who put all that crap in your head?/You know what it's like to be dead/And it's making me feel like my trousers are torn."

Taxman The Beatles

(George Harrison) ✳ Parlophone ✳ 1966 ✳ Appears on: *Revolver*

Harrison wrote in his autobiography, "'Taxman' was when I realised that even though we had started earning money, we were actually giving most of it away in taxes." The song is not entirely serious, with delightful backing vocals name-checking Mr Wilson and Mr Heath (the leaders of the Labour and Tory parties at the time). It was clearly a subject dear to the Beatles' hearts given that they were paying up to 90 per cent of their earnings to the internal revenue.

'Taxman' opens *Revolver*, the Beatles' most mature and complex to date, and arguably their best overall disc. (Starr suggested the album be titled *After Geography* because the latest Rolling Stones album was called *Aftermath*.) Harrison has a killer riff here – played by Paul McCartney – over a tough soul rhythm pattern, and the record has a live feel that would soon disappear from the Beatles. Perhaps not Harrison's most enduring lyric, but the riff certainly is durable – the Jam copped it wholesale fifteen years later.

Spicks & Specks The Bee Gees

(Barry Gibb) ✳ Spin ✳ 1966 ✳ Appears on: *Monday's Rain*

The Gibb family migrated from Manchester to Australia in 1958, settling in Brisbane. Hughie Gibb was a sometime musician. His three sons took to performing and were discovered singing at a local Brisbane car racing event. They were soon in Sydney appearing on TV. While still a teenager, Barry Gibb was writing songs for other singers and the Bee Gees were themselves recording artists, although not making much headway in the charts.

Nat Kipner is an American record producer and songwriter who worked with the Bee Gees in a shed-cum-studio in the Sydney suburb of Hurstville.

The studio was owned by Ossie Byrne and the Bee Gees spent a lot of time there working on material.

While cutting a track for another singer, Maurice Gibb started vamping out a chord progression that caught Barry Gibb's ear and in less than twenty minutes he had written a song based on it.

'Spicks & Specks' is a monumental ballad. The Gibb voices climb above a menacing, dramatic piano figure that is coloured by a simple horn line. It was here that Gibb had found the Bee Gees' forte – the desperate love song with heartbreaking male harmonies. 'Spicks & Specks' has a piano part that is so rigid in its insistent rhythm that you can't help but feel the force of desire and then the vocals on top bring home the turmoil.

With 'Spicks & Specks' finally breaking the Australian charts, the Bee Gees were ready to board the *Fairsky* and return to England and thence conquer the world.

Ballad of a Thin Man Bob Dylan

(Bob Dylan) ❋ Columbia ❋ 1998 ❋ Appears on: *Live 1966*

My brother used to tell me stories of seeing Bob Dylan at the Sydney Stadium in 1966, and how on that night the singer was so stoned that he had to be led to the microphone by a roadie. There, in a battered old boxing shed with a creaky revolving stage, Dylan played a set of songs accompanied only by his acoustic guitar. Then, after intermission, he resumed with his backing band. My cousin Robyn's memory of the night was that she slept through most of it and was rudely woken by the raucous noise of the backing band. Or perhaps it was the sound of the folkies jeering the electric music. Whatever, Dylan's 1965–66 tour was a pivotal moment in history: the point where the pop phenomenon of the Beatles met academic literary tradition and suddenly the beat had a meaning and vice versa.

This tour was the culmination of an eighteen-month burst of creativity in which Dylan recorded three albums, each a masterpiece and each a departure from the last. For those years he lived on cigarettes, coffee and amphetamines. Those albums notwithstanding, it was the live performances that defined the future sound of rock & roll.

When Dylan first went electric at the Newport Folk Festival and then shortly thereafter at a concert in New Jersey, it's said that there were howls of abuse. When plugging in his Fender Telecaster, Dylan drew a generational line in the sand. Any criticism from the guardians of good taste only encouraged him.

In a moment of pure serendipity, Dylan was introduced to a Canadian bar band, the Hawks, who had never heard of him. According to guitarist Robbie Robertson, "We met Bob and he said he was playing the Hollywood Bowl, would we like to play? And we said when and he said 'Saturday'".

The relationship continued, although without drummer Levon Helm who couldn't take the constant booing of the audiences and was replaced by session drummer Mickey Jones. Dylan's advice to the band when faced with boos from the audience was "play louder". He said he was looking for "that wild mercury sound". Robertson described the music as simply "violent".

The 1966 tour ended at London's Royal Albert Hall. A tape of a concert at Manchester's Free Trade Hall two nights previously was illegally pressed and distributed as 'Live at the Royal Albert Hall', one of the first rock bootlegs. Dylan has restored and remastered those tapes as the complete concert, dubbed simply *Live 1966*. Even better than the bootleg versions, *Live 1966* captures Dylan standing on the ledge of creative brilliance, the energy of his revolution pumping through his veins.

On the first, acoustic disc, there is so much clarity that you can hear his every breath. Dylan's singing has rarely sounded so strong. 'Fourth Time Around', 'Visions of Johanna', 'Just Like a Woman' and 'Mr Tambourine Man' roll around in his mouth like perfect luscious cherries. You can almost touch the fast ladies in the museum, feel the death squad's hand on the back of your neck or taste the contempt and sadness that Dylan felt as she broke just like a little girl. As the first disc closes Dylan plays his harmonica in an extended reverie as though he has really gone tripping to the skipping reels of time.

The second record in the set is rock & roll at its most raw. Robbie Roberston's guitar lines burst out like machine gun fire as he embellishes the lyric. Meanwhile the rhythm section and organ swirl around, sometimes elegiac and other times sleazy. Against the force of the music, Dylan sings the songs of a man out on the edge: "When your gravity fails and negativity won't pull you through/Don't put on any airs when you're down on Rue Morgue Avenue". He may well be on the brink of insanity, but the words just pour forth.

The songs themselves are full of spite toward ex-lovers or in the case of 'Like a Rolling Stone', 'Ballad of a Thin Man' and 'Leopard Skin Pill Box Hat', toward a society just then emerging. The contempt in his lyric is softened in the studio but out in front of the raging band it's venomous. 'Ballad of a Thin Man', a diatribe against the media in particular, and an older generation that can't sense the changes in the world, is like a thunderstorm, a warning for the darkness that was to come in the latter half of the century.

A matter of days after this concert Dylan retreated from the world. Rumours of a motorcycle accident masked what was essentially rehab. His backing group became the Band and earned their own place in history and Dylan continued to make groundbreaking music. But no-one ever again tore the world of music apart.

Just Like a Woman   Bob Dylan

(Bob Dylan) ❋ Columbia ❋ 1966 ❋ Appears on: *Blonde on Blonde*

Dylan claims the he wrote this song in Kansas City one Thanksgiving. The *Blonde on Blonde* album was a cycle of songs mostly about the changes that were happening in Dylan's life. He was cleaning house – saying farewell to old lovers and celebrating his new marriage. 'Just like a Woman' falls into the former category. There has been much speculation about which ex-lover Dylan addressed with this song – Joan Baez perhaps, although its been suggested that Warhol starlet Edie Sedgwick can be seen here (the line "With her Fog,
her amphetamine, and her pearls" – the Fog being a London Fog raincoat).

Melodically, 'Just Like a Woman' is one of Dylan's finest – the arrangement of the musicians playing against Dylan's syncopated vocal is exceptional. It was on this album that Dylan claimed he reached his ideal sound. "It's that thin, that wild mercury sound. It's metallic and bright and gold, with whatever that conjures up. That's my particular sound," he said in 1978. As with the rest of the album, the musicians are Nashville studio cats plus New Yorker Al Kooper and the songs are cut pretty much live.

'Just like a Woman' caused some controversy on its release. It was attacked as being misogynist, although it's hard to see how. Dylan relished 'Just Like a Woman', especially the way he could play with the words. The version on *The Concert for Bangladesh* is a particularly good example of the elastic phrasing of the words and the way the tune can be teased – the song can be spiteful or compassionate depending on the circumstances of the night.

Sad Eyed Lady of the Lowlands   Bob Dylan

(Bob Dylan) ❋ Columbia ❋ 1966 ❋ Appears on: *Blonde on Blonde*

Well, this is a track that blew everyone's minds. Dylan's double album *Blonde on Blonde* was a big gambit. He had changed the course of music less than two years earlier with *Bringing It All Back Home*, then gone on a blistering world tour and delivered another masterpiece in *Highway 61 Revisited*. The two-record set of which the last entire side was one song of hallucinatory imagery.

We now know, courtesy of Dylan's own pen, that 'Sad Eyed Lady of the Lowlands' was written late at night in the Chelsea Hotel. Its subject is Sara Lowndes, Dylan's future wife. The title suggested as much.

The studio band was called for two in the afternoon on one day but Dylan kept them waiting into the night as he polished the words. By the time he was ready, most of the players were falling asleep. Kooper was on organ, the guitarists were Jerry Kennedy, Charlie McCoy, Wayne Moss and Joe South, the pianist was Hargus 'Pig' Robbins, Henry Strzelecki was on bass and Kenny Buttrey on drums. Dylan began the country waltz in 6/8 time, strumming his acoustic guitar. The verses just kept coming. According to Buttrey, "I was playing left-handed, looking at my watch and it kept on and kept on". There's a halting, lurching quality to the song which may be in part because the band were expecting to reach a crescendo at each verse not realising that there was more to come.

The sheer size of the song (eleven minutes) and the potency of its images piled on each other, images that owed more to Rimbaud than rock & roll, put Dylan in an entirely new class of his own. This was a piece of rock & roll that had never been attempted before or probably since. When finally completed, 'Sad Eyed Lady of the Lowlands' took up one entire side of the album – the longest song yet recorded in popular music.

Visions of Johanna Bob Dylan

(Bob Dylan) ✳ Columbia ✳ 1966 ✳ Appears on: *Blonde on Blonde*

'Visions of Johanna' is one of Bob Dylan's masterpieces. It's mysterious, brimfull of vivid images and ultimately inscrutable. Set in the Chelsea Hotel, it's the late-night musings of a man with one woman in his arms and another on his mind. The song veers from the prosaic ("In this room the heat pipes just cough/The country music station plays soft") to the surreal ("On the back of the fish truck that loads/While my conscience explodes"). All kinds of meaning have been attributed to these abstruse lines – is it about ex-girlfriend Joan Baez, his wife Sara? Is it about God or the Devil? It's unlikely that we will ever know. Trying to decipher the literal meaning of 'Visions of Johanna' is a fruitless task. The meaning is there in the narcotic mood of the music, which is dense and opaque and drifting like smoke. The clanging of the plumbing, the faint hum of the radio and the reflections of the world of straight people going about their lives go on whilst in the night Dylan goes through his sweet turmoil.

Originally titled 'Seems Like a Freeze Out', 'Visions of Johanna' was one of the few songs that had been in Dylan's repertoire before he went to Nashville for the *Blonde on Blonde* sessions. Keyboard player Al Kooper and guitarist Robbie Robertson accompanied Dylan; the other players were all country music sessioneers. It was the highpoint of an amazingly fertile period in Dylan's work, where he refashioned the shape of rock music.

Most of the songs on the album were written in Dylan's Chelsea Hotel period, where he ended his relationship with Joan Baez, hung around the fringes of Warhol's Factory crowd, possibly had a romance with starlet Edie Sedgwick and fell in love with Sara Lowndes, whom he married shortly after. It was also the culmination of a creative surge that took Dylan from the folk scene to the centre of rock & roll music.

The answer to the riddle of Johanna's visions isn't to be found in anything beyond itself.

Season of the Witch Donovan

(Donovan Leitch) ✳ Epic ✳ 1966 ✳ Appears on: *Sunshine Superman*

DA Pennebaker's film *Don't Look Back* captures the meeting between Bob Dylan and Donovan Leitch, whom Dylan reputedly feared to be his English competition. Within a few minutes of first contact, Dylan vanquishes the Brit folkie who never knew quite what hit him. A handy tunesmith with a sweet voice, Donovan was never other than a pop performer.

His early folk pop on *Pye* has some real gems: 'Catch the Wind', 'Colours', 'To Sing for You' and, notably, 'Hey Gyp (Dig the Slowness)', which has been covered formidably by Ed Kuepper, the Animals and others. However, Donovan found his best voice with Mickey Most, England's super-pop producer.

Sunshine Superman was the beginning of the new Donovan and his most consistent album. There's still a strong pulse of British blues in tracks such as 'The Fat Angel' (key line: "Fly Jefferson Airplane, get you there on time"), 'Ferris Wheel' and 'Bert's Blues'. On songs like the title track and the self-explanatory 'The Trip', Donovan brought the Haight Ashbury experience right into your suburban living room. The centrepiece of the album is the spiky, psychedelic 'Season of the Witch', which is both fey and threatening in its ambiguity.

Produced by Mickie Most, the track features future Led Zeppelin bass player John Paul Jones and guitarist Jimmy Page working up a psychedelic storm. It's unclear what the "season of the witch" will bring other than rabbits running in a ditch, but mostly it doesn't sound too good. The song is a vision of the darkness that came with the summer of love – madness, death and degradation – though few saw it at the time.

You Don't Have to Say You Love Me Dusty Springfield

(Giuseppe Donaggio/Simon Napier-Bell/Vito Pallavicini/Vicki Wickham) ❋ Philips ❋ 1966 ❋ Appears on: *Golden Hits*

Dusty Springfield discovered 'Io Che Non Vivo (Senza Te)' at the San Remo Festival. On returning to England she asked Vicki Wickham to write an English lyric. According to Simon Napier-Bell, Wickham and he penned a lyric one evening after dinner. Springfield and her producer Johnny Franz were both a little unsure of the quality of the words but had a shot nevertheless.

"Dusty was insecure about her singing ability," Napier-Bell writes in his memoir *Black Vinyl White Powder*. "When it came to recording she would accept nothing less than perfection and always presumed she could come nowhere near it. The night she recorded our song she complained that the echo on her voice wasn't right. The engineer ran downstairs to the basement to adjust the inputs to the echo chamber. As he did, he noticed how good the echo sounded in the stairwell of the seven-storey circular staircase. Five minutes later, Dusty was halfway up it, singing into a mike hanging in space in front of her. What she sang was one of the great pop performances of all time. Sheer perfection from the first breath to the last."

Springfield's insecurity probably had much to do with the power of this recording. It's a song that carries the entire yearning drama of a person bereft of self-esteem. It's a song of enormous emotional truth just laid bare. Songs like this tend to disappear in their own pathos and kitsch dramatics but Dusty Springfield sings it like a confession and it's impossible to look away from his honesty.

Trouble Comin' Every Day

Frank Zappa & the Mothers of Invention

(Frank Zappa) ❋ MGM/Verve ❋ 1966 ❋ Appears on: *Freak Out!*

Freak Out! is significant as the second rock-era double album and as the only interesting album Frank Zappa ever made.

Zappa grew up in the suburbs of Los Angeles entranced by R&B and doo-wop music, which he understood perfectly. However, Zappa could never trust his love. He also had a hankering for "real" art as expressed by modern classical composers, in particular, Edward Varese. Although he fronted a number of garage bands in the very early '60s, Zappa was never satisfied. He wanted to be taken seriously according to his square definition of what a real composer did. So he tried to marry the two. One can't help suspect that perhaps he wasn't really up to serious composition and that passing ineptitude off as satire was his best option.

Zappa had a gift for controversy. His target was hypocrisy, always an easy mark. His barbs were aimed not only at the Establishment but also at the counter culture – his audience. Zappa's tirades were full of self-righteousness and overbearing egomania. No-one but Zappa followed the one true path.

The cover of *We're Only In It for the Money*, the third Mothers of Invention album, was a grotesque parody of the Beatles, implying that they had sold out and that Zappa (who was much more financially savvy than any of the Fabs) was in it for the art.

Zappa's occasional glimpses of astute satire were outweighed by his lumbering caricatures of social types and an increasing tendency towards scatology.

Over time Zappa's attacks on the hippies smacked of self-loathing and fear. Although he had a curious moustache, Zappa led a very moralistic and straight life. More disturbing, however, was the misogyny that ran through all his work. He was obsessed with ridiculing sexually independent women. The modern composer had the perspective of a redneck who repressed himself because he had to live in the rock & roll world.

Tom Wilson, the producer of Bob Dylan and the Velvet Underground, signed Frank Zappa and the Mothers of Invention to Verve/MGM. (It's notable that the Velvets elegantly played avant-garde rock & roll without having to bang on endlessly about their credentials. Basically, Frank Zappa never did get the point.)

In early 1966 Zappa made *Freak Out!* as an extension of the Mothers' live act – some R&B mixed with dadaist noise experiments that were given obtuse names. Wilson was apparently delighted with the exuberance of it all and blew the budget out to a whopping (in those days) $21,000.

The saving grace of the disc is the dirty garage R&B track 'Trouble Comin' Every Day'. Written in response to the Watts riots that set the Los Angeles ghetto on fire, this is Zappa at his most unselfconscious. The song ranks with 'Satisfaction' as a description of the turmoil of the times and it still resonates now.

In the long run Zappa is known by his disciples – a bunch of nerds, generally without girlfriends, who can spout Zappa lyrics as easily as they recite the scripts of early Monty Python. Zappa will be remembered for discovering Alice Cooper and Captain Beefheart. The former he championed because he thought Alice epitomised all that was terrible with rock & roll – childishness, theatricality and amateurism. Little did Zappa know how great his protégés were. Beefheart, aka Don Van Vliet was a school friend who had a unique take on the blues. He was what Zappa aspired to be – except that Zappa died a very wealthy control freak and Van Vliet lives in a trailer in the desert. Who was only in it for the money?

River Deep, Mountain High Ike & Tina Turner

(Jeff Barry/Ellie Greenwich/Phil Spector) ❋ Phillies/A&M ❋ 1966 ❋
Appears on: River Deep, Mountain High

Phil Spector was in a slump when he signed up Ike and Tina. Ike Turner – one of the most innovative producer/songwriters of the '50s – was in a slump too, and agreed to sit out the sessions which Spector assured him would put Ike and Tina Turner back on top.

The track was from the recently divorced team of Jeff Barry and Ellie Greenwich. "Phil wanted to make this definitive rock & roll anthem symphony," said Greenwich. "What happened was that all of us had individually started different songs. We sat down at the piano and it was, 'What about this? What about that?' And you can hear the different versions."

"I went over to Phil's house," string arranger Jack Nitzsche recalled. "And we went over the arrangement note by note. Phil said, 'I've got a song for Tina.' I knew who she was. I had seen them perform at the California Club. When he played me 'River Deep, Mountain High' on the piano I knew it was great song. We did the rhythm track in two different three-hour sessions."

Spector had worked with the Ike and Tina Turner Revue on a special he produced (the Big TNT Show) and had subsequently bought them out of their old recording deal. Spector's vision was to utilise Tina Turner's explosive sexuality and the power of her delivery in the way that he made ingénues of the Ronettes and the Crystals some years earlier.

The recording took place in Spector's favourite studio, Gold Star. Nitzsche brought Mick Jagger along to watch the proceedings.

Spector built one of his typically epic arrangements for the song: massive walls of pianos and strings and percussion. The song was triumphant in the way that it contrasted the tender verses with the faux naïveté of a girl's rag doll or puppy, with the monumental chorus that featured the full-bodied sensuousness of Turner's vocals.

"I must have sung that 500,000 times," Turner said. "I was drenched with sweat. I had to take my shirt off and stand there in my bra to sing."

"It was amazing to watch 'River Deep' grow," said Nitzsche. "Even during the cutting of the track, when she was putting on a scratch, Tina was singing along as we cut it and was so into it she was holding her crotch on the high notes. Oh, man, she was great, doing a rough, scratch vocal as the musicians really kicked the rhythm section in the ass. Once in a while a vocalist would run through a song, but this time Tina made everybody play better."

Surprisingly, the song was Spector's first real flop, failing to even crack the Top 40 in the US, although it was a hit in Europe and Australia. As a consequence of the record's failure, Spector announced his retirement – from which he was soon coaxed by John Lennon.

"Phil antagonised some people," opined Nitzsche. "He had thirteen hits in a row without a miss. Around 'River Deep, Mountain High', people started to want him to fail. That's how it is with sports and everything. You get too good and people don't like it, too successful and people don't like it.

"I thought 'River Deep, Mountain High' would be the biggest record Phil ever made. I thought it was an obvious number one. I couldn't believe it didn't happen here. I was happy it charted in England. But even before 'River Deep', Phil felt that it was starting to come to a close. The enthusiasm was gone. We had done it so many times. The musicians were changing. It was a combination of things, and it just stopped being so much fun. The Beatles were coming."

"I think when it came out, it was like my farewell," said Spector. "I was just sayin' goodbye, and I just wanted to go crazy for ... four minutes on wax."

The Loved One The Loved Ones

(Ian Clyne/Gerry Humphreys/Rob Lovett) ❋ In ❋ 1966 ❋ Appears on: *Magic Box*

Gerry Humphreys was a true star. His eccentric stage manner and his gorgeous blues voice was the perfect instrument to front a band like the Loved Ones. Half of the group came from the Red Onions Jazz Band and the other half from the R&B garage outfit the Wild Cherries. This supergroup – by the standards of backwater Australian rock in the mid-'60s – played mostly covers until their first recording session, where they worked up a riff by guitarist Rob Lovett that has become one of the few Australian classics from the period. 'The Loved One' has a chord progression that moves inexorably through a simple cycle while Humphries wails over the top in an orgiastic fury supported by a rising intensity in the guitar and organ lines.

Red Onions organist Ian Clyne had a relationship with W&G records that scored him three hours in the studio. The group decided they needed an original song in a hurry and, according to Lovett, he offered a chord progression he had lying around. "Well, I had been playing these three chords, so when Gerry asked if anyone had anything I nervously mentioned it and Ian said, 'Well, how does it go?'" Lovett told journalist Christopher Hollow. "So I played it. I had been interested in the big chord music by the Who's Pete Townshend and when Gerry asked, 'What's the melody?' I mumbled that the idea was that it had 'sort of – you know, no melody ...' To my relief he took this on board, but said he'd need another sequence because there wasn't enough in this one. I think, 'It's a bit boring' was how he, tactfully, put it. So I came up with the second one. 'That's more like it, I can work with that.' Ian came up with the bass line and the lead guitar line. He played guitar as well as piano, in fact he played guitar far better than I did.

"Then Gerry said that it was going along OK but it needed a chorus, a real sing-along, and just wrote down the most obvious lines he could think of. Ian asked how it would go and he sang it while Ian worked out the chords. It still didn't have enough for Ian, and on the night before recording he went to the Winston Charles nightclub and had a long talk to the organist.

"Yeah, the organist said he liked it but he thought we should put some handclaps in so the audience didn't get lost. In those days most people were brought up with 'easy listenin'' music – country and western, very straightforward. In the end, the handclaps were more dominant than the two-beat pattern so the whole thing sounded a bit like a crazy waltz. As it turned out the organist was absolutely right. It would never have made it without his suggestion and the way he played. He really gave it some atmosphere and suspenseful excitement – building up on the first chord sequence till it burst out into the second and Gerry screamed out his, 'Yonder she's walking'.

"It's so crazy. I mean, who says 'yonder' any more? But Gerry was good like that. He didn't give a shit if it made sense as long as it was easy to sing and with his rough voice it didn't sound dorky."

'The Loved One' is one of the few Australian records of the era to remain continuously in print and was recorded by INXS on their second album. English producer Chris Thomas liked the song so much he suggested it be re-recorded for the *Kick* album.

The title of the song was pretty much serendipity, based on the brief fashion for appropriating the titles of classic novels. According to Lovett, "When Lindsay, the engineer, asked what he should write on the tape, we didn't have a title, so he simply wrote on it 'The Loved One', which is the actual name of the Evelyn Waugh book. No-one ever thought to change it."

California Dreamin' The Mamas & the Papas

(John Phillips) ❋ Dunhill ❋ 1966 ❋ Appears on: *If You Can Believe Your Eyes and Ears*

Hal Blaine, who had drummed for every major group in the Los Angeles area in the '60s, described a session with the Mamas & the Papas as like "a visit from the angels". No doubt he was referring to their voices – their personal lives were quite the opposite. Journalist Lillian Roxon wrote in her famous *Encyclopedia*, "The Mamas and the Papas were the royal family of American rock ... because they were the first, with the Spoonful, of the big American groups, the first, that is, since the Beatles."

The Mamas & the Papas were folkies from the early-'60s coffeehouse circuit. Their friends included Roger McGuinn (the Byrds), Barry McGuire, John Sebastian and Zal Yanovsky (the Lovin' Spoonful). Of the four, Cass Elliott and Denny Doherty had the voices, John Phillips wrote the songs and his wife Michelle Phillips looked beautiful.

While scuffling around in the New York winter of 1963, Phillips wrote a song about wishing he were in warmer California. In any event, they took off for the Virgin Islands where they stayed until the credit card was maxed and they wound up in Los Angeles in the office of Lou Adler, who cut the song for Barry McGuire and offered the Mamas & the Papas a deal. "What we really want is a steady flow of money from your office to our house," said Phillips. They then re-did the vocals on McGuire's record with Doherty singing lead. The song was an instant classic.

I'm a Believer The Monkees

(Neil Diamond) ✳ Colgems ✳ 1966 ✳ Appears on: *More of the Monkees*

'I'm a Believer' was the third most popular song of the '60s. It was recorded in October 1966 and a month later was the number one single in the US and became the biggest selling single of 1967.

The key to the Monkees was their connection, through executive producer Don Kirshner, to the Brill Building. This songwriting factory based in New York was under siege once the Beatles broke. Almost overnight the fashion changed towards groups who wrote their own material. The Monkees were a group through whom the Brill Building writers could fight back.

Neil Diamond left school to become a songwriter in the Brill Building tradition. He came under the wing of producer Bert Berns and the production/songwriting duo of Ellie Greenwich and Jeff Barry. His first session with Barry yielded three hit songs, one of which was 'I'm a Believer'. Barry produced the track in New York and then Monkey Mickey Dolenz added his vocal. The song has an amazing garage-rock energy, a touch of the Beatles in the long guitar runs and a touch of the Phil Spector sound in the percussion, the backing vocals and the harmonies. Pop doesn't get any more perfect.

Try a Little Tenderness Otis Redding

(Jimmy Campbell/Reginald Connelly/Harry Woods) ✳ Stax ✳ 1966 ✳
Appears on: *The Very Best of Otis Redding*

"Otis made a better musician out of you," bass player Donald 'Duck' Dunn told Barney Hoskyns. "He just brought out things you didn't know you had in you. You got happier, you felt better, and your hands and fingers moved better. He was a star. He wore the halo. Elvis, Sinatra, the Beatles ... Otis was one of 'em."

Redding was a big man whose voice matched his size. 'Try a Little Tenderness' is his most complex song – emotionally and musically. It goes through a number of changes from supplication to intense passion in about three minutes. Part of the dynamic structure of the song came from drummer Al Jackson switching around the beat. "We didn't know he was gonna do that," said Dunn. "It was amazing."

Where Redding's songs had been powerful soul grooves, 'Tenderness' itches. It's tense and nervous and uncomfortable, starting out as a whisper that's desperate to become a scream. It was originally a hit for Bing Crosby and later for Sam Cooke, but Redding fills up the song and then moves around in there until it's ready to burst at the seams.

'Try a Little Tenderness' was a very mature song for the period and it reflected Redding's own personality.

"His love for people showed up in his songs," guitarist Steve Cropper told *Hit Parader* magazine. "He was always trying to get back to his baby or he missed her – she was the greatest thing in the world. He always had a positive approach. It's hard to convince the public with a negative song, 'You did me wrong.' Otis showed me the best way is to write positive. Otis didn't get to be with his wife and three children as much as he wanted. He had a definite thing for them. Whenever he had time, he'd think about them. He brought his wife and kids to recording sessions quite often."

Mais Que Nada   Sergio Mendes & Brasil '66

(Jorge Ben) ❋ A&M ❋ 1966 ❋ Appears on: *Sergio Mendes & Brasil '66*

Sergio Mendes cut his teeth as a jazz pianist in Brasil working with Antonio Carlos Jobim and João Gilberto pioneering the bossa nova. Mendes was certainly well regarded as an instrumentalist and arranger playing with visiting American jazz masters such as Stan Getz, Dizzy Gillespie, Charlie Byrd and Roy Eldridge. While visiting New York in 1962 he cut an album with Cannonball Adderley. Mendes was astute enough to balance his more adventurous playing with commercial sessions and recordings.

In 1964 he moved to the US and a year later formed his own combo – Brasil '65 which, a year later, became Brasil '66 and came to the attention of trumpeter and impresario Herb Alpert who signed Mendes to his A&M label. Brasil '66 had a string of easy-listening hits, regularly charting in the Top 10 pop charts of the time. Often their hits were bossa nova versions of Beatles' songs and the like but equally they had Latin tunes that found an audience. Mendes ran a tight band of three instrumentalists and two very winsome female vocalists. 'Mais Que Nada' is typical of the supple, swinging ensemble playing with Mendes' witty piano and the breathless voice of Lani Hall bringing the romance of South America into the suburban living room.

"It's good that Brasil '66 has succeeded, because it confirms one's belief that, musically, these are fluid times, with more openings than ever before for contemporary creative endeavour," wrote Derek Taylor in his liner notes to the album. "I cannot see how substantial international achievement can elude this group who have marketed, with considerable taste, a delicately-mixed blend of pianistic jazz, subtle Latin nuances, Lennon-McCartneyisms, some Mancini, here and there a touch of Bacharach, cool, minor chords, danceable up-beat, gentle laughter and a little sex."

Wild Thing The Troggs

(Chip Taylor) ✳ Fontana ✳ 1966 ✳ Appears on: *From Nowhere*

Chip Taylor was a professional songwriter and record producer (and brother to actor Jon Voight) when he knocked off 'Wild Thing' in a 1965 afternoon on assignment for a group named Jordan Christopher and the Wild Ones. He improvised the song and engineer Ron Johnson added the whistling solo. "I was on the floor laughing when I was through," he said. "As soon as I did it I said 'What is this monster?' Because, basically, it was just a guttural expression, some kind of sexual thought."

'Wild Thing' is the foundation stone, the Rosetta Stone and the Magna Carta of rock & roll.

The original recording stiffed, as did a version by British studio outfit Hedgehoppers Anonymous. Then manager/producer Larry Page thought it might be good for the Troggs. Fronted by Reg Presley, the Troggs were considered to be not very bright. However, Presley's limited but powerful voice was perfect for the simple yet powerful song.

"We recorded 'Wild Thing' and 'With a Girl Like You' at the same sessions," said Presley. "And they were recorded really fast because we only had about three-quarters of an hour to get our gear set up, get a balance, do the record and then move out."

Instead of whistling, the Troggs supplemented an ocarina solo. The ocarina is a musical toy mostly used by children and this is its first and only appearance on a number one record. Not only did 'Wild Thing' top the charts, it set the benchmark for perfect raw rock & roll and has never been bettered. In 1966, pop music ventured off into the world of concept albums and art. The Troggs were the conscience of rock & roll. 'Wild Thing' remains a stellar classic now that the Moody Blues and their ilk have, thankfully, vanished.

"It's not like the chords don't sound like a thousand other songs," said Taylor. "But there's something within the simple structure that's magical. It's still inspired, even in its dumbness."

Respect Aretha Franklin

(Otis Redding) ✳ Atlantic ✳ 1967 ✳

Appears on: *I Never Loved a Man the Way I Love You*

On Valentine's Day 1967 Aretha Franklin walked into Atlantic Studios in New York City as a promising singer with six years of unfulfilled promise on her back. She left the room Lady Soul – the absolute queen of pop, the greatest female R&B singer in the history of the world. Her crowning glory was 'Respect'.

Franklin had been signed to Columbia for six years, where she made respectable jazz and R&B sides but failed to set anyone's inspiration alight. Jerry Wexler, house producer at Atlantic, heard the gospel power in Franklin's voice and brought her to Atlantic, where he matched her abilities with the southern sensibility of the Muscle Shoals sidemen – organist Spooner Oldham, guitarist Jimmy Johnson, bass player Tommy Coghill and drummer Roger Hawkins. Wexler and his team of engineer Tom Dowd and arranger/ engineer Arif Mardin had created a particular brand of soul music that was harmonically sophisticated, rhythmically completely perfect and dripping with the sensuousness of R&B and the grandeur of southern gospel.

Franklin's first Atlantic side, 'I Never Loved a Man the Way I Love You', was released in February 1967 and was already on the radio. Wexler knew he was on to something. He had two other singles in hand and towards the end of the 14 February date, they turned their attention to a version of a song that had already been a hit for Otis Redding. "The song lines are great," said Redding of his version. "The band track is beautiful. It took me a whole day to write it and about twenty minutes to arrange it. We cut it once and that was it. Everybody wants respect, you know."

Everybody understood the implication of a black person demanding R-E-S-P-E-C-T in the racially charged climate of the mid-'60s. Aretha understood the repercussions of switching gender on the song. "It could be a racial situation," said Tom Dowd. "It could be a political situation, it could be just the man–woman situation. Anybody could identify with it. It cut a lot of ground. If the issue was universal, it was the particular talent that Franklin brought to the tune."

First of all Aretha sings the hell out of the tune. She's supported by her sisters Carolyn and Erma on those incredible backing vocals that just burn off the track, particularly the "sock-it-to-me" breakdown and the spelling of the title, which lifts the track into a revivalist meeting. The vocal arrangement came from Franklin herself.

According to Wexler, "She had a piano at home and she would sit there with her sisters. I put the song together with the rhythm section, but it wound up being a realisation of an arrangement that already existed in her mind.

"Aretha added another dimension to the song. This was almost a feminist clarion – whenever women heard the record, it was like a tidal wave of unity. 'A little respect when you come home' doesn't only connote respect in the sense of having concern for another's position; there's also a little lubricity in there – respect acquires the notion of being able to perform conjugally in optimum fashion. It was just a very interesting mix: an intuitive feminist outcry. A sexual statement and an announcement of dignity. And a minority person making a statement of pride without sloganeering."

The production and the playing on the track is perfect, from the opening sound of the call and response between King Curtis' sax and Johnny Johnson's guitar with the drum beat skipping across the top like a stone on a pond. The track jumps from the start and just builds from there with Aretha's piano and the backing voices. Wexler added an instrumental bridge by using a riff from 'When Something is Wrong with My Baby' and inserting it. Everything is perfectly judged. But nothing sounds laboured or sterile.

Wexler played the finished track to Otis Redding. "He looked at me with a big grin and said, 'That girl done stole my song.'"

A Day in the Life The Beatles

(John Lennon/Paul McCartney) ✳ Parlophone ✳ 1967 ✳
Appears on: *Sgt. Pepper's Lonely Hearts Club Band*

This was one of the pivotal moments in 20th-century music. The Beatles incorporated bits of poetry and puerile lyrics with techniques of randomness, modern atonal orchestration, and then at the end of it all a death-like falling tone. It's all there in a magnificent soundscape. The *Sgt. Pepper* album was a watershed in music when it was released, but it was this last track that was shocking. The Beatles had certainly used complex orchestration but never with such conceptual breadth and not usually with such a morbid theme. What could have sounded kitsch still sounds startling.

The song began with two fragments – one is Paul McCartney's story of an ordinary day, based he said on his schooldays. The other is Lennon's random collection of thoughts, mostly taken from newspaper stories, his recent film role in *How I Won the War*, and the death of a friend, Tara Browne. The Beatles and producer George Martin stuck these two unrelated ideas together. The song doesn't resemble any pop music, as it had been known, with its shifting tempos and moods and its gradual increase in intensity and momentum until the final release at the end of the piece.

The crucial element to the success of the whole venture is Martin's scoring.

In the initial recording the instrumental sections were left open to be recorded later. The end of one of these sections was marked with an alarm clock, the sound from which was eventually left in.

Eventually the orchestra was added, in costume as it happened.

"What I did there was to write, at the beginning of the twenty-four bars, the lowest possible note for each of the instruments in the orchestra," the producer said. "At the end of the twenty-four bars, I wrote the highest note each instrument could reach that was near a chord of E major. Then I put a squiggly line right through the twenty-four bars, with reference points to tell them roughly what note they should have reached during each bar ... Of course, they all looked at me as though I were completely mad.

"Come the night, I discovered that they'd also invited along all of their way-out friends, like Mick Jagger, Marianne Faithfull, and Simon and Marijke, the psychedelic artists who were running the Apple Shop in Baker Street. They were wandering in and out of the orchestra, passing out sparklers and joints and God knows what, and on top of that they had brought along a mass of party novelties. When I came back into the studio the sight was unbelievable. The orchestra leader, David McCallum, who used to be the leader of the Royal Philharmonic, was sitting there in a bright red false nose. He looked up at me through paper glasses!"

Lennon, McCartney, Starr, Martin and Mal Evans banging simultaneously on three pianos and holding the note for fifty-three seconds did the final piano chord.

Lennon's summation: "I thought it was a damn good piece of work."

I Am the Walrus The Beatles

(John Lennon/Paul McCartney) ✲ Apple ✲ 1967 ✲ Appears on: *Magical Mystery Tour*

The fact that most of 'I Am the Walrus' was written while John Lennon was on acid should come as no surprise. The fact that it is utter nonsense enhances rather than detracts from it as one of the Beatles' more interesting songs.

"The first line was written on one acid trip one weekend. The second line was written on the next acid trip the next weekend, and it was filled in after I met Yoko," Lennon said in 1980. "Part of it was putting down Hare

Krishna. All these people were going on about Hare Krishna, Allen Ginsberg in particular. The reference to 'Element'ry penguin' is the elementary, naïve attitude of going around chanting, 'Hare Krishna', or putting all your faith in any one idol. I was writing obscurely, a la Dylan, in those days."

According to Lennon's school friend Pete Shotton, much of the more nonsensical lyrics were prompted by a fan letter.

"I just dipped into a sack," Shotton said, "and pulled out a letter that happened to be from our old school, from a pupil at Quarry Bank. He said his English teacher was getting them to read and analyse Beatles lyrics, find out hidden meanings, what they were really all about. This got John off remembering lines we used to recite when we were at school."

This was the poem – "Yellow matter custard, green slop pie/All mixed together with a dead dog's eye/Slap it on a butty, 10 ft thick/Then wash it all down with a cup of cold sick."

Lennon riffed on those ideas and some other free association. The walrus section simply came from the Lewis Carroll verse 'The Walrus and the Carpenter'. Lennon later noted that on rereading the poem it occurred to him that, in fact, it was the Carpenter who was the hero but it was too late for him to change it.

The first fragment of the tune comes from a police siren that passed his window. The second fragment relates to "sitting in a country garden", and the third is more offbeat to match the surreal lyric. George Martin welded these ideas together masterfully, adding a cheesy singing group and allowing the sound of a BBC production of *King Lear* to bleed into it.

The free associations of lyric, tune and sound effects work together to make their own kind of logic. Then there is the finale where Lennon declares himself "the eggman, coo coo ca choo". It's worth remembering that Martin's claim to fame before he produced the Beatles was as producer of the Goons and Peter Sellers. This piece of English absurdism fits into that tradition. It's also worth noting that for all the nonsense, 'I Am the Walrus' became one of the Beatles' most popular songs and has well outlasted the putative A-side 'Hello Goodbye'.

"It actually was fantastic in stereo," said Lennon. "But you never hear it all."

Strawberry Fields Forever The Beatles

(John Lennon/Paul McCartney) ❋ Parlophone ❋ 1967 ❋
Appears on: *The Beatles 1967–1970*

The real Strawberry Field was a Salvation Army orphanage near Lennon's childhood home in Menlove Avenue, Liverpool. As a child he played in the extensive grounds of the large Victorian building. Its almost Gothic design and large grounds were otherworldly for an imaginative child like Lennon.

While in Spain filming *How I Won the War*, Lennon started a song reminiscing about his childhood and innocence. He was now one of the most famous people on the planet and perhaps he missed those innocent days. The song started out as melancholy blues but was gradually transformed into the most complex pop song of its time.

The first few run-throughs, featuring extensive use of the Mellotron, failed to yield the song that Lennon heard in his head. It's worth noting that he was using a lot of drugs at this point, especially hallucinogens.

According to George Martin, "Before the very first recording of 'Strawberry Fields Forever' John stood opposite me in the studio and played me the song on his acoustic guitar and it was absolutely wonderful. Then when we actually taped it with the usual instruments it started to get a bit heavy. John didn't say anything but I knew it wasn't what he had originally wanted. So I wasn't totally surprised when he came back to me a week or so later and suggested we have another go at recording it, perhaps even bringing in some outside musicians. Together we worked out that I should score the song for trumpets and cellos."

The Beatles kept at the song, keeping versions as they went.

In early December they were back in the studio with only engineer Dave Harries on deck. "We recorded Ringo's cymbals, played them backwards. Paul and George were on timpani and bongos, Mal Evans played tambourine, and we overdubbed the guitars."

According to Mark Lewishon's book on the Beatles' sessions, George Martin and engineer Geoff Emerick returned later that night and edited together the first three-quarters of take fifteen with the last quarter of take twenty-four and mixed it to become take twenty-five.

In 1966 recording studios only had four tracks on which to record so parts were progressively mixed or bounced down to one track to leave space for further overdubs.

Percussion, including backward cymbals and an Indian instrument called a swordmandel, cellos and trumpets were added. The song was now a cacophony of edgy strings and winds with a thick, heavy percussion on the bottom end and a tense, speedy feel.

Lennon then added his lyrics. What was a reverie about innocence had become a questioning of existence and reality. If that wasn't enough, he added random phrases like "cranberry sauce," which was misheard as "I buried Paul".

After a month of recording, Lennon was still not happy. "John told me he liked both versions of 'Strawberry Fields Forever', the original, lighter version and the more intense, scored version," Martin recalled. "He said to me, 'Why don't you join the beginning of the first one to the end of the second one?' I told him that there were two problems. One was that they were both in completely different keys and two was that they were both running at different tempos. He said, 'Well you can fix it.'"

Martin sped up the first section and slowed down the second to compensate for the difference in keys and then decreased the pitch of the first version at the join, sixty seconds into the song.

'Strawberry Fields' was released as a single with McCartney's ode to his Liverpool childhood, 'Penny Lane', on the other A-side. The disc demonstrated the divergence that was happening in the Beatles. Lennon's track is still a benchmark in pop history.

Within You Without You The Beatles

(George Harrison) ✳ Parlophone ✳ 1967 ✳
Appears on: Sgt. Pepper's Lonely Hearts Club Band

The Beatles' concept album has attracted way more attention and been given far more artistic baggage than the disc can carry. The Beatles were obviously taking their work to a new level. Hailed as a concept record, there is no discernible theme – musical or lyrical – through the songs. By Beatles' standards they're not particularly good songs at that. The production techniques were interesting. The artwork was unusual and the album was a phenomenon. It's now almost fifty years since Sgt Pepper taught the band to play and pretty much only three of the tunes have lasted, Harrison's 'Within You Without You' being one. Where 'A Day in the Life' deconstructed pop, 'Within You Without You' really opened pop up to ethnic influence in a whole new way. Not only were the Beatles using non-Western instruments, they were doing it in conjunction with non-Western spirituality.

The impact of George Harrison's interest in the East cannot be overstated. When he became interested in the Maharishi and then Hindu mysticism, the world followed. After George the world suddenly had heard of Krishna. The influence in the West of transcendental meditation and meditation in general, the Hare Krishnas, the Orange People, the gurus Muktananda and Maharaji is a direct result of Harrison. India suddenly became hip. The hippy highway from London to Kathmandu was open for business and all things Indian were popular.

Harrison came to mysticism by way of music. In August 1965, David Crosby, then with the Byrds, introduced Harrison to the music of sitar virtuoso Ravi Shankar. He was immediately intrigued and by December that year was adding sitar licks to the *Rubber Soul* album. Six months later he met Shankar and went to India for six weeks of intensive study.

This song was written early the following year. According to writer David Fricke, Harrison was at Klaus Voorman's house for dinner when the first line came to him: "We were talking – about the space between us all." Voorman, a friend of the Beatles since the Hamburg days, had a new harmonium and Harrison was "doodling on it, playing to amuse myself when 'Within You' started to come."

The lyric reads on the one hand as an interpretation of Hindu notions of being and nothingness, but on the other it also sounds like a song about estrangement from the Beatles. None of the other Beatles appear on the track – an Indian ensemble, an orchestra and Beatles' confidant Neil Aspinall accompany Harrison.

'Within You Without You' stuck out amongst the novelty tracks but it was also the first time that what would be called world music was thrust into the mainstream. It has lasted much better than 'Being for the Benefit of Mr Kite'.

"It was an interesting song," said George Martin. "I find it more interesting now than I did then."

To Love Somebody The Bee Gees

(Barry Gibb/Robin Gibb) ✳ NEMS/Atco ✳ 1967 ✳ Appears on: *Bee Gees 1st*

By the time the Bee Gees arrived in London in 1967, they had been professional entertainers for almost ten years – and none of them had reached twenty-one. The Bee Gees had the good fortune to have Australian expatriate impresario Robert Stigwood as their major fan. Stigwood had taken over Brian Epstein's empire (except for the Beatles) and saw limitless potential in the three Gibb Brothers. Stigwood signed them to NEMS and Atlantic.

The Bee Gees recorded their first album between 7 March and 21 April 1967. Their first single was the unlikely named 'New York Mining Disaster 1941 (Have You Seen My Wife Mr Jones?)', which was a sizeable hit in the US and the UK.

The next single from the album was not a hit. 'To Love Somebody' was written that March, not for the Bee Gees but for Otis Redding.

"Robert Stigwood had brought me to New York," Barry Gibb recalled. "I'd never been to New York before so it was a great thrill for me. I met Otis Redding early in the evening and Robert Stigwood had sort of suggested I write a song for Otis Redding, and I said I would try. I was inspired because I had just met him. That first flash you get – you meet somebody like that who you really admire and something happens. The rest of the evening I was alone and I sort of concocted most of it in that time. But the song was finished with Robin and Maurice."

Despite its unexpected failure as a single for the Bee Gees, 'To Love Somebody' has been wonderfully covered by the Flying Burrito Brothers, Janis Joplin and best of all by Nina Simone, who smoulders through a soul reading of the tune.

All Along the Watchtower Bob Dylan

(Bob Dylan) ❊ Columbia ❊ 1967 ❊ Appears on: *John Wesley Harding*

At a time when the Beatles were at their most baroque and the world was going psychedelic with the opportunities offered by new recording studios, Bob Dylan recorded his album *John Wesley Harding* accompanied only by a bass player and drummer with pedal steel on two other tracks. It was a complete about-face. For some months Dylan had been recording demo tapes with the Hawks. Over a hundred songs had been written. Dylan went to Nashville, however, to cut his new album and used none of them.

John Wesley Harding is full of ancient images from the Wild West and the Bible. The characters in these songs deal with eternal truths, in oblique ways.

'All Along the Watchtower' is an apocalyptic song set in a mythical landscape of castles and horsemen and strange portents. It's a song with images that don't lend themselves to a literal reading. The vampiric businessmen probably refers to manager Albert Grossman whom Dylan felt was exploiting him. The sense of paranoia probably comes from the hordes of hippies who besieged Dylan's property at this time. There was a sense that this generation of freaks and hippies and dropouts was leading somewhere and the most prescient commentators such as Joan Didion had started to speculate about the dark side of the social anarchy of the '60s.

Despite its obscure imagery, 'All Along the Watchtower' was a song that spoke to its time. The song's biggest fan was guitarist Jimi Hendrix who, upon hearing it, booked a studio with his band the Experience and guitarist Dave Mason and cut a version on the spot. Hendrix rearranged the tune and added his own tempestuous guitar lines – swirling around like the gathering storm. Hendrix had a major hit with the song. Dylan, too, preferred the cover version over the original and when playing live he uses the Hendrix arrangement rather than his own.

Sunshine of Your Love Cream

(Pete Brown/Jack Bruce/Eric Clapton) ❋ Polydor ❋ 1967 ❋ Appears on: *Disraeli Gears*

'Sunshine of Your Love' launched the era of the heavy riff in rock & roll. This is all about the riff zigzagging up and down the fret-board. Jack Bruce screams the lyrics as though he's chained to this guitar sequence.

'Sunshine of Your Love' was a perfect title for 1967 – meaningless but with the right catchphrases. According to journalist Ritchie Unterberger, lyricist Pete Brown came up with the line "It's getting near dawn" because while Jack Bruce was playing his bass part he looked out the window and it *was* getting near dawn. But the whole track has that explosive serendipity. Clapton's guitar sounds like it's on fire. Most important, however, was Ginger Baker's wild syncopation. The difference between Cream and their heavy metal imitators was Ginger Baker's drumming and his capacity to move around the kit with the dexterity of a crazed jazz player (which he was) and that kept the song buoyant. 'Sunshine of Your Love' influenced every rock band of the day and every blues-based band since.

"I'm very fond of this simply because it's a riff that has entered the consciousness," said Bruce. "It's very nice if you can write something that gets across to everyone. It was, I suppose, a kind of synthesis of things that were around at the time – there's a bit of 'You Really Got Me' in there – but the unusual thing about it was the way it syncopates towards the end of the riff, which is more of a Latin thing, a very un-British, un-pop thing to do.

"I just got a thing commemorating a million plays of it in America. It has been covered by many people. A lot of Latin bands like Tito Puente have done it and there's a really good version by Ella Fitzgerald, sung live with a trio. The song gets used in films a lot. My favourite is *GoodFellas* where

Robert De Niro slices a guy up to it. You can't get any better recognition than that."

Light My Fire The Doors

(Robbie Krieger/Jim Morrison/Ray Manzarek/John Densmore) ✷ Elektra ✷ 1967 ✷
Appears on: *The Doors*

In 1967 few people took the Doors seriously. They were regulars at the Whiskey Au Go Go nightclub where their bluesy, psychedelic Oedipal epic 'The End' got them a bit of a reputation. Then there was Jim Morrison – stunningly handsome and fucked-up on drugs – always an attractive combination. Behind Morrison the band struggled to develop a version of jazz rock. Although all the compositions were jointly credited, the bulk of the songwriting was split between Krieger, whose tastes veered towards pop music, and Morrison, whose lyrics were mostly inane babblings.

Jac Holzman signed the group to Elektra and assigned producer Paul Rothchild who cut their eponymous debut in ten days. The album was split between Morrison's dark poetic musings and Krieger's powerful pop tunes. The former gave them some credibility but it was the latter that turned the group into a chart success and made them more than a footnote in an anthology of cult acts. Morrison and the Doors needed each other. Without him they were a bunch of fairly bloodless would-be jazz players. The combination, however, was very potent.

'Light My Fire' was a perfect synthesis of all that was best about the Doors – a swinging drum part and deliciously melodic work from Krieger and organ player Ray Manzarek. On top of that the lyrics that Morrison delivered positively dripped with sexual desire.

It was a brilliant debut for Krieger, who had never attempted writing before. "Jim had been writing all the songs and one day he said, 'We don't have enough tunes. Why don't you guys try to write some?' That night I wrote my first song ever, 'Light My Fire'. I brought it into rehearsal the next day and everyone liked it. Ray wrote the intro keyboard part in just a few minutes.

"And working with Jim made me write a certain way because I had to compete with his songs, which were pretty heavy. He was really cool about it, too."

An edited version of the seven-minute track was a major hit single and put the Doors on the national map. Which was just as well because they had been banned from the Whisky Au Go Go.

Now on the world stage, Morrison could come up with his statement to Michael Lydon, "Maybe you could call us erotic politicians. We're a rock & roll band, a blues band, just a band, but that's not all. A Doors concert is a public meeting called by us for a special kind of dramatic discussion and entertainment. When we perform, we're participating in the creation of a world, and we celebrate that creation with the audience. It becomes the sculpture of bodies in action.

"That's politics, but our power is sexual. We make concerts sexual politics. The sex starts out with just me, then moves out to include the charmed circle of musicians on stage. The music we make goes out to the audience and interacts with them, they go home and interact with the rest of reality, then I get it back by interacting with that reality, so the whole sex thing works out to be one big ball of fire."

Fair enough, but it was the sultry pop of 'Light My Fire' that made it possible.

Friday on My Mind   The Easybeats

(Harry Vanda/George Young) ✳ Alberts ✳ 1967 ✳
Appears on: *Nuggets, Vol. 2: Original Artyfacts From the British Empire & Beyond*

Easyfever swept through Australia in the mid-'60s. With the screaming, kinetic hobbit Stevie Wright out front of a pile-driving mod sound, the Easybeats were the real deal at the wrong end of the world. Five British and Dutch expatriates who met around the Villawood Hostel, the Easybeats not only mastered the sound from Swinging London but had their own spin on it courtesy of guitarist George Young and his partners Wright and fellow guitarist Harry Vanda. By the time they moved to the UK, Wright was so overcome with fame that he had stopped writing, so it fell to the others to sit in the bedroom and come up with the hits.

They hooked up with the producer of the day, Shel Talmy, who had made hits for the Kinks and the Who amongst many others. Having presented him with a hundred ideas, he thought there might be some promise with one, 'Friday on My Mind'.

"We actually got stuck on that song. It almost didn't make the grade," Vanda said in the documentary *A Long Way to the Top*. "There was a devil of a part to get to the chorus 'cause there was a key change problem that finally fell into place. We played it to Shel and he said, 'That's the one.' We said, 'OK Mr God, Sir.'

"So he took us in the studio and said, 'Play big guys, run through it.' Then he said, 'Thanks'. We were thinking of going through this long drawn-out creative process where the skies would open and revelations would come and that was it, one take."

'Friday on My Mind' has a raga-like ascending guitar riff that appears effortless over the top of a rhythm section that plays like their life depends on it. The mastery of the song though is in its lyrics – the working man's daydream of the delights of the weekend. It's a perennial theme that goes back to the roots of rock & roll, but the Easybeats give it a new cast that is a little bit psychedelic but mostly just urgent.

The song was not only an inspiration to working-class kids but also to David Bowie, who covered the track on *Pin Ups*, and Bruce Springsteen, who performed it live.

"I guess it was a good omen," said Vanda, "that when we left the studio a guy was walking through the hall humming it. It was just one of those songs, it took off with a vengeance."

Carrie Anne The Hollies

(Allan Clarke/Tony Hicks/Graham Nash) ❋ EMI ❋ 1967 ❋
Appears on: *The Hollies' Greatest Hits*

The Hollies first claim to fame was that they took over the Beatles' gig at the Cavern Club when the moptops moved on to bigger and better things. The Hollies, who named themselves in honour of Texan singer/songwriter Buddy Holly, were one of the better groups of the British beat boom. History has passed them by, largely because they were so nice. The Hollies' sound was based on harmony singing and especially the beautifully blended voices of Allan Clarke and Graham Nash. Their sweetness was no match for the Rolling Stones or other more colourful artists. The Hollies, however, could really sing and at their best they were amongst the leaders of their field. Their best-known song is the Graham Gouldman penned 'Bus Stop'. But it was on 'Carrie Anne' that the voices really flew.

'Carrie Anne' was one of their first compositions to become a hit in the US and the UK. It is squeaky clean but it's also built on amazing vocal dynamics over a three-chord melody. In its way it's at least as clever as anything the Byrds were doing. Indeed, guitarist Tony Hicks was listening to the Byrds on the Hollies' 1965 tour of Norway when he got the idea for this masterpiece. The song was finally cut on 3 May 1967 in two takes.

The Dark End of the Street James Carr

(Dan Penn/Chips Moman) ✻ Vivid Sound ✻ 1967 ✻
Appears on: *The Essential James Carr*

Dan Penn is one of the most gifted southern songwriters. Growing up as a white kid in segregated Alabama, his only contact with black music – R&B, rock & roll and jazz – was from the radio. Nonetheless, once he heard Ray Charles, his course was set. He made his way to Memphis, where he started writing country songs for Conway Twitty, and befriended Spooner Oldham and Arthur Alexander and was seminal in establishing the Muscle Shoals Sound. In bridging country and R&B, Penn was instrumental in founding the southern soul sound.

"We were only in there for about thirty minutes," Dan Penn told Barney Hoskyns when recalling the writing of the song. It was specifically penned for James Carr to sing. "I guess 'Dark End of the Street' was the culmination of two or three years of thinkin' about cheatin'," he said.

'The Dark End of the Street' is an aching ballad about forbidden love – perhaps the definitive word on adultery. The song has a touch of country and a big dollop of soul and there's also a hint of gospel that only adds to the plaintive nature of the tune. The singer laments being forced to meet up in the shadows and to hide his feelings. It's a record that drips with guilt and with dark passion and the song has proved durable enough to be covered by men and women across the disciplines.

White Rabbit Jefferson Airplane

(Grace Slick) ✻ RCA ✻ 1967 ✻ Appears on: *Surrealistic Pillow*

Singer Grace Slick retold Lewis Carroll's Alice stories as a metaphor for the hypocrisy of the straight world in the mid-'60s. The comparisons were all there and the connection between Alice's eat-me cake and the new drug LSD was too rich to ignore.

The key line in the song is "feed your head," which not only implied taking mind-expanding drugs but also finding a new awareness whether that be spiritual, political or sexual.

"It also means you gotta feed your brains," said the now-retired Slick recently. "Our parents wanted us to get educated, and we did. We found that you could either get married and live in a suburb with a station wagon and two bratty kids, or you could live like Alice B Toklas, Picasso or Diaghilev.

We chose the latter, to live a relatively free and artistic life. The phrase is: 'Fuck you, we do what we want.'"

Slick wrote the song when in her first band, the Great Society. When she joined the Airplane for their second album, *Surrealistic Pillow*, the Airplane adapted it. Jorma Kaukonen brought his acidic, sharp guitar tones to the tune and Spencer Dryden's staccato drumming made it a very unsettling. Most of all, though, there was Slick's caustic, banshee voice that just tore down the melody. To hear Slick scream "feed your head" is to have a psychedelic experience.

Hey Joe The Jimi Hendrix Experience

(Billy Roberts) ❄ Track ❄ 1967 ❄ Appears on: *Smash Hits*

Billy Roberts remains an obscure figure in the California music scene. However, in 1962 he copyrighted a song 'Hey Joe', which has been covered some 800 times. David Crosby of the Byrds claims that he was taught it by Dino Valente of Quicksilver and the Youngbloods in 1965 before Valente went to jail on a drug bust. The song is attributed to Billy Roberts who has never been heard of or from apparently. In any case, 'Hey Joe' was a big hit on the folk scene and amongst garage rock bands in the mid-'60s. Between 1965 and 1968 it was recorded by Love, the Byrds, Tim Rose, Leaves, Shadows of Knight, Mothers of Invention, Wilson Pickett, Deep Purple, King Curtis, Cher and the Music Machine.

Chas Chandler, who was in the Animals and also a manager, liked the song, as did his client, Jimi Hendrix. According to legend, Chandler heard Hendrix doing the song at the Café Wha? in New York and that's what convinced him to take on the guitarist. Hendrix played the Tim Rose arrangement from the folkie's 1967 debut LP.

In any case, on 23 October 1966 the Jimi Hendrix Experience recorded 'Hey Joe'. At that moment the song became his. The Experience was three weeks old. Chandler had brought Hendrix back to London where they had found drummer Mitch Mitchell and bass player Noel Redding.

'Hey Joe' is a murder ballad – a man resolves to shoot his unfaithful lover. The lyric here is full of suppressed rage and Hendrix's guitar is similarly holding back, but you can feel the pressure. There's a heavy, almost ponderous feel at work, a sense of doom.

The version that became the Experience's debut was the first take of the first song attempted by the group in the studio. "I'm sure not a lot of time was spent on 'Hey Joe'," Mitch Mitchell recalled. "Studio time was expensive and there simply wasn't the budget for endless recording."

Little Wing The Jimi Hendrix Experience

(Jimi Hendrix) ✳ Track ✳ 1967 ✳ Appears on: *Axis: Bold as Love*

The sessions for the Jimi Hendrix Experience's second album were rushed. His whole life was going at break-neck speed. 'Little Wing' was an idea begun in 1966 when Hendrix was still playing Greenwich Village haunts and the song has that floating quality. Its sound is gently enhanced by putting the guitar through a Leslie speaker, which gives a floppy distortion, and also by the use of glockenspiel. The song is full of beautiful bits of filigree that are simply delightful.

Only two verses long with no chorus, Hendrix described the song as "like one of those beautiful girls that come around sometimes."

Purple Haze The Jimi Hendrix Experience

(Jimi Hendrix) ✳ Track ✳ 1967 ✳ Appears on: *Smash Hits*

"I had these dreams that something was gonna happen, seeing the numbers 1966 in my sleep, so I was just passing time till then," Hendrix said. "I wanted my own scene, making my music, not playing the same riffs."

Legend has it that 'Purple Haze' started out as a poem, 'Purple haze – Jesus saves', to which Hendrix added this incredible riff and finished the song backstage in a club on Boxing Day 1966 just as their first single, 'Stone Free' (backed with 'Hey Joe'), was crawling up the charts.

It's clear that 'Purple Haze' is a homage to LSD. The song kicks off with a fuzzed-out two-note riff and then the guitar goes crazy and the lyrics follow – with the immortal line, "'Scuze me while I kiss the sky". On this track Hendrix was doing things with his upside-down guitar that nobody had ever dreamed of. He was inventing a new vocabulary for the guitar in the same way that Charlie Parker had done for the saxophone. According to engineer Eddie Kramer, Hendrix was so much in command of his own instrument that he could literally create those sounds without the use of a studio. He could make himself sound backwards even though he wasn't.

'Purple Haze' was recorded on 11 January 1967. "Hendrix came in and kind of hummed us the riff and showed Noel the chords and the changes," said drummer Mitch Mitchell. "I listened to it and we went, 'OK, let's do it.' We got it on the third take as I recall."

Released on 17 March that year, 'Purple Haze' became Hendrix's signature tune.

Suzanne Leonard Cohen

(Leonard Cohen) ❋ 1967 ❋ Columbia ❋ Appears on: *The Songs of Leonard Cohen*

Leonard Cohen is a Canadian poet and novelist who in the mid-'60s fell into the folk scene. His is a singular style of songwriting – his voice almost monotonous and his tunes reeking of flamenco dancers and cantors.

'Suzanne' was his first hit. It's startling in its accurate rendition of places like the sailor's church – Notre-Dame-de-Bon-Secours – by the harbour and poetic in ways that not even Bob Dylan had approached – sensual and sacred all at once.

"Suzanne Vaillancourt was the wife of a friend of mine. They were a stunning couple around Montreal at the time," Cohen told the BBC. "But there was no ... well, there was thought, but there was no possibility, one would not allow oneself to think of toiling at the seduction of Armand Vaillancourt's wife.

"I bumped into her one evening, and she invited me down to her place near the river. She had a loft, at a time when lofts were ... the word wasn't used. She invited me down, and I went with her, and she served me Constant Comment tea, which has little bits of oranges in it. And the boats were going by, and I touched her perfect body with my mind, because there was no other opportunity. There was no other way that you could touch her perfect body under those circumstances."

"He got such a kick out of seeing me emerge as a young schoolgirl I suppose, and a young artist, into becoming Armand's lover and then wife," Suzanne recalled some thirty years after the first meeting with Cohen. "So, he was more or less chronicling the times.

"With Leonard, it happened more in the beginning of the '60s. I was very much interested in the waterfront. The St Lawrence River held a particular poetry and beauty to me and [I] decided to live there with our daughter, Julie. Leonard heard about this place I was living, with crooked floors and a poetic view of the river, and he came to visit me many times. We had tea together many times and mandarin oranges.

"I would always light a candle and serve tea and it would be quiet for several minutes, then we would speak. And I would speak about life and poetry and we'd share ideas.

"He became a big star after the song was launched and he became a songwriter. Our relationship did change with time. I travelled, went to the US, and we'd see him and bump into him. In Minneapolis for instance, he did a concert there and he saw me back stage and received me very beautifully, 'Oh Suzanne, you gave me a beautiful song.'"

In 1966, folk singer Judy Collins was looking for material and Cohen offered her some of his songs, including 'Suzanne', which he sang to her over the telephone. Word spread of Cohen's abilities and he was invited to New York to audition for Columbia's legendary talent scout John Hammond (who signed Billie Holiday, Bob Dylan and many of the other key jazz, folk and blues artists from the '30s to the '60s).

Hammond recalled discovering Cohen: "A friend of mine said, 'John, there's this poet from Canada, who I think you'd be interested in. He plays pretty good guitar, and he's a wonderful songwriter, but he doesn't read music, and he's sort of very strange. I don't think Columbia would be at all interested in him, but you might be.'

"So, I listened to this guy, and he's got a hypnotic effect. I thought he was enchanting ... because that's the only word you can use. He was not like anything I'd ever heard before. I just feel that I always want a true original, if I can find one, because there are not many in the world; and the young man set his own rules. They all looked at me at Columbia and said, 'What, are you ... A forty-year-old Canadian poet? How are we going to sell him?' I said, 'Listen to him ...' and, lo and behold, Columbia signed him."

Within two weeks, Cohen (who was thirty-two at the time) was in the studio recording his first album. Cohen's one request was for a mirror to be set up in front of his microphone so that he could serenade himself. At one point in the sessions, Hammond shouted out, "Watch out Dylan!"

"It was a small studio we had at 49 East 52nd Street," Hammond recalled. "He was alone, in the studio, and it used to be lit with incense and candles; and we had no lights on in the studio, and it had a very exotic effect. He had a hypnotising effect on everybody. And he felt comfortable with the mirror.

"So, the record came out, and it sold remarkably well. And I had a lot of fun with him. He was a completely weird guy, who liked to go around the streets of Montreal and play pinball. And I liked to play pinball, too, so that was a great bond that we had. The only thing I could do was to stay out of his way, and give him whatever reassurance he needed, and I could do that pretty well."

'Suzanne' sparked Cohen's career and a thousand imitators. Randy Newman wrote a parody but the song itself defies the ravages of imitation and time.

Suzanne Vaillancourt became a masseuse and New Age therapist in Los Angeles, near the Mt Baldy monastery where Cohen lived for a time. Although their paths crossed, he never did touch her perfect body.

"Once when he was visiting Montreal, I saw him briefly in a hotel and it was a very, very wonderful, happy moment because he was on his way to becoming the great success he is," she recalled. "And the moment arose that we could have a moment together intimately, and I declined. I forget that Leonard is more than just an amazing poet and philosopher. He's also a human being who happens to be a man.

"I'm flattered somewhat. But I was depicted, I think, in sad terms too in a sense, and that's a little unfortunate. You know I don't think I was quite as sad as that, albeit maybe I was and he perceived that and I didn't."

Undecided Masters Apprentices

(Bower/Harrison) ❋ Astor ❋ 1967 ❋ Appears on: *Hands of Time*

"Our songs were a mishmash of styles," said Masters Apprentices singer Jim Keays. Mishmash or not, they got off to a very good start with their first single, 'Undecided'. The flip side ('Wars and Hands of Time') was a psychedelic anti-war masterpiece but the A-side was a burning, rocking garage classic straight out of Adelaide, Australia, sounding like the Rolling Stones in a bad mood. Snarly, crunching guitar riffs over Keays' sex-starved vocals brought a unique urgency to 'Undecided'. The song is still fresh and it was most recently covered – faithfully – by Silverchair jamming with Radio Birdman guitarist Deniz Tek.

"So we got a letter from Astor Records saying, can you put down some demos and send them to us," said Keays. "So we went into a little studio in Adelaide. In fact I put the vocals down in a warehouse across the lane because the echo in there was monstrous. Anyway we did the songs and sent them over to them and basically forgot about it. I was at the drive-in with my girlfriend one night and in between the two movies I put on the car radio and 'Undecided' came on, one of the songs we'd recorded as a demo. And I couldn't believe it; it was just a shock. And it was a monstrous hit for us, it thrust us from the garage band virtually straight into a national band, virtually overnight."

The track was written in the studio by guitarists Mick Bower and Rick Harrison in less than fifteen minutes. In his memoir *His Master's Voice*, Keays notes, "It had no real chorus line and no lyric that seemed to jump out as a title. 'What shall I write on the tape box?' inquired Max Pepper, studio proprietor. 'I don't know I'm undecided', I said. That was it. 'Undecided' was boldly printed on the tape box as song number four."

Mama Tried   Merle Haggard

(Merle Haggard) ❋ Capitol ❋ 1967 ❋ Appears on: *Mama Tried*

Merle Haggard was raised on the grapes of wrath. The Haggard family was part of the Okie diaspora who came to California in the Dust Bowl years. The family lived in a converted boxcar in Bakersfield, California. When Merle was nine his father died and the son went off the rails.

He told *Lost Highway* author Peter Guralnick: "I was a child that needed two parents and there was a period that came up that my mother just couldn't handle. My dad wasn't there and my older brother tried to step in and of course I resented that. It just got all confused and messed up. Mama certainly did try."

Haggard's mama tried everything to control her wayward son, even committing him to a juvenile facility for a time. Throughout his teens he was involved in petty theft until at age twenty in 1957 he was sentenced to a maximum of fifteen years for attempted armed robbery. Possibly it was Johnny Cash's 1968 concert at San Quentin; possibly it was the memory of his father's fiddle playing. For whatever reason, when Haggard was released in 1960 he determined to make a go of it as a musician.

Haggard quickly became a key player in the Bakersfield country scene. His style was taken from a touch of western swing added to a honky tonk style. The influences of Jimmy Rodgers, Hank Williams and Lefty Frizzel were strong. His outlaw songs had the verisimilitude of a hard life to them, none better than 'Mama Tried'.

To be Young, Gifted and Black   Nina Simone

(Weldon Irvine/Nina Simone) ❋ RCA ❋ 1967 ❋ Appears on: *The Essential Nina Simone*

"To most white people, jazz means black and jazz means dirt and that's not what I play," said Nina Simone. "I play black classical music. That's why I don't like the term 'jazz', and Duke Ellington didn't either – it's a term that's simply used to identify black people.

"My original plan was to be the first black concert pianist – not a singer.

"Because I was hired to play the piano for forty-five minutes out of each hour for six hours a night, and since I hadn't played any popular music before, I had to incorporate jazz and classical motifs into what I was doing, and that developed into the difficult role I'm playing now. I didn't start singing until the manager of the bar told me that just playing wasn't good enough."

Nina Simone was not an easy person. A self-confessed diva, Simone's fractious temper and wildly inconsistent behaviour were tolerated for thirty-five years because she was one of the truly magnificent talents of the 20th century. Rightly dubbed the High Priestess of Soul, Simone was capable of pulling out breathtaking performances. A masterful reinterpreter of songwriters, Simone was also capable of classics herself.

In 1968, at the height of the civil rights movement, Simone and co-writer Weldon Irvine penned 'To be Young, Gifted and Black' in honour of her friend, playwright Lorraine Hansberry.

Released as a single in November 1969, it became her biggest RCA hit, reaching the Top 10 on the R&B charts and was covered by Aretha Franklin, Donny Hathaway and Dionne Warwick.

The song became an anthem for black America and the Congress of Racial Equality declared it to be the black national anthem.

"Yes," said Simone, "and then black America promptly refused it."

Interstellar Overdrive Pink Floyd

(Syd Barrett/Nick Mason/Roger Waters/Richard Wright) ✳ Harvest ✳ 1967 ✳
Appears on: *Piper at the Gates of Dawn*

Dubbed "space rock," this instrumental was recorded at the Floyd's sessions for their debut single, 'Arnold Layne', and then revisited on their debut album, *Piper at the Gates of Dawn*. The song marked the transition from psychedelic pop group to something else – an English jamming band heading off into their own universe. At this stage, Syd Barrett was still at the helm, having not yet disappeared into his own psychotic cosmos.

According to legend the song started from manager Peter Jenner humming Love's 'Little Red Book' at Barrett, who picked the melody out on his guitar and brought it to the Floyd, who improvised the rest.

Barrett named the group after two obscure blues musicians and their initial interest was in emulating American records. However, as Nick Mason has observed, they weren't particularly accomplished musicians. Nonetheless, they were lauded by the London underground scene of the late '60s, with newspapers like the *International Times* and venues like UFO London emulating the hip scene of San Francisco. Pink Floyd became the house act. This freeform environment and accessible LSD encouraged the group to stretch out and play to their strengths – no matter how long it took (in the case of this track, 9:41). Richard Wright's keyboards laid epic textures for Barrett's idiosyncratic guitar, and Mason's steady hand on the tempos allowed for the Floyd to create free-flowing, elegant and sometimes unsettling pieces. This might have been the beginning of British psychedelia but it was also the inspiration for a million insufferable ambient tapes.

'Interstellar Overdrive' was, then, the template for the Floyd's first golden era and it was followed by similar favourites – 'Saucerful of Secrets' and 'Set the Controls for the Heart of the Sun'. Syd Barrett was soon gone, replaced by David Gilmore, who encouraged a more sober approach.

"Syd was fantastic, a great guy, but the Pink Floyd he was in was a completely different band to the one that came afterwards," said Gilmore. "If people say we weren't the same after Syd left, fair enough. The first album was English whimsy at its best, with large slices of psychedelia thrown in, but it bears very little resemblance to anything we've tried to do since." 'Interstellar Overdrive' was the bridge to that gap.

A Whiter Shade of Pale   Procol Harum

(Keith Reid/Gary Brooker) ❋ Regal Zonophone/Deram ❋ 1967 ❋
Appears on: *Procol Harum*

Keith Reid was a nerdy twenty-something in 1967 who, having studied English literature, fancied he'd like to write lyrics. Gary Brooker played journeyman piano in the R&B band the Paramounts. Hipster DJ and record producer Guy Stevens introduced them. Brooker added JS Bach's 'Suite no. 3 in D Major' to what were, in Reid's words, "a lot of abstract phrases," and together they wrote 'A Whiter Shade of Pale' – the perfect record for the summer of 1967. It sounded like a happening. It was mysterious – why were the sixteen vestal virgins leaving for the coast? What the hell is a vestal virgin anyway? It alluded to Chaucer and was therefore literary while sounding like what most people thought was going on at these LSD parties they were reading about in the Sunday papers. Even this group's name, Procol Harum, sounded groovy (it was borrowed from Stevens' cat).

The song went to number one around the world immediately.

Brooker called on former colleague Robin Trower and Matthew Fisher, who had played the haunting organ lines of 'Pale', to be the core of the band and they knocked out a debut album under the ear of producer/manager Denny Cordell.

While never coming close to the heights of that first magnificent single, Procol Harum continued to make interesting albums. Their third, *A Salty Dog* (1969), was possibly the best of them. The group also launched solo guitar virtuoso Robin Trower. However, they will always be remembered for those vestal virgins who launched progressive rock on an undeserving world.

D-I-V-O-R-C-E Tammy Wynette

(Bobby Braddock/Curly Putman) ❊ Epic ❊ 1967 ❊

Appears on: *The Essential Tammy Wynette*

One of Tammy Wynette's early hits, 'D-I-V-O-R-C-E' was a subject with which she was familiar. She was at the time parting from her second husband and about to enter a tumultuous marriage with country star George Jones. She would eventually divorce him too.

'D-I-V-O-R-C-E' was one of the songs that really reflected the way that country music was picking up on the changes that were happening in society. It was a 'countrypolitan' style song, in tune with the '60s. Wynette brought the soap opera of her life to the song and to her career. That adds to the camp quality of 'D-I-V-O-R-C-E' and the image that country had – trailer trash white people with big hair and drunken husbands – through the '70s.

"I just don't understand how a young person of twenty-one or twenty-two can sing about walking out and hearing the baby cry," Wynette told *MOJO*. "I just don't understand how they can put their heart and soul into it because it's never happened to them. It happened to us."

All Tomorrow's Parties The Velvet Underground

(Lou Reed) ❊ Verve ❊ 1967 ❊ Appears on: *The Velvet Underground & Nico*

The Velvet Underground's only screen appearance was in the film *Midnight Cowboy* where they're seen playing at one of Andy Warhol's Happenings.

Warhol's understanding of subculture recognised the genius in the Velvet Underground. He became their mentor and gave them the courage to pursue what was a decidedly uncommercial style of music.

Warhol's atelier was the Factory, a downtown New York warehouse where he made his films and artworks and where he encouraged a group of people who belonged nowhere else. Warhol called them superstars even though they hadn't the change for the subway. He glorified them and their lifestyles and he forever changed the way that people considered the concept of beauty.

It was a heady scene at the Factory and the Velvet Underground captured its quicksilver ambience of art and drugs and sex.

"I didn't appreciate what we were doing," said guitarist Sterling Morrison. "I never considered what it meant to be doing something with Andy Warhol and seeing all these weird people marching by and hanging around the loft. I just worried about little songs and how well they were played.

"We used to practise at the Factory and hang out there every day for a couple of years, from '66 to '68. We would arrive some time in the afternoon and every day would begin with the same question: 'What parties shall we go to tonight?' A thousand, thousand parties ... reflected on from a distance, they were almost unimaginable. Real high rolling affairs, with a lot of energetic depravity going on."

One of the flotsam starlets who drifted through the factory was Nico, a model and actress who had appeared in Fellini's La Dolce Vita. Despite the fact that she couldn't sing, Warhol suggested that the Velvets use her as vocalist.

"Andy suggested we use Nico," Morrison recalled. "She'd made a couple of singles with [Rolling Stones manager] Andrew Loog Oldham in London and one of them was not bad – sort of like early Marianne Faithfull. So we said fine, she looks great, and just gradually tried to work her in. There were problems from the very beginning because there were only so many songs that were appropriate for Nico and she wanted to sing them all – 'Waiting for the Man', 'Heroin', all of them. And she would try and do little sexual politics things in the band. Whoever seemed to be having undue influence on the course of events, you'd find Nico close by. So she went from Lou to Cale, but neither of those affairs lasted for very long."

She did a fine version of 'All Tomorrow's Parties', which has the perfect wistfulness to capture that innocent and decadent moment.

Heroin The Velvet Underground

(Lou Reed) ❋ Verve ❋ 1967 ❋ Appears on: *The Velvet Underground & Nico*

This was not the first song about hard drugs in the canon of popular music. It was the first song that told it like it was. The innovation of Lou Reed's writing in this song was the dispassion; there are no moral judgements, simply a statement of the experience.

After leaving college, Lou Reed worked for a music publisher, Pickwick, turning out anonymous would-be Top 40 tunes. It was here that he wrote 'Heroin'. Unsurprisingly, Pickwick thought there was little commercial potential. The Velvet Underground, though, was ideal for this literary material because they mixed in art circles (the group comprised a couple of English graduates and a fine music graduate in John Cale). The song is worked up in an organic warm style that belies the subject matter.

The group had also found it difficult to get a recording deal. According to guitarist Dr Sterling Morrison, "Ahmet Ertegun liked it, but said, 'No, no, no, none of this – no drug songs.' Then we took it over to Elektra, who said some of the content was unacceptable and the whole sound was unacceptable. 'This viola – can't Cale play anything else?'

"So then we talked to Tom Wilson, who was still at Columbia. He told us to wait and come and sign with him when he moved to Verve because he swore that at Verve we could do anything we wanted. And he was right. We gave something up of course because there was no effective marketing on Verve; we were stuck there with the Mothers of Invention and Richie Havens."

Artist Andy Warhol financed the making of the album at a reported cost of $2500. The recording conditions were difficult in that one studio was barely finished and didn't work properly.

Tom Wilson, one of the great producers of the '60s, signed the group to Verve largely because he was romantically interested in singer Nico but played very little part in the recording of the record.

According to drummer Mo Tucker, "'Heroin' is such a good song but it's a pile of garbage on the record. The guys couldn't have their amps up loud in the studio so I couldn't hear anything. When we got to the part where you speed up it became this mountain of drum noise. I couldn't hear shit. So I just stopped and, being a little wacky, they just kept going. And that's the one we took."

Frank Zappa delayed the release of the Velvet's album to avoid the release of the Mothers of Invention. No radio stations would touch it and according to Morrison, "They wouldn't even accept advertising for the album, because it was about drugs and sex and perversion."

So what? 'Heroin' changed the way rock & roll songs were written ever after.

I'm Waiting for the Man The Velvet Underground

(Lou Reed) ❊ Verve ❊ 1967 ❊ Appears on: *The Velvet Underground & Nico*

If 'Heroin' on the first Velvets album told you of the experience of taking the drug, 'I'm Waiting for the Man' told you where to get it – the corner of Lexington Avenue and 125th Street. Also the price – $26. It also told you that while waiting you would experience withdrawal and the Velvet Underground made a sound like that.

The churning rhythm guitar on 'I'm Waiting for the Man' is the prototype for what became punk rock. They grind through the changes – where there are changes – oblivious to the demands of R&B, just straight chording and overtones. It's extraordinary playing and was hugely influential on the development of heavy rock as it occurred in the '70s, particularly with David Bowie. Where 'Heroin' was an epic poem, this is more urgent and minimal. It remains one of the great rock & roll songs.

The critic Lester Bangs said in the late '70s, "modern music starts with the Velvet Underground". In fact, it starts with this track.

1, 2, 3, Red Light 1910 Fruitgum Company

(B Trimachi/S Trimachi) ❊ Buddah ❊ 1968 ❊ Appears on: *1, 2, 3, Red Light*

"Well, we were the ones," Jeff Katz recalled in *Goldmine* magazine, "when we were talking about different things, we would gear 'em toward a certain audience, and we figured it was the teenagers, the young kids. And at the time we used to be chewing bubblegum and that, and my partner and I used to look at it and laugh and say, 'Ah, this is like bubblegum music.'

"Bubblegum music, in the real sense of sort of kiddie records, was around for quite a while, like various artists doing various songs. But there were very few that were doing it on some continuity where it was the same type of style or whatnot. We were gearing with all our writers for, as I said, a specific kids' [appeal]. We want hits, obviously; but we want these type of things, and we want our artists to be known for these type of things. And that's what we were knocking out."

Jerry Kasenetz and Jeff Katz met at the University of Arizona and had no interest in music. However, in 1966 the pair took on the Rare Breed and then had a number two hit with 'A Little Bit of Soul' by the Music Explosion – a bona fide garage rock classic. By 1967 they were working with Neil Bogart at Buddah Records. Katz's father came across a garage band then called Jeckyll and the Hydes in a New Jersey diner. Kasenetz and Katz renamed them the 1910 Fruitgum Company, gave them a song, 'Simon Says', and launched bubblegum music.

The Fruitgum Company was followed by the Ohio Express and others and a rush of imitators like the Archies.

It was a teen antidote to the pretensions that had swamped rock & roll in the late '60s, and to the political upheaval that engulfed America. Bubblegum had a slightly trippy tone to it and a deep suburban conservative take on the revolution that was happening in the streets.

Bubblegum was all about sex. Innuendo was never deep below the hook, especially in cases such as the '1, 2, 3, Red Light'. Male passion has rarely been better expressed in under two minutes.

The Fruitgum Company were at first a band but shortly devolved to singer Mark Gutkowski. Even he lost his berth if he wasn't at the Super K factory when the session commenced.

Despite the disparaging commentary Bubblegum received from the under-ground press, it has survived much better than progressive rock and its traditions have been upheld by no less than the Ramones and Kylie Minogue.

I Say a Little Prayer Aretha Franklin

(Burt Bacharach/Hal David) ✳ Atlantic ✳ 1968 ✳ Appears on: *Aretha Now*

Written for Dionne Warwick, Jerry Wexler produced Aretha Franklin's version and substantially changed the song – altering the tempo and pumping up the gospel flavour. Where Warwick had been wistful, Aretha just let it all hang out. This was the only time that Burt Bacharach felt a cover version had improved on his original arrangement.

"We'd sit in a room," said lyricist Hal David, "and start with maybe a line that I had, or four bars of Burt's music, and we'd build a song sort of like we were building a house. Very often we were writing three songs at a time.

"There are a lot of songs where the music is fine and the lyric is fine, yet they seem to come in, get in front of you and just fly away. They don't hold on. What I try to do is to find something that's a little rougher, something that's not so smooth that it evaporates. Often, in searching for that feeling, you go almost against the grain.

"In 'I Say a Little Prayer' where the chorus is 'forever forever', that's where the title would ordinarily be, and yet the song for me took place in the verses, so that's where I put the title."

Franklin, whose father was a minister and who sang in church before she could talk, brought her enormous power to this song. Bacharach's tunes tended to be based around tonal colour, where Franklin just "took it back to church".

(You Make Me Feel Like) A Natural Woman
Aretha Franklin

(Gerry Goffin/Carole King/Jerry Wexler) ❊ Atlantic ❊ 1968 ❊ Appears on: *Lady Soul*

"There was a sadness, and you couldn't define it. It was ungraspable, like quicksilver. But it was my job to furnish the most nurturing context for the music, to get the kind of players who were alert to the little changes or improvisations that Aretha might throw in there," said Jerry Wexler.

Wexler had been in love with Franklin's voice ever since he first heard her sing gospel on a Chess record in the '50s. The producer waited out her contract with Columbia where she was cutting polite jazz. As soon as it expired, Wexler signed Aretha Franklin to Atlantic, a label he co-owned, and he "took her back to church". This was one of the stellar partnerships in pop music. With Wexler at the board, she cut 'I Never Loved a Man the Way I Loved You' then 'Respect' and suddenly Aretha Franklin was the Queen of Soul.

Franklin had grown up in church – her father was a preacher. By the time Wexler found her, she had lived a little as well. On the sides they cut together at Atlantic, Aretha married the sacred and the profane.

'(You Make Me Feel Like) A Natural Woman' was written for Franklin by Gerry Goffin and Carole King – the greatest husband and wife writing partnership in pop. Wexler suggested the title as a brief for Goffin and King. Where 'Respect' is a song that asserts and demands, 'Natural Woman' is more sensual. It's not any less powerful or feminine than 'Respect' but certainly it's a softer lyric.

Wexler enlisted Wilson Pickett's band for the backing. 'Natural Woman' has an organic build to it, and that's the key. Franklin allows the song to swell and evolve and she goes with it, rising to the occasion rather than pushing the arrangement. Many have tried this song but only Franklin and Carole

King have done it justice. They're the only singers who have allowed the song to make its 'natural' way.

I Shall Be Released The Band

(Bob Dylan/Richard Manuel) ❋ Capitol ❋ 1968 ❋ Appears on: *Music from Big Pink*

The Basement Tapes were the most famous bootleg in rock history. Dylan and the Band were living in upstate New York playing songs together and recording them on a reel-to-reel tape recorder. There was no agenda or deadline. Possibly the songs would be used in the future. Possibly they would be shopped to other performers or none of the above. Such was Dylan's stature, however, that once the rumour mill started, the "Basement Tapes" soon became indistinguishable from the Holy Grail. Copies of the tapes began to circulate and were among the first bootleg albums.

"Maybe 150 songs were recorded in a seven or eight month period," said bassist Rick Danko referring to the Basement Tapes. "Bob would come and bang the songs out on his typewriter and we'd go down into the basement and make some music up for them. The tapes were part of Bob's rehabilitation – he was getting stronger and feeling better. And from that we started getting our writing chops together a little bit."

Although the Basement Tapes are discussed in terms of Bob Dylan's work, the transformation in the Band was way more profound. Over those months, the Band went from being a singer's backing group to a complete ensemble with its own sound.

"Bob helped us more than anybody ever did," said drummer Levon Helm. "What Bob was doing, it's easy to see now, was showing us how to construct songs, how to put songs together, and he was doing it right there with us, in front of us. He and Rick were writing 'This Wheel's on Fire', and he and Richard had written 'I Shall Be Released'. Bob had set the Band on fire, and everybody was starting to write, Richard and Robbie especially."

'I Shall Be Released' is one of the gems to emerge from those sessions. This was one of the few songs to be rerecorded for the Band's first album. It's a disconsolate cry for redemption – spiritual or physical.

The troubled Richard Manuel with his plaintive falsetto was the ideal singer to take the lead on this track with Danko and Helm backing up the lower registers.

"Up to this point I've been harping on Bob Dylan, on everybody, about this sound, and I don't mean electronic trick sounds," said Robertson. "All

ROCKWIZ DECADES

96

of that plays a part, but there's a vibe to certain records, a quality, whether it's a Motown thing or a Sun Records thing or a Phil Spector thing. [Bob] was saying, 'Who cares about that? I'm only interested in the lyrics.' Well, that's not the way I felt about it all.

"I wanted to discover the sound of the Band. So I thought, I'm gonna do this record and I'm not gonna play a guitar solo on the whole record. I'm only going to play riffs, Curtis Mayfield kind of riffs. I wanted the drums to have their own character, I wanted the piano not to sound like a big Yamaha grand. I wanted it to sound like an upright piano. I wanted these pictures in your mind, I wanted this flavour.

"I didn't want screaming vocals. I wanted sensitive vocals where you can hear the breathing and the voices coming in. This whole thing of discovering the voices – don't everybody come in together. Everybody in records is working on getting all the voices together until it neutralises itself. I like voices coming in one at a time, in a chain reaction kind of thing like the Staple Singers did. But, because we are all men it will have another effect.

"All of these ideas come to the surface and what becomes the clear picture is that this isn't just clever. This is emotional and this is storytelling. You can see this mythology."

Long Black Veil The Band

(Marijohn Wilkin/Danny Dill) ✻ Capitol ✻ 1968 ✻ Appears on: *Music from Big Pink*

Perhaps the most famous "murder ballad," this song has been extensively covered by country, folk and rock artists including Lefty Frizzell (from whom the Band learnt it), Johnny Cash, Joan Baez, Nick Cave and the Bad Seeds, Marianne Faithful, Jerry Garcia, Burl Ives, Jason & the Scorchers, the Kingston Trio, Bill Monroe, the Move, Fred Neil, the New Riders of the Purple Sage, the Proclaimers, the Seldom Scene, the Sir Douglas Quintet, the Stranglers, Barry White and many others. As you can see from the diversity of artists who have covered the song, it has a universal quality.

The simple waltz here carries a powerful story told from beyond the grave. The narrator was unable to use the alibi that would have saved him from the gallows – he was in the arms of his best friend's wife. Now six feet under he watches as his lover tends his grave. 'Long Black Veil' is romantic and Gothic and stark. It suited Rick Danko's plaintive voice and the style to which the Band aspired on their first album. As Jaime Robbie Robertson said, "I thought it was a great song. It was in the tradition that I wanted to begin writing in."

According to producer John Simon, "It's much more of a country wail or moan. [This] was more of a wail from the heart or gut."

Tears of Rage The Band

(Richard Manuel/Bob Dylan) ✳ Capitol ✳ 1968 ✳ Appears on: *Music from Big Pink*

'Tears of Rage' opened an album that changed music. Bootleg copies of the song had circulated on *The Basement Tapes* – the rehearsal tapes of Bob Dylan and the Band in their basement at the Big Pink House. *The Basement Tapes* made George Harrison want to split the Beatles and Eric Clapton to split Cream. "I got hold of a bootleg tape of *Big Pink* at the end of the last Cream tour," recalled Eric Clapton. "I used to put it on as soon as I checked into my hotel room, do the gig and be utterly miserable, then rush back and put the tape on and go to sleep fairly contented until I woke up the next morning and remembered who I was and what I was doing. It was that potent!" For Clapton, "the sound of music changed drastically after that first album."

Rather than competing over solos and threatening to burn down the world, the Band proposed a return to family values and togetherness. 'Tears of Rage' was a song about a relationship between a father and daughter.

"It's from a parent's side of view," said Robertson. "So what if your parents did you wrong? Maybe they did, but so what? Everybody's just doing what they can do, right or wrong. I'm just tired of hearing all of this – that little girl Janis Ian. You know, Jim Morrison and those people. I just think they're a drag. Even if that is their situation, who cares? That's got nothing to do with music."

Dylan arrived at Big Pink with the lyric and gave it to Manuel, who swiftly added a piano melody. "I had a couple of movements that seemed to fit, so I just elaborated a little," said Manuel.

It's really Manuel's soaring and desperately sad vocal that makes this track work, however. The languid pace of the arrangement gives enormous space to what is an extraordinary vocal.

The song was cut live on A&R's four-track studio in New York. The majestic sound of Garth Hudson's organ and Robertson's guitar, fed through a Leslie speaker, and Helm's muffled drums all serve Manuel's voice. It's something not completely rock & roll nor country but ancient and dark and sad.

As Robbie Robertson put it, "It's the most heartbreaking performance he ever sung in his life."

The Weight The Band

(Jaime Robbie Robertson) ❋ Capitol ❋ 1968 ❋ Appears on: *Music from Big Pink*

'The Weight' became a signature song for the Band, although no-one much thought it would be at the time. "'The Weight' was another one that after we recorded it, it became what it was," Robertson told *Musician* magazine. "It was like, 'OK, this doesn't have a very complicated chord progression, it's just kind of traditional, so we'll cut that when we get stuck for a song.' And then we cut it and we thought, 'Gee, it's kind of effective when you hear if back at you like that.' It happens sometimes. A song takes on a character after you've done it."

This song was loaded up with characters and semi-religious allegories that went nowhere much in an opaque story. Over time, and as a result of its powerful melody, the song has accumulated a sense of profundity. If you break it down, however, it sounds like Robertson was copying Bob Dylan's style in search of his own voice.

Later in interviews, Robertson would ascribe more meaning to its lyric, likening it to the films of Spanish anarchist filmmaker Luis Buñuel.

"He did so many films on the impossibility of sainthood," said Robertson. "People trying to be good in *Viridiana* and *Nazarin*, people trying to do this thing. In 'The Weight' it's the same thing. People like Buñuel would make films that had these religious connotations to them but it wasn't necessarily a religious meaning. In Buñuel there were these people trying to be good and it's impossible to be good.

"In 'The Weight', it was this very simple thing. Someone says, 'Listen, will you do me this favour? When you get there will you say 'Hello' to somebody or will you pick up one of these for me? Oh, you're going to Nazareth, that's where the Martin guitar factory is. Do me a favour when you're there.' This is what it's all about. So the guy goes and one thing leads to another and it's like, 'Holy shit, what has this turned into? I've only come here to say "Hello" for somebody and I've got myself in this incredible predicament.' It was very Buñuelish to me at the time."

The literal meaning of the song is elusive, however. Levon Helm's vocal and the ensemble playing is completely in the pocket with Robertson's avowed inspiration from Curtis Mayfield on the guitar and the steady rambling arrangement.

"You pick things that come to mind and [they] sometimes have to do with personal experiences and people that you have known. But, they are not 'specific' stories," said Robertson. "It was North American folklore in the making."

Helter Skelter The Beatles

(John Lennon/Paul McCartney) ✳ Apple ✳ 1968 ✳ Appears on: *The Beatles*

Paul McCartney supposedly heard that the Who had made the noisiest record ever and took that as a challenge, his response being this noise fest driven by his best Little Richard voice and a dive-bombing bass guitar.

This was one of the few songs at the time that was recorded by the Beatles as a band. Having stopped touring they beavered away in the recording studio, often individually, and their music tended towards the mid-tempo rather than the supercharged rock & roll of their early years.

A helter skelter is a child's playground slide built in a corkscrew shape and that's pretty much what the song is about – going up and down and turning around. The first take of the song lasted thirty minutes of intense jamming – Harrison's guitar matching the zooming bass from McCartney and Starr's amped-up Motown feel. The song's apparent dumbness added to the tornado effect. It rises and falls and then rises again until it comes to a stop and then goes straight back into it. The song captures that sense of being out of control.

Unfortunately 'Helter Skelter' will be forever associated with Charles Manson, who used the phrase in his crazed, homicidal spree in 1969. However, the memory of Manson fades and 'Helter Skelter' remains, as McCartney intended, to be one raucous piece of music.

Hey Jude The Beatles

(John Lennon/Paul McCartney) ✳ Apple ✳ 1968 ✳ Appears on: *Hey Jude*

Paul McCartney's consolation note to John Lennon's son Julian evolved into an epic that transcended the specifics of the Lennon family.

The lyric and tune came to McCartney on a trip to visit the estranged family after Lennon had set up house with Yoko Ono. "I originally thought of it whilst driving my car out to visit Cynthia and Julian after John's divorce from them," McCartney said in *Many Years from Now*. "We'd been very good friends for millions of years and I thought it was a bit much for them to suddenly be persona non grata and out of my life, so I decided to pay them a visit and say, 'How are you doing? What's happening?' ... I always feel sorry for kids in divorce. The adults may be fine but the kids ... I had the idea by the time I got there. I knew it was not going to be easy for him. I started with the idea 'Hey Jules', which was Julian, don't make it bad, take a sad song and make it better. Hey, try and deal with this terrible thing, you know."

Being egocentric, Lennon heard the lyric as a message to him. "I heard it as a song to me," he said. "If you think about it … Yoko's just come into the picture, and Paul's saying, 'Hey Jude – hey, John'. I know I'm sounding like one of those fans who reads things into it, but you can hear it as a song to me. The words 'go out and get her' – subconsciously he was saying, 'Go ahead, leave me'. On a conscious level he didn't want me to go ahead. The angel in him was saying, 'Bless you'. The devil in him didn't like it at all, because he didn't want to lose his partner."

This seems unlikely given the many times McCartney has talked about the beginnings of the song. It is perhaps typical, though, of Lennon's distant parenting of his first child.

"I've never really wanted to know the truth about how dad was with me," Julian said. "There was some very negative stuff talked about me – like when he said I'd come out of a whisky bottle on a Saturday night. Stuff like that. You think, where's the love in that? Paul and I used to hang about quite a bit – more than Dad and I did. We had a great friendship going and there seems to be far more pictures of me and Paul playing together at that age than there are pictures of me and my dad."

McCartney felt proud of the song and was very strict about its arrangement. The bulk of the tune is straightforward – although Lennon misses a backing vocal and can be faintly heard to exclaim "Fuckin' hell!" – and then at the end comes a repeating phrase with a massed choir made up of Beatles and the orchestra providing hand claps and vocals. The mantra-like vocals are set against McCartney's scat singing, which owes more than a little to James Brown and Little Richard. The tension here between the melody and the beat is wound as tight as any soul session. The vamp at the end builds over four minutes – more than the length of time a radio station would ordinarily allow for one song. Despite its modal nature, there's such spirit in the tune and the performance that it's hard to cut.

As the first release on the Beatles' custom imprint Apple (with 'Revolution' on the flip side) it was decided to promote the single with a TV performance on which they were introduced as "the greatest tea-room orchestra in the world".

While My Guitar Gently Weeps The Beatles

(George Harrison) ❋ Apple ❋ 1968 ❋ Appears on: *The Beatles*

This was where the quiet Beatle became less so. The Beatles (aka *White album*) was a confusing, unfocused sloppy mess. Only two tracks – 'Helter

Skelter' and 'While My Guitar' – had the solidity and presence expected of the Beatles. Lennon's material was increasingly self-obsessed and McCartney's twee, but 'While My Guitar' couldn't be denied.

Harrison was never given his due by Lennon, McCartney or producer George Martin. When he presented this song to the others it received a lukewarm response.

After working on the track, Harrison was still dissatisfied. While giving Eric Clapton a lift he suggested that the Cream guitarist come in to do the electric guitar part. Clapton agreed and the song was cut with Harrison on organ (so it wasn't strictly his guitar that wept) and acoustic engineer Chris Thomas was enlisted to wobble an oscillator through Clapton's guitar part to give the track a sadder sound.

Ball and Chain Big Brother & the Holding Company

(Willie Mae Thornton) ✳ Columbia ✳ 1968 ✳ Appears on: *Janis*

In DA Pennebaker's film of the concert, Janis Joplin takes the stage on the Sunday night of the Monterey Pop Festival in her nicest evening wear – slingback shoes and a gold lame pantsuit and she looks a little try-hard, like a girl on her best behaviour for a cocktail party. Then she took it all off. Joplin sang naked emotion.

Big Brother, a rough garage blues band, starts the song with rudimentary bass, drums and guitar slipping and sliding through the blues changes. Then Joplin comes in with a smooth reading of the verses ratcheting up the emotional content. As she reaches the chorus suddenly the floodgates open and the pain and the hope and joy just come screaming out. The song goes from a blues into a soul arrangement with its stop-start dynamics and Joplin gets higher and higher every time and crashes further down in the breaks. The esteemed jazz writer Nat Hentoff said he had been in contact with "an overwhelming life force". Joplin told writer Michael Lydon, "When I sing I feel like when you're first in love ... I feel chills, weird feelings, slipping all over my body, it's a supreme emotional and physical experience." Big Mama Thornton may have written the song, but Janis Joplin made it her own – in eight minutes she has the highs and the lows; the joy and the pain and the need and desire and shame. Entertainment is about simulated emotion. Janis Joplin can get so far into a song that artifice evaporates. This is real.

'Ball and Chain' was a favourite blues of Joplin's even as a teenager. She identified with the great women blues singers such as Big Mama Thornton and Bessie Smith and brought that sensibility to Big Brother & the Holding Company's psychedelic rock. The band was on the lowest rung of the burgeoning San Francisco scene, regarded, with some truth, as dopers with a thin grasp of tunefulness. With Joplin, however, they had a natural resource.

According to drummer Peter Albin, "We changed Big Mama Thornton's 'Ball and Chain' to a minor-key blues. We used the slash-and-burn method of arranging. The chainsaw method." This was necessity rather than invention. Nonetheless there is a raw charm and excitement to the Big Brother recordings that is true to the blues, and which has definitely lasted beyond the '60s. At the end of the day, though, it was only ever the Janis Joplin show.

This version of 'Ball and Chain' was recorded on the Saturday night at Monterey and they were given a second spot the following night so that Pennebaker could include them in his film. Big Brother was a largely unknown band that had nothing to lose and everything to gain from the showcase at Monterey. Everything depended on a great set. At the end of it, as the crowds went wild, so did Clive Davis, the head of Columbia, who signed them on the spot, and Albert Grossman, manager of the Band and Bob Dylan, who then took on Janis Joplin.

Monterey introduced Janis to the world. There has never been a singer who has even come close.

Spoonful Cream

(Willie Dixon) ✳ Polydor ✳ 1968 ✳ Appears on: *Wheels of Fire*

Cream introduced the extended improvisation into mainstream rock & roll. Prior to Cream's 1967 tours, extended improvisation was not an element in rock & roll music that was built around concise songs with a carefully defined structure. Extended instrumental workouts were not part of the blues lexicon either. Improvisation was a jazz concept that required musicianship way beyond the capacity of most rock & roll bands. Once jamming became fashionable, everyone did it whether they had the ability or not. On *Wheels of Fire*, Cream also introduced the drum solo – something that Cream drummer Ginger Baker and perhaps a dozen others have been able to carry out but which plagued concerts for the next fifteen years.

"The Windsor Jazz and Blues Festival 1966, which was almost our first gig, we found that we ran out of numbers so quickly that we just had to improvise," said guitarist Eric Clapton. "So we just made up twelve-bar blues and that became Cream. That became what we were known for. I liked it up to a point, but it wasn't what I wanted."

Cream's most successful recorded jam is this version of Howlin' Wolf's 'Spoonful', which goes for about seventeen minutes. The three virtuosos in Cream all battle it out over the riff without disappearing. This is close to a jazz logic but with a very, very heavy arrangement.

Clapton found that the live shows were losing their charm when he noticed that the individuals were soloing without reference to the others.

"I just experimented one night," he said. "I stopped playing halfway through a number and the other two didn't notice, you know! I just stood there and watched and they carried on playing 'til the end of the number. I thought, well fuck that! You see, Cream was originally meant to be blues trio, like Buddy Guy with a rhythm section. I wanted to be Buddy Guy, the guitarist with a good rhythm section.

"With Cream we had our ups and downs. We had good gigs and bad gigs. We had gigs when you could have mistaken us for Hendrix, it was that good, and other times we were like the worst band in the world. It was this kind of inconsistency that relied upon the improvisation factor. All our songs had a starting theme, a finishing theme, and a middle that was up to us. On a good night it was great and on a bad night it was awful. I couldn't take this kind of up and down."

'Spoonful' was recorded on a good night.

Do You Know the Way to San Jose? Dionne Warwick

(Burt Bacharach/Hal David) ✳ Scepter ✳ 1968 ✳ Appears on: *Valley of the Dolls*

"When I was doing those songs with Dionne [Warwick], I was thinking in terms of miniature movies, you know?" said Burt Bacharach. "Three and a half minute movies with peak moments and not just one intensity level the whole way through. I never liked it where there's only one intensity from the singer, from the musical content, from the tracks and orchestration – it tends to beat you up."

Amongst Hal David's many gifts as a lyricist was his ability to tell a complete story. 'Do You Know the Way to San Jose?' is a precise, poignant story of a girl who is seduced by the bright lights of Hollywood. She finds that Hollywood Boulevard is crowded with girls just like her and that she will not be one of the chosen few. Armed with this self-knowledge she returns to her small-town life. It all happens in two verses.

"Sometimes I'd write against the mood," said David. "For instance, 'Do You Know the Way to San Jose?' is bright and rhythmic, and because of that you'd think it was instinctively happy. But it wasn't to me.

"I do labour over these things. I spend inordinate amounts of time deciding whether 'and' or 'but' is the right word. To a certain extent, lyrics flow easily, but no matter how much they flow at a given time, by the time you get it together, finished and refined to the best of your ability, it's a lot of work."

I Walk on Gilded Splinters Dr John the Night Tripper

(Dr John) ❉ Atco ❉ 1968 ❉ Appears on: *Gris Gris*

Mac Rebennack literally grew up in the New Orleans music scene alongside Fats Domino and Dave Bartholemew and the blues and R&B artists who played the New Orleans clubs and bordellos. In the mid-'60s he moved to Los Angeles, where he teamed up with another Crescent City native, Harold Battiste, who was working with Sonny Bono. Using some Sonny and Cher downtime, Battiste and Rebennack collected other New Orleans émigrés and cut the *Gris Gris* album – a deep, swampy and funkified version of New Orleans music that was way further out than the acid rock on FM airwaves.

For the album Rebennack assumed the persona of Dr John the Night Tripper – a characterisation of a voodoo priest.

"I had been working on some kind of voodoo idea for a couple of years," said Rebennack. The album closed with the epic 'I Walk on Gilded Splinters', which bubbles along on a sly funk bass and deep, ghostly, echoed percussion hanging back way behind the beat while Dr John mumbles his incantations. This is a very spooky and beautiful record.

"Atlantic reacted to it like, 'What the fuck is this? What are we gonna tell our promotions people'," said Harold Battiste. "None of us thought of a name for what we were doing but I knew the press would do that, call it Voodoo Rock or Swamp Rock or whatever. It was a tongue-in-cheek thing for me. It was the psychedelic period out in California and I said, 'Well, we're gonna give 'em some new shit to go underground with!'

"I had always wanted to do that sort of Afro-centric stuff. Really it was just a gathering of things that went with our heritage: the Indians, the Africans, the Cajuns, everybody that was making up our culture."

On 'Splinters' Dr John incants his voodoo lyrics and the mysterious sensuality of the song's groove is as strong as ever.

My Way Frank Sinatra

(Paul Anka/Claude François/Jacques Revaux/Gilles Thibault) ❊ Reprise ❊ 1968 ❊
Appears on: *My Way*

Paul Anka was only fourteen when he cut his first single. A year later his parents gave him $1000 to go to New York to try his luck in showbusiness. He struck gold, getting a record deal and hit record, 'Diana', the following year. Anka had reasonable success as a teen heartthrob but he never lost sight of the big picture and that included songwriting. He placed songs with Buddy Holly (and narrowly missed catching the fateful flight on 3 February 1959).

By the time he was twenty, Anka was playing Vegas. He had 200 copyrights to his name and a million dollars in the bank. He wrote the theme song to Johnny Carson's *The Tonight Show*.

Anka was one of the first rock & roll stars to be big in France. In the early '60s he married a French model and in 1966 they were on holiday in France when Anka heard 'Comme d'Habitude' sung by Claude François.

The love gone wrong song appealed to Anka, who bought the copyright with the intention of writing English-language lyrics. In 1968 Sinatra was planning one of his many retirements. He approached Anka about writing him a swansong. 'My Way', based on the tune of 'Comme d'Habitude', was the result. Anka claimed that the lyric expressed the individualistic spirit of the late '60s as much as it did Sinatra's personality. The song suited Sinatra perfectly, however, and became one of his signature tunes.

"He always thought that song was self-serving and self-indulgent," the singer's daughter Tina told the BBC. "That song stuck and he couldn't get it off his shoe. He didn't love it."

Wichita Lineman Glen Campbell

(Jimmy Webb) ❊ Capitol ❊ 1968 ❊ Appears on: *Wichita Lineman*

"Jimmy Webb is my favourite songwriter," Glen Campbell said. "I think Jimmy's the best musical poet to come out of America."

Webb was the master of sad. His songs were complex, erudite pop masterpieces. Webb was lavishly melancholic with a sort of existential Americana – loners out in the vast American night.

'Wichita Lineman' is his most concise and powerful lyric – the telephone guy out in Kansas, isolated by the immenseness of the Great Plains but still connecting lovers across the country. The imagery here is so clear and simple that it only takes two verses to break your heart.

In 1968 Glen Campbell was an in-demand session guitarist around Los Angeles. He had worked with the legendary studio players of the '60s, and for a time joined the Beach Boys as a vocalist. His solo career really took off with his version of a Jimmy Webb song, 'By the Time I Get to Phoenix'. He turned to Webb again. The songwriter had been driving through the midwest when he saw a man repairing telephone wires.

"I had been driving around northern Oklahoma, an area that's real flat and remote – almost surreal in its boundless horizons and infinite distances," he told *Blender*'s Johnny Black. "I'd seen a lineman up on a telephone pole, talking on the phone. It was such a curiosity to see a human being perched up there in those surroundings."

The song took approximately two hours to write, but was still unfinished – hence its brevity – when Campbell called for a track. Using his friends from the LA session pool, Campbell cut the track in ninety minutes. Carol Kaye provided the distinctive bass notes that open proceedings and Campbell played the guitar solo on her bass. Producer Al De Lory did the string arrangement that gently mimics the morse code signals down the wire.

The most difficult part of the production was Campbell's attempts to reproduce the sparse lonesomeness of Webb's demo recording. The songwriter had a large electronic organ that was brought into the studio to add ambience. "I had a Gilbranson," said Webb, "which had a humming, resonating, reverberating electronic sound with a tremolo quality, but also an echo, so there was a lot of sustain. Kind of a bubbling noise. Just three notes, but it produced a kind of electronic chiming – which might be a telecommunications sound, a satellite sound or something of that nature."

Campbell gave a flawless reading of the track, his voice quivering and cracking with sadness and resignation and desire.

A Very Cellular Song The Incredible String Band

(Mike Heron/Robin Williamson) ✳ Elektra ✳ 1968 ✳
Appears on: *The Hangman's Beautiful Daughter*

The cover says it all. This was the utopian dream of all hippies – great clothes, out in the woods with winsome girlfriends who had very long hair and names like Rosie and Liquorice. Can't beat that. The Incredibles were, for a while, the epitome of cool. Their number one fan was Robert Plant; Bob Dylan and

Marianne Faithful sang their praises, and the Grateful Dead covered their songs.

The Incredibles – Mike Heron and Robin Williamson – were folk singers who jumped head-on into the counterculture. They took the roots of British folk, a touch of American music and dollops of what Robert Plant called Bulgarian scales and transformed them into something completely their own.

The music was eclectic enough. The lyrics touched on Celtic traditions and a smorgasbord of spirituality including, finally, Scientology.

The Hangman's Beautiful Daughter, produced by Joe Boyd, pulled everything together in the most concise way while still being right out there. There is some self-deprecating humour here, but most of the album is fey and ephemeral. Musically the Incredibles were on fire. Between the two of them they played organ, dulcimer, bass, guitar, harpsichord, horn, sitar, harmonica, mandolin, percussion, piano, violin, harp and oud. They also had a gimbri and they knew how to use it. The melodies and tempos flew off on tangents only to resolve themselves in unlikely ways.

The closing track of *Hangman's*, 'A Very Cellular Song', was their finest moment. "Part of 'Cellular Song' was written on acid actually," said Heron. "Most of it on one trip, kind of through the night, before the dawn. It wasn't personal though. I was writing a song for the world while on acid." The song is a suite built around an old hymn, which evolves into a chant that became a global incantation, the national anthem of communes: "May the long time sun shine upon you/All love surround you/And the pure light within you/ Guide you all the way on."

Voodoo Chile The Jimi Hendrix Experience

(Jimi Hendrix) ✳ Track Record ✳ 1968 ✳ Appears on: *Electric Ladyland*

This fifteen-minute epic blues track had a very simple start. Hendrix had fought with his bass player Noel Redding while recording the *Electric Ladyland* album. At Steve Paul's the Scene nightclub, where Traffic was playing, Hendrix ran into Jefferson Airplane bassist Jack Casady. Hendrix invited Casady and Traffic's Steve Winwood and Chris Wood to come to the studio and cut a tune along with regular Experience drummer Mitch Mitchell.

Hendrix had block booked New York studio the Record Plant – an unheard of concept in those days – and simply recorded as much as possible. Hendrix's explorations led to tensions with his manager Chas Chandler, who had to bail out halfway through the project because he couldn't stand the wasted studio time. Nonetheless, *Electric Ladyland* is a landmark recording – indulgent, sprawling and innovative at every turn.

There were three versions of 'Voodoo Chile': the first run-through; the second, on which Hendrix broke a string; and the third, which was a charm.

"'Voodoo Chile' is really a straight improv in a blues format," said Casady. "Jimi sketched out the chords, everybody got it, and counted it off. And we didn't stop 'til 7.30 a.m. There was no sign of how monumental it was after we'd finished. It was just, 'Hey, that was fun to do. See you later, I got to catch a plane.'"

Deportee (Plane Wreck at Los Gatos) Judy Collins

(Woody Guthrie/Martin Hoffman) ✳ Warner Bros. ✳ 1968 ✳
Appears on: *A Tribute to Woody Guthrie*

Woody Guthrie wrote songs about those whose own voices could not be heard. Guthrie frequently took stories from the newspapers and turned them into ballads, immortalising folk heroes and events. One of his last great songs was inspired by a plane crash over Los Gatos Canyon in California where a plane, packed with poor, illegal immigrant workers, crashed, killing all on board. The twenty-eight Mexican farm workers were on their way back to Mexico. It's likely that they would be processed through the red tape and then make their way back to California to do it all again. The fruit industry exploited the law as a mechanism to keep labour costs low. The practice continued into the '60s when Ceasar Chavez finally brought union power into the industry. The practice of exploiting and endangering the poor for the benefit of the wealthy continues, though.

Guthrie penned a poem after reading reports in the newspaper on 29 January 1948. In 'Deportee' he simply chronicles the tragedy of the plane crash and highlights the anonymity of the victims ("You won't have your names when you ride the big airplane/All they will call you will be deportees"). Guthrie's lyric is both universal and particular.

A schoolteacher, Martin Hoffman, wrote a melody to Guthrie's words and Pete Seeger added it to his set in 1959. It has since become one of Guthrie's most performed works – in no small part due to Hoffman's contribution, which is more tuneful than most of Guthrie's own compositions.

Stoned Soul Picnic Laura Nyro

(Laura Nyro) ❊ Columbia ❊ 1968 ❊ Appears on: *Eli and the Thirteenth Confession*

Laura Nyro was only nineteen when Blood, Sweat and Tear's version of her song 'When I Die' became a number one hit record. The daughter of a piano tuner and sometime trumpet player, Laura Nyro had a delicate gift for pop songs. The early success and the fragility of her temperament contributed to her early retirement. Within three years of her second album, she was already withdrawing from show business. But it was precisely this delicacy that comes through on her own records and has made her a legend. She was David Geffen's first client. He arranged for her to audition for Clive Davis at Columbia and she insisted that all the lights be turned off as she played by the light of a TV set. Davis then advanced her $3 million to record at Columbia.

Nyro's is a particularly New York sensibility. Doo-wop, the girl groups of the early '60s and R&B all informed her pop sensibility, while there was a strong dose of jazz in her elegantly romantic harmonies and melodies.

"From the time I could read, from six years old, I always loved poetry," she told Bill Flanagan in the '80s. "I would find these little books of the poets of different countries. I just always loved it, I trusted it, and I found it to be a pure expression of something that was going on. And all the music that was happening when I was a kid was, I think, *luscious* music. John Coltrane was really happening, and very late-'50s rock & roll, very romantic, melodic stuff. I loved the guys' voices then – the street singers – they had beautiful voices. Then the very early-'60s R&B – there was a lot of music and poetry in life. And I think it influenced me."

'Stoned Soul Picnic' from her second album became a smash hit for the Fifth Dimension and was covered by Sinatra and Aretha Franklin amongst many others. Her own version, though, is more fragile. The joy of getting a little high on wine on a sunny afternoon has a delicious quality when she sings of it and a sense of how fleeting joy can be. Floating on the breeze of this melody we can faintly hear the Shangri-Las and the soulfulness of Nina Simone. Mostly what you hear in this track is the sound of a perfect moment.

Paralyzed The Legendary Stardust Cowboy

(Norman Carl Odam) ❄ Mercury ❄ 1968 ❄

Appears on: *Texas Music, Vol. 3: Garage Bands and Psychedelia*

Norman Carl Odam was born in Lubbock, Texas, where he was a schoolmate of Joe Ely. While the latter became one of the most respected songwriters of his generation, Odam combined his two interests – the Wild West and space exploration – into the persona of the Legendary Stardust Cowboy.

"When I was fourteen," he wrote in 1969, "I started doing Rebel yells and Indian whoops because I am part Shawnee. I taught myself to do birdcalls and jungle sounds. I figured that by singing I was able to attract all the girls."

Music, in the conventional sense, was not his forte, but he did record one timeless single. 'Paralyzed' is a demented yowl of Indian war whoops, cat calls, yelps and chanted lyrics recorded at a breakneck pace. Suddenly the guitar stops and he picks up a bugle and blows a free jazz solo. "The band was just me on drums, and he had a Dobro with a broken neck, so he could only play on the first fret," said T-Bone Burnett who, as a trainee engineer at the studio, was assigned the session. "We just set up two microphones. Norman gave me some instructions – 'Play drums in the same tempo I'm singing in' – and I said, 'I could do that.' Maybe probably. Then he said he was going to take a bugle solo, and he wanted me to take a drum solo, and I found that all agreeable. It was explosive, to say the least."

'Paralyzed' became a hit single, and Odam appeared on national TV. Three more songs were recorded but real stardom proved elusive.

The Ledge, as he is known, has had many influential admirers, but none so public as David Bowie, who heard 'Paralyzed', 'Down in the Wrecking Yard' and 'I Took a Trip on a Gemini Spaceship' in 1971. "The integrity, honesty and innocent, brutal focus entranced me," he wrote in *MOJO*. In admiration, Bowie took the surname for his alter ego, Ziggy Stardust, and eventually recorded 'I Took a Trip on a Gemini Spaceship' for his *Heathen* album.

"For me, he's up there with people like Wild Man Fisher – it's the original outsider music," said Bowie in 1996. "Music by people probably not playing with a full deck. He played guitar, and he had a drummer and a one-legged trumpet player. They assembled their music without any awareness that there are supposed to be rules to follow. And so they go in directions that wouldn't occur to even a semi-trained musician. And it's such a freeing exercise, listening to them commit to those performances with full integrity – knowing that they are not joking."

Dream a Little Dream of Me The Mamas & the Papas

(Gus Kahn/Wilbur Schwandt/Fabian Andre) ✳ Dunhill ✳ 1968 ✳

Appears on: The Papas and the Mamas

Gus Kahn was a songwriting machine. With his wife Grace at the piano playing the tune, Kahn added words to suit. In 1931, a tune came to him from journeymen musicians Wilbur Schwandt and Fabian Andre, who reckoned they knocked up the melody in a ten-minute break between sets at a date in Paw Paw, Michigan. With the addition of Kahn's lyric, the song attracted many covers from Frankie Laine, Kate Smith, Nat King Cole and Frank Sinatra.

"My dad always tried to keep his lyrics simple," his son Donald Kahn told NPR. "But he also said that young men and women do not know how to say 'I love you' to one another so we say it for them in thirty-two bars."

In 1950 a six-year-old girl called Michelle was introduced to Fabian Andre, then playing piano in Mexico City. Eighteen years later she was one of the Mamas and Papas, one of the most successful recording groups of its time. They were in the studio when they heard the news that Andre had fallen down a mine shaft in Mexico City and died. The childhood incident was recalled and there was nothing for it but to run through the song, with Cass Elliott singing lead. According to Michelle Phillips, Cass Elliott always envied Barbra Streisand but, Phillips told NPR, "Streisand could never match the sweetness and love in Cass' voice."

I Heard It Through the Grapevine Marvin Gaye

(Barrett Strong/Norman Whitfield) ✳ Tamla ✳ 1968 ✳ Appears on: In the Groove

Motown put the factory in 'hit factory'. Songwriter/producers cut tracks with the house band and then allocated the house stars to the particular tunes. No song illustrates the process better than 'I Heard It Through the Grapevine', which Barrett Strong initially gave to Gladys Knight and the Pips. Fellow inmates the Isley Brothers and the Miracles also cut the song.

A month after the Pips had recorded 'Grapevine', producer/writer Norman Whitfield recut the track for Marvin Gaye, accenting a more churchy, Ray Charles feel. Whitfield replaced the acoustic piano with an electric Wurlitzer. For the drums he wanted an 'Indian' sound with the accent on the toms. He slowed the track down to a voodoo chant pace and built a powerful groove.

"I came up with a little idea on the piano, the bass-line figure," said Barrett Strong. "We thought it was great, and I thought of this title, 'I Heard It Through the Grapevine', because I'd heard people saying it so much but nobody had ever written a song about it. We just went from there."

With Gladys Knight's version reaching number two on the charts, the Gaye version was shelved and it took a year of insistence before Motown supremo Berry Gordy agreed to release the track. He's reported to have said to Whitfield, "Mention that fucking record again and you're fired".

The song stayed in the vaults until uncovered by archivist/quality control manager Billie Jean Brown who needed a filler for a Gaye album. A Chicago radio station began playing the album track and it took off. 'I Heard It Through the Grapevine' became Motown's biggest hit of the label's first twenty years. The song was also reinterpreted by Creedence Clearwater Revival into a swamp rock jam.

Even Marvin himself was apparently ambivalent about the song at first. "I was being a good artist at the time," he said in 1972. "They tell you, 'Marvin, you gotta come in and do this tune, because this song is a good song for you and it was written by so and so, and so come right in there and be a good guy and cut it, OK?' And that always bugged me. Generally I say go take your song and stuff it. But this particular time I said, 'Oh. Hell, I'll be a good artist'. But it was the Lord who was working and He knew I should have gotten to do it so I did. And that's why it became a big hit."

(Sittin' On) The Dock of the Bay Otis Redding

(Otis Redding/Steve Cropper) ❋ Stax ❋ 1968 ❋ Appears on: *Dock of the Bay*

"Elvis was the king of rock & roll and Otis was the king of soul," said Steve Cropper. "Had he lived, I think he would have been king of them all."

With the backing of Booker T and the MGs, Redding was the most versatile singer in the Stax stable and a performer of immense charisma. His show-stopping set at the 1967 Monterey Pop Festival had poised him to step out from a strictly soul and R&B market into the pop charts. 'Dock of the Bay' was the song that could do it.

Redding began the song in August 1967 while living on a houseboat in Sausalito, outside San Francisco. Back in Memphis in December, MGs' guitarist Steve Cropper helped him to finish it. "I'm not sure he knew, but my trick was always to write about Otis. So I came up with the lines 'I left my home in Georgia/Headed for the 'Frisco Bay.' It was so easy," said Cropper.

"When he came in with it, he played me the melody and he had almost one whole verse completed. We sat down in the studio by ourselves and within two hours we had the completed song. I helped him with part of the second verse and the bridge and the changes. Then I did the arrangement.

"Right before the accident, he came into the studio for one whole week and then off and on for another two weeks," Cropper told *Hit Parade* magazine. "We cut a lot of stuff on him then. At the time, he was going out on weekend dates. He'd come back and cut from Monday to Thursday. This time we cut some final horn lines of a Friday morning. He said, "I'll see ya'all." He went off to Nashville to do *Up Beat* and then the next night he left for Wisconsin. He was due back here Monday to cut more songs."

The track was recorded in one day including an improvised whistling part at the end and Redding's vocal. The MGs were in perfect form. The song is ostensibly a homesick ballad but there's a deep forlornness there that is mirrored by Cropper's guitar line, which weaves a majestic melody underneath Redding's wistfulness.

Redding never finished the track. Four days later while on tour, his plane crashed into a lake killing everyone on board.

Cropper spent three weeks mixing the song and it did give Otis Redding his number one in the pop charts.

Street Fighting Man The Rolling Stones

(Mick Jagger/Keith Richards) ❊ Decca ❊ 1968 ❊ Appears on: *Beggars Banquet*

'Street Fighting Man' is an ambivalent call to arms recorded while students in Paris, London and across the US were literally building the barricades for a revolution.

The song began life as 'Did Everybody Pay Your Dues'. Keith Richards had cut a cassette demo with Charlie Watts playing a '30s toy drum kit and Richards on acoustic guitar. That set up, complete with cassette player, was replicated at Olympic studios, where the track was redone. The song has a massive drum sound that sits just behind the beat, layers of churning and ringing acoustic guitars all piled up by Richards, and bass, also from Richards.

These were the first sessions with American producer Jimmy Miller. It was a relationship that produced their golden run of classic Rolling Stones albums.

Richards and Jagger both felt they were in the eye of the storm of history. They were being persecuted by the British police and for a time locked in Wormwood Scrubs prison. Meanwhile the aristocracy invited them to the best parties. At the same time, intellectuals and radicals around the world saw the Rolling Stones as the spearhead of a revolution. It's not surprising that the sentiments in the song are somewhat confused.

'Pay Your Dues' was scrapped as a single release, replaced by 'Jumping Jack Flash'. The lyrics were rewritten and vocal redone by Jagger to emerge as 'Street Fighting Man'.

"'Street Fighting Man' is a funny song to play on stage in an era when you don't fight in the street any more," said Charlie Watts. "To play the song is fantastic, but the lyrics are very much about the events of 1968 in Paris, which is when Mick wrote it. It was political; not that it was going to change the world, but it was extremely influenced by what was going on – a very strong song about what was happening at the time."

Sympathy for the Devil The Rolling Stones

(Mick Jagger/Keith Richards) ❋ Decca ❋ 1968 ❋ Appears on: *Beggars Banquet*

"'Sympathy' was one of those sort of songs where we tried everything," drummer Charlie Watts said. "The first time I ever heard the song was when Mick was playing it at the front door of a house where I lived in Sussex. It was at dinner. He played it entirely on his own, the sun was going down – and it was fantastic. We had a go at loads of different ways of playing it; in the end I just played a jazz Latin feel in the style Kenny Clarke would have played on 'A Night in Tunisia' – not the actual rhythm he played, but the same styling. Fortunately it worked, because it was a sod to get together."

The recording of 'Sympathy for the Devil' at Olympic studios in London was documented by the French director Jean Luc Godard in his film *One Plus One*. Godard captured the laborious process the group went through – trying different arrangements – to get the song to work. Godard cut this footage with storylines about the coming revolution, and the whole makes some kind of sense. Keith Richards plays the guitars and bass, Brian Jones is sidelined in a corner with his guitar disconnected from the recording machines, Nicky Hopkins plays piano and Rocky Dijon plays congas while everybody is finally drafted into singing the haunting backing vocals.

Jagger's lyric came from the Mikhail Bulgakov novel *The Master and Margarita*. It reflected the singer's growing interest in the occult. The book is about Satan's visit to Russia after the Bolshevik revolution. In a time of optimism about a future of peace and love, Jagger was pointing out the evil that lurks in the hearts of men.

Oscillations Silver Apples

(Simeon/Warren Stanley) ✳ Kapp ✳ 1968 ✳ Appears on: *Silver Apples*

For a moment in 1968, Silver Apples looked like the future of music. The duo of Dan Taylor and Simeon played (respectively) tuned drums and the Simeon, which was an assemblage of oscillators and other electronic junk wired together to make music. This was a garage version of what serious music composers had been doing since Percy Grainger left his country garden. But Silver Apples lived in a rock & roll context. They took their name from a Yeats poem. And as Simeon noted, "The silver part reminded us of the solder that held all the junk together, and the apples we felt linked us to New York."

The Simeon was made of at least nine oscillators, each tuned differently, making rhythmic noise and rough melodies accompanied by the drums, and sometimes poetry. For a time the Silver Apples toured widely and held down a residency at the ultra-hip Max's Kansas City. The Mayor of New York commissioned them to write and perform a piece celebrating the first moonwalk in 1969. The Apples were briefly the toast of the underground, performing the scores to off-off-Broadway theatre. "Theatre producer and director John Vacarro had a reputation for putting on the most outrageous theatrical experiences in New York. He was producing a musical called *Cockstrong* and wanted Silver Apples to create the music for it," Simeon recalled. The star of the show was to be one of New York's most famous trans-vestites named Jackie Curtis. There was one dance number called 'The Kama Sutra' where we were allowed to improvise for ten minutes while the players, in their clothes, tried to accomplish all the sexual positions, both couples and groups. One night the audience seemed to be very into it and Danny and I decided to keep it going a while longer. I didn't realise how physically demanding it was for the actors and after a while they started screaming for mercy. I thought they were just acting and kept going. Soon there was open rebellion on the stage and the actors, while still in their contorted Kama Sutra positions, were shaking their fists at me and giving the 'cut' sign with their fingers across the throat. They were really glaring at me and the audience was roaring with delight. I finally gave in, and Jackie Curtis went into her final number, 'Cockstrong', during which this enormous, erect, papier-mâché penis slowly expanded out over the stage pointing at the audience."

Surprisingly, commercial success never came their way after that. Instead they have gone into history as the precursors of Suicide, Orchestral Manoeuvres in the Dark, the Human League, Brian Eno, Kraftwerk, the Prodigy and electronica acts everywhere.

Dance to the Music   Sly & the Family Stone

(Sylvester 'Sly Stone' Stewart) ❋ EPIC ❋ 1968 ❋

Appears on: *Dance to the Music*

The first Sly & the Family Stone record had not done well. The pressure from the record company had got to the point where Epic was trying to tell Sly Stone what to record. According to sax player Jerry Martini, this got Sly's back up.

"I remember Sly and I going over to CBS Records," Martini recalled. "They gave us some shit and Sly threw it down and he looked at me and said, 'OK, I'll give them something.' And that is when he took off with his formula style. He hated it. He just did it to sell records. The whole album was called *Dance to the Music*, dance to the medley, dance to the shmedley. It was so unhip to us. The beats were glorified Motown beats. We had been doing something different, but these beats weren't going over. So we did the formula thing. The rest is history and he continued his formula style.

"On 'Dance to the Music', one of the sub-hooks was my clarinet. We used it on the medley. It was snowing in New York and if we wanted to get paid by the union, which was so strong, you had to bring an instrument to the session. If a union guy came in, you better have your horn. I was freezing and just wanted to carry my small clarinet. I had already done my horn parts. I was in the back room, just fucking around with the tune. Sly walked by the studio and called me over. So then, on a lot of things, I used clarinet. That is how hits happen. He was smart. He heard something unique and it was the sound of a clarinet. When is the last time you heard of somebody in rock using a clarinet? I used to take my clarinet on the road for a long time until we got too fucked up, then I just played the lick on my sax. A lot of people thought that it was a soprano sax on that, but it was B flat clarinet."

'Dance to the Music' built on the soul plus gospel that the group had developed in its years in Vegas and on the road. Sly & the Family Stone were one of the greatest live acts in the country and with material like 'Dance to the Music' they conquered every venue they played. One of the crucial dates was Woodstock, where the medley that starts with 'Dance to the Music' completely stole the show and the Woodstock film.

"Our songs would segue one into the other and many times there wasn't a place where you could get a big audience response," said bass player Larry Graham recalling the Woodstock gig. "When we did stop playing, there was this tremendous roar unlike anything we had ever heard. It was dark and you couldn't see all those people, but to hear that was like, wow. To go back out and play the encore after hearing that, it made us rise to a level we had never been musically. There was so much energy; everybody reached deep down inside and pulled out some stuff we didn't know was there. From that point on, once you tap into a certain zone, you know you can go back there because you have now tasted that. The audience might not be as big as Woodstock, but to play anything after that, you know you have capabilities beyond. So that took our concerts up to a whole other giant notch, to where the concerts became an experience, for the audience and for us. We started playing in this new zone we had never played in before and it was some of heaviest stuff I had ever been involved in."

Born to be Wild Steppenwolf

(Mars Bonfire) ❄ Dunhill ❄ 1968 ❄ Appears on: *Steppenwolf*

'Born to be Wild' is one of the great, greasy riffs in rock. It's ugly, dirty, sexy. With the chugging guitar and swirling organ on top of a funky rock beat, it has it all.

John Kay, guitarist and singer, was born in Germany and raised in Canada where his band Sparrow played the circuit before moving to Los Angeles. They met producer Gabriel Mekler, who named the group after the Herman Hesse novel and then gave them a sound that was darker and more sleazy than most of the rock bands of the period. When it was fashionable on the Sunset Strip to freak out, Steppenwolf had this churning, almost demonic funk happening. Their debut album featured a brilliant and scary version of Hoyt Axton's 'The Pusher' and the quirky 'Sookie Sookie'.

'Born to be Wild' was written by Sparrow Dennis Edmonton under the pseudonym Mars Bonfire. The lyrics included the famous line, "I like smokin' lightning, heavy metal thunder," which it was said named the genre. 'Born to be Wild' was not heavy metal – it was too fast and too complex for that.

The song was a hit in 1968. Dennis Hopper rightly picked the track for his film *Easy Rider* and used it to denote the spirit of rebelliousness and freedom that was at the core of the film. The combination of that riff and chopped Harley Davidson motorcycles was the iconic partnership of the era. Ever since then 'Born to be Wild' has been associated with motorcycle clubs in particular and outlaw behaviour in general.

"'Born to be Wild' reached global anthem status," said singer John Kay. "It's one of those things that just outgrew its constraints and became its own animal."

Stand By Your Man   Tammy Wynette

(Billy Sherrill/Tammy Wynette) ✳ Epic ✳ 1968 ✳ Appears on: *Stand By Your Man*

Tammy Wynette was the first lady of country music, in large part because of this song. Her Nashville twang grows to epic proportions here. It's an iconic image of absolute love and devotion. It's also a sentiment that is deeply conservative – the comfort zone of the perfect union no matter how imperfect the participants.

Wynette was still new to the game when she cut the track. Coming from the poor white background that breeds so many country greats, Wynette was discovered in 1966 by producer Billy Sherrill who put her on the charts with 'Apartment #9'.

Sherrill had 'Stand By Your Man' for about a year before he recorded the track with Wynette.

"All that time, the world was barraged by ERA and Women's Lib so I decided that I wanted the song to be for all women everywhere who did not agree," he said. "I wanted it to be a tune for the truly liberated woman; it was for women who were secure enough in their own identity to enjoy it.

"Some people thought the song was about chauvinism, but that's their problem. They can like the song or lump it! It's just another way of saying I love you with no strings attached."

Crimson and Clover   Tommy James & the Shondells

(Tommy James) ✳ Rhino ✳ 1968 ✳ Appears on: *Anthology*

Tommy Jackson (aka James) cut one of the great singles of all time when he was just thirteen and working in a record shop. It wasn't until three years later in 1966 that 'Hanky Panky' became a national number one. The song has that classic 'Louie Louie' progression behind James' twangy voice. James teamed up with producer/writers Bo Gentry and Richie Cordell for a string of exquisite pop songs including 'I Think We're Alone Now' and 'Mony Mony'. James' sweet and sexy material had him tagged as a bubblegum artist.

Then, in 1968, he released his first self-produced single, 'Crimson and Clover'. Pure psychedelic pop with groundbreaking production, the 45 sold five million copies and the album had liner notes from Vice President Hubert Humphrey. "I never set out to make a so-called psychedelic record," James said. "I was just having fun with the new technology. I wanted to make sounds swim, make 'em wiggle a little bit." The trippy vocal sound came from James singing through his guitar amp with the tremolo turned up. Add layers of guitar and echo and in one session the classic was recorded and mixed.

The album also featured the equally trippy 'Crystal Blue Persuasion'. By 1970, James had cut nine albums in three years and collapsed on stage in Montgomery, Alabama. He recuperated enough to have another hit with 'Draggin' the Line' in 1972. While his legend has not lived large, the songs have – each one has been a hit for at least one other artist. The originals remain works of staggering pop beauty.

Love Is All Around The Troggs

(Reg Presley) ❊ Fontana ❊ 1968 ❊ Appears on: *Love Is All Around*

After pumping out some of the best pop in Britain in the '60s, the Troggs came out with this massive ballad. Its modal guitar riff has a faintly Elizabethan feel to it against the inexorable rhythm. Singer Reg Presley, although trying to be sweet, still has that deeply sexual undercurrent in his vocal. The Troggs had followed 'Wild Thing' with their own 'I Can't Control Myself', which was even more wild than the first track. 'Love Is All Around' puts that brutish past behind the Troggs. This is a real chocolate box ballad. There's so much personality here, especially in the ham-fisted but well-meaning backing vocals.

'Love Is All Around' was yet another hit in Britain and their second smash in the US, although none of this transferred into long-term success for the band. 'Love Is All Around' has lived on through cover versions by R.E.M., Everything But the Girl and the bloodless but popular version by Wet Wet Wet on the soundtrack for the film *Four Weddings and a Funeral*.

Rag Mama Rag The Band

(Jaime Robbie Robertson) ❊ Capitol ❊ 1969 ❊ Appears on: *The Band*

For the recording of their second album, the Band moved to Los Angeles with their families to escape the harsh Woodstock winter. They rented Sammy Davis Jr's mansion and turned the pool house into a studio. The five players set up their equipment much as it had been in Big Pink with the musicians together in a large room, generally playing at the same time.

"Everything in rock was kind of going in that high-end direction," said Robbie Robertson. "We wanted something different, a kind of woody, thuddy sound." Robertson played guitar and engineered while producer John Simon also played on some tracks. All the other musicians played multiple instruments. This swapping of instruments gave *The Band* a distinctive sound. It was particularly important for Levon Helm, who had to phrase his vocals around his drumming, giving many of the songs a country funk feel.

"I started thinking that the music was finally taking shape with the second album," said Helm. "We had actually figured out some methods of how to really turn the heat up and get the music to cook: how to blend our voices three different ways, how to get the track together and not make it so complicated. We'd sit and talk about medicine shows and, shit, the tune would just come to us. A lot of those good lessons Dylan had given us started to manifest themselves."

The Band's imagery suggested a 19th century ambience of pre-Civil War backwoodsmen and God-fearing patriarchs. In fact, the Band was anything but that. They were a group who had been playing tough rock & roll for a decade in bars and clubs across America. They were not familiar with folk music and not much accomplished with country. The group's bass player, Rick Danko, for instance, took his style from jazz virtuoso Ron Carter and the Motown sound of Chuck Rainey and James Jamerson.

However, Robertson's myth was the context for everything. Part of that myth relied on the voice and the personality of Levon Helm, who was at least from the backwoods of Arkansas and gave a veracity to songs like 'Up on Cripple Creek', 'The Night They Drove Old Dixie Down' and 'Rag Mama Rag'.

The latter song was a perfect example of the Band's modus operandi. Helm moved to mandolin. Richard Manuel played the drums in his own loping, behind-the-beat style, Danko moved to fiddle and John Simon played the bass part on tuba even though he hadn't previously played the instrument.

"'Rag Mama Rag' was like, 'Well, this is an extra one and if we don't have anything better to do we might as well cut this one'," said Robertson. "It didn't have very much importance to it until after we recorded it. It showed something else that we could do: Richard plays the drums, Rick played violin – we got to show something else that we do in a style that doesn't exist. You know – 'Name this music!'"

The song had the appearance of an old folk song but it is, in fact, pure funk.

"Me and a bunch of guys from New Orleans would listen to *The Band* all the time," said Mac 'Dr John' Rebennack. "The music sounded to me like a cross between Memphis and New Orleans. It was really in the pockets of those places without ever copying the original stuff."

Come Together The Beatles

(John Lennon/Paul McCartney) ✳ Apple ✳ 1969 ✳ Appears on: *Abbey Road*

One of the darkest and most funky of Beatles' songs, 'Come Together' rides on Paul McCartney's dirty bass parts that slide into the song and make it swing. The treated percussion sounds and details bejewel this track. The groove here comes from Chuck Berry's 'You Can't Catch Me' – undeniably a lift for which Lennon confessed. The lyrics for the chorus come from acid guru Timothy Leary, who used the slogan 'Come Together' in a Californian gubernatorial race and for whom Lennon whipped out a campaign song along those lines.

'Come Together' is much, more than just a rehash of Chuck Berry. The sounds here are layered and the studio effects are carefully manipulated for a Beatles sound unlike any other. The sheer fatness over the top of a boogie beat here prefigures the glam rock that was only two years away.

The lyrics are a typical Lennon word salad, fitting in with the swamp groove of the track without meaning anything in particular. Whatever the case, it's perhaps the funkiest they ever got.

Hey Bulldog The Beatles

(John Lennon/Paul McCartney) ✳ Apple ✳ 1969 ✳ Appears on: *Yellow Submarine*

Written and recorded in one day, 'Hey Bulldog' is an oft-neglected Beatle classic. The Beatles were short one of the four songs they were obliged to deliver to United Artists for the animated film *Yellow Submarine*. While filming a clip for 'Lady Madonna', McCartney suggested they cut a track and Lennon proffered this one. It's the group at their least self-conscious and Lennon at his least pretentious. The lyric, while not specific, is more acute than the word salads he came up with around this period. The performance, though, is top notch, including a rare lead solo from Lennon. There is no bulldog mentioned in the song. The title comes from impromptu barking by McCartney as the song fades.

I Want You (She's So Heavy) The Beatles

(John Lennon/Paul McCartney) ✳ Apple ✳ 1969 ✳ Appears on: *Abbey Road*

In the '60s, rock & roll music created pop culture. Essentially unschooled musicians and lyricists were taken seriously as artists for the first time in history and this upward cultural mobility meant that rock musicians rubbed shoulders with, and were influenced by, more serious and academic artists and they started to incorporate those ideas into pop. When one of the Beatles was involved in that exchange then the result immediately went out into the culture at large.

Yoko Ono's influence on John Lennon was significant – her minimalist theory and practice in the visual arts and the avant-garde milieu from which she came reinvigorated Lennon's work. Often the results were unimpressive, but 'I Want You (She's So Heavy)' is a masterstroke. The minimalist lyrics are sung almost as a mantra over swirling layers of noise.

Lennon's guitar and the bluesy melody build up, improvising and adding as they go, then moving into a jazzy section and finally into the ascending guitar riffs at the end of the song with the Beatles' voices blending and spiralling upwards. The Beatles also used an early Moog synthesiser on the track and brought in Billy Preston to add organ licks.

Lennon plays against the lack of lyric by using his voice to run through a whole gamut of emotions from petulance to pleading to screaming. The band, too, mirrors these emotional shifts. Then the song just ends.

The End The Beatles

(John Lennon/Paul McCartney) ✳ Apple ✳ 1969 ✳ Appears on: *Abbey Road*

The Beatles assembled *Abbey Road* as a farewell (*Let It Be*, the final album, was already recorded and at this point discarded) so it's an entirely appropriate note on which to end. Most of the second side of the album was an extended medley of half-formed songs patched together by Paul McCartney that rises up to 'Carry That Weight' – one of the many songs the Beatles wrote about the trials of being in the Beatles. Then comes Ringo Starr's only recorded drum solo followed by a farewell guitar solo taken by the other three Beatles in turn. As John Lennon said, "There's a nice little bit I played on *Abbey Road* … Paul gave us each a piece, a little break where Paul plays, George plays and I play. It stops, on 'Carry That Weight', then suddenly it goes boom-boom-boom on the drums and we all take it in turns to play. I'm the third one on it. I have a definite style of playing, always had. But I was overshadowed. They call George the invisible singer, I'm the invisible guitarist."

Finally there's a brief lyric – "The love you take is equal to the love you make" – which even had the approval of Lennon himself. Not a big hit, 'The End' has a delicate, concise sweetness and is a fitting farewell. Lest anyone get too serious, the song is undercut by the twee 'Her Majesty'. The perfect ending to a perfect career.

Presence of the Lord Blind Faith

(Eric Clapton) ✳ Polydor ✳ 1969 ✳ Appears on: *Blind Faith*

Never before has an album with so much riding on it been so rushed and half-baked. Blind Faith was the first supergroup. It combined Ginger Baker and Eric Clapton from Cream with Steve Winwood from Traffic and the little known Rick Gretch. Clapton's friend David Litvanoff had played the guitarist a bootleg copy of *The Basement Tapes* and Clapton immediately disbanded Cream in search of something more pastoral and song-based.

Baker invited himself along and Clapton, in fear of the drummer, allowed him to stay and psychologically left the room himself. The first album was assembled hastily. Six songs running a total of less than three-quarters of an hour (and one-third of that being a drum solo) is the sum total of *Blind Faith*. But Clapton was right – the combination of his melancholic persona and guitar style with Steve Winwood's keening bittersweet voice and beautiful, delicate melodies was extraordinary.

The songs expressed the sense of being wasted. There's an eerie sense of a search for meaning – almost all the tracks are mid-tempo ballads.

Clapton's contribution, 'Presence of the Lord', was in tune with the new Christianity that was overtaking the charts at the time. He said he unfolded two posters of Humphrey Bogart and James Cagney and a picture of Jesus dropped out. A moment later two Christians appeared at Clapton's hotel room door. He told *Uncut* recently, "I remember playing it one night with Blind Faith. The audience turned into devils or angels according to what I played." One suspects the 'Clapton is God' graffiti had gone to his head and perhaps drugs played a part too.

Time Is Tight   Booker T & the MGs

(Booker T Jones/Steve Cropper/Al Jackson/Donald Duck Dunn) ✳ Stax ✳ 1969 ✳

Appears on: *Booker T and the MGs Greatest Hits*

The funkiest and best known instrumental of the '60s grew out of a jam amongst the session players in the Stax studio. "We were trying to think of something as funky as possible," said Steve Cropper of the song 'Green Onions'. And they did. The song went Top 5 and suddenly the session cats needed an identity – hence the MGs (Memphis Group). Now not only were they the most in demand session team for soul tracks but they had their own career.

The MGs' funkiness drips out of all the classic sides by Eddie Floyd, Aretha Franklin, Otis Redding and Wilson Pickett to name but a few. In 1964 the tougher Duck Dunn replaced Lewis Shinberg and the MGs continued to have hits like the spectacular, sexy and slightly jazzy 'Hip Hug Her'.

Their final hit, 'Time Is Tight' reflected the jazz touch but was still with the funky, bluesy sound. The key to the record is its simplicity – not a move is in haste or misjudged. Everything sits perfectly in the pocket.

By 1969 they were still powering but the mood at Stax and amongst the group had changed. The one constant, however, and the secret to their success was drummer Al Jackson.

"Al was just the cleanest drummer in the world," Dunn told Barney Hoskyns. "The pocket where Al put everything was the real secret of Stax. Every time we recorded, he was ninety-eight per cent correct on just about everything we did. And even today, every drummer I play with asks me, 'What was it like to play with Al Jackson?'"

"I can't really define it as a secret formula, but we did make a concerted effort to keep things simple through the years," Booker T Jones told Hoskyns. "That was the one kind of unspoken and sometimes spoken agreement among the Stax producers. It just happened to be the chemistry of the time and the players."

Loan Me a Dime   Boz Scaggs

(Fenton Robinson) ✳ Atlantic ✳ 1969 ✳ Appears on: *Boz Scaggs*

Texan-born Scaggs moved to San Francisco – "after the summer of love, in the winter of mild discontent" – to play with the Steve Miller Band where he had a reputation as a hot shot blues guitarist. *Rolling Stone* editor Jann Wenner produced his first solo album.

"At that time he [Wenner] was being courted by a lot of key people in the industry who saw the emergence of *Rolling Stone* as very important," said Scaggs. "He was meeting the likes of Jerry Wexler and Ahmet Ertegun and Clive Davis – and at some point he took a tape of my work to Jerry, and Jerry liked it. We decided to do the album at Muscle Shoals, with Barry Beckett, Roger Hawkins, David Hood, Eddie Hinton, Pete Carr and Duane Allman."

With those people involved the record was going to be very strong on R&B and soul grooves. Allman was only then getting a reputation as a guitar virtuoso. His work on the thirteen-minute 'Loan Me a Dime', where he duets with Scaggs, is one of his finest pieces. Unlike many blues improvisations, the song never gets indulgent and never loses its groove.

"He was a powerful guy in a low-key way, and he added a real spark to everything we did – on 'Loan Me a Dime' his solo was a real catalyst," said Scaggs. "There's real magic in those guys, a chemistry to the way they play. They leave room for just that one quality of the other player that fits, and they take that space knowing that the other guy's going to give way. Jann just directed traffic and called the big shots." The record was not a hit of any magnitude, but it has stood the test of time.

Fortunate Son Creedence Clearwater Revival

(John Fogerty) ❀ Fantasy ❀ 1969 ❀ Appears on: *Willie and the Poor Boys*

Even the critic paid to write the sleeve notes on their first album damned Creedence Clearwater Revival with faint praise. The quartet from the suburbs never fitted into the hip San Francisco scene. Their ability to knock out astounding, powerful 45s rather than unfocused and rambling jams had them consigned to the Top 40 bin. Nonetheless, Creedence is one of the few San Francisco groups of the period whose records now sound as vital as when they were cut.

John Fogerty, who wrote, produced, sang and played most of the instruments, is a formidable writer. Coming from a dysfunctional working-class family, there's a lot of anger in his tracks. He's one of the few American rock writers to raise the issue of class. 'Fortunate Son' then, isn't just another hippie anti-war song, but a critique on the American aristocracy sending the poor to fight and die "in a war no-one even pretends to believe in".

"I see things through lower-class eyes," said Fogerty. "If you sit around and think about all that money, you can never write a song about where you came from."

The song took twenty minutes to write. Recording took a couple of hours and the entire *Willie and the Poor Boys* LP was done in less than ten days.

The venom of the lyrics is matched by stinging guitar lines from Fogerty and the rhythm section of Doug Clifford (drums), Stu Cook (bass) and Tom Fogerty (rhythm guitar) going hell for leather. While many of Creedence's songs to this point had been southern boogie music and good-time rock & roll, there was no ambiguity about the meaning of 'Fortunate Son'.

Creedence didn't appeal to the cognoscenti; their audience was precisely the kind of white kids who were in the Vietnam jungles. As Fogerty said, referring to the children of the Republican Party's aristocracy, "Julie Nixon was hanging around with David Eisenhower, and you just had the feeling that none of these people were going to be too involved with the war."

Space Oddity David Bowie

(David Bowie) ✳ RCA ✳ 1969 ✳ Appears on: *Space Oddity*

He had been a mod and then an acoustic troubadour with a Bob Dylan fixation. Then Stanley Kubrick's space epic *2001* gave David Bowie the idea of a lifetime. It was the year of the moonwalk and space definitely seemed the place. 'Space Oddity', in its production, its lyric and in David Bowie, signalled the end of one decade of rock and the beginning of a new mannerist period. Bowie's song, rather than celebrating the conquest of the void, is a haunting ballad about alienation.

Inspired by *2001* and a "flirtation with smack," 'Space Oddity' has the now-immortal line "Ground control to Major Tom". The astronaut is trapped in his spacecraft with no hope of returning to Earth. Essentially it's a folk song strummed on acoustic guitar. Bowie took the performance to another level – his deadpan, world-weary singing was quite unlike anything that had come before. There was a whole new slant on ambivalence here.

George Martin and Tony Visconti turned down the opportunity to produce this track. Visconti thought it an attempt to cash in on the Apollo mission. Gus Dudgeon was enlisted and brought along string arranger Paul Buckmaster and Rick Wakeman on the Mellotron. Dudgeon's use of strings and keyboards made the record sound slightly futuristic and trippy without losing its sense of the narrative.

The song was recorded in one day – 20 June. It was played to the public at the Rolling Stones' free concert in Hyde Park on 5 July and released as a 45 a week later. The BBC adopted 'Space Oddity' as its theme for its coverage of the first moonwalk that summer and the song became a hit.

In the Ghetto Elvis Presley

(Mac Davis) ✻ RCA ✻ 1969 ✻ Appears on: *From Elvis in Memphis*

In 1969 Elvis Presley made a dramatic career turnaround. For the past decade he had appeared in a series of increasingly silly films and his recordings were limited to inane soundtrack songs. Even Elvis Presley could see that he was no longer King and was in danger of being the court jester. His solution was to get back to his roots. Having grown up in Memphis, steeped in southern music, Presley felt like going home.

Everything about *From Elvis in Memphis* was surprising. But Presley kept the best for last. The final track was a soulful ballad about poverty and struggle.

'In the Ghetto' is almost political. It's an empathic story of hardship and honest toil. While Presley was now wealthy, his family had been dirt poor and it didn't take much for him to reach back and pull out the memory of those hard times. There was no question that Presley could call on the emotions. It was surprising that after so long he did.

Mac Davis, then a promising young singer/songwriter who had contributed to songs for Presley's film soundtracks, had written the ballad not intending it for Elvis. However, the singer insisted.

"With 'In the Ghetto', he was just really into it," said guitarist Reggie Young. "I remember it being stopped a few times – he just wanted to do it better. It was like he was finally doing a song with some meaning to it, with some soul – it would have to turn him on. By this time he was really enthused about what he was doing, he really cared … Instead of it just being a party, you know, go to the studio and have a party, he was really trying."

Suspicious Minds Elvis Presley

(Mark James) ✻ RCA ✻ 1969 ✻ Appears on: *From Memphis to Vegas*

Elvis Presley's self-reinvention in the late '60s was an extraordinary achievement. The greatest rock & roll star, the King was in decline as a consequence of ten years of song choices and increasingly poor films. Elvis was pretty much finished as a recording artist until he returned to Memphis for the 1968 *From Elvis in Memphis* album and a subsequent TV special.

By the late '60s, Memphis was a music capital with its writers turning out country-soul hits. The field was there for Presley to claim. What he needed, though, was the right material.

Lincoln 'Chips' Moman, an esteemed songwriter and producer, was one of the fathers of country soul. He had made a record with singer/songwriter Mark James that had flopped but did have a song for Presley, 'Suspicious Minds'. Usually the singer demanded a cut of the songwriting royalties but, whether out of perversity or cunning, Moman refused to split the track with Presley and finally the King conceded.

The song was cut at Moman's American studios. The sessions, over two days, yielded thirty-five songs. Somewhere between four and seven in the morning of the first session Presley captured 'Suspicious Minds' on the fourth take. The song is full of speedy paranoid energy. The band is well oiled and Presley sings as if everything depends on it. He allows his vulnerability to come through as well; it's a remarkably open performance. The success of 'Suspicious Minds' sealed the King's comeback and it remained a centrepiece of his repertoire until his final concert.

A Sailor's Life Fairport Convention

(Traditional) ❋ Hannibal ❋ 1969 ❋ Appears on: *Unhalfbricking*

In America the rock groups were taking traditional music – blues and country – and exploding it. In that spirit, singer Sandy Denny, drummer Martin Lamble, bass player Ashley Hutchings, and guitarists Richard Thompson and Simon Nicol formed Fairport Convention to do the same thing with English folk.

"The climate in Britain at that time was bad music *à la* Geno Washington, and blues bands – and a sheen of psychedelia was creeping in over the top," said Thompson. "By the time we turned professional we had what might be called a 'psychedelic' audience. You'd have a light show, an attempt to recreate the kind of environment that was being so successful in America with the Fillmores and the Avalon Ballroom. The audiences were basically fashion-conscious.

"Probably since about '65 we'd been playing the odd British traditional tune, and when Sandy joined she brought with her a fairly good traditional repertoire that she'd been singing around the folk clubs, and we started to incorporate that into what we were doing.

"There was a certain amount of scholarship in it. We thought because we were British we should be playing the indigenous music. This was something at which we could excel, whereas we may never excel at being second-rate BB Kings or third-rate Waylon Jenningses. We also saw that there was a need for the traditional music in this country to be revived. It was unpopular with British people, so we wanted to bring it up to date. We were white liberal intellectuals, I suppose."

Vocalist Sandy Denny was already a veteran of the English folk scene when she joined Fairport Convention. One of the songs she brought was a very old tune full of moral complexity.

'A Sailor's Life' is a love story in which the sailor is the romantic figure who loves and travels on. One woman, however, follows him to her own doom.

Denny learnt the song from Martin Carthy and taught it to the band backstage at Southampton University. Fairport Convention took to the song and ran with it; Richard Thompson and Simon Nicol stretched out the guitar parts, competing with Dave Swarbrick's violin. A sea shanty became an epic voyage and a grand passion. The tune runs for over eleven minutes. It completely refashioned Fairport Convention and the sound of British music.

Who Knows Where the Time Goes?
Fairport Convention

(Sandy Denny) ❋ Hannibal ❋ 1969 ❋ Appears on: *Unhalfbricking*

Sandy Denny was the unquestioned queen of British folk music. Her clear soprano voice rang like a bell through tunes already centuries old. Denny also turned her hand to songwriting.

Fellow singer Linda Thompson recalls that in the '60s, women didn't write. That was a man's work. Nonetheless, Denny persevered. "'I'm going to write some songs', she said to me," Linda Thompson recalled to Jim Irvin. "I said, 'What do you mean write songs?' It's hard to believe, but it never occurred to us to write back then. The next thing I knew we were watching the TV in her attic in Gloucester Road and a butter ad came on, this voice singing, 'We're all a lot better for butter.' And it was Sandy! She said, 'Promise me you won't tell Richard [Thompson] I did this, he'd kill me! But I got £40!' Then she played me 'Who Knows Where the Time Goes?' and I was stunned."

Her second attempt, 'Who Knows Where the Time Goes?', made at the age of nineteen, was placed with traditional act the Strawbs and also quickly covered by Judy Collins before finding its definitive home on this 1969 recording by Fairport Convention.

This is a song about the big issues – mortality, the worth of a life – but Denny sounds neither naïve nor twee. The metre is often eccentric and the melody wanders into difficult areas that only Richard Thompson's guitar can navigate to support her, but that only serves to make this one of the most captivating tracks of its era.

Albatross   Fleetwood Mac

(Peter Green) ✳ Epic ✳ 1969 ✳ Appears on: *Pious Bird of Good Omen*

This beautiful and beguiling instrumental built around the languid guitar of Peter Green was Fleetwood Mac's first hit.

Green wrote the song while playing in John Mayall's Bluesbreakers – filling the vacancy left by Eric Clapton's departure. The initial guitar part came, he said, "from a phrase that Eric Clapton played when he was with John Mayall, one of the groups of notes."

"When 'Albatross' came out, we were still very much a blues band," said drummer Mick Fleetwood. "It was an extension of 'The Supernatural', an instrumental Peter wrote when he was with John Mayall. Obviously it was influenced by Santo & Johnny's lap steel hit 'Sleep Walk'. It went to number one during our first tour of the States, and when we came back it was all over the music papers: 'They've sold out.' It signposted what was going to happen; *Then Play On* epitomised that vision Peter had of going forward. We just didn't want to keep treading water, and that album was the real start of Fleetwood Mac."

'Albatross' floats through the airwaves, picking up touches of blues and jazz and calypso. It has an ethereal quality, too, that transcends any particular style.

"We had four or five hit records," Green said in 1983, "so I know the audience received us. They knew us from 'Albatross'. 'Albatross' is a kind of symbol for a hit record."

Black Magic Woman Fleetwood Mac

(Peter Green) ❊ Epic ❊ 1969 ❊ Appears on: *Pious Bird of Good Omen*

Guitarist Peter Green and drummer Mick Fleetwood were fired from John Mayall's Bluesbreakers in 1967. With second guitarist Jeremy Spencer and bass player John McVie, Fleetwood Mac was born as a backing group for Green's erudite blues playing. Green was one of the early guitar heroes, guaranteed to pull a crowd. Fleetwood was a distinctive showman drummer, so the enterprise got off to a flying start.

The combination of blues guitar and percussion was no doubt attractive to Santana, who covered 'Black Magic Woman' and had a hit with it in 1970.

"I actually wrote 'Black Magic Woman' when I was with John Mayall," Green recalled in a 1983 interview. "I was living in John Mayall's house when I started to write that. John Mayall started me writing the blues things; he said that I could do what he did sometimes. If you're singing or playing someone else's song and you really, really like it, if you're bubbling over with it, then you should take the first line and write another song. I took something out of Otis Rush's 'All Your Love'. It wasn't really like 'All Your Love' in the end, it was more like BB King's 'Help the Poor'."

Oh Well Fleetwood Mac

(Peter Green) ❊ Reprise ❊ 1969 ❊ Appears on: *Then Play On*

Initially a purist blues group, Fleetwood Mac followed the eccentricities of guitarist Peter Green and drummer Mick Fleetwood into uncharted territory. This almost nine-minute song was a stretch into what would become heavy metal. Green leads the band through a series of moods from the violent to the serene. While building on blues, the guitarist allows in a number of flavours from Africa, Spain and the Caribbean. Green's inspiration for the song was in part Muddy Waters who, according to Green, frequently used the phrase, "Oh well, oh well".

"The following that Peter had was a very strong movement," said Fleetwood. "These people in the clubs and ballrooms would travel all over the place. Fleetwood Mac was their band. Then other bands got drawn into it; even Jethro Tull were categorised as a blues band, but with all due respect they were never a blues band. Peter was, in the nicest possible sense, very ambitious. He knew what was right, which is why his legacy, even in the short amount of time he made it, is still very much alive."

Little Girl Blue   Janis Joplin

(Lorenz Hart/Richard Rodgers) ✳ Columbia ✳ 1969 ✳

Appears on: *I Got Dem Ol' Kozmic Blues Again Mama*

Joplin takes her cues on this from Nina Simone's arrangement of the song from the musical *Jumbo*. The song was written for a middle-aged character reflecting on her life but Joplin, barely in her mid-twenties, sings the song with a lifetime of experience in her voice.

Sam Andrew's guitar has a beautiful counterpoint to Janis' melody line and producer Gabriel Mekler dresses the song with gorgeous strings and organ parts, but everybody keeps their distance from Janis' vocal. Joplin was a singer that usually went for the epic emotion and the big note, but here she hangs back in total control.

Joplin not only discards Lorenz Hart's first verse, but many of the other lines as well and twists the syntax to make this song an autobiography. Even though the delivery is measured, there's a raw quality here – Joplin's opening up her heart – and the disappointment and pain and rejection and confusion which was so much a part of her short life is there for all to see.

21st Century Schizoid Man (Including Mirrors)
King Crimson

(Robert Fripp/Michael Giles/Greg Lake/Ian McDonald/Peter Sinfield) ✳ Island ✳ 1969 ✳ Appears on: *In the Court of the Crimson King*

Possibly the best progressive rock band (if that isn't an oxymoron) opened their account with '21st Century Schizoid Man', the first track from their 1969 debut album, *In the Court of the Crimson King*. Crimson was the brainchild of guitarist Robert Fripp with Ian McDonald on the reeds, woodwinds and Mellotron, bassist Greg Lake, drummer Michael Giles and lyricist Peter Sinfield. Together they created a sludgy portentous music that aspired to be Wagnerian. "At the time," Sinfield recalled, "the music was very weighty and red. It was very majestic."

'21st Century Schizoid Man' was a kind of Orwellian sci-fi epic. Sinfield foresaw the rape and pillage of families, death and destruction and prophets ignored. It was a world described by a freak-out Mellotron played backwards with phasing effects. Progressive rock acts could typically never settle on a time signature and that is certainly the case with Crimson. This leads into a passage of angular and nasty guitar work from Fripp before the apocalypse descends on the whole thing.

"I find it easier to write when I'm angry, sad or depressed," said the lyricist/poet Sinfield. "When I'm happy the things I write are banal and trite. I've nothing to say. It's the state of mind I want to be in so I just enjoy it."

Six years later when Fripp disbanded Crimson to better prepare himself for the collapse of the West he predicted, "The transition will reach its most marked point in the years 1990 to 1999. Within that period, there will be the greatest friction and, unless there are people with a certain education, we could see the complete collapse of civilisation as we know it and a period of devastation that could last, maybe, 300 years. It will be comparable, perhaps, to the collapse of the Minoan civilisation."

'21st Century Schizoid Man (Including Mirrors)' is the apex of British progressive rock, it certainly didn't get any better – especially with bassist Greg Lake's next project Emerson, Lake and Palmer. The best thing about the group was Barry Godber's painting on the front cover of *In the Court of the Crimson King* – one of the best covers of the LP era.

Whole Lotta Love Led Zeppelin

(John Bonham/Willie Dixon/John Paul Jones/Jimmy Page/Robert Plant) ❋ Atlantic ❋ 1969 ❋ Appears on: *Led Zeppelin II*

"From the release of the first album, and our first tour in the States when we supported Vanilla Fudge, all of a sudden the name of the band travelled like wildfire," Jimmy Page recalled in *MOJO*. "We were supporting bands and they weren't turning up, because we were really quite an intimidating force.

"We toured on the strength of the first album, and we just toured and toured and toured. In between times, we fitted in a small amount of recording at Olympic, where we did part of 'Ramble On' and 'Whole Lotta Love' and a couple of others, and the rest of the album was recorded at various times, and finally I mixed it with Eddie Kramer in New York. And then we were touring on the strength of the second album. And it wasn't until we had a real break, and that break was probably only a couple of months, but to us it seemed an eternity."

Everything about Zeppelin was bigger than life. They looked like they didn't give a fuck about anyone. As soon as they started headlining they dispensed with support acts and took to the stage with three hours of loud rock. Plus they had the charisma between Plant and Page at the front of the stage radiating cool.

The second album, called, of course, *II*, didn't break new ground but it did take them up a notch from the first.

Robert Plant comes more to the fore with his immense voice. By this time he was more comfortable in the role of sex god, enjoying the sleaze and the double entendres of the blues idiom.

Most of all, however, the album is known for its opening track. 'Whole Lotta Love', based on Muddy Waters' 'You Need Love', is pretty much five minutes and thirty-five seconds of the sound of a man having sex. It was recorded in an afternoon.

"It came from, if memory serves, it came just from just having a perfect symmetry of musicianship, where we could just go off on a tangent, just go off here, there and everywhere, and come back together again," Plant explained. "Jimmy had just discovered the theremin, that sort of 'whoop-whoop-whoop', and it just got into the groove. And it worked perfectly. But that was the way we played. That was how we felt we expressed ourselves best, with all the emphasis, and then having the abstraction in the middle of it. It broke it up in order to turn people's heads."

Against the band's initial wishes, 'Whole Lotta Love' was edited and released as a single, which simply increased their audience.

Led Zeppelin were the prototype of the third generation of rock & roll bands. They were apolitical, and boasted of huge appetites for sex, drugs and money. They were removed by their management and their wealth from their fans. They were the first band to become gods.

Kick out the Jams MC5

(Michael Davis/Wayne Kramer/Fred 'Sonic' Smith/Dennis Thompson/Rob Tyner) ☀ Elektra ☀ 1969 ☀ Appears on: *Kick out the Jams*

'Kick out the Jams' is the absolute pinnacle of high-energy rock & roll. The Detroit-based MC5 slammed their way through their first album. Very few groups start out with a live album, but the MC5 were totally correct here. They had done a few lame studio singles for independent labels but when they signed to Elektra they intended to blow the lid off the music business.

The MC5 – the name stands for Motor City 5 – were managed by John Sinclair, a local Detroit activist who formed the White Panther Party to get in on some of the revolutionary action that the Black Panthers were stirring up. He declared MC5 the cultural arm of the White Panther Party. Not only did they bankroll the White Panthers but also they gave a national spotlight to a local revolution. But then it would be hard for young men to resist a revolutionary front whose manifesto was "dope, guns and fucking in the streets".

"The phones were always tapped – you could hear them clicking and popping – the police would come by our house and run their siren at night while we were sleeping, flash their spotlights on the windows," guitarist Wayne Kramer recalled. "And anytime we stepped out, we were subject to search and the vans were always pulled over. The police would come up onstage and tell us we couldn't play that song. It was really out of control. And that was only the tip of the iceberg, we found out later that clearly there was a plan in place, coming from the highest offices of power, to destroy us."

The main venue in Detroit in 1968 was the Grande Ballroom and this is where the MC5 took the stand for their first album. The energy in the Grande Ballroom was everywhere in the air, bouncing around off the walls. The guitars of Wayne Kramer and 'Sonic' Smith crunched against each other in wild squalls of electric noise while the bass and drums pounded out a Motown-meets-metal beat.

But all that White Panther rhetoric has been lost in the winds of history. There was a lot of hype that the group were trying to emulate free jazz but they are nowhere near that. What we have here is absolute high energy rock & roll, which has seldom been matched and never bettered.

"We were struggling how to learn our instruments and play songs to be able to perform for people," Wayne Kramer told *Perfect Sound Forever*. "We gravitated to a certain kind of material, like the music of Chuck Berry and instrumental records and certain records that had a ... what we'd call ... 'high energy'. We later became articulate enough to define it as music that was real visceral. It was about a lot of heat and energy, like the music of James Brown, black gospel music."

Their fervour was aided by the fact that they were on a cosmic mission.

"Pure sound energises," the late Rob Tyner told a magazine at the time. "The more energy in the sound, the bigger the sound that gets to you, and the more intense the experience is, the more intense reality is – your metabolic reality at that moment, you know, an intensive feeling of your metabolism – that's where you find your reality. And music is equated on that level too, because it does make metabolic changes. Like on the stage, I notice metabolic changes at every instant. So fast – your heartbeat and your respiration and everything, because you're using your body one hundred per cent – that's what music is supposed to make you do. It's supposed to use your body one hundred per cent, so that you can force yourself out, put out as much energy as possible and make a perfect circuit so that there's an energy flow between the music and the audience, it all becomes one big thing, and it reinforces itself and everybody feels pure and clean. We send it out, and they send it back to you, and we send it out harder and it culminates in a reaction – things happen in the room.

"It's necessary, it's the killer experience and the purge: purification and a resensification on all levels. Resensify you back to your meat, because that's the way you take it in. Your meat is your senses, because your senses are made out of meat. And if you don't keep into contact with your meat … that's why all these straight people are so fucked up, man, 'cause they let their meat loaf – and it just rots, it rots."

'Kick out the Jams' by contrast is still as fresh as the day it was performed.

"The MC5 always played with reckless abandon and I think we were probably the first band that did that," said bassist Michael Davis. "We were always reaching into the unknown and I think that's it. No-one else played that way before and that's really what hardcore punk was all about – playing with reckless abandon with no regard for the safe things that you know about. And that's it. We were bad."

Rivers of Babylon   The Melodians

(Brenton Dowe/Trevor McNaughton) ❋ Mango ❋ 1969 ❋
Appears on: *The Harder They Come*

The story of the Israelites taken in bondage from their homeland to toil in Babylon was a potent story for the descendants of Africans enslaved to work on the plantations in Jamaica. This track by the Melodians is one of the best songs of its type, certainly for western tastes. Producer Leslie Kong has crafted a masterful backing track that flows like a great river behind the vocal skills of the Melodians, rich with intertwined voices. The tempo of the track is stately like a hymn rather than a reggae hit. Nonetheless, the song was a success upon its release and after its inclusion on the soundtrack for *The Harder They Come* it became a classic. It even survived a Euro disco version by Boney M in the late '70s. The lyric is a transcription of Psalm 137 from the Old Testament in which the Israelites bemoan their imprisonment and vow to keep alive the memory of Zion – the Promised Land.

In a Silent Way Miles Davis

(Joe Zawinul) ✳ Columbia ✳ 1969 ✳ Appears on: *In a Silent Way*

Although he was the emperor of jazz in 1968, Miles Davis also had an ear cocked to what was happening across town in R&B and rock. He was aware of James Brown and Jimi Hendrix and Sly Stone. He was intrigued by the possibilities of electronic instruments. On 18 February 1969 Miles Davis took his musicians – Chick Corea, Herbie Hancock, Dave Holland, John McLaughlin, Wayne Shorter, Tony Williams and Joe Zawinul – into the studio to rewrite jazz. One Zawinul piece in particular, 'In a Silent Way', stood out. Building on the fusion of previous years and his background in acoustic jazz, Miles just stretched out on this record.

There's a dreamlike quality to 'In a Silent Way' that comes from the three electric keyboards, all competing with one another, and the percussion. This is the kind of ethereal soundscape that Davis touched with *Kind of Blue* – a late-night meditation that glimpses the eternal.

Much credit for 'In a Silent Way' goes to Teo Macero who, with Davis, edited the improvisations into some kind of logic.

"You wouldn't know where the splices are," he said. "And those days we still were doing it with a razor blade. Joe Zawinul should give us half of his money for fixing it all up. Because, at the end, I didn't know, I thought it was all Miles' music. But apparently Joe Zawinul claimed it was his. So we paid him all the royalties.

"But I think *In a Silent Way* is really a remarkable record for what it is. I mean for a little bit of music it's turned into a classic. And we did that with a lot of other records of his where we would use bits and pieces of cassettes that he would send me and say, 'Put this in that new album we're working on.' I would really shudder. I'd say, 'Look, where the hell is it going to go? I don't know.' He says, 'Oh, you know.'"

Way to Blue Nick Drake

(Nick Drake) ✳ Hannibal ✳ 1969 ✳ Appears on: *Five Leaves Left*

Nick Drake was still a student at Cambridge when Fairport Convention's bass player Tyger Hutchings came across the singer/songwriter at a twelve-day festival at London's Roundhouse. Hutchings alerted producer Joe Boyd, who asked to hear some tapes.

"I've always had a very strong taste for melody and it has obviously been reflected in the people I have worked with," said Boyd. "It was Nick's melodies that really impressed me. There was also a considerable feeling of sophistication and maturity about his songs and the way they were delivered. While the tapes were in the office, I was playing them to someone who came in, and he made a remark to the effect that they sounded like Donovan, and although a lot of people went on to echo that sentiment it was one that had never occurred to me. I really did feel that I was listening to a remarkably original singer. And from the point of view of a producer, I felt that they lent themselves perfectly to good arrangements. So when he came into the office we decided to do an album."

Boyd signed Drake to Witchseason, his production company. They spent an entire year developing Drake's first album, *Five Leaves Left*, with enthusiastic help from Fairport guitarist Richard Thompson and Journeyman bassist Danny Thompson.

Still only twenty years of age, Drake had strong ideas about how to develop his melancholy folk songs. He insisted his friend Robert Kirby work on the strings, which are central to the gorgeous 'Way to Blue'. The song has the sense of theatre and drama that is central to Drake's songs and lifts them from a mire of self-pity. There are also touches of jazz and blues here. Unfathomably, *Five Leaves Left* was a commercial disaster and may well have cast a pall over Drake's brief life.

Cowgirl in the Sand Neil Young & Crazy Horse

(Neil Young) ✳ Reprise ✳ 1969 ✳ Appears on: *Everybody Knows This Is Nowhere*

There is a story of a monk going to monastery in search of enlightenment and being given a broom and told to sweep. After a year of sweeping he asks the master what is the secret of enlightenment and he's told not to ask but to go back and sweep and ask again in five years. Five years later the same thing happens and he goes back to sweeping and then one day he understands enlightenment.

Young said of Crazy Horse, "A lot of people think we play simple and there is no finesse. But we're not trying to impress anybody; we just want to play with the feeling. It's like a trance we get into."

Supposedly Neil Young had a fever while he was writing his second solo album and three songs came to him then – 'Down by the River', 'Cowgirl' and 'Cinnamon Girl'. The former two are showcases for Young's particular guitar architecture – long and drawn-out lines that play with distortion and chaos. What he's doing in these songs is mining the four-chord rock song for its last possible nuance. He finds a groove and then mines it back and forth like the proverbial Zen monk and the broom.

The First Time Ever I Saw Your Face Roberta Flack

(Ewan MacColl) ❈ Atlantic ❈ 1969 ❈ Appears on: *First Take*

Ewan MacColl was a Communist folk singer who deplored pop music. He led the ridiculous British protest against Bob Dylan's electric music and publicly campaigned against the hit parade. Ironically, his enduring legacy is firmly in pop. His daughter, Kirsty MacColl, was a talented writer and singer of pop songs and MacColl himself will be forever remembered for 'The First Time Ever I Saw Your Face'.

'The First Time' was penned on the spot at the request of MacColl's second wife, Peggy Seeger, in 1957. It entered the folk songbook and was covered by Peter, Paul & Mary, Marianne Faithfull, Gordon Lightfoot and Bert Jansch before Roberta Flack gave it the definitive reading on her debut album, *First Take*, in 1969. Every major interpretive singer has covered it since that time, never as well as Roberta Flack (although Peter Blakeley did a sublime version on *Harry's Café De Wheels*).

Flack was a jazz and soul singer who brought her classical training to her piano and vocals. *First Take* is a masterpiece of controlled emotion. Flack makes much use of the spaces and silences to give the emotions a genuine space to play on. Her reading of 'The First Time' is devastating in its architecture. She sings as though she is in a rapture, floating above the real world. The first time to which she refers in the song is a moment outside of time, as we know it. It's Flack's phrasing that brings the lyrics to life and transforms a prosaic folk melody into something timeless and full of flesh and blood. It's one of the glorious monuments of pop. Clint Eastwood recognised the power of the song and included it in his 1972 film *Play Misty for Me*. Consequently the song was released as a single and spent six weeks at the top of the charts.

Gimme Shelter The Rolling Stones

(Mick Jagger/Keith Richards) ❋ Decca ❋ 1969 ❋ Appears on: *Let It Bleed*

According to writer and sometime confidante Stanley Booth, Keith Richards wrote the words and music to 'Gimme Shelter' while alone in Robert Fraser's London flat. Mick Jagger was nearby, shooting the film *Performance* with Richards' girlfriend Anita Pallenberg as his co-star. The love scenes were all too actual for Richards' taste and he refused to go anywhere near the set or contribute to the soundtrack. But Richards was not only consumed by jealousy. He faced a prison sentence for drug possession. No wonder the song sounds paranoid.

"It was a grey afternoon," Richards recalled. "It was basically just like a chord structure at first. It just keeps going up and down. It's a strange sort of scale."

The song is about a coming storm; an apocalypse. To add to the mood, producer Jimmy Miller added an incredible vocal from session singer Merry Clayton as a banshee howl on top of Richards' layers of guitar. Musically it was a progression from 'Jumping Jack Flash' and 'Sympathy for the Devil'. However, the song soon acquired a tragic and even darker context.

'Gimme Shelter' was the lead track for the last Stones album of the '60s. The Woodstock Nation was born in August of 1969, the same summer that Charles Manson ordered his homicidal rampage and less than five months before the Rolling Stones concert at Altamont where the Hells Angels fatally knifed a crazed fan. The Beatles sang 'All You Need Is Love', the Rolling Stones responded with, "Storm is threatenin'/My very life today/If I don't get some shelter/Oh, I'm gonna fade away". It's obvious now who was the most prescient.

The Rolling Stones 1969 tour on the back of *Let It Bleed* finished at Altamont and the film of that tour, made by the Maysles Brothers, was titled *Gimme Shelter*. It set the tone for the coming decades.

1969 The Stooges

(Iggy Pop/Dave Alexander/Ron Asheton/Scott Asheton) ❋ Elektra ❋ 1969 ❋ Appears on: *The Stooges*

"Last year I was twenty-one/I didn't have a lot of fun/Now I'm gonna be twenty-two/I say 'Oh my and a boo-hoo'".

Like millions of other white, working-class kids in the suburbs, the '60s revolution passed the Stooges by.

The local kings, the MC5, however, looked like they were starting a Detroit movement and the Stooges were signed to Elektra on their coat-tails. John Cale, recently departed from the Velvet Underground, was assigned to produce them and what he captured was the inarticulate aggression of the band. The fact that all the songs were two-chord riffs made sense to him, although it wouldn't to the rest of the world for some time to come.

Guitarist Ron Asheton maintains that the group was heavily influenced by Ravi Shankar, Gregorian chants, John Coltrane and avant-gardist Harry Partch – but you wouldn't know it from hearing the record. The Stooges album is big and dumb.

As writer Lenny Kaye said at the time, "By any formal criteria, [the Stooges] are a retrogressive group, a pale copy of the early Rolling Stones. Their music revolves around one modified Bo Diddley chord progression, and neither the singing nor musicianship on their album attains any memorable level of competence ... The world of the Stooges, simply, revolves around boredom. Not only a mere lack of something to do, but rather a total negation of anything to do ... this is 1969 now, when the hope that came out of Haight Street is nearly dead, when the protest has been neatly swept up and glorified by the mass media. In consequence, the only stance that seems to be left is that of Iggy Stooge ... If 1967 was the year of the Beatles and 'Get Together', if 1968 was the year of the Band and *Beggar's Banquet*, then 1969 may well be the year of the Stooges. You might not like it, but you can't escape it."

In time, of course, the Stooges turned out to be more right than any number of protest singers.

Tecumseh Valley Townes Van Zandt

(Townes Van Zandt) ❋ Tomato ❋ 1969 ❋ Appears on: *For the Sake of the Song*

"I think of Townes as the greatest folk songwriter that my native state of Texas ever gave birth to," said Nanci Griffith. "Some of us songwriters are just lyricists, but he was definitely a poet."

In the mid-'60s, Van Zandt, born into a wealthy Texas oil family, forsook the family business to become a singer and songwriter. His was the world of the road and the American archetypes to be found there. He transformed these stories with an eye for detail and a poetic sense that owed a debt to both Bob Dylan and Elvis Presley. Johnny Cash's producer Jack Clement recorded his first album, *For the Sake of the Song*.

Van Zandt's influence was to transform Texas songwriting for Guy Clark, Lyle Lovett, Steve Earle, Joe Ely, Jimmie Dale Gilmore and others. His influence can also be heard in Rosanne Cash, Paul Kelly, Emmylou Harris and countless more who are better known than Townes will ever be.

'Tecumseh', on his first album, is a perfect example of a Townes song – full of tragedy and pain, a kind of wilfulness to live and a story line that is saved from cliché by the rhythm of its telling.

Pinball Wizard The Who

(Pete Townshend) ❋ Track ❋ 1969 ❋ Appears on: *Tommy*

Kit Lambert, co-manager of the Who, was the son of composer and conductor Constance Lambert, one of the leading lights of the British cultural Establishment. Almost from the start of the Who's career, Kit urged Pete Townshend to write something grander than a pop song. It was largely his influence behind the mini-opera *A Quick One*. Finally in 1968 Townshend wrote *Tommy*, the first rock opera. It's not an opera in the formal sense but closer to a sacred cantata.

"It was Kit Lambert's idea to do the full rock opera," said Daltrey. "Basically the story line of *Tommy*, the holiday camp, was Keith's idea. The actual story line is more Kit Lambert than Pete Townshend. You don't very often hear Kit Lambert's name mentioned when it comes to *Tommy* these days but I haven't forgotten."

The *Tommy* book is completely preposterous. A young boy sees a murder; goes deaf, dumb and blind; is molested by an uncle; given LSD by a witch; becomes a pinball champion and is elevated to god-like status; recovers his senses; and eventually, after various spiritual realisations, the idol falls.

"It's about life," said Townshend.

Operas are frequently preposterous, as are pop songs. This one is particularly so, especially when surrounded by so many philosophical allusions. It would have been much better if it didn't take itself so seriously.

At the time, Townshend was deeply involved in the teachings of Indian guru Meher Baba. He struggled with his fame and with the demands the Who placed on him as writer and leader. He was a man who had always struggled with himself. His friend Nik Cohn, one of the best commentators on rock & roll, was a pinball fanatic. All of these factors plus the suggestions of the band (Entwistle contributed the child molesting, Moon the holiday camp) went into writing *Tommy*. At the end of the day they had a double album of mostly extraordinary songs, beautifully recorded and strung together with a flimsy scenario. Townshend's extensive analysis mostly just gets in the way of the record.

This might have been an opera but the Who were a rock & roll band and they needed singles. The obvious choice on *Tommy* was 'Pinball Wizard'.

"The whole point of 'Pinball Wizard' was to let the boy have some sort of colourful event and excitement," Townshend explained. "'Pinball Wizard' is about life's games, playing the machine – the boy and his machine, the disciples with theirs, the scores, results, colours, vibration and action.

"People play their own pinball in other ways, like I muck around with tape recorders all the time. Most people's pinball machines are their cars. The car obsession is overwhelming, but it's there and I imagine it can only increase. I think it's groovy – why not? I thrive on modern things – good hi-fi, amplifiers, tape recorders, colour TV. A lot of them look like they're all padding, but there's far less than you'd imagine."

Whatever the context, 'Pinball Wizard' is an extraordinary piece. Townshend uses a wall of acoustic guitars in an almost flamenco style of lightning-fast strumming to set the atmosphere, which is then pierced with fat chords of electric guitar peeled off and then allowed to float through the air. (The arrangement bears a similarity to the Pretty Things' 'Old Man Going'.) Townshend plays his guitars off against each other like an argument with himself that can never be resolved. Daltrey is at the top of his form, for once not fighting with the others but allowed get inside the melody.

When performing *Tommy* live, Keith Moon would on occasion wave his drum sticks like a conductor and was known to yell, "Stop laughing! This is serious. It's a fucking opera."

The Seventies

NEW WAVE

Marquee Moon
Television

Another Girl Another Planet
The Only Ones

Radio Radio
Elvis Costello & The Attractions

This Is Pop
XTC

She's So Tough
Mink DeVille

Teenage Kicks
The Undertones

She Does It Right
Dr. Feelgood

When You Find Out
The Nerves

Living in the Land of Oz
Ross Wilson

Lust for Life
Iggy Pop

Ever Fallen in Love
The Buzzcocks

Shake Some Action
The Flamin' Grooviest

Land
Part I: Horses
Part II: Land of a Thousand Dances
Part III: La Mer(de)
Patti Smith

**You Can't Put Your Arms
Around a Memory**
Johnny Thunders

Neat Neat Neat
The Damned

Roadrunner
Jonathon Richman and
the Modern Lovers

Looks
The Student Teachers

Dream Baby Dream
Suicide

Germ-Free Adolescents
X-Ray Spex

Tell That Girl to Shut Up
Holly and the Italians

Money Changes Everything
The Brains

Goodbye Girl
Squeeze

Dream Sequence
Pauline Murray &
The Invisible Girls

Misty Eyes
Richard Lloyd

Heat Treatment
Graham Parker & The Rumour

Breakin' In My Heart
Tom Verlaine

JO'K / Shout
XL Capris

(I Wish It Could Be) 1965 Again
The Barracudas

Planet Claire
The B-52's

Whole Wide World
Wreckless Eric

No Matter What Badfinger

(Pete Ham) ✻ Apple ✻ 1970 ✻ Appears on: *No Dice*

Badfinger were Britain's first '70s power pop act. Originally called the Iveys, they were one of the first acts signed to the Beatles' Apple label and their first single, 'Come and Get It', was written and produced by Paul McCartney. It was a national smash but placed Badfinger forever in McCartney's shadow. It was a pity given that Pete Ham and Tom Evans were accomplished songwriters themselves.

The Badfinger quartet – Pete Ham, Tom Evans, Mike Gibbins and Joey Molland – lacked a clear frontman. Ham was an exceptional guitarist and both he and Evans wrote catchy, intricate pop songs. As well as working with McCartney, Badfinger were used by George Harrison on *All Things Must Pass* and they appeared in the Concert For Bangladesh.

'No Matter What', from their second album, *No Dice*, was a muscular piece of pop music with elegant harmony vocals filling out the sound. The melodies were sophisticated and the harmonies delightful. "A lot of it is a load of rubbish," said bassist Molland in 1970 of the contemporary pop scene. "They play a guitar riff and write a number round it. They should try writing a number and finding a guitar riff to fit it. That's much harder. I think people will get back to more melodic things soon. They have all learned to improvise now and they will use this in writing good songs. That is what we are trying to do."

The record was a major hit and the album did well. However, music in the early '70s was moving into a heavier phase and Badfinger seemed a little twee. The group struggled along until 1975 when leader Pete Ham committed suicide.

Across the Universe The Beatles

(John Lennon/Paul McCartney) ✻ Apple ✻ 1970 ✻ Appears on: *Let It Be*

An often overlooked small masterstroke from John Lennon, 'Across the Universe' was written in 1967 and recorded in 1968 as a possible single (it lost out to 'Lady Madonna') and subsequently turned up on a charity record. Spike Milligan was in Abbey Road when the song was first recorded. He asked if he could have a song for a benefit album he was compiling for the World Wildlife Fund and the Beatles added some animal noises to this one and gave it away. Sixteen-year-old Brazilian Lizzie Bravo and seventeen-year-old Gayleen Pease, two Apple scruffs who camped on the steps of the Apple offices, supplied backing vocals. When working on *Let It Be*, Phil Spector took the original tapes and erased the sound effects and backing vocal and added strings.

There is a dreamlike quality to the song as it veers off into the cosmic. The Beatles at the time were studying with the Maharishi and the chorus name checks his guru, Dev.

Lennon was ultimately never satisfied with the Beatles' version of the song, telling a magazine in 1980, "The Beatles didn't make a good record of 'Across the Universe'. I thought Paul subconsciously tried to destroy my great songs. We would play experimental games with my great pieces, like 'Strawberry Fields', which I always felt was badly recorded. It worked, but it wasn't what it could have been. I allowed it, though. We would spend hours doing little, detailed cleaning up on Paul's songs, but when it came to mine – especially a great song like 'Strawberry Fields' or 'Across the Universe' – somehow an atmosphere of looseness and experimentation would come up.

"Paul will deny it, because he has a bland face and will say this doesn't exist. This is the kind of thing I'm talking about where I was always seeing what was going on and began to think, 'Well, maybe I'm paranoid.' But it is not paranoid. It is the absolute truth. The same thing happened to 'Across the Universe'. The song was never done properly. The words stand, luckily."

Lennon claimed the lyric came to him when he was trying to sleep and wouldn't go away until he had written it down.

"I was lying next to her in bed," he said. "And I was irritated. She must have been going on and on and on about something, and she'd gone to sleep and I kept on hearing these words over and over, flowing like an endless stream. I went downstairs and it turned into a sort of cosmic song rather than an irritated song. It drove me out of bed. I didn't want to write it, but I was slightly irritable and I went downstairs and I couldn't get to sleep until I put it down on paper, and then I went to sleep."

Get Back The Beatles

(John Lennon/Paul McCartney) ❄ Apple ❄ 1970 ❄ Appears on: *Let It Be*

Paul McCartney borrowed the line "Get back to where you once belonged," from George's song 'Sour Milk Sea' as sung by Apple recording artist Jackie Lomax. An early version of the song contained a quote from Conservative politician Enoch Powell, who ran a virulent racist line against Pakistani immigration. McCartney wisely dropped the reference. Lennon, however, thought it to be an attack on Yoko. He told a magazine shortly before his death, "I've always thought there was this underlying thing in Paul's 'Get Back'. When we were in the studio recording it, every time he sang the line 'Get back to where you once belonged', he'd look at Yoko."

Initially it was to be the title of the album but by the time that record was finished, so were the Beatles, and McCartney's wishful thinking was less appropriate as a title than the requiem *Let It Be*.

There are two main versions of the song – a studio version, which was a hit single, and the album version, which closes *Let It Be* and which was recorded on the roof of the Apple office.

The rooftop version has a certain sloppiness and warmth and finishes with the faint voice of a policeman saying, "I'm afraid it's just too long." Then Lennon chimes in with the greatest understatement of the century, "I'd like to say thank you on behalf of the group and ourselves, and I hope we passed the audition."

I Me Mine   The Beatles

(George Harrison) ❋ Apple ❋ 1970 ❋ Appears on: *Let It Be*

The last song recorded on the final Beatles recording session (although John Lennon wasn't there) is George Harrison's critique of ego. An Austrian marching band he saw on TV inspired the melody. The words were inspired by his interest in Indian mysticism. As the Beatles were in turmoil about each other's egos and battles over money, it's likely that this impacted on the lyric as well.

The song, as finished in the studio, was only a ninety-second riff that Phil Spector edited into double that length. The tune's saving grace is the melancholic guitar lines from Harrison in the chorus, which work against the pushy and testy mood of the verses. The quiet Beatle, it appears, had the best perspective on what was tearing apart the Fab Four.

Up Around the Bend   Creedence Clearwater Revival

(John Fogerty) ❋ Fantasy ❋ 1970 ❋ Appears on: *Cosmos Factory*

If you want to hear what match fitness sounds like, Creedence's *Cosmos Factory* is it. Recorded in ten days, it was their fifth album in two and a half years. When not in the studio they were on the road. Every single they made in those years went to the top of the charts, as did the albums. *Cosmos Factory* also saw the group shift gear, away from the swampy feel of previous records into a muscular, versatile and hyped-up quartet, paying tribute to Little Richard, Marvin Gaye and Roy Orbison, but with a rust-proof edge. By the time they recorded *Cosmos Factory* there was no question but that Creedence were immortals and that Fogerty had the other great white rock & roll voice (alongside John Lennon).

"*Cosmos Factory* may actually be our best record," said Fogerty. "I always thought it was the culmination. By that time, Creedence had all these records and we looked back and put everything on it. It was almost redemptive, you might say. We'd done all these things and it was like 'Boom! There, I said it again.'"

Cosmos touches on the blues workouts and anti-war songs of previous albums but on this LP they let their hair down more. 'Up Around the Bend' is a furious slide guitar boogie pursued at breakneck pace. It was like taking on Little Richard at his own game.

Serious rock groups in 1970 rarely released singles that were viewed as a teeny-bopper medium. Creedence blew that right out the window with their often biting songs and their superb musicianship. This song celebrates the joys of rock & roll and its simplicity remains as thrilling now as it did a generation ago.

Move on Up Curtis Mayfield

(Curtis Mayfield) ❊ Curtom ❊ 1970 ❊ Appears on: *Curtis*

Mayfield's first solo album away from the Impressions is sublime soul funk and, on this track, a hint of gospel. Mayfield's grandmother was a minister and he grew up in a church environment while also listening to the blues that was so much a part of his hometown Chicago. The positive message that ran through the Impressions' work continued on *Curtis*.

"I came up in the church, and heard her words of inspiration and her ability to speak to the people of matters that would make them think and inspire or motivate them. Living with a grandmother who is trying to earn her ministry, you certainly stay in church," he said. "Anyway, a combination of common sense and growing up in that area with those women probably helped to mould what I'm about lyrically."

The soulful, feel-good funk of 'Move on Up' shows off Mayfield's guitar playing. He finds here a sublime little groove to match the lyrical message and he inflects with an individuality that few soul singer/songwriters had, other than Hendrix and Marvin Gaye, at that time. Mayfield's guitar playing was a significant inspiration to both Hendrix and Robbie Robertson of the Band and influenced scores of players in between.

'Move on Up' is a defiant song without militancy. Like Dr King, the lyric doesn't guild the lily or make light of the task, but stresses a positive outlook and faith as the solution to the problems of black people in America. Of course, the song can have wider implications and it has been greatly covered.

The Jam covered 'Move on Up' and then Paul Weller jazzed it a bit with the Style Council and put Mayfield on the map for a later generation who came up through acid jazz and new soul groups. Primal Scream's 'Movin' on Up' shows a clear influence. American singer and songwriter Mark Eitzel has also done an interesting '90s version. 'Move on Up' has also been sampled to the point of ubiquity.

"I was observing things, what happened politically, what was in the paper, what was on TV," Mayfield said of his influences in the early '70s. "Asking what things were wrong that oughta be right. It was just straight from the heart and I didn't have answers all the time. The songs were food for thought, I hoped my music was inspirational in manner. It could speak in a dialogue that makes you think for yourself. What would I do if I seriously gave this some thought?"

Layla Derek & the Dominos

(Eric Clapton/Jim Gordon) ✳ Atco ✳ 1970 ✳ Appears on: *Layla and Other Love Songs*

"I'm terribly proud of that song," said Eric Clapton of 'Layla'.

"To have ownership of something that powerful is something I'll never be able to get used to. I've tried to recapture the sense of that again and again. And it cannot be done. I've realised it's pointless. Just leave it be."

In the summer of 1970 Eric Clapton had a new band, dubbed the Dominos. They were the cream of young American players – Carl Radle on bass, drummer Jim Gordon and keyboard player Bobby Whitlock were veterans of Leon Russell's Mad Dogs and Englishmen project and Delaney and Bonnie. They found themselves in the UK hanging out with Eric Clapton and working on George Harrison's *All Things Must Pass*.

At the time Clapton was obsessively in love with his close friend Harrison's wife, Patti Boyd. All of the songs he would write in this period were songs of unrequited love and most of the cover versions he played were on this topic.

"Well, it was the heaviest thing going on at the time so, yeah, I suppose it came about like that," said Clapton. "I didn't consciously do it, though, it just happened that way. That was what I wanted to write about most of all."

In August 1970 Clapton and the Dominos moved to Criteria Studios in Florida, where producer Tom Dowd worked. Dowd was then producing the Allman Brothers Band and had a history going back to the great Atlantic R&B sides of the '50s.

At Criteria the group just jammed. Then Dowd introduced Duane Allman to the mix. Allman had been doing sessions for Wilson Pickett and Aretha Franklin on the side and his band had a reputation for their extended improvisations on stage. At the time Allman was just becoming recognised as one of the great innovative guitarists of his generation.

Dowd took Clapton to an Allman Brothers Show and introduced them. "It was love at first sight," the producer recalled. "And that's how the whole *Layla* thing got to be, because they just sat at the back of the studio and traded instruments and licks for the next five days, and that made an album."

"I went down there to watch them make that record because I was interested in it," said Allman. "I've been an admirer of Eric Clapton for a long, long time; he inspired me a lot and I always just personally dug his playing. Figured I'd get a chance to meet him and watch this thing go down, y'know. So when I saw him he acted like he knew me, like I was an old friend. And he said, 'As long as you're here we want you to get on this record and make it with us, we need more guitar players anyway,' so I did. I was real flattered and glad to be able to do it."

"He took it from being an all-right record to being something completely extraordinary," said Clapton. The key song was recorded almost last. The lyric came from a Persian story of the tragic love affair between Layla and Mahoun. "I had no idea what 'Layla' was going to be," said Clapton. "It was just a ditty."

Duane Allman opened the proceedings with a riff adapted from Albert King's 'The Years Go Passing By' and speeded up into a torrent of guitar. From there the guitars are layered up with acoustic and electric lines crammed on top of each other. The track is as close to perfect as a rock & roll song can be.

Two months after the recording had finished, the Dominos told Dowd they wanted to add a coda to 'Layla'. Jim Gordon had a piano instrumental that he had been jamming on for some years.

Although primarily a drummer, Gordon was an accomplished multi-instrumentalist much in demand. Gordon recorded his instrumental at some point during the *Layla* sessions and they asked Dowd to mix it into the end of the song. "And that's how it went on," said Dowd. "The piano portion at the back of it was added months after the initial composition, but the rest of it was the way it was done in initial concept and pursuit. The last part came in during a playback session, when the album was all mixed, so we had to remix 'Layla', but that was no problem, it was a pleasure."

'Layla' clocked in at seven minutes – too long for a single, so an edited version eventually went to radio. The record was not well received. The general public weren't aware that this was a Clapton project and the double album was long and intense. It took two years before the record finally started selling and the song 'Layla' became Clapton's signature tune.

Your Song Elton John

(Elton John/Bernie Taupin) ❋ DJM ❋ 1970 ❋ Appears on: *Elton John*

Elton John was the singer that Britain just had to have. His piano playing was so intimate and his singing so intense that one couldn't help but think that the lyrics, sent in the post by Bernie Taupin, must mean something at least as profound as those of the American singer/songwriters who were all over the charts. John was different from the other singer/songwriters inasmuch as not only did he not write the lyrics but he paid no attention to their meaning – a good thing since mostly they were oddball fantasies and often a little puerile. Elton has a knack for being able to find a tune on the spot for any string of words. This instant response gave immediacy to his delivery, which was often captivating.

The former Reg Dwight had an exceptional gift for a tune. His trade had been learnt the hard way, touring with third-division blues bands and pounding out covers for supermarket albums. A first album died. Then came the eponymous second LP.

'Your Song' is the track that put Elton John on the map. Much of the credit for this breakthrough goes to producer Gus Dudgeon and string arranger Paul Buckmeister, who wrapped Elton with a lush soundscape that was neither saccharine middle-of-the-road nor too avant-garde. They were helped, too, by an unusually direct lyric from Taupin. The mood of the song was quite ethereal as befitting this romantic tale. The details were odd but potent. According to the producer, "No-one else had ever attempted to fuse a rock rhythm section with an orchestra on the scale and standard of sophistication of arrangement that we were attempting."

All Right Now Free

(Andy Fraser/Paul Rodgers) ✳ Island ✳ 1970 ✳ Appears on: *Fire & Water*

The first concert I ever saw was the beginning of the end for Free. It was on 9 May 1971 at Randwick Racecourse for $3 with Manfred Mann's Earth Band opening and Deep Purple closing. Free took the day with their unassuming, workmanlike rock. This working-class quartet was never going to achieve the grand heights of Zeppelin or the Rolling Stones. Their virtue was their ordinariness.

Paul Rodgers had an impressive high register that brought Robert Plant to mind and Paul Kossoff had an interesting if limited blues style, but mostly it was their modesty that was Free's charm. For a while it seemed as though they would adopt the mantle of the next big British band, but they never lived up to it.

Free had their admirers, not least of whom became Prime Minister. "Paul Rodgers was the man whose voice I most wanted to emulate," Tony Blair told the BBC. "If I could have sung like that I would probably have stuck with being a rock musician."

Bassist Andy Fraser had the distinction of having briefly played with John Mayall when he met Simon Kirke and the other members of the band. They were a traditional British blues-rock band at that time until venereal disease laid up the singer and he and Fraser began writing songs. Their best work betrayed their teenage years with its simplistic lyrics while the lugubrious tempos and simple if soulful bottom end went perfectly with cheap wine and Mandrax.

They hit their stride with the third album, *Fire & Water*, which contained the anthems 'Mr Big', 'Fire & Water' and their signature tune 'All Right Now'. This was a big dumb album with massive choruses. Rodgers described the writing of 'All Right Now' to Mat Snow as, "I just put myself in the position of your average bloke chatting up your average chick and that's timeless."

Uncle John's Band The Grateful Dead

(Jerry Garcia/Robert Hunter) ✳ Warner Bros. ✳ 1970 ✳
Appears on: *Workingman's Dead*

The Grateful Dead were an electric blues band given to jamming for up to six hours at a time. Their music was often formless, closer to jazz than to rock & roll and decidedly uncommercial. Despite a devoted live following, the group's albums were epic financial disasters. In 1969 the group's leader, guitarist Jerry Garcia, junked the formless rock. He picked up on a trend towards country that was happening at the time and drew on his own roots as a bluegrass banjo player. Garcia wanted to make an album of songs and to cut it quickly so as to have some chance of paying off the group's debts.

Workingman's Dead was sort of country although the songs by Garcia and lyricist Robert Hunter tackled themes close to them. Hunter's lyrics were uncharacteristically direct while Garcia's tune respected the conventions of pop music.

The first track, 'Uncle John's Band', was almost a statement of purpose. It was inspired by the folk music that Hunter and Garcia loved as teenagers, especially the bluegrass and folk of the New Lost City Ramblers.

Hunter assembled the lyrics from old folk and bluegrass tunes: 'Buckdancer's Choice', 'Stories the Crow Told Me' and others. Hunter references the 1776 Revolutionary War and the tradition of baptism. Like so many artists of the late '60s – Dylan, the Byrds, the Band – the Dead were hoping to get in touch with traditional American values.

'Uncle John's Band' had its debut at the Fillmore Auditorium on 4 December 1969, two days before the Dead played the fateful Altamont Concert at which their friends the Hell's Angels stabbed a man to death in the crowd and brought the hippie dream crashing down. The Dead recorded 'Uncle John's Band' shortly thereafter. It remains one of their most tuneful and positive songs.

The Revolution Will Not Be Televised   Gil Scott-Heron

(Gil Scott-Heron) ✻ Flying Dutchman ✻ 1970 ✻
Appears on: *Small Talk at 125th and Lenox*

Gil Scott-Heron was a prodigy, publishing poetry and prose while still a teenager. He identified with the Harlem Renaissance movement and was influenced by the writers Langston Hughes and LeRoi Jones. While at university in 1968, he met jazz musician Brian Jackson. They started putting the words and music together and formed the Midnight band. Producer Bob Thiele recorded Scott-Heron's work using some of the finest jazz and funk musicians for his Flying Dutchman label.

'The Revolution Will Not Be Televised' is his best known work. It's very funny as a satire on mass media and white-dominated culture, but it is also a very angry call to arms for African Americans. No-one is spared.

"We as black people haven't had the proper forums to display our art," said Scott-Heron of his role in showbusiness. "We've had to be dependent on society at large to provide these forums and they're often more interested to show Elvis Presley than Little Richard, or the Osmonds than the Jacksons.

"It's consistently been an issue. And going back, the Tommy Dorseys and the Benny Goodmans and the Stan Kentons were hailed as innovators when in actuality you have to look at Count Basie and Duke Ellington as the springboards for that whole feeling that swept America and continues to sweep the world."

Brian Jackson provided the funk but it was Scott-Heron's adept way with words that made 'The Revolution' a classic. The mixture of funk and rhymes – especially in militant verse like this – was the prototype for rap that was to come fifteen years later.

"You know the consciousness is first. In any movement for change," Scott-Heron said, "education comes before organization and action, so you would like to see a continuing period of enlightenment and awareness going around so people know exactly where they are and what they're dealing with. We live in a world now where communication and information and stuff is readily accessible for people who have their antenna up trying to pick up on those types of vibes, the information is there. Those are the people who inevitably relate ideas that bring change about, people who are conscious initially are springboards for other periods of consciousness."

God John Lennon

(John Lennon) ✳ Apple ✳ 1970 ✳ Appears on: *John Lennon/Plastic Ono Band*

At the end of the '60s John Lennon should have been a happy man. He was one of the most esteemed artists of his time, wealthy, powerful and respected, and married to the woman he loved. Lennon, however, seemed at a loss. He and Yoko Ono had been in and out of heroin addiction, he was confused and tormented by the success of the Beatles, and he had issues with his parents that were still unresolved. As part of his search for happiness, he tried therapy, including primal scream – a technique developed by Arthur Janov for letting pent-up feelings out. So Lennon's first real solo album, written while using Janov's techniques, is known as the primal scream record.

'God' is one of the album's cornerstones. It's a litany of the things that Lennon once held dear but now has seen through. These include the Beatles and Bob Dylan and, of course, God in all his incarnations. Lennon finally concludes with the phrase "the dream is over," meaning the Beatles. The phrase has gone into the popular vernacular as a summation of the idealism of the '60s.

Although 'God' is not a pop song or even an easy song to listen to, it is, as Yoko Ono has said, "as important as Sgt Pepper". Mostly for the daring arrangement and the strength and minimalism involved.

Working Class Hero John Lennon

(John Lennon) ✳ Apple ✳ 1970 ✳ Appears on: *John Lennon/Plastic Ono Band*

John Lennon wasn't a working-class hero. He was a lower-middle-class hero but that doesn't have the same ring to it. This, one of the centrepieces of his first solo album, is a spare and dark and blunt song that attempts to erase his past.

Lennon's album was all about settling scores with himself.

He wanted to turn away from the super pop sound of the Beatles and find something more elemental. To this end, Lennon had only Klaus Voorman on bass, Ringo Starr on drums and Billy Preston on occasional keyboards through the whole album.

According to Voorman, "Just the fact that he asked Ringo and myself to play on the album meant to me that he wanted it to be a real close, intimate atmosphere. He did not say much about what we played.

"The playing itself, to him, was not important. It was more important to capture the feeling. We did mostly one or two takes. There's a lot of mistakes on there and timing changes, but it was exactly like a pulse, exactly what John wanted. He loved it."

'Working Class Hero' is both an attack on the class system in general and on capitalism. It's also a piece of self-loathing as Lennon vents his ambivalence at the experience of the Beatles.

"One has to completely humiliate oneself to be what the Beatles were," Lennon said at the time. "And I resent it."

What is Truth? Johnny Cash

(Johnny Cash) ✳ Columbia ✳ 1970 ✳ Appears on: *The Essential Johnny Cash 1955–1983*

The Vietnam War and permissive society polarised the United States. The Union was again divided across the Mason–Dixon line. By and large the country Establishment aligned itself with Richard Nixon and his Silent

Majority. The rest of the music business challenged the values and the authority of the Establishment.

Johnny Cash was somewhere in between. His song 'What is Truth?' starts out wondering why the music is so different. Over subsequent verses Cash questions the war effort and the judicial system and the suspicion of the younger generation. It's an update and an improvement on his friend's 'The Times They Are A-Changin''.

Cash recalled that the song had its genesis backstage while watching Kenny Rogers and the First Edition.

"Merle [Haggard] made a – it wasn't a derogatory comment – he made a complimentary comment," Cash recalled. "He said, 'Boy, the young people are really coming up with some unusual chord changes in their songs these days.' He said, 'We didn't go from so and so to so and so back when I was learning to play the guitar.' He said, 'It was kinda hard to get used to.' And I said, 'They're terrific. I really like it.'

"So then about that same time, that same night, the producer of my show asked me if I would write a song especially for a campus special we were going to do, which I believe was one of my last network shows. It was near the last *Johnny Cash On Campus*. We had all the Vanderbilt University of Nashville in the Ryman Auditorium the night we taped, so I said, 'Well, I'll write a special song for the college' and so I wrote 'What is Truth?'. And I started off with Merle Travis' 'kids sure play funny music these days'."

Big Yellow Taxi Joni Mitchell

(Joni Mitchell) ✳ Reprise ✳ 1970 ✳ Appears on: *Ladies of the Canyon*

One of Joni Mitchell's most well known songs, 'Big Yellow Taxi' combines the global and the personal in a playful, jaunty song that nonetheless makes its point.

Mitchell told journalist Alan McDougall that the song was inspired by waking up in the Royal Hawaiian Hotel on Waikiki Beach.

"Living in Los Angeles, smog-choked LA, is bad enough but the last straw came when I visited Hawaii for the first time," she said. "It was night-time when we got there, so I didn't get my first view of the scenery until I got up the next morning. The hotel room was quite high up so in the distance I could see the blue Pacific Ocean. I walked over to the balcony and there was the picturebook scenery, palm tree swaying in the breeze and all. Then I looked down and there was this ugly concrete car park in the hotel grounds.

I thought, 'They paved paradise and put up a parking lot' and that's how the song 'Big Yellow Taxi' was born."

The world was only starting to recognise the threats to the ecology in 1970 when the song was written. Fears about pollution and industrialisation were regarded as part of the hippie fringe. Over the ensuing thirty years Mitchell's song has, of course, become prescient.

Mitchell was a folk singer in the early '60s and the melody and arrangement reflect that light folk pop feel, although Mitchell has said, "The first music that I made that was my own, when I stopped singing folk songs, was rooted in Chuck Berry. 'Big Yellow Taxi' is rooted in Chuck Berry."

The final verse of the song brings the problem back to the personal and if you treat your lover as we treat the planet they will leave in a big yellow taxi.

While Mitchell's versions are hard to beat, the song has been a hit for a number of other artists, including the Counting Crows, who recently put it back into the charts.

Help Me Make it Through the Night   Kris Kristofferson

(Kris Kristofferson) ❋ Monument ❋ 1970 ❋ Appears on: *Kristofferson*

"He brought country music songwriting into its own. Before Kris, most of the songs didn't have that much depth to them," said the late Waylon Jennings. "His songs were about sex, but the undercurrent all the way through was love."

'Help Me Make it Through the Night' became a major hit for Sammi Smith in 1971, and following Janis Joplin's cover of 'Me and Bobby McGee', assured Kristofferson's reputation as a songwriter. This version on his first solo album had none of that triumph in his voice. At the time he was a scuffling singer/janitor/ helicopter pilot and his life was in desperate straits. Kristofferson brings that history to bear on the tune.

"I fell in love with the whole life, of songwriters hanging out writing songs to each other, and seeing people that I had heard of on the Grand Ole Opry since I was a little kid," said Kristofferson. "I decided to get out of the army and go back there. To the horror of my parents, my wife, my peers. For about four years they thought I had lost my mind."

Kristofferson eventually came to the attention of Johnny Cash who could relate to the songwriter's hell-raising lifestyle and the deep poetic sensibility behind the lyrics. Kristofferson has a deep empathy for the struggle in life, the temptations and pain.

"I think so far what I've had to contribute has been a certain way to look at things, at emotions," Kristofferson said of his work. "And I think in general my work has been human and made people respond to the things I like to respond to. That's the way my brain responds to my experience. It works it out in lines when it's working the best. It doesn't always work it out like that, but it works it out in lines that make sense. It makes more sense than you think it would. But I do think you can wear your heart on your sleeve, and mistakes I've made in that direction have usually been when I was under the influence of something that made me more confident of my surroundings than I deserved.

"But when I decided I was going to write songs, I decided I was gonna do it right – be true to the best of it – and I think I was pretty idealistic. I thought I would show, in the best way I could, all the emotions I could."

Wake Up, Niggers The Last Poets

(Jalal Mansur Nuriddin) ✳ Douglas ✳ 1970 ✳ Appears on: *The Last Poets*

Before there was rap there was poetry and jazz and rhythm. The Last Poets were poets operating in the African-American traditions of poetry and jazz like Amiri Baraka (Le Roi Jones). Their verses were revolutionary, in the spirit of the times, and not adverse to a violent revolution to overthrow the racist ruling paradigm. The most significant difference between the Last Poets and Public Enemy was the accent had moved from the four-beat to the one-beat. Otherwise it's a pretty clear lineage.

Jalal Mansur Nuriddin met Omar Ben Hassan and Abiodun Oyewole while in jail for refusing to serve in Vietnam. They grew to a larger ensemble including Gylan Kain, Felipe Luciano and Suliamn El Hadi and called themselves the Last Poets after a poem by South African Little Willie Kgositsile. "When the moment hatches in time's womb there will be no art talk," Kgositsile wrote. "The only poem you will hear will be the spearpoint pivoted in the punctured marrow of the villain ... Therefore we are the last poets of the world." The ranks of the Last Poets swelled and their style of performance poetry gained a lot of attention. One person who took notice was Jack Douglas, producer of jazz records, another was Jimi Hendrix, who saw the Poets doing a TV spot.

"I called the station immediately and got a number for them," Douglas told writer David Dalton. "There was a lot of distrust between blacks and whites at that time, a lot of tension. Going up to Harlem was intense. Around two the next afternoon I drove up there in my silver Jaguar. The address turned out to be a basketball court: there were about twenty black guys standing around. As I walked across the court they parted until there were only four guys left, the three poets and the conga player. Jalal was standing under the hoop – no net – and when I came close he said, 'Stand there, on the foul line'. And then for the next forty minutes they played their repertoire. When they were done I asked them if they wanted to make a record. They said they would and we all piled into the Jaguar and went down to a little studio on 77th and recorded the whole album then and there in four hours."

While the Last Poets were ready for war with white society, they weren't letting blacks off the hook either. Tracks on the first album like 'Wake Up Niggers' are critical of black apathy. The song broke into the hip white arena with its appearance in the film *Performance*.

"But with the Poets, we were angry and we had something to say," explained Abiodun Oyewole. "We addressed the language. We just put it right in front of your face. We parented to the hip-hop generation. I can't deny that. I worked with a lot of them and they have the same rage and I understand that. There was a movement back then with the Panthers and other organizations, trying to secure human rights for the community. We had these guidelines and guard rails. These kids don't have these guard rails. The rage is going every which way. It's self-destructive."

After the Goldrush   Neil Young

(Neil Young) ❋ Reprise ❋ 1970 ❋ Appears on: *After the Goldrush*

"But, in all modesty, *After the Goldrush*, which was kind of the turning point, was a strong album," Neil Young told Cameron Crowe. "I really think it was. A lot of hard work went into it. Everything was there. The picture it painted was a strong one. *After the Goldrush* was the spirit of Topanga Canyon. It seemed like I realised that I'd gotten somewhere. I joined CSNY and was still working a lot with Crazy Horse ... I was playing all the time. And having a great time. Right after that album, I left the house. It was a good coda."

The album, or at least the title track, was written as the theme for an independent film to be made by actor Dean Stockwell. The film, or at least what can be gleaned from interviews and the lyrics of this title song, involved the destruction of the planet and the human race's escape into space. The film was never made. This song remains as an exquisite ecology hymn. That the lyrics are somewhat obscure adds to the mystery. The accompaniment by Young and some horns is perfect and the tune is haunting. This is some of Young's best singing – before he became self-conscious about his voice – and he's really stretching out to the limits of it. *After the Goldrush* cemented Young's reputation before the next album, *Harvest*, made him a superstar and he had to commit thirty years of career suicide.

Love in Vain The Rolling Stones

(Robert Johnson) ❋ Decca ❋ 1970 ❋ Appears on: *Get Yer Ya Yas Out*

Robert Johnson's 'Love in Vain' was cut for the *Let It Bleed* album, but this version recorded on the 1969 tour – probably at Baltimore Civic Centre – is the best blues recording the Rolling Stones ever made. The Taylor and Richards team that was first tested on this tour was the most fertile period for the Rolling Stones. Taylor was a very talented player, particularly with fluid and inventive melodic lines to counterpoint Richards, and they bring a completely new life to Robert Johnson's delicate blues song. The rest of the album sounds like a hurricane of slashing guitars and horns. Then, on this song, they pull it right back to a funeral march pace, Charlie Watts keeping time like the clock of doom. Mick Jagger's vocal is full of dragged out, vulnerable, yearning syllables working against the beat. As he draws the note, Watts' kick drum thumps in punctuation. Then the guitars slowly come up behind with gorgeous notes left to float in the ether or to slide against each other. There's a wonderful to-and-fro effect, a tension and release that transcends the song itself.

Wild Horses The Rolling Stones

(Mick Jagger/Keith Richards) ❋ Rolling Stones Records ❋ 1970 ❋
Appears on: *Sticky Fingers*

Keith Richards wrote the bulk of 'Wild Horses' as he was preparing for the Rolling Stones' 1969 American tour. His first son, Marlon, was born in August 1969, less than two months before the band was to leave for an extensive tour. The birth of Marlon was one of the most profound experiences of Richards' life. "You've never felt so loved in your life," he said. "And you realise, 'I've just been given the first two or three years of my life back.'" Jagger's verses for the tune were written about his break-up with Marianne Faithfull.

'Wild Horses' is one of the Rolling Stones' most vulnerable and gentle love songs and represents the beginning of a mature direction they would take in the future.

Richards' new best friend at the time was American country rocker Gram Parsons and it has been suggested that Parsons had something to do with the genesis of the song, but that's hard to demonstrate. Richards had the tune, the title and most of the lyrics worked out, and Jagger finished the song.

Recording of the song was mostly done at Muscle Shoals, Alabama, in early December 1969, three days before the tour finished at Altamont. The legendary producer Jim Dickerson played tack piano.

"When they cut at Muscle Shoals studio, where they did 'Brown Sugar' and 'Wild Horses', that was kinda my idea," Dickson recalled. "Stanley [Booth, journalist and friend to the Rolling Stones] called while they were on the road and asked if the Stones could record in Memphis. They had three days at the end of the '69 tour – 'cause they wanted to record when they were, hot from playing together. With [Musicians] Union regulations back then you could get either a touring or a recording permit but not both. They were in a position where they could tour but not record and had been prevented from recording in Los Angeles. So, they were looking for a place where nobody would care and I told 'em about Muscle Shoals.

"When the Stones got to Muscle Shoals I was the only outside person who was allowed to stay. On the third day, they recorded 'Wild Horses', which began with a minor chord, and Ian Stewart [Stones pianist and road manager] wouldn't play minor chords. Stew finally told me one day, at a hotel in New York, about his thing of not playing minor chords, and I thought 'thank god' man. But for that, I would have no claim to fame.

"That was a fantastic week," said Charlie Watts. "We cut some great tracks, which appeared on *Sticky Fingers* – 'You Gotta Move', 'Brown Sugar' and 'Wild Horses' … it's one of Keith's things to go in and record while you're in the middle of a tour and your playing is in good shape."

Oye Como Va Santana

(Tito Puente) ❋ Columbia ❋ 1970 ❋ Appears on: *Abraxas*

When Michael Goldberg asked Mexican guitarist Carlos Santana for the secret to his two-decade career, he answered, "They say it's the merging of the congas and timbales with the electric guitar. But I feel the main reason, the prime motivation that gets people out of their houses to see us and buy our albums, is the cry." The cry is Santana's unique guitar style – part blues, part fusion and a lot of Latin.

Carlos Santana lived in San Francisco in the Summer of Love and started playing his Latin blues at the same time as the Jefferson Airplane and the Grateful Dead were doling psychedelic rock. Unlike the white groups, Santana's mostly Hispanic band relished intricate melody lines and polyrhythms.

The group appeared at Woodstock and their eight-minute workout of 'Soul Sacrifice' was a highlight of the subsequent film. On the back of that promotion Santana became a massive hit. A self-titled first album was a smash and its sequel, *Abraxas*, spent a year in the charts. On *Abraxas*, Santana perfected the merging of Latin, jazz and blues styles together, bringing songs such as Tito Puente's 'Oye Como Va' to a rock audience.

"*Abraxas* was the peak of that band on that level I would say," said Santana. "When I hear the word 'Abraxas', it brings to mind Miles Davis – he was hanging around a lot and calling us up, and he liked the direction of the band. And Jimi did too – a lot of people were becoming aware that this bunch of guys had something to say that musically was made in Chicago … and the Rolling Stones got congas and cowbells and all kinds of things. So that album is very significant, mainly because of the colours and the instruments that it brought to rock & roll. It injected a whole lot of stuff – Bo Diddley led to that beat, which comes from Latin music to the blues, and I feel we did it again to rock & roll, to a certain extent. Not that we were the first, but we were just there in a way that nobody was doing it – Motown already had congas, but they didn't have them upfront, or timbales, and they didn't have a guitar upfront. That's what *Abraxas* reminds me of – a group of people who became significant, if you will."

Bridge over Troubled Water Simon & Garfunkel

(Paul Simon) ❋ Columbia ❋ 1970 ❋ Appears on: *Bridge over Troubled Water*

Bridge over Troubled Water is one of the great statements about modern relationships. The friendship between Simon and Garfunkel – ripped apart by ego and competing careers – and Simon's relationship with his wife, with his audience and with music are laid out in perfectly measured melodies, decorated by massed voices over the course of an LP.

The album as a whole is a masterpiece of pop, its production (by Simon, Garfunkel and Roy Halee) is flawless, and the lyrics are multi-dimensional, wry and often heartbreaking.

'Bridge over Troubled Water' was written in Los Angeles, in the same house George Harrison immortalised in 'Blue Jay Way'. Simon was listening to a Swan Silvertones' recording of 'O Mary Don't You Weep' and thinking about his wife Peggy.

Two verses came quickly and he presented the song to Garfunkel, who initially declined the lead vocal.

"We were all renting this house. Me and Artie and Peggy were living in this house with a bunch of other people throughout the summer," Simon recalled. "I said, 'Here's a song; it's in G, but I want it in E flat. I want it to have a gospel piano.' Each night we'd work on the piano part until Larry Knechtel really honed it into a good part. Now, the song was originally two verses, and in the studio, as Larry was playing it, we decided – I believe it was Artie's idea – to add another verse. I always felt that you could clearly see that it was written afterwards. It just doesn't sound like the first two verses.

"Then the piano part was finished. Then we added bass – two basses, one way up high, the high bass notes. Then we added vibes in the second verse just to make the thing ring a bit. Then we recorded the drum with a tape-reverb that made the drum part sound different, because of that after-beat effect. Then we gave it out to have a string part written. This was all in Los Angeles and then we came back to New York and did the vocals. Artie spent several days on the vocals.

"I didn't think it was a hit, because I didn't think they'd play a five-minute song on the radio. Actually, I just wrote it to be two verses done on the piano. But when we got into the studio, Artie and Roy wanted to add a third verse and drums to make it huge. Their tendency was to make things bigger and lusher and sweeter. Mine was to keep things more raw. And that mixture, I think, is what produced a lot of the hits. It probably would have been a hit with two verses on the piano, but it wouldn't have been the monster hit that it became. I think a lot of what people were responding to was that soaring melody at the end.

"Funny, I'm reminded of the last verse. It was about Peggy, whom I was living with at the time: 'Sail on, silver girl ... Your time has come to shine' was half a joke, because she was upset one day when she had found two or three grey hairs on her head."

The song was the crowning glory on an album about mixed feelings. Two of the best tracks were about the separation of Simon & Garfunkel ('The Only Living Boy in New York' and 'So Long Frank Lloyd Wright'). 'The Boxer' was a harrowing piece of self-laceration but elsewhere Simon affirmed his passion for music of all kinds.

'Bridge' was to be their biggest hit. But for many years it was a sore point with Simon, in part because of its ubiquity.

"When I wrote and first sang the line 'Like a bridge over troubled water, I will lay me down,' I burst into tears," Simon revealed in an interview some ten years after the fact. "I was thinking of Peggy. That I would lie down and be a bridge for her. It was an overwhelming feeling coupled with that melody. Now it's been sung so many times by so many people that I have no feeling whatsoever for it. But at the moment of creation, it was huge."

Shakin' All Over The Who

(Johnny Kidd) ✳ Track ✳ 1970 ✳ Appears on: *Live at Leeds*

'Shakin' All Over' was the first British rock & roll hit as such. Johnny Kidd wrote and sang the song with his group the Pirates and topped the UK charts in 1960. It was a big deal for Roger Daltrey and his mates. Ten years later it was in their set when they made the greatest live album of the rock era. It's big and loud and incredibly exciting.

"*Live at Leeds* is my favourite album by the Who and it's the only Who album I still play," said John Entwistle shortly before his death.

It's hard to explain just why *Live at Leeds* is such a perfect record. The Who are down to the basic quartet. Listening to it you can feel the room. Townshend rips big chords from his guitar and then lets them boom around the walls. You can feel the energy coming off Keith Moon as he flails around the kit not keeping the beat so much as pushing the song forward. Then there's Entwistle carrying the melody on his bass guitar.

The Who were not a band so much as four soloists who agreed on a tune, each retaining the right to do it their way. On *Live at Leeds* you can hear the interplay as Townshend calls the shots and you can feel, almost touch, the empathy between the players.

'Shakin' All Over' kicks off like a taut boogie carried by Entwistle's bass riff. But Kidd's song is just a jumping-off point and the Who explode the tune with flashes of brilliance coming from all quarters.

"*Live at Leeds* is the best and most exciting Who live stuff I've heard," said Townshend. "It may be a bit of a head-banging album. It's not pretty or brilliantly performed or anything, it's just energy."

I Can't Get Next to You Al Green

(Barrett Strong/Norman Whitfield) ✳ Hi ✳ 1971 ✳ Appears on: *Gets Next to You*

Al Green was a struggling soul singer on the Chitlin Circuit when he met Willie Mitchell in 1969. Mitchell, then a trumpeter and bandleader, found Green at a gig in Texas and when the show was over he offered the singer the chance to record. "I suggested he come back to Memphis with me and cut a record," Mitchell recalled. "He said, 'How long will it take before I become a star?' I told him about eighteen months. He said, 'I don't have that long.'"

It was in fact 1970 when Green and Mitchell hit on their perfect sound and put Al Green on the charts with a remake of the Temptations hit, 'I Can't Get Next to You'.

Where there were five parts, Green pulled them all into one. Where the song was forceful and pushing, Green held it all back into a love groove. The Hi Records band that consisted of Al Jackson on drums and the Hodges brothers on everything else had the perfect light touch for Green's airy voice.

Al Green and Willie Mitchell found another way to make soul records and Green stepped into the space left vacant with the death of Otis Redding.

"To me," Green said, "Otis was like GATTA-GATTA-GATTA, you know, very choppy, which was very effective but a little rougher than me. I'm usually tinkling with the high notes and floating between the chords ... trying to create some, uh, colour."

Tired of Being Alone Al Green

(Al Green) ✳ Hi ✳ 1971 ✳ Appears on: *Gets Next To You*

"I wrote 'Tired of Being Alone' about 5 o'clock one morning," Al Green recalled. "I was dreaming about me singing this weird song and I'd never heard that song before. I woke up and it kind of frightened me. I was singing these lyrics, "I'm so tired of being alone," and wondering, where did that come from? So I took a pen and paper and my guitar, and wrote it. I guess I got done about 7:30 that morning and I went back to sleep."

Flush with the success of 'I Can't Get Next to You', Green lobbied hard for this track as his next hit. When Hi Records finally did put the song out and it wasn't getting airplay, Green took matters into his own hands. "Three months passed. Nothing happened. Four months. Five months," Green said. "I said, 'Look, I need to go to New York – tonight!' So I went to London Records. I says, 'I gotta call a general house meeting of everybody in here!'

I was nuts. I don't see how I did that. This big, huge company, these people looking at this kid. I says, 'I want this record 'Tired of Being Alone'. You've just gotta hear it.' So they played it and they really liked it."

Green's charisma overpowered the staff and they got behind the single, pushing it to radio stations. Once people heard Al Green's distinctive style, they were converted. It was to be his first million-seller.

The band is in wonderful form. Drummer Al Jackson, one of the greatest soul timekeepers, sits the tune right in the pocket. Teeny Hodges' guitar is ultra smooth and also just colouring the groove. It's here too that Al Green finds his real voice, taking producer Willie Mitchell's advice. "Al always sang really hard," said Mitchell. "And I used to tell Al, 'You've got a good falsetto, you need to soften up some.' I said, 'You need to settle this music down.'"

Is It My Body? Alice Cooper

(Michael Bruce/Glen Buxton/Alice Cooper/Dennis Dunaway/Neal Smith) ❋
Warner Bros. ❋ 1971 ❋ Appears on: *Love It To Death*

Once Alice Cooper dumped his first mentor Frank Zappa and moved to Detroit in 1970 things started to get interesting. With the help of producer Bob Ezrin, Alice's sound became a stripped back, lean and shining metal machine with beautiful gleaming guitar riffs and solid, muscular rhythms. He picked up on the Motor City madness of the MC5 and the Stooges, but they could play real well.

'Is It My Body?' is a beautiful, slinky mess of power chords and snappy time changes. The song is kind of complex for Alice – it's a rock star wondering about the interests of a groupie and it plays on the identity issues involved: "What have I got/That makes you want to love me/Is it my body?/Someone I might be?"

In calling himself Alice Cooper, the one hundred per cent straight Vincent Furnier raised gender issues that had long been taboo – especially in the US. He was the first man to adopt a woman's name and to publicly wear drag while doing so. Because he wasn't gay or a transvestite, and indeed because he had nothing to lose, Alice pulled sexual fetishes and lifestyles out of the closet and put them on *American Bandstand*.

Alice didn't care about the politics of sex. He just wanted to shake things up.

"Like, we're taking sex, which is probably another half of American entertainment, sex and violence, and we're projecting it, and we're saying this is the way everything is right now," he said in 1969. "Biologically, everyone is male and female, so many male genes and so many female. And so what it is we're saying is 'OK, what's the big deal.' Why is everybody so up tight about sex? About faggots, queers, things like that. That's the way they are. That's like making fun of a maniac because his brain isn't completely right, because he isn't in the norm.

"People don't accept that they are both male and female, and people are afraid to break out of their sex thing because that's a big insecurity that's doing that. Consequently, people will make fun of us. We don't mind that, that's making them accept more, making fun that we accept that. The thing is this is the way we are. We think it's a gas."

I'm Eighteen   Alice Cooper

(Michael Bruce/Glen Buxton/Alice Cooper/Dennis Dunaway/Neal Smith) ❋
Warner Bros. ❋ 1971 ❋ Appears on: *Love it to Death*

It's hard now, after all we've been through, to understand what Alice Cooper really meant in 1971 when 'I'm Eighteen' put him under the noses of nice middle-class people. Here was this greasy guy from Detroit with a girl's name, women's clothes and a snake for a pet. That was all shocking enough – in the '70s the conservative parties in the federal parliament tried to have Alice Cooper kept out of Australia. But the question on the minds of right-thinking people everywhere was: what was his agenda? And the answer was disturbing – he didn't have one. He just wanted to turn civilisation on its head for the hell of it. Alice Cooper was all that trash coming right out of the TV set, right back at ya!

"People that haven't seen us yet are shocked because they think that Alice Cooper must be a female folksinger," said Alice. "They don't expect the whole thing. And the whole thing is a direct product of TV and movies and America, 'cause that's where America's based. That's where their heart is from – the sex and violence of TV and the movies, and that was our influence.

"We weren't brought up under a blues influence. We were brought up under an electronics influence – the bomb (I'm not knocking the bomb, I think the bomb's a gas), but TV has been the main influence for this generation, and that's why this whole thing is happening.

"You just let your lower self go, and then it takes on all these aspects of the society – the city with horns blowing, the people yelling things at each other, and the all-in-all violence and chaos of the city. Put that on stage with music, and that's what this is.

"It's like this – these five members have been influenced of course by other groups, because that's where this generation's groups came from – an environment like the Beatles, the Rolling Stones, the Yardbirds, and the Who. People like that. They were five years ago, and when they first came out, we were influenced by them – Zappa and people like that.

"So now we've taken that influence – we've done that whole trip, the sounding-like-other-people trip – and now we're applying it to a theatrics basis, to a statement and what the statement is, is nothing."

There had been teen anthems before. 'I'm Eighteen' was the teen anthem for the kids in the 'burbs loaded on TV and mandrax.

"I got a baby's brain and an old man's heart/Took eighteen years to get this far/Don't always know what I'm talkin' about/Feels like I'm livin' in the middle of doubt/'Cause I'm eighteen."

Whipping Post The Allman Brothers Band

(Gregg Allman) ✳ Mercury ✳ 1971 ✳ Appears on: At Fillmore East

'Whipping Post', from their first album, was a live favourite of the Allman Brothers. "I had this girlfriend in LA," said Gregg Allman about the song's inspiration. "She was using this pseudo love on me like an M16. She kept putting me through all kinds of tricks."

The Allman Brothers Band put this song through all kinds of tricks. To its blues-based structure they added the jazz inflections of their two guitars/ dual drum attack.

"The stage is really our natural element," said guitarist Duane Allman. "We kind of get frustrated doing the records, so consequently our next album will be for the most part a live recording to get some of that natural fire on it. We have rough arrangements, layouts of the songs, and then the solos are entirely up to each member of the band."

To that end, producer Tom Dowd recorded the group's two dates (12 and 13 March 1971) at the Fillmore East in New York. "My favourite album of theirs," said Dowd, "is when I did them at the Fillmore. They were at their absolute peak, the playing just flowed. It's the greatest fusion album I've ever heard."

The album closes with a twenty-two-minute version of 'Whipping Post'. The song is in six/eight time, led by Berry Oakley's firm but fluid bass attack and then follows the swelling, surging organ against the firestorm of guitars. Dickey Betts pulls out a hint of his 'Les Bres in A Minor', which was inspired by John Coltrane, and Duane Allman answers. This was the closest that rock got to jazz in the '70s and it's unlikely that many of the fans who sent the record into the Top 10 realised it.

Jim Marshall's cover photo of a long-haired group of southerners surrounded by road cases was an iconic image of the sublime beauty of rock music in the early '70s. 'Whipping Post' is its aural equivalent.

Surf's Up The Beach Boys

(Van Dyke Parks/Brian Wilson) ✳ Caribou ✳ 1971 ✳ Appears on: Surf's Up

As if being beaten and betrayed by his father and losing his hearing and then going insane wasn't enough, Brian Wilson has been subjected to more ridiculous journalism than any musician deserves. Much of the verbiage revolves around the lost album Smile.

The legend goes like this: Wilson, the pop genius of the Beach Boys, creates the masterpiece song cycle in Pet Sounds in 1966. He then embarks on his masterwork, Smile, which he refers to as a symphony to God. The lyrics, by Van Dyke Parks, are an extended meditation on the birth of the United States. In any case, things get too weird. The other Beach Boys, especially cousin Mike Love, hate the project and want the songs to get back to the beach.

The Smile album was eventually abandoned. Bits of it surfaced, notably the singles 'Good Vibrations' and 'Heroes and Villains' and also this song, 'Surf's Up', which was rerecorded and appears on the Surf's Up album.

In 2004 Smile was reconstructed and it's easy to see why the project was abandoned – it's completely uncommercial. Wilson and Parks weren't just trying to outdo the Beatles and Phil Spector now; they took on Aaron Copeland and Leonard Bernstein and the real heavyweights.

So, 'Surf's Up' is magnificent, but let's not attribute to it qualities it doesn't have. The melody is a gorgeous nocturne. Its notes soar off into the darkened sky, and the vocal melody, sung with exquisite grace by Carl Wilson, flits through this dreamscape. The lyrics are nonsense, but that doesn't matter, they add to the dreamlike mood.

"We were taking LSD and marijuana and amphetamines," said Brian Wilson. "So our heads were, like, spaced, and we got into some very advanced, avant-garde music. And we started creating some of the songs for Smile, and we got about two movements done, and then we decided to junk it, because we thought it was too advanced for people."

So he clearly wasn't that stoned. *Smile was* too advanced. Wilson, in his quest to compete with some of the greatest musicians of the time, had pushed the possibilities of pop beyond their envelope. *Smile* remains a glorious folly with some moments of near perfection, and 'Surf's Up' is one of them.

Iron Man Black Sabbath

(Geezer Butler/Tony Iommi/Ozzy Osbourne/Bill Ward) ※ Vertigo ※ 1971 ※
Appears on: *Paranoid*

Heavy metal starts here. The big, dumb riff under big, dumb lyrics and a monster beat delivered at a funereal pace. 'Iron Man' is one of the cornerstones of '70s rock.

Is the Iron Man of the song just the Marvel cartoon character or does it represent the real feelings of male teenagers who need to build the psychological defences that they will need in adulthood? Isn't there an Iron Man inside every boy?

"When we started writing things we didn't want to present bullshit like 'I'm gonna see my chick and we're gonna get it on.' It's all hypocritical," said Ozzy Osbourne. "This love trip is so grossly distorted. One week you fall in love, the next week you fall out and start doing dope and blow your mind out. I don't believe there's anyone in this world that is one hundred per cent in love. I don't think anyone is totally happy; you can't really wake up in the morning free of hassles and do what you want as long as you don't harm anybody else. If you wanna stick needles into your arm it's your own life. Like, I'm not into taking heavy dope although I have taken dope. People who take it just have hang-ups that they can't deal with.

"If you haven't got your own mind and can't do what you want, you're not an individual, just part of a mass. The society trip in England is that you go to school, then get a job, and at the age of twenty-one you get married. You work the rest of your life in a factory and when you retire at the age of sixty-five you get a gold watch; forty-five years in a factory with stinking oil, polluting the land. I used to work in a factory and I used to see these blokes dying on their machines. That just blew my mind.

"They're saying you should cut your hair and get a good job – for what? So people can suck off you? They're picking your bones, getting all that energy out of you, when it could be put to so much better use."

By the time Sabbath cut this, their second album, they had devised a sound that was simplistic and direct. The tempo of 'Iron Man' was set not for dancing but for banging one's head, especially when imbibing the downer drugs that were plentiful in the '70s or, indeed, marijuana and cheap wine.

Black Sabbath were initially not taken seriously by the rock critics, but young boys understood and from this small acorn grew the first wave of British heavy metal and, later, Nirvana and grunge rock.

I Feel the Earth Move Carole King

(Carole King) ❊ Ode ❊ 1971 ❊ Appears on: *Tapestry*

In the late '50s, while studying to become a teacher, Carole Klein was drawn into the Brill Building scene where she met her future husband, Gerry Goffin. Goffin/King were a hit-making machine from the bobbysoxing '50s through to the hippie era of the mid-'60s: 'Will You Love Me Tomorrow', 'The Locomotion', 'Up on the Roof', 'Chains', 'I'm into Something Good', 'Don't Bring Me Down', 'Wasn't Born to Follow', 'Pleasant Valley Sunday' and '(You Make Me Feel Like a) Natural Woman'. The hits kept coming until the couple divorced in 1967.

It was a feminist fairytale when the newly unshackled King recorded her own songs. Recorded in 1970, *Tapestry* was the female equivalent of her friend James Taylor's *Sweet Baby James*. It was like a calming coda to the turbulent '60s. The cover photo says it all – hair long and natural, blue jeans, casual shirt, bare feet and tabby cat. Here was a genuinely natural woman for the post-Woodstock era. Casual, sexy and real. King reworked two of her Brill Building hits: 'Will You Love Me Tomorrow' and '(You Make Me Feel Like a) Natural Woman', which laid a bridge between the songcraft of the pre-Beatles era and the cynical Nixon years. Her mellifluous piano matched her singing voice, which was sensual and mature.

'I Feel the Earth Move' is a mature version of the breathless love songs of her youth, powered by a very funky band and King's joyous vocal. The song was perfect for the liberated woman.

Her first solo album shifted five thousand copies. *Tapestry*, her third, moved over ten million, making it the largest selling album by a female artist until Alanis Morissette's *Jagged Little Pill*. King also spearheaded a movement towards the confessional singer/songwriter that was to dominate rock & roll for decades. King once said, "Until I met Gerry, I was just a musician who wrote bad lyrics." *Tapestry* proved otherwise.

Superstar The Carpenters

(Leon Russell/Bonnie Bramlett) ❋ A&M ❋ 1971 ❋ Appears on: *The Carpenters*

Tragedy and darkness haunted the Carpenters. The brother and sister act with the perfect hair and shiny teeth looked like they were cast by David Lynch. Richard Carpenter's spare, gentle, middle-of-the-road arrangements, which featured his piano and generally a mournful saxophone, sounded positively haunted. In the light of Karen Carpenter's 1982 death by anorexia it just seems all too sad.

Growing up in the white-bread middle class suburbs on both coasts, Richard Carpenter was a piano-bar jazz player, eventually bringing his sister in to sing and play drums. Their second single for A&M, the Bacharach/David song 'Close to You', was a massive global hit. Richard Nixon's Silent Majority now had a voice. The Carpenters, with their apple-pie grins and Karen's neck-to-knee gowns, were the antidotes to a decade of free love, sexual revolution, flower power, civil rights and student power.

"The thing is, it had to do with what we represented, Middle America and all. We weren't trying to stamp down rock. I like rock. We just made the records we wanted to make, and it so happened that radio was ready for it and it clicked," Richard Carpenter said. "But they would throw these barbs at us, clawing at us. I'm not saying everyone should like it, but no-one can ever tell me those records weren't well made."

They were exquisite in their pain. Carpenter was meticulous in a kitsch way. All the parts fitted so smoothly together there was a soft-focus sentimentality to each bar. Karen was perpetually wistful and discreet. Her songs were sung like a girl alone in her bedroom imagining the prince that would one day come to rescue her from the soft toys. There was not a touch of lust or passion on a Carpenters' track. Dionne Warwick, that other Bacharach medium, brought desire and pain to his torch songs; the Carpenters channelled sentimentality.

Their third album is much like its predecessors; tributes to Bacharach and Henry Mancini give a sense of its direction. The album's chocolate box hits, 'Rainy Days and Mondays' and 'For All We Know', are Karen at her most passive and warm. There is one out-of-character song here – Leon Russell and Bonnie Bramlett's 'Superstar'. Richard Carpenter heard Bette Midler perform the song and persuaded Karen to cut a version. Legend has it that it was done in one take to protect Karen's sensibilities. It's the story of a groupie waiting for her rock star boyfriend to return – a modern take on *Sleeping Beauty*.

Richard Carpenter is right when he points to the singularity of the Carpenters. Although it was probably their other-worldliness and the sense of panic in Karen's voice rather than the bulk of the songs. "I really think we were unique," he told Joe Smith. "I really do. We made good records, the songs were great, and Karen was a fabulous singer. The public knew. Maybe they couldn't articulate it, but they knew." Of course they couldn't articulate it; they were the Silent Majority.

Southern Man Crosby, Stills, Nash & Young

(Neil Young) ❋ Atlantic ❋ 1971 ❋ Appears on: *Four-Way Street*

Neil Young's take on racial issues in the south is one of the highlights of his end-of-the-world album *After the Goldrush*. As with many of his apocalyptic tales, this is filled with images of burning estates and a society in flames. Its Crazy Horse-style loping tempo and Young's burning guitar lines made 'Southern Man' an instant live favourite. It also alienated southerners like Lynard Skynard, who penned the anti-Young song 'Sweet Home Alabama'.

'Southern Man' had its best reading, though, on *Four-Way Street*, the live double album from Crosby, Stills, Nash & Young. Over thirteen minutes the song evolves into a ferocious guitar duel between the ragged, spastic guitar lines from Young and the more considered but no less violent solos coming from Stephen Stills. Despite its length, not a note is superfluous.

Four-Way Street encapsulates the excess that was beginning to overtake rock during this period. The audience had grown exponentially in only a couple of years and the pockets and the egos of the arts had swelled accordingly. Plus, in the wake of Cream, extensive improvisation was regarded as an essential part of the concert experience. This lasted only a couple of years before improvisation was beyond the capacities of artists and the concert experience became too large to effectively accommodate such an intimate discourse. On 'Southern Man', however, Young and Stills go over the top together. The volatile relationship between the two friends becomes an on-stage competition full of surprising thrusts and unexpected parries, veering off into new directions never touched again.

What Are Their Names? David Crosby

(David Crosby/Jerry Garcia/Phil Lesh/Michael Shrieve/Neil Young) ✳ Atlantic ✳
1971 ✳ Appears on: *If I Could Only Remember My Name*

David Crosby's talent is so fleeting that its moments in full flight are absolute treasures. Crosby had been a founding Byrd and later of Crosby, Stills, Nash and Young, where his harmonic sense was so subtle it has rarely been given its due, but it has lifted both these enterprises to a higher level. Crosby's songs tend to be the weird, political and edgy ones that put the backbone onto the platitudes of his comrades.

Crosby's other talent is his affability. His friends were legion and many of them dropped by the sessions for this first solo album. Jefferson Airplane's Jack Casady, Grace Slick, David Freiberg, Paul Kantner, Jorma Kaukonen, the Grateful Dead's Jerry Garcia, Mickey Hart, Bill Kreutzmann, Phil Lesh and Santana's Gregg Rolie, Michael Shrieve along with Joni Mitchell, Graham Nash and Neil Young all appear on these songs, which are about as free form as American rock has ever been. These are mysterious tracks unlike anything else before or since.

At the time of recording Crosby was accelerating the drug binge that dominated the first half of his life. His girlfriend, Christine Hinton, had been killed in a car crash. Crosby, Stills, Nash and Young were imploding under their own egos.

"The studio was almost the only place I felt I could function," Crosby told *MOJO*. "So I would go there every night and my friends would come. A lot of really wonderful people would just show up and I would start a song and whoever had come that night would join in. Sometimes it made magic and sometimes it made mud."

'What Are Their Names' starts out very clearly as a guitar duel between Jerry Garcia and Neil Young – both at the height of their powers and feeding off each other until the vocal comes in with an acidic taunt to the Establishment (with help from Grace Slick).

On this record, Crosby fulfilled the hippie dream of musicians getting together. But only Crosby could pull it off.

LA Woman The Doors

(Robbie Kreiger/John Densmore/Ray Manzarek/Jim Morrison) ❋ Elektra ❋ 1971 ❋

Appears on: *LA Woman*

Over three years, the Doors recorded five albums, became one of the hottest groups in the world and then after Jim Morrison exposed himself to an audience in Miami, a target for police everywhere. Drugs and alcohol fuelled the already unstable Morrison. He thought himself a poet but was regarded as a teenage girl's pin-up idol.

For their sixth album, producer Paul Rothchild walked away from the group, promoting engineer Bruce Botnick to co-producer. Then they built a studio in their rehearsal space to make what Morrison promised the *LA Free Press* would be a blues album. "That's what we do best. Just your basic blues."

When Morrison wasn't in a fog of drugs he was dealing with police charges relating to the Miami incident. The rest of the Doors carried on. Within three months of the album's release, Morrison was dead.

"At the time of *LA Woman* the Doors were looking like a doomed thing and I felt like Paul was a rat deserting a sinking ship," said guitarist Robbie Krieger. "We couldn't play anywhere, *Morrison Hotel* didn't do that well, Jim looked bad and was getting fat. And I think we came up with something so loose exactly because there was no pressure. We figured we were already screwed, so we were having fun again."

"As his self destruction, alcoholism and drug abuse increased, it became more and more obvious just how crazy he was," said Densmore. "Unfortunately, we had to pull away, and it became three and one instead of four great friends in a great band. But that was personal. Musically, I think we had a sweet democracy that somehow survived all the madness. It's really odd, but there was some wonderful kind of thing that happened when we were together writing and rehearsing."

This was the last album under the Doors' contract and Morrison contemplated leaving rock & roll to be a full-time poet. Perhaps that sense of freedom was part of the special kick of *LA Woman*.

The title track is the crowning glory in the Doors' career – an ode to Los Angeles, the city that had nurtured them. The song began life as a slow blues but the tempo picked up, reflecting the images of cars on an endless night-time freeway.

"'LA Woman' was completely live, and I think that could be the quintessential Doors song," said Krieger. "The way we came up with it was amazing. We just started playing and it came together as if by magic. Jim made a lot of it up as he went along, and I think it's one of his most poetic songs."

Keyboard player Ray Manzarek also cites 'LA Woman' as a career peak. "It represents to me a drive across the great American South West," he said. "Driving on the freeways and highways through the desert – Arizona or New Mexico – or driving up the coast of California on Highway 1, from Los Angeles to San Francisco. It's alive, it's free, it's young and it's wild."

Tiny Dancer   Elton John

(Elton John/Bernie Taupin) ✳ DJM ✳ 1971 ✳ Appears on: *Madman across the Water*

One of Bernie Taupin's best songs, 'Tiny Dancer' was written on John and Taupin's first American tour. The tiny dancer in question is Maxine Feibelmann, Bernie Taupin's future wife and a sometime "seamstress for the band".

Taupin evokes that early '70s mythology of life on the road, which in those days was more along the lines of a travelling gypsy caravan than the well-oiled machine that it has become. Cameron Crowe obviously picked up on this and used the song for that purpose in his film *Almost Famous*.

Until that point, most of Taupin's lyrics had been fantasies based on his tales of the old West or ephemeral pop confections. On this fifth Elton John album, Taupin is taking greater risks. So did Elton. The production and Paul Buckmaster's string arrangements are lavish and ornate but not overbearing. Within this luxury, 'Tiny Dancer' is a beautifully crafted gem.

Maggot Brain   Funkadelic

(George Clinton/Eddie Hazel) ✳ Westbound ✳ 1971 ✳ Appears on: *Maggot Brain*

The opening gambit on Funkadelic's breakthrough third album was a dark piece of acid-inspired protest at the war in Vietnam.

"That was originally a comment on the war in Vietnam, but it really took in the world at large," said Funkadelic commander George Clinton. "While I'm not trying to be goody goody, I'm saying we got to acknowledge the fact that we have a part in this shit just by the fact that we enjoy certain things without knowing the chain of events that leads to our comfort. Protest that and eat yourself fat, ain't you deep in your semi-first class seat. You can't take the bow without taking the blame. The whole point of Funkadelic was not to tell people what to think, just tell them they could think.

"There was a lot of black groups getting mad, because we had Vietnam hitting the black communities hard, and life in the ghettoes was meaner than a muthafucka. I could get mad enough at the world and how it was treating people to wait in an alley with a brick and kill some muthafucka and, like anybody else in the ghetto, if somebody made me mad I was ready to fight. But there ain't no winning in a situation like that, so once we got out of there I'd take acid to make sure I didn't get that mad no more. I'd start looking at, you know, alternative realities.

"There wasn't no other black groups taking acid at that time. At the time I didn't realise that we were doing what we were doing because we were doing so much acid, but I can see that now."

'Maggot Brain' is one of the finest pieces to come out of the Mothership – a catch-all that covered the work of Parliament, Funkadelic, Bootsy Collins and others. It confirmed George Clinton's place alongside Sly Stone and Jimi Hendrix as a R&B visionary.

The song is an extraordinary ten-minute jam that is part rock and part funk and part just out there. Recorded live in one take, there's an amazing guitar solo from Eddie Hazel. The guitarist was directed to "play like yo' mama just died". It worked. This is one of the saddest pieces of electric guitar of the era.

A Good Year for the Roses George Jones

(Jerry Chesnut) ❋ Musicor ❋ 1971 ❋ Appears on: *George Jones with Love*

George Jones is generally regarded as the best balladeer in country music. Heartbreak was his stock-in-trade and 'A Good Year for the Roses' is a classic of Jones' middle period.

By 1971 he had met Tammy Wynette and they were being marketed as the King and Queen of Country. Jones' more longstanding romance with the bottle was also in full swing at this point.

"In the '70s, I was drunk the majority of the time," Jones wrote in his autobiography. "I had drunk heavily for years and had pitched benders that might last two or three days, but in the '70s, I was drunk the majority of the time for half a decade. If you saw me sober, chances are you saw me asleep. It was a five-year binge laced with occasional sickness from sobriety ... Some folks think they're in pain if they've had one too many cocktails the night before. They have no idea how it feels to have one too many pints. It's like going through a violent food poisoning with an axe in your skull."

'A Good Year for the Roses' then is a song of great regret. It's a song about losing it all and the narrator is prepared to shoulder the blame. Produced by Pappy Daily, who had given Jones all his hits to this point, the song's lyric is economical and the sadness, because it's understated, is eternal: "When you turn to walk away, as the door behind you closes/The only thing I know to say, It's been a good year for the roses."

Theme from Shaft Isaac Hayes

(Isaac Hayes) ❈ Enterprise ❈ 1971 ❈ Appears on: *Shaft*

Isaac Hayes was an integral part of Stax/Volt records and the Memphis scene in the '60s. He was one of the best keyboard players and arrangers at Stax even before he started writing in partnership with lyricist David Porter. Their hits included Carla Thomas' 'B-A-B-Y' and Sam and Dave's 'Soul Man', 'Hold On, I'm Comin'', and 'When Something is Wrong with My Baby', among others.

Shaft was an early blaxploitation film for which Hayes was employed to write the score. Hayes sets the film up with one of the most dramatic pieces of film music. The track starts out on the high hat and then in comes a scratchy Curtis Mayfield-style guitar with a scratch wah wah theme drenched in reverb and the groove just doesn't quit. Hayes eventually comes in crooning praise for Shaft in his rumbling bass voice: "the private dick who's a sex machine to all the chicks".

The theme from *Shaft* increased the seismic shift in R&B towards funk and towards a jazzier, blacker sound. The song embodies this new idea of the African-American as a cool guy, brimming with machismo – proud and lethal and righteous.

'Theme from Shaft' won an Academy Award and the score won Hayes an Oscar as well – the first black composer to take the statue.

Imagine John Lennon

(John Lennon) ❈ Apple ❈ 1971 ❈ Appears on: *Imagine*

John Lennon's musing here has become something more than a pop song. It has become an anthem that people sing when they need hope for mankind. It is unlikely that many of the song's fans have listened to the lyric. Lennon is advocating an atheistic, anarchist utopia. Lennon regarded the song as a sugar-coated version of the bilious 'Working Class Hero'.

"So you think 'Imagine' ain't political?" Lennon told the *Melody Maker*. "It's 'Working Class Hero' with sugar on it for conservatives."

Lennon wrote the song on the white piano at home at Ascot, his English estate. A strange place to be "imagining no possessions". The lyric, which was effectively written on the spot, was a fusion of Lennon's pacifism and his wife Yoko Ono's art statements from her book *Grapefruit*.

"The lyric, the concept, came from Yoko, but in those days I was more selfish, more macho, and omitted to mention her contribution," he said. "But it was right out of her *Grapefruit* book – there's a whole pile of pieces about imagine this and imagine that."

Lennon produced the track with Phil Spector, who was uncharacteristically restrained but lush enough to sugar-coat the minimal backing from Klaus Voorman on bass and Ringo Starr on drums.

Ultimately the word – imagine – wins out over everything. It's another word for hope.

Jealous Guy John Lennon

(John Lennon) ❋ Apple ❋ 1971 ❋ Appears on: *Imagine*

John Lennon was not a particularly easy person to get along with. He admitted to being violent and to being insanely jealous. Just on the basis of its remarkable candour, Lennon's 'Jealous Guy' would have to rank with one of his finest songs.

The song had been begun for the *White Album* sessions and was originally titled 'Child of Nature'. Lennon revisited the tune for the *Imagine* album and recast the lyric.

Over the top of a beautiful and beguiling melody, Lennon admits to his feelings of jealousy and the violence that wells up within him. He sings with such an openness that one can't help but marvel at his passion – of which the jealousy simply seem to be the reverse of his real feelings. It's the most tender of nasty songs.

A Case of You Joni Mitchell

(Joni Mitchell) ❋ Reprise ❋ 1971 ❋ Appears on: *Blue*

Few records in popular music are as intimate as Joni Mitchell's *Blue* album. Mostly the record documents the end of her relationship with singer/

songwriter Graham Nash. Mitchell, at age twenty-seven, was also coming to terms with the rest of her life – the success and fame and the loss of the daughter she gave up for adoption.

"By the time of my fourth album, I came to another turning point – the terrible opportunity that people are given in their lives. The day that they discover to the tips of their toes that they're assholes," she said. "And you have to work on from there. And decide what your values are. Which parts of you are no longer really necessary? They belong to childhood's end. *Blue* really was a turning point in a lot of ways."

'A Case of You' is the album's finest moment. Spare and delicately drawn, this song spells out absolute devotion while the singer knows full well that the love she needs will never come.

Mitchell's language is carefully balanced in the rhythm of the song. When asked once who she considered to be her peers she replied, "Dylan, Leonard Cohen … that's about it as far as lyricists go. I'm influenced by Shakespeare, not so much by the reading of him as by the idea that the language should be trippingly on the tongue, and also by the concept of the dark soliloquy, with a lot of human meat in it." This is her best and darkest soliloquy. It's also a song that has enormous resonance to anyone that has lost love or found it unrequited.

"I was beginning an emotional descent at the time of *Blue*," said Mitchell. "They'd call it a nervous breakdown in this country – and when you're depressed, everything is up for question. You see how unbelievably phoney the world is and most of your survival mechanisms fall away. So that album was made at a time when I had no defences at all. As many a person has pointed out, *Blue* works really good if you're really low. These five girls came up to me once in a bar and said, 'Joni, before there was Prozac, there was you.'"

The Last Time I Saw Richard Joni Mitchell

(Joni Mitchell) ❊ Reprise ❊ 1971 ❊ Appears on: *Blue*

The closing track of the harrowing journey that is the *Blue* album is kind of uplifting. 'The Last Time I Saw Richard' is a song about Chuck Mitchell, Joni's first husband. They were a folksinging duo who met in 1965 and married the following year. According to the *Detroit News*, which reported their union: "Chuck said, 'Joni and I have developed our act. We are not just folk singers now. We do comedy, sing some ragtime and do folk rock. We're ready for the big clubs.' Joni nodded her approval, as any dutiful wife would do."

By the following year they had split and Joni had moved to New York while Chuck remained singing folk and telling jokes in Detroit. Judging by Mitchell's note of their last meeting it seems that things hadn't worked out too well for her former partner. His love had turned to poison, his romance for life had turned to cynicism. He inhabited a dark bar drinking undistinguished cocktails while playing sappy love songs on the jukebox. Chuck had sold himself out for a dishwasher and a coffee percolator. He had run from love and life.

'The Last Time I Saw Richard' comes at the end of Mitchell's *Blue* journey and part of its power (and the album's) is that whatever she has been through, she's not prepared to stay in the dark café.

Mitchell has moved on from folk music too. The rhymes in the song are sprung brilliantly. The vocal melody dances around phrases like "he put a coin in the Wurlitzer/and the thing began to whirl". The backing is simple but the melody is delightful.

"My chords," she said. "Nobody in the coffeehouses ever played chords like those. And they're not jazz chords either. Harmonically speaking, I'm in my own kind of world."

When the Levee Breaks Led Zeppelin

(Jimmy Page/John Paul Jones/Robert Plant/John Bonham/Memphis Minnie) ✳
Atlantic ✳ 1971 ✳ Appears on: *untitled fourth LP*

On their fourth album, Zeppelin created their masterpiece, one of the highpoints of rock music. Having spawned heavy metal and then gone bucolic the year previously, on this untitled album they pulled all their influences together in an entirely new way.

The album was recorded at Hedley Grange, a three-storey Victorian workhouse. Its large stairwell became the drum booth with a microphone two storeys up.

John Bonham, particularly, shines here. The closing track, 'When the Levee Breaks', is the biggest and heaviest drum part in all of rock. It's a twisted blues-like Howlin' Wolf on steroids.

"I recall Page and I listening to Electric Mud at the time by Muddy Waters," said bass player John Paul Jones. "One track is a long rambling riff and I really liked the idea of writing something like that – a riff that would be like a linear journey. The idea came on a train coming back from Page's Pangbourne house. From the first run-through at the Grange we knew it was a good one." Bonham's slow, insistent groove is unique and was one of the most popular drum samples in the early days of hip-hop.

Beware of Darkness Leon Russell & the Shelter People

(George Harrison) ❋ Shelter ❋ 1971 ❋ Appears on: *Leon Russell and the Shelter People*

Leon Russell was the pivotal figure in rock & roll between 1969 and 1971. He brought together the discipline of a studio musician and his raw southern rock and soul music. He was the bandleader extraordinaire. For those few years, the south infatuated the superstar elite – especially Brits like Eric Clapton – and a new generation of southerners came through. Russell moved effortlessly between the parties. He was a catalyst for some of the best records of the period.

He was raised in Tulsa, Oklahoma, and in his teens Russell's band backed Jerry Lee Lewis as the Killer barnstormed across the south. He wound up in Los Angeles playing piano and bass in Hal Blaine's Wrecking Crew – the session men for Phil Spector, Terry Melcher and other producers. He appeared on thousands of hits by the likes of Frank Sinatra, Ike and Tina Turner ('River Deep, Mountain High'), the Rolling Stones, the Byrds ('Mr Tambourine Man'), Bobby Darin, Sam Cooke, the Beach Boys ('California Girls' and the album *Pet Sounds*) and Herb Albert and Tijuana Brass to name just a few. Russell never lost his sense of southern-fried soul and gospel music. In the late '60s he hung out with Delaney Bramlett, another southerner in a similar position.

"I think the first record experience where I really did just what came off the top of my head was the Bonnie and Delaney album [*Accept No Substitute*]," he said. "We just all got around and had a party. That's what it sounds like."

The party continued a few months later when Joe Cocker landed in Los Angeles looking for a band. Having just recorded a Russell song, 'Delta Lady', the connection was easily made and Russell assembled the Mad Dogs and Englishmen, which in turn made him famous as indeed it did almost every player on the tour. Over the next year he made his own records, produced Bob Dylan's single 'Watching the River Flow' and featured heavily in the Concert for Bangladesh.

The Shelter People suggested a return to the holy rolling anarchy of the Mad Dogs. Russell was at the prime of his career, fired up on gospel and soul, and the Shelter People were in fact made up of players from either the Mad Dogs or the Muscle Shoals, aided by incredible soul backing singers and a few guests.

"We mainly went down to Muscle Shoals to record the new Shelter People album because that's where everybody goes for a certain type of music that we like," Russell said in one of his rare interviews. "It's mainly the musicians. They have that unique experience of playing together for quite some different artists, and they really are easy to work with. I also cut a George Harrison song in London with the Dominos over there, which is nice, and there was one that I just kind of wrote on the spot, so there'll be two songs with the Dominos on the album.

"I did one session with George and Ringo in London, but I haven't gotten around to writing the words for it. The music on the album is considerably more laid-back than in the first album. The songs are just a diary of what I was into at the time."

The album starts with 'Stranger in a Strange Land', adapted from Robert Heinlein's sci-fi novel which had been co-opted by the counterculture as a metaphor for themselves. There's 'Crystal Closet Queen', an ode to Little Richard. There are the semi-autobiographical 'Ballad of the Mad Dogs and Englishmen', which is curiously poignant, 'Home Sweet Oklahoma' and one of Russell's better songs, 'Of Thee I Sing'. Three Dylan songs include a soulful 'Hard Rain'. The album's best moment comes at the end with the definitive reading of George Harrison's 'Beware of Darkness'. Gospel and southern Gothic were never far from the surface, or each other, and he brings chiaroscuro to this song about Eastern mysticism.

Coal Miner's Daughter Loretta Lynn

(Loretta Lynn) ❋ MCA ❋ 1971 ❋ Appears on: *Coal Miner's Daughter*

Born a coal miner's daughter in Butcher Hollow, Kentucky, Lynn Webb married Doolittle Lynn at fourteen. A grandmother at age twenty-nine, their daughter Loretta Lynn embodied all the clichés of country – teenage marriage to a philandering drunkard. Lynn was able to write and to sing evocatively of her struggle and that struck a real chord amongst American women who had the same problems, though perhaps somewhat less intensely. Lynn was one of the early women country singers who wrote her own material. She started out in 1959 with 'I'm a Honky Tonk Girl' and by 1962 was appearing at the Grand Ole Opry and had a song in the country Top 10.

Country singer Tanya Tucker said Lynn "was one of the first to tell it like it is." Tammy Wynette also said, "Loretta definitely paved the way for me, I was always so proud of Loretta, she was so honest, she was so sincere." Lynn was never afraid to tackle the difficult subjects: 'Don't Come Home A-Drinkin' (with Lovin' on Your Mind)', 'Fist City', 'Your Squaw is on the Warpath' and, later, 'Rated X' about divorce, and 'The Pill', which was denounced from pulpits around the US.

So much of Lynn's work comes from her own experience as summed up in 'Coal Miner's Daughter' and she never forgot her dirt-poor upbringing.

"My early childhood memories probably are some of my best," she said. "They stuck with me more, and if they didn't I probably wouldn't be who I am today. If you don't remember who you are or where you come from, you get lost in the shuffle as you get older.

"Back in the mountains they wrote about everything that happened. If anybody got killed they wrote about that, if anybody died they wrote about that, if anything happy happened or if there was a day that was a good day, like Christmas, they wrote about that. There was always mountain music."

What's Going On Marvin Gaye

(Renaldo Benson/Marvin Gaye/Al Cleveland) ✳ Tamla ✳ 1971 ✳
Appears on: *What's Going On*

"Something happened to me in that period. I felt the strong urge to write music and to write lyrics that would touch the souls of men," said Marvin Gaye. "In that way I thought I could help."

His brother, Frankie, had recently returned from Vietnam with tales of horror, and his good friend and Motown label-mate Tammi Terrell had been slain by a brain tumour. When Obie Benson of the Four Tops showed him a song he'd written with Al Cleveland it reflected like a slow, shiny river Gaye's feelings of quiet despair. He tinkered with the lyrics, adjusted the melody, enlisted a session band of Motown's finest and insisted on producing the song himself, which was unheard of at the hit factory. The result was also revolutionary: powerful, pure-hearted protest with a mournful, mellow jazz-inspired groove. Bass player James Jamerson went home from the studio and told his wife that he'd just cut a classic.

The label refused to release it. Gaye (the 'Prince of Motown') dug in his heels and refused to record anything else until they did. His stubbornness paid off. 'What's Going On' shipped 700,000 units in its first week and was one of the label's fastest selling records. Its stay in the charts exceeded even that of 'Grapevine', Gaye's giant hit of 1968, and no record company suit attempted to mess with Gaye's creative process thereafter.

I Think It's Going to Rain Today Randy Newman

(Randy Newman) ❊ Reprise ❊ 1971 ❊ Appears on: *Randy Newman Live*

This emotionally charged track was a little out of place in Randy Newman's songbook. It was a song worthy of Bacharach or Gershwin – it's the introspection and melancholy that jars with the rest of Newman's songwriting. Judy Collins had a hit with the track in 1966 bringing a folky wistfulness and poignancy to the piece. It was also a minor hit for Barbra Streisand and was well interpreted by Dusty Springfield and Nina Simone.

On his live set, Randy Newman achieves that time-stopping moment. The appreciative audience who had been talking throughout the set fall completely silent. Newman's piano is so spare that he seems to be sketching the melody with Zen brushstrokes.

While the humour in many of Newman's songs has worn thin through familiarity, 'I Think It's Going to Rain Today' remains as poignant and powerful as ever.

"I used to think that it was just sophomore, college-boy romantic misery somehow," Newman said recently of the tune. "But it's not bad. You know, 'Scarecrows dressed in the latest style ...' Just the fact that the song uses the word 'implore', it's almost outside the vocabulary you use for pop music nowadays."

Maggie May Rod Stewart

(Rod Stewart/Martin Quittenton) ❊ Mercury ❊ 1971 ❊
Appears on: *Every Picture Tells a Story*

Let's face it, if 'Maggie May' was released in our current century, the singer would be hounded to death by tabloid headlines declaring "Rod Stewart: the victim of child sexual abuse!" It's the story of a teenager seduced and abandoned by an older woman, his innocence lost forever and a deep scar left on his soul. Times have changed. In the context of *Every Picture Tells a Story*, this was just another adventure for a young man in search of a good time.

Stewart was a lad before the word became a demographic: liked his soccer, liked a pint and a dolly bird, liked music. Stewart the songwriter wore his heart on his sleeve, not in the manner of American lyricists who aspired to be literary, but because he couldn't be bothered making stuff up.

Everything came together on *Every Picture* – American folk music, full tilt R&B, straight rock and pastoral English folk. The sheer size and expansiveness of the album comes from Stewart's synthesis of diverse styles. Although many of the songs were American and others used American motifs, there was something quintessentially English about Rod Stewart. 'Maggie May' itself was based on an old Liverpudlian folk song and given an R&B feel.

Every Picture says it all in the first seconds of the LP. A reflective, melancholy guitar theme opens the title track and then as the last note hangs suspended, gently fading, Mickey Waller's drums thump it down like a thousand-pound hammer. Then Stewart comes in with the lyric, "Spent some time feeling inferior/Standing in front of my mirror/Combed my hair in a thousand ways/Came out looking just the same". On this note of self-discovery, the singer embarks on his world tour; the odyssey of this album.

The key to Stewart's classic period was his sidemen. The importance of Ronnie Wood can't be overestimated. Wood was a versatile musician whose guitar and bass parts complemented Stewart in a way that no other collaborator has. Mostly it's Wood's style – loose and funky one minute, driving hard the next and then soft and reflective. He wove the melodies around Stewart's humour – relaxing him and stopping him from taking himself too seriously. The moment that partnership ended, so did Stewart's golden age.

With Wood playing the Sundance Kid the rest of the hole-in-the-wall gang represented the best aspects of British rock from the late '60s: acoustic guitarist Martin Quittenton; drummer Mickey Waller, whose rambunctious style matched Wood; Pete Sears on piano. If all else failed there was the Faces.

Every Picture is not just the high point of Rod Stewart's career but the foundation of British rock as something more than just a regurgitated version of American music. Having achieved that, within a couple of years Stewart made his Atlantic crossing and never looked back. He would have bigger hits but, like Maggie's schoolboy, he lost his innocence.

Sister Morphine The Rolling Stones

(Mick Jagger/Keith Richards/Marianne Faithfull) ☀ Rolling Stones Records ☀ 1971 ☀ Appears on: *Sticky Fingers*

'Sister Morphine' was begun in May 1968 during the sessions for *Beggars Banquet* and Marianne Faithfull released her own version in January 1969. By the time the song appeared on *Sticky Fingers*, Faithfull had broken up with Jagger and had a heroin habit, and Keith Richards was well on the way down that track.

The song is literally about the victim of an accident hanging out for painkillers. However, in the context of this album and the Rolling Stones at this point in time, 'Sister Morphine' is one of the most harrowing and powerful drug songs.

It starts with an unsettling dream against an acoustic guitar and then the other instruments slowly come in, as the lyric becomes more deranged. Ry Cooder's jagged, bluesy guitar answers the vocal with a continuous melody line. Jack Nitzsche's piano turns the dream into a nightmare with sheets of treated sound playing off against Charlie Watts' delightfully sloppy but hard drums. Rather than playing as an ensemble, each of the notes here accentuates the lyric and builds into the most sophisticated arrangement the Rolling Stones had yet tried.

While drugs had long been a part of the rock & roll scene, 'Sister Morphine' made it clear, in no uncertain terms, what was going on.

Family Affair   Sly & the Family Stone

(Sylvester Stewart) ❋ Epic ❋ 1971 ❋ Appears on: *There's a Riot Goin' On*

Apparently there was a riot goin' on in Sly Stone's mind during the making of this album. In previous years Sylvester Stewart (aka Sly Stone) had revolutionised soul with his rainbow coalition bands and his futuristic gospel sound. This was fresh and powerful music.

Unfortunately, Sly developed a taste for the drug angel dust, also known as PCP, and his life went off the rails. He stopped turning up for concerts and his behaviour became increasingly erratic.

The recording of *Riot* went months over time. Bobby Womack, Miles Davis and Billy Preston all showed up for sessions but there is no evidence that their parts were kept or any proof of their visits. Sly Stone was endlessly recording and rerecording tracks.

The album budget blew out to a massive $1,000,000 – unheard of in those days. The party atmosphere of previous records was played down in a fog of paranoia.

Through it all came 'Family Affair' – a beautiful piece of funk and one of the first hits to feature electronic drums. The song was elastic enough to be shaped by the listener into a song of paranoia or a song of love. Depending on where your head is.

Respect Yourself The Staple Singers

(Mack Rice/Luther Ingram) ✳ Stax ✳ 1971 ✳
Appears on: *The Best of the Staple Singers*

As a child in the Mississippi Delta in the '20s, Roebuck Pops Staples heard the original Delta blues legends. After moving to Chicago and embarking on his own career with his family – including his daughter Mavis – he took a more gospel bent with a large dose of R&B. They signed to Stax in the mid-'60s and recorded extensively with the strong and muscular Muscle Shoals rhythm section and other legendary Memphis session bands.

'Respect Yourself' was a perfect Staples Singers vehicle. The message of the song centres on non-violent black pride and it brings together the urgency of R&B with vocal arrangements evolved from gospel.

"Still, on this particular album, Al [producer Al Bell] and I talked a lot about all the different styles we wanted to incorporate," engineer Terry Manning told *Mix* magazine. "I was trying to bring in some rock elements – fuzz tone and various things. And Al was trying to bring in a Jamaican feel. He'd been on a trip to Montego Bay and he'd heard some of the early reggae and he brought that back with him: 'We need to get this feeling in with the R&B and the funk and the rock.' That may sound a bit grandiose because maybe you listen to that and think, 'It's just the Memphis sound, it's just R&B.' But it's not. It was a big thing to us at the time. I can hear Jamaican ska types of jumps that are on the drums, especially on 'I'll Take You There' – that off-beat, not all the way to reggae, mixed with R&B."

Manning had recently acquired a Moog synthesiser, then a new invention, and used it on the record as well – the first time a synthesiser appeared on an R&B record.

"At the time, they were just more sessions," Manning said. "I mean I always loved them, but we didn't know they were so great that we'd be hearing them still thirty years later."

Song to the Siren Tim Buckley

(Tim Buckley/Larry Beckett) ✳ Bizarre/Straight ✳ 1971 ✳ Appears on: *Starsailor*

Tim Buckley was a restless soul and equally itinerant with his music. Starting out in the mid-'60s as a folkie, he embraced rock and R&B but increasingly wandered towards jazz. He was gifted with an extraordinary voice – a six-octave range that in its baritone registers could sound like pure sex.

At the time Buckley was making the *Starsailor* album he had just started a romance with his last wife and was living happily in California, while spinning, according to friends, sides by Olivier Messiaen, Satie and Penderecki.

"I even started singing in different languages – Swahili, for instance – just because it sounded better," Buckley later wrote. "An instrumentalist can be understood doing just about anything, but people are really geared for hearing only words come out of the mouth … The most shocking thing I've ever seen people come up against – besides a performer taking off his clothes – is dealing with someone who doesn't sing words. I get off on great-sounding words. If I had my way, words wouldn't mean a thing. It shocked the hell out of the people. It was refreshing."

The *Starsailor* album, produced by the Lovin' Spoonful's Jerry Yester, was expected to be the breakthrough album for Buckley after a couple of promising LPs and a solid cult following. Instead it was jammed with experimental epics and jazz flavours and judged by the public and his own fans to be unlistenable. All except 'Song to the Siren', which has an appropriately haunting atmosphere to it. It was the song that most resembled Buckley's early work: ephemeral and moody and full of melodic texture. Buckley agreed that it was one of his best tracks.

In 1983, the song became a major cult hit in Britain when Liz Fraser of This Mortal Coil reinterpreted it and, of course, a terrible Brit rock band called themselves *Starsailor*. Nonetheless 'Song to the Siren' remains enchanting four decades on.

"Sometimes you're writing and you know that you're not going to fit," Buckley said at the time. "But you do it because it's your heart and soul and you gotta say it. When you play a chord, you're dating yourself … the fewer chords you play, the less likely you are to get conditioned, and the more you can reveal of what you are."

The Low Spark of High Heeled Boys Traffic

(Jim Capaldi/Steve Winwood) ✳ Island ✳ 1971 ✳
Appears on: *The Low Spark of High Heeled Boys*

Actor Michael J Pollard (cult star of *Bonnie & Clyde*) came up with the phrase "the low spark of high heeled boys," which the Traffic lyricist used as the title of one of his best songs.

Lyrically the song seems to be about the commodification of youth culture. However, the key here is the twelve-minute exposition by Winwood and Chris Wood, and borrowing a little from later Miles Davis. There are plenty of other flavours in this stew, including some African percussion, some blues and always Winwood's expressive soulful voice.

The song develops in a very organic manner from a bass, sax and piano figure. The jamming is getting very jazzy when suddenly the group crunches into rock & roll and finally finds its way back, guided by Winwood's piano.

"We were testing the boundaries of musical reality like the Doors were testing the boundaries of reality, period," Capaldi told *MOJO*.

"I mean, such little preparation before the recording, but capturing such a great spontaneity, yet not overly investigating a song to a point where the song ain't fresh any more either."

"Of everything Steve's done, that title track always seems to me to be the song that's most like him – bizarre, clever, complex, loose, not well formulated, but with a great groove," said Muff Winwood, his brother and sometime record producer. "Depending on my mood, it's my favourite and least favourite track. It kind of sums him up for me."

Baba O'Riley The Who

(Pete Townshend) ✳ Track ✳ 1971 ✳ Appears on: *Who's Next*

Peter Townshend crammed multiple obsessions into this track. The title is an amalgam of the names of his guru Meher Baba and avant-garde composer Terry Riley. Then at the end Townshend returns to his perennial theme of youth culture, in this case a "teenage wasteland".

Having had massive success with his first rock opera *Tommy*, Townshend turned his attention to a more complex concept album based on the teaching of Meher Baba. The project, Lifehouse, was never finished but fragments of the work turned up in a number of places. 'Baba O'Riley' was originally a nine-minute track recorded for Lifehouse. This truncated version recorded by the Who opens *Who's Next* with a dramatic flurry of notes from the ARP synthesiser, then a very new instrument that Riley was teaching the Who guitarist to play. The cascaded riff is one of the more dramatic moments in '70s rock. The Who then come in behind with a massive, muscular sound and singer Roger Daltrey at the absolute top of his form. In a song about spiritual poverty, the music has a very different message.

Won't Get Fooled Again The Who

(Pete Townshend) ✳ Track ✳ 1971 ✳ Appears on: *Who's Next*

Townshend was a big believer in youth movements but his natural scepticism meant he kept his distance from the counterculture revolution in the '60s. When activist Abbie Hoffman, then one of the most famous men in the world, interrupted the Who's Woodstock set to make some political comment, Townshend famously hit him over the head with his guitar.

'Won't Get Fooled Again' was written for Townshend's Meher Baba project, *Lifehouse*, but it came to signify the end of the '60s movement.

"The people who were trying to harness rock in order to break down the right-wing British and US Establishments are now all dead or rich like Felix Dennis," Townshend said recently. "I am not a pacifist, but I felt my guitar sound, and the band's edge, came from and reflected its essentially working-class audience of non-intellectuals who knew they might have to fight and die like their fathers. They would not be fooled by university graduates telling them what to think. Even the ever-gorgeous Germaine Greer."

The song rides on the frenzied riffs of the ARP synthesiser. Townshend backs it up with fat chords from his acoustic guitar and a war whoop from Daltrey. "That big scream I did was totally instinctive, but it became a focal point of the song," said Daltrey.

Much of the album was recorded in the Rolling Stones' mobile studio parked at Mick Jagger's house, Stargroves. "What's great about *Who's Next* is that it was the only album where we played all those songs over and over again. They were our songs. They weren't just Pete's songs. That's the difference with *Who's Next*. We had that freedom to do that. We were never allowed that freedom after that."

I've Seen All Good People Yes

(Jon Anderson/Chris Squire) ✳ Atlantic ✳ 1971 ✳ Appears on: *The Yes Album*

"Three-quarters of the way through we realised that for the first time we were making something that might possibly last," is how Jon Anderson described the making of *The Yes Album* to journalist Penny Valentine. "I'm never sure that the things I've written are going to last any kind of time, so much music seems a momentary thing. We were only talking the other day about the possibility of rock music – in the next ten years – really developing into a higher art form. Building up the same way classical music did into huge works that last and stand the test of time. Rock musicians will make music that will last a hell of a lot longer in the future."

Which explains why this album is about half good and what happened to make a perfectly fine little progressive rock outfit into the most faintly ridiculous behemoth that it became.

Classical-rock fusion was at best a daft idea.

It had been a promising beginning back in 1968 when singer Jon Anderson and bass player Chris Squire bonded over Simon & Garfunkel and determined to form a group modelled on the 5th Dimension. Their pop sensibility was augmented by drummer Bill Bruford, Tony Kay on organ and Peter Banks playing guitar. By this, their third album, Steve Howe had replaced Banks.

No doubt in a desire to emulate classical music Yes began to forsake songs for suites. They abandoned love songs for space operas and heavy themes (and generally impenetrable ones at that).

What Yes had on *The Yes Album* was chemistry and discipline. Bruford is one of the finest drummers – subtle and fluid to match Squire's bass lines. Steve Howe's complex and elegant guitar, however, makes the record spark.

The album's best cut is the single 'I've Seen All Good People'. The track sparkles with the light from Anderson's voice. 'Good People' was their first hit, and it was downhill ever after. Kaye was replaced by the classically trained, unspeakably pretentious keyboardist Rick Wakeman. In their search for the kudos of art, Yes honed their technique and lost their soul.

In the Street Big Star

(Chris Bell/Alex Chilton) ❈ Ardent ❈ 1972 ❈ Appears on: #1 Record

Alex Chilton was on the run from pop stardom when he formed the band that for so many rock critics defined pure pop for now people. Chilton had been the singer for the Box Tops and had a number of hits while still a teenager. By 1971 he had dropped out, been to New York and returned to Memphis looking to record. Through Ardent studios Chilton met songwriter Chris Bell and, with Jody Stephens and Andy Hummel, Big Star was born.

They took their name from the supermarket across the road from the studio and they took their sound from the Kinks, the Beatles and the Velvet Underground, with some soul and country. Mostly though it was jangly guitars. At the time the radio was dominated by southern boogie, Led Zeppelin or progressive rock, and Big Star wrote concise pop songs with innovative guitar textures. Nowhere was this better caught than on 'In the Street'. The riff for the song was copped from Blind Willie McTell and the recording sounds like Paul McCartney backed by the Rolling Stones.

The sound of the first Big Star album was the template for R.E.M. and the Replacements and indeed most of the first wave of college rock artists. According to Robert Gordon's *It Came From Memphis*, "Though they are ostensibly a pop band, there's an underlying menace to Big Star's work. They meld the winsome with the twisted."

Woman's Gotta Have It Bobby Womack

(Darryl Carter/Bobby Womack/Linda Womack) ❋ United Artists ❋ 1972 ❋

Appears on: *Understanding*

Bobby Womack was never much of a joiner. His initial training was in gospel. He played guitar for the Five Blind Boys of Jackson, Mississippi, before working with Sam Cooke. Through the '60s he was mostly a session guitarist and songwriter based out of Memphis and Muscle Schools. Those two towns had particular house bands and particular "sounds". Womack developed his own brand of funky soul music, which came to the fore on a number of records he made under his own name for United Artists.

"I'm bridging the gap, if you like," he said. "R&B is one thing, but I also believe in rock, using electronics, but in good taste, not to the point where it distorts what you're tryin' to say. A lot of blacks tell me that I'm a strange cat; that I sing funky but hang out with some of the differentest cats, one minute with Donald Byrd, the next minute with Segovia. But to me all music makes sense. I can't stand to hear no one thing constantly."

'A Woman's Gotta Have It' was a wonderful deep soul track that chimed perfectly with the era of women's emancipation.

The inspiration for the song came from Darryl Carter, an engineer at Chips Moman's American Sound Studios in Memphis. It was based on a real couple's marital difficulties, and he and the Womacks intended the track for Jackie Wilson. It was Bobby Womack's version that went to number one in the R&B chart though. The track has since been covered by a number of artists including Wendy Matthews, the Neville Brothers, James Taylor and Prince.

Return to Forever   Chick Corea & Return to Forever

(Chick Corea) ✳ ECM ✳ 1972 ✳ Appears on: *Return to Forever*

Chick Corea, yet another alumnus of Miles Davis' Bitches Brew sessions, took fusion into his own direction. With bassist Stanley Clarke, Joe Farell on flute and sax, percussionist Airto Moreira and Airto's wife, Flora Purim, singing, Corea knew he had something unique.

The pianist was particularly interested in putting a strong rhythmic Latin colour to his music. Stan Getz offered the opportunity to keep the band together as his backing, while in downtime Corea recorded this album. The group Return to Forever was to be one of the most enduring fusion or jazz-rock groups of the early '70s.

Like many of his contemporaries, Corea saw his future not in terms of the increasingly esoteric world of jazz but in crossing over into rock. It was not to be.

"I have a very clear intention now, which is shared by the others: to present very high quality music and to communicate to a lot of people," he said at the time. "Right now we've been working the standard jazz circuit, because that's what we're mainly known as. But more and more, as we play this music, we're getting opportunities to play to the audiences that we feel would like what we do more – colleges, concert dates, and pop audiences also."

Corea's problem was that he was too intellectual a composer and his music too sophisticated for even the progressive rock market of the time.

"Forever is a word which means a duration of time without ending, you see, and it implies a place where people are when they're not thinking about time, not embroiled in the world, and they're very much themselves," he said of the title song. "Where time just passes without being noticed. And it's a very beautiful place to be; it's a very light, happy place, where a lot of production and creativity happens. It's not really a place or a time – it's just a way of being; and it's a return to that, you see.

"Returning to it is necessary because I think this is a basic goal that all people share – just to be happy, to be very creative, and to communicate with one another very freely. Such a way of existence smacks of truth. But people have moved away from the awareness of this. All you have to do is take a look around you, and inside you, to observe how far we've travelled from it."

Corea was an inspired pianist and composer but he lacked the aggression of John McLaughlin or the spacey styling of Weather Report, and so somehow fell between the cracks. His solo piano work would ultimately last longer. But on this first album the fluid, innovative bass playing of Clarke, Corea's own work and the Latin colours of Airto make it a classic.

Suffragette City David Bowie

(David Bowie) ❋ RCA ❋ 1972 ❋

Appears on: *The Rise and Fall of Ziggy Stardust and the Spiders from Mars*

David Bowie raised the stakes in 1972 by declaring to the *NME*, "I'm gay". He has subsequently remarked it was the best thing he ever said. There is an irony in a heterosexual man claiming to be queer, but it was a great publicity stunt. Bowie then invented himself a character complete with a concept album. While other rock stars of the era were struggling to get out a dozen songs, Bowie was playing on a whole new field.

"It's one of those instantaneous vision things you get," said Bowie of his inspiration for the concept album. "It all came to me in a daydream about what this whole thing was about." The character Ziggy Stardust was loosely based on an American rock & roll singer, Vince Taylor, who had moved to Paris and become something of a cult figure. That was added to the Legendary Stardust Cowboy, the singer of 'Paralysed', often thought to be the worst single ever recorded. There was possibly also a nod to Iggy Pop, who was one of Bowie's idols at the time. This pastiche of rock iconography was tied into a science fiction storyline. What mattered in the end was the playing on the *Spiders from Mars*.

'Suffragette City' was a homage to the Velvet Underground. Lou Reed's driving guitar was mimicked and embellished by the more adroit Mick Ronson, who added sweetness and light to the mix. "He provided this strong, earthy, simply-focussed idea of what a song was all about. And I would flutter around on the edges and decorate," said Bowie.

'Suffragette City' rocked. It was pure energy. At an early performance Bowie dropped to his knees and gave Ronson's guitar oral pleasure, which not only looked exciting and dangerous but added to the already loud furore over Bowie's sexuality.

Ziggy Stardust made Bowie a superstar. "I packaged a totally credible plastic rock star," said Bowie. "Much better than any sort of Monkees fabrication. My plastic rocker was much more plastic than anybody's."

Smoke on the Water Deep Purple

(Ritchie Blackmore/Ian Gillan/Roger Glover/Jon Lord/Ian Paice) ❊ Harvest ❊ 1972 ❊
Appears on: *Machine Head*

This is the classic air guitar song and for over thirty years the epic three-chord riff has blown the minds of millions of teenage boys in black T-shirts.

Guitarist Ritchie Blackmore, a refugee from Screaming Lord Sutch's band, formed Deep Purple in the mid-'60s. A short jab at the pop charts with 'Hush' led to a fascination with progressive rock. The arrival of Hammond organist Jon Lord brought some pretensions towards classical music while singer Ian Gillan had a banshee's range. In one of the dumbest conceits by a rock band, Deep Purple booked the London Philharmonic for the *Concerto For Group and Orchestra*. Fortunately they quickly abandoned such affectation for savage, hard-edged rock on their excellent *Deep Purple in Rock* (1970). Within two years they were Led Zeppelin's poor cousins and doing well enough to make a record in Switzerland.

The *Machine Head* sessions in December of 1971 were scheduled to take place in the Casino at Montreux. On the night they were to start, a fan at a Frank Zappa gig in the venue ignited a flare, burning the Casino to the ground. The occasion was quickly committed to song: 'Smoke on the Water'.

"Everybody was running out of the place, but I didn't know why," Blackmore recalled. "I thought it was an intermission or something, because I had got tired of Frank Zappa within the first ten minutes, and I was more interested in this girl who was quite well endowed. I took her outside and was talking to her, and all these people were running past me with white faces, and I presumed it must be an intermission and that they were going to get ice creams until I saw the smoke coming out and realised something was wrong.

"It's a good job I realised it, because otherwise I'd have been with this certain young lady somewhere, in some kind of cupboard, up to some sort of mischief, and I would have been burnt down with the place, because it was a habit of mine to disappear into cellars and places ...

"We had already recorded the backing track before the fire, and we did it in about four takes because we had to – the police were banging on the door, and we knew it was the police, but we had such a good sound in this hall that we were waking up the neighbours about five miles away because the sound was echoing through the mountains. We had just finished it when the police burst in and said we had to stop, and since we'd finished it, we did. Then Ian wrote the words after the fire."

Debris The Faces

(Ronnie Lane) ❊ Warner Bros. ❊ 1972 ❊

Appears on: *A Nod is as Good as a Wink ... to a Blind Horse*

They saw themselves as the wild cards of the second division although they put most of the premier league teams to shame. Few groups have had so much promise and then been too lazy to fulfil it. Few groups have understood and communicated the joy of playing rock & roll quite as well as the Faces did.

The problem was Rod Stewart. The singer joined the former Small Faces while maintaining his solo career and when that took off, in no small part because of the Faces, Stewart kept his best stuff for himself and hamstrung the group.

A Nod is as Good as a Wink, the third Faces studio album, is as perfect as Stewart's albums of the time – boozily sentimental, socially gormless, laddishly sexist but enormously charming – with a recurring theme of missing the late night bus. The Faces sounded like they really didn't care.

The Faces may have been loose but they were one of the most powerful live acts of the time; Wood's fuzzed-out guitar and buzzing slide-work against Kenny Jones' massive drumming made them the equal of any of their contemporaries. The Faces were much maligned in their time as sloppy and ill-focused but they were also the template for Squeeze, the Black Crowes, Oasis and, more recently, Jet. Interestingly, the back-to-basics movements tend to draw on the Faces more than any others.

While the Rolling Stones and the Who grappled with metaphysics and jet set models, the Faces lived in the suburbs trying to make a go of it – even for a night – with plain birds. On 'Too Bad' they crash a trendy party but are shown the door "before we could shake a leg". "Well let me please explain/'Cause we're not to blame/We just don't have the right accent," sang Stewart.

The soul of this album is bass player Ronnie Lane though. His kitchen-sink stories of couples married too young and now failed ran through the album. The best of them is the magnificent 'Debris', which flows along as two lovers drift apart. It's a concise portrait of stagnation in an affair, using once again buses as a metaphor for passion:

> There's more trouble at the depot,
> With the general workers union
> And you said, "They'll never change a thing."
> Well, they won't fight and they're not working.

Sung in Lane's small, cracking voice, the melody is overpowering.

By the time *A Nod* came out Stewart was ready with *Never a Dull Moment* to make him a superstar and then it became Rod Stewart and the Faces and it was pretty much last orders please. But this remains a classic.

Morning Dew The Grateful Dead

(Bonnie Dobson/Tim Rose) ❊ Warner Bros. ❊ 1972 ❊ Appears on: *Europe '72*

'Morning Dew' is one of the most durable of folk songs. It was written by a Canadian folksinger, Bonnie Dobson, who sang it on the coffeehouse circuit in the early '60s. The song came to the attention of Elektra recording artist Fred Neil, who was an estimable songwriter himself. Folksinger Tim Rose also recorded the song and incidentally added his name to the songwriting credits without ever meeting Dobson or talking to her. From there came the Jeff Beck Group's cover of the song with Rod Stewart singing.

Dobson wrote the words after seeing the film *On the Beach*, which is set after a nuclear holocaust.

"It made a tremendous impression on me, that film," said Dobson. "Particularly at that time because everybody was very worried about the bomb and whether we were going to get through the next ten years.

"I remember I was singing in Los Angeles at the Ashe Grove. I was staying with a girl named Joyce. She went to bed and I just started writing this song. I had never written anything in my life. I'd written some poetry as a kid. I'd never written songs and this song just came out. Really it was a kind of re-enactment of that film where at the end there is nobody left and it was a conversation between these two people trying to explain what's happening.

"The first time that I know that I performed it where it actually made an impact was at the first Mariposa festival in Toronto. I remember vividly the review in the *Globe & Mail*, they said some things about me and a mournful dirge called 'Morning Dew'. That's what it was really about, it was really about that film and the feelings, the fearful feelings we had at that time. And then things got better and then they got worse and we are where we are now. Actually I think that the song, if anything, is more of this time, of the present than it ever was then."

The Grateful Dead recorded the song on their first album with a lacklustre reading. It entered their set, however, generally as the closing number. 'Morning Dew' became one of their great jam songs. *Europe '72* closes with a twenty-minute free form improvisation that slowly resolves itself into the blues changes of 'Morning Dew' and it becomes a beautiful showcase for the lyrical guitar playing of Jerry Garcia. The guitar weaves its way through the melody until the final verse where Garcia's guitar explodes with a glissando of high chords and then the song crashes to an end. The end of the world could not be as sweet as these transcendental few moments.

I Am Woman   Helen Reddy

(Helen Reddy/Ray Burton) ❋ Capitol ❋ 1972 ❋ Appears on: I Am Woman

Australian singer Helen Reddy had one hit in the US with 'I Don't Know How to Love Him' but was struggling to establish herself there when she came up with an anthem for the burgeoning women's movement. The phrase 'I am woman, hear me roar' has since become part of common parlance.

"I wanted songs that reflected the very positive sense of self that I had gotten from the women's movement," she said. "I thought about the women in my family, how strong they all were, how, during the world wars and the depressions and the pretty-much-useless husbands, they had been the glue that held the family together.

"I wanted a song that reflected that, that was my idea of womanhood. I realised I was going to have to write it myself. I'd never thought about being a songwriter. I was lying in bed one night and the phrase, 'I am strong, I'm invincible, I am woman', kept going over and over in my head. I wasn't even sure what 'invincible' meant, but it sounded like the beginning of something.

"I had the lyrics and I was trying to write music to go with them, but I needed somebody to come in. The Executives was an Australian group I used to hang out with, we used to play water polo and stuff. I asked one of the guys in the band, Ray Burton, would he take a shot at it. So he wrote the music for the song.

"It was on my first album and it was mentioned In reviews but it never got any airplay. Then, as the women's movement became more and more popular, a producer at Columbia decided to make a film to exploit what they thought was a hula-hoop fad, this fad of women's lib. They put a script together out of Robyn Morgan's book Sisterhood is Powerful, which was a series of anecdotes. They wanted to use 'I Am Woman' under the opening credits. That version was on my third album and that was the version that became the hit."

"Helen used to have a dozen of her girlfriends sometimes come up on a Sunday and no guys allowed," Burton recalled. "I was allowed up there a couple of times. But there I was – one guy with a dozen girls and they're all whingeing about their husbands and their boyfriends. They went home and I'm still there with Helen having a wine and I said, 'look, if you're really serious about this why don't you write some words down and I'll take it away and make a song out of it?' That's basically what happened. She wrote it out on a piece of paper. The next day I took them home and worked on it and then 'I Am Woman' evolved from it.

"I find it very disheartening that Helen never mentioned my name in any interviews."

"'I Am Woman' is my legacy," said Reddy. "I have so many women, to this day, who will come up to me in public and say, your song gave me the courage to get out of an abusive relationship, or it was because of your song I went to law school or things like that."

The Harder They Come Jimmy Cliff

(Jimmy Cliff) ❋ Mango ❋ 1972 ❋ Appears on: *The Harder They Come*

The film *The Harder They Come*, written and directed by Perry Henzell in 1971, captured the gangster life in the Trenchtown ghetto amongst the black youth of Jamaica. Jimmy Cliff, who had already had a hit in the UK, starred as Ivan – a country boy who comes to the city in search of fame as a singer. The film was the first real introduction to Rastafarianism and the thriving music culture of Jamaica.

"I went into that movie with a positive mind, not really having any idea of the impact that it would have, but I did have high hopes," said Cliff. "It seemed as though some of my subconscious dreams really did come true. But there was some dissatisfaction with it too. My character portrayed an innocent guy from the country that came into the city to experience the hard ways of the city. He found himself having to do things that were not really pretty. I wanted to show more of the positive stuff that goes on in the ghetto too. I wanted to be able to show that you can really survive in the ghetto without having to take up a gun or becoming violent." 'The Harder They Come', produced by Jimmy Cliff, is a song of defiance that became a rude boy anthem in Jamaica and a reggae standard elsewhere.

Easy to Slip   Little Feat

(Lowell George/Martin Kibbee) ❋ Warner Bros. ❋ 1972 ❋ Appears on: *Sailin' Shoes*

Intended originally for the Doobie Brothers, 'Easy to Slip' opened Little Feat's second album with their trademarks – elliptical lyrics, bittersweet slide guitar and funky rhythm patterns. 'Easy to Slip' was begun by Martin Kibbee, whose wife had recently left him. It's a gorgeous song of bereavement, of bad things happening just because that's the tragedy of life. It's a sensibility that George got from the blues. The other thing he got was a slide guitar technique. George could make his guitar shine and cry at will. Using a socket wrench rather than a thinner bottleneck produced his distinctive tone.

Nothing with Little Feat was quite what you expected. The musical parts were syncopated in ways that no-one else could do. The lyrics were always a little oblique but the emotional content was always straight and true.

"I think he had the audacity of a schizophrenic, which I associate with great work, whether it's Van Gogh or Ravel," said Van Dyke Parks, who frequently worked with George in the early '70s. "Lowell had a madness in his work that he wanted to explore, and he had the integrity to do it. That is what makes him an artist. I see the physical comedy in Lowell George that you get out of Buster Keaton. It's the tragicomedy of man in crisis – that's what Lowell did for me. He filled a void, because it takes a lot of intelligence to get away with that."

Willin'   Little Feat

(Lowell George) ❋ Warner Bros. ❋ 1972 ❋ Appears on: *Sailin' Shoes*

The story of a lonely truck driver kicked off the career of one of America's most interesting, if short-lived, writers. 'Willin'' is sung from the perspective of a truck driver trapped on the perpetual highway of life. Superficially it's a country song but George makes this scenario into an existential condition. George's command of the language lifted the song from the typical truckdriver lament into something that was more gorgeous, more poetic.

"The whole West Coast of the United States is going to look like the whole East Coast – one hamburger stand right after another," George said. "I admit I have a thing about truck drivers. After all, they're stuck like the rest of us. He might enjoy himself, the freedom of the road, but he's been through hell too."

George, a native of Los Angeles, wrote the song during his tenure as singer in Frank Zappa's Mothers of Invention. Keyboardist Bill Payne believes that the drug references in the song got him fired because of Zappa's notorious paranoia about drugs.

Everyone else who heard it loved it. Clarence White heard a version and took it to the Byrds, who cut it. Linda Ronstadt did a version. As a result of this interest, in 1971 Lenny Waronker at Warner Bros. signed the group and made three of the best albums of the decade.

George may never have driven a rig himself but he was behind the wheel in 'Willin''. Most of his life he battled demons. He was famously overweight with a healthy appetite for drugs. By the mid-'70s he was withdrawing from the group unable to write any longer. He was eventually fired from his own band and shortly after completing a solo album, weighing 300 pounds, he died of a heart attack.

Cabaret   Liza Minnelli

(Fred Ebb/John Kander) ✳ MCA ✳ 1972 ✳ Appears on: *Cabaret*

The writing team of Fred Ebb and John Kander was described as "a little sassy and with mustard". Their work was often political, sexually ambiguous and morally complicated and some of the most vigorous material to come out of Broadway. In 1966 they were contracted to write songs for a musical based on the unlikely topic of Christopher Isherwood's memoirs of Weimar Berlin. Isherwood lived in the demimonde of whores, entertainers and poets. One of his characters, Sally Bowles – a nightclub singer and goodtime girl – became the centre of a story about Berlin, libertarians and the Nazi storm that was brewing.

Isherwood's stories are not overly sentimental, nor is the play, nor its songs. The screen adaptation was in the inspired but troubled hands of director Bob Fosse and starred the brilliant but troubled Liza Minnelli.

The result was a masterpiece. Not least of all due to Kander and Ebb's songs.

The title song is a triumph of ambiguity and will. When she sings it, Sally has had an abortion and she knows that the life she leads is quite probably killing her. She belts out "Life is a cabaret" full of irony. It's a song that Liza Minnelli owns in every way. She is full of regret and fear and yet she gets up and pounds out this belief that:

> What good is sitting alone in your room?
> Come hear the music play
> Life is a cabaret, old chum
> Come to the cabaret

It's an extraordinary moment and one of the few times in a Broadway song when the real ambiguities of life at its most raw all come together. "'Cabaret' is one of the happiest memories I have," said Ebb. "Because it was mostly what I had in mind, and I think mostly is the best you can do."

Walk on the Wild Side Lou Reed

(Lou Reed) ✳ RCA ✳ 1972 ✳ Appears on: *Transformer*

The cultural impact of this song is only matched by its perfection as a pop track. Lou Reed put the downtown Manhattan scene – the hustlers, whores, transvestites and desperates – into the mass media and he did it without romanticising them.

The best description of the inspiration for this track is from Reed himself on the *Take No Prisoners* live album. He describes, with many asides, how he ran away from the imminent success of the Velvet Underground and while unemployed and with no prospects was commissioned to write songs for a stage musical version of Nelson Algren's novel *Walk on the Wild Side*. The project faded but Reed kept the title and wrote a talking blues about the people who hung around Andy Warhol's Factory – stud actor Joe Dallesandro, the transvestite/transsexual superstars Holly Woodlawn, Candy Darling and Jackie Curtis. Warhol's enduring creation was to take these flowers in the dustbin and call them superstars – he glamorised outsiders and turned the notion of status on its head. Warhol's view of what was glamorous or cool eventually became everybody's. Of course, one of his first makeovers was the Velvet Underground and Reed remained forever (mostly) grateful.

When he made the *Transformer* album Reed was pretty much nobody. The Velvets were never popular. Reed's first solo album was a flop. The fact that David Bowie agreed to produce was a key factor in this record being made at all. Bowie's production is masterful. The sweet touches in the vocal harmonies, and the quick and deceptively simple arrangements are in large part due to Bowie.

The hook in 'Walk on the Wild Side', though, belongs to Herbie Flowers. It's the most famous bass line in pop music. Flowers, an old session hand, played a simple, stripped-back double bass. He claims that he suggested adding an electric bass part so he could double his fee. With the electric bass counterpointing the acoustic part and this wonderful fairy story lyric, the whole song is virtually there.

Now with the Top 40 audience he had so long claimed he craved, Reed followed the sexy and witty *Transformer* with a concept album about junkies dying. So much for success. "It was a fluke anyway," he deadpanned.

The Needle and the Damage Done Neil Young

(Neil Young) ❋ Reprise ❋ 1972 ❋ Appears on: *Harvest*

Neil Young once tellingly introduced the song on stage with this speech: "This is a serious song I'd like to do about some people you know, some people I know and some people that neither one of us knows. It's about heroin addiction. Somewhere in the universe there's probably a place where all the great art is that didn't get out. A museum of incredible lost art that didn't get out because of heroin."

Neil Young is rarely this blunt. The song is one of the most famous anti-heroin songs because it is so simple and so direct. It was written for Crazy Horse guitarist Danny Whitten, who was then a heroin addict and would soon be dead. With the escalation of the Vietnam War in the late '60s and into the early '70s, when GIs returned from South-East Asia, heroin became increasingly commonplace in American cities. Shortly before this song went into Young's live repertoire Janis Joplin, Jim Morrison and guitarist Al Wilson died from heroin overdoses. Then Jimi Hendrix died from an overdose of drugs – the number of junkies around the music business was increasing rapidly.

This track was recorded live and has that stark beauty. Young was not used to being so prosaic in his lyrics, but when he does he's very forceful.

Pink Moon Nick Drake

(Nick Drake) ❋ Hannibal ❋ 1972 ❋ Appears on: *Pink Moon*

This is Drake's finest moment. The singer/songwriter had been through hell and his sensitive mental health had declined steadily over the three years he had been recording. Then there was the frustration of not selling records. Drake was too sophisticated for the folk and the middle-of-the-road crowd and not in tune with the rock audience. The fact that he was a recluse and barely played in public didn't help.

"The most startling conversation I ever had with him was when we were making *Pink Moon*," said John Wood, who produced the album. "As you've probably read we made the record in, I think, two evenings. Nick was determined to make a record that was very stark, that would have all the texture and cotton wool and sort of tinsel, that had been on the other two, pulled away. So it was only just him. And he would sit in the control room and sort of blankly look on the wall, and say: 'Well, I really don't want to hear anything else, I really think people should only just be aware of me and how I am. And the record shouldn't have any sort of tinsel.' That wasn't the word he used, I can't remember exactly how he described it. He was very determined to make this a very stark, bare record and he definitely wanted it to be him more than anything. And I think, in some ways, *Pink Moon* is probably more like Nick is than the other two records."

It's a singular season in hell, which has out-lasted so many pretenders. Drake brought the tapes in unannounced to Island. He stayed for a cup of tea and left the tapes with the receptionist on his way out.

Shortly afterwards, at the age of twenty-six, Nick Drake died of an overdose.

Will the Circle Be Unbroken   The Nitty Gritty Dirt Band

(AP Carter) ❊ EMI ❊ 1972 ❊ Appears on: *Will the Circle Be Unbroken*

In the '20s, AP Carter, one of the first and most prolific country songwriters, took 19th-century Scottish and English ballads and the folk music of his time, spiced them with some jazz and blues and pushed them through a string band arrangement. This formula has remained true to this day. As country music evolved and grew in popularity, hillbilly music remained a backwater, notable mostly for giving us the theme for *The Beverly Hillbillies*. Perhaps then it's fitting that the film *O Brother, Where Art Thou?* spurred the most recent bluegrass revival. In amongst the hokey settings and the clichés there are timeless truths to be discovered.

Which is exactly what the Nitty Gritty Dirt Band (John McEuen, Jeff Hanna, Jimmie Fadden, Les Thompson, and Jim Ibbotson) were searching for six days in August of 1971 when they assembled the living legends of country for what became a three-album disc appropriately titled *Will the Circle Be Unbroken*.

You have to cast your mind back to a time when guys like the Dirt Band, with hair down their backs, stood across a chasm of the ages from rednecks. *Easy Rider* was only two years in the can and the sentiments in that film's finale as the rednecks murdered the longhairs were not far from anyone's mind.

By the time tape rolled, the players on this album included Roy Acuff, Earl Scruggs, Randy Scruggs, Merle Travis, Doc Watson and Mother Maybelle Carter, three generations of country royalty, to which they added some newcomers: Norman Blake and fiddler Vassar Clements. Of these characters, Earl Scruggs invented bluegrass banjo when he was with Bill Monroe, while Mother Maybelle Carter made her first record in 1928 with the Carter Family. Her daughter June was to marry Johnny Cash and their children Carlene Carter and Roseanne Cash continued the family business. Doc Watson, a blind guitarist from North Carolina, was one of the three most influential guitar pickers of the last century. The other one, Merle Travis (after whom Watson named his son), was also at these sessions (it was the first time the two had met). Family, the real rock of ages, runs through every moment of this album. There's a palpable sense of time being conquered, of the thickness of both music and blood.

The tracks here are often familiar: 'Keep on the Sunny Side', 'Tennessee Stud', 'Wreck on the Highway', 'I Saw the Light', 'Nine Pound Hammer', 'Honky Tonkin'', 'Orange Blossom Special', 'Wabash Cannonball', 'Lost Highway', 'I'm Thinking Tonight of My Blue Eyes', 'I Am a Pilgrim', 'Wildwood Flower' and 'Soldier's Joy'. These renditions have the freshness of truly sublime art. The album's penultimate song is, appropriately, the Carter Family's hymn, 'Will the Circle Be Unbroken', performed with three generations of musicians who loved their country music pure.

Political Science Randy Newman

(Randy Newman) ❋ Warner Bros. ❋ 1972 ❋ Appears on: *Sail Away*

In an unfortunate foresight, Randy Newman put George W Bush's foreign policy to music back when W was still organising keg parties and reputedly avoiding military service.

Newman could be Texas' favourite son when he sings over a jaunty piano figure: "No-one likes us, I don't know why/We may not be perfect, but heaven knows we try/But all around, even our old friends put us down/Let's drop the big one and see what happens."

You can hear Donald Rumsfeld chiming in: "Asia's crowded and Europe's too old."

The premise of the song is that the rest of the world doesn't understand America, so America might as well stop apologising for itself and realise its Manifest Destiny.

Boom goes London and boom Paree
More room for you and more room for me
And every city the whole world round
Will just be another American town
Oh, how peaceful it will be
We'll set everybody free

"When I wrote it, I thought, 'Well, all that is a joke.' But that kind of ignorance and arrogance and jingoism is actually out there, to some extent," the songwriter said recently. "Saying 'old Europe'. Who would have ever dreamed that anyone would say that in public? God knows what they've said in private, or what was done, like with Allende. Secret stuff that you find out twenty years later. But they're keeping it right out in front now. Since we became one world power, we've been acting like Rome."

As a songwriter and satirist, Newman is notoriously unpopular although his soundtrack work for Pixar is massively commercial. Perhaps he's too close to the bone.

"I don't have any great hopes that any one song will change anything, but it's intended to get people to feel superior to the jingoistic sentiments expressed in the song," he said. "With a lot of my songs you can certainly feel better about yourself, because you're definitely better than the people in them."

It's not just the crisp production with Newman's ragtimey piano to the fore that has kept 'Political Science' so fresh. Unfortunately.

Happy The Rolling Stones

(Mick Jagger/Keith Richards) ❋ Rolling Stones Records ❋ 1972 ❋
Appears on: *Exile on Main Street*

"*Exile on Main Street* is not one of my favourite albums, although I think the record does have a particular feeling," Mick Jagger said. "I'm not too sure how great the songs are, but put together it's a nice piece. However, when I listen to *Exile* it has some of the worst mixes I've ever heard. At the time Jimmy Miller was not functioning properly. I had to finish the whole record myself, because otherwise there were just drunks and junkies. I was in Los Angeles trying to finish the record, up against a deadline. It was a joke."

Exile on Main Street is the apotheosis of the rock & roll album. It is perfect in its imperfections. Jagger is right in observing that the mix is dirty and there are no hits, but it does have a particular quality all of its own.

In 1971 the Rolling Stones moved to France to avoid the punitive British tax rates. Keith Richards set up a base in Nellcote on the Mediterranean. A studio was set up in his wine cellar and much of *Exile* was recorded there. There's a myth the album reflects life in Richards' house but most of the tracks had been sitting in the vaults, some going back to the *Beggars Banquet* sessions of 1968. What *Exile* really represented was the culmination of their golden era: *Beggars Banquet*, *Let it Bleed* and *Sticky Fingers*.

'Happy', recorded almost entirely by Keith Richards and sung by him with some gusto, is autobiographical: "Well I never kept a dollar past sunset/It always burned a hole in my pants/Never made a school mama happy/Never blew a second chance". It is a true outlaw song that just bristles with the simple joys of defiance and indifference, and captures the ragged dirty feel of *Exile* so perfectly.

"The basic track was Bobby Keyes on baritone sax, myself on guitar and Jimmy Miller on drums. 'Happy' was cut in one afternoon," Richards explained. "We were basically doing the sound check and the track just popped out. I had this idea for a song, but it really was like a warm up."

Hey Porter   Ry Cooder

(Johnny Cash) ❋ Reprise ❋ 1972 ❋ Appears on: *Into the Purple Valley*

Ry Cooder's guitar sound is one of the most distinctive of the last forty years, whether that be with the Rolling Stones, Little Feat or dozens of soundtracks. It was based around his inventive tunings and his distorted tone combined with a sly and witty use of bottleneck guitar.

Born a white middle-class baby boomer to bohemian parents, Cooder developed an obsession with folk blues in the early '60s. What set him apart from the hundreds of other white kids learning blues from the old masters was that Cooder didn't try replicating the old songs and style but adapted them into something entirely particular.

Cooder did his time at the arthritic knees of the greats. At times he was paying for lessons from artists such as Gary Davis.

"You absorb by watching a guy and you learn where it's coming from. Not so much how it's played, because who knows how anybody plays anything, but you get a feeling of what kind of energy's in it, and what the people look like and how they move around, which was very illuminating. People like Gary Davis were fantastic ...

"You give the guy some money – what are you going to do, not give him money? It comes down to a question of what the rewards are for folks like that, who have been poor beyond your wildest imagination for their whole life, and still were that poor, except that they happened to be playing for middle-class white kids like me. Which doesn't change the fact that they're still poor beyond your wildest imagination. So you just say, 'Here's five bucks – how do you play that song?', and it seems like the right thing to do, money being about the only way you can show any kind of appreciation to such people. One by one, these guys died poor – John Estes, they had to borrow dirt to bury him, and Gary Davis and everyone died so destitute ... But it had never changed. On one side, you've got a group of people indulging their sensibilities in the warm bath of ethnic purity, and on the other, you've got the guys who actually do it, but who can't afford firewood, and that creates a certain kind of ambivalence that you can never resolve."

Cooder's bottleneck style was learnt from another white blues fan, John Fahey, who had actually been south and seen many of the Delta players using the necks of wine bottles.

Cooder also adapted the attitude, the funky slapping drum sound and the loose swinging rhythm of folk blues. His mandolin playing, which adds even more sweet, high vibrato to the tunes, generally complements the vibrato in his slide playing.

Cooder's second solo album, *Into the Purple Valley*, was designed loosely around the concept of the Great Depression and the journey that the Okies made from the dustbowl of the Midwest to the promised land of California. Many of the tunes were from that era, augmented by other travelling songs such as 'Hey Porter'. The irony of the similarity between being poor in the Depression and being part of the underclass in modern California was pretty much lost on the public who regarded Cooper as some kind of musicologist.

"A fair amount of money was spent on that album in terms of promotion, which resulted in a lot more visibility," said Cooder. "But that presented certain problems, because you can't forge a career based on social-type music in an era when that music is becoming less and less current, and less interesting to people. But I still thought it was the sort of stuff I should do, and I still think it's good."

'Hey Porter', although not from the '30s, is a masterful compilation of Cooder's talents. With Jim Dickinson's tack piano grounding the track, Cooder's mandolin dances around the melody solo and partners with the guitar and piano.

'Hey Porter' has a brief acoustic postscript to 'Great Dream from Heaven' by Joseph Spence. "There's a handful of guys that have something to do with the way I play now, in particular Joseph Spence, the Bahamian guitarist," said Cooder who in describing Spence pretty much explained his own style. "He always played in a melodic and rhythmic way that I found exotic, intricate and fascinating, with bass, melody, chord and this interior syncopation all going on at the same time, like juggling. He played mostly church music, old Protestant hymns. But he'd sit down with a hymn that everybody knew and twist it up so even his own wife can't sing along with him. He could play 'Jingle Bells' and make it sound unrecognisable, but it's how he likes to hear it. As far as he's concerned, everyone else is wrong."

Mama Weer All Crazee Now Slade

(Noddy Holder/Jim Lea) ✳ Polydor ✳ 1972 ✳ Appears on: *Slayed?*

"The beat is the main thing with us. We like to hit their guts with the beat and get some feeling going through their bloodstream into their hands," Slade singer Noddy Holder told *Melody Maker*. "If you want to come and sit down and delve into the music, it's no good coming to see us. I think we could play like that if we wanted to, but we don't want to. We get our kicks from pulsating music."

Coming out of Birmingham and the industrial midlands of Britain at the turn of the decade as Ambrose Slade, the shortened Slade were unashamedly a people's band. Not for them the arty sounds of progressive rock or the charms of Ancient Albion. Slade – guitarist Dave Hill, bassist Jimmy Lea and drummer Don Powell – were here to rock. Initially a skinhead group, Slade distanced themselves from the violence associated with skinheads and they started dressing in glam outfits with nose-bleed platform shoes and silver jumpsuits.

"Basically we're known in England as the people's group," Dave Hill said, "being as we've worked with the working class people – they're the ones who're with us now that actually made us in England. It seems to me they go for our kind of music 'cuz it's mixed. We're not puttin' out the same kind of thing every record. We've got a style, a sound and we're in with 'em. And we don't mind mixin' with our fans whereas most groups usually get to the stage where they don't even talk to 'em."

Slade's sound – which barely varied from one hit to the next – was typical of the English glam sound, which was big on simple, massive beats designed for clubfooted dancers wearing boots. The drums fought their way through a heavy sludge of guitar, piano and bass. It was simple and powerful. It grew from ham-fisted versions of '50s rock & roll and developed into a style all Slade's own. Their songs were misspelt anthems to a good time – 'Get Down and Get with It', 'Cos I Luv You', 'Look Wot You Dun', 'Take Me Bak 'Ome.'

Holder was inspired to write 'Mama Weer All Crazee Now' when he contemplated a typical Slade rave up. "I thought, 'Christ, everyone must have been crazy tonight'," he said.

"You see, everyone was so hip and cool in England that when anything would come out big, it was a hype or something," Hill said. "A section of the population was hairies, you know, who didn't want to know any kids comin' out that way. To them, any group with short hair ... you couldn't play guitar or couldn't play this. You know what I mean? That's the way they thought, which was ridiculous really. You're still a bloke. Hair's got nothing at all to do with it."

Children of the Revolution T. Rex

(Marc Bolan) ✳ EMI ✳ 1972 ✳ Appears on: *Tanx*

'Children of the Revolution' broke T. Rex's stride as a hit machine in 1972. Like all the T. Rex songs, this was a twelve-bar boogie tune that updated the classic '50s styles into something more appropriate to the '70s. Marc Bolan was T. Rex (the drummer and bass player notwithstanding). The whole enterprise had one purpose, which was to turn Marc Bolan into a true star. Like a true star, the message was peripheral. If he was required to be a hippie mystic, then he was. If it was required that he be a retro rocker then he was that and if he had been required to be a protest singer, he would have been that too. The excitement that he felt as a pop star was infectious, and we felt it too.

Perhaps it signified the beginning of apathy amongst the hippie movement, perhaps the song wasn't sexy enough – it was slightly more '50s and a little less taut than previous T. Rex songs. Its faltering in the charts didn't of course deter Bolan who just went back to the well for another series of hits. Ironically though, 'Children of the Revolution' is probably Bolan's best-remembered song, having been revived well by the Violent Femmes and less well by others, and having been used in TV commercials.

"But it's not all just fun, there's substance as well," said Bolan of his lyrics. "It really makes me cry to know that I can't explain the stuff to people who purchased the LP. I don't write nonsense as some of the English papers have inferred."

'Children of the Revolution' is thus a heavy song, its final verse declaring, "Well you can bump and grind/And it's good for your mind/I drive a Rolls

Royce/'cause it's good for my voice/But you won't fool the children of the revolution". Whether this is meant as a critique of the aristocracy of rock or simply a boast is not clear. It probably wasn't for Bolan either.

Get It On T. Rex

(Marc Bolan) ❊ Fly/EMI ❊ 1972 ❊ Appears on: *Electric Warrior*

Like Chuck Berry and most of the '50s rockers on whom he styled himself, Marc Bolan really only had one song. The trick is to have that one song versatile enough for lots of re-renderings and Bolan had a number of hits with his. Sometimes they were called 'Telegram Sam', sometimes 'Jeepster' – all very much the same, but the details made them soar to the heavens.

Bolan's boogie was a cornerstone of glam rock. Bolan and producer Tony Visconti made the blues changes even more simple, riding along on a light-footed boogie style and guitars that sounded like they were distorted by fairy dust.

Like all of Bolan's best work, the lyric was less than minimalist. A phrase, preferably nonsensical, but one which could, with a teenage imagination, be salacious, would suffice. Bolan's vocal was sly and sexy without ever being threatening. The music was all about the groove, and for that reason it is as glorious now as ever.

Visconti, who produced this and most of Bolan's work, recalled the session as being easy. "Bolan was very much a feel person," he said. "If the feel was there, we'd get it down in two or three takes."

Ramblin' Man The Allman Brothers Band

(Dickey Betts) ❊ Capricorn ❊ 1973 ❊ Appears on: *Brothers and Sisters*

The Allman Brothers Band really took off once its founder Duane Allman died. Allman was considered to be one of the supreme guitar players of the day. The group's dual guitar/dual drum sound had been their calling card and yet with Duane gone they blossomed. Second guitarist Dickey Betts stepped up to the plate, writing an album's worth of tunes, and they shifted the group from blues jams into a country tempo that eventually became known as southern rock.

"Duane was a very strong leader," said the manager and proprietor of Capricorn records Phil Walden. "After he died there was a real struggle between Dickey Betts, who leaned very strongly towards country, and Gregg, who probably found country music offensive."

The Allman Brothers were mostly an electric guitar rock band although Betts and Allman were leaning towards acoustic music when Duane died. Betts had played Allman his song 'Ramblin' Man' as early as 1971.

"You get a hint of 'Ramblin' Man' on *Eat a Peach* with 'Blue Sky'," said producer Johnny Sandlin. "Generally their harmonies had been very pentatonic and blues-based, and when Dickey wrote 'Ramblin' Man' it was very major, very up-sounding, and it took a while to enjoy that."

It didn't take the public long. The song was a smash. The *Brothers and Sisters* album had a positive message – right from the picture of a blonde hippie child on the cover through to the country-style photography. The sounds of the record were strong on traditional values – lots of dobro and slide guitar and warm piano. 'Ramblin' Man' was a country lyric – the notion of the hobo on the road was a southern stereotype and the world was ready for the rise of the south. More than any of the other Allman records this sets the template for the success of Lynard Skynard, the Charlie Daniels Band and a resurgence of interest in bluegrass and country.

But 'Ramblin' Man' was to prove the end of the Allman Brothers. Almost immediately after its release they vaulted into the top echelon of American groups and one of the most popular live acts. But the Olympic-level drug taking continued, as did the personal squabbles. Their subsequent records were just a pale imitation of past glories.

"I remember certain high spots, but what I really remember is bein' afraid a lot," said Gregg Allman. "I don't know, when my brother went . . . you never know how much you're leanin' on somebody 'til they die. And that pissed me off with myself, and pissed me off with him for dyin'. It was just a whole circus of changes, man."

When the group's roadie and drug courier Scooter Herring was busted for drugs, Gregg Allman testified against him. The rest of the group fired the last Allman brother from the Allman Brothers Band.

Knockin' on Heaven's Door Bob Dylan

(Bob Dylan) ✳ Columbia ✳ 1973 ✳ Appears on: *Pat Garrett & Billy the Kid*

Sam Peckinpah's film *Pat Garrett & Billy the Kid* was a retelling of the Wild West story in which Billy the Kid is hunted down and killed by his old friend Garrett. Bob Dylan had a small role in the picture and was asked to write the soundtrack. A song was called for in the scene where the old sheriff, played by Slim Pickens, dies in his wife's arms. Dylan came up with a masterpiece that outshone the rest of the film. In a movie that is largely about doom and fate, Dylan, then in his early thirties, expresses it all in a few spare lines. Dylan's melody moves at a funereal pace and the lyrics are spare, but the song says it all.

This is one of Dylan's most covered songs. In 2003 Warren Zevon did perhaps the most emotional reading for his album *The Wind*. Diagnosed with lung cancer and with only weeks to live, Zevon recorded the song, finding in it not only an acceptance of death but also a resolution of life.

In the outtakes from the *Pat Garrett* sessions you can hear Dylan light-heartedly call for another run through of the track. "OK, let's do it without the vocal," he says. "It's the last time I work for anybody though, on a movie. With music."

Stir It Up Bob Marley

(Bob Marley) ❄ Tuff Gong ❄ 1973 ❄ Appears on: *Catch a Fire*

The *Catch a Fire* album was the beginning of Bob Marley's infiltration of the West. With the help of Island's Chris Blackwell, he took the long and rambling Trenchtown jams and crafted them into an album that would be intelligible to rock & roll fans.

In 1971, Bob Marley and the Wailers met with Chris Blackwell who owned Island and he advanced them £8000 to make an album in Jamaica. Blackwell saw in Marley an artist whom he could market to a rock audience; Marley too was ready to cross over. For Vivien Goldman, who joined Island as a press officer in 1974, *Catch a Fire* "altered the landscape of reggae completely and irrevocably". "We're talking about an era in which the notions of the singer/songwriter and the album were paramount in the critical hierarchy," she told *MOJO*. "Chris knew this and knew Bob was capable of extended work rather than just singles, so the two of them made it happen. There was a great mutual respect and trust there: they were in it together."

Back in Jamaica the Wailers jammed out the songs. Many of them lasted up to twenty minutes. The tracks went back to London, where Blackwell supervised their editing, in consultation with the Wailers. American keyboard player John 'Rabbit' Bundrick and guitarist Wayne Perkins were brought in to sweeten the tracks a little for rock fans.

'Stir It Up' was one of the hits from the record, in as much as there were hits. It's close to an R&B groove with a rock-steady feel. It's long, slow burn makes it one of the most seductive reggae tracks, using all the usual blues and R&B motifs for the same end.

Search and Destroy Iggy & the Stooges

(Iggy Pop/James Williamson) ✲ Columbia ✲ 1973 ✲ Appears on: *Raw Power*

Hard to believe, but Elektra dropped the Stooges after two albums. Admittedly the Stooges were considered something of a joke by the music business and most critics ... and somewhat less than that by the public. Their pure, desperate noise was ten years ahead of its time. In hindsight we can see that a handful of rock critics and musicians were right and the Stooges were one of the most exciting and revolutionary rock & roll bands of all time. The only influential fan they had was David Bowie, who took the Stooges under his wing. He persuaded Columbia to commission this album and persuaded singer Iggy Pop to reform the band that was then in tatters.

Raw Power delivers exactly what the title promises, right from its opening cut, 'Search and Destroy' – from the open shards of screeching torn notes from James Williamson's guitar and Iggy singing, "I'm a street walking cheetah with a heart full of napalm/I'm a runaway child with a nuclear A bomb/I am the world's most forgotten boy/The one who searches to destroy."

Iggy teamed up with old pal James Williamson and then sent for the other Stooges, Ron and Scott Asheton. Ron was moved to bass and Scott provided his usual monolithic beat.

Once in London the Stooges rehearsed six hours a day and then went into the studio for two months in the height of the 1972 summer. Iggy, who claims he was on serious drugs (the others claim the band was mostly clean at the time), produced the album and it sounds like semi-structured chaos.

"At the time when we were over in England, we had just gotten off of drugs," Williamson said. "We were actually pretty good almost the entire time, at least through most of *Raw Power* there was very little drugs involved. A lot of drinking and just the regular dope scene but by the end of the album we'd met a few people and sort of slid back ... by the end we were playing around with that, but I wouldn't say that was our heavy period of drug abuse."

The songwriting was the sharpest the Stooges had ever done. Sheer, cold aggression and bitterness had replaced the unformed improvisations of their early albums. Williamson's guitar playing on 'Search and Destroy' is like being attacked by a switchblade. It tears through the rhythm section like it's carving live flesh. Iggy's lyrics are funny and also poetic and focused. This is a song not just of an alienated white trash junkie; these are the words of a man who has crossed the line, and they would come to bear on the cultural nemeses of the next twenty years; whether they be named Travis Bickle or Mark Chapman or Osama Bin Laden.

The album was, by the end of the sessions, a mess, and Bowie took the tapes and mixed them for release. Much criticism has come subsequently for the mix and its treble sound (Iggy remixed it himself a couple of years ago) but that high, thin, rapier sound is part of its intensity.

'Search and Destroy' was an anthem of the punks some years later but they never captured its elemental force.

"This new album by the Stooges – aptly titled *Raw Power* – had the very same effect on me the first time I heard it," critic Ben Edmonds wrote in 1973. "It's like your first hard-on or the first time you got really high: an experience so over-powering that it forces new definitions for even the most familiar things."

I'd Rather Be the Devil John Martyn

(Skip James) ✳ Island ✳ 1973 ✳ Appears on: *Solid Air*

The Glasgow-raised Martyn went to London at age seventeen and was quickly recognised as a prodigy on the London folk scene of the mid-'60s. He was welcomed as a guitar virtuoso – in a town that was full of highly original stylists. Martyn's temperament kept him a little aside from John Renbourn, Bert Jansch, Richard Thompson and others but he was widely respected and on this 1973 album is backed by Fairport Convention.

Martyn's technique is derived from the blues but interpreted through jazz and traditional English folk music to have a sound entirely his. 'I'd Rather Be the Devil' was written by American blues artist Skip James with an obvious gospel overtone. In Martyn's hands it's completely transformed. Using the echo effects and his manic, highly stylised picking style the song is stripped of its American roots and becomes decidedly English. It's as though the tune has been taken out of the southern Baptist church and translated into the Presbyterian. What is left is Martyn's feverish personality creating great walls of guitar harmonics that rise and clash against each other and his frantic vocal, which struggles against the tune as though wresting the Devil inside.

Let's Get It On Marvin Gaye

(Marvin Gaye/Ed Townsend) ❋ Motown ❋ 1973 ❋ Appears on: *Let's Get It On*

Like all of Marvin Gaye's transcendental work, 'Let's Get It On' is both seductive and a suggestion to himself to hold his life together.

The song was recorded at Motown's Hitsville West in March of 1973. Gaye used a group of musicians from the Motown house band (notably guitarist Melvin 'Wah Wah' Ragin) plus some of the era's best funk and jazz players, such as Joe Sample and Wilton Felder, as the basic tracks for the song were cut live.

Nine days later Gaye returned to the studio to put on his vocal. Writer Ben Edmonds noted that one of Gaye's acquaintances brought along sixteen-year-old Janis Hunter. For Gaye it was love at first sight. According to Edmonds, "The presence of this young girl compelled him to perform the song to her, and in so doing, it was transformed into the masterpiece of raw emotion we know so well."

Gaye and Hunter were married as soon as Gaye's divorce from his first wife was finalised. No doubt this new love brought a heightened focus to the album.

"I can't see anything wrong with sex between consenting anybodies," Gaye wrote in the liner notes to the *Let's Get It On* album. "I think we make far too much of it. After all, one's genitals are just one part of the magnificent human body ... I contend that SEX IS SEX and LOVE IS LOVE. When combined, they work well together, if two people are about the same mind ... Have your sex, it can be very exciting, if you're lucky."

All the Young Dudes Mott the Hoople

(David Bowie) ❋ CBS ❋ 1973 ❋ Appears on: *All the Young Dudes*

As one onlooker tells it, "Dave was trembling when he knocked at Mott's dressing room door." It should have been the other way around. In 1972, when Bowie approached Mott the Hoople the group was about to disintegrate. They had been dropped from their label (Island) and three years of gigging had given them little more than the reputation as the best live band in Britain. They were beloved by rock critics and students who believed that Mott had achieved the perfect British rock sound. They were raw and sloppy and loud and quirky. David Bowie was an unabashed fan.

Mott was conceived and named in 1969 by record producer Guy Stevens to be a British synthesis of the Rolling Stones and Bob Dylan. In reality they would be neither but Ian Hunter was a charismatic enough singer and Mick Ralphs had the psychotic guitar-slinger pose down pat.

'All the Young Dudes' focused Mott's shambolic charm with Bowie's very determined production style. The song picked up on the British tradition of male bonding and identification in a '70s update of the Who's mod leanings. The song gave Mott a place to be in the rock scene rather than just another great live band with progressive rock overtones. Bowie's production especially brought Ian Hunter's vocals to the fore. The song was a hit in the UK and broke the group briefly in the US. However, subsequently left to its own devices, Mott slipped away to irrelevance.

"All we ever had," said Hunter, "at least in the beginning, was our ability to relate to audiences."

Band on the Run Paul McCartney & Wings

(Paul McCartney/Linda McCartney) ✳ Capitol ✳ 1973 ✳ Appears on: *Band on the Run*

As Beatles fans will know, McCartney treasured the idea of being in a band more than any of the other Beatles. He believed that the way forward for that group was to behave like a band and get in front of people with pop and rock songs. On the demise of the Beatles, McCartney formed his own group, Wings, and tried to approximate the chemistry of the Fab Four.

It came together for a few brief years. The best of the work was *Band on the Run*, which appeared to be a loosely themed album. 'Band on the Run' itself is a wonderful homage to the idea of the rock band as travelling gang. McCartney here finds the balance in the group – the song has a more steady and propulsive theme than much of his work and it is, in short, a delight.

Killing Me Softly with His Song Roberta Flack

(Norman Gimbel/Charles Fox) ✳ Atlantic ✳ 1973 ✳ Appears on: *Killing Me Softly*

Surprisingly, this song is a true story. Well, not literally the killing bit. The songwriter/protagonist is Don McLean and the song in question is neither of his hits ('American Pie' and 'Vincent') but an album track, 'Empty Chairs'.

"I was going through some difficult things at the time, and what he was singing about made me think, 'Whoa! This person knows me! How could he know me so well?'" poet Lori Lieberman told journalist Johnny Black. "I went home and wrote a poem and showed it to the two men I was working with at the time. Never having written a song, I didn't know how to put my poem into lyric form. Norman was able to do that. The finished lyrics are Norman's, but he was very careful to make sure that all of the feelings were coming from me."

Gimbel changed the last word in the title from 'Blues' to 'Song' and helped Lieberman record the track. Her original version was not a hit. However, singer Roberta Flack heard the song on an in-flight program.

"I was flying from Los Angeles to New York," Flack said. "Looking at the in-flight magazine, I saw the picture of this little girl, Lori Lieberman, and the title of the song. Before I heard the song, I thought it had an awfully good title, and when I heard it, I loved it. By the time I got to New York I knew I had to do that song and I knew I'd be able to add something to it.

"My classical background made it possible for me to try a number of things with it. I changed parts of the chord structure and chose to end on a major chord. It wasn't written that way."

Flack's producer Quincy Jones worked with the singer and the writers to develop a lushly romantic and forlorn atmosphere. The track shot to the top of the charts in February 1973, which is when McLean heard about his fan's obsession.

When Roberta's version came out, McLean told *Blender*, "Somebody called me and said, 'Do you know there's a song about you that's number one?' I said, 'What – are you kidding?' And they said, 'The girl who originally recorded it had it written for her after she saw you at the Troubadour in Los Angeles. She went on TV and talked about it.'"

'Killing Me Softly' was rearranged yet again in 1996 when the Fugees gave it a hip-hop treatment, and it surfaced again in 2002 when it featured in the film *About a Boy*. According to *Blender* magazine, 'Killing Me Softly' is the eleventh most performed song of all time.

Angie The Rolling Stones

(Mick Jagger/Keith Richards) ✳ Rolling Stones Records ✳ 1973 ✳
Appears on: *Goat's Head Soup*

Despite years of speculation on the matter, it's unlikely that the song 'Angie' is evidence that Mick Jagger was having an affair with David Bowie's wife Angela, or indeed David Bowie. Keith Richards suggested the title because it came to him with the tune. Richards' second child, Dandelion, who was born around this time, was later called Angie and if there is a personal connection for the title, this would seem to be the more likely source. 'Angie' is one of the better Rolling Stones' ballads with a lush melody and a very vulnerable Mick Jagger singing.

This entire album was written and recorded in two months in between tours. While there might not have been a close relationship between the principals, the group itself was in sharp form. *Goat's Head Soup* was the beginning of a new era. The Stones were now more complex and less sure of themselves. The centre was lost but there were still flashes of brilliance such as on *Goat's Head Soup*, a record that has improved with age like fine cheese.

"I sort of remember the album *Exile on Main Street* being done in France and also the United States, and after that going on tour and becoming complacent and thinking, 'It's '72. Fuck it. We've done it'," Mick Jagger once confessed. "We still tried after that, but I don't think the results were ever that wonderful. Maybe some people liked *Goat's Head Soup*, *It's Only Rock & Roll* and *Black and Blue*, but basically those albums do not represent the best of the Rolling Stones."

Do the Strand Roxy Music

(Bryan Ferry) ✳ Island ✳ 1973 ✳ Appears on: *For Your Pleasure*

"It's the most complete. The one that captured what I wanted to do most clearly," is how Bryan Ferry summed up *For Your Pleasure* for *MOJO* magazine.

Roxy Music's second album is built on the creative tension between Ferry and Brian Eno: the former a traditionalist and the latter at the absolute edge of pop music. This would be their best work but at the end of it, Eno was out of the group.

"I saw Bryan's songs in the context of pop art," said Eno. "That was the period when pop music became self-conscious, in the sense that it started to look at its own history as material that could be used. We wanted to say, 'We know we're working in pop music, we know there's a history to it and we know it's a showbiz game.' And knowing all that, we're still going to try to do something new."

A retro futurism infected Roxy Music and the group revelled in the stupidity of the paradox. On the one hand they co-opted titles from serious

British artists ('Every Dream Home a Heartache') and on the other made up silly dance songs ('Do the Strand').

In 1973 Roxy Music were out on their own limb, conceptually miles ahead of every would-be art band. Then with 'Do the Strand' they reached out and touched a Top 40 audience. A significant amount of credit must go to producer Chris Thomas who, with an innate sense of song craft, has a capacity to make pop out of any cloth.

"We had so many ideas that it was like, 'Christ! Let's get them all down before they go away'," Ferry said in 1997. "Later you start to compromise, for fear of your music going over people's heads. On Roxy Music it was like, 'Let's do this thing right next to that, edit straight in from this to that ...' and so you never got bored with it. I mean, there are many flaws on that first album – the singing is terrible, and the recording isn't very good – but it's also incredibly exciting. I think we enjoyed making *For Your Pleasure* more, because we felt a little more in control. We still had a producer, but I think Brian had a lot more to do with the sound. And I think I underestimated what a help Brian was to me when we split up."

Higher Ground Stevie Wonder

(Stevie Wonder) ❋ Motown ❋ 1973 ❋ Appears on: *Innervisions*

Stevie Wonder hit a creative peak on *Innervisions*. He unlocked new possibilities for the synthesiser and, particularly on 'Higher Ground', made the new electronics sound funky. The album and this song also expressed some of Wonder's spiritual beliefs perhaps better than he had done before. Wonder had taken to writing, playing and producing his albums all by himself, as was the case here. *Innervisions* was named after his creative process: "For the most part I've listened to just what's in my head," he said at the time. Nonetheless, the album also had some acute things to say about the state of the world on 'Living in the City'. 'Higher Ground' pulls these strands together.

On 6 August 1973, shortly after this album was completed, Wonder was in a car accident that put him in a coma. Malcolm Cecil, who was one of the synthesiser programmers on the *Innervisions* album, and tour manager Ira Tucker Jr visited Wonder in hospital and sang 'Higher Ground' to Stevie. At this point the singer moved a finger in time. That's truly the mark of an exceptional R&B groove.

I Shot the Sheriff The Wailers

(Bob Marley) ✻ Tuff Gong ✻ 1973 ✻ Appears on: *Burnin'*

This was the song that introduced reggae to the west via Eric Clapton's version on his *461 Ocean Boulevard* album. After Clapton's hit in 1974, the rock audience started to take notice of what was happening in the Caribbean. Clapton's rock arrangement, of course, lacked the steaming Jamaican groove and the ambience of Harry J's ganja-filled studio. This comic tale of a battle with the police had a strong narrative but lacked the rebel fire of the best Wailers music. The fact that it was slightly rebellious and the stoned ambience in the lyric and tempo were obviously appealing to teenagers. This was a pop song for the Wailers, picking up on the theme of *The Harder They Come*, the tune had sprightly groove.

Burnin' was a difficult album to make in as much as the Wailers were falling apart. Marley was clearly the dominant force in the group and his rapid ascendancy alienated his former friends Peter Tosh and Bunny Livingston. After *Burnin'* the releases became Bob Marley and the Wailers.

La Grange ZZ Top

(Frank Beard/Billy Gibbons/Dusty Hill) ✻ Warner Bros. ✻ 1973 ✻
Appears on: *Tres Hombres*

Billy Gibbons grew up the son of an orchestra conductor in Houston, Texas. His first band, the Moving Sidewalks, were a psychedelic garage band in the footsteps of the 13th Floor Elevators. His big teenage moment came when the Sidewalks opened for Jimi Hendrix, who praised his playing, gave him a guitar and advised him, "The best thing you can do is turn it up as loud as it will go."

This he did in February 1970 when he, Dusty Hill and Frank Beard formed ZZ Top, a blues rock bar band. They play twelve-bar boogie with a dynamic rhythm section on top of which Gibbons lays witty, sharp guitar lines that sound deceptively simple.

Mostly, though, it was the attitude that broke ZZ Top out of Texas – mindless, sexual, irreverent beer-drinking music is what they specialised in. That style met its pinnacle with 'La Grange' from *Tres Hombres*. The track became a teenage boy classic and its riff is as powerful as a Chuck Berry hook. The album features other classics such as 'Waitin' for the Bus', 'Jesus Just Left Chicago', 'Beer Drinkers & Hell Raisers' and 'Hot, Blue and Righteous'.

"We're still attempting to qualify as interpreters," said Gibbons of the band's blues roots. "Which is a posture I can rest comfortably within because, fortunately, there are still plenty of living exponents who qualify as originators. We're at a place in time – it shouldn't even be called history – where we can still expose ourselves to those kinds of resources, and if one is really willing to understand it, then maybe the original attitude – the original intention – can be embraced. And I think, without meaning to sound too I-know-it-all, that so far we've been pretty successful."

Waterloo ABBA

(Benny Andersson/Stig Anderson/Björn Ulvaeus) ✳ Polygram ✳ 1974 ✳
Appears on: *Waterloo*

The Battle of Waterloo was a defining moment in the relations between England and wider Europe, with England reigning victorious. ABBA reversed the result with this piece of corny pop. First they conquered that bastion of naff music TV, the Eurovision Song Contest, and then marched on to the British charts and from there to world domination.

The song's title was changed from 'Honey-pie' to the sexier 'Waterloo' by manager Stig Anderson, himself a songwriter. Already occupying the Euro charts, ABBA developed a long-term invasion strategy with 'Waterloo', spending the winter of 1973–74 working on the arrangement. The challenge for ABBA was no mean one. Sweden had a minor pop industry; mostly, the radio broadcast politically correct symphonic music. They also battled against history – traditionally the Europeans can do everything well except rock and pop music. "You have to realise that, in Sweden, we don't have the rock & roll background that there is in Britain or America," said Benny Andersson. "We listened to Chuck Berry and the Rolling Stones, of course, but we didn't quite grow up with them in the same way that you did."

ABBA's rhythmic and melodic sensibility was based on different parameters to most pop – something more aligned with the traditional music of Northern Europe. "Our folk songs sound like that," Andersson said. "The first instrument I ever had was an accordion. My parents bought it for me when I was about ten." But years poring over the Beatles and Phil Spector showed through.

Take Me to the River Al Green

(Al Green/Mabon 'Teenie' Hodges) ❋ HI ❋ 1974 ❋

Appears on: *Al Green Explores Your Mind*

Success wasn't enough for Al Green. Raised in the church, as his secular success increased so too did the spiritual need. In 1973, Al Green was saved.

"I was 'born again'," he said. "I had flown my girlfriend to Los Angeles, done a show in San Francisco in the evening, then another at midnight at Disneyland. So when she got there, I says, 'Man, I am pooped. I am tired. So good night, right? In the other side of the suite, right? 'Cause I am gonna hit it, right?' Man I went in there, and I got in bed and I went to sleep, simple, like the rest of the twenty years I'd went through. About 4:30 that morning, man I woke up praising and rejoicing. And I had never felt like that before, and I have never felt like that again. So many things were changing so fast, and I had this input, like a charge of electricity. To create a new 'person-all' and I do mean all. To come in and just change your whole personality. I said, 'Man I don't understand.' So I ran into the bathroom. My girlfriend is knocking on the door wondering what's happening. I'm saying, 'Thank you Jesus, hallelujah, praise God.' I says, 'Huh? I never said that before.' I tried to cover my mouth, to keep from saying this stuff, because she's going to hear me. And I heard a voice saying, 'Are you ashamed of me?' And man, I had to come out of there. I came out of there saying, 'No, I am not ashamed. I am not ashamed and I never will be ashamed.' And I kept that. I was feeling so good, I've tried to keep that feeling for as long as I could.

"I'm trying to do my best to be a rock & roll, R&B artist, and I had no control over what was happening. We were all kind of dumbfounded. So I told my mom and I told my dad, 'I don't know what to do, I'm totally confused.' My dad said, 'What's the problem?' I said, 'I've been born again.' He said, 'Well, thank God.' So he went into tears. My mother says, 'Oh Hallelujah', so she went into tears. I said, 'Y'all are not much help, I gotta figure out what to do!' I've got a million dollar career going here, and I'm telling folks they need to be born again. I mean this is tripping me out. On stage, I'd be doing great. I'd be singing 'Love and Happiness', 'I'm Still in Love', all that stuff, then something starts happening, I'd get this impulse – vroom vroom – all of a sudden: scriptures."

The 1974 sessions were a transitional time for Green as he shed the secular songs. 'Take Me to the River' is obviously a baptism song – John the Baptist rebirthing his flock in the holy waters.

Green drew on his gospel roots here and his past as an R&B singer. The song has one of the most powerful and memorable grooves in pop music. Mabon 'Teenie' Hodges rightly gets credit for the tune. It's a harder edged song that reflects Green's turmoil and need for salvation. But there's also strength in the bottom and a sensuality that was so much a part of Green's best work.

"I'm good and bad. I'm right, I'm wrong. I'm light and I'm darkness, I am spiritual and I love to hold my old lady's hand and walk on the beach," said Green. "God made us like that to love. I had to build on 'Take Me to the River'. People see me and say, 'He sure did seem a little rock & roll.' I can't help being like I am. That's the way I am."

Pick Up the Pieces   The Average White Band

(Roger Ball/Malcolm Duncan/Alan Gorie/Robbie McIntosh/Onnie McIntyre/Salazer/ Hamish Stuart) ✳ Atlantic ✳ 1974 ✳ Appears on: AWB

"The name of the band started out as an 'in' saying among us, you know, we'd be listening to a track and say 'not bad for an average white band'. I guess it just stuck from there," said singer and bassist Alan Gorrie. "The slums of Dundee aren't pretty places to be either. They produce tough people who demand tough music. The same is true of the American ghettoes."

The Average White Band came out of Scotland to debut at Eric Clapton's Rainbow Concert in 1973 and surprised everyone who heard them with the authenticity of their soul/funk sound.

Guitarists Hamish Stuart and Onnie McIntyre aided Alan Gorrie with horn players Malcolm Duncan, Roger Ball and drummer Robbie McIntosh (who died soon after this breakthrough album).

The key was 'Pick Up the Pieces' – one of the most perfect soul/funk riffs, which was arranged and produced by Arif Mardin into a track that would become ubiquitous. The Average White Band had a musical dexterity to match the American masters. They brought a certain Scottish toughness, some jazz and rock feel to the party, and that gave them a distinction all their own.

"We're not out to be superstars, just to be a good, working band," said McIntosh. "In fact the biggest compliment you could pay us is to say that our sound is in the same bag as James Brown or the Temptations." They achieved those not so humble ambitions.

Forever Young Bob Dylan

(Bob Dylan) ✳ Asylum ✳ 1974 ✳ Appears on: *Planet Waves*

In his notes for the *Biograph* album, Dylan said, "'Forever Young' I wrote in Tuscon. I wrote it thinking about one of my boys and not wanting to be too sentimental. The lines came to me; they were done in a minute. I don't know. Sometimes that's what you're given. You're given something like that. You don't know what it is exactly that you want but this is what comes. That's how that song came out. I certainly didn't intend to write it – I was going for something else, the song wrote itself . . ."

Dylan's son Jakob was about to reach his fourth birthday at the time. Howard Sounes in his book *Down the Highway* also notes that Keats used the phrases "For ever painting and for ever young" in his 'Ode to a Grecian Urn'. That sentiment would accord with this extraordinary blessing.

The *Planet Waves* album, on which the song appears in two versions, was recorded in three days with the Band. Much of the record appears to be about the commitments of family. On this track the skipping reels of Robbie Roberston's guitar sit like jewels in the song.

'Forever Young' is remarkable amongst Dylan's songs in as much as it is so naked. The imagery is simple and spare and touched with a little of the Divine. It's a beatitude.

The Lamb Lies Down on Broadway Genesis

(Tony Banks/Phil Collins/Peter Gabriel/Steve Hackett/Mike Rutherford) ✳ Charisma ✳ 1974 ✳ Appears on: *The Lamb Lies Down on Broadway*

The concept album, or rock operetta, was an almost exclusively British quirk. It's an odd form, suited best to the British because they care about artistic respectability. Thus you have concertos for groups and orchestras and grandiose statements like this two-album set from Genesis. Being private school boys, Genesis had something to prove.

'The Lamb Lies Down on Broadway' opens proceedings in the operetta of the same name. The story unfolds with homeless urchin Rael emerging from the subway into the light of New York accompanied by the cascading tinkling of Tony Banks' piano. Then Genesis pounds into a rock track that simulates the excitement of Gotham.

Gabriel here is picking up on a change in mood in the music audience, looking for something more visceral than the overblown art rock of the mid-

'70s. However, guitarist Steve Hackett opined at the time, "We tend to keep away from the present. We're very hesitant to make any commitment to how we feel about what's happening now." That would soon be their undoing. Gabriel meanwhile was hoping that "spending time in America might well change our music for the better by making us seem less isolated in our opinions. Soul music excites me more than rock & roll. There's more emotion and I like the rhythm better. A lot of rock & roll seems to be working at a high speed, but not a high intensity." 'The Lamb Lies Down on Broadway' starts out with the best of intentions and contains the most intensity that Genesis would manage for some time. But it was downhill from there

Fountain of Sorrow   Jackson Browne

(Jackson Browne) ❋ Asylum ❋ 1974 ❋ Appears on: *Late for the Sky*

Even before Jackson Browne had made his first album, David Crosby described him to *Rolling Stone* as, "one of the probably ten best songwriters around ... he's got songs that'll make your hair stand on end; he's incredible". The most hair-raising of Browne's album was his third, a picture of apocalypse.

Browne's first two albums put him into the first rank of confessional singer/songwriters. His work had already been recorded by the Eagles, Gregg Allman, the Jackson 5 and Nico. Browne, with his high mellifluous voice and waifish, sensitive features could easily have become a major heartthrob. However, *Late for the Sky* was a complex series of songs about death and loss, with jazz inflections coming into his idiosyncratic pop tunes, and it was clear that the Eagles would have the country-pop-rock field all to themselves.

Browne's arty piano tunes dominate the tracks, aided by David Lindley on guitar, violin and slide, and organist Jai Winding, and David Crosby adding his incomparable harmony vocals. Bud Scoppa called it "the first genuine innovation in what has become known as the LA Sound since the Byrds recorded 'Mr Tambourine Man'."

'Fountain of Sorrow' is a masterpiece of Browne's lyric writing, playing around with images of death and loss and love and pain with a literary touch far more sophisticated than any of his contemporaries. 'Fountain of Sorrow', like most of the rest of this LP, is disquieting. The mixture of hyper-charged romanticism with particular, prosaic details has rarely been handled so well.

"I certainly don't cultivate disappointment in order to write," he said shortly after 'Fountain of Sorrow' was released. "I even had a song at one point in which my accountant comes up to me and slaps me round the face and says 'This is no time to get happy. You're making too much by being sad and serious.' That actually occurred to me. It's in my notes somewhere but I think it'd be a little too indulgent writing about that kind of thing. The audience wouldn't really relate to it. Most of them don't have accountants!"

Autobahn Kraftwerk

(Ralf Hütter/Florian Schneider/Emil Schult) ❋ Elektra ❋ 1974 ❋ Appears on: *Autobahn*

Florian Schneider and Ralf Hütter first met as classical music students at the Dusseldorf Conservatory. They joined the experimental music community in Berlin and in 1970 adopted the name Kraftwerk (Powerplant). The pair early on embraced the advantages of a mechanised future – "our drummers don't sweat!" they proudly exclaimed.

After three albums Kraftwerk hit on the idea of recording the street. They drove around Berlin and recorded the sounds of traffic and ambient noise and then constructed music from their experiments. "What we are doing is making sound-pictures of real environments, what we call tone-films. We strive for clarity, not nebulosity; we are trying to recreate realism, not vague images. In our music we make the machines sing: in 'Autobahn' the cars hum a melody."

The song was, to everyone's surprise, a massive global hit. Certainly there was a novelty factor to the song's success. Essentially no-one had conceived of using the synthesiser and drum machine to create songs in this way. The instruments were no filler or ersatz versions of other instruments, but exploring their own melodic and harmonic possibilities.

'Autobahn' was a new palette for popular music.

Lady Marmalade Labelle

(Bob Crewe/Kenny Nolan) ❋ Epic ❋ 1974 ❋ Appears on: *Nightbirds*

A meeting of exceptional talents made 'Lady Marmalade' the best single of the '70s. Although it has been tarnished of late through overuse and poor cover versions, 'Lady Marmalade' exploded on the airwaves in 1974 with funk and disco and pop all burning through the track and the scorching vocals of Labelle over the top. Producer Allen Toussaint brought New Orleans music into the space age.

Labelle – Patti Labelle, Nona Hendryx and Sarah Dash – had been Patti Labelle and the Bluebelles doing the R&B circuit since 1962 when they had their first hit 'I Sold My Heart to the Junkman'. By the early '70s they had moved to New York and were working with the likes of Laura Nyro. They started to do more music by contemporary artists and Nona Hendryx began writing. In the early '70s, they took over Bette Midler's residency at the Continental Baths in New York and suddenly had a gay following. Then someone suggested they record with Allen Toussaint in New Orleans.

The *Nightbirds* album is pure sex on wax. Labelle channelled the era – gay lib, women's lib, hedonism. They were all for liberation. "I don't wear tampons [on stage] because if it run down my leg, that's what you see and that's what you git," said Dash. "We told our band, 'We like to reach orgasms on stage' ... I really came in Philadelphia."

New York notwithstanding, Labelle decided to record with Allen Toussaint in the Crescent City (New Orleans). Toussaint was the John the Baptist of the New Orleans sound since the days of Fats Domino right through to Dr John.

"What a record is all about is the singer – a showcase for the voice," he said when quizzed about his production style. "Whatever else goes on in a track, is *for* the voice. We build all the other instruments with the singer in mind. I prefer the highlights of a voice. Most singers have particular highlights and the way to record them is to move towards the highlights, bringing them out."

To bring out Labelle's highlights, Toussaint assembled a cast of the best New Orleans musicians, including local legends the Meters. Among the songs chosen was this story of a prostitute and voodoo queen, Lady Marmalade. The backing track was built out of a deep, funky bass, piano and percussion and the whole thing was syncopated within an inch of its life. The rhythm tracks are deeply in the groove but playing with verve and spontaneity.

This is as good as pop gets – dirty and sleazy and funny and impossible to avoid. Over the top of that Labelle wail the lyric, reaching choruses like they're about to explode with pleasure.

'Lady Marmalade' broke out first in the discos and amongst the gay community. It soon transferred to pop radio – despite efforts by church groups to have the track black-listed.

"I like appealing to both men and women. I have no preferences," said Nona Hendryx. "I don't limit myself. I'm all sexes, I don't know what a heterosexual or a bisexual or a homosexual or a monosexual is. I don't understand the differences."

These were strong words in 1974.

But then, as Hendryx said, "Labelle was ahead of our time because we did something opposite from what was happening for a black girl group."

Chelsea Hotel #2   Leonard Cohen

(Leonard Cohen) ❊ Columbia ❊ 1974 ❊ Appears on: *New Skin for the Old Ceremony*

Leonard Cohen introduced this song at a concert in San Francisco in 1993 with this anecdote: "I was in the manager's office downstairs and on the wall I saw a picture of a woman. It remembered to me the time that I left Montreal for New York City. My mother said to me, even though I was a grown man, 'Watch out for those people, Leonard, they aren't like we are.' I was deeply offended by her presumption of giving a man of such years this advice but after I'd lost the copyright to 'Suzanne' and 'The Stranger Song' and 'Dress Rehearsal Rag', I think I knew what she was talking about.

"There were, however, some compensations, some consolations, a sophisticated hotel on 23rd Street. You could enter with a pygmy and a polar bear and not an eyebrow was raised, the key was just shoved across the counter. I used to ride the elevator late at night, up and down. I noticed that there was a young woman in that elevator. I did not know the great fame, the renown she had attained. All I knew was that she was a nightrider like myself, trying to pass the hours of the early morning. I gathered my courage and I summoned the most razor-like approach that I could carve for her presence and I said, 'Are you looking for someone?' She said, 'Yes I'm looking for Kris Kristofferson.' I said, 'Lady, you're in luck tonight. I'm Kris Kristofferson.'

"Well, such was the generosity of those times that she never called me on it. A couple of years later after she passed over to the other side, I found myself at this bar in a Polynesian restaurant in Miami Beach. Life leads the thoughtful man on a path of many windings. I was drinking a cocktail out of a ceramic coconut.

"This was an imponderable mystery because the entire place was frothing with actual, authentic coconuts. I hold these mysteries on the level of the Trinity. Not only can they not be penetrated but there is no need to penetrate them. They are comforting in their obscurity. The very obscurity is what offers such solace.

"I think we can take a lesson from this. Many of the mysteries that seem to beset us, just lie back on them and relax. The thought of the young woman came to me very strongly as I sat at that bar and I wrote this song for Janis Joplin."

'Chelsea Hotel #2' documents the evening and includes the immortal lines: "You were giving me head/On an unmade bed/While the limousine waits in the street."

Janis Joplin was the most fragile of performers with a deep pool of loneliness. The performances she gave were of extraordinary power and beauty and selflessness for which she received less love in return than she needed.

"Janis Joplin would sing to twenty or thirty thousand people who were drooling at her feet and I'd see her wandering around the Chelsea Hotel at three in the morning trying to find somebody to have a cup of coffee with," Cohen said in an interview. "So how do you reconcile those things? I don't know. She stood for something beautiful and nervous and high, and surrendered completely, and yet she couldn't have those things, she couldn't manifest simple things, simple beautiful things in her own life, that's really what I mean."

Rock & Roll Lou Reed

(Lou Reed) ❋ RCA ❋ 1974 ❋ Appears on: *Rock & Roll Animal*

This anthem first appeared on *Loaded*, the fourth Velvet Underground LP. In the booklet accompanying the Velvets' box set, *Peel Slowly*, Lou Reed wrote, "'Rock & roll' is about me. If I hadn't heard rock & roll on the radio, I would have had no idea there was life on this planet. Which would have been devastating – to think that everything, everywhere was like it was where I come from. That would have been profoundly discouraging. Movies didn't do it for me. TV didn't do it for me. It was the radio that did it."

The definitive version, however, exists on Reed's solo *Rock & Roll Animal* album. That tour followed Lou's hit single 'Walk on the Wild Side' and his *Berlin* album, which was recorded by Alice Cooper and KISS producer Bob Ezrin. For the tour Reed retained the *Berlin* musicians – especially the guitarists Steve Hunter and Dick Wagner. Their sound was hard, shiny and impenetrable, and that fitted Lou Reed's style at the time.

"*Rock & Roll Animal* is still one of the best live recordings ever done," said Lou Reed, and it's impossible to dispute him. "I've got enough distance on it now that I can hear it today. Those songs were made for that. And there's also a vibe on there that's – phew! I can't listen to any of it, it's just too difficult to relate to."

Sneakin' Sally Through the Alley Robert Palmer

(Allen Toussaint) ❋ Island ❋ 1974 ❋ Appears on: *Sneakin' Sally Through the Alley*

The elegantly tailored suits and beautiful grooming obscured Robert Palmer's love for dirty R&B and sleazy funk. Palmer will forever be remembered for the iconic video 'Addicted to Love' and for the relatively bland pop tunes of his '80s heyday.

Palmer was, at his best, an interpreter of songs and grooves. His first album, *Sneakin' Sally Through the Alley*, was recorded with the Meters and it remains the best hybrid of Crescent City funk and white rock. The grooves are deep and long and Palmer knows how to make the best out of them. The title track is an Allen Toussaint number and Palmer brings a witty but sensual vocal to the steamy groove.

Most of the material is by Palmer and it's short on lyrics but deep on feel. He glides along with the rhythm section, allowing his voice to be buffed by the keys and guitar. It all sounds effortless, like a breeze, but the mastery of his instrument and the discretion with which he uses it are impeccable.

Although his upbringing was strictly working class, Palmer assumed the couture of a gentleman and that characterised his career – discreet, appropriate and tasteful. But under the Armani was a heart of funk.

It's Only Rock & Roll   The Rolling Stones

(Mick Jagger/Keith Richards) ❋ Rolling Stones Records ❋ 1974 ❋
Appears on: It's Only Rock & Roll

Ron Wood's sessions for his first solo album were a house party. At one session Mick Jagger offered to help Wood with his track 'I Can Feel the Fire' in return for Wood's assistance on 'It's Only Rock & Roll', which he cut at Wood's home studio with David Bowie on backing vocals, Andy Newmark on bass and Kenny Jones of the Faces on drums. It's symptomatic of the state of the Rolling Stones at this point – Mick Taylor was hardly present and about to quit, Richards was mostly stoned and producer Jimmy Miller was cracking up.

But then, rock & roll in general was in pretty bad shape in 1974. All of the first wave of rock stars from the '60s were well past their prime – all the groups were disbanded or should have been and not one of the '60s stars was making records even close to their past form. The new generation were mostly caught up in glam rock and metal – David Bowie and Elton John and Alice Cooper dominated the era. Mostly, though, the excitement and the sense of being on the edge of a social change had all but completely dissipated by the early '70s. The revolution was over and in place of zeal there was irony and cynicism. 'It's Only Rock & Roll' was Jagger's most cynical song – denying any response to his work other than the most superficial. Jagger was fortunate that such a fickle lyric was matched with a killer riff that made him a liar.

I Can Feel the Fire Ron Wood

(Ron Wood) ✳ Warner Bros. ✳ 1974 ✳ Appears on: I've Got My Own Album to Do

The real title of this album should be I've Got My Own Album to Do and It's Better than What My Superstar Mates Are Doing. Ron Wood is the most gregarious man in British rock and his first solo album features Rolling Stones, George Harrison, David Bowie (uncredited), Rod Stewart and the Faces, aided by some of the best sidemen of the era. Unlike so many similar albums, Wood's solo venture sounds like a house party. The groove, mostly from Andy Newmark and Willie Weeks, is pretty much unstoppable, especially on tracks like the opener 'I Can Feel the Fire' with Jagger and Richards helping out. This is arguably the last great Rolling Stones cut. And on top of that is layered the work of the cream of British rock. These sessions in the early spring of 1974 at Wood's Richmond house occurred just as the British invasion artists ran out of steam, and the album sounds like the going away party. The egos, including George Harrison, Rod Stewart and Paul McCartney, had been checked at the door and the rhythm section is left to shine. If Wood had more than a thin and rasping voice, perhaps this track might have been a hit, but that would have destroyed the bonhomie.

Rikki Don't Lose That Number Steely Dan

(Walter Becker/Donald Fagen) ✳ ABC ✳ 1974 ✳ Appears on: Pretzel Logic

"By the time we were ready to start work on our third album, we were no longer the enthusiastic amateurs of the Can't Buy a Thrill period, champing at the bit to have our first real chance to get in the studio and record an album of our songs," wrote Steely Dan's Walter Becker and Donald Fagen. "Nor were we the shell-shocked road warriors of the Countdown to Ecstasy period, leading our little troop through the jazz-rock underbrush. Rather, we had settled into a comfortable writing and working groove, which was based on a calculated reversion to our pre-West Coast schizotypal tendencies and tastes. As it turned out, the sunny clime and prefab cookie-cutter robo-culture in which we now found ourselves only served to heighten our paranoia and alienation. We had our songs, some nice axes, good girlfriends, brand new drivers' licenses, lots of twenty-four-track studio time, and a warm place to compose."

Steely Dan occupies its own oddball corner of the pop world. They see themselves more in a jazz tradition than a pop one and their music is witty and antiseptic, intellectual rather than visceral.

Given all that, Steely Dan turned out hot singles through the '70s and none better than 'Rikki Don't Lose That Number'.

The bass line is taken from Horace Silver's 'Song For My Father' and drummer Jim Gordon powers the track along with a muscular but unobtrusive drum pattern. The melody is playful and joyous, perhaps despite Becker and Fagen's intentions.

The Rikki is a girl whom Fagen had an adolescent crush on while at college. The song is not about drugs or Eric Clapton or any number of pothead rumours that have circulated in the past thirty years.

Bloody Well Right Supertramp

(Rick Davies/Roger Hodgson) ❊ A&M ❊ 1974 ❊ Appears on: *Crime of the Century*

At the risk of being accused of hyperbole, it should be said that Supertramp were probably the worst rock & roll group, and at the very least the embodiment of everything that threatened to destroy the genre in the '70s. They were a progressive rock band with duelling keyboards that played complex melodies underneath banal lyrics. Supertramp – essentially a vehicle for Rick Davies and Roger Hodgson – had pretensions to reshape music and the world at large. Their vaguely conceptual albums like *Crime of the Century* looked at the "big picture" in a not very amusing manner. They suffered from schoolboy lyrics in tricked-up pop songs. They reached their nadir with 'Bloody Well Right' simply because the hook to the song was so indelible, stupid and charmless. Supertramp could claim a series of equally irritating and infectious songs that sold millions of copies. Thank Christ it's over.

(Looking for) The Heart of Saturday Night Tom Waits

(Tom Waits) ❊ Asylum ❊ 1974 ❊ Appears on: *The Heart of Saturday Night*

The title track of Tom Waits' second album is a powerful piece of Americana. Waits wanted to be a beatnik. He had read up on the Beat Generation and his verse style was clearly based on that tradition – melancholy, nostalgic, working class, celebrating the essential virtues of American mass culture (e.g. the car).

Waits' blue-collar beatnik was out of step with most American singer/ songwriters in 1973. Indeed, the only other practitioner of this kind of lyric was Bruce Springsteen. Waits' voice is appropriately described as having escaped from Alcatraz, and this song goes right to the heart of loneliness.

"It's a new song," he said by way of introducing the piece on a radio show back in 1973. "I'm anxious to play it. It's kind of about driving down Hollywood Boulevard on Saturday night. Bob Webb and I were kicking this around one afternoon, Saturday afternoon. It was, the idea of looking for the heart of Saturday night, hadn't really worked on any tune about it yet, we're both real Jack Kerouac fans and this is kind of a tribute to Kerouacians I guess".

Cypress Avenue Van Morrison

(Van Morrison) ✳ Warner Bros. ✳ 1974 ✳ Appears on: *It's Too Late to Stop Now*

It's Too Late to Stop Now is one of the few indispensable live rock & roll albums. Morrison's live band, the Caledonia Soul Orchestra, had the classical sensibilities of violinist Nathan Rubin and the jazzy edginess of guitarist John Platania, pianist Jeff Labes and the seamless rhythm section of David Hayes on bass and Dahaud Shaar on drums. This was Morrison's most consumate ensemble. They could cover all of his moods with ease and the instrumental flourishes brought these songs alive in ways that the studio versions never did.

Mostly Morrison here was on an R&B trip. He sounds like he's enjoying himself and he's recasting the folk and soul jazz of his early '70s work in the style of Ray Charles. It's invigorating to hear the eleven-piece band go through the paces of 'Cypress Avenue'. In its original form on *Astral Weeks* it's full of suppressed emotion and pain. It was a song about a desire that could never be consummated. With the Soul Orchestra it's a triumph of love and passion. Morrison puts the group through all the changes – the false stops, the wild flights of melody. Morrison sings the hell out of it, competing again and again with the strings and horn section with a James Brown dramatic line. Unlike so many live albums, where the material is made simpler and more bombastic, Morrison opens up 'Cypress Avenue' and lets new things into the arrangement. What had seemed morbid in 1968 was by 1974 transformed into a breathtaking combination of rock, pop and soul.

I'm Not in Love   10CC

(Eric Stewart/Graham Gouldman) ❈ Mercury ❈ 1975 ❈

Appears on: *The Original Soundtrack*

"We dream in clichés, we dream in parodies," said popmeister Graham Gouldman in a 1975 interview. 10CC were the masters of immoderate studio production – as were so many others who tried to outdo George Martin and the Beatles' arrangements. However, 10CC had a vicious sense of irony that gave a bite to the otherwise soppy strings.

Essentially a studio conceit from the start, Eric Stewart, a refugee from Merseybeat, had a studio in Manchester where with Kevin Godley and Lol Crème he had a 1970 novelty hit, 'Neanderthal Man', as Hotlegs.

By 1972, with the addition of Graham Gouldman who wrote many of the biggest hits of the '60s for the Yardbirds, the Hollies, Herman's Hermits and others, they became 10CC. A first album full of satiric pastiches was an instant hit. By 1975, when they released this, their third album, they were busting with ideas. The best of them was the track 'I'm Not in Love', notable for its 256 vocal parts.

Stewart explained the genesis of the song in *MOJO* magazine: "It was a silly phase I was going through with my wife, about not wanting to say 'I love you' every day because it lost its meaning. I mentioned this to Graham, because we were going to write a love song, and we came up with the idea of saying, I'm not in love – but here are all the reasons why I am. That's basically the start of the song. We wrote it in about three hours.

"We actually recorded thirteen notes of a chromatic scale onto a sixteen-track machine and fed them through the control desk with the four of us – myself, Graham, Kevin and Lol – all working the faders like a keyboard down onto a stereo pair."

In an age of overdubbing excess, 10CC's dry wit under pop craftsmanship gave their discs a rare longevity. There was one more album (*How Dare You*) and Godley and Crème left to pursue concept albums and, ultimately, pop videos. Gouldman and Stewart continued 10CC and racked up even bigger hits but never matched the understated glory of 'I'm Not in Love' or the opening track,

'Une Nuit à Paris: One Night in Paris, pt. 1/The Same Night in Paris, pt. 2'.

The esteemed critic Ken Barnes noted that "10CC's *Original Soundtrack* is a fascinating record. Musically there's more going on than in ten Yes albums ..." This was the triumph of British art rock.

It's a Long Way to the Top
(If You Wanna Rock & Roll) AC/DC

(Bon Scott/Angus Young/Malcolm Young) ❊ Alberts ❊ 1975 ❊ Appears on: *TNT*

This was Bon Scott's life story. He had been a singer with pop group the Valentines in the '60s, topping the Australian charts, then a member of bluesy progressive rock collective Fraternity on the hippie trail in London. Bon had tasted success and failure. Mostly the latter. When he joined AC/DC they were punk kids playing a circuit of suburban dances, high schools, rough pubs and the like for no money and less glory. Although the group were related to Australian rock royalty (Angus and Malcolm were brothers of George Young, member of the Easy Beats), their early years were a tough grind of loud music, abuse and poverty. As Scott wrote to his wife around this time, "I just wanna be famous I guess. Just so when people talk about you it's good things they say."

Things changed in 1975 when the group began recording and having some radio play. Quite clearly the Young brothers had a unique chemistry as guitar players and through the months of solid touring had developed their own style. With the first album getting some serious attention, perhaps Scott felt there was some hope.

Produced by Harry Vanda and George Young, 'Long Way' was recorded at Alberts Studio One in King Street, Sydney. "It was very small," said bass player Dave Evans. "We used to record in the side room, had two Marshall stacks and bass rig pointing towards the wall and miked up, and in what used to be the kitchen, drums in there – everything put down at once, generally the fire was in the first couple of takes."

'It's a Long Way to the Top' had the addition of Bon Scott playing a bagpipe solo – the first one on a rock & roll record. The track captures a particular battler spirit that reflects the Australian roots of the song and is one of the reasons why it has become an iconic number in Australia. When they wrote the song, AC/DC could have no idea how close to the top they would get. It's unfortunate Scott wasn't with them when it happened.

Toys in the Attic Aerosmith

(Joe Perry/Steven Tyler) ❊ Columbia ❊ 1975 ❊ Appears on: *Toys in the Attic*

Aerosmith's Stephen Tyler didn't always respond well to criticism. When a reviewer in *Creem* magazine suggested that the group's album *Toys in the*

Attic lacked "class," Tyler was not happy. "Class. I'll give him some fuckin' class. Obviously, anyone who writes about class is looking for a rock & roll band with class, right? So he's got the wrong group. Our music is rock & roll, and rock & roll is rock & roll. Some people would never admit they still masturbate. I think class is puttin' something over really well. That's what class is."

"We were drug addicts dabbling in music, rather than musicians dabbling with drugs," said singer Joe Perry by way of explaining his singer's behaviour.

'Toys in the Attic' is classy. In a trashy classy way.

This was the opener for Aerosmith's second album. It was a rock & roll track that was raw and dirty and ragged. The track sounds strung out on speed, like it was made in cheap hotels. At the time Aerosmith aspired to be the Yardbirds but sounded more like the New York Dolls. They were living the rock & roll dream – all of it. Aerosmith in 1975 were determined to be the next Led Zeppelin or die trying. They almost accomplished both those things and this is what it sounds like.

Jive Talkin' The Bee Gees

(Barry Gibb/Maurice Gibb/Robin Gibb) ✳ Polydor ✳ 1975 ✳
Appears on: *Main Course*

The Bee Gees were going nowhere fast in the mid-'70s. Their heyday as pop balladeers was pretty much over. The siblings had already been through tumultuous years of bickering and drug and alcohol problems. Their ace in the hole was working with Arif Mardin, an arranger/producer who had worked on many of the classic R&B sides from Atlantic right through the '60s. Mardin was also hip to the groove-based flavour that was changing R&B and he introduced the Bee Gees to that style. The *Mr Natural* album had been a step in the right direction. Things started to come together with their next project, which was recorded at Criteria studios in Miami. The rhythm of tyres on a bridge gave the brothers Gibb a new groove.

"Arif was an R&B man; the Bee Gees were balladeers. They were writing but they still hadn't quite come up with that new formula," said David English, who worked with the group at the time. "We were going home to [the house at] 461 Ocean Boulevard. Fanny got the meal ready already and we're in the station wagon. We went over the Sunny Isles Bridge and all three of them looked at each other, this is the important thing. It was always a three thing. They saw something. Barry said, 'Let's go back'. They went back to the studio and said, 'Arif, we've got an idea'. They got the guitar and they wrote 'Jive Talkin'' and that was the riff and that's how it all came about and that drive back in the station wagon changed their whole career."

On that bridge the Bee Gees discovered blue-eyed soul for the '70s.

Idiot Wind Bob Dylan

(Bob Dylan) ❋ Columbia ❋ 1975 ❋ Appears on: *Blood on the Tracks*

Dylan's mid-'70s resurgence hit its high point with the album *Blood on the Tracks*. As has been extensively reported, the album coincided with the break-up of Dylan's marriage to Sara Lowndes.

Most of the songs on the record are love songs of one sort or another. The exception is 'Idiot Wind', a seven-minute epic of elegantly phrased bile. Line readings of the lyrics tend to fall short. This is not a song based on logical exposition. Rather, here Dylan piles up a list of frustrations, public and private. It's a song that expresses a man's disgust as to where his life has lead and he lashes out at the barking dogs of gossip that have bedevilled the protagonist. No-one is excused "from the Grand Coolle Dam to the Capitol". The idiot wind would seem to be the words that come from people's mouths.

"That was a song I wanted to make as a painting," said Dylan of 'Idiot Wind'. "A lot of people thought that song, that album *Blood on the Tracks*, pertained to me. Because it seemed to at the time. It didn't pertain to me. It was just a concept of putting in images that defy time – yesterday, today, and tomorrow. I wanted to make them all connect in some kind of a strange way. I've read that that album had to do with my divorce. Well, I didn't get divorced till four years after that.

"I thought I might have gone a little bit too far with 'Idiot Wind'. I might have changed some of it. I didn't really think I was giving away too much; I thought that it seemed so personal that people would think it was about so-and-so who was close to me. It wasn't. But you can put all these words together and that's where it falls. You can't help where it falls.

"I didn't feel that one was too personal, but I felt it 'seemed' too personal. Which might be the same thing, I don't know. But it never was 'painful'. 'Cause usually with those kinds of things, if you think you're too close to something, you're giving away too much of your feelings, well, your feelings are going to change a month later and you're going to look back and say, 'What did I do that for?'"

'Idiot Wind' is an older and wiser companion piece to 'Like a Rolling Stone'. It's a song that contains much of Dylan's most scathing and acute observations fractured through a crumbling consciousness.

Dylan recorded 'Idiot Wind' with steel guitar, organ, and bass on 12 September 1974. A week later he redid the song without pedal steel. He then returned to the song in December in Minnesota when he recut the song and each time he changed the lyrics. It's a song about a state of mind rather than a specific incident.

"Yeah, you know, obviously, if you've heard both versions you realise, of course, that there could be a myriad of verses for the thing. It doesn't stop," Dylan told writer Bill Flanagan. "It wouldn't stop. Where do you end? You could still be writing it, really. It's something that could be a work continually in progress. Although, on saying that, let me say that my lyrics, to my way of thinking, are better for my songs than anybody else's. People have felt about my songs sometimes the same way as me. And they say to me, your songs are so opaque that, people tell me, they have feelings they'd like to express within the same framework. My response, always, is go ahead, do it, if you feel like it. But it never comes off. They're not as good as my lyrics. There's just something about my lyrics that just have a gallantry to them. And that might be all they have going for them. However, it's no small thing."

The Lonesome Death of Hattie Carroll Bob Dylan

(Bob Dylan) ✳ Columbia ✳ 1975 ✳ Appears on: *The Bootleg Series: 1975 Live*

Hattie Carroll, fifty-one, was a maid at a charity ball in Baltimore, Maryland, on the night of 8 February 1963. William Zantzinger, then twenty-four, was a guest at the ball. Annoyed at the service he was getting, Zantzinger struck Hattie Carroll with his cane, killing the mother of eleven children. Zantzinger, a local landowner and tobacco farmer, was charged with her manslaughter and received six months' jail. Zantzinger was, of course, wealthy and white and Hattie Carroll, the opposite.

Dylan's retelling of the events is remarkable for its detail – the behaviour of the participants, the atmosphere of the Baltimore Hotel and later the courtroom. Dylan has a keen eye for the issues here, which are class and justice.

Many of Dylan's songs of this period were ripped from the news. Dylan learnt of this case from newspaper reports – Zantzinger was jailed on 15 September, and Dylan recorded the song on 23 October 1963. He wrote the song while staying with Joan Baez at her house in California. 'Hattie Carroll', however, is most notable for the economy of its writing.

The song first appeared on Dylan's third album, *The Times They Are A-Changin'*, with just Bob on guitar and harmonica. He reprised the track for the Rolling Thunder tour where the starkness of the original was replaced by the fire and the passion of the Rolling Thunder ensemble. This is a song where righteousness surges up with each chorus to be defeated by the dismay at the injustice of Hattie Carroll's life. It was twelve years between versions, but the tragedy had not diminished. (Zantzinger eventually went into real estate. He was charged with fraudulently collecting rents from poor black tenants but was acquitted.)

Tangled Up in Blue Bob Dylan

(Bob Dylan) ☀ Columbia ☀ 1975 ☀ Appears on: *Blood on the Tracks*

Bob Dylan often refers to 'Tangled Up in Blue' in terms of it being a painting. Part of the mystery in the song is the shifts in perspective as though the narrator is sometimes a protagonist and sometimes an observer, and the action takes place in the present and the past simultaneously. It's an ambitious lyric to say the least.

Dylan recorded the seven-minute epic twice in September 1974, and then re-recorded it in late December 1974 in Minnesota. Each time there were subtle changes in the lyric. Dylan, who claims the version on 1984's *Real Live* is the best, has frequently altered the song's words. The details in the song are flexible. It's the emotional core that's constant.

Whether the song somehow documents the writer's relationship with his wife is impossible to know. His son Jakob has said that the *Blood on the Tracks* album is like listening to his parents arguing. In any case, Dylan has certainly disguised the characters enough to remove it from the historical to the metaphysical. Dylan here again refers to getting a woman out of a jam as he has referred to Sara ten years previously. The scenes down on Montague Street, however, recall his years in the Village before he became famous.

The gist of 'Tangled Up in Blue' is that we live lives governed by the winds of fate. Change is constant – who we are and where we are and what happens to us is in the lap of the gods.

"That was another one of those things where I was trying to do something that I didn't think had ever been done before in terms of trying to tell a story and be a present character in it without it being some kind of fake, sappy attempted tear jerker," said Dylan. "I was trying to be somebody in the present time while conjuring up a lot of past images. I was trying to do it in a conscious way. I used to be able to do it in an unconscious way, but I wasn't into it that way any more. That particular song was built like that, and it was always open to be cut better. But I had no particular reason to do it because I'd already made the record.

"See, what I was trying to do had nothing to do with the characters or what was going on. I was trying to do something that I don't know if I was prepared to do. I wanted to defy time, so that the story took place in the present and past at the same time. When you look at a painting, you can see any part of it or see all of it together. I wanted that song to be like a painting."

No Woman, No Cry Bob Marley & the Wailers

(Vincent Ford/Bob Marley) ❋ Tuff Gong ❋ 1975 ❋ Appears on: *Live!*

Bob Marley & the Wailers had taken their rebel music to the verge of superstardom. Reggae, which had been bubbling out of Jamaica through white rock & roll for three years or so, was no longer completely exotic. However, the real reggae experience of a large and soulful band grooving on their version of R&B was an experience that was confined to the Jamaican diaspora and a few white fans. 'No Woman, No Cry' appeared on 1974's *Natty Dread*, credited to Vincent Ford, a Jamaican cook, who had fed Marley when he was impoverished. The song is a tribute to solidarity and generosity.

Partly it was the politics and the Rastafarianism that put the public off reggae music at first. Marley was a committed Rasta but he also understood R&B music. What he delivered on the live version of 'No Woman, No Cry' was the Rosetta Stone of reggae. It was a love song with a romantic flavour that transcended all cultural boundaries.

Bob Marley & the Wailers' two-night stand at the Lyceum in London on 18 and 19 July 1975 was a turning point in the history of music.

"The first night at the Lyceum, the intensity and the vibe were just nuts," Steve Smith, who co-produced the live recording with Chris Blackwell, told *MOJO*. "They opened up the roof because it was so hot. After the gig, Chris asked if I wanted to record the following night's show. I said, 'Get the Rolling Stones' Mobile and I'll do it.' The recording would never have been as good as it was if it hadn't been for Dave Harper, who mixed the live sound out front. So much of the mix is to do with those live hall mikes, and you can hear that in 'No Woman, No Cry', the ultimate sing-along.

"And it was bizarre. Blackwell took the tapes back to Basing Street, and Phill Brown mixed it as a live performance. Phill set up all the EQs, and he and Chris did a performance, in the same way the band had walked onstage, plugged in, and played to the end of the set. It was pretty fucking brave. After that, the Tim Clarks and Brian Blevins took over, and they just beat up on Blackwell to put out a single. About six weeks later he reluctantly agreed, and released 'No Woman, No Cry'. The damn thing just jumped off the radio. Someone said there were only ever three great live albums: Ray Charles at Newport in 1958, James Brown at the Apollo in 1962, and Bob Marley at the Lyceum in 1975. I tend to agree."

Thunder Road   Bruce Springsteen & the E Street Band

(Bruce Springsteen) ❋ Columbia ❋ 1975 ❋ Appears on: Born to Run

Bruce Springsteen wrote his first masterpiece, Born to Run, as the post-war boom faded. As he wrote in Songs, "There was a continuing gas crisis … no gas … no cars. People were contemplating a country that was finite, where resources and life had limits." The characters on the Born to Run album defied those limits. Gas crisis or no, they took to the road in a sometimes desperate crusade for deliverance.

The song that was to open this new volume was originally called 'Wings for Wheels' until it was rightly renamed after a New Jersey drag strip. According to Springsteen, "'Thunder Road' opens the album, introducing its characters and its central proposition: Do you want to take a chance? On us? On life?"

This album was a make-or-break for Springsteen. His first two had established a cult audience, but Columbia was not satisfied with the level of sales. Springsteen was not satisfied with his recorded sound. He spent five months in the studio reworking and layering parts. He was also not satisfied with his producer/manager Mike Appel and they fought frequently. Eventually Springsteen brought in his friend, the rock critic Jon Landau, to co-produce. It was on 'Thunder Road' that Landau showed he had a vision and aptitude to match the singer/songwriter's own. This was a transitional song – an epic like he used to do, but it's stripped back, less jazzy and more forceful. Unlike the title anthem, 'Thunder Road' is very much of its time – two people acknowledging their imperfections, abandoning romance and also looking back to the '50s. Springsteen builds the lyric with small details into a very full character sketch and then, in impatience, demands that Mary get in the car because: "It's a town full of losers and I'm pulling out of here to win!"

According to keyboard player Roy Brittan, "He wanted a record where the singing sounded like Roy Orbison and the music sounded like Phil Spector."

Marcus Garvey Burning Spear

(Philip Fullwood/Winston Rodney) ✳ Mango ✳ 1975 ✳ Appears on: *Marcus Garvey*

Marcus Garvey was born in 1887 in St Ann's Bay, Jamaica. He became radicalised by the poverty and racism he encountered in his youth. To redress the balance, Garvey developed an ideology of economic independence for black people. In August 1914 he established the Universal Negro Improvement Association (UNIA) and African Community's League (ACL). In 1917 he relocated his organisation to a base in Harlem in New York where he found a receptive audience amongst the West Indian community and the African Americans. Garvey's organisational skills were not up to the resistance he encountered and his organisation faltered. Nonetheless, the ideology he promoted was an important part of black culture in Jamaica and the US.

Burning Spear vocalist Winston Rodney was also born in St Ann's Bay. Rodney was a strong supporter of Garvey's ideas. On this first track he attempts to put Garvey's message to a smouldering reggae beat. The song was originally recorded just for sound system play but was released as a single and quickly established Spear as one of the leading reggae acts of the mid-'70s.

Young Americans David Bowie

(David Bowie) ✳ RCA ✳ 1975 ✳ Appears on: *Young Americans*

According to Tony Visconti, Bowie's third reinvention of the decade came to him in a phone call out of the blue. "David said, 'I've got the most fantastic band lined up for this next album, and I'm really into black music.' This was by trans-Atlantic phone call, and I said, 'Great, who have you got?' and he said, 'Willie Weeks on bass, Andy Newmark on drums, and this new guy from New York called Carlos Alomar', and I said, 'Say no more, I'll be on the next plane'."

Bowie was sitting on a string of three hit albums in the US, each bigger than the last. His stage show was state of the art. His band had reinvented rock. Then Bowie discovered disco.

The *Young Americans* album picked up on the sounds of Philadelphia; the funky but chic new style of R&B was pretty much off the radar for most rock fans but Bowie embraced it fully. His cocaine addiction might also have helped the taste for fast and choppy guitar.

Essentially, though, Bowie was simply doing what all good mods do and picked up on what American R&B artists were doing.

The first song recorded was 'Young Americans'.

"However, despite the fact that I was so tired, there was an electrifying atmosphere that night, and we recorded the 'Young Americans' track, and the next week or two went down like a breeze. But towards the end, that album did get very strange because we didn't know what we were doing – David did mostly live vocals, and although all the songs were written, they were being heavily rearranged as time went on, but nothing was organised, and it turned out to be one enormous jam," said Tony Visconti.

During his stay in New York, Bowie befriended John Lennon and they recorded a new version of the Beatles' 'Across the Universe' and a collaboration, 'Fame', which was Bowie's first number one US single. 'Young Americans', however, topped the R&B charts. The song gave a whole new lease of life to an artist who was beginning to burn out.

"'Young Americans'," said Bowie, "is about a newly-wed couple who don't know if they really like each other. Well, they do, but they don't know if they do or don't. It's a bit of a predicament."

Bowie's departure from dress-up annoyed his fans but showed his sense of the winds of change. In the next two years disco would change the face of popular music. But by then Bowie would have gone from disco too.

Love to Love You Baby Donna Summer

(Pete Bellotte/Giorgio Moroder/Donna Summer) ✳ Casablanca ✳ 1975 ✳
Appears on: *Love to Love You Baby*

Boston-born LaDonna Adrian Gaines wound up in Germany in the early '70s in the cast of *Hair*. She married, took an Anglicised version of her husband's name and met Giorgio Moroder, an Italian-born producer. With co-writer Pete Bellotte, Moroder and Summer created the absolute disco epic 'Love to Love You Baby'. Moroder structured the song as a DJ would play the track in a club – all seventeen minutes of it. Summer provided the moaning and groaning of simulated sex over the Eurodisco beat and the record notched the disco phenomenon up a little.

Moroder's production of 'Love to Love You' brought Eurodisco to the US in a big way and radically altered the way records sounded for the next ten years right up through techno and house music. It's a masterpiece.

'Love to Love You' with its unabridged sexuality (she has said that she was inspired by Marilyn Monroe) was a hit in gay clubs and brought straight white people into discos as never before. The song captured the hedonism of the time.

"You were coming out of the Vietnam War, the '60s, the protest era, and I was coming out of it as well," she said recently. "I think people were just in a different mind set. When dance music came out, with that beat and that movement, it was a switch. In that period, people were in a dance mood. They wanted to be lifted up, they wanted to have fun, they didn't want to think."

She Does It Right Dr Feelgood

(Wilco Johnson) ❋ United Artists ❋ 1975 ❋ Appears on: *Down by the Jetty*

"How can anyone be so basic in 1975? Are they really four zombies who fell asleep in the early '60s and snored happily through the 'progressive' rock era? After ten years of remorseless rock progress from psychedelia to sophistication to decadence to degeneracy, until every other band is carting around its very own oratorio about the downfall of civilisation, Dr Feelgood turn up looking like hoodlums from some long forgotten B picture, and sounding as though the idea of musical progress had quite simply never occurred to them," wrote Mick Gold in *Let It Rock*.

Dr Feelgood were ahead of their time. That description of the skanky R&B quartet could be read as a manifesto of the punk tsunami that overtook London a year and half later. In 1975 the Feelgoods were the cure for what was rotten in British rock. Formed in Canvey Island, in London's industrial wasteland, Dr Feelgood were one step better than a bar band due to the riffs, hooks and songs that spewed from Wilco Johnson's guitar.

On stage, Wilco played like a zombie strutting back and forth, zigzagging, twirling around with his eyes permanently fixed in a thousand-yard stare. Lee Brilleaux's vocals had that alcohol-soaked heft of early Van Morrison as he lurched around like a deranged bank clerk (his description).

This first album sounded like John Lee Hooker on an amphetamine bender. The opening cut is the deepest: 'She Does It Right' has a blistering riff that just bounces out. To honour the creative debt to both Hooker and the Animals, the Feelgoods rip into 'Boom Boom' before taking off into another eight Johnson originals before closing with a slamming version of 'Tequila'. Like the Ramones, Dr Feelgood's monochrome cover with the industrial end of the Thames in the background is a statement of intent – stripped back, no nonsense, go for the throat, classic R&B. Only the Rolling Stones' first album matches this for lean, mean rocking blues.

The beauty of Dr Feelgood was their singularity. They reeked of the time and place of their birth. As their pal Nick Lowe said, "They're the greatest local band in the world." *Down by the Jetty* is so redolent of its time and place that you can positively smell the pollution. It's one of the classics of British rock & roll.

Sin City Emmylou Harris

(Chris Hillman/Gram Parsons) ⁂ Reprise ⁂ 1975 ⁂ Appears on: *Elite Hotel*

Emmylou Harris was content being a folksinger until one day Chris Hillman of the Flying Burrito Brothers saw her sing in a club and suggested to his partner Gram Parsons that they hire her. Parsons caught her act the next night in Baltimore. Harris became Parson's muse and after his death in 1973, picked up the torch he had lit. Parsons was a gifted songwriter who was refashioning country music away from the hayseed Nashville archetype. His lyrics were more sophisticated, his moods more complex.

"It's hard to pinpoint any one quality about Gram," said Harris at the time. "It was a collective talent – the vision, the songs, the voice and the feel. Most people have one or two of those things but there is always something lacking. He really had everything. Someone needed to take country music and not change it but lift it up and over and say kind of 'look at this'. He brought it to a new audience and to a completely new level."

Having the torch, Harris had little choice other than to run with it. She engaged the Hot Band – including James Burton on guitar and Rodney Crowell on keyboards – and proceeded to put some of her own style into country.

Elite Hotel captures Harris and the Hot Band in concert at their peak. 'Sin City' was a signature tune for the Burrito Brothers but, here, Harris is clear about the dark goings on in Sin City and she takes it all in with equanimity. She is sexy and strong and her voice is a pure wonder.

Rhiannon Fleetwood Mac

(Stevie Nicks) ✳ Reprise ✳ 1975 ✳ Appears on: *Fleetwood Mac*

"'Rhiannon' was not written about the mythological mebanogian from Wales," Stevie Nicks told VH1. "She was written about a name that came up in a book that I read that somebody gave me. A little paperback novel. It was called *Triad* [by Mary Leader]. You can trace it down and find it. There were two women in it; they were named Rhiannon and Branwen.

"So, when everybody wants to say, 'Oh you write premonition, premonitions, you know you have premonitions', I don't think that I consciously have premonitions, but I do seem to have some sort of a psychic knowledge of what's gonna happen in the future. The whole thing about the birds and the sky and the, all this, this is all intricately woven through the myth. So I always think it's pretty interesting I play it that I had no idea about any of this when I wrote it. I just thought it was a beautiful name and I thought if I ever have a little girl maybe I'll name her Rhiannon, and that's really what I took to the piano to write the song.

"I also wrote this song in Aspen, same time I wrote 'Landslide'. There must have been a very creative force going on in Colorado at that moment that night."

Stevie Nicks will be forever identified with this song that is part New Age mysticism and part a song of great romance. Initially intended for her next album as part of Buckingham Nicks, she recorded the song with Fleetwood Mac and this song gave that group a new lease of life.

Let's Get Funky Hound Dog Taylor & the Houserockers

(Hound Dog Taylor) ✳ Alligator ✳ 1975 ✳ Appears on: *Beware of the Dog*

"Hound Dog was sort of a throw back," said Bruce Iglauer, who started Alligator Records specifically to release the Hound. "He didn't use a bass because bass players couldn't keep up with him. Like what had happened before in other blues bands, he used a second guitar for bass lines. There was a drive that you couldn't get out of a Fender bass. The sounds were so raw and distorted – Hound Dog played on $50 Japanese guitars through Sears amplifiers and cracked speakers. The whole attitude was 'Who gives a damn? We're just playin' for fun.' The music basically could have been played at a juke joint in Mississippi next door to where Muddy Waters was playing in 1949. It was totally unvarnished by virtue of the energy level and the distortion."

In my opinion, 'Let's Get Funky' as recorded here is the absolute apotheosis of rock & roll. It doesn't get more joyful, more raw, more Zen than this. Taylor sets up an insistent riff and then just rides it for absolutely all its worth. This is music that is pointless to intellectualise about and impossible to deny. It's sexy and dirty and irresponsible and pure.

Theodore Roosevelt 'Hound Dog' Taylor was fifty-five when Bruce Iglauer discovered him playing reckless slide guitar in clubs with Brewer Phillips hanging on to the bass lines on guitar and Ted Harvey pounding out a houserocking beat for $15 a night.

Iglauer set up Alligator for a first eponymous album, which was an enormous hit, and then followed it with *Natural Boogie*. The songs are perfect, snappy vehicles for lewd lyrics and incredible slide guitar.

Compositionally, *Natural Boogie* has the best tracks: 'Hawaiian Boogie', 'Roll Your Moneymaker', 'See Me in the Evening' and 'Sadie', but it's this live album, released shortly after his death in 1975, that captures the sheer insanity (and does include the classic 'Give Me Back My Wig').

It's worth noting that Hound Dog's two guitars and no bass have become a template for alternative blues acts in the '90s such as the Jon Spencer Blues Explosion and more famously the White Stripes.

"They didn't rehearse," said Iglauer. "That was sort of a rule. They followed that rule very closely. They also followed the rule that you *really* shouldn't perform unless you'd had a reasonable amount of alcohol. He set an example for that. In that regard, he was sort of an exemplary bandleader."

The Hissing of Summer Lawns Joni Mitchell

(Joni Mitchell) ❋ Asylum ❋ 1975 ❋ Appears on: *The Hissing of Summer Lawns*

Joni Mitchell's 1973 album *Court and Spark* was a massive hit and the singer/songwriter was suddenly a superstar. She had also shaken off her folkie past and embraced a soft jazz style. With Tom Scott and the LA Express she found musicians who could give form to her melodic ideas. Mitchell went running into a jazz future but her folkie fans who just wanted sensitive lyrics were left somewhere behind.

"*The Hissing of Summer Lawns* is a suburban album," she said. The title refers to sprinklers and the implication is that this track and much of the album will be looking at what is happening behind the white picket fences.

"About the time that album came around I thought, 'I'm not going to be your sin eater any longer.' So I began to write social description as opposed to personal confession," she told Cameron Crowe. "I met with a tremendous amount of resentment. People thought suddenly that I was secure in my success, that I was being a snot and was attacking them. The basic theme of the album, which everybody thought was so abstract, was just any summer day in any neighbourhood when people turn their sprinklers on all up and down the block. It's just that hiss of suburbia.

"I had stopped being confessional. I think they were ready to nail me, anyway. They would have said, 'More morose, scathing introspection.' They were ready to get me; that's the way I figure it."

'The Hissing of Summer Lawns', however, is one of Mitchell's strongest pieces of work. The interplay between the jazz backing and her lyrics is completely unique in rock music. It's funny and carefully observed and complex. Mitchell drew some influence from African music, which was still novel in the west, and that further changed her sound. The tonal sophistication that Mitchell introduced on this record had a great influence, particularly in Los Angeles with artists like Steely Dan.

"There was a big stink about that. It was taboo," she said. "I don't think I realised how culturally isolated we were until the release of that record. In white culture it was problematic, but it got good reviews in the black magazines, where it was accidentally reviewed because there was an illustration of a black person on the cover. I thought it was adventuresome, but it was shocking how frightened people were of it. I think the record was inadvertently holding up a mirror to a change that people were on the brink of in this hemisphere, and people were disturbed by the teetering they were experiencing. The Third World was becoming more important and they were disoriented."

Rock & Roll All Nite KISS

(Gene Simmons/Paul Stanley) ❉ Casablanca ❉ 1975 ❉ Appears on: *Alive!*

'Rock & Roll All Nite' had lain dormant on KISS' third album. Indeed, in 1975 KISS were going nowhere fast. To stimulate his label's cash flow, Neil Bogart of Casablanca records enlisted producer Eddie Kramer to record a KISS live album. Imaginatively titled *Alive!*, KISS couldn't sell the records but they knew how to stage a show. Their music benefited from the exchange of a great live room. 'Rock & Roll All Nite', like most anthems, was dumb and it too benefited from the energy of a concert audience.

Simmons and Stanley had cobbled the song together from an old tune ('Drive Me Wild') and a general desire to reproduce the dynamics of a rave-up like Sly Stone's 'I Want to Take You Higher'.

KISS' audience was out in the suburban wasteland, the kids who were alienated from the arty superstar rockers and really just wanted colour and movement and drama. The credo "I want to rock & roll all nite and party everyday" was a spot-on description of their wildest dreams. It fulfilled KISS' dreams too – the album went Top 10 and sold over five million copies.

Cortez the Killer Neil Young & Crazy Horse

(Neil Young) ✳ Reprise ✳ 1975 ✳ Appears on: *Zuma*

'Cortez the Killer' makes little or no sense as a lyric. A meeting between the explorer and the doomed king – Montezuma may be a metaphor for the '70s superstars living like kings in southern California, sacrificing virgins to their godlike egos and not knowing what is about to hit them. Perhaps this is a prefiguring of punk or perhaps it's all another fever dream from Neil Young. It matters little. The song is a three-chord template for some of his most incendiary guitar playing.

A power failure during the recording cut into the song. "They missed a whole verse, a whole section," said Young. "You can hear the splice on the recording where we stop and start again. It's a messy edit. But yeah that's true ... it was a total accident. But that's how I see my best art, as one magical accident after another.

"My guitar improvisations with Crazy Horse are very, very Coltrane-influenced," he said to Nick Kent. "I'm particularly taken by work like 'Equinox' and 'My Favourite Things'. Miles I love just because of his overall attitude towards the concept of creation, which is one of constant change. There's no reason to stay there once you've done it. You could stay for the rest of your life and it would become like a regular job."

The *Zuma* album came as the sky was breaking in Young's life – he had left his second wife and had finished mourning the loss of his friends. He was back with Crazy Horse making a huge sound. *Zuma* was his release and a return to form. As Lou Reed said, summing up Young's career, "He's done it once – 'Cortez the Killer'."

"It was a combination of imagination and knowledge," said Young. "What Cortez represented to me is the explorer with two sides, one benevolent, the other utterly ruthless. I mean, look at Columbus! Everyone now knows he was less than great and he wasn't even there first. It always makes me question all these other so-called 'icons'."

Tonight's the Night Neil Young & Crazy Horse

(Neil Young) ❉ Reprise ❉ 1975 ❉ Appears on: *Tonight's the Night*

The *Harvest* album put Neil Young in the middle of the road and as he famously sang, he "headed for the ditch". Young and his friends were indulging and two of those close to him – guitarist Danny Whitten and roadie Bruce Berry – died as a result of drugs.

"'Tonight's the Night' is like an OD letter," Young said around the time of the album's release. "The whole thing is about life, dope and death. When we [Nils Lofgren, Talbot, Molina and Young] played that music we were all thinking of Danny Whitten and Bruce Berry, two close members of our unit lost to junk overdoses.

"The *Tonight's the Night* sessions were the first time what was left of Crazy Horse had gotten together since Danny died. It was up to us to get the strength together among us to fill the hole he left. The other OD, Bruce Berry, was CSNY's roadie for a long time. His brother Ken runs Studio Instrument Rentals, where we recorded the album. So we had a lot of vibes going for us. There was a lot of spirit in the music we made.

"It's funny, I remember the whole experience in black and white. We'd go down to SIR about five in the afternoon and start getting high, drinking tequila and playing pool. About midnight, we'd start playing. And we played Bruce and Danny on their way all through the night. I'm not a junkie and I won't even try it out to check out what it's like … but we all got high enough, right out there on the edge where we felt wide-open to the whole mood. It was spooky. I probably feel this album more than anything else I've ever done."

The album was shelved for more than a year until manager Elliot Roberts added some live tracks and other songs from the vault. It still lay dormant until Young was about to release another country-style album, *Homegrown*, and played the two albums back to back. He then shelved the country record for the less commercial *Tonight's the Night*. A wise move, as it's one of his greatest moments. The loping title song captures the essence of the album – collapsing and getting up again.

"I know the first time I listened back on *Tonight's the Night* it was the most out-of-tune thing I'd ever heard," he said. "Everyone's off-key. I couldn't hack it. I took *Tonight's the Night* because of its overall strength in performance and feeling.

"I fully expect some of the most determinedly worst reviews I've ever had. I mean if anybody really wanted to let go, they could do it on this one. And undoubtedly a few people will. That's good for them, though. I like to see people make giant breakthroughs for themselves. It's good for their psyche to get it all off their chests.

"I've seen *Tonight's the Night* draw a line everywhere it's been played. People who thought they would never dislike anything I did fall on the other side of the line. Others who thought 'I can't listen to that cat. He's just too sad,' or whatever ... They listen another way now."

Gloria Patti Smith

(Van Morrison/Patti Smith) ✳ Arista ✳ 1975 ✳ Appears on: *Horses*

Writing about the conception of the Patti Smith Group in 1974, the singer said 'Gloria' was bred of this time, crossing the poem 'Oath', written in 1970, with the Van Morrison classic. It was to be the first Patti Smith Group single and in the words of writer Paul Williams, "a declaration of existence. 'Gloria' gave me the opportunity to acknowledge and disclaim our musical and spiritual heritage. It personifies for me, within its adolescent conceit, what I hold sacred as an artist. The right to create, without apology, from a stance beyond gender or social definition, but not beyond the responsibility to create something of worth."

'Gloria' opens with the unforgettable statement, "Jesus died for somebody's sins but not mine", which is pure teen arrogance in the style of the most surly of French teens, Arthur Rimbaud. 'Gloria' is a play on the Latin use of the name in worship and in Van Morrison's hymn to desire, 'Gloria', which also has a lineage through its many reinterpretations by '60s garage bands.

"A lot of songs started off as jams and soon we found that things would organically come together," said guitarist Lenny Kaye. "'Gloria' started as a jam. We'd do chordal riffs over which Patti would chant, poeticize, and tell stories. We never thought about it becoming as big as it did. We were satisfied playing for local art audiences. We just liked doing what we were doing. It didn't have a category. It was an attitude."

It's all here – God, sex and great rock & roll 45s. There's no coincidence in the fact that the flipside was a reworking of the Who's 'My Generation'. *Horses* was one of the first albums in what was to be called punk rock, not only because there was an outsider attitude and a penchant for black and white photography, but because it placed a new sensibility and rawness into the context of the classic, stripped back '60s music. Not only did Patti Smith help to build (literally) the stage at CBGB, with 'Gloria' she gave an intellectual backbone to the music that was to come out of there.

Land: Horses/Land of a Thousand Dances/ La Mer (de) Patti Smith

(Chris Kenner/Patti Smith) ❋ Arista ❋ 1975 ❋ Appears on: *Horses*

"It's time to figure out what happened in the '60s," Patti Smith said in 1976. Smith chose John Cale to be the producer of her first album. Cale had been a member of the Velvet Underground and had produced records for the Stooges and Nico. She could not have chosen a more sympathetic ear, but the collaboration was not a happy one.

According to Cale, the group's instruments were all warped and they had to get new instruments and then learn how to play them in tune. "As a producer," he wrote. "You've got to be a catalyst, an ally, a co-conspirator. Sometimes you have to introduce conflict in order to resolve it."

"All I was really looking for was a technical person," said Smith of Cale. "Instead, I got a total maniac artist. I went to pick out an expensive watercolour painting, and instead I got a mirror. It was really like 'A Season in Hell', for both of us. But inspiration doesn't always have to be someone sending me half a dozen American Beauty roses. There's a lotta inspiration going on between the murderer and the victim."

'Land' started out as a poem about the relationship between a murderer and victim. Its rambling epic journey touches on the power of '60s R&B with the soul anthem 'Land of a Thousand Dances.'

"At first it was just me and Lenny Kaye on electric guitar farting around at poetry readings," she said. "Then it started to gather force. We advertised for a piano player. And finally Richard Sohl came in wearing a sailor suit, and he was totally stoned and totally pompous. We said, 'This guy's fucked up.' Lenny gave him the big cosmic spiel and Sohl said, 'Look, buddy, just play.' So we just brought him in.

"And then we started looking for another guitarist. We'd make them do forty minutes of 'Gloria'. I'd go off on this long poem about a blue T-bird smashing into a wall of sound or some shit like that and Lenny would keep the same three chords going, louder and louder. And we'd see who dropped out first. If the guy auditioning dropped out first, that meant he wasn't any good. So finally Ivan Kral came in. This little Czechoslovakian would-be rock star. So we did 'Land of a Thousand Dances' and it went on so long I thought I was gonna puke. But Ivan was so nervous he wouldn't stop, and we figured that was really cool.

"Now it's at the point where I really love the group. I did a solo reading the other week in Philadelphia. I went great, but I was so lonely. I read 'Land Without Music', and right away I'm thinking, here's the part where Lenny always fucks up; here's where I'd look at Sohl and tell him to stop sleeping on the keyboard. I missed them so much I didn't want to ever again perform without them. They give me tremendous energy. I get like a little kid, and it's beautiful."

Piss Factory Patti Smith

(Patti Smith) ❋ Ork ❋ 1975 ❋ Appears on: *Land*

Patti Smith grew up listening to Bob Dylan and James Brown and reading the poetry of Arthur Rimbaud and William Blake. She gave herself an education in visionary artists. In the late '60s she moved from New Jersey to New York where she lived amongst the artists and hipsters, writing poetry and looking for her voice. A friendship with critic Lenny Kaye, who also played guitar, led to poetry readings on St Mark's Place in New York's East Village. One of these poems/songs was called 'Piss factory'. Clearly autobiographical, the song detailed her journey thus far and was also clearly a masterpiece of rock & roll. One of the patrons of the downtown scene, Terry Ork, recorded and released the song backed with a version of 'Hey Joe' and a star (or stars) was born.

"Repetition makes me carsick. I used to get carsick when I did piecework at the factory in south Jersey," she told Nick Tosches. "I'd have to inspect baby buggy bumper beepers – no shit – y'know, beep, beep, beep, and I'd wind up puking in the bathroom. I'd have to take those little yellow pills. I inspected beepers, steel sheets. It depended, it changed every week. I cut leather straps for baby carriages, made big cardboard boxes for baby mattresses. Toys, strollers, all that stuff.

"Some people told me that 'Piss Factory' was immoral, that it was base; it's not immoral, it's total truth. To me that little 'Piss Factory' thing is the most truthful thing I ever writ. It's autobiography. In fact, the truth was stronger than the poem. The stuff those women did to me at that factory was more horrible than I let on in the song. They did shit like gang up on me and stick my head in a toilet full of piss. People like beauty and purity. They pretend that's what it's all about. I don't like that. *That's* immoral."

Shine on You Crazy Diamond Pink Floyd

(David Gilmour/Roger Waters/Richard Wright) ❊ EMI ❊ 1975 ❊
Appears on: *Wish You Were Here*

Pink Floyd's best track was an elegy to founder Syd Barrett, who went insane shortly after the release of their first album in 1968.

"I think the whole album sprang from that one four-note guitar phrase of Dave's in 'Shine On'," keyboard player Rick Wright told *MOJO*. "We heard it and went, 'That's a really nice phrase.' The wine came out, and that led to what I think is our best album, the most colourful, the most feelingful."

Wright recalled being in the studio as the track was being finished and meeting a disassociated Syd, now a shadow of his former self. Dave Gilmour's melancholy guitar part was developed into a lengthy portrait of Syd – the manic and the tragic sides of his personality. The song also reflected the mixed feeling of Waters about having continued so long in his shadow.

The song had been worked up in concert and, at Waters' suggestion, the final twenty-five minute studio version is split into two parts, opening and closing Floyd's only listenable album of the '70s.

Hurricane Bob Dylan

(Bob Dylan/Jacques Levy) ❊ Columbia ❊ 1976 ❊ Appears on: *Desire*

The sound of Dylan's *Desire* album, of which 'Hurricane' is the best song, was a consequence of the way the album was made. Dylan was separated from his wife and children and revisiting the haunts of his youth, writing songs with another lyricist and recording with pick-up bands. The violin that dominates the sound of the album was played by Scarlett Riviera whom Dylan had seen walking down the street and then asked along to the sessions. This was the first time Riviera had been in a recording studio but her playing gives a gypsy wind to the album.

'Hurricane' is based on the experiences of Ruben 'Hurricane' Carter, a boxer. In 1966 he and another person were convicted of the triple murder of three people in a bar. Carter was sentenced to life in prison for the crimes.

While incarcerated he wrote a book, *The 16th Round*, which Dylan read and responded to.

"I think I ran into Jacques [Levy] downtown and we went off and just wrote some songs," said Dylan. "The people from the Hurricane Carter movement kept calling me and writing me. And Hurricane sent me his book, which I read and which really touched me. I felt that the man was just innocent, from his writings and knowing that part of the country. So I went to visit him and was really behind him, trying to get a new trial. So that was one of the things I brought to Jacques, too. I said, 'Why don't you help me write this song and see if we can do something?' So we wrote 'Hurricane', and then we just wrote a bunch of others. An album came out of it."

The Hurricane Carter story had so many of Dylan's themes already – racism and unfair imprisonment had been subjects of his songs going back to his early folk days.

Dylan and Levy, a playwright, recast the story and trial of Hurricane. It's an amazing piece of songwriting with a multitude of characters and action. Clearly it's part of a tradition going back to Guthrie and the old folk ballads. However, Dylan and Levy provide so many layers to the narrative that the song is completely unlike any other.

The extensive narrative flows on the violin line. The melody rushes forward, maintaining the tension and the sense of frantic activity.

'Hurricane' was a major hit single for Dylan in November 1975. As a result of the publicity from Dylan's crusade, Carter was freed in March 1976. In November 1976 Carter was retried and found guilty. In 1985 Carter's appeal against his sentence was upheld on procedural grounds and he was released from prison after nineteen years. The story was recently made into a feature film with Denzel Washington in the lead.

Two Sevens Clash Culture

(Roy S Dayes/R Gordon/Joseph Hill/Delroy Thompson/Albert Walker) ✳ Mango ✳ 1976 ✳ Appears on: *Tougher Than Tough*

Marcus Garvey was an intellectual who, in the early part of the 20th century, promoted the idea of Africa as a utopian vision for the African diaspora created by slavery. Garvey was a principal architect of Rastafarianism and the belief that Ethiopia was the promised land. Culture singer Joseph Hill developed the idea that the apocalypse would start and Jah would return when the two sevens clash – the 7th day of the 7th month of the 77th year. The song combines Garvey's prophecies with some extemporising by Hill.

In 1976, when Culture penned the tune, the nation was in complete turmoil as a consequence of endemic poverty and lawlessness. According to legend, Hill's claim of Garvey's prophecy was sufficiently potent that on the appointed day the army was put on alert and businesses closed.

The song is one of the classics of the golden age of reggae and is uplifting rather than doom-laden. Joseph Hill's energised vocals are ably supported by Ralph Walker and Kenneth Dayes' harmonies.

Not only was the track a hit in Jamaica but it gave bassist Paul Simenon the name of his band – the Clash.

Beth KISS

(Peter Criss/Bob Ezrin/Stan Penridge) ❊ Casablanca ❊ 1976 ❊
Appears on: Destroyer

One of the first power ballads, 'Beth' is the story of the eternal struggle between a man's band and his girlfriend. Drummer Peter Criss wrote the song in 1971 when he was in a band called Chelsea with Stan Penridge. The inspiration being a mate's nagging girlfriend interrupting their rehearsals.

"She was the world's greatest hypochondriac," said Criss in a 1994 interview recalling the woman in question. "She was always sick. And she was continually calling up and interrupting our rehearsals. So after a month, six weeks, of this going on, we'd know it had to be her when the phone rang. So I would start writing down what Michael was saying back to Beck. He would literally say, 'Beck, I heard you calling but I can't come home right now'. He'd be pissed off, you know. 'Me and the boys are playing here and we've got to get the sound together. Give me another hour and I'll be there'".

The song lay dormant until the sessions for Destroyer. Initially titled 'Beck', Gene Simmons suggested a change in title to avoid confusion with guitarist Jeff Beck and he suggested that Criss submit the song for the next album. Producer Bob Ezrin made some minor changes and orchestrated the song with monumental string arrangements performed by the New York Philharmonic Orchestra. Originally the flipside to 'Detroit Rock City', a radio station started playing the track and it was eventually issued as a single in its own right and became KISS' first Top 10 single.

Metal Machine Music, Part 1 Lou Reed

(Lou Reed) ✳ RCA ✳ 1976 ✳ Appears on: *Metal Machine Music*

Riding high on the back of the pop success of *Transformer* and *Rock & Roll Animal*, Lou Reed made the most unlistenable album of all time. Then he made it a double.

Metal Machine Music is exactly what it says – the sound of machines. While it may be uncomfortable and while not even Lou Reed can listen to it in its entirety, *Metal Machine Music* is one of the most important albums made during the rock era.

The late great critic Lester Bangs put it best when he wrote in *Creem* in 1976: "If you ever thought feedback was the best thing that ever happened to the guitar, well, Lou just got rid of the guitars. I realise that any idiot with the equipment could have made this album, including me, you or Lou. That's one of the main reasons I like it so much ...

"In his excellent liner notes, Lou asserts that he and the other speed freaks did not start World Wars I, II, 'or the Bay of Pigs, for that matter'. And he's right. If everybody took amphetamines, all the time, everybody would understand each other. Either that or never listen or bother with the other son of a bitch, because they'd all be too busy spending three days drawing psychedelic lines around a piece of steno paper until it's totally black, writing eighty-page letters about meaningless occurrences to their mothers, or creating MMM. There would be no more wars, and peace and harmony would reign ...

"I have heard this record characterised as 'anti-human' and 'anti-emotional'. That it is, in a sense, since it is music made more by tape recorders, amps, speakers, and microphones and ring modulators than any set of human hands and emotions. But so what? Almost all music today is anti-emotional and made by machines too. From Elton John to disco to *Sally Can't Dance* (which Lou doesn't realise is one of his best albums, precisely because it's so cold) it's computerised formula production line shit into which the human heart enters very rarely if at all. At least Lou is upfront about it, which makes him more human than the rest of those middle-of-the-road dick-noses. Besides which, any record that sends listeners fleeing the room screaming for surcease of aural flagellation or, alternately, getting physical and disturbing your medications to the point of breaking the damn thing, can hardly be accused, at least in results if not original creative man-hours, of lacking emotional content. Why do people go to see movies like *Jaws*, *The Exorcist*, or *Lisa, She Wolf of the SS*? So they can get beat over the head with baseball bats, have their nerves wrenched while electrodes are being stapled to their spines, and generally brutalised at least every once every fifteen minutes or so (the time between the face falling out of the bottom of the sunk boat and the guy's bit-off leg hitting the bottom of the ocean). This is what, today, is commonly understood as entertainment, as fun, as art even! So they've got a lot of nerve landing on Lou for *Metal Machine Music*. At least here there's no fifteen minutes of bullshit padding between brutalisation. Anybody who got off on *The Exorcist* should like this record. It's certainly far more moral a product.

"All landlords are mealy-mouthed bastards who would let the ruins of Pompeii fall on your four-poster before they'd lift a finger. They deserve whatever they get, and *Metal Machine Music* is the all-time guaranteed lease breaker. Every tenant in America should own a copy of this album. Forearmed!

"My pet land hermit crab, Spud, who sometimes goes for days at a time curled up inside his shell in a corner of the cage so you gotta check to see if he's dead, likes *Metal Machine Music* a lot. Every time I put it on, he comes out of his shell and starts crawling happily around the sand and climbing the bars. It is, in fact, the only time I ever see him get any exercise. Either that or he's dancing ...

"I played it for President Idi 'Big Daddy' Amin of Uganda when he flew me and Lisa Robinson over there to interview him for upcoming cover articles in *Creem* and *Hit Parader*, and he absolutely loved it. I gave him a copy, and now by special edict he has it piped through the Muzak vents of every supermarket (all thirty-five of them) and doctor's waiting room (all eight) in his great nation, so that the citizens there may be inspired to ever fiercer heights of patriotism for his regime and all that it stands for. He wanted to declare it the Ugandan national anthem, but I told him that I would have to check with the American teenage shock vets first, and being a wise, fair, graciously diplomatic politician, he of course immediately assented, and then, genial host that he is, whisked us off to see a live multiple snuff film done sans cameras and celluloid. 'We can't afford them', he explained. 'And besides, the next time you have a dangling conversation with Paul Simon, you can inform him that the theatre is not really dead.'

"It is the greatest record ever made in the history of the human eardrum. Number two: *KISS Alive!*"

Roadrunner The Modern Lovers

(Jonathan Richman) ✳ Berserkeley ✳ 1976 ✳ Appears on: *The Modern Lovers*

"By the time I was fifteen years old I was pretty lonely," Jonathan Richman wrote in the early '70s. "High school and I didn't understand each other well at all. So I heard the Velvet Underground, got inspired, took up guitar and drove into Boston from my suburb of Nantick to terrorise Boston audiences with my four-and-a-third-note vocal range and crude guitar playing.

"Well, I got lonely doing that, so I put a band together when I was nineteen and called it the Modern Lovers. I've been changing and growing ever since".

Richman's first Modern Lovers (Ernie Brooks, bass; David Robinson, drums; Jerry Harrison, keyboards) was perfect. The songs were prosaic in the best Lou Reed style but instead of writing about junkies in New York he wrote about the world in which he lived – suburbia. It was a neat inversion of the Velvets delivered in monochromatic style.

'Roadrunner' is Richman's classic. It's a driving song in the rock & roll tradition, but rather than having a flash car, the singer is on a bicycle. He records, not the glamorous Route 66, but rather, the stores on Route 128.

The song is a one-chord riff that hits a perfect groove and floats Richman's vocal on top of Harrison's cheesy organ line and the unbeatable enthusiasm when Richman shouts out "Radio on!" Its honesty and its innocence are impossible to beat.

John Cale recorded the Lovers' debut album in 1973 for Warner Bros., who could make neither head nor tail of it and it was shelved until Berserkeley Records bought the tapes back and the album became a cult hit. By then the band was disbanded and Richman off on his idiot savant trip. But 'Roadrunner' is the real deal.

Blitzkrieg Bop The Ramones

(Joey Ramone/Johnny Ramone/Tommy Ramone/Dee Dee Ramone) ✳ Sire ✳ 1976 ✳ Appears on: *The Ramones*

"What they want I don't know/All revved up and ready to go."

Straight out of CBGB in New York, the Ramones set the template for punk rock. They had the look – torn jeans, motorcycle jackets, bangs and sneakers. They had the sound – stripped back rock & roll that was big and dumb. They had the good fortune to stumble on the downtown New York scene of

Max's Kansas City and CBGB where their primitive rock could be recast into a movement complete with an aesthetic and a momentum.

"We came first," said Johnny. "We did what came naturally to us."

The four Ramones had met in the suburbs. They liked the Spector sound and they liked bubblegum and big rock, the Bay City Rollers and '60s garage band rock. What they didn't like was the limpness that had overcome most of the superstars of rock and the fact that it had become so removed from the audience.

"We were having fun," Joey Ramone said shortly before his death in 2001. "The Ramones were always about having fun. Fun disappeared in 1974, there were too many serious people out there at the time.

"I always felt like I was a rock fan first, because I am. So I just remembered what I loved about rock & roll and put that into the Ramones. When the Ramones got together that was pretty much all gone from music. I just loved the excitement, the dare, the challenge, the passion, and the sincerity. Having a point of view on things. Nobody cares about that any more, it's all about business today."

The Ramones took to writing songs about dumb things mostly – sniffing glue, cartoon ideas, violence. There were also some heavy subjects such as Dee Dee's years as a prostitute and junkie. By and large the Ramones were ground zero.

'Blitzkrieg Bop' was the opening salvo from the first Ramones album and it is the perfect call to arms. It was such a good song that the Ramones kept on recording it. As have a million groups ever since.

"The first time we went to CBGB to audition, Hilly [Kristal, proprietor] said, 'Nobody's going to like you guys but I'll have you back'," Joey recalled. "He knew we had something. Our first show was just the bartender and his dog, but then we got the Warhol, arty crowd. It always seems to be gays who pick up on things first."

Blank Generation   Richard Hell & the Voidoids

(Richard Hell) ✳ Ork ✳ 1976 ✳ Appears on: *Blank Generation*

Richard Hell and school friend Tom Verlaine came to New York to be poets and rock stars. In the downtown scene of the mid-'70s they found themselves scuffling around trying to make music, first as the Neon Boys and later as Television. Hell, making the best of his poverty, restructured his T-shirts and jeans with safety pins and knocked out his versions of garage rock-via-symbolist poetry. London clothes designer Malcolm McLaren picked up on Hell's style and formed a band in his image. He called them the Sex Pistols.

Meanwhile Hell had been kicked out of Television and the Heartbreakers. Which was fortunate because he formed one of the best groups of the era – the Voidoids. Robert Quine's prickly, lyrical lines danced guitars with Ivan Julian and Mark Bell's heavy drums. Hell squirmed his way through vocals.

The lead track became a catchcry for the New York scene. Its title was a throwaway idea Hell had for a line in a poetry book.

"As for the song, I liked the idea of doing my versions of sorta genre songs, and a 'generation' song was one of them," Hell told Barney Hoskyns of Rocksbackpages.com. "I was way into the Who's first album [*The Who Sings My Generation*], and Tom had this funny, kitsch single by Rod McKuen called 'I Belong to the Beat Generation', so it just seemed like a perfect conjunction to use that classic 'Hit the Road Jack' chord sequence as the structure of that song.

"For me, it was an awareness of, like, Andy Warhol and Beckett and a whole bunch of people that I identified with but that were actually very different from each other. Samuel Beckett and Andy Warhol had very little in common, except that you could imagine applying the word 'blank' to them. But ultimately, when anything was discussed long enough, my conclusion was that I didn't care! It was kind of a defensive thing that kids that age will use. I think I felt just overwhelmed by input: the Vietnam war and the collapse of the '60s and the proliferation of media … it just felt like everything was too much to handle and you just tuned out. Blank seemed appropriate to me, because my own feeling was of sensory overload."

Memory Motel The Rolling Stones

(Mick Jagger/Keith Richards) ✳ Rolling Stones Records ✳ 1976 ✳
Appears on: *Black and Blue*

Black and Blue is the least rock & roll album the Rolling Stones ever recorded. Most of the songs tend towards funk, reggae and R&B with none of the linear, knockdown rock tracks or pop tunes. With three new guitarists – Harvey Mandel, Wayne Perkins and Ron Wood – plus Billy Preston's keyboards, the Rolling Stones here stretch their boundaries. Much derided on its release, *Black and Blue* holds up remarkably well.

The rehearsals and recording took place in Munich so that Richards could be close to his girlfriend Uschi Obermeier, with whom he was besotted. The songs were only half formed, mostly just funk jams or obscure covers. The outstanding cut on the album is 'Memory Motel', with Richards on electric piano and Jagger on acoustic piano, and both Perkins and Mandel playing guitar. It is one of the Stones' last epics.

'Memory Motel' was very likely inspired by Obermeier, although Jagger told Jonathan Cott, "The girl in 'Memory Motel' is a real, independent American girl. Actually, the girl in 'Memory Motel' is a combination. Nearly all the girls in my songs are combinations."

Cherry Bomb The Runaways

(Kim Fowley/Joan Jett) ✳ Mercury ✳ 1976 ✳ Appears on: *The Runaways*

That they couldn't play very well at all is incidental to the significance of the Runaways. They were the second all-women rock & roll outfit but the first to break through to the public. Five very suburban girls with bad attitudes, or rather good/bad but not evil, the Runaways were a great rock & roll band.

Kim Fowley, a Los Angeles scenester, was the music business equivalent of Roger Corman. He made B-records and exploitation records that were trashy and low rent and he excelled himself with the Runaways.

Fowley and his coterie of Anglophiles like DJ Rodney Bigenheimer and journalist/record maker Greg Shaw had an acute appreciation for the glam-metal pop that had come out of England with the Sweet, Mud, Slade and the like, which was right off the radar of the serious rock fan but dear to the hearts of the kids in the vast suburban teenage wasteland.

"They're young, white, suburban American girls, a segment of society that hasn't had anyone to identify with," said Fowley, describing the Runaways in 1976. "When a boy takes his girl to a Black Sabbath concert, the girl has to keep quiet because it's his show really. And what do the girls have to relate to? Joni Mitchell singing about Laurel Canyon? Now the guys can drool over the girls and enjoy the music, and the girls can identify with the young white chicks on stage."

The group was assembled around guitarist Joan Jett, a Suzi Quatro neophyte. They were not intimidated by their limitations but, rather, rushed headlong into a fantasy world. To quote from *Bomp* magazine, "The Runaways are the quintessence of everything that's great about teenage girls – not the giggly demure saps, but the aggro ones who never came to school because they were out too late at Rodney's the night before. And they're living it right now; they don't write songs from idyllic memories that gain romantic scope over the years.

"The Runaways are as real as getting beat up after school. Their songs are about juvenile delinquent wrecks, sex, pressure, and anything incidental like drugs and parties. Sometimes the reflections on these are good, often bad, but there's always the underlying, understood agreement that the state of Teenage is what it's all about. They take all the elements of their lives, punch 'em up into catchy anthems set to the beat of the street, plug it into their amps and sing it all out loud to your crotch or your feet or your head; whichever they hit first."

The Runaways' first single, 'Cherry Bomb', was written on the spot by Fowley and Jett in imitation of Suzi Quatro. The song exploded with the suggestion of illicit sex and the loss of virginity while also referring to the homemade explosives favoured by American teenage boys. The sound was pure third-generation Chinnichap – big unison voices and a British beat. With it, the Runaways kicked down the door and a generation of women have followed.

(I'm) Stranded The Saints

(Ed Kuepper/Chris Bailey) ✳ Fatal ✳ 1976 ✳ Appears on: (I'm) Stranded

Modern Australian rock began here.

"I've got very kind of fond memories of my first ever recording session and it's stupid but I actually don't remember the recording too much," said Chris Bailey. "I remember going to it; I was wearing my girlfriend's coat and for the first time and probably the last time I actually felt like a pop star for the day. My other lingering memory is when we got the record and I was playing it. I'd never been so happy, and I'm sure this is true for everyone but it was just fun to hold the thing."

The first recording, '(I'm) Stranded' (the flipside was 'No Time'), on the Fatal label, launched the Saints from the obscurity of the Brisbane backwaters into the international limelight. The Saints drew on a number of influences. The massive chording of Kuepper's guitars showed the influence of the Stooges and the Missing Links. The jazzy drum feel from Ivor Hay and Chris Bailey's sardonic bar room vocals was perfect punk even though it had been conceived and executed 15,000 km from Soho or CBGB. The self-financed single was sent to the British music press who jumped on it: *Sounds* newspaper declared it single of the week. EMI London despatched orders to the colonies to find and track down the Saints – to make up for the ignominy of having fired the Sex Pistols.

"When you're sixteen or seventeen there's heaps of things that you get angry about – your parents, school, job if you've got it, police," said Bailey. "You're at an age where you want to be doing a whole range of things and you're restricted 'cause of the age that you are. Especially in Brisbane at the time there was active harassment from the police force. There was a political agenda at that stage too if you were in the least bit left-leaning and the Saints were quite blatantly left-leaning."

"One of the things I find that I'm drawn back to the most about Brisbane in the '70s is an overwhelming feeling of possibility," said Bailey. "For youngsters like me from the wrong side of the tracks coming into the city, you didn't need that much money to get mind-numbingly drunk, have fun, do lots of middle-class girls who seemed very keen on sexual exploration. [There were] massively fantastic parties and you could get away with feeling that you were a dyed-in-the-wool committed socialist while having this incredibly wonderful bourgeois life. That was Brisbane to me in the '70s."

The Saints, however, were determined to be original. The more resistance from the squares, the more they were reassured they were on the right path. Eschewing booking agencies or even the alternative radio station 4ZZZ, the Saints played mostly at parties at their house in Petrie Terrace, dubbed Club 76.

"I'm meant to be mocking and humble and I s'pose that's an alternative to lack of success and picking up sheilas but I won't be mockingly humble," said the singer. "Hindsight colours this. I think that we quite seriously thought that we were really quite good."

"Yeah, initially the reaction of the group of people who were supporting us in Brisbane was pretty positive," said Kuepper. "But that was only maybe a couple of dozen people. The response here was generally negative and in some cases violently so. Until the overseas response happened and that came in very quickly afterwards and then suddenly there was a shift in opinion. The early reviews in the pop press that we got here were abysmal ... so abysmal that we used them in our own publicity."

Anarchy in the UK The Sex Pistols

(Steve Jones, Paul Cook, Johnny Rotten, Glen Matlock) ❋ EMI ❋ 1976 ❋

Appears on: *Never Mind the Bollocks*

Few records have had the impact of the Sex Pistols' debut 45. The London punk rock quartet signed to EMI records for a record advance of £40,000 on the basis of the buzz generated by the group's live shows and by the groundswell that was clearly building in the London music scene for snotty, amateurish rock bands.

With the encouragement of manager Malcolm McLaren, the musicians' natural bad behaviour was turned into a sociopathic political statement, best exemplified by their tune 'Anarchy in the UK'.

Image to the contrary, the Pistols were very serious about music. Guitarist Steve Jones rehearsed obsessively and bass player Glen Matlock, who wrote the bulk of the tunes, was also dedicated to his instrument.

"'Anarchy in the UK' was several of his tunes put together," Rotten told journalist Caroline Coon at the time. "I came in a bit late and they'd already put the basic melody and I just said 'I'll call it "Anarchy!"'" The rest of the words came quite easily."

"We're more anti-social, than political," said Matlock.

The Sex Pistols' agenda was inchoate, to say the least. It was a general call to rebellion that falls apart at the slightest scrutiny. The real rebel yell came from Jones' guitars: a mass wall of sound based on the most simple, retro guitar riffs. Essentially, the Sex Pistols reinforced what the garage bands of the '60s had demonstrated – you don't need technique to make rock & roll. In a time when music had been increasingly complicated and defanged, the Sex Pistols' generational shift caused a real revolution.

The first attempt at recording had been poor. Then Chris Thomas was brought in as producer and he layered up the band's sound with take after take of the riff. The sheer size of the sound was breathtaking.

A month after release the record hit number twelve on the British charts. The group agreed to a TV interview, but somewhat drunk they were cajoled into swearing on TV and their performance caused an outrage. The Sex Pistols were front-page news. EMI workers refused to handle the stock and a month later EMI terminated their contract.

The bull was out of the gate, however. The Sex Pistols were no longer a band but a cultural phenomenon.

"If the single ['Anarchy in the UK'] gets into the charts then it will show that it's been worth it," Rotten told Caroline Coon. "That there are thousands of people who are pissed off with everything. And I really think they are. I can't see how they can put up with it. People say we're not the alternative. But we never said we were. We're just one alternative. There should be several."

The Boys Are Back in Town Thin Lizzy

(Phil Lynott) ❋ Mercury ❋ 1976 ❋ Appears on: *Jailbreak*

Phil Lynott wanted to be a rock & roll star. He just never really knew what kind. He guided Thin Lizzy through hard rock and revamped Irish folk songs and finally found his biggest hit by imitating Bruce Springsteen. Lynott was charisma in search of a muse. By dint of his personality and the band's strong live shows, Lizzy had a following. Then Lynott took the riff from Springsteen's 'Kitty's Back' and adapted it to a lyric about a returning Vietnam veteran. The subject matter had no resonance and the verses evolved into a song about male bonding and camaraderie – a subject to which the Irish Lynott could relate. This was a great working-class anthem. The rousing sentiments and the massed harmonies and guitars made 'The Boys Are Back in Town' a perfect rock song for its day. The year 1976 was a notoriously soft time for rock & roll – the calm before the storm of the New Wave – and Thin Lizzy were one of the few rocking voices standing out against the mellowness.

"I just like blood and guts," said Lynott. "I've seen every Clint Eastwood movie goin'. I get off on aggression. One of the main reasons I get up on a stage is to let the aggression out, to put the aggression to a good purpose like rock & roll. I'm sure I'd be fookin' locked up now if I didn't play in a group. I'd be in this jail I'm always singin' about."

American Girl Tom Petty & the Heartbreakers

(Tom Petty) ❋ Shelter ❋ 1976 ❋ Appears on: *Tom Petty & the Heartbreakers*

In 1976, Tom Petty single-handedly saved American rock & roll.

Born and raised in Florida, Petty moved to Los Angeles where he and the Heartbreakers worked as a bar band. It was good honest craft in an era of gigantism. Even Springsteen had ascended to Olympus, New Jersey. The singer/songwriters were, as Neil Young famously remarked, in the middle of the road. Heavy metal and radio rock was all puff and studio production. The more authentic groups were lost in endless jamming. Tom Petty was a dose of salts.

In New York there was a groundswell of new traditionalists at CBGB and Max's but that was way too arty to move beyond downtown. Petty, on the other hand, wasn't art school at all.

Tom Petty & the Heartbreakers were signed to Shelter Records, former home to Leon Russell. They were produced by Russell's former partner Denny Cordell, who understood how to get a tough, bright sound in just fifteen days. "That first album was a real oddity to everyone – I remember takin' it all around and people would just listen and say, 'How weird, what is it?'" he recalled. "At ABC [Shelter's distributor], it was 'We don't know what this is, I guess it's punk rock.' Which was because I happened to be wearing my leather jacket and the songs happened to be short. At that point the only 'rock bands' were playin' long guitar solos – heavy metal stuff."

Petty's short, sharp songs were as unsentimental as John Fogerty was and as rich texturally. Most distinctive was the use of twelve-string Rickenbacker guitars, a direct homage to the Byrds – this rooted Petty in the mainstream American tradition. As did the songs themselves.

The icing on the cake was Petty's gift as a lyricist. He could freshen a cliché – teen love, rock & roll. On tracks like 'Breakdown' he created an apparently effortless classic of chiming guitars and Stonesy feel. The best, however, came at the close with 'American Girl'. Here, over the sound of cascading, chiming guitars layered up into an epic, Petty puts the entire paradox of manifest destiny and the American Dream into the moment of a girl's life as she considers jumping to her death.

"The 'American Girl'," Petty told journalist Cynthia Rose, "is just one example of this character I write about a lot – the small-town kid who knows there's more out there for them but gets fucked up trying to find it. Like the song says, she was raised on promises. I've always felt sympathetic towards her."

At that point Petty reached out to the kids of America and led rock & roll back to the people.

Tom Traubert's Blues (Four Sheets to the Wind in Copenhagen) Tom Waits

(Tom Waits) ✳ Asylum ✳ 1976 ✳ Appears on: *Small Change*

Playing in Sydney in May 1979, Tom Waits introduced 'Tom Traubert's Blues' with this ambiguous patter: "This is a song where I kinda borrowed your unofficial national anthem on this whole thing ... I'll give it back when I'm done. Well I met this girl named Matilda. And eh, I had a little too much to drink that night. This is about throwing up in a foreign country." This is a song about heartbreak and love and alcohol and that moment when they all come together. The foreign country is specifically Denmark.

'Tom Traubert's Blues (Four Sheets to the Wind in Copenhagen)' includes a version of 'Waltzing Matilda', which was written by Banjo Patterson and Christina McPherson in the late 19th century. The tune was adapted from an old Scottish air, 'The Bonnie Wood of Craiglee' but all of this is somewhat irrelevant. The Matilda with whom Waits dances is Mathilde Bondo, a Danish violinist who entertained the American singer on a drunken Copenhagen evening in June 1976.

The following month he finished writing the songs for his *Small Change* album and no doubt Mathilde was somewhat on his mind as was Waits' itinerant lifestyle at the time: "A Matilda is a, eh, backpack. So 'Waltzing Matilda' just means, really just to take off, you know? Like blow town, you know? And eh, you know, that's what the song means, maybe ..."

According to producer Bones Howe, Waits was interested in drunkenness and investigating skid row. Howe recalled a phone conversation with Waits in the early hours on one morning: "He said the most wonderful thing about writing that song. He went down and hung around on skid row in Los Angeles because he wanted to get stimulated for writing this material. He called me up and said, 'I went down to skid row ... I bought a pint of rye. In a brown paper bag – hunkered down, drank the pint of rye, went home, threw up, and wrote 'Tom Traubert's Blues'. Every guy down there ... everyone I spoke to, a woman put him there.'"

As a writer Waits put together disparate ideas that all revolved around the journey from heartbreak to delirium. The song is rich with vignettes and character studies and the notion that really when you're drunk you're travelling in a foreign country where your bearings are lost and your language is useless.

The *Small Change* album was recorded in five days, from 15–20 July 1976, at the Wally Heider Studios in Hollywood and it was on the streets in September.

The elements of the song are identifiable; however, the piece has a mystery in it that's more than its component parts. As the songwriter himself said in 1990, "It's funny eh. This is one of those songs that I never quite figured it out. It's just one of those songs that puzzles me. And so I sing it and I get further puzzled. Eh, alcohol and, eh, writing don't mix. If they do it takes a long time to unravel them ..."

Dancing Queen ABBA

(Benny Andersson/Stig Anderson/Björn Ulvaeus) ✳ Polygram ✳ 1977 ✳
Appears on: *Arrival*

Like any mega pop group, ABBA was not going to buck a trend. So when disco ruled the American airwaves, ABBA went disco. 'Dancing Queen' was ABBA's only number one record in the US.

According to the *All Music Guide*, 'Dancing Queen' was originally called 'Boogaloo' and was based on George McCrae's 1974 disco single 'Rock Your Baby'. Over the course of some months, 'Dancing Queen' evolved with lyrics, partly contributed by ABBA manager Stig Anderson. Benny Andersson and Björn Ulvaeus gradually developed the rhythm track, which is a Euro pop version of American disco – supposedly with a New Orleans influence care of Dr John. Essentially ABBA was replicating the "wall of sound". The major difference between ABBA and Spector is the grandeur of the vision. Where Spector built a monument to passion and romance, 'Dancing Queen' was more filigree and immediate. Where Spector created a mansion, ABBA had a nightclub. Which is not to take anything from 'Dancing Queen'.

The vocals were layered so that Frida Lyngstad and Agnetha Faltskog were entwined in the mystery of the dancing queen. The dynamism of the vocal track is enhanced by the fact that the vocal is brought in halfway through a chorus. 'Dancing Queen' was the ultimate in Euro pop; seductive but not sexy. Like all good pop it was filled with the promise of a Saturday night in your best dress

Stayin' Alive The Bee Gees

(Barry Gibb/Robin Gibb/Maurice Gibb) ✳ Polydor ✳ 1977 ✳
Appears on: *Saturday Night Fever*

Robert Stigwood moved into film production in the '70s sensing not only the excitement of Hollywood but the opportunities for film and music tie-ins. He got involved with the production of a film based on a magazine article by journalist Nik Cohn called 'Tribal Rites of a New Saturday Night'. Cohn's story was set in the world of the 2001 Disco in Bay Ridge, just across the bridge from Manhattan. Although Cohn made up most of the details, he described a vigorous subculture of working-class kids, mostly from European immigrant backgrounds, who loved to dance. These were people whose cultural life was not represented in film and TV. Their preferred style of music – disco – was regarded as somewhat low-rent and gimmicky.

Stigwood read the article in *New York* magazine, called Cohn and within twenty-four hours had made a deal for the movie rights for $10,000.

While Stigwood put the film together, the Bee Gees were in France making their next album. Stigwood picked 'Stayin' Alive', 'Night Fever', 'How Deep is Your Love', 'More than a Woman' and 'If I Can't Have You' for the soundtrack.

This was not a musical in the traditional sense of the term – none of the cast broke into song – but music was central to the film in a way that it had never been expressed before.

Saturday Night Fever was a low-budget film with a gritty, not particularly romantic story. It was Stigwood's genius that put John Travolta with the Bee Gees and caused a massive ruction in the otherwise smooth, and then colourless, worlds of music and film. To see Travolta as Tony Manero striding down the Bay Ridge street to the beat of 'Stayin' Alive' is to get that astonishing rush when you see the collision of a groove and an attitude.

Stigwood had given the Bee Gees an outline of the film, but essentially the Bee Gees were just getting on with it.

"We never really knew what was going on," said Robin Gibb. "It just so happened that the songs worked, especially 'Stayin' Alive'. It's a very straightforward song about survival in the city. That's what it was and that's the statement."

Saturday Night Fever was a massive phenomenon that broke disco wide open. It became the biggest selling soundtrack in history with over thirty million copies sold. It was a true cultural milestone and no-one will ever think of the '70s without an image of Travolta in a white suit with one hand in the air and one on his hip.

Police and Thieves The Clash

(Junior Murvin/Lee Perry) ❋ Epic ❋ 1977 ❋ Appears on: *The Clash*

The Sex Pistols may have started punk rock but the Clash made it mean something. Their songs of dispossessed youth forgotten in the shadows of capitalism were better said and better played than any of their comrades down at the 100 Club.

The Clash's first album is a stone classic. The song 'White Riot' is a perfect teenage anthem. It also suggests that the Clash, and singer Joe Strummer in particular, had a wider view of the social and political hierarchy than most rock singers. 'White Riot' is a song about identifying with the underclass, especially the non-whites.

The album included a track lasting longer than three minutes and with a non-rock rhythm, which announced that the Clash were not going to be confined to any category – not even a punk one.But the key track on *The Clash* is their blistering cover of Junior Murvin's Jamaican hit 'Police and Thieves'.

"The poor blacks and the poor whites are in the same boat," said Strummer at the time. "They don't want us in their culture, but we just happen to dig Tapper Zukie and Big Youth, Dillinger and Aswad and Delroy Washington. We dig them and we ain't scared of going into heavy black record shops and getting their gear. We even go to heavy black gigs where we're the only white people there.

"We'd just like to bridge the gap between the two things, I'd like to have black people coming to hear us, right, but primarily we gotta be concerned with young white kids because that's what we are. But we ain't nothing like racist, *no way.*"

The Clash was recorded over three weekends by their live soundman, who had never made an album before. The essence of the record was the group's live sound – the fiercely slashing guitars over Strummer's screams and the deep dub bass from Paul Simonon. The song's simple message of paranoia about police fitted perfectly with the rest of the album. Mostly, though, it's a great groove – not so much reggae as a hybrid that sounds complete and confident and undeniable. "It was just a wild idea I had one night. I wanted to play reggae when the band first started but I was talked out of it. Rightly so," said Strummer. "And we can't really play reggae. Who the hell could play them reggae drums apart from a black man? We just did it within our limitations. If it had sounded shitty we'd have dropped it. But it sounded great. There's hardly any reggae in it at all – just a few offbeat guitars thrown in for a laugh – it's all rock & roll. I think it's an incredible track."

Neat Neat Neat The Damned

(Brian James) ❊ Stiff ❊ 1977 ❊ Appears on: *Damned Damned Damned*

The Damned were the clown princes of punk rock. They were not spearheading any revolution. They didn't care about the monarchy or the oppression of the working classes; they were out to drink the old order into submission. They were anarchists because they weren't sober enough to subscribe to any other ideology.

The Damned were drawn into the punk movement then by default. Had punk not happened, the Damned – Brian James, Dave Vanian, Rat Scabies and Captain Sensible – would have been catcalled off the stage and returned to the dole queue.

Their garage-band virulence was recognised by Dave Robinson of Stiff and with Nick Lowe they quickly cut a single, 'New Rose', which became "the first punk single ever". It's one of the most pure and entertaining 45s of the era. With that in mind they recorded a debut album, *Damned Damned Damned*, in one day with Lowe again producing. He used Elvis Costello's demo tapes to record the album and it's claimed that there are still snatches of acoustic guitar to be heard faintly in the background.

"Compared with the Pistols album, which was very polished, ours was gnarled and beaten up. To me it was the punk rock sound," the Captain told *MOJO*.

The first single from the album was 'Neat Neat Neat', almost identical to 'New Rose'. The song is pumped up by Scabies' Spectoresque drumming. The lyrics are almost indecipherable and once deciphered are nonsensical, but it's all there in the mood, the almighty racket.

"It sounds like Eddie Cochran as played by a bunch of cider-fuelled crazies in a garage," Sensible said. "'Cause that's what it was."

Sound and Vision David Bowie

(David Bowie) ✳ RCA ✳ 1977 ✳ Appears on: *Low*

In 1977, David Bowie moved to Berlin to save his life. Bowie had changed his identity so many times in seven years that he no longer knew exactly who he was. Taking cocaine didn't help. In Berlin, near the Wall, Bowie found Hansa studios. There, he strained the pop out of his music with the help of Brain Eno.

Bowie and Eno created songs out of small riffs and ambient moods, unafraid to be self-consciously arty.

"We both work in very different ways," said Eno. "David works very fast. He's very impulsive and he works like crazy for about two hours or sometimes three-quarters of an hour – and then he takes the rest of the day off. And in that time, he does an incredible amount, very well, very quickly and faultlessly. He just puts on track after track and they're all just right and then he goes away, and that's it for the day. Quite often that's how it works.

"Whereas what I do is to – quite slowly – build things up over a period, you know. Since I'm using a monophonic synthesiser, it's incredibly tedious putting on one line at a time, 'da-da-da-da ...' like that. Very slow. So I get terribly nervous about working with other people around because so little seems to be happening."

Bowie and Eno played with the texture of contemporary music and on 'Sound and Vision' gave the rock world the opportunity to hear the mixture of ambience, melody, voice and machine in new ways. While 'Sound and Vision' was not a hit, this track and the album *Low* deeply affected the direction music would take in the '80s.

"I don't think people realise how finely he can tune his singing, in terms of picking a particular emotional pitch," said Eno. "It's really scientific the way he does it, very interesting. He'll say, 'I think that's slightly too theatrical there, it should be more withdrawn and introspective' – and he'll go in and sing it again, and you'll hear this point-four of a degree shift which makes all the difference. It's one of the very few times you get to see real craftsmanship, where someone will tell you about what they're going to do, then do it. He picks up the mood of a musical landscape, such as the type I might make, and he can really bring it to a sharp focus, both with the words he uses and the style of singing he chooses."

Mongoloid Devo

(Gerald V Casale) ❊ Stiff ❊ 1977 ❊ Appears on: *Hardcore Devo*

Devo started out angry. Based in the industrial city of Akron, Ohio, Devo was a bunch of art students (or should have been) who developed a group that satirised the straight world of Middle America. They did it with primitive guitars and synthesisers and a few riffs. Their first sessions took place in December 1976 with a four-track Revox tape recorder in the garage. It was so cold that Mark Mothersbaugh played guitar with his gloves on.

Mittens notwithstanding, Devo's sound on their first release was jerky and angular and squeaking. The beats were speeded up and the time signatures suggested a sort of spastic rock sound. It fitted perfectly with the deconstructed fashion of punk rock. Nonetheless, Devo got their first single, 'Jocko Homo', and 'Mongoloid' out of it.

When asked by Jon Savage to describe the smell of the song 'Mongoloid', writer Jerry Casale replied, "Pabulum and bacon frying. Hospitals."

Devo – Jerry Casale, Mark Mothersbaugh, Jim Mothersbaugh, Bob Casale and Alan Myers – were very big with the concepts. The idea of Devolution suggested that the human race was getting more stupid or de-evolving. 'Mongoloid' is about a man with an extra gene who just fits right into the button-down-world of the modern post-industrial society.

"Devolution's a big idea about the way things are," said writer and bass player Gerald Casale. "Everyone has a big idea about the way things are. Whether they admit it or not, a lot of people's ideas masquerade themselves as non-ideas, which we find the most dishonest.

"Devo just has the biggest, best and most interesting idea about reality that allows people to discover things, which is exactly what other ideas don't allow. Other ideas begin by ignoring what's there so their idea doesn't account for the whole picture. It's like when people thought that the earth was at the centre of the universe but the movement of certain planets didn't really match up to that idea – they couldn't make it match because their idea of what was happening was at basis wrong. And when the premise is wrong, everything else that follows is sick."

Hotel California The Eagles

(Don Felder/Glen Frey/Don Henley) ❋ Asylum ❋ 1977 ❋ Appears on: *Hotel California*

The Eagles started as a humble country-rock outfit riding the coat-tails of Jackson Browne. By 1976 when they recorded 'Hotel California' they had become, mostly, a drug dependent parody of decadent rock stars. Camaraderie had become open hostility yet the high, keening vocals and the gnarly, meshing guitars were the sound of modern America.

'Hotel California' was their finest moment, in part for the extended Joe Walsh and Don Felder guitar tussle, but also for its self-loathing and its unsentimental appraisal of what was happening to America and to the Eagles.

The starting point of the song was drummer Don Henley's break-up with girlfriend Loree Rodkin. From there it got more universal. Henley told *Uncut* recently, "It's about loss of innocence, fading glory and decadence. I was trying to use California as a microcosm for the rest of the nation ... I think it was about the dark underbelly of America at large." There's also a dig at Steely Dan: "They stab it with their steely knives but they just can't kill the beast."

No-one could. The chugging groove with a touch of reggae was largely from Felder.

The process of recording this album took seven months in between touring and commuting to the studio in Miami where it was recorded. The song itself is weighted down by the excess – too many drugs, too much money, too many concerts and too much pressure. By the end of the process the Eagles were over their peak and on the way out.

Go Your Own Way Fleetwood Mac

(Lindsey Buckingham) ✳ Warner Bros. ✳ 1977 ✳ Appears on: *Rumours*

Much has been written about the circumstances of recording Fleetwood Mac's *Rumours* album. The relationships in the group were all irrevocably breaking down. They were taking too much cocaine. They were not talking. Yet at the end of the day they made a pop album that sold more than thirty million copies. At the end of the day, though, it wasn't the soap opera that made *Rumours* a masterpiece, it was guitarist Lindsey Buckingham's production.

"The only two instruments that were actually played together on that album was the guitar solo and drum track on 'The Chain'," said co-producer Richard Dashpot. "It wasn't necessary or even expedient for them all to be in the studio at once. Virtually every track is either an overdub, or lifted from a separate take of that particular song. What you hear is the best pieces assembled, a true aural collage. Lindsey and I did most of the production. That's not to take anything away from Ken or the others in the band – they were all involved. But Lindsey and myself really produced that record and he should've gotten the individual credit for it, instead of the whole band.

"I'd worked with Lindsey Buckingham and Stevie Nicks since their debut album, *Buckingham Nicks*. After they joined Fleetwood Mac, Lindsey invited me to do their live sound. They started recording *Rumours* in Sausalito, across the bay from San Francisco, with the Record Plant's engineer, but they fired him after four days for being too into astrology. I was really just around keeping Lindsey company, then Mick takes me into the parking lot, puts his arm around my shoulder and says, 'Guess what? You're producing the album.' The funny thing was, I never really wanted to be a producer. I brought in a friend from Wally Heider's studio in Los Angeles, Ken Caillat, to help me, and we started co-producing. Mick gave me and Ken an old Chinese I-Ching coin and said, 'Good luck'."

Best of all is Buckingham's farewell to Nicks: 'Go Your Own Way'. His vocal is impassioned and urgent and his wall of guitars is worthy of Brian Wilson. Mostly though, the song rests on Mick Fleetwood's drumming, which runs heavy on the tom toms with a galloping tempo that sparks the entire group while holding it together.

"'Go Your Own Way''s rhythm was a tom-tom structure that Lindsey demoed by hitting Kleenex boxes or something," Fleetwood said. "I never quite got to grips with what he wanted, so the end result was a mutated interpretation. It became a major part of the song, a completely back-to-front approach that came, I'm ashamed to say, from capitalising on my own ineptness."

Sex & Drugs & Rock & Roll Ian Dury & the Blockheads

(Ian Dury/Chaz Jankel) ❋ Stiff ❋ 1977 ❋ Appears on: *New Boots and Panties*

This phrase is now part of everyday speech. Ian Dury was a painter by trade, a bit of a poet and bit of a jazz buff, when he fell into rock & roll. He was a mature-age rocker, forming the Blockheads in the mid-'70s at the age of thirty-five. Prior to that he had scuffled around with music and began writing his often amusing lyrics with a Cockney slant. The Blockheads, who revolved around keyboardist Chaz Jankel, were a versatile bunch with a taste for classic R&B and jazz rather than rock. They were, unlike most other bands of that period, funky. The Blockheads' feel and Dury's Cockney spoken rhyming basically laid the way for British hip-hop – especially acid jazz, which was for the most part a poor imitation of what the Blockheads were doing in 1977.

"The first thing we recorded was 'Sex & Drugs & Rock & Roll'," Dury told Chris Welch before his death in 2000. "It had a sound and a simplicity, because it's basically just three people, with Chaz on guitars and pianos, Charlie [Charles] and Norman [Watt-Roy] on drums and bass. It was long before the age of click tracks. We just played and if it sped up a bit, so what.

"'Sex & Drugs' started as a mild admonishment and ended as a lovely anthem. When me and Jankel wrote this song we stole the riff from a Charlie Haden bass solo on a 1960 Ornette Coleman album called *Change of the Century*. I met Charlie Haden later and he told me that he'd nicked the riff too, from a Cajun folk tune. It was banned by the BBC when we released it as a single but it sold about 18,000 copies.

"With this song I was trying to suggest there was more to life than either of those three – sex, drugs and rock & roll, or pulling a lever all day in a factory.

"I was saying, 'If all you think about is sex and drugs and rock & roll, there is something wrong.' The title was used in headlines all over the world. I wish I'd got a quid every time that title has been used."

In the City The Jam

(Paul Weller) ✳ Polydor ✳ 1977 ✳ Appears on: *The Jam*

They were the junior partners in the British punk invasion. Where the Sex Pistols and the Clash demanded the abolition of the class system and the destruction of the rock superstars, Paul Weller's band the Jam were more nostalgic. They wore mod suits and aped the sounds of Swinging London albeit with a tough punk attitude.

Like all bands of the era, the Jam started out with a manifesto. Because Weller, then still a teenager, was the sole composing force in the Jam, their songs right from the start tended towards the personal.

This first single was really about shaking off their lower-middle class suburbia and getting amongst the action. It was originally titled 'In the City There's a Thousand Things I Want to Say to You'. "London was where it all seemed to be happening," said Weller. "Life there seemed so removed from sleepy Woking ... and that was the feeling that we were trying to capture."

The song is fast and furious, based as it is on the Who-ish bass line from Bruce Foxton and the explosive drums from Rick Buckler. This had the amphetamine energy of the mod era. The whole first album was made in one hundred hours. Like most of Weller's material at the time, it was tied into this notion of a dynamic youth wanting to grasp the future with both hands and shake it.

Flash Light Parliament

(George Clinton/Bootsy Collins/Bernie Worrell) ✳ Casablanca ✳ 1977 ✳
Appears on: *Funkentelechy vs the Placebo Syndrome*

'Flash Light' was one of the funkiest tracks of the '70s. George Clinton's Parliament – one version of his umbrella for musicians – was looking for something that could be both political and danceable. This track is powered by the synth bass lines of Bernie Worrell working off a Bootsy Collins groove in the belief that after freeing the ass the mind would follow.

"As far as Parliament was going, we wanted to be saying something to black people," said Clinton. "I figured all I had to do was give black people something to be proud of, and as long as the music's slick and funky then it'll start working on its own. We got a momentum going that don't logically hold up, but once that momentum steps in you ain't got to explain shit.

"Parliament is more vocal, more disco with horns, and a bit more conservative. Funkadelic is more guitars, no horns, more free-form feelings, and more wild. Sometimes there's a criss-cross, but generally Funkadelic gets more pussy than Parliament.

"We made it cool to be funky again, like James Brown had done."

Solsbury Hill Peter Gabriel

(Peter Gabriel) ✳ Charisma ✳ 1977 ✳ Appears on: *Peter Gabriel*

Peter Gabriel quit the progressive rock band Genesis for a career as an art rock star. At the time of his departure, Genesis was poised to become one of the most popular groups in the world. England had been conquered and the US beckoned. Much of their success came from the theatrical and confronting live show that Gabriel had developed. Then Gabriel jumped ship. Genesis continued and became huge in America and indeed one of the most successful groups of the '80s.

'Solsbury Hill' was Gabriel's statement of intent, his explanation for leaving Genesis. Allegedly the inspiration was a Bruce Springsteen concert. Be that as it may, he needed the excitement of a solo life. He also, one suspects, needed to start again. 'Solsbury Hill' is that place.

Producer Bob Ezrin brought a Detroit rock connection – Steve Hunter, Dick Wagner – and Gabriel brought along the best of British boffins – Kate Bush, Robert Fripp, Peter Hammill and Paul Weller. The record sounded quite unlike anything else in its time. 'Solsbury Hill' also featured a peerless vocal from Gabriel – he sounds like a man with the wind in his hair. He knows that "open doors will be shut" but seems not to care.

Ca Plane Pour Moi Plastic Bertrand

(Lou Deprijk/Lou Lacomblez) ✳ Vogue Belgium ✳ 1977 ✳ Appears on: *Ca Plane Pour Moi*

Plastic Bertrand was the first rock star I ever interviewed and he was perhaps the most revealing. In halting English he made no attempt to create a mystique around this hit punk rock song, and even less attempt to establish any punk credentials at all. It was, he announced, the work of a production company that churned out hits in many genres (including the Euro electronica of Telex) but mostly disco. 'Ca Plane Pour Moi' was a pastiche of the Sex Pistols sound (that being the most slick of punk recordings). Of course there is none of the angst, none of the anti-social themes of punk rock, but in its cheekiness and energy it made sense. Even better, of course, was the fact that they used the same backing track for another song, the English-language 'Jet Boy Jet Girl' by Elton Motello – its lyrics making no more sense than the French 'Ca Plane Pour Moi'.

According to the Clash's Joe Strummer in 1978, "By purist rules, it's not allowed to even mention Plastic Bertrand. Yet this record was probably a lot better than a lot of the so-called punk records."

I-94 Radio Birdman

(Deniz Tek/Chris Jones) ❉ Trafalgar ❉ 1977 ❉ Appears on: *Burn My Eye*

Guitarist and songwriter Deniz Tek was raised in Michigan but moved to Sydney, Australia, with a white Epiphone guitar that had once belonged to Fred Sonic Smith of the MC5. The sound of the MC5 permeated Radio Birdman, the group Tek formed in 1974. There were plenty of other styles in there too – the New York Dolls, the Stooges, Jan and Dean, the Velvet Underground, Alice Cooper, the Blue Oyster Cult, the Missing Links and the Rolling Stones, but pretty soon they had a sound and style all their own. In 1977 Radio Birdman was shaking Sydney apart just as the Clash was doing in London and the Ramones did in New York.

'I-94' was Tek's homesick note, name checking the interstate highway between Chicago and Detroit. It also contained the line "I got Garland Jeffreys on the car radio/You know I don't need you," which is among my very favourite couplets in rock & roll – especially when spat out by Birdman's singer Rob Younger. (The reference is to Jeffreys' single 'Wild in the Streets', which had been a regional hit in the early '70s.)

Financed by Anthony O'Grady, the editor of *RAM* magazine, Radio Birdman's first recording was an EP cut live just as the group was beginning to hit its straps. Teenage guitarist Chris Masuak added a melodic touch that complemented Tek's fierce, intense guitar playing and Ron Keeley's swinging drums while bass player Warwick Gilbert held the fire fight together and Younger seethed.

Tek told Birdman biographer Vivien Johnson, "I remember one day in Detroit, it was winter time and so many clouds and so much mist, you could look at the sun and all you could see was great distant sky behind the clouds. It was cold and bitter. It was like all snow and ice, grey streets and grey sun. I remember just looking at that and thinking it was a really powerful image and it came out in that song. I find those kind of days and those kind of landscapes moving. They make me feel kind off sad and kind of happy at the same time and I guess they show in my songs quite a bit. I actually wrote this song 'cause I was really homesick. I'd been in Australia about a year-and-a-half and I really wanted to go home bad, and I wrote some songs that are just full of Michigan references – this is one of them."

Frankie Teardrop Suicide

(Alan Vega/Martin Rev) ❋ Red Star ❋ 1977 ❋ Appears on: *Suicide*

Alan Vega and Martin Rev started Suicide in 1971 in New York playing the downtown circuit with just Vega singing and Rev playing primitive synthesisers and drum machines. Suicide took the Stooges and the Velvet Underground and some Elvis Presley and Otis Redding and then reinterpreted it as if they were Kraftwerk. They were rightly regarded as true pioneers and when punk rock moved above ground in 1976 and 1977, Suicide surfaced with it. The Clash and Elvis Costello both added Suicide to their tours and caused riots at their concerts. The world was not yet ready for industrial techno. Suicide's heirs – Devo, Ultravox, Depeche Mode, Jesus and Mary Chain, Sisters of Mercy, Daft Punk, Air, Chemical, Nick Cave to name but a few – benefited from their pioneering sheets of industrial music.

The '70s certainly weren't ready for 'Frankie Teardrop' – a ten-minute epic about a man trapped in a factory. Rev's keyboards are angry and agitated and frustrated and desperate. Vega's singing walks the line between despair and madness until the song ends in violent tragedy.

"That's what's happening all over the place," said Vega. "Everybody's blowin' everybody else away, and who are these people? They're not maniacs. They're just ordinary people gone a little berserk because life just got too hard for them."

'Frankie Teardrop' is hard in the way that the Velvets' 'Sister Ray' is hard. The key to it is that amongst Vega's screams and crooning pain is a pumping heart. It's not a song you're going to want to hear a lot, but it will stay with you.

Psychokiller   Talking Heads

(David Byrne/Tina Weymouth/Chris Franz) ✳ Sire ✳ 1977 ✳ Appears on: *Talking Heads '77*

The most frightening song of the punk rock era came from a quartet who tried their hardest to look normal. In 1977, when most would-be rock & roll stars had leather jackets and clothes designed for shock and awe, Talking Heads had slacks and nice, pressed shirts as if playing rock & roll was another day at the office. Their signature tune, however, was a chilling monologue from a psychopath.

'Psychokiller', with its minimal chord changes and swinging, minimal groove, was a very spooky song.

"When that was the song that drew all the attention, it used to bother us," said singer David Byrne. "But we rationalised it by telling ourselves that it was that driving meter of the bass line and chord changes that had the appeal.

"I realise now, that the idea of a personality close to the edge has something to do with the song's attraction. I don't mean that in a sensational way – it's just a normal human attraction for something a little out of the ordinary."

Byrne wrote 'Psychokiller' while still at the Rhode Island School of Design and it was in the group's repertoire while they were still a trio (Tina Weymouth on bass and drummer Chris Franz) playing at CBGB in New York, alongside Television and the Ramones.

"That was the first song that actually got performed," said Byrne. "I attempted, when I was much younger, to write some songs. Gosh, they were really terrible! They were like fake Bob Dylan songs. And I never finished them. That one was the first one that got finished. It was a way to see if I could do it. And we all worked together on it."

"David came in and said, 'I've got this song, it's like an Alice Cooper song – sort of'", Franz recalled. "He started to play it, saying, 'This is as much as I've got'. Between the three of us, we managed to make it complete."

The hook line is the refrain sung in French, as translated by Weymouth.

"David had asked somebody else to do it in another language because he wanted to create a split personality," said Weymouth. "He was trying to recreate a person who has a criminal mind. The people who he originally approached to do it said, 'It's about a psycho killer? No, we won't contribute to that song'. They were socially minded. So he came to our studio where we were painting, because I knew French. So I put in the stuff that sounds like a Napoleonic complex. Then David said, 'OK, we've got this French. So what would a French band do with this rock & roll song?' I said, 'Well, the French right now are really into what they call "Yeah Yeah" music, because of the Beatles.' So he put in all those 'Fa fa fa's' instead of 'Yeah yeah'."

Marquee Moon Television

(Tom Verlaine) ❋ Elektra ❋ 1977 ❋ Appears on: *Marquee Moon*

Patti Smith accurately described Tom Verlaine's guitar playing as "a thousand bluebirds screaming". This song features the best piece of electric guitar since Jimi Hendrix. Verlaine's long, snaky and abstract lines create their own logic and resolve the melodies in all kinds of obtuse but exciting ways. This is like rock & roll reinvented, but the achievement was so singular that it has never been copied.

Tom Miller took the name of French Symbolist poet Paul Verlaine when he came to New York to be a rock star in the early '70s. He scuffled through the downtown music scene for five years, gradually assembling Television and building a stage at a Bowery bar – CBGB – that would later attract the New York punk crowd.

Verlaine's milieu was the bohemian downtown scene. His musical influences included Dylan and the Rolling Stones, the psychedelic sounds of the Nuggets era bands and especially the 13th Floor Elevators, plus he liked a lot of jazz. Verlaine had a jazz approach to making rock & roll – a rhythm section that could swing behind two guitar players improvising off each other. Television played long songs but the ingenuity of Verlaine and second guitarist Richard Lloyd was the main attraction. Verlaine's songs had a dry romanticism about them – more florid and abstract than Lou Reed but something of that order.

A first single, 'Little Johnny Jewel', attracted attention with its jagged guitar attack against a jazzy, spastic drum pattern. For their major-label debut, Television settled on producer Andy Johns, fresh from working with the Stones. Johns set up a commercial rock sound for Television and Verlaine told him to dismantle it.

The centrepiece of it all was 'Marquee Moon', the strange story of a night on the town. The narrative is elusive and dreamlike to match the music. It's a song of the city – all hard pavements and neon lights and bright spots polka-dotting the night air. The song flows along, pushed by the loping and lazy beat of Billy Ficca's drums and Fred Smith's shy bass playing. The narrative is in the guitar lines – sometimes percussive jabs and at other times languid meditations on the state of the night. There's a conversation going on between Verlaine and Lloyd here unlike anything else before or since.

The take of 'Marquee Moon' on the first album was recorded in the first run down of the song – Ficca thought it was a rehearsal. Johns wanted to have another crack at the song but Verlaine announced that he was done. And he's right.

"I generally end up following something in a dreamlike sort of way," said Verlaine of his method. "It's like watching pictures unfold. I don't really have any ideas, not even about the guitar. A lot of it has to do with developing what the physical sound of that guitar is, coming off the amp. Time and time again the music is about returning to the physicality of the sound, and maybe that in itself generates ideas."

Oh Bondage, Up Yours X Ray Spex

(Poly Styrene) ✳ Virgin ✳ 1977 ✳ Appears on: *Germ Free Adolescents*

The London punk scene prided itself on female empowerment. Prior to punk rock, the role of rock star was an almost exclusively male preserve.

Marion Elliot was still a teenager when she saw the Sex Pistols and took up the microphone for herself as vocalist and songwriter Poly Styrene. The sheer force of her personality, her voice and the oddball quirkiness of X Ray Spex put a decidedly softer, but no less critical slant, on the punk movement.

Poly Styrene's songs just poured forth in the excitement of it all. Many of them dealt with issues of image and consumerism. She told *MOJO*, "I was trying to do a diary of 1977, to write about everyday experiences.

"One of the first songs we did was 'Oh Bondage, Up Yours'," she said at the time. "It was about being in bondage to the material life. A call for liberation. I was saying, 'Bondage? Forget it, I'm not going to be bound by the laws of consumerism.'"

Germ Free Adolescents was one of the better albums of the period, and of course the issues remain as relevant as ever.

Is This Pop? XTC

(Andy Partridge) ✳ Virgin ✳ 1977 ✳ Appears on: *White Music*

"I'd like to think we're the Vasco de Gamas of popular music," said XTC bass player Colin Moulding. The five-piece from the provincial English town of Swindon had formed in 1973 as the Helium Kids in a pathetic attempt to be a glam rock band from the suburbs. Then punk rock hit. Although guitarist Andy Partridge claimed to be underwhelmed by first exposure to the Sex Pistols, punk rock opened doors for their high-energy, eccentric pop music.

Recorded in a week, *White Music* deconstructs pop music. It's angry and angular, zigzagging across the stereo with half-formed ideas. The album credits three producers, including three British superstars of the desk, Robert John 'Mutt' Lange, Steve Lillywhite and John Leckie, who more than compensate for the group's furious youth.

It's a much better record than Partridge, who was the main composer, recalls. "The first album, *White Music*, was just snotty, naked baby photos," he said in the early '80s. "I don't know if I'd want to see them now. Don't get them out, Mother, I'm not like that any more. I get embarrassed by *White Music* now because I was really trying too hard to find a style in which to say these things. But the paradox was, at that point in time I had nothing to say. I was just writing lyrics and they never gave me any pictures other than the total thing of that sort of modern, loud, noisy guitar, bass, drums, organ mess.

"The chords were picked because they upset more than they were musically well crafted. After *White Music* I started to feel like I really wanted to get out cohesive ideas."

Its lack of cohesion is its strength. He was more accurate when he described it as "Captain Beefheart meets the Archies ... I can see now it's just everything we'd ever listened to. The Beatles are in there, Sun Ra, Atomic Rooster in there, anybody who'd done anything we liked in the previous lifetime. We just thought it was real, dead original."

The single 'Is This Pop?' was, in its own way, a manifesto on the state of the art. Their confusion about the nature of pop was an important step, spearheading a movement that, for want of any better phrase, was called power pop and later, of course, New Wave.

Partridge's vision has always guided the group and he saw himself in the eccentric tradition of Ray Davies and Syd Barrett. As time went on, he became better at the craft and the singles were better, but the weirdness developed into self-consciousness and was less and less powerful.

XTC probably made better records as time went on, but this first one – right down to the pop art style of the cover, the typeface, and the clothes they wore – had a unique bravery. The kind of blind nerve that it takes to explore the ends of the Earth. Moulding was right when he said, "The most impressive thing about it is the energy."

1/1 Brian Eno

(Rhett Davies/Brian Eno/Robert Wyatt) ✳ EG ✳ 1978 ✳
Appears on: *Ambient 1: Music for Airports*

The opening track on *Ambient 1: Music for Airports* heralded a whole new phase for popular music – music without tunes. Eno recognised the existence of tuneless music and then gave it a name. From there followed all kinds of permutations from the New Age noodling of hippies wanting meditation soundtracks to ambient house music and all kinds of dynamics in between.

Perhaps then, it's not surprising that the idea came while Eno was recovering from a head injury after being knocked over by a taxi.

"A friend came to visit and, as she was leaving, I asked her to put a record of harp music on the stereo," he recalled. "Well, one channel wasn't working. It was very quiet, pouring with rain outside and I thought, 'Oh shit, I'll have to wait for the next visitor to turn it up.' Then I started to listen to it ..."

Eno had achieved his ambition of taking the musician out of the music-making process and he was "very, very pleased" with the result.

"It was done," he admitted, "with a minimum of good intentions. I didn't go into it thinking, 'I'm going to make a very interesting piece of music here'. I went into it thinking I just wanted to make something that would work in an airport, that would actually make you think that flying was a pleasant thing to do instead of an unbearably uncomfortable thing, as I think it generally is."

Eno's instruments were a series of very long tape loops – some as long as 20 minutes.

"There were twenty-two loops," he explained. "One loop had just one piano note on it. Another one would have two piano notes. Another one would have a group of girls singing one note, sustaining it for ten seconds. There were eight loops of girls' voices and about fourteen loops of piano. I just set all these loops running and let them configure in whichever way they wanted to, and in fact the result is very, very nice."

In fact, for a piece of music composed by machines, the effect is surprisingly organic.

"The interesting thing," Eno noted, "is that it doesn't sound at all mechanical or mathematical. It sounds like some guy is sitting there playing the piano with quite intense feeling. The spacing and dynamics of 'his' playing sound very well organised. That was an example of hardly interfering at all. When the piece was finished I listened to it and there was just one piano note I didn't like. It seemed to appear in the wrong place, so I simply edited it out. A lot of the so-called systems composers have this thing that the system is always right. You don't fiddle with it at all. Well, I don't think like that. I think that the system is as right as you judge it to be. If, for some reason, you don't like a bit of it, you must trust your intuition on that. I don't take a doctrinaire approach to systems."

Surrender Cheap Trick

(Rick Nielsen) ✳ Epic ✳ 1978 ✳ Appears on: *Heaven Tonight*

Cheap Trick was like a fifth column in the British Invasions, a group from America's mid-west who loved British pop. Guitarist Rick Nielsen was an Anglophile with a deep understanding of the quirky British bands such as the Move with their musical witticisms. They also envied the British ability to frock up and present a visual as well as musical package. For all of that, though, Cheap Trick was from the Midwest and on 'Surrender' they recorded the first 'dysfunctional family' hit.

"Mommy's all right, Daddy's all right/They just seem a little weird," sang Robin Zander in a beautifully high voice. He posed the question of what to do when your parents are smoking pot and making out on the couch. The answer – get out the KISS records. Cheap Trick outlined the slacker manifesto.

'Surrender', a song that had been around since the group's first album (*Cheap Trick*, 1977), was on their third. It was given the power pop treatment by producer Tom Werman. The combination of big power chords and repetitive sixteenth-note passages recalled the Who's 'Baba O'Riley'. This was indeed a teen anthem. Cheap Trick put the power back into pop.

Le Freak Chic

(Bernard Edwards/Nile Rodgers) ✳ Atlantic ✳ 1978 ✳ Appears on: *C'est Chic*

The biggest selling single in Atlantic's history came about after Chic was refused entry to the chic Studio 54. The pair – Bernard Edwards and Nile Rodgers – left their date Grace Jones and walked down the street chanting "Aw, fuck off," which evolved into the hook "Freak out!" Once in the studio Rodgers and Edwards jammed the rest of the song into place with the help of drummer Tony Thompson.

The Chic style started when Rodgers was in London at a Roxy Music concert.

"I went to see Roxy. I thought this shit is happening," said the guitarist. "If we could take this sophisticated, cerebral stuff, put a beat to it, make it black and our own thing, we could really be happening, too.

"We also idolised KISS. When KISS were on stage, they had a certain vibe and image, and once they left that stage, you had absolutely no idea who they are. That's what Chic was like. Our costumes made us look like bankers and business people. To us, it was just as over-the-top and flamboyant as KISS."

Chic had the songs too – whether for Chic records or for artists such as Sister Sledge ('We are Family'). They weren't the first disco band but they took disco from being a dance craze into a lasting musical style. Their influence is still heard on the radio.

"It was a three-piece band playing all the rhythm tracks and then we started overdubbing," said Edwards, who played the bass. "When you're first laying down the rhythm track, you want it to be tight and the less people playing, the tighter. If it's just me and Nile and the drummer, we know the rhythm track's going to be solid.

"My main role is to keep the bottom there, keep the groove solid and steady. I play a lot on the E and A strings and I play down in the first five frets mainly to keep a really fat, chunky sound. I usually start more basic – I don't like to get too note-y and it's usually a reaction to some rhythm that Nile's playing. He'll start playing a chord and I'll pick up on it and put notes to the rhythm.

"A lot of times there's no melody so I have total freedom as to what I'm going to play – just knowing whether it's a major or minor mode and then I can go with it. I'll come up with a line and maybe we'll write around that line."

Of course, the irony is that no group defined the disco era so well as Chic. Rodgers and Edwards had a groove that was both rock and R&B, that was light and heavy. This was disco. Dance music with wit. Rodgers' snappy, rhythmic guitar style perfectly complemented Edwards' heavy bass lines. "Our philosophies defined our personalities. I had my bohemian lifestyle and Bernard was the family man," said Rodgers. "Everything that was systematic about Bernard was exactly what my anarchy needed."

Goodbye Astrid Cold Chisel

(Don Walker/Jimmy Barnes) ❋ WEA ❋ 1978 ❋

Appears on: *You're 13, You're Beautiful and You're Mine*

Jimmy Barnes wrote all three chords and Don Walker the lyrics to this classic small piece of misogyny. At the time of first writing, Cold Chisel was to all intents and purposes, five Adelaide boys going nowhere fast and loudly so. Living in dive hotel rooms and playing three sets a night in any bar that would have them, Chisel lived the rock & roll dream. What set them apart, however, was impeccable taste in dirty rock & roll.

'Astrid' was a twelve-bar thrash in the style of the Troggs, although even with a tune as rudimentary as this, Chisel brought a unique touch. Foremost is Ian Moss' sandpaper guitar lines.

Don Walker's tale of marriage break-up is full of wit and attitude. There's no melancholic, wistful sense of lost possibility; just "seven long years of give a little, take a little, put a little money away". This is the Australian version of *Men are from Mars, Women are from Venus*. The narrator lets fly his scorn for the woman's lifestyle. All the bottled-up anger spews out, all the feelings he has suppressed are vomited up. "Turn up the tears/And make sure you let the neighbours see/What a lowdown deal you got/When you married me".

'Astrid' lent itself to the full force of Chisel on stage – Ian Moss' breakneck guitar leading the way for a tightly swinging rhythm section of Steve Prestwich's versatile drumming and Phil Small's solid bass with Walker's Jerry Lee Lewis piano playing. Then there was Jimmy Barnes who let fly on this song like his life depended on it. His vocal here was a tsunami of emotion way beyond the usual scope of rock & roll and completely his own. Cold Chisel wrote more literate songs and more sophisticated tunes but taking three chords and a simple story and transforming them into a unique and confronting piece like this takes real genius.

Killing an Arab The Cure

(Michael Dempsey/Robert Smith/Lol Tolhurst) ✳ Fiction ✳ 1978 ✳
Appears on: *Standing at the Sea: the Singles*

Robert Smith started the Cure like many other young Englishmen as a kind of art school statement. Encouraged by punk rock, which was then the rage, the Cure was gloomy, dark, perverse and funny. Smith's vocals were fey and his tunes were obtuse to disguise their early amateurishness. But clearly early on he had a gift. The first two songs, '10:15 Saturday Night' and 'Killing an Arab', displayed a unique talent for songwriting, which was literate and whimsical.

The Cure's early sessions were conducted in the Jam's studio downtime, using their instruments.

They were sufficiently striking to make it to the head of the post-punk pack. "People picked up on it, because it sounded very different from anything else at the time," said Smith in retrospect. "The whole LP did. Because Lol couldn't drum very well, we had to keep everything very, very simple. Our sound was forced on us to a certain extent."

Albert Camus' novel *L'Étranger* inspired the single 'Killing an Arab'.

"When I wrote the song I realised it was a very inflammatory title taken out of context," said Smith. "But I never imagined that the two could be divorced. 'Killing an Arab' is a title of a song which is about a certain prescient event which happened in a book written by Albert Camus. Otherwise, you might as well give titles purely for shock value like heavy metal bands do. I found it absurd that a group like the Cure should be singled out for that kind of attack."

The title created a significant controversy in the US where the group had hitherto been largely ignored.

"For a couple of days we made the national news in America," said Smith. "And it was the last thing in the world I wanted to get caught up in. Debating Camus on American cable TV was totally surreal."

Heroes   David Bowie

(David Bowie/Brian Eno) ✳ RCA ✳ 1978 ✳ Appears on: *Heroes*

"I had no statement to make on *Low*," David Bowie said of his groundbreaking 1977 album. Bowie moved to Berlin with a bad drug habit, a chaotic home life and a need to get rid of the cobwebs of stardom. Collaborating with Brian Eno, he fashioned an entirely new type of rock & roll music, which bore fruit a year later with the *Heroes* album. "The strange thing that came out of *Low* is that in my meanderings in new processes and new methods of writing, when Eno and I listened back to it, we realised we had created new information without even realising it and that by not trying to write about anything we had written more about something or other that one couldn't quite put one's finger on than we could have had we actually gone out and said, 'let's do a concept album'.

"It was quite remarkable so we thought, great, fine, let's do that again, it's quite exciting, so we did that with *Heroes*. We used an immense amount of imagery and juxtaposed one against the other and used incredibly startling methods of writing, anything from random selections out of books. Musically as well – I mean, chord changes. We were quite arbitrary sometimes and the total effect astonished both of us when we sat back and listened to the finished thing."

It's surprising that Bowie and Eno had not worked together before. However, in Berlin they made up for lost time. Eno brought his ambient textures to the highly compressed sound. Guitarist Robert Fripp added an arty, angular counterpoint to the more soulful Carlos Alomar, while Tony Visconti played bass and mixed the project.

"We did *Low*," Tony Visconti recalled. "David wasn't too keen on recording any more if it would mean sustaining that Ziggy Stardust image, that monster he'd created, and he said he wanted to make an album of music which was very uncompromising and reflected the way he felt.

"Then we came to 'Heroes' – what we started to do on *Low*, we developed into a fine art on 'Heroes'. It was more expansive. We used a bigger studio, the Hansa Studio, which is just five hundred yards from the Wall, from East Berlin, and every afternoon, I'd sit down at the desk and see three Russian Red Guards looking at us with binoculars with their sten guns over their shoulders, and the barbed wire, and I knew there were mines buried in that wall – that atmosphere was so provocative and so stimulating and so frightening that the band played with an incredible amount of energy, because I think they wanted to go home, actually.

"The sound's so vast and so massive on that album, and a lot of the echo comes from that ambient sound; we didn't have to add much in the mix. By the time it got to 'Heroes', he had conquered the low period and he felt like a hero – every minute of the day he was in the studio, he'd get up to the microphone and sing at the top of his lungs. You can hear it on 'Heroes', his own particular style of yelling and screaming, which he calls 'Bowie histrionics'."

The title track saw Bowie at his unsentimental best yet somehow deeply emotional. It is the most ironic moment in this very ironic artist's repertoire.

The production of the album is ripe; saturated in ambient noise. Inside there are seductive riffs from Fripp breaking through the pea soup. Bowie's vocal is vulnerable and beseeching – yet it's hard to tell whether this is just a camp put-on. The lyrics too are some of the least oblique words Bowie has written.

Amidst the density of the track, Bowie sings of undying love in such a way that you believe him – and believe that he's putting you on.

Sultans of Swing Dire Straits

(Mark Knopfler) ✳ Vertigo ✳ 1978 ✳ Appears on: *Dire Straits*

It's indeed fortunate that Mark Knopfler is such an erudite guitar player because he has to be the most inexpressive singer in the history of rock. My friend Amanda who worked on the Straits' multi-month Australian tour remembered that the same notes were played in the same place every single night. If Mark Knopfler ever had a bad day, you wouldn't know it from the concert.

Dire Straits were initially regarded as a New Wave band. They landed in this company having come up through the London pub scene with a vaguely gloomy name. But you can't imagine them getting so worked up that they slashed into a power chord in sheer frustration at the blandness of the straight world or whatever it was that got New Wavers going.

Dire Straits were, in fact, the perfect representation of the '80s – an era of post-modernism. They played long songs that appeared to have flights of improvisation but were tightly scripted. The lyrics had a Dylanesque obscurity but lacked poetry or much meaning.

Dire Straits, however, did have their moments. The first of them is 'Sultans of Swing' on the debut album. The lyric is about some long-lost band and is inconsequential. The thing here is the hook that Knopfler lays down with fluid and inventive guitar runs while the rhythm section maintains a gentle funk undertow. Knopfler's voice is ethereal and laid back, as befits the lyric. He's not upset that the Sultans are no longer here, just passing the information on.

Ultimately, if he doesn't care, why should we?

April Sun in Cuba Dragon

(Paul Hewson/Marc Hunter) ✳ CBS ✳ 1978 ✳ Appears on: *Running Free*

Dragon was one of the great pop bands of all time. Five New Zealanders with a background in progressive rock and fans of Lou Reed found themselves as teen sensations. This was largely due to the enormous charisma of singer Marc Hunter and the pop craftsmanship of pianist and writer Paul Hewson.

Their finest moment came in what is effectively a nonsense song with a massive hook and a stop--start, funky tempo.

Hewson was a chess fiend and idea for the lyric came from a story that chess champion Garry Kasparov, during a tournament in Cuba, claimed that the sun was putting him off his game.

"Paul had 'April Sun in Cuba' in the bag," said guitarist Robert Taylor. "It only took him about five minutes to write. We played it live once at the Rooty Hill RSL and the first time people heard it they went berserk so we knew people loved that riff. We recorded it in a couple of days."

The sessions were interrupted by a car accident that put Taylor out of action and the Divinyls' Mark McEntee plays the slide part while Dawkins added sound effects – to the band's ire. Nonetheless, the single went to number two and it remains an enigmatic classic.

"I think that annoying 'da da, da da' and the fact that it's 'April Sun in Cuba' just sounds like a happy pop song," said bass player Todd Hunter. "In 1957 Kasparov is complaining about the April sun in Cuba ruining his game and the whole missile crisis thing – it's all these layers underneath. So who knew? It's just this, you can just tell it's got that thing about it.

"Somebody said to us when we first came to Australia, 'OK you guys, in this country you've got to have fuck-you money or a fuck-you attitude.' It was obvious to us we were never going to get any fuck-you money so we just had the attitude."

Down in the Tube Station at Midnight The Jam

(Paul Weller) ❄ Polydor ❄ 1978 ❄ Appears on: *All Mod Cons*

The third Jam album in less than two years started inauspiciously. The initial demo tapes presented to Polydor were rejected and singer Paul Weller was persuaded to record a Kinks song ('David Watts') as filler. Then Weller found himself as a writer; firstly with 'A Bomb in Wardour Street', which captured the paranoia, violence, anger and the siege mentality of London then undergoing an IRA bombing campaign.

Weller's first single with the Jam was 'In the City' and he made London a core part of his writing. It was the landscape on which he projected his emotional life. While contemporaries the Clash and the Sex Pistols drew their inspiration exclusively from across the Atlantic, Weller was steeped in British sounds and rhythm and the lyrics were too particular in their detail to come from anywhere else.

'Down in the Tube Station at Midnight' is a complex narrative telling the story of a man on his way home to suburbia with a takeaway curry who gets mugged in the train station. The detail is so acute you can picture the thugs and feel his humiliation as he hits the concrete. Weller turns the perfectly ordinary location of a train station into a horror show. So much of it is in the carefully chosen detail – the Queen on the coin, the graffiti "from some atheist nutter," the toffee wrappers, "wormwood scrubs/And too many right wing meetings". These are the details that make up a life. The telling of them here speaks of both the hopelessness of daily life and the black futility of taking it.

Then there's the chilling coda "They took the keys/She'll think it's me" and with just that couplet you can picture the whole *Clockwork Orange* scenario. 'Tube Station' is powered by the Jam hitting their straps and moving out of the punk thrash of their first two albums. Here there's light and shade and a steadily increasing tension. 'Tube Station' marked the point where the Jam and Paul Weller came out of the shadows of their '60s forefathers and laid the ground for a new era of British rock that carried right though to the Brit pop of the '90s and beyond.

Wuthering Heights Kate Bush

(Kate Bush) ❋ EMI ❋ 1978 ❋ Appears on: *The Kick Inside*

"I was brought up on movies: love, revenge and death," said Kate Bush. It's all there in her first single, a retelling of Emily Brontë's Gothic epic in four and a half minutes. Bush was then only eighteen years old and had lived a comfortable middle-class English life. The doomed, passionate romance of *Wuthering Heights* appealed to her, as to so many teenage girls, and she adapted it to song, partly no doubt because she had not yet experienced that level of romantic passion herself. Sharing the same name as the heroine of the book probably increased her identification.

"I felt that to actually get your name anywhere, you've got to do something that is unusual, because there's so much good music around and it's all in a similar vein," she said after the release of 'Wuthering Heights'. "It was, musically, for me, one of my strongest songs. It had the high pitch and it also had a very English story-line, which everyone would know because it was a classic book."

'Wuthering Heights' is a magnificent artifice of trembling vocals and breathless choruses. The entire track overflows with nervous energy. There is a Gothic sexuality that comes panting out of 'Wuthering Heights'. "Don't you think art is a tremendous sensual-sexual expression? I feel that energy is often ... the driving force is probably not the right way to put it," she said, more than a little disingenuously. "I felt very flattered that those people should think of me in those sex symbol terms. That was my first reaction, but it can be very destructive. For a start, there are so many incredibly good looking women around, and their craft is in that. They're either models or acting, so their physical image is important. What I really want to come across as is as a musician, and I think that sort of thing can distract, because people will only see you on a superficial level."

'Wuthering Heights' was an instant hit, which Bush backed up with the equally idiosyncratic 'The Man with the Child in His Eyes' and she has continued to follow her own star since.

Another Girl, Another Planet The Only Ones

(Peter Perrett) ✳ CBS ✳ 1978 ✳ Appears on: *The Only Ones*

A truly great piece of rock guitar, 'Another Girl, Another Planet' is one of the most dynamic rock songs of all time. It's a guitar duel between John Perry and singer/songwriter Peter Perrett that simply takes off into the stratosphere.

Perrett was a Dylan and Lou Reed devotee who formed the Only Ones in punk-dominated London. Their colleagues were the Pretenders and the Heartbreakers, with whom Perrett shared drug habits. Unlike most London bands of the period, the Only Ones were accomplished musicians who found that technique was no barrier to raw power when necessary. American guitarist John Perry had played with Robert Hunter and the Grateful Dead while drummer Mike Kellie was in the forgettable British '70s band Spooky Tooth. The combination of innocence and experience enlivened the Only Ones, especially on their early albums. Perrett's heroin addiction, however, drastically compromised his career. His world-weary vocals complemented his opiate verse and contrasted with the fire that came out of the guitar stacks.

'Another Girl', their second single, gets some of its excitement from being recorded live to tape. The long intro from the guitars is pushed along at punishing speed by the rhythm section, which steadily mounts the tension until Perry goes screaming up the guitar neck with a kind of banshee wail and then the song kicks into overdrive. The lyrics, more likely about heroin as a woman, are sly and witty and careless as only a Lou Reed fan could do.

Many groups have tried to replicate the messy brilliance of this track but none have. You had to be there.

Miss You The Rolling Stones

(Mick Jagger/Keith Richards) ❋ Rolling Stones Records ❋ 1978 ❋
Appears on: *Some Girls*

"A lot of these songs like 'Miss You' were heavily influenced by going to the discos," said Charlie Watts. "Mick and I used to go to discos a lot. A great way to hear a dance record was by listening to it in a dance hall or disco. In the '70s there were some fantastic dance records out. As dopey as their clothes might have looked, the actual records that Earth, Wind & Fire released, for example, were fabulous."

Jagger was clearly plugged into the changes that were overtaking the charts. Meanwhile, Keith Richards was fighting legal battles and perpetually detoxing from heroin. After three less than stellar albums, the Rolling Stones put themselves under pressure. The *Some Girls* album was hailed as a return to form.

'Miss You' is one of their more enduring tracks. It has the four-on-the-floor of the Philadelphia sound but still maintains a rock & roll feel. Along with Blondie's 'Heart of Glass', it was an important step in breaking down the the rock audience's antipathy towards dance music.

While Richards struggled to get his life back together, Jagger took control of the Rolling Stones and *Some Girls* is very much his album. The record both satirises and applauds the decadent New York of the late '70s with its disco and champagne and trash aristocracy. The lyrics mock not only Andy Warhol but also Jagger's wife ("You're the easiest lay on the White House lawn"), and the record acknowledged New York as the new centre of the universe.

On 'Miss You' the Rolling Stones reconnected with the people. The groove is driven by Jagger's guitar style, and his playful vocals, especially in the upper register, are some of his best. 'Miss You' is a modest proposal, not to be the greatest band in the world, but just to be on the dance floor once more.

The Big Country Talking Heads

(David Byrne) ❋ Sire ❋ 1978 ❋ Appears on: *More Songs about Buildings and Food*

Talking Heads may have been able to claim the prize for best album title but that would have meant little had not the music been right. The previous year they were awkward art-school geeks. On *More Songs* they were confident arty rock musicians.

They give some credit to Brian Eno, who is the most artful of record producers. "Eno taught us to relax in the studio," said bass player Tina Weymouth. "Which I think was his intention all along. He found that we were very willing to be experimental, as he was, and he was delighted with that … to find a band that would allow him to race everybody's track and not get artistically sensitive and precious about it.

"What makes Eno a great leader is that he's willing to share everything he knows. Eno thinks our albums are hoovering music, which was suggested by David's manner of moving around in the studio," Weymouth said. "David moves around the studio as if he were a janitor cleaning up and vacuuming while whistling an idiotic tune. His second description of our music is 'music to do your housework by'."

This contrast between normalcy and the avant-garde is the crux of the album's best song, 'The Big Country'. Bryne sings a beautiful songlike poem to suburbia and its geometric harmonies and the glories of the economic and social forces that have created it. Then he undercuts it with the line "I wouldn't live there if you paid me".

There's a tension in Talking Heads' music, a twitch in the grooves between Byrne's affection for the button-down world and his need to escape from it. So much of rock & roll, and especially punk rock, is about breaking free into unbridled self-expression, but so much of that is really a cartoon pastiche in which neither the artist nor the listener really understand what is being said. That wasn't the case with Byrne in this song or many others where he floats dispassionately above the shopping malls of the world observing the straight people in their cages.

"I think people confuse coldness and unfeelingness with the fact that we're aware of what we're doing," said Byrne. "I know that may suggest arrogance or awkwardness, but I mean it in just the literal sense of being aware of what you're doing, like: 'Look at the funny place we're in, we're in front of people doing this'. That might seem cold to some; to me, it just seems realistic."

YMCA Village People

(Henri Belolo/Jacques Morali/Victor Willis) ✳ Casablanca ✳ 1978 ✳
Appears on: *Can't Stop the Music*

It is still hard to believe that a song about promiscuous sodomy has become a popular dance anthem sung by school children and adults in all walks of life.

Henri Belolo and Jacques Morali were two French songwriters and record producers attempting to crack America. They worked with Casablanca Records, the home of mainstream disco in the mid-'70s, where they hit upon the idea of writing disco songs for the gay community. A first try, 'Macho Man' was a hit. To promote the record they cast straight singer Victor Willis and a group of actors and singers, each of whom was costumed according to the then current gay 'clones': the mechanic, the GI, the construction worker, the cowboy, the leather man, the cop, the Indian.

The gay bar scene was at the time taking off in New York and San Francisco and much of the good time was fuelled by disco music. A perfect marriage. Disco music and clubbing presented a wide-open field.

Then one day the pair – Morali was gay and Belolo just a fellow traveller – walked past the 23rd Street YMCA, then a popular beat for cruising. "Jacques asked what they did in there," said Belolo. "We went inside, saw what was happening and started humming the song." Willis helped with the lyrics. Belolo and Morali recorded the track mostly in Philadelphia. "So much fun," Belolo told *MOJO* magazine in 1998. "We knew it was a hit straightaway. We had those goose bumps. We tested it at Studio 54 and it killed the room. Killed it."

The song was an instant smash hit. Most of the public didn't understand the gay imagery of the Village People, let alone the culture stereotypes of cruising, and those that did simply thought the joke too delicious to pass up. The characters of the Village People, as much as they represented gay culture, did so in a non-threatening way.

However, the outfits, the jokes – all would have meant nothing had the record itself not had a perfect groove. "I've been a DJ for more than ten years and I can't remember not playing it," Broadway Disco's Darren Reuben told *MOJO*. "Nor can I remember having to teach anyone the actions

Werewolves of London Warren Zevon

(LeRoy Marinell/Waddy Wachtel/Warren Zevon) ✳ Asylum ✳ 1978 ✳
Appears on: *Excitable Boy*

It was an odd irony that many of the really exceptional lyricists of the '70s only ever touched the charts with novelty songs. It happened to Loudon Wainwright III with 'Dead Skunk' and to Randy Newman with 'Short People' and it happened to Warren Zevon with 'Werewolves of London'. Zevon's tune had some interesting cover versions from the Grateful Dead and the

Flamin' Groovies and some notable appearances in films – not least of which was the film based on the song: *An American Werewolf in London*.

According to Zevon, the track was entirely Phil Everly's idea. Zevon had been part of the Everly Brothers' band. He and his wife were living with Everly, who suggested he write a dance song.

"So we were staying in Phil's guesthouse. And he said, 'I'm working on this solo album. Why don't you guys write a song for me? Write a dance song. Like, 'Werewolves of London''. That's exactly what he said. I just said, 'O-kaayy ...'

"I was over at Roy Marinell's house, and Roy started playing the figure. And Waddy walked in and said, 'What are you guys doing?' And I said, 'We're doing the 'Werewolves of London''. And Waddy, without batting an eye, said, 'You mean, "Aah-Ooh! Werewolves of London"?' And we said, 'That's right.' And he sat down and we wrote it in twenty minutes. But it was entirely instigated by Philip.

"I think most of the first verse was entirely Waddy. I thought it was pretty remarkable that he spontaneously delivered himself of this sort of Paul Simon-esque verse. No sooner had we told him we were 'doing the Werewolves of London', than he said, 'I saw a werewolf with a Chinese menu in his hand/ Walking through the streets of Soho in the rain'."

Guitarist Waddy Wachtel headed up an ensemble that recorded the song, including the Fleetwood Mac rhythm section of Mick Fleetwood and John McVie.

Zevon regarded the song as a tribute to one of his best friends. He describes it as, "one three-minute song that still seems funny, that was and is an homage to Hunter Thompson, I don't mind playing it. That's a fact that seems to elude most journalists because, I guess, it's so obvious. And it wouldn't occur to Hunter, because he's too much of a southern gentleman to consider the fact that he's been ripped off."

Gotta Serve Somebody Bob Dylan

(Bob Dylan) ❄ Columbia ❄ 1979 ❄ Appears on: *Slow Train Coming*

"Jesus put his hand on me. It was a physical thing," Bob Dylan told Karen Hughes in 1980, shortly after his conversion to Christianity. "I felt it. I felt it all over me. I felt my whole body tremble. The glory of the Lord knocked me down and picked me up. Being born again is a hard thing."

At least Dylan chose an easy selection of people to lead him into his next life. If you're going to make a gospel record you could choose a lot worse producers than Atlantic's Jerry Wexler and Muscle Shoals keyboard player Barry Beckett. Dylan augmented them with Mark Knopfler and Dire Straits drummer Pick Withers. On 'Gotta Serve Somebody' they find themselves a nice groove and then lay back in it as the singer/songwriter rains down the fire and brimstone. It's a long walk from "Don't follow leaders/Watch the parking meters" to "It may be the Devil or/It may be the Lord/But you're gonna have to serve somebody".

Although this song would win Dylan his first Grammy and top the charts, it was the beginning of Dylan's most wretched decade as he sought answers artistic and spiritual. It was the path that almost killed him.

"At every point in my life I've had to make decisions for what I believed in," he said. "Sometimes I've ended up hurting people that I've loved. Other times I've ended up loving people that I never thought I would.

"It's Him through you. 'He's alive', Paul said. 'I've been crucified with Christ, nevertheless I live. Yet not I but Christ who liveth in me.' See Christ is not some kind of figure down the road. We serve the living God."

Ever Fallen in Love   The Buzzcocks

(Pete Shelley) ✳ United Artists ✳ 1979 ✳ Appears on: *Love Bites*

'Ever Fallen in Love' is the definitive love song of the punk era. "It's the whole reason I started writing intelligent love songs," said Pete Shelley. "I realised that most of the times I fell in love I'd end up being hurt and I'd hurt other people as well.

"If I'm a modern romantic, it's because I'm trying to find out what modern romance is. It's not that I'm a new version of the old kind of romantic – I'm trying to find something new.

"All the old kinds of romance are self-destructive because they don't take account of realities."

Good Times   Chic

(Bernard Edwards/Nile Rodgers) ✳ Atlantic ✳ 1979 ✳ Appears on: *Risqué*

"During the late '70s we were going through the greatest recession since the depression," said Chic guitarist Nile Rodgers. "During the Great Depression they wrote 'Happy Days are Here Again', because they could drink booze again. Every lyric in the song was a throwback to depression-era songs. I even ripped off 'Happy days are here again/The time is right for making friends' (the opening verse of 'Good Times'). Then I took an Al Jolson song that said 'The stars are going to twinkle and shine this evening, 'bout a quarter to nine' – so I went 'let's get together, about a quarter to ten.'"

It's unlikely that the millions around the world who did the Bump and the Hustle to 'Good Times' in the late '70s in their white suits picked up on Rodgers' commentary. Rodgers grew up in a semi-bohemian atmosphere in New York. As a youth he hung with R&B combos and the Black Panther party. His songs may have been disco but they were informed by cultural politics.

"It was all about authenticity," the guitarist explained. "Being African Americans, because our skin is black, we've never been able to assimilate into culture the way other races have. During the Harlem Renaissance, people who were descendants of slaves came up with their own class system and royalty to beat this: 'Duke' Ellington, 'Count' Basie, 'King' Pleasure.

"We were paying tribute on *Risqué* to people who were oppressed and not having any voice apart from their music and their art. Everything had to fit the vibe. We got the Nicholas Brothers to dance on 'My Feet Keep Dancing'. We were saying 'thank you' to the aristocrats in the ghetto, and their form of dancing was tapping. We thought no-one would know why we did it, but we didn't care."

Chic's third album, *Risqué*, was one of the highpoints of 20th-century pop. Its lead single, 'Good Times', provided the bass line for the seminal rap track 'Rapper's Delight' by the Sugarhill Gang and was also appropriated for Queen's 'Another One Bites the Dust'. It was the riff that kept on giving.

'Good Times' was the sound of the era though, with its minimal, precise bass riff and its showy lyrics celebrating the superficial, kitschy wealth of the era. It was a fantasy as big as the groove.

London Calling The Clash

(Mick Jones/Joe Strummer) ❄ Epic ❄ 1979 ❄ Appears on: *London Calling*

You couldn't have a better war cry. Or a more accurate one. On this magnificent double album, the Clash landed the third Great British invasion. There was subterfuge – the album's cover rips off Elvis Presley's first LP – but mostly it was sheer force. And nowhere was that more evident than on the opening track.

'London Calling' is a call to arms – to resist oppression, to resist drugs and to confront the apathy and materialism and mostly the nostalgic state of pop culture. The riff is taken from the BBC World Service call sign. It's a song that takes on the terror of nuclear war (then a possibility) and thumbs its nose. For the past four years the punk rockers in London had been saying the same thing, preaching loudly to the converted. 'London Calling' reached out beyond that ghetto.

'London Calling' had none of the amateurish noise of punk rock. Strummer was here shaking off the pretensions of London at the time and acknowledging the fact that the music of his heart was part Woody Guthrie and part pub rock. His lyrics and vocals then came into sharper focus. Fortunately he had Mick Jones and Paul Simonon to lift the music out of his limitations.

The sound is a hybrid of roots rock and dub but there is nothing here to get in the way of the message. Simonon's deep, rich bass punctuates the marching beat – kept by Jones' and Strummer's guitars, which sound like weapons rather than instruments. By the third verse, 'London Calling' is a firefight.

Jones said of the sessions that producer Guy Stevens was "exhorting us to make it more, to increase the intensity, to lay the energy on." They succeeded in that.

Tusk Fleetwood Mac

(Lindsey Buckingham) ❊ Reprise ❊ 1979 ❊ Appears on: *Tusk*

Fleetwood Mac was stunned by it all in 1978. They were the biggest group in the world. Rich beyond their dreams. On expensive drugs. Thinking, "what do you do now?" Lindsey Buckingham – songwriter, singer, guitarist and producer – was the craziest of them all. He wanted to turn into Brian Wilson. Fleetwood Mac would record their songs and Buckingham would take them away and do whatever was necessary to make them little symphonies.

"He was a maniac," said engineer Ken Caillat. "The first day, I set the studio up as usual. Then he said, 'Turn every knob 180 degrees from where it is now and see what happens.' He'd tape microphones to the studio floor and get into a sort of push-up position to sing. Early on, he came in and he'd freaked out in the shower and cut off all his hair with nail scissors. He was stressed. And into sound destruction."

"*Tusk*, from my point of view, was an attempt to derail the machine that kicked in after *Rumours*," said Buckingham. He was dealing with his inner turmoil; his pop obsessions and the New Wave and punk groups coming through threatened to make Fleetwood Mac artistically obsolete.

The *Tusk* album is a large sprawling pop edifice that has been appreciated more as time has caught up with it. The title track, a euphemism, was the album's crowning glory.

'Tusk' was a riff worked up by Mick Fleetwood and Buckingham at sound checks. Producer Richard Dashut turned it into a twenty-second tape loop as the basis of the song. The riff was then recorded with 112 members of the University of Southern California Marching Band in Dodger Stadium. With the rhythm as the core of the song it only remained to embellish the track with snatches of melody and vocal.

One of the great singles of the '70s, 'Tusk' did throw the Mac audience a curve ball and delight pop connoisseurs. It also probably saved Fleetwood Mac from irrelevance.

"My thought was, let's subvert the norm," said Buckingham.

Anthrax Gang of Four

(Dave Allen/Hugo Burnham/Andrew Gill/Jon King) ❋ EMI ❋ 1979 ❋
Appears on: *Entertainment!*

Michael Hutchence described the Gang of Four as "art meets the devil via James Brown". The Gang of Four pretty much rewrote the book of rock with their debut album. It had the strident leftist politics of the best punk, but then deconstructed rock music to its core and added some funk. The album closed with 'Anthrax', a perfect example of a song that had a hook that was profoundly disturbing.

Andy Gill used his guitar like a machete, taking to the beat and slashing it to pieces. The music was best described as "itchy": scratching guitar over beats that came and went. There were ominous hollow spaces in the music and shouted epigrams. It was clearly a balancing act of startling proportions.

The funk and rock four-piece was the brainchild of singer Jon King and guitarist Gill, who saw the group as a vehicle for leftist political agitation. The title of this album suggests that entertainment was a tool of the ruling class but that it could also be used to subvert the dominant paradigm (as one said in those days).

"If you think of the first crop of punk stuff, it was all just tedious guitars cranked up through Marshalls," Andy Gill said recently. "In the wake of the Damned and the Sex Pistols, it was heavy metal but faster and not as well played.

"Gang of Four was radically different from that. The guitar was very staccato, very stripped down, very repetitive, loop-based. The drumming was basically funky but not through copying various icons of black music, more through simply deconstructing the nature of drumming and where you place the beats. It was like starting from ground zero with the drumming. Anything that sounded like rock drumming, I would change ...

"The same thing happened with the melodies. The tunes had vocals to it but it was very rhythm- and phrase-related. You could tell by listening to Gang of Four music that punk had happened. But it definitely wasn't punk music."

Gang of Four saw the construction of rock music in political terms.

Having had some success with an indie single, Gang of Four signed with EMI, a political contradiction perhaps. The upshot was that it gave them the opportunity to have free rein in the studio to develop the masterpiece that is *Entertainment*.

"It's a very accurate representation of where the band was at," said Gill. "You pretty much get the whole picture there. It's not all one thing. There's a variety of things going on. 'Anthrax' is a cool track. It was just this idea to have these very simple elements, like the guitar is just going to do feedback and the drums are going to play this weird pattern and they're just going to stop and they're just going to start. That's really its strength – to take the idea to a logical point and not get distracted and to avoid the frills and really just take it to its conclusion.

"I love its directness, simplicity, the minimalism of it, the powerfulness of it. The guitar is so simple and spare through the whole track and it rocks."

As Bono put it, "Andy Gill's chin is the very black hole of '90s music we should have all disappeared into ... if we had sense ... a dimple atop the body politic, a pimple on the arse of pop. A Gang of Four metal guru, a corporation of common sense, a smart bomb of text that had me 'at home feeling like a typist'."

Hindu Gods of Love   Lipstick Killers

(Lipstick Killers) ❋ Lost In Space ❋ 1979 ❋

Appears on: *Do the Pop: the Australian Garage-Rock Sound 1976–87*

Let's face it, most of what passes for rock & roll these days is rubbish. On the one hand you've got the emaciated bleating of fey little alternative rock boys whining in their bedsits about fuck knows what because they're not honest enough to say that they just can't get laid. On the other hand you've got the noise boys also full of self-important self-flagellation, but they're doing it "because it's the genre, man" and they've studied the form, and they can make the same cardboard cut-out records that the other guys make, their heads full of marketing plans, their best friends their lawyers. It's all so dull and self-serving. Where's the excitement, the flash, the dumb moves that haven't been suggested by their publicist? And the fake rebellion, the tatts and the piercings as badges of outsiderness? Please give us a break. Where's the spontaneity? When was the last time that you played a record and were *surprised*? Who was the last act that blew your mind wide open? Which was the last act whose sound didn't match their trousers? And don't start talking about punk rock. Jesus Christ, I'm glad the last punk revival is over now. That was the worst of it. People are still carrying on about the Sex Pistols and the wretched-looking Johnny Rotten as though they had anything to do with punk rock – of course, all the '90s punks picked up on the hair style and didn't get the point of punk at all. The Lipstick Killers' 'Hindu Gods of Love' may be the best Australian rock & roll single ever.

One Step Beyond Madness

(Cecil Campbell) ❋ Stiff ❋ 1979 ❋ Appears on: *One Step Beyond*

"Hey You! Don't watch that! Watch this!" exclaimed Chas Smash as he introduced the "heavy, heavy monster sound of Madness". The seven-piece ska band were the ideal antidote for the often self-righteousness of punk rock in Britain. When the pop world was locked into a battle for the soul of the nation, then came Madness. They had pork pie hats and mod suits and they kicked up a real storm. Like an Ealing comedy with a Jamaican soundtrack, Madness was unafraid to look stupid in their vaudeville poses and crazy dances. This was entertainment. The nutty boys were a breath of fresh air and they had more than a dozen chart-topping hits in four years.

Madness evolved from a ska party band into writing their own material, which turned out to be celebrations of suburban England, in the manner of Ray Davies but lower-brow. They were gentle celebrations of ordinariness. When asked to define the Madness credo, backup singer Smash said, "It's alright to be ordinary. Everything around you is beautiful". The sound gradually developed too as Mark Bedford added Motown influences and traditional British pop arrangements to the pumping ska beat in his tunes.

'One Step Beyond' was a ska classic as recorded by Prince Buster. Madness play the track like it was a party – pounding out the sax and pumping up the tempo. Here was where the blueprint for the nutty, nutty sound of Madness started.

The Ballad of Lucy Jordan Marianne Faithfull
(Shel Silverstein) ❋ Island ❋ 1979 ❋ Appears on: *Broken English*

In the '60s, Shel Silverstein was what was termed "a humorist". He drew amusing illustrations for *Playboy* magazine, wrote humorous poetry and sold folk and country songs. Silverstein's best known number was 'A Boy Named Sue', made famous by Johnny Cash. In the early '70s he was associated with the band Dr Hook for whom he penned a number of ribald lyrics and some hits ('Sylvia's Mother'). Silverstein gave them the out-of-character 'The Ballad of Lucy Jordan' for their 1973 album *Belly Up!*. Marianne Faithfull, who was a hopeless junkie at the time, liked the track enough to commit it to record herself.

In one of those strange show business coincidences, Silverstein contributed to the soundtrack on Tony Richardson's film *Ned Kelly*, in which Marianne Faithfull was cast. Upon arriving in Sydney to begin shooting, Faithfull took an overdose of drugs. This precipitated the end of her relationship with Mick Jagger and her quick descent into drug addiction. Faithfull had been a very delicate beauty with a similarly fragile voice and as her habit worsened (and the smoking and drinking) she tore her instrument apart.

By the time she returned to singing she was a very different kind of artist. The *Broken English* album actually sounds more German than British with the brooding synthesiser textures and dark atmospheres. The songs too have that cast – they possess little hope and they're big on coming to terms with the existential questions.

'The Ballad of Lucy Jordan' is about a housewife who realises at the age of thirty-seven that she will not have romance or excitement or exhilaration and so jumps off the roof of her house. Marianne Faithfull sings the song with the parched passion of someone who has stood on that roof and looked over the edge. However, there is the redemptive tone in her voice – she didn't do it and in that knowledge we can feel the warm wind in her hair.

The Nips Are Getting Bigger   Mental As Anything

(Martin Plaza) ✳ Regular ✳ 1979 ✳ Appears on: *Get Wet*

In the '60s, art schools were the crucibles of blues bands. Mental As Anything were the epitome of an art school band, given that they met at Alexander Mackie, Sydney's leading art school in the mid-'70s. Reg Mombassa (Chris O'Doherty), his brother Pete, Martin Plaza (nee Murphy), Wayne 'Bird' Delisle (David Twohill) and Andrew 'Greedy' Smith had the most humble of intentions – drinking beer pretty much – behind forming the group. Their Monday night stand at the Unicorn Hotel, however, soon became a hive of hipsters paying $0.80 to hear versions of Roy Orbison, the Monkees or Michael and the Messengers' 'Just Like Romeo and Juliet'. Gradually original songs began to appear in the set.

The Mentals' signature tune, 'The Nips Are Getting Bigger', was an ode to alcohol and heartbreak coloured by a primitive, cheesy organ sound and the Zen bass of Peter O'Doherty. The song is witty and true. A perfect power pop anthem and possibly the best 45 to come out of Australia in the entire decade.

The fledgling Regular Records hastily put the Mentals into the studio for their debut album, produced by regular co-supremo Cameron Allen. "The first two records that we made were Darlinghurst records," Martin Plaza said. "They were badly executed and not that well considered but with a naïve charm." He is being typically and unnecessarily modest.

Mental As Anything celebrated laziness and dissolute behaviour with songs like 'The Nips' and 'Business and Pleasure Don't Mix'. They had their finger on the pulse of the modern world as only a bunch of slack art students could.

Hey Hey, My My (into the Black)
Neil Young & Crazy Horse

(Neil Young/Jeff Blackburn) ✳ Reprise ✳ 1979 ✳ Appears on: *Rust Never Sleeps*

Punk rock really took the rock royalty by surprise. The '70s superstars were mostly dismissive of the snotty new generation, failing to recognise their younger selves or understand the attraction of feeling over technique. Neil Young was one of the few among his generation who embraced punk rock, because he'd been feeling that way himself.

He appreciated the attitude of the Sex Pistols and the wacky theories of Devo, from whom he took the concept of rust as it relates to cultural icons as well as the phrase "rust never sleeps".

"When you look back at the old bands, they're just not that funny," he said. "People want to have a good time. That's why the punk thing is so good and healthy. People who make fun of the established rock scene, like Devo and the Ramones, are much more vital to my ears than what's been happening in the last four or five years."

He said as much in 'Hey Hey, My My (into the Black)', where he had the temerity to compare Johnny Rotten with Elvis Presley: "The King is gone but he's not forgotten/This is a story about Johnny Rotten/It's better to burn out/'Cause rust never sleeps/The King is gone but he's not forgotten."

The companion song 'My My, Hey Hey' contains the line, "It's better to burn out than to fade away." Tragically Kurt Cobain used the phrase in his suicide note fifteen years later.

Young recorded the song once as an acoustic ballad and then a second time with the full-on attack of Crazy Horse. Everything here is subsumed by a massive drum beat from Ralph Molina (who claims he was imitating Queen). This is truly a great monument to the enduring power of rock.

Girlfriend's Boyfriend The Passengers

(Jeff Sullivan) ❋ Phantom ❋ 1979 ❋ Appears on: *It's Just That I Miss You*

'Girlfriend's Boyfriend' is the most perfect power pop record made in Australia. The Passengers lit up the Sydney rock scene for a nanosecond in 1978. The members of the five-piece band were mostly acolytes of Radio Birdman – singer Angie Pepper, guitarist Jeff Sullivan, drummer Alan Brown, keyboard player Steve Harris and bass player Jim Dickson.

The centrepiece of the Passengers' set was their version of the Shangri-Las 'Remember (Walkin' in the Sand)', which they delivered with all the fragile passion of the original but a strangely more dry and knowing modernity. Much of the credit goes to Pepper's arid, distant delivery that hit the emotional notes dead on.

'Girlfriend's Boyfriend' was the first song Sullivan wrote for this, his first band, and it's an absolutely perfect riff in a song about the perils of love, dressed up in the context of a '60s pop tune. Angie has an ocean of hurt and desire in her voice – tender and tough. The song just sparkles. It's the sound of love in first blush.

Dancing Barefoot Patti Smith Group

(Ivan Kral/Patti Smith) ✳ Arista ✳ 1979 ✳ Appears on: *Wave*

The fourth album from the Patti Smith Group marked the end of a journey. In 1975, high on Symbolist poetry and the Rolling Stones, she had kicked off her *Horses* album with a defiant challenge to Christ. She embraced her own theology of mystical rock & roll like Joan Of Arc with a Fender Duo-Sonic. By 1979, when she wrote most of the fourth album, Smith was devoting her life and beliefs to her husband-to-be Fred and to Jesus Christ.

'Dancing Barefoot' is a song that brings together mysticism and her subservient love for Fred together. It's a song about submission in the same way that the Sufis regard their twirling dance as a submission to the Divine.

The melody of 'Dancing Barefoot' (which seems to owe a debt to the Go-Betweens' 'Karen') has a vertiginous quality; a modal meditation on love in all its forms.

Todd Rundgren (whose early work Patti Smith had reviewed in the pages of *Rolling Stone*) produced the album. It's probably the best recording the group made.

"I thought it might be the last album I did," she said. "I felt it was time for me to evolve as a human being. I hadn't ever really planned to make records. I came to that organically, and I felt that I had really expressed everything that I knew how to express. So I had a lot of thoughts doing that record: both joyful thoughts and ...

"Todd's an old friend of mine, I thought that it would be nice to work with a friend and also he's a great musician and I knew that he would contribute to the musical sense of the record. He was very good with using keyboards, he was a pianist himself and a lot of those songs evolved around that. It was not an easy record to make and Todd works very quickly – I work quickly too but not as quickly as Todd, but I think the sound of that record is beautiful."

Comfortably Numb Pink Floyd

(David Gilmore/Roger Waters) ✳ EMI ✳ 1979 ✳ Appears on: *The Wall*

Pretty much the last significant gasp from Pink Floyd, *The Wall* was, like so much of Floyd's work, on the brink of insanity. Roger Waters conceived the album in an epiphany of self-hatred and contempt for his audience while on stage. He spat on a fan. Then this huge double album was gradually vomited out. The tale of a rock star whose fame had sent him mad is also an essay on alienation.

Waters had his demons – troubled childhood, father who died in WWII – and he thought the rest of the group were not much better. He fired keyboard player Rick Wright during the sessions for this album and producer Bob Ezrin owed his job to an ability to keep some peace between Waters and guitarist Dave Gilmore.

Insanity had dogged the band since it lost its founder, Syd Barrett, but Waters also empathised. "On the couple of occasions in my life where I have felt myself approaching mental breakdown it has felt like delirium," he said.

As the group was facing bankruptcy at the time, there was a pressing need for a new album, so whoever had the idea was bound to get a green light.

"But there were things about it where I thought, 'Oh no, here we go again – it's all about the war, about his mother, about his father being lost.' I'd hoped he could get through all this and eventually he could deal with other stuff, but he had a fixation," keyboard player Rick Wright told MOJO. "Every song was written in the same tempo, same key, same everything. Possibly if we were not in this financial situation we might have said, 'We don't like these songs,' and things might have been different. But Roger has this material, Dave and I didn't have any, so we'll do it."

"Initially I had two images – of building a wall across the stage, and of the sadomasochistic relationship between audience and band, the idea of an audience being bombed and the ones being blown to pieces applauding the loudest because they're the centre of action, even as victims," said Waters. "There is something macabre and a bit worrying about that relationship – that we will provide a PA system so loud that it can damage you and that you will fight to sit right in front of it so you can be damaged as much as possible – which is where the idea of Pink metamorphosed into a Nazi demagogue began to generate from."

Ezrin constructed a scenario from the songs at the beginning of the project around which the album could be built. As part of the process Gilmore also contributed ideas while the others sat on the sidelines.

The album's centrepiece is the last real collaboration between Gilmore and Waters: 'Comfortably Numb'.

"Things like 'Comfortably Numb' are really the last embers of Roger and my ability to work collaboratively together – my music, his words," Gilmore told MOJO. "I had the basic part of the music done. I gave Roger the bits of music, he wrote some words, he came in and said, 'I want to sing this line here, can we extend this by so many bars so I can do that,' so I said, 'OK, I'll put something in there.'"

"'Comfortably Numb' started off as a demo of Dave's – a piece in D with a lovely, soaring chorus and a very moody verse," said Ezrin. "At first Roger had not planned to include any of Dave's material but we had things that needed filling in. I fought for this song and insisted that Roger work on it. My recollection is that he did so grudgingly, but he did it. He came back with this spoken-word verse and a lyric in the chorus that to me still stands out as one of the greatest ever written. The marriage of that lyric and Dave's melodies and emotionally spectacular solo – every time I hear that song I get goosebumps."

Chuck E's in Love   Rickie Lee Jones

(Rickie Lee Jones) ✳ Warner Bros. ✳ 1979 ✳ Appears on: *Rickie Lee Jones*

Discovered by Little Feat's Lowell George, Rickie Lee Jones was not much more than a kid when she wrote 'Chuck E's in Love' for the bass player Chuck E Weiss. The song had a smoky, swinging jazz feel with a touch of R&B. Rickie Lee Jones sounded like a beatnik waif. "I was pretty much just winging it," she told Andy Gill. "Looking to the next day to see if you would have money for gas, looking to the next week to see if you would get a job; always thinking about what you have to do to escape poverty, to create art that is going to catch the world on fire. You have to live in the moment totally to create a moment that is compelling, and though it may be kind of bohemian, it does make the earth of your soul richer."

Jones was then a little under the wing of Los Angeles hipsters such as her ex-boyfriend Tom Waits. Her songs, like his, were populated by the characters of the American underbelly, and Jones had seen plenty of that in her time. Her mother was a waitress, her father a waiter and her grandfather a vaudevillian. They had moved a lot through her childhood and this transitory lifestyle had made Jones both strong and a little lonely. There's an affection in Jones' singing – celebrating a friend's romance, rather than writing about her own love life. That vulnerability comes through on this track but it's subsumed by the playfulness of the lyric – and Chuck E's warm, rich bass playing.

A Message to You Rudy   The Specials

(Lee 'Scratch' Perry/Lee Thompson) ✳ 2 Tone ✳ 1979 ✳ Appears on: *The Specials*

With punk rock in full flight in the UK, reviving the past glories of the early rock & roll years, it was only a matter of time before the mods and their musical accessory, ska, returned also. Ska (with its variations of blue beat and rock-steady) is a limited style of Jamaican music, which was popular for a couple of years before it evolved into reggae. It fell to keyboardist Jerry Dammers to start the ska revival with his outfit, the Specials. They came properly accessorised with the tight suits and the small hats, the scooters and the attitude. Their sworn enemies were the skinheads who similarly recreated the look and racist ideology of the original skins ten years earlier. Unfortunately the skins too had loved ska so, right from the start, the music came with its own tension.

England has always been a land of subcultures. Tribes of skinheads, mods, teddy boys and rastas had existed since the '60s. After punk rock and its new tribes arrived under a media spotlight, culture wars erupted, sometimes violently. Jerry Dammers well understood British pop culture. He created a new tribe – the modern rude boy – and the Specials came not just with a sound but an ideology. Dammers also formed his own label, 2 Tone, and developed logos and design ideas to brand both band and label. Other groups – notably Madness and The Beat – sprung up in The Specials' wake. Both went on to significant success over the next decade.

Ska drew out the pus on the simpering wound of racism that existed in the UK at the time. The Specials were proudly multi-racial and they talked it like they walked it. They were a ferocious live band with two singers and a horn section; the insistent beat of ska hopped up a few notches in honour of the punk years. Their music was less laid-back, more passionate and darker than classic ska. There was a real intensity to the Specials that matched the agit-rock of the Clash and Elvis Costello. 'A Message to You Rudy' was their second single and, produced by Elvis Costello, it had a raw power missing from Dandy Livingstone's rock-steady original

Goodbye Girl Squeeze

(Chris Difford/Glenn Tillbrook) ☀ A&M ☀ 1979 ☀ Appears on: *Cool for Cats*

Chris Difford and Glenn Tillbrook, the songwriting team behind Squeeze, are regularly compared with Lennon and McCartney, Leiber and Stoller and any manner of songwriting couples. The comparisons are more relevant to the structure of the partnership than to its output. Difford wrote the lyric and Tillbrook the music and together, at their best, they captured that whimsical Bristishness – their songs were often populated by recognisable everyday English people just trying to make the best of things. In short, Squeeze was perfect at kitchen-sink drama.

Difford claimed Bob Dylan as a formative influence. "I just loved the way he could create an imaginary story that would be right there in your mind as you're listening to the song," he said. "'Lily, Rosemary and the Jack of Hearts' for me, is the most fantastic lyric for that particular scene within your mind. Where you can play the track and you can see the film running by. And I thought I'd like to be able to do that sort of thing, to be able to create a mini film in someone's head."

His writing blossomed on *Cool for Cats*, Squeeze's second album. So many of the songs had beautiful vignettes. The best of them is 'Goodbye Girl', a story of a bloke who scores a one-night stand and wakes up with his wallet gone and some apologising to do.

Difford captures so many shades and particulars in the space of this short narrative – the excitement of picking up a girl, the abandon of a night on the turps, the terrible consequences for his relationship when he returns home, the betrayals. It's all there in that moment of waking and realising the terrible truth of the daylight. There's a bittersweet quality to the song too, as the narrator distills the pureness of the passion in a one-night stand.

Squeeze have many such moments, including 'Black Coffee in Bed', 'Up the Junction' and 'Tempted', but none has quite the quality of this track.

Life During Wartime   Talking Heads

(David Byrne) ❋ Sire ❋ 1979 ❋ Appears on: *Fear of Music*

"We were under a lot of stress and pressure so [the title] *Fear of Music* seemed perfect," said bass player Tina Weymouth of the Talking Heads' third album. The group developed very fast from its minimalist garage folk beginnings at CBGB. Within two years they had moved on from itchy rock to a new kind of funk. Producer Brian Eno had encouraged the group to experiment more and so for the third album they began with a blank slate.

The first two albums were written before the group had a recording deal. For the third they started with bass and drum grooves that were worked into songs and then recorded over two days, after which Byrne added his lyrics and the songs were polished.

'Life During Wartime' is a particularly disturbing song, sung from the point of view of a character trying to survive in the middle of a war zone. The singer is saying that "this ain't no party/this ain't no disco" as he sorts through the rubble. It's a song that mocks the nightclub lifestyle and the political grandstanding of rock stars who sing about wars and foreign affairs; it's also a perspective that's probably true for thousands of people all over the Third World.

The legacy of Talking Heads will be the way that they brought a particular style of funk to white rock and no-one has dug that groove better.

"I think Jerry puts it best," said Weymouth. "When we were discussing this record ... Brian wanted to say it was his record, David wanted to say it was his record. They both thought it was the greatest venture of their lives. But Jerry said, 'No, we didn't all have the same idea. We all came in with different ideas of what we were going to do. It was the collective influences that created the result.' No-one could put an individual claim to it.

"Plus, Eno had always said that he wanted to go into the studio cold with us, without any material, so that we could learn the way he makes albums, simple things layer upon layer. It's really not novel at all, it's just the old idea of jamming, one key, no chord changes ... and everybody played and everybody produced. The songs were written by the five of us."

Many of the phrases from 'Life During Wartime' have entered the vernacular and the song is still as fresh as its scenario is perennial.

The Eighties

Wide Open Road
The Triffids

I Hear Motion
The Models

Burn for You
INXS

Saturday Night
Cold Chisel

No Second Prize
Jimmy Barnes

A Touch of Paradise
John Farnham

Blue Sky Day
Died Pretty

Everything I've Got Belongs to You
Ed Kuepper

Trust Me
I'm Talking

Still Hanging 'Round
Hunters & Collectors

Trust
Tall Tales and True

If You Leave
Hummingbirds

Ocean Liner
Lighthouse Keepers

Shivers
Boys Next Door

Live it Up
Mental As Anything

Blackfella/Whitefella
Warumpi Band

From My Eyes
No Fixed Address

**When Love Comes Back
to Haunt You**
Stephen Cummings

Don't Need Love
Johnny Diesel & The Injectors

Electric Lash
The Church

Into Temptation
Crowded House

Fraction Too Much Friction
Tim Finn

To Her Door
Paul Kelly & the Coloured Girls

Taxi Mary
Jo Jo Zep

I Want You Back
Hoodoo Gurus

Daughters of the Northern Coast
Australian Crawl

Warakurna
Midnight Oil

Kitchen Man
The Reels

Too Hot to Move
The Takeaways

Average Inadequacy
Machinations

You Shook Me All Night Long AC/DC

(Brian Johnson/Malcolm Young/Angus Young) ❊ Alberts ❊ 1980 ❊
Appears on: *Back in Black*

When Bon Scott died of misadventure in February 1980, the Young brothers, Malcolm and Angus, resolved that AC/DC wasn't going to stop there. The group was by then a success in Europe and Australia and poised to crack the American market. Perhaps a fresh start was required anyway. Bon Scott was possibly too raunchy and wild for the United States. New singer Brian Johnson had the voice to carry the music but no discernible personality. Let alone an attitude.

'You Shook Me All Night Long' was in many ways a classic AC/DC sound – big solid riffing guitars without too much subtlety. The group was now working with Robert 'Mutt' Lange, the most polished and powerful metal producer in the history of rock. He took the rough diamond band and buffed them to perfection. There's still enough grunt in the tune to satisfy the black-shirted heavy metal kids, there's enough swing to know that the Youngs have heard their share of Chess blues, but it's also clean and large enough to fit into commercial radio.

The lyrics, like classic AC/DC, were naughty and sexual. However, 'You Shook Me' has none of the sleaze of earlier AC/DC. It's not overly sexist, it's not demeaning to anyone and there's nothing really R-rated.

This was the new AC/DC and *Back in Black* became one of the biggest selling records of all time, and one of the most loved.

The Tide Is High Blondie

(John Holt) ❊ Chrysalis ❊ 1980 ❊ Appears on: *Autoamerican*

Originally recorded as a reggae ballad by the Paragons, Blondie added their own pop interpretation including a horn section and the superlative feel of drummer Clem Burke. Mike Chapman, who had produced the group's breakthrough, was again behind the board.

Guitarist Chris Stein recalls the sessions as intense, writing in the group's fan club newsletter, "Chapman hunches over the console into the wee hours. People are pressed flat against the back wall by his playback volume. Gallons of Jose Cuervo Gold are consumed ... Finally, the basic tracks wind down, and we move a block down the Strip to Studio B. The move marks the home stretch; the vocals, overdubs and finally the orchestral horns and what have you. Here is Mike Chapman's little magic room. In days gone by, these burlap walls saw the likes of the Righteous Brothers, Jan & Dean, the Beach Boys ... Now the control room is filled with a gigantic blue console that's hooked up to computers, satellites and atomic submarines off the coast of Maine. Here the songs get the 'chrome' put on."

'The Tide Is High' retained its reggae groove, although with Deborah Harry singing, it had a kind of ironic distance. The *Autoamerican* album saw the group playing with roots styles – including 'Rapture', the first rap track recorded by a white band.

According to engineer Lenise Bent, "Magical things did happen; there was room for those spontaneous-combustion kinds of things."

Shivers The Boys Next Door

(Rowland Howard) ❋ White ❋ 1980 ❋ Appears on: *Door Door*

The Boys Next Door were pimply schoolboys high on art rock in the late '70s. With the nascent talents of Nick Cave and Mick Harvey still very wet behind the ears, it was apparent early on that something was happening here. Mostly it was Cave's ability to find the limit and push everything to it. As time went on the envelope just got bigger. The Boys Next Door were swept up in a quick frenzy by White Records and put into the studio with Greg Macainsh, who had been an enfant terrible only eight years before but was now a grumpy old man. With engineer Tony Cohen, the Boys Next Door and Greg Macainsh tried to find common ground. Halfway through the making of the record Rowland Howard, guitarist for the Young Charlatans, joined and brought some of his songs.

'Shivers' was a haunting ballad, a teenage mediation on narcissism, vanity, cruelty and beauty that was built around Howard's guitar figure – a style that had evolved from Robert Fripp.

'Shivers' was a powerful piece of songwriting. Majestic, sad pop music. Naturally and rightly, the Boys Next Door repudiated the song almost immediately and moved on to harsher ground. Despite their best endeavours to bury the track, it has become a classic.

Stolen Car Bruce Springsteen & the E Street Band

(Bruce Springsteen) ❋ Columbia ❋ 1980 ❋ Appears on: *The River*

Cars had been a sustaining metaphor for Bruce Springsteen since the early days. By 1980, all the cars on *The River* were either wrecked or stolen; their only destination was to take the singer back to see his faded dreams.

In 'Stolen Car' the character rides the streets at night in a stolen car in the hope, which is never satisfied, of being arrested in order to prove that he exists. It's perhaps the most existential piece of writing in rock. If Kafka had been a hot rod enthusiast, this is what *The Castle* would have been.

According to Springsteen, "'Stolen Car' was the predecessor for a good deal of the music I'd be writing in the future. It was inner-directed, psychological; this was the character whose progress I'd soon be following on *Tunnel of Love*. He was the archetype for the male role in my later songs about men and women."

The music here is so quiet. It's minimal and held back like the early hours in which the car drives. The keyboards are like a fog on the road and the voice is just drifting in the murk, barely alive.

It was the single 'Holiday', a much more club-oriented track produced by Madonna's boyfriend and DJ Jellybean Benitez, that became a breakout hit. Suddenly Madonna was on her way, and she never lost control again.

"I think it stands up well," she said of her debut album. "It just took a long time for people to pay attention to me – and I thank God they did."

I Can't Stand Up for Falling Down
Elvis Costello & the Attractions

(H Banks/A Jones) ❋ 1980 ❋ Radar ❋ Appears on: *Get Happy!!*

Elvis Costello's fourth album featured a frantic, almost berserk embrace of soul music. The centrepiece is this cover of a Sam & Dave track that positively sweats cocaine.

"Speaking quite frankly, I'm amazed that no-one at the time exposed the fact that I was into almost totally wrecking myself on drink and chemicals for … well, three years virtually non-stop," Costello told journalist Nick Kent. "I was into a daily thing of artificial stimulation – drinking myself into a stupor, fuelling myself on cocaine, but no-one suspected a thing.

"But it got carried away and in the process I became falsely 'enigmatic', if you like, and very contrary. At the same time I don't want this to sound schizophrenic because I'm not, and the person who wrote those songs has always been me. Plus I was very, very bitter and angry and … well, the first year I played with the Attractions I was performing live almost exclusively on this level of anger and just incredible nervous energy. And then it got to that stage where I would be functioning on mental or, y'know, 'artificial' energy. But I found that as I continued, it became automatically a thing of me never letting my guard down."

Costello reaped the whirlwind. Phenomenal success in the press and in the charts, at least in the UK, played significantly with his head – the former geek with poor social skills and low self-esteem was overnight the voice of a generation. As well as the drugs, Costello attracted some of the world's most beautiful women. Not surprisingly, his marriage collapsed.

When he sang 'I Can't Stand Up for Falling Down' it was pretty much the simple truth.

"*Get Happy!!* was made under extreme self-inflicted emotional stress," he said. "It was a very extreme record from the point of view of the condition that I and the rest of the band were in. The aftermath of what happened in America and just generally very emotional, you know, shattered nerves. Too much drinking. That's why it sounds unfinished – because it's about all we were capable of doing."

That's Entertainment The Jam

(Paul Weller) ❋ Polydor ❋ 1980 ❋ Appears on: *Sound Affects*

Paul Weller was never bashful about his reverence for the Kinks' Ray Davies. According to the Jam's singer/songwriter, "He was the only person writing in that way at the time – writing about basic, ordinary life. And it's very pure English language that he uses – there are never any Americanisms in it." Weller achieved his own 'Waterloo Sunset' with a song that he claims he knocked off in just ten minutes after returning from the pub.

'That's Entertainment' has the wonderful, rich and dreamy melody of classic Kinks. However, where Davies saw an urban pastorale of the working classes going about their daily business in a divine and sunny Britannia, untroubled about the future or the world, Weller's London was entirely different. It starts with "A police car and a screaming siren/A pneumatic drill and ripped up concrete/A baby waiting and stray dog howling" and gets more bleak from there. The refrain "That's entertainment" is the key to the track, prefiguring the media overload that was to come in the next decade, the pornography of misery churned out on cable news channels so that the audience is eventually immune to the pain on the screen. Weller and the Jam captured the darkness, paranoia and disappointment of the modern city.

The singer and songwriter based the lyric on a poem, 'Entertainment', which he had previously published. The music was a step forward for the group, which three years earlier had pounded out lightning fast punk rock. 'That's Entertainment' was built around a wall of acoustic guitar that allowed the melody room to flow. The *Sound Affects* album took all of three months in the studio – about three times the length of any previous albums – and it shows. Reportedly the Jam's inspirations for these sessions were the Beatles' *Revolver* and Michael Jackson's *Off the Wall*.

'That's Entertainment' is Paul Weller's masterpiece, as powerful today as when it was recorded in the summer of 1980.

Biko Peter Gabriel

(Peter Gabriel) ❊ Charisma ❊ 1980 ❊ Appears on: *Peter Gabriel*

Steve Biko was a black South African who was tortured and killed for his anti-apartheid activism. His story provoked Peter Gabriel to pen a song that added to the international pressure on South Africa to end its apartheid policy.

"It's a white, middle-class, ex-public schoolboy, domesticated, English person observing his own reactions from afar," Gabriel said. "It seemed impossible to me that the South Africans had let him be killed when there had been so much international publicity about his imprisonment. He was very intelligent, well reasoned and not full of hate. His writings seemed very solid in a way that polarised politics often doesn't."

The simple potency of the track made it an international hit and helped make Biko a martyr of the anti-apartheid movement and to focus attention on the South African regime. This attention, ignited partly by Gabriel, ran through most of the rest of the decade – leading to films like *Cry Freedom* and *Biko* – until the final release of Nelson Mandela and the fall of the regime.

"I was quite uncertain about getting engaged in a political song," Gabriel said. "I'd never directly taken on an issue in that way. I just tried some ideas, and I felt the spine tingling. That to me is the musician's rubber stamp."

Games Without Frontiers Peter Gabriel

(Peter Gabriel) ❋ Charisma ❋ 1980 ❋ Appears on: *Peter Gabriel (3)*

Peter Gabriel's third, eponymous solo album cemented his career as an artist of the first rank. The project was off to a difficult start, however, when Atlantic deemed the album uncommercial and dropped Gabriel. "I gather Ahmet Ertegun, the chairman, thought it was quite arty but the A&R department told him it was undesirable, too esoteric," he told Phil Sutcliff in 1980. "An Atlantic guy who came over to hear us in the studio asked me to make one song sound more like the Doobie Brothers."

Gabriel was not heading anywhere near Doobie Brothers territory. Certainly not with guest performers such as Paul Weller, Tony Levin, Robert Fripp and Kate Bush. These were the crème of British art rock and the album's strength is that tension between the outré and Gabriel's strong melodic and rhythmic instincts.

Gabriel has said that this was "the album on which I discovered a style." Certainly the single 'Jeux Sans Frontières' ('Games Without Frontiers') was the beginning of a new phase for Gabriel.

Brass in Pocket The Pretenders

(James Honeyman-Scott/Chrissie Hynde) ❋ Real/Sire ❋ 1980 ❋
Appears on: *The Pretenders*

"I have no illusions," Chrissie Hynde told the NME's Chris Salewicz shortly after the release of The Pretenders' eponymous debut. "I know how low the standards are. I'm aware of why things happen in the music business. I know why the album did so well; we got our timing right.

"The market was wide open for a band like ours with a girl vocalist and solid, simple, straight ahead rock songs. It sounds perfect on the radio, too, which is a large reason why it happened in America. And that is the exact reason why it sold 300,000 copies in California alone. I mean, why should we sell records there? Because, quite simply, it doesn't jar when it's played next to Foreigner or Styx.

"That said, though, I hated 'Brass in Pocket' with a vengeance. Fuckin' Ada. I hated it so much that if I was in Woolworth's and they started playing it I'd have to run out of the store."

The Pretenders were absolutely the right band at the right time. Their rightness was largely due to Hynde.

Originally from Akron, Ohio, Hynde was in London for the birth of British punk – she worked at Malcolm McLaren's Sex Shop, taught guitar to Johnny Rotten, palled around with the Clash's Mick Jones and the superstar rock journalist Nick Kent.

"I'd arrived in England naïvely thinking that I'd bump into Marc Bolan or Jeff Beck on every street corner," she said. "All I had was a coupla hundred dollars and three albums by Iggy and Lou Reed, and of course it was instant disillusion – I was living in these really cheap, skuzzy hotels, having to sell leather handbags in one of those sucker tourist markets on Oxford Street and modelling at St Martin's School of Art. And, like, no-one knew what the hell I was talking about when I mentioned the Stooges or Lou Reed."

Once Hynde had her band together – James Honeyman-Scott on guitar, Pete Farndon on bass and drummer Martin Chambers – Nick Lowe spent a day in the studio recording a single. The A-side, a cover of an obscure Kinks song, 'Stop Your Sobbing', was an instant hit.

Hynde's songs were carefully observed vignettes of life made spectacular by Honeyman-Scott's guitars and Hynde's elegantly detached delivery. Hynde, sometimes bitchy, erotic or wistful, told it like it was in the spirit of punk but without the alienated trappings.

The album cruised from one hook to another. Producer Chris Thomas specialised in taking melodic garage bands (including the Sex Pistols) and casting their vignettes as epics. Under pressure to follow up the hits – each of the first three Pretenders 45s was a smash hit – Hynde's entire repertoire went onto the record. Meanwhile the group was finding its feet after fewer than a dozen shows. All these elements cooked *The Pretenders* into one of the best pop albums of all time.

The Pretenders had the perfect sound – they had the '60s pop moves and the punk rock credibility but unlike most other punk groups they could play. Honeyman-Scott's guitar parts bristled with ideas – sparkling melodic touches that complemented Hynde's prickly lyrics. Chambers and Farndon put a soulful bedrock under Hynde whether she was bitter or wistful – as is the case with 'Brass in Pocket', which secured their place at the top of the tree.

"We're all on £50 a week," she said when quizzed about her instant stardom. "I've got to leave my flat tomorrow and move in with a friend, I've got no bank account, no publisher and no management – at least nothing signed, it's all on a trust basis. I'm not really that concerned with whether I'm being ripped off. I'm in too much of a fizzy, I'm too busy writing songs."

When You Were Mine Prince

(Prince) ❊ Warner Bros. ❊ 1980 ❊ Appears on: *Dirty Mind*

"Prince's third album for Warner Bros. continues his safari through the jungle of teenage lust and heavy breathing." (*Minneapolis Tribune*, 7 November 1980.)

Prince's second album had sold over a million copies, mostly to a black audience. For his third, *Dirty Mind*, Prince was determined to cross over. He was seen as an oversexed junior Rick James who couldn't keep his clothes on. Few pundits could see the influence that Prince would have on music after this.

There was some curiosity value in the fact that this man with only one name wrote, recorded and produced almost every note on his records, and had been doing so since his teens. Beyond the curiosity value though, Prince was clearly imparting a singular vision more strongly than most.

Sure Prince wrote about sex – oral pleasure, incest, multiple partners. Prince pushed the boundaries. According to keyboard player Matt Fink, "That really was him at the time. He was rejoicing in his own sexuality. He was saying 'Sex is a reality. Don't be afraid of it.'"

Songs like 'When You Were Mine', however, were not only sexually adventurous, but also sonically so. The production borrowed from Curtis Mayfield and New Wave pop but had, at its core, a hook that couldn't be beat.

"He knew he was entering some hot soup. Anytime you do when you're pushing the envelope, you know?" said drummer Bobby Z. "He really found himself with that album. I think he wrote better songs. And the roughness of it gave it an edge – it was a little more garage sounding."

The cover – a stark black-and-white photo of Prince against bed springs, wearing a military outfit over nothing more than his underwear – is a statement of intent.

"Of course it was a risky record," co-manager Bob Cavallo said. "Some thought we were losing our minds."

Another One Bites the Dust Queen

(John Deacon) ❊ EMI ❊ 1980 ❊ Appears on: *The Game*

"We did hate each other too for a while," said Queen guitarist Brian May. "Recording *Jazz* and those albums we did in Munich, *The Game* and *The Works*, we got very angry with each other. I left the group a couple of times, just for the day, you know. I'm off and I'm not coming back! We've all done that. You end up quibbling over one note." Apparently one major bone of contention between bassist John Deacon and drummer Roger Taylor was a tune based around a very simple funk bass line. According again to May, "Roger, at the time, certainly felt that it wasn't rock & roll and was quite angry at the way it was going. And Freddie said, 'Darling, leave it to me. I believe in this'. John had written the song. But it took Freddie's support to make it happen."

Mercury clearly understood that Queen's horizons could extend beyond operatic pop and hard rock. 'Another One Bites the Dust' took them into funk and gave them a crossover hit on all radio formats in America. The track sold three million copies.

The funk/hard-rock crossover was an important step in building the bridge between rock and R&B – swinging rock songs and toughening up R&B. The 'Dust' riff was picked up by Grandmaster Flash for his 'Adventures on the Wheels of Steel' and became one of the first and most recognisable break beats in rap.

I Got You Split Enz

(Neil Finn) ✳ 1980 ✳ Mushroom ✳ Appears on: *True Colours*

Tim Finn had led Split Enz through five years of the storm and tempest of art rock and pop music. Things were looking grim until his little brother Neil popped out with a very simple pop song that had a slightly menacing melody.

"Tim and I were living in a house in Sydney, in Rose Bay, and we were throwing titles at each other every day, in readiness for recording *True Colours*," said Neil. "He gave me 'I Got You'. I think he did anyway. I wrote the verse and the chorus actually as it is, but in my mind the chorus was always too corny and I'd have to come back and try and change it and fix it up. Which is probably one of the reasons why it's a smash hit single, it was because it was corny. I felt intimidated by its directness, but as soon as the band played it, I realised it had something very strong about it. But on the day, I remember liking the verse but thinking the chorus sucked."

Split Enz had twisted time signatures into pretzels for some years. Faced with this naïve tune they arranged it as plainly as possible yet still there's a sense of dark tension in the verses, which is released with the impossibly catchy hook. On the back of this track Split Enz became a pop band with a twist and went on to sell over a million albums. This song remains one of the enduring pop songs of the decade.

As for the perfectly paced guitar riff that opens the track? "That was the only one I knew how to play at the time," Neil admitted. "That was me learning how to play electric guitar."

Once in a Lifetime Talking Heads

(David Byrne/Brian Eno/Chris Frantz/Jerry Harrison/Tina Weymouth) ❊ Sire ❊ 1980 ❊
Appears on: *Remain in Light*

Remain in Light was part of Talking Heads' African period. Head chief David Byrne and producer Brian Eno had already made an album of found sounds and African rhythms. The band's fourth album expanded on that, putting enormous weight on the polyrhythms while getting more esoteric in the lyric.

They were also listening to a lot of funk and to the just then breaking rap and hip-hop scene. Three years earlier they had been a preppy garage art rock band playing CBGB. By the time of *Remain in Light* they were ready to turn into a funk machine.

On 'Once in a Lifetime' Byrne piles on all his obsessions. The words were taken in part from an evangelist radio broadcast. The polyrhythms that underscored the track were based on African drumming and the character who sings the song is a white-bread suburban guy trapped in a metaphysical dream about his own life, as though he had been transported from Ghana to Connecticut.

"We weren't trying to do African music," said Byrne. "We were trying to use some of the things we thought we'd learn from that in making a newer version of our own music. I don't think it's like putting on a new set of clothes and 'here we are, it's all new'. It's saying, 'This might be a clearer version of what we've been trying to do anyway' – or a more refined version."

I Will Follow U2

(Bono/Adam Clayton/The Edge/Larry Mullen Jr) ❊ Island ❊ 1980 ❊ Appears on: *Boy*

On U2's first American tour they played 'I Will Follow' twice in their set because they didn't have enough songs. The Irish group's first single and the opening track of *Boy*, their first album, was a strong if inchoate debut. What is immediately apparent is the way that drummer Larry Mullen Jr and bass player Adam Clayton have essentially taken their patterns from the Factory sound of Joy Division and given them a sense of uplift rather than doom. The

Edge's spiky guitar owes a direct lineage to Tom Verlaine of Television. U2 adopted the innovations of the first wave of punk rock and adapted them. Bearing in mind that their level of musicianship wasn't of the highest order.

Bono said that the song was a response to his childhood – his lack of contact with his father and his mother's death, which occurred when he was fourteen.

"To be honest, I don't remember that much about my mother," he told *Rolling Stone*'s David Breskin in 1987. "I forget what she looks like. I was fourteen or fifteen when she died, but I don't remember. I wasn't close to my mother or father. And that's why, when it all went wrong – when my mother died – I felt a real resentment, because I actually had never got a chance … to feel that unconditional love a mother has for a child. There was a feeling of that house pulled down on top of me, because after the death of my mother that house was no longer a home – it was just a house. That's what 'I Will Follow' is about. It's a little sketch about that unconditional love a mother has for a child: 'If you walk away, walk away I will follow', and 'I was on the outside when you said you needed me/I was looking at myself I was blind I could not see'. It's a really chronic lyric."

Turning that pain into an epic is what made U2 great.

King Ink The Birthday Party

(Nick Cave) ❋ Missing Link ❋ 1981 ❋ Appears on: *Prayers on Fire*

The Birthday Party pulled down the house of rock & roll, made a pyre and watched it burn. Their sound was huge and dark with the spastic beats of Mick Harvey counterpointing the massive bass rumble from Tracey Pew and the elliptical, electrical fragments from Rowland Howard's earring scratching guitar. Over which Nick Cave declaimed rather than sang tales of fire and brimstone as if his guts were burning.

It reflected on the one hand their love of aggressive anarchic music from the likes of the Pop Group and Suicide, while reacting against the self-importance of the likes of Echo and the Bunnymen.

The Birthday Party had grown up playing the Australian pub scene in the wake of the Saints and Radio Birdman. By contrast they found the British music scene to be too genteel.

"Compared to the gigs in Australia, especially in Sydney, they're nothing," Cave told the *NME*. "In Australia, you really feel you're turning decent people into monsters. But look, we're not setting ourselves up as some kind of demonic force, it's just that things are generally more successful when they become blind and unconscious, when you feel anything could happen.

"Coming to London has been one of the most disillusioning experiences of my life, partly for a lot of obvious reasons, like everything closing down at eleven o'clock, but more important, because when we came here we thought here at least people were doing more than standing around twanging their guitars. I was really shocked. When we arrived, we saw this package show at the Lyceum, with Echo and The Bunnymen, A Certain Ratio, Teardrop Explodes and so forth and ... Well, I've never been able to take English music seriously since. It was horrible."

But then the Birthday Party were never a happy bunch. "*Prayers on Fire* stinks, quite honestly," Pew told the *NME*. "The engineer slept through the entire session for a start."

"*Prayers on Fire* was a kind of reaction to the major disappointments we felt when we went to England," Cave said in retrospect. "I think the members of the Birthday Party began to see a vision and I don't think we were really that positively influenced by things, more negatively influenced. There were a lot of things we didn't want to be like, we didn't want to be like the English New Wave pop groups of the time."

The album was recorded in Melbourne with engineer Tony Cohen also producing. As the group struggled with creating their own identity some of them also began indulging an appetite for alcohol and heroin.

"I think with this particular record we were digging for something and we kind of just found it with certain songs," Cave said. "Some of the songs on that record are quite horrible. 'Zoo Music Girl' is a massively embarrassing song. But it also has a song like 'King Ink' on it and I think we knew by the end of *Prayers on Fire* that we'd discovered a certain kind of sound that we wanted to work with on records after that."

Critic Ed St John summed *Prayers on Fire* up best: "It's well played, but that's hardly the point, for this is an expression which ebbs out beyond the confines of proficiently played music. Listening to this album is akin to watching a film of Jackson Pollock painting or listening to Dylan Thomas in full alcoholic flight."

Girls on Film Duran Duran

(Simon Le Bon/Nick Rhodes/Andy Taylor/John Taylor/Roger Taylor) ❊ EMI ❊ 1981 ❊
Appears on: *Duran Duran*

After all those depressing years of dressing in black and worrying about the government, the British working classes rebelled. Throughout the provinces the boys got out the grease paint and the sewing machines and descended on London for a good time. In London the clubs were playing European disco and hip-hop and soul music. Roxy Music and David Bowie were the new role models.

It was colourful. It was exciting. The synthesiser replaced the guitar as the instrument of the day.

Duran Duran, a quintet from Birmingham, was very much of the moment. "The whole London scene seems very superficial," said keyboard player Nick Rhodes. "In Birmingham, people really look forward to the weekends when they can get dressed up and go to somewhere like the Rumrunner, which is the hip club there. And it's all sorts of people – office workers, factory workers, students. The London lot seem very tense."

"What we're doing is European white disco," said bassist John Taylor.

"What we wanted to do," added Rhodes, "was just pick out all the elements of various musics. Disco's pretty good on its own, but a lot of the vocals wreck it. We've got really strong melody lines. I think that's something that disco's lacking. In general, melodies have been missing over the past couple of years."

Whatever their intention at the time may have been, Duran Duran were an instant sensation amongst teenage girls. They were pop gold. Amid all the hype, though, are some excellent grooves and tunes, perhaps the best of them being 'Girls on Film', which just oozed shop-assistant sexuality. It combined the notion of illicit sex with the erotically charged medium of the day – photography.

The fact that a risqué film clip accompanied the song only added to the excitement.

From there it was a steep ride to the top and then a steep ride down.

"We had been forced by our own desire for success into a stereotype of a teen-idol group. We were spending far more time worrying about clothes, make-up and photo sessions than we were about writing songs," said Simon Le Bon recently. He is, however, relaxed about the whole ride. "Many of my friends from school now spend a lot of their time in pubs swilling down beer and getting big bellies. They go home at night to watch TV and are hassled with mortgage payments."

Our Lips Are Sealed The Go-Go's

(Terry Hall/Jane Wiedlin) ❄ IRS ❄ 1981 ❄ Appears on: *Beauty and the Beat*

"I get really annoyed when I see these periodic women-in-rock articles, and the Go-Go's are not even mentioned," said bass player Kathy Valentine. "I don't see how you can omit a band that was the first female band to play all their instruments, write their own songs – and we were on a little label ..." In fact the first all-girl rock & roll band was Fanny some ten years earlier than when the Go-Go's hit the charts, but no previous group had made such a spectacular impact on the music scene as this punk rock band from Los Angeles.

Original bass player Margot, singer Belinda Carlisle and guitarist Jane Wiedlin were all part of the formative Los Angeles punk scene, living with the other scenesters/dropouts at the Canterbury apartment house in Hollywood, determined to get a band together.

By all accounts their first two years showed enthusiasm rather than talent but by 1980 the group had started to find its voice.

"When I joined the band, they had a lot of songs that were politically oriented," said guitarist Charlotte Caffey. "I can remember asking them why not take advantage of the word Go-Go? You don't have to do sweet, power-pop stuff. We started writing songs using the idea of the name of the band rather than the hard-core punk we played in the beginning because, I imagine, it was the easiest to play."

Just the existence of an all-girl band without a male svengali was a political statement. Like other punk groups of the period, they knew their '60s pop and for their first album enlisted producer Richard Gottehrer, whose credits went back to the Angels' 'My Boyfriend's Back' and the Strangeloves' 'I Want Candy' and forward to the first Blondie and Richard Hell albums.

The Go-Go's stayed true to punk rock even as they improved their playing and writing. Their songs had the energy and excitement of punk rock – they were still far from slick. The album *Beauty and the Beat* featured great tunes, especially 'Our Lips Are Sealed', written by Wieldin and Specials singer Terry Hall after the two groups had toured together and a romance ensued. 'Our Lips' had the hallmarks of classic girl group pop updated to the '80s.

The Go-Go's announced girl power before it was fashionable. "The first reviews we got that really made me feel that this band was going to work said, 'The Go-Go's are to punk rock what botulism is to tuna'," said Caffey. "Stuff like that really inspired me. We wrote our best songs after we heard that."

I Love Rock & Roll Joan Jett

(Alan Merrill/Jake Hooker) ❈ Boardwalk ❈ 1981 ❈ Appears on: *I Love Rock & Roll*

As a teenage Suzi Quatro wannabe, Joan Jett formed the Runaways on Los Angeles' Sunset Strip. On New Year's Day 1980, she was a solo artist. With one solo album under her belt, Jett teamed up with producers Kenny Laguna and Richie Cordell. The latter had been a major force in British music at the end of the '60s, producing Joe Cocker and then teaming up with Leon Russell.

Jett had found 'I Love Rock & Roll', a song performed by English New Wave band the Arrows.

The song lent itself to a big glam rock anthem, which was essentially an update of the Chinnichap sound as made famous by Suzi Quatro. Laguna and Cordell built a huge sound from handclaps and layered vocals that was big, dumb and fun. At a time when rock was suffering from pretentious art music, 'I Love Rock & Roll' was an irresistible return to core values. The song went to number one in early 1982 and has sold more than ten million copies.

"Well, it was an obvious way to do it," engineer Glen Kolotkin told Blair Jackson. "I knew it was going to be a hit and I wasn't going to let it slip away. We wanted the vocal overdubs to be almost like an audience.

"It took us almost no time to get a basic track on 'I Love Rock & Roll'. I thought it was a smash hit from the beginning. Then Laguna came in and Cordell came in and they were as knocked out as I was, and we finished the record up in one day. It just came together.

"We just kept building it up and up and up. I knew it was right when the hair stood up on the back of my neck."

Love Will Tear Us Apart Joy Division

(Ian Curtis/Peter Hook/Stephen Morris/Bernard Sumner) ❈ Factory ❈ 1981 ❈
Appears on: *Substance*

Inevitably and forever this song will live in the shadow of Ian Curtis' suicide. Shortly after its recording the singer and principal lyricist, father of a one-year-old daughter, hung himself in the kitchen at home near Manchester in the early hours of 18 May 1980. In March, the group had spent two weeks in London's Britannia Row Studios, recording what would become their second LP, *Closer*. Although it's likely that Joy Division would have forever broken out of their Mancunian provincialism anyway, Curtis' death just added to the story. These weren't just English boys moaning in their bedsits.

Joy Division began in June 1976 when the Sex Pistols played Manchester and bassist Peter Hook and guitarist Bernard Sumner resolved to form a band. They asked an acquaintance, Ian Curtis, to be the singer.

"Ian brought a direction," Sumner told Jon Savage. "He was into the extremities of life. He wanted to make extreme music: he wanted to be totally extreme on stage, no half measures. Ian's influence seemed to be madness and insanity.

"Everyone says Joy Division's music is gloomy and heavy; I often get asked why this is so. I can only guess why it was heavy for Ian, but for me it was because the whole neighbourhood that I'd grown up in was completely decimated in the mid-'60s. At the end of our street was a huge chemical factory: where I used to live is just oil drums filled with chemicals.

"When I left school and got a job, I was chained in this horrible office: every day, every week, every year, with maybe three weeks' holiday a year. The horror enveloped me. So the music of Joy Division was about the death of optimism, of youth."

The first album, *Unknown Pleasures*, was described by Jon Savage as "a definitive northern Gothic statement: guilt-ridden, romantic, and claustrophobic." Great wads of keyboard and guitar surrounded Hook's melodic bass lines and Curtis' strangled voice.

Closer was the next step for the group. A substantial leap.

Curtis had severe epilepsy that he was medicating with Benzedrine. He was chronically depressed and had been threatening suicide since his teens and tried three times before finally succeeding. Added to all this, his marriage was failing, he was in a relationship with another woman and there was a new child. The world was closing in on Curtis.

"The mood he was in when he wrote that stuff is a very big question," Factory boss Tony Wilson told Savage. "It's almost as if writing that album contributed to his state: he immersed himself in it, rather than just expressing it."

According to his wife, Deborah Curtis, "I think he [Ian] enjoyed being unhappy, that he wallowed in it. When we were kids, lots of people were miserable; they grew out of it. I thought Ian would."

One of the last things recorded before Curtis' death was the single, 'Love Will Tear Us Apart', which became one of the great love ballads of the decade. The album *Closer*, however, was the epitaph for Joy Division and set the tone for serious young bands for the future.

O Superman (for Massenet) Laurie Anderson

(Laurie Anderson) ❊ 110 ❊ 1981 ❊ Appears on: *Big Science*

Laurie Anderson is referred to as a performance artist, which means that her work usually appears in serious art contexts such as galleries, museums and festivals. Which is where it would have stayed except that legendary BBC DJ John Peel began playing an excerpt of one piece on the radio and put 'O Superman (for Massenet)' at the top of the charts.

An eight-minute poem set to electronic loops plus abstracted voice and minimal instruments, it was actually a very catchy version of the kinds of things that Eno and Talking Heads had been doing. For this reason, Anderson wasn't thought of as art by the pop audience and was still taken as art by the art audience. Incidentally, the 'for Massenet' refers to Jules Massenet, the French operatic composer whose 'O Souverain' influenced this track.

'O Superman (for Massenet)' is about paranoia and communication and technology and it's put into a sound-scape that is both deliciously inviting and slightly unnerving. She has taken the self-consciousness of Brian Eno and made it warm and melodic. She used voice as both abstract and percussive and treated it with electronics – the heavy breathing underneath the poem pushed the boundaries of popular recording. Robert Christgau called 'O Superman (for Massenet)' "the pop event of the year".

Quasimodo's Dream The Reels

(Dave Mason/Craig Hooper) ❊ Polygram ❊ 1981 ❊ Appears on: *Quasimodo's Dream*

"I suppose it was original and it was ahead of its time for Australia," said singer and songwriter Dave Mason. "We were pretty free in those times to do what we wanted, and we did. So it was like an adventure."

Having arrived in Sydney as a jumpy, quirky New Wave act, on their second album the Reels revealed a much darker sensibility. There were plenty of pop songs: 'After the News', 'Stand and Deliver' and 'According to My Heart'. The sequined synth melodies from Polly Newham and Craig Hooper shone brightly against the prevailing winds of Oz rock. Beneath that was an itchy, unhappy mood.

Between squabbles amongst the band and the record company, it took almost a year for the record to be released and the conflicts pretty much finished the group thereafter.

However, the real gems on the album were the deeply melancholy 'Kitchen

Man' and the title track. The former captures the existential dread of suburban loneliness over a sweet and seductive keyboard line. The latter, which has often been covered and is greatly admired by other songwriters, is a grim but beautiful tale of alienation and self-hatred.

Or is it? "I don't consider it to be my best song," said Mason. "The whole lyric just doesn't make sense. But that's what I'm like in the studio. I never finish my lyrics until the last minute. It's just annoying. I think it was one of those things that people took to their hearts."

Super Freak   Rick James

(Rick James/Alonzo Miller) ❊ Motown ❊ 1981 ❊ Appears on: *Street Songs*

The late Rick James achieved immortality with a bass line. James conceived the riff as a humorous parody of a dance beat, then he added some fat synthesiser sounds, the Temptations on backing vocals, and salacious lyrics. The result was debauched and playful at the same time.

James had a truly tragic life – he was destroyed by an addiction to crack cocaine and involved in sadomasochistic sex, which eventuated in kidnapping and assault charges and jail time. However, 'Super Freak' is a classic. The bass line was revisited by MC Hammer on his global number one hit 'U Can't Touch This'.

"I am trying to make multi, multi-millions of dollars, I am trying to make Paul McCartney white boy money, so I can sit back and have a big house in Spain and not ever work again," said James. "Right now I got a few million dollars and I'm doing all right; I hope to have twenty million soon, so I can sit back real fat like Mick Jagger and Rod Stewart and all them other assholes who sit out there and talk shit and procrastinate and talk that hypocritical ass bullshit about their 'art' ..."

Start Me Up   The Rolling Stones

(Mick Jagger/Keith Richards) ❊ Rolling Stones ❊ 1981 ❊ Appears on: *Tattoo You*

Mick Jagger and Keith Richards were no longer speaking in 1980, making recording a new album difficult. It fell to engineer Chris Kimsey to sort through ten years of out-takes to find the basis of the *Tattoo You* album. 'Start Me Up' was originally recorded at the *Some Girls* sessions on the same day as the disco hit 'Miss You', and promptly binned.

"'Miss You' took quite a time to come together," said Kimsey. "Bill [Wyman, bassist] needed to go to quite a few clubs before he got that bass line sorted out. But he did sort it out, and bless him, it made that song. Then, immediately after 'Miss You' was recorded, 'Start Me Up' got straightened out. They'd been throwing it around as a reggae song, but they rearranged it and, within twenty-four hours of 'Miss You', 'Start Me Up' was recorded.

"However, when I played it back, Keith said, 'Nah, it sounds like something I've heard on the radio. Wipe it.' Of course, I didn't, but he really didn't like it, and I'm not sure whether he likes it to this day. I don't think it's one of his favourite songs, although it's obviously everyone's favourite guitar riff; his guitar riff. Maybe because Keith loves reggae so much, he wanted it to be a reggae song.

"'Start Me Up' took about six hours to record. If they all played the right chords in the right time, went to the chorus at the right time and got to the middle eight together, that was a master. Don't forget, they would never sit down and work out a song. They would jam it and the song would evolve out of that. That's their magic."

Three years after the *Some Girls* sessions, Jagger returned to the track to put on vocals and a lyric, much of which was improvised with the music.

"He'd give it the full performance, moving all over the place," Kimsey told *Mix* magazine. "It was great to watch and equally great to record. He knows how to work a microphone. He might be at the back of the control room, just a bar before the verse, and all of a sudden he's in front of the mic. He backs off in the chorus when he's singing loud, he gets in close when he's singing soft, and he knows what to do. Keith, on the other hand, is the complete opposite. You need a shotgun to get him in front of the mic. He'll wander all over the place while singing, taking an attitude of 'You do your job, you record me.'"

Whatever Richards' reservations, if any, 'Start Me Up' made *Tattoo You* the Rolling Stones' most successful album and has been one of their signature tunes ever since.

Tainted Love Soft Cell

(Ed Cobb) ❋ Phonogram ❋ 1981 ❋ Appears on: *Non-Stop Erotic Cabaret*

"I've always loved the idea of glamour in squalor – filth and squalor and sleaziness and seediness – there's always something really glamorous and sort of really sparkling," Marc Almond told *Face*. "That's what I ... I find it curious, I have a fetish about those places. It's a bit like ... I always feel like a spectator, which is wrong but, I like it anyway." Almond should know: as the singer for the duo Soft Cell he mixed both glamour and sleaze together and topped the charts with a cover of 'Tainted Love'.

Almond and keyboard player David Ball were familiar with northern soul, a strand of R&B popular in the north of England in the early '70s. Marc Bolan's wife Gloria Jones had a northern soul hit with 'Tainted Love', which Soft Cell covered in their electronic style. Most synthesiser artists of the time were making clinical, clever and sweet tunes with the new technology. Soft Cell made the keyboard as dirty and sexual an instrument as any other. The computerised rhythm track didn't have the supple play of a live band but the pressing, uncompromising, insistent beat had an emotional message of its own.

Almond brought a sleazy sexiness to the song. His camp reading also intimated other kinds of polymorphous perversity – the listener was invited to let their imagination wander in the knowledge that everyone dreams of the forbidden. There was something in the way that Almond's seduction played against the synthesiser – and of course the strength of the song – that made this track irresistible.

Ghost Town   The Specials

(Jerry Dammers) ❋ 2 Tone/Chrysalis ❋ 1981 ❋ Appears on: *The Singles Collection*

Having started a ska revival, the Specials keyboardist Jerry Dammers pushed the genre into a new shape. Using the bouncing, slightly spastic ska rhythm and drenching it in lashings of dub echo, Dammers made a requiem with what was essentially party music.

'Ghost Town' was written in the wake of the massive riots in the Jamaican ghetto of Brixton and in the context of the rampantly conservative Thatcher government, the rising unemployment and the climate of racism that engulfed Britain at the time. The Specials' gigs had been targeted as recruiting sites for right-wing groups such as the National Front, which led to confrontations between mods and skinheads. Their shows were regularly stopped because of violence on the dance floor. 'Ghost Town' became an urban anthem in Britain in the summer of 1981.

The paranoia that positively seeps out of 'Ghost Town' was also a consequence of the deteriorating relationships in the band. Shortly after the song's release singer Terry Hall, Neville Staple and Lynval Golding jumped ship for the less dictatorial collective Fun Boy Three. 'Ghost Town' sounds like its name – it's spare and haunted and frightening.

Happy Man Sunnyboys

(Jeremy Oxley) ✳ Mushroom ✳ 1981 ✳ Appears on: *This Is Real*

Few rock groups have been better named than the Sunnyboys. You couldn't meet guys who were more easygoing than Richard (guitar), Bil Bilson (drums) and Peter Oxley (bass). In fact, in my whole life I don't think I've met a better character than Pete. The singer Jeremy, though, gave the name an ironic twist . . .

Jeremy Oxley, barely nineteen, and Bil Bilson. They'd been playing with brother Pete since they were kids in Kingscliff, near Byron. Jeremy had been writing songs and now he got a really strong batch. Pete, Richard, Bil and Jeremy found themselves in an old warehouse on the western edge of Sydney. Then suddenly in August 1979 the Sunnyboys were born. Great name – courtesy of artist Liz Croll.

That first Sunnyboys album is a complete gem. It's hard as a diamond but it's got a great spirit and is complete and pure in the way that too few albums ever are. The single 'Happy Man' is the distillation of the Sunnyboys – bright but filled with the confusion of being a teenager. The trials of adolescence writ into an epic frame.

Jeremy was prone to mental illness. At a very tender age he had his ego blown. He went from shy art student surfer to the spokesman for a generation in no time flat. And, of course, there were temptations and who wouldn't . . . the options for self-medication probably didn't help things and they probably masked deeper problems. But you only have to listen to the lyrics to know that Jeremy was a complex guy crying out for some understanding.

This is still one of the best rock & roll tracks of that era. It's bound so tight that you can't see the seams and sounds so fresh you'd think it was plucked just as it flowered.

Genius of Love Tom Tom Club

(Tom Tom Club) ✳ Sire ✳ 1981 ✳ Appears on: *Tom Tom Club*

"We had just finished the big *Remain in Light* tour with Talking Heads, and David had announced that he was going to do a solo project and Jerry [Harrison] had announced he was going to do one, and I thought, 'Well, what do we do?' So we decided to do a record, and Chris Blackwell of Island, whom we had met while working with the Talking Heads down in Nassau, said, 'Why don't you come down to my studio ...'" That's how Chris Franz, Talking Heads' drummer, explained the genesis of the Tom Tom Club, a side project that threatened to eclipse the mother ship.

Franz and his wife, Talking Heads' bassist Tina Weymouth, set up some grooves with a Caribbean flavour – some reggae, a hint of calypso and some hip-hop – and then added vocals from Weymouth and her sisters.

The first single, 'Wordy Rappinghood', was heavily influenced by the early Bronx rap (which had yet to move out of Manhattan) but with a childlike quality. Not only was it endearing but it was a hit.

The Tom Tom Club brought their arty friends (including guitarist Adrian Belew) and their own art school backgrounds to bear.

Their funky version of 'Under the Boardwalk' was a beautiful culture clash for pop R&B. The other lead track, 'Genius of Love', was even better and remains much sampled today. The funkiness of the band, with cheesy keyboards and breezy vocals, was a pure delight and a precursor to hip-hop from the likes of De La Soul and Deee-Lite. The Tom Tom Club was essential club music in the early '80s.

As Weymouth said at the time: "It's pushing it to the extreme, because we're extremely light with Tom Tom Club. If Talking Heads wasn't so extremely serious on the other side, I don't think we ever could have come up with such light music."

Highway Patrolman Bruce Springsteen

(Bruce Springsteen) ✳ Columbia ✳ 1982 ✳ Appears on: *Nebraska*

No-one in 1982 is reported to have heard *Nebraska* and announced: "I have heard the future of folk music!" No-one, it has to be said, was looking for the future of folk music. Certainly not from Bruce Springsteen. Viewed by the industry as career suicide and shunned by most of his fans, *Nebraska* is a high point in Bruce Springsteen's career. It has inspired one classic film (*The Indian Runner*) and a sublime cover version by Johnny Cash ('Johnny 99') amongst many other tributes. *Nebraska* has survived the slings and arrows of fashion. It has been consistently magnificent.

Although the '80s album *The River* had been Springsteen's strongest work to date, his personal life was a mess. He was depressed and isolated. He was also picking up on the pall that had fallen over America as a consequence of the recession and Reaganomics. Springsteen was reading Flannery O'Connor and watching films about the American soul – Louis Malle's *Atlantic City*, Terence Mallick's *Badlands*, John Huston's *Wise Blood*, and *True Confessions*, written by Joan Didion and John Gregory Dunne.

In January 1982, at home alone with his tape recorder, he recorded *Nebraska* in less than three hours (the same sessions also produced the songs 'Born in the USA' and 'Pink Cadillac'). With minimal backing over a spare vocal and guitar, this was a bleak album with none of the redemptive moments Springsteen had previously supplied. Moreover, the songs failed to respond to the band and in the end it was the home recordings that became *Nebraska*. Fifty years previously, Alan Lomax had taken primitive tape recorders into the depths of America and returned with songs that became the billion-dollar rock & roll business and superstar brands of which Bruce Springsteen was the apotheosis. Now, in his bedroom, Springsteen reversed the journey.

Springsteen was looking at the core of his own beliefs and family. There are tales like 'Used Cars' and especially 'My Father's House' which come literally from that experience. From there he was able to extrapolate more generally; the moral dilemma of family has rarely been as well expressed as on 'Highway Patrolman'. Nihilism has rarely been better expressed as on the album's final cut, 'Reason to Believe', which opens with a vignette of a man poking a dog's carcass by the side of the highway hoping that the animal will come back to life.

"When I wrote *Nebraska* ... I'd found the record's centre. The songs tapped into white gospel and early Appalachian music, as well as the blues. In small detail – the slow twirling of a baton, the twisting of a ring on a finger – they had found their character," Springsteen wrote in his book, *Songs*.

"If there's a theme that runs through the record, it's the thin line between stability and that moment when time stops and everything goes black, when the things that connect you to your world – your job, your family, friends, your faith, the love and grace in your heart – fail you. I wanted the music to feel like a waking dream and the record to move like poetry. I wanted the blood on it to feel destined and fateful."

Sweet Dreams (Are Made of This) Eurythmics

(Annie Lennox/Dave Stewart) ✳ RCA ✳ 1982 ✳

Appears on: *Sweet Dreams (Are Made of This)*

It wasn't singer Annie Lennox's sexual ambiguity that made 'Sweet Dreams (Are Made of This)' the most controversial single of 1982. It was the fact that the song, which topped charts all around the world, was made, effectively, in a home studio. Forget the gigantism that had taken over show business. This was do-it-yourself delivering on its promise.

Then there were the sounds – all electronic drums and layers of synthesiser – that for once didn't sound cold and synthetic. With one single, guitarist Dave Stewart created a new direction for pop to go in.

Stewart and Lennox had been in New Wave band the Tourists. When that combo split they began working with friends from the German electronic scene – Conny Plank, members of Deutsche Amerikanische Freundschaft, Can drummer Jackie Liebezeit and Holger Czukay all contributed to the first Eurythmics album. Stewart quickly moved on, however, creating a new style of synth-pop that owed a debt to Kraut rock but was more in the style of British pop.

"People think that album is so high tech," said Stewart. "But we couldn't even afford a claptrap – the classic disco thing, you know, that goes ckkk-ckkk-ckkk! It's just me and Annie, banging on the wall with a handful of picture-frames. If we'd had the money, of course, we would have used a claptrap. But not having it made us a lot more inventive.

"That was basically Conny and Holger's influence. They'd always say, 'If there's no fun involved, if you just press a button and *that* does that, then you tend to just say, oh, we'll use that button to do that and this one to do this.' And your music just goes further and further away from you."

For the second album, Stewart and Lennox extracted themselves from their management and incurred a huge burden of debt. 'Sweet Dreams' was their DIY manifesto.

"We had been so stitched up when we started out as the Tourists in '78, and even as Eurythmics at the beginning, we just had to take things into our own hands," recalled Annie. "That line in 'Sweet Dreams' about being 'used and abused' refers directly to my own experiences. Not just in love, but in this business too. Right at the beginning Dave said to me, 'Annie we must have a manifesto', so we wrote down all the things we liked to do on a big sheet of paper."

The Eurythmics also understood how to present themselves through video. MTV was then still a novelty and Stewart and Lennox were among the first to use videos to break records internationally.

"We discovered that America was very reactionary about how somebody looked. I suddenly became this threatening entity, which I quite liked but I'd never intended it to be that controversial," said Lennox. "I thought the ambiguity gave me a degree of power, because up to that point women had been portraying – and betraying – themselves in an overtly sexual way, which is fine, but it didn't suit me. We also felt there should be something different about Eurythmics' presentation. We weren't too sure if we were a group or not and at one point said categorically we weren't. We wanted to wear the same sorts of clothes so we could say that, at least visually, there was no difference between us.

"'Sweet Dreams' kicked things off in a big way. It was a definite hit, and a hit everywhere. You no longer had to prove yourself to anybody. All of a sudden it felt like a lot of doors were flung open, like the world wanted to know you, and I got a bit scared. It really was like going on a roller coaster. Our tour seemed to go on forever, and though I could have chosen not to, I wanted to see how far the thing could go."

The Message   Grandmaster Flash & the Furious Five

(Duke Bootee) ❉ Sugarhill ❉ 1982 ❉ Appears on: *Louder than a Bomb*

Block parties where a DJ set up a sound system and played records were a feature of life in the Bronx in the mid-'70s. A group of DJs began beat matching – extending the music by mixing two songs together on the beat. MCs improvised verse over the top – and there you have the beginnings of rap. By the turn of the decade DJs were becoming stars – Cool Herc, Afrika Bambaataa and Grandmaster Flash were the three innovators leading the charge.

Joseph Saddler (aka Flash) was a master of the break. He collected a group of MCs – the Furious Five (Melle Mel, Kid Creole, Cowboy, Scorpio and Raheim) – and invented much of the hip-hop style right there.

Sugarhill Records put Flash in the studio to make 'Adventures on the Wheels of Steel', which was the first record made solely from mixing other records.

"It took three turntables, two mixers and between ten and fifteen takes to get it right," he recalled. "It took me three hours. I had to do it live. And whenever I'd mess up I would just refuse to punch. I would just go back to the beginning."

Sylvia Robinson, co-owner of Sugarhill, then pressed a tune written by the house band percussionist Ed 'Duke Bootee' Fletcher. Flash and the Five were unconvinced by the political message and just plain didn't like the song. Robinson insisted and the record was cut with Melle Mel on the lead vocal.

The rest is history. 'The Message', with its stark images of ghetto life, also has the killer hook, "Don't push me 'cause I'm close to the edge," which had universal appeal. The record was a Top 10 smash around the globe and sold over half a million 12-inch singles. So much broke out with that one record – scratching, angry political rap lyrics and the nascent hip-hop style were all introduced on that single. What had once been a party trick became the most significant cultural movement of the next three decades. 'Adventures on the Wheels of Steel' opened the way; 'The Message' brought rap to the world.

"I was first," Flash told the *Guardian* newspaper. "I don't care who's better, who's worse. My contribution is first. Because first is forever."

Billie Jean Michael Jackson

(Michael Jackson) ❋ Epic ❋ 1982 ❋ Appears on: *Thriller*

Michael Jackson's solo album *Thriller* had an air of unreality to it at the time. It was the apotheosis of pop music – the most popular album of all time with fifty million copies sold around the world. No other album (discounting greatest hits packages) has come close to its ubiquity. Yet in hindsight it has the hallmarks of a Greek tragedy. It made Michael Jackson the King of Pop but cost him his soul. Quincy Jones said, "It felt like entering hyperspace at one point. It almost scared me. I thought maybe this is going too far."

Produced at a cost of $750,000, producer Quincy Jones and Jackson laboured for a year over the album, sorting through 300 songs, casting the right cameos (Paul McCartney for a duet and Eddie Van Halen for a guitar solo). Then the marketing really took off with the videos. Jackson worked hard to make an album that would get played on MTV and rock radio – hence Van Halen – and he saw, before most, the possibility of MTV. None of that really explains why *Thriller* was so huge.

Much of the credit, of course, goes to Jackson. Although Quincy Jones is a producer of extraordinary vision dating back to his work with Miles Davis, it was Jackson's enigma that made *Thriller*. Things look different in retrospect, but listening to these songs now, there's a haunted, tortured quality – parodied perhaps in the title track but most present in the first single, 'Billie Jean'.

On the face of it, 'Billie Jean' is a song about a paternity suit. There's a funk bass line that dances around, pulsing the song forward with the seductive grip of the best R&B. On top of that is Jackson's almost sexless vocal – pleading innocence. Jackson makes this a song not about sex but identity. It's about the power of a rock star to break young girls' hearts. It's about conceiving a child without a relationship. It's about being hunted by the public. If the lyrics weren't enough, the 'Billie Jean' video reinforces all of the eerie qualities of this song. The fact that you can faintly hear Jackson dancing in the studio as he sang only adds a further ghostly layer to the track.

'Billie Jean' raises more questions than it answers. There's a suspicion here in the layers of vocal about the layers of Jackson's own personality and how they will come off. Listening to 'Billie Jean' is like hearing a train wreck in the middle of the night.

The Power and the Passion Midnight Oil

(Rob Hirst/Jim Moginie/Peter Garrett) ❊ CBS ❊ 1982 ❊
Appears on: *10, 9, 8, 7, 6, 5, 4, 3, 2, 1*

No-one, not even Midnight Oil, saw *10–1* coming. The group had made three albums of blistering agit rock. Angry, straight ahead, drums and guitars to the floor, pub rock. Then they took it all apart and started from scratch.

In 1981 Midnight Oil were one of the most popular bands in Australia, having dominated the pub rock scene with their massive rock & roll sound and their strident, individualistic attitude. Then just as it was about to pay off, they moved to London to work with a new producer and a whole new sound. The risks were substantial. Everything that the group had was reinvested into the project and they were living on subsistence wages, barely enough to eat. Drummer Rob Hirst recalled the reaction to his fear, "I'd come into the studio and just bash out my aggression."

Hirst and the rest of the band were also responding to the global paranoia that then engulfed the world. At the height of the Cold War, nuclear missiles were being deployed in Britain. A holocaust appeared not just possible but likely. The album took its title from such apocalyptic times.

Producer Nick Launay had come to the Oils' attention through his work with Killing Joke, Public Image and the Birthday Party, although this was his first solo production job.

Having been liberated from the live sound, as Hirst put it, the acoustic guitars came to the fore on songs like 'The Power and the Passion' and 'US Forces'. Elsewhere a breakneck rock track, 'Read about It', slammed biased media with their most short, sharp lyric, and the atmospheric keyboards of Jim Moginie established moods that were quietly doom-laden and at other times sensual.

'The Power and the Passion' is a song about apathy. The lyric points to the urgency of the time with growing US militancy and the decline of the left while the singer laments the 'I'm all right Jack' indolence of the Australian public. It's a call to arms in a nation put to sleep in a sunburnt complacency.

Koyaanisqatsi Philip Glass

(Philip Glass) ❊ Nonesuch ❊ 1982 ❊ Appears on: *Koyaanisqatsi*

Avant-garde composer Philip Glass operates in the twilight world between high art and popular taste. His music, which borrows from Indian traditions as well as the West, relies on repetition and minimalism and electronics. Somewhere in the middle he meets up with the art side of rock & roll. There's a common language here. Glass' most successful popular work is the soundtrack to Godfrey Reggio's 1982 film *Koyaanisqatsi*. The original release of the music on the soundtrack album was edited for time considerations. In 1998 Glass re-recorded the score.

The film's title is a Hopi Indian phrase meaning "life out of balance". The eighty-seven minute film is a selection of images from around the globe – from deserts to cities and all manner of life situations. Although there are no words, Reggio's intent was clear: nature=good; urbanisation=bad.

Central to the film and somewhat more ambiguous is Glass' music. Without any other narrative, the score certainly gives a particular take on the images. It's rare for a composer to be given this sort of opportunity and Glass made the most of it.

"We didn't mean to spend that much time on it, but it took three years to get the money to finish the film," said Glass. "Godfrey and I would work on a few things, then he'd get more money and go out and shoot some more. He'd come back five months later and we'd work on a few more things. It gave us a long gestation period with a lot of time to think about it, to look at and reflect on it.

"Godfrey came in with a very strong, almost political, social, and ideological construction. He had a film language he wanted to work with. He had a concept of the piece. And he even had a whole ideological background that he could supply me with – books, articles and lectures. He's sort of a full-service intellectual. So we had an opportunity to wed the parts of the film together very organically. In a sense you could say the text ... although the text never appears ... the text, the image, and the music become very organically intertwined."

Writers have called it a "tone poem" but it's really just the longest art music video ever made. The film was a success and introduced post-modern minimalist composition to a mass audience. Glass' hypnotic keyboard passages entered the vocabulary of popular instrumental music, especially techno and ambient in the '80s and beyond.

"The piece kind of became a classic without our realising it," said Glass.

Love My Way The Psychedelic Furs

(John Ashton/Richard Butler/Tim Butler/Vince Ely) ✳ Columbia ✳ 1982 ✳
Appears on: *Forever Now*

This is a song about what to do when your girlfriend is bisexual. The Psychedelic Furs, according to singer and writer Richard Butler, spearheaded the second wave of the New Wave in the early '80s. Butler's influences were primarily the Velvet Underground, Bob Dylan and David Bowie.

The sound and atmosphere of their early records – energetic, slightly speedy and dreamy – had been established with the help of producer Steve Lillywhite. For their third, they moved to Bearsville to work with the auteur of art rock, Todd Rundgren.

"I was supposed to have been working on a song which I hadn't done," Butler said. "I had one of those stylophone things and I had this 'dadadadadada nananananana' – just those two changes. I'd been listening to [David Bowie's] *Scary Monsters*, that must have informed it a bit, and came up with this vocal melody and all the words within the space of about an hour. We put it down, and then Ed Bueller, a friend of ours, came round with his keyboard and put the marimba part on. We sent it off to Todd who said, 'Well, the vocals sound a little bit angry, why don't you try singing a little bit more,' and I was like, 'Yeah, OK.'"

Unlike the Bunnymen and their other British contemporaries, the Furs were more intimate, more flesh and blood and more sexy. There is an effeteness to Butler's singing that betrays a degree of honesty. As the name implies, they're looking for heightened experience and not simply art for art's sake.

"The sound of the band really came together completely by accident," said Butler. "We weren't very good musicians. We still aren't, it's an ideas thing."

Don't Renege on Our Love Richard & Linda Thompson

(Richard Thompson) ✳ Hannibal ✳ 1982 ✳ Appears on: *Shoot Out the Lights*

Break-up records are rarely pretty affairs. After ten years and three children, the Thompson's marriage was cracking and shortly after this album's completion, Richard left Linda for another woman. Their union was announced by the album *I Want to See the Bright Lights Tonight* and it's impossible to hear the opening song of *Shoot Out the Lights* other than in the context of their marital lives. It's an approach that Richard is wary of, but not dismissive. "Songs are very much a product of imagination," he said. "They may be founded in reality; they're certainly founded in experience. But they're an imaginative projection beyond that. It devalues the songs to say that they're just soap opera. I think the songs have a broader meaning than that."

The album was recorded quickly by producer Joe Boyd and the austerity of the sound complements the hard edge of the sentiment in most of these relationship songs. Thompson's guitar brings that home. His jazz inflected folk style is pitiless, wiry and taut with tension, anger and shame. There's a bitterness to his playing that is breathtaking. Linda Thompson was later to describe their marriage as "abject misery". 'Don't Renege on Our Love', however, is the complete antithesis of that.

More Than This Roxy Music

(Bryan Ferry) ✳ Island ✳ 1982 ✳ Appears on: *Avalon*

"The whole thing of trying to write something that is from the heart and is hopefully going to be popular and successful and all the rest of it is very stressful," Bryan Ferry said, giving a quick capsule of his recording career through the '70s and '80s. "And as the years go by it gets harder and harder – at least that's how it seems to me. Then I got sort of fed up with the group thing for a while and I thought I'd like to do some of my own songs under my own name. So I did a couple of albums like that – and then I missed the group thing again and went back to doing a couple of group albums. We did three – finished with *Avalon*. And then I got fed up with the constrictions of the group. Groups always end up bickering – because, if you think about it, it's unnatural to work with the same people forever."

Sessions for *Avalon*, the last studio effort from Roxy Music, took place over 1981 and early 1982. Produced by Chris Thomas, this was as slick and high-tech as was possible to get. Thomas encouraged the group to experiment with sounds and layering up sounds almost to the point of abstraction. And as guitarist Phil Manzenera noted, "for the last three albums, quite frankly, there were a lot more drugs around as well, which was good and bad. It created a lot of paranoia and a lot of spaced-out stuff."

As the album's title suggests, this was dreamscape, with a sense of myths and phantoms.

The record's lead track has an ethereal quality although it started out as a full-bodied pop song. "Halfway through, Bryan rebelled," Manzanera said. "It was all scrapped and simplified incredibly."

"I think Bryan decided he wanted a more adult type of lyric," said Manzanera. From the early days of Roxy Music, Bryan Ferry stated his intention to emulate American soul music and here in the last days he came closest.

Here Comes the Rain Again Eurythmics

(Annie Lennox/Dave Stewart) ✳ RCA ✳ 1983 ✳ Appears on: Touch

"Dave and I wrote 'Here Comes the Rain Again' one afternoon in a room in the Mayflower Hotel in New York," said Annie Lennox of the writing session that involved a wrestling match on the hotel room floor. The phenomenal success of the Eurythmics was due to Stewart's innovative approach to pop songs and Lennox's soul-bearing singing.

'Here Comes the Rain' moves on from the synth-pop of earlier records with the addition of a string section. But you still have the quirky arrangement with its absence of a chorus. You have a melody that borrows from torch songs but doesn't quite go to the same places.

Lennox is at her finest here. Most of her best work deals with her struggle with anxiety and depression. "I lived like that for years, sort of verging on suicide," she said. "I certainly don't mean I'd ever do away with myself, but it's as if I did toy with the idea for a long time. And now, I feel I'm coming out of it.

"No matter how much you want to get out of that sort of thing, or how much help you get, it's a very hard thing to crack. And, in the end, it has to come entirely from within yourself.

"But, although these bad experiences can be horrific, with a bit of luck and a lot of grit, you can also turn them into something creative. I do believe in self-improvement and I don't think one is always a victim, not at all."

Rockit Herbie Hancock

(Michael Beinhorn/Herbie Hancock/Bill Laswell) ❋ Columbia ❋ 1983 ❋
Appears on: *Future Shock*

"The last few records I don't consider jazz at all," Herbie Hancock said in relation to his groundbreaking 1983 album. After a long journey from bop to fusion and funk, Hancock enlisted Bill Laswell to help him find a relationship with hip-hop.

Laswell was an important player in the art rock scene of New York with his own group, Material. Laswell's tastes went from classic jazz and fusion though to European art rock, disco and hip-hop. *Future Shock* embraces all of these styles in a completely original sound.

Laswell enlisted his Material partner Michael Beinhorn and a group of downtown art rock stars including Anton Fier, Bernard Fowler, Nicky Skopelitis, plus Fred Frith and drummer du jour Sly Dunbar. He then added DJ Grandmixer D.ST on turntables. This crew, plus Hancock's particular sense of funk and jazz vocabulary, created a techno/electro/hip-hop crossover. The song 'Rockit', with its MTV-friendly video, became a smash hit.

"I had just finished doing a series of hip-hop records and I was very tired," Laswell recalled in Stuart Nicholson's *Jazz Rock: A History*. "I wanted to do something crazy and experimental." Laswell cut a track, 'Rockit', with Grandmixer D.ST and took it to Hancock, who wasn't certain how to react. Laswell directed Hancock's parts and in less than three hours had finished the track. He took it to an audio shop to test out some speakers and after a few moments of play, "for a few weird seconds there was a feeling in the room like something was happening. I turned around and there was literally like a hundred kids going, 'What was that.' At that moment we realised what we had done. And then it blew up."

Cattle and Cane The Go-Betweens

(Grant McLennan) ❋ Stunn ❋ 1983 ❋ Appears on: *Before Hollywood*

Precious fans of Bob Dylan and the Gang of Four, the Go-Betweens were ostensibly a semi-acoustic punk band with two naturally gifted songwriters in Forster and McLennan. A first album of dysrhythmic New Wave saw the group floundering. On the second album they returned to their strengths as folk rockers. But it all fell into place with 'Cattle and Cane' with its gorgeous melody on the bass guitar.

"We had all the tracks for the album," McLennan recalled. "But I was at a party where Nick Cave and Tracey Pew were living in London. Nick had brought this acoustic guitar and at that stage he couldn't play guitar very well. Neither could I but I picked it up and weird chords came to me and the phrase, 'The railroad takes him home', came straight away. So I worked on it and it became 'Cattle and Cane'. I knew that I wanted three verses and I wanted a different point of view to come in at the end of the song so I asked Robert to contribute an overview character. We nailed that song. I still get such a rush when I hear it because it's such a different sounding song and you don't write many songs like that."

With the addition of Lindy Morrison's rolling, militant drum pattern, the song was full of hooks and wistfulness and a young man's sense of purpose.

According to McLennan, "'Cattle and Cane' was a reaction to where I'd grown up in north Queensland, near the coast surrounded by sugar cane farms and then moving out to a cattle station and being surrounded by Hereford cattle and dirt roads and then finding yourself in London at twenty, twenty-one, playing music, such personal music."

Death Defying Hoodoo Gurus

(Dave Faulkner) ✳ Big Time ✳ 1983 ✳ Appears on: *Mars Needs Guitars*

Dave Faulkner was once asked whether the Hoodoo Gurus, the band he sings and plays guitar for, had left an influence. "I know we have," he replied. "I see it in lots of things going on, but whether it's our influence or people that we were influenced by, who can tell? I see our way of thinking, which is something that when we started I didn't see as much of."

Sixties garage rock, the music that was the original punk rock, wasn't about tattoos and Mohawks. It was garage bands – young bands trying to work out what this new music called rock & roll was all about. Typically the best of them made one single or one album and then disappeared, only to be reborn on the Nuggets compilation – an absolutely essential album. In Australia, combos like the Throb, the Missing Links, the Easybeats and later the Masters Apprentices all made great rock & roll. It was devil-may-care music, garage punk sounds as if the Beatles tried to cover *The Rolling Stones Now!* album.

The Gurus' first masterpiece was *Mars Needs Guitars*. Less self-consciously pop culture than their debut, the album had killer songs, the best of which was the ballad 'Death Defying'. As powerful a lyric as you're likely to hear, it was matched by a melody. Dave Faulkner once told me that one of his heroes was Cole Porter. It sounded incongruous coming from the leader of a garage band, but then a track like this makes him a contender in that league.

Pills and Soap The Imposter

(Elvis Costello) ✳ Imp/Demon ✳ 1983 ✳ Appears on: *The Very Best of Elvis Costello*

Elvis Costello is generally in danger of entangling his work in his own puns and the sheer weight of his record collection. One album followed the next with stylistic twists, but by the mid-'80s the world was suffering Elvis Costello overdose.

Then he rose again. The occasion was the 1982 Falklands War; a military adventure, the sole purpose of which was increasing support for Margaret Thatcher. Costello penned 'Shipbuilding' about the effect of the war on the average English person and how the dockyards would come back to life on the blood of soldiers and sailors in the southern Atlantic. Sung by Robert Wyatt, it was a deeply affecting song.

The following year, he followed it up with 'Pills and Soap'.

"Lyrically speaking, it carried on in a sense from 'Shipbuilding'," he said. "The intention behind releasing it at such a time was that some people might sympathise with it. That's all."

Costello's panoramas of modern Britain under Thatcher were stark and spare, filled mostly with Steve Naive's funereal organ and piano against the lament of Costello's voice:

> The king is in his counting house, some folks have all the luck
> And all we get is pictures of Lord and Lady Muck
> They come from lovely people with a hard line in hypocrisy
> There are ashtrays of emotion for the fag ends of aristocracy ...
> Give us our daily bread in individual slices
> And something in the daily rag to cancel all the crises ...

Costello wanted the record out quickly and his deal with Warner Bros. was not concluded so he released the track himself, as the Imposter. The disguise was somewhat blown though when Costello personally delivered the record to radio and the press.

"I wanted the song to be heard at this particular time," he said. "It couldn't wait the month or two that it will take to finalise legal matters."

It was further asserted that the single would only be pressed in a limited edition of 15,000 copies.

"'Pills and Soap' had already been a hit," said Costello. "Albeit with a bit of a con trick on the retailers and the BBC, when we threatened to delete it in a week, which helped catapult it into the charts. But in effect it was a broadside, a protest song."

Pink Houses John Cougar Mellencamp

(John Mellencamp) ✳ Riva ✳ 1983 ✳ Appears on: *Uh-Huh*

"I looked down and saw this old man early in the morning, sitting on the porch of his pink shack with a cat in his arms. He waved, and I waved back. That's how the song started." John Cougar Mellencamp is recalling 'Pink Houses', the song that gave him his real name back.

Johnny Cougar had tried to become a pop idol of sorts. Then in 1982 he went back to his Midwestern roots for the *American Fool* album and tapped into the perfect Reagan-era album. On its sequel, he found his voice as the poet of acceptance. Mellencamp made it all right to be comfortable with middle-class America. He was not complacent, however, and in songs like 'Authority Song' and 'Crumbling Down' he addressed the decline of traditional values. Mellencamp's genius was in the way he phrased his dissent – not as an intellectual leftist from Hollywood or New York but as a true-blue American who despised the big-city capitalists as much as the big government. Mellencamp touched a strong vein of rugged individualism and his personal narrative of trying to be a pop star in the big city and then rediscovering himself in the heartland reinforced the lyrics.

As befits the subject matter, the album was recorded on an Indiana farm over sixteen days. He warmed the studio up by producing an album for Mitch Ryder, a Detroit blue-eyed soul star from the '60s, and then ploughed right in.

Borderline Madonna

(Reggie Lucas/Madonna) ✳ Sire ✳ 1983 ✳ Appears on: *Madonna*

Madonna was a downtown dancer who couldn't sing very well when she signed to Sire. She was assigned producer Reggie Lucas, who had impeccable credits stretching back to his stint with Miles Davis and more recently with soulful R&B acts such as Mtume. Madonna was awed by Lucas' pedigree.

"Reggie, I thought, might be able to push me, having worked with Phyllis Hyman and Roberta Flack. The only problem was that he wanted to make me sound like them," Madonna told Barney Hoskyns. "I now know what I want on my next record. The production won't be so slick, because where Reggie and Mtume come from is a whole different school. I want a sound that's mine. There will be a more crossover approach to it this time. Maybe I should work with a British producer."

The best example of their working relationship is 'Borderline', which was a balance between the two creative impulses. Lucas pushes Madonna to find some emotional depth in the song and he provides a backing that is icy and contemporary but with a deep warm heart. 'Borderline' hinted at the range that Madonna's next twenty years would cover.

Holiday Madonna

(Madonna) ❋ Sire ❋ 1983 ❋ Appears on: *Madonna*

"For me, it was superstardom from the word go, and I thought, what is this shit? It's just a home away from home. So I left and came back to New York, and it was ... hell. New York is good to me now, but it was a really horrible in the beginning," Madonna told Barney Hoskyns back in 1983 when she was just another downtown girl with black roots in her hair and an overload of cheap jewellery.

Madonna would be the first to admit that she's no great singer but she knows two things. First of all, she knows what's going to happen next in music. Second, she knows that nothing so insignificant as a meagre vocal range is going to stop her.

In the early '80s, Madonna was a girl from the suburbs who wanted to make it in the downtown New York scene. She danced, she modelled, she acted and she sang. She met all the right people, including Sire Records' president Seymour Stein, who, legend has it, signed her contract while laid up in a hospital bed.

Stein put Madonna with Roberta Flack's producer Reggie Lucas, who described the sessions as "very informal and casual. It was my first pop project, and she was just a new artist. I had no idea it would be the biggest thing since sliced bread."

The record initially had a lukewarm reaction.

Mad World   Tears for Fears

(Roland Orzabal) ✳ Mercury ✳ 1983 ✳ Appears on *The Hurting*

Psychologist Arthur Janov had his primal scream therapy placed on the pop map by John Lennon who claimed that Janov's techniques had enabled him to be brutally honest with himself and as a consequence he wrote his purgative eponymous solo album. Ten years later, out of the town of Bath comes Roland Orzabal, fired up on Janov, and produces the primal whispering album of sensitive pop all about unnameable suffering. The key track here being the melodically rich 'Mad World'.

Take for instance the lyric from 'Mad World' – "the dreams in which I'm dying are the best I've ever had". Orzabal claimed this means that if dreams release tension, then the ones in which you have an intensely emotional experience, like dreaming of death, will release the most tension. Heavy.

Orzabal was happy to drop names like Sartre and Freud in interviews with the pop press and engage in deep philosophical discussions about the meaning of it all. "What Freud says is it's not so much what happened to you during childhood that's important, it's more how you experienced it," he told *Melody Maker*. "But where Janov comes from is, you were a victim, you were born innocent and they did this to you. I suppose the truth is somewhere in between. What I believe is that at some point you have to take account of your own actions. We can't keep on saying the problem is capitalism or communism or poverty or the ecology. Of course, these things have to be dealt with, but we have to stop blaming the Other and look inside."

Gorgeous, complex melodies and Curt Smith's sweet vocals ameliorated the pain of it all. "Primal therapy isn't a religion, a cult, a sect, a mythology," Orzabal explained to the readers of teenybopper mag *Smash Hits*. "It isn't anything weird at all, just a theory about the importance of relationships between children and their parents. We're not into primal therapy. We're just into living life to the full."

Blue Monday   New Order

(Gilbert/Hook/Morris/Sumner) ✳ Factory ✳ 1983 ✳ Appears on: *Power, Corruption & Lies*

The reverberations from this song were still being felt in popular music twenty years later.

New Order, born from the ashes of Joy Division, developed their distinctive, gloomy Manchester rock on their debut, *Movement*. This was the sound of the industrial wasteland of Britain's north country viewed through the prism of Bowie's Berlin recordings. The songs were humourless, relentless and thick with guitar and keyboards. There was a singularity to New Order's vision that made it compelling, especially to troubled teens.

The key to New Order wasn't, however, their sombre lyrics but rather the erupting rhythm section of Peter Hook on bass and drummer Stephen Morris. The monochromatic Joy Division groove – part Kraut Rock, part industrial and part metal – was an entirely new approach to rock and became the industry standard for post-punk rock. There were thick slabs of synthesiser propelled by the molten bass lines from Hook and coloured by the keyboards of Gillian Gilbert, who replaced the late Ian Curtis. The ghost of Curtis hung around the early years of New Order giving a gravitas to their monotonous, bleak songs. Paul Rambali put it well in *Face*: "Their music has reached deep into the sensitive isolation of nineteen-year-old male bedrooms. Playing a kind of refined, high-tech heavy metal, stripped of all the stucco frills but not lacking in melodrama . . ."

The change in the group's sound came with Peter Hook and Stephen Morris investing in computers and sequencers.

"With guitar, bass and drums you've got limited horizons," said Hook. "We'd like to increase our range of sounds and rhythms. If you come up with an idea for a song, you know exactly what you want the machine to do. You want a machine that can do everything! But that hasn't been built yet. We thought the Emulator was going to be it – but you get one and you soon find it has its limits."

So with their new toys and an appreciation of nightclubs, the song 'Blue Monday' gave New Order its first hit single, a dance floor anthem and a new purpose in life. The 12-inch is a perfect synthesis of German and industrial music with a pop melody. This is one of those moments where the shape of popular music was altered forever.

New Order then teamed up with New York remixer Arthur Baker, who had fused hip-hop and Kraftwerk so seamlessly with Afrika Bambaataa. Baker and New Order remixed this rock/dance music fusion so well that 'Blue Monday' became the template for dance music to come.

New Order was very much a live rock & roll band with a "heavy" sound. Their live shows brought a rock credibility to dance music. The sales of over 250,000 12-inch singles of 'Blue Monday' were evidence of the change in audience tastes. They retained a simplistic, punk attitude to their progressive rock styling and that simplicity was crucial to their popularity. "There's not one of our songs that uses a black note on the keyboard," said Hook. "That's true!"

Every Breath You Take   The Police

(Sting) ❊ A&M ❊ 1983 ❊ Appears on: *Synchronicity*

Sting famously announced, "I do my best work when I'm in pain and turmoil." This was his best work and he did it sitting at the desk on which Ian Fleming wrote the James Bond books. If one is in pain and turmoil, it's nice to be in the Bahamas.

Sting had come to the end of a seven-year marriage to Frances Tomelty and his even longer relationship with Andy Summers and Stuart Copeland was over for all but the shouting. The sessions for the *Synchronicity* album were, according to the players, fraught with conflict. Perhaps that's why the songs were so dark.

'Every Breath You Take' is Sting's finest moment, if only because he's not trying to be clever. A simple R&B chord progression, played with finesse but always understated, seduces the audience into a sense of wellbeing. The lyrics come up. A desperate tale told by a paranoiac stalker, this is more malevolent than mellow. Yet this song has launched a thousand weddings. Finally Sting has some irony.

Little Red Corvette   Prince

(Prince) ❊ Warner Bros. ❊ 1983 ❊ Appears on: *1999*

Like Chuck Berry thirty years before, it was a car song that crossed Prince's funk/soul and rock style over to a mainstream audience. The song was written in a pink Ford Edsel belonging to Lisa Coleman from Prince's backing band, the Revolution. The *1999* album accelerated the momentum that Prince had begun only three years before. He installed a state-of-the-art studio in his house and the next day cut 'Little Red Corvette'.

At the time Prince was putting together careers for Vanity 6 and the Time as well as his own full touring and recording schedule. Perhaps in the spirit of time management, Prince also bought an early drum machine. "I felt like an auto assembly worker looking at a robot for the first time, wondering if I still had a job," said drummer Bobby Z. "Prince said, 'Here it is, figure out what you're going to do with it'".

'Little Red Corvette' like Berry's 'Maybelline' eroticised the automobile, taking the metaphor one step further. Prince's presentation, both vocally and in the video clip, was pure sex. "He was trying to become as mainstream as possible," said the Revolution's Matt Fink, "without compromising".

This Charming Man The Smiths

(Johnny Marr/Morrissey) ✳ Rough Trade ✳ 1983 ✳ Appears on: *The Smiths*

"Many people who go into this business think that they have to have a very aggressive machismo or a very aggressive stage image," singer Morrissey told Jon Savage in January 1984. "It's time for a different version: not everybody is like Ozzy Osbourne. The normal rock & roll terminology sounds like a chant of agony. I think we need more brains in popular music."

'This Charming Man' was a manifesto of the fey, the twee, the alternative bookish types of the '80s versus the bombastic rock stars. Kicking off with the spiky, spine-tingling guitar of Johnny Marr against the cartoonishly wimpy voice of Morrissey, the Smiths' second single was a war cry for passive aggressives. Morrissey's vocal and his word play emboldened thousands of fans who later became the alternative nation.

"Up until then, either you were a chart group with no substance or you were an indie group no-one got to hear," said Johnny Marr. "'This Charming Man' found a happy compromise. It brought a real commercial sound together with interesting lyrics and a good groove.'

Just Be Good to Me The SOS Band

(James Harris/Terry Lewis) ✳ Tabu ✳ 1983 ✳ Appears on: *Rise*

Jimmy Jam and Terry Lewis were members of the Time, one of Prince's subgroups and doing production work on the side for the SOS Band. They had slipped off tour to make a recording date in Los Angeles and their flight to Texas was waylaid by a freak snowstorm causing them to miss a date. Prince suggested that it was time they were encouraged to move on. As it turns out, they would have been happy to go; the SOS Band hit number two with 'Just Be Good to Me' and Jam and Lewis became one of the most successful production teams of the '80s and '90s.

Led by Mary Davis' measured but sweet vocal, 'Just Be Good to Me' has a glorious deep groove lined with layers of sweet synthesiser pads. A gently funky drum track and a melodic, honeyed bass line complement the ambiguous situation of the singer ("I don't care about your other girls/Just be good to me"). She's in some pain but stoic and desperate. Jam and Lewis defined their own style, which owed something to Prince's funk but with the warmer feel of the Philly sound of Gamble and Huff. They went on to produce Janet Jackson and many other platinum artists while 'Just Be Good to Me' was revived by Fatboy Slim's Beats International as 'Dub Be Good to Me'. It remains one of the defining grooves of the '80s.

16 Shells From a Thirty-Ought Six Tom Waits

(Tom Waits) ✳ Island ✳ 1983 ✳ Appears on: *Swordfishtrombones*

Having started out as a wordsmith who produced metaphors to order by the tonne, Waits learnt the value of brevity. Capable of sentimental heart tug and wistful melody, in the '80s Waits transformed his sound yet again.

'16 Shells From a Thirty-Ought Six' is Waits' attempt to write a chain gang song. It's full of old time imagery – a thirty-ought six is a shotgun made in 1906, a Washburn is an old make of guitar – and the percussion includes a locomotive's brake pad.

"I tried to get a chain gang/work song/field holler," Waits told an interviewer in 1983. "Get a low trombone to give a feeling of a freight train going by. It's Stephen Hodges on drums, Larry Taylor on acoustic bass, Fred Tackett on electric guitar, Victor Feldman on brake drum and bell plate and Joe Romano on trombone. So, I wanted to have that kind of a sledgehammer coming down on an anvil.

"Originally I saw the story as a guy and a mule going off looking for this crow. He has a Washburn guitar strapped on the side of his mule and when he gets the crow he pulls the strings back and shoves this bird inside the guitar and then the strings make like a jail. Then he bangs on the strings and the bird goes out of his mind as he is riding off over the hill. So I tried to make the story a bit impressionistic but at the same time adding some very specific images in there.

"I worked a long time on this. The feel of it was really critical. I added snare and we pulled the snare off 'cause it made it shuffle too much. I liked the holes in it as much as I liked what was in them. It was a matter of trying to get that feeling of a train going. Originally I tried it just with organ and bass. Then I was afraid to add too much to it 'cause sometimes you get a feel that's appropriate. If you try to heap too much on it then it crumbles into the strain."

Sunday Bloody Sunday U2

(Bono/Adam Clayton/The Edge/Larry Mullen Jr) ❋ Island ❋ 1983 ❋ Appears on: *War*

On Sunday 30 January 1972 soldiers from the British Army's 1st Parachute Regiment opened fire on unarmed civilian demonstrators in the Bogside, Londonderry, in Northern Ireland. Thirteen demonstrators were killed protesting the British policy of internment without trial. Bloody Sunday highlighted the butchery and uselessness of the British occupation of Northern Island in the public consciousness. It was a turning point in the struggle for a republic. The first Bloody Sunday was 21 November 1920. Republican activist Michael Collins assassinated fourteen British intelligence officers known as "the Cairo Gang". In response the British army descended on a football game at Croke Park in Dublin, slaughtering hundreds of spectators, some as young as eleven years old.

In 1983 U2, who were Protestants from Eire (the south), put their views on the issue into this song.

The Edge began writing the lyric while Bono was away on his honeymoon. The initial take on the song was stridently anti-violence. The original first line was, "Don't talk to me about the rights of the IRA". Together they made the lyrics more general and concentrated on the central existential question, "How long must I sing this song".

"It means so much to me, that song, because ... I'm not sure I got it right," Bono told the late Timothy White. "I mighta got it wrong, I'm not sure. I originally wanted to contrast the day, Sunday Bloody Sunday, when thirteen innocent people were shot dead in 'Derry by the British army, with Easter Sunday. I wanted to make this contrast because I thought that it pointed out the awful irony of the fact that these two warring faiths share the same belief in the one God. And I thought how ... it's so absurd, really, this Catholic and Protestant rivalry. So that's what I wanted to do. In the end, I'm not sure I did that successfully with the words. But we certainly did it with the music. The spirit of the song speaks louder than the flesh of it."

Born in the USA Bruce Springsteen

(Bruce Springsteen) ❋ Columbia ❋ 1984 ❋ Appears on: *Born in the USA*

'Born in the USA' was written as an acoustic protest song for his earlier album, *Nebraska*, but Springsteen "electrified" it with the E Street Band and created one of the great (if often misunderstood) anthemic moments in rock.

"The sound of 'Born in the USA' was martial, modal and straight ahead," said Springsteen of the song's central contradiction. "The lyrics dealt with the problems Vietnam vets faced when they came back home after fighting 'the only war that America had ever lost'. In order to understand the song's intent, you needed to invest a certain amount of time and effort to absorb both the music and the words ...

"The first guy I played the finished version for was a Vietnam veteran ... He came into the studio and sat between two large speakers at the front of the console. I turned up the volume. He sat there for a moment listening to the first couple of verses, and then a big smile crossed his face.

"On the other hand, for years after the release of the album, I had little kids in red bandannas knocking on my door with their trick-or-treat bags, singing, 'I was born in the USA ...' They were not particularly well versed in the 'had a brother at Khe Sahn' lyric but they all had plenty of lung power when the chorus rolled around. I guess the same fate awaited Woody Guthrie's 'This Land is Your Land' around the campfire. But that didn't make me feel any better."

The song became the title track to Springsteen's follow up to *Nebraska*. The album was two years in the making and dominated the charts for more than a year after release. It was on this album that Springsteen translated his skill with personal, raw, folk-inspired material into full-tilt, electric rock & roll.

Time After Time   Cyndi Lauper

(Cyndi Lauper) ❉ Portrait ❉ 1984 ❉ Appears on: *She's So Unusual*

Cyndi Lauper was a goddess to all those girls who didn't fit in. This was the era of the teen misfit (as portrayed so eloquently by John Hughes in the film *The Breakfast Club* or Francis Ford Coppola's *Rumble Fish*). Lauper was a perfect fit. She was also very televisual just as MTV kicked off and was looking for kooky, quirky and colourful.

It might have been a case of right time, right place, but Cyndi Lauper was also the right girl. She was a wonderful interpreter of songs, notably the chick-lib anthem 'Girls Just Want to Have Fun', Prince's 'When You Were Mine' and the Brains' brilliant New Waver 'Money Changes Everything'. She can go from being Lucille Ball on one number to Judy Garland on another. Furthering the cause of women's emancipation is the first hit single about female masturbation – 'She Bop'. The real core of the album, however, is Lauper's own composition 'Time After Time' – a gorgeous stately ballad of heartbreak. The song was covered by Miles Davis and became his last hit.

Producer Rick Chertoff enlisted the appalling Philly rock band the Hooters to supply most of the backing on the album and it's a mark of Lauper's personality that she transcends their synthesiser sludge.

Lauper, who had already made an album with her band Blue Angel, put her heart and soul into *She's So Unusual* and it had a force that was simply undeniable. It was one of the few really great pop records to come out of the '80s and it happened because Lauper's Brooklyn whine and her personality cut through. And there was that haircut.

The Boys of Summer Don Henley

(Mike Campbell/Don Henley) ❋ Geffen ❋ 1984 ❋ Appears on: *Building the Perfect Beast*

As the singing drummer for the Eagles, Don Henley saw the liberal possibilities of the '70s dissolve into consumerist apathy. 'The Boys of Summer' from Henley's solo album is a companion piece to 'Hotel California'. However, where in the latter the characters sink into decadence and lethargy, in 'Summer' the symbols and icons and ideas of a progressive generation are transformed into cheap baubles and knick-knacks. The art that helped to change the world was now little more than a bumper sticker. Henley got all that information into a pop song of under four minutes.

"I was driving down the San Diego freeway," he told the *NME* of the genesis of the song. "I got passed by a $21,000 Cadillac Seville, the status symbol of the right-wing upper-middle-class American bourgeoisie – all the guys with the blue blazers with the crests and the grey pants – and there was this Grateful Dead 'Deadhead' bumper sticker on it."

Henley didn't look back when recording the track. Rather than replicate the country-rock style of the Eagles, Henley embraced synthesisers and drum machines to get a modern sound to the record.

"'Boys of Summer' was one of those great, rare moments where I got so inspired by the track that Mike Campbell had given me that it just sort of wrote itself," he told Bud Scoppa. "It came just screamin' out of me. And I was jumping up and down in the car 'cause I knew I had something there."

The song was a massive hit, though it perhaps didn't do much to stop the commodification of revolution. Henley's despair just became more name-checking of consumer brands.

"I wonder what happened to my generation," Henley mused. "All those great liberal ideas we had. Now everything's swung back to the right, the TV preachers with their own networks ... it's pretty scary."

John Coltrane Stereo Blues Dream Syndicate

(D Mehaffey/Karl Precoda/David Provost/Kendra Smith/Steve Wynn) ✳ A&M ✳
1984 ✳ Appears on: *The Medicine Show*

Dream Syndicate had the misfortune to be labelled the leaders of a movement. The term Paisley Underground loosely grouped cutting edge guitar bands together. Their common influence was nothing paisley but, rather, the Velvet Underground, the Byrds and early Neil Young. Dream Syndicate leader Steve Wynn acknowledged those influences but added some more – specifically free jazz.

'John Coltrane Stereo Blues' was a free-form improvisation. Intense, sprawling, reckless, hypnotic and cathartic. 'John Coltrane' took a gutsy rock and blues riff and just went with it. It wasn't jazz but experimental rock & roll that paid off.

"It's a free for all," said Wynn of the song. "But it isn't just an obligatory measure of wildness, it's for a band that knows it well enough to jam on. It's probably my favourite song on the album, but it's got to be right."

'Coltrane' appears on the group's second album. They had moved from the indie Slash to the more corporate A&M and had hard rock producer Sandy Pearlman (Blue Oyster Cult, the Clash) at the helm to make an album that was harder and slicker. 'Coltrane' was the moment when it all came together for them.

"When we formed we went out there playing whatever you'd call it – psychedelic garage or indie/underground noise – and we weren't seeing it anywhere," said Wynn. "I think it just opened a lot of people's ears to some alternatives at the time – to Duran Duran or Haircut 100 or whatever people thought was hip and groovy at the time. We just say, 'Nahh. There's another darker, weirder, deeper, creepier side of underground music. Check this out!' We were advocates for this music that excited us. And I think we had something to do with bridging the gap with what came before – the Stooges, the Velvets, the Modern Lovers, Big Star – and all the things that came afterwards – Yo La Tengo, Nirvana, and bands like that."

Original Sufferhead Fela Kuti

(Fela Kuti) ✳ Shanachie ✳ 1984 ✳ Appears on: *Original Sufferhead*

Fela Anikulapo Kuti is Nigeria's superstar. A child of the Nigerian ruling classes, Kuti went to Britain in 1969 for his education and gave something back. Even then he was playing highlife, popular dance music from Africa to English audiences. In the west he discovered jazz, R&B and rock & roll – all influences he transformed into a sound he called Afrobeat. In the '60s he travelled to the US where he came in contact with the Black Power movement and was himself politicised.

"I did not know about African music," he said to Barney Hoskyns. "It was up to you to trace, to decipher what was happening, and how modern jazz came from Africa. After I went to America, I went home and decided to get deep, and thought maybe I'll start looking for the link. At that time I didn't even know that Africans had wind instruments, because at school they did not teach us these things."

Back in Nigeria his outspokenness caused trouble with the authorities. In November 1977 his house was attacked by the local military and sacked, resulting in multiple deaths including that of his mother. Kuti spent more than two years in jail. With over fifty albums to his name, he has remained steadfastly political and an outspoken critic of corruption and cronyism in Nigeria.

His music is heavily based around African highlife and the syncopated power of a large ensemble. Kuti, who sings and plays saxophone and trumpet, builds massive grooves that grow organically out of a theme, meander around and are finally resolved some twenty minutes later (as in the case of 'Original Sufferhead'). It's a worthwhile journey.

Relax Frankie Goes to Hollywood

(Peter Gill/Holly Johnson/Mark O'Toole) ❋ ZTT ❋ 1984 ❋

Appears on: *Hollywood's Welcome to the Pleasuredome*

Trevor Horn's father was a professional musician who played in show bands. Horn followed in his father's footsteps, spending the '70s performing in ballrooms around Britain. In the '80s he moved behind the desk and became an über producer who embraced the innovations computers offered to recording. His first hit, with the Buggles' 'Video Killed the Radio Star', was a smash. Then, Phil Spector-like, he manipulated or created a number of entities including the Art of Noise. Perhaps his most famous work, however, was with a Liverpool band called Frankie Goes to Hollywood, whom he completely reshaped in the studio.

"I saw how people reacted to songs that made them dance, because of my big band job, so I made 'Video Killed the Radio Star', a single that you could dance to," Horn said. "'Relax' was the same. It has exactly the same beat as *Saturday Night Fever* because that's what I was playing with my band every Saturday night at the Hammersmith Palais."

Frankie was mostly singer Holly Johnson – the only member of the group to make a significant contribution to the first Frankie album. Johnson was openly gay, which make the highly sexual 'Relax' all the more controversial.

Horn used members of Ian Dury's Blockheads and Steve Howe of Yes (of which he was a sometime member) for the instrumental work. Johnson provided the personality. The end result was a massive hit. The heavy breathing and the stuttering musical passages owed a debt to Giorgio Moroder's singles with Donna Summer.

"When I used to go to the dances in Durham with my dad in the early '60s the beat groups were appearing and everyone was afraid," said Horn. "On the one hand you had men who could read music and knew what they were playing, and on the other you had guys banging a guitar around. When we started making electronic music I imagined that the reaction we got from the rock musicians must have been similar to the one the beat groups got from people like my dad."

'Relax', with its Hi-NRG (a genre that was very popular in clubs in the mid-'80s) feel and its joyful, tongue-in-cheek lasciviousness, was indeed the shape of things to come – and it still sounds great.

I Can't Live Without My Radio LL Cool J

(LL Cool J/Rick Rubin) ✳ Def Jam ✳ 1984 ✳ Appears on: *Radio*

On 'I Can't Live Without My Radio' LL Cool J showed himself to be a lover, not a fighter. Indeed he was a gawky, geeky teenager when *Radio* became a landmark hip-hop album. The album's opening salvo and key track, 'I Can't Live Without My Radio', was a perfect summer anthem – strong beats with resprung hooks and a dexterous rhyme jumped LL to the front of the queue. 'Radio' was a major step in recasting the vocabulary of rap music away from toasting and boasting over extended jams to being something else again.

Elsewhere on the album LL professes his love and pretty much nails the claim to be the first rap heartthrob. Working with producer Rick Rubin, LL Cool J shows the range and diversity that a rap artist could explore. Until this point most rappers had developed a single persona and rarely strayed from it. With *Radio* stretching the boundaries, Rubin and LL Cool J showed that rap was going to develop into a multifaceted musical form just as profound as jazz or rock.

Like a Virgin Madonna

(Tom Kelly/Billy Steinberg) ✳ Sire ✳ 1984 ✳ Appears on: *Like a Virgin*

This track told the world that Madonna was not here to mince words. It's about sex. The startling thing was how untroubled Madonna seemed to be about the whole affair. She took what could have been a torch song and just played with it. The production and the beats are light and airy and tossed off in a flirting style. Working with Chic producer Nile Rodgers the record had a masterful pop sheen and an innate sense of where the beat lay.

Mostly it's attitude that put Madonna into a class of her own. She was an icon to a generation of emancipated women. She sexualised everything. That "Boy Toy" buckle was pure irony and in taking control of her sexuality, Madonna was a leader in the next wave of emancipation.

'Like a Virgin' was controversial, with the Christian Right trying to keep it from the airwaves. Nonetheless it was Madonna's first number one single.

"I mean ... there's a lot of really narrow-minded people," Madonna told MTV Europe, "I really can't predict how far-reaching that can be and how many people I can change and how much tolerance will grow of the messages I put in my music."

When Doves Cry Prince & the Revolution

(Prince) ✳ Warner Bros. ✳ 1984 ✳ Appears on: *Purple Rain*

Surreal, psychedelic and sexy, 'When Doves Cry' was Prince reaching a new level of maturity as a writer and performer.

The song bears the influence of his band at the time, the Revolution. Its arrangement is somewhat more pop and sophisticated than the funk of the previous album.

According to engineer Peggy McCreary, Prince "came in, cut it and mixed it in a day. He was listening to it playing back and just popped the bass out." It was unheard of for any major album to go without a bass part, especially one in the R&B field, but Prince insisted. His whole process in recording the song was to pile up a complete and conventional arrangement of the song and then to nip and tuck so that the spaces created tensions and made the single sound unsettling.

Unlike so much of Prince's previous work, 'When Doves Cry' is almost baroque in its romanticism. It was the peak of his Purple period – characterised, of course, by the film *Purple Rain*, which Prince was conceiving as he wrote the music to the album of the same name. The music is closer to traditional R&B and jazz than funk and initially caused some fear in the Warner Bros. ranks. "They were a little afraid," said engineer David Z. "They didn't know what to do with it because it was drastically different."

The public did though. It was the biggest selling single of 1984 ahead of Springsteen and Jackson.

It's Like That Run-DMC

(Darryl 'DMC' McDaniels/Joe 'Run' Simmons/Larry Smith) ✳ Profile ✳ 1984 ✳
Appears on: *Run-DMC*

The marriage of metal and rap has been a longstanding affair, which began here. The trio from Queens, New York, were the first hardcore rappers, whose tough lyrics over tougher, spare beats set the template for the rap explosion that was to come. They took the rhyming that had been going on with Bronx parties and gave it a new form, especially with integration of metal guitar riffs over their beats. With this album they showed how rap could translate to an LP form rather than 12-inch singles and live performances.

Run (Joseph Simmons) and DMC (Darryl McDaniels) had a unique style of rapping over each other, finishing the other's sentences and using their dual syntax as syncopation with the beats from DJ Jam Master Jay. Their first single, 'It's Like That', was an R&B hit.

Where other rappers were there to toast the party or brag, Run-DMC had a confrontational approach to urban tales of life as it is on the streets. According to Run, "It's good to be raw."

Producer, manager and elder brother Russel Simmons brought freshness to the rap sounds on the album and put it into the R&B charts. The addition of some guitar made 'It's Like That' acceptable for MTV. According to Run, "I was trying to get a record that was positive because I knew that radio didn't want to play anything negative."

Your Love Is King Sade

(Sade Adu/Stuart Matthewman/Gordon Matthewman) ✳ Epic ✳ 1984 ✳
Appears on: *Diamond Life*

Everything about Sade is exotic. Her looks. Her birthplace – a village outside Lagos, Nigeria's capital. Her name – Helen Folasade Adu. Most of all, though, her music oozes exotic, languid Latin motifs and jazz stylings. Sade's first album, *Diamond Life*, swept through the airwaves of 1984 like a sublime perfume on a quiet night's breeze.

Sade had been the singer for the eight-piece soul and jazz band Pride, which included Stuart Matthewman, Paul Denman and Andrew Hale for some three years before signing with Epic records. Sade's obvious influences – Donny Hathaway, Billie Holliday, Curtis Mayfield and Marvin Gaye – were subsumed by the jazz influences in the band, especially Matthewman's playing and the demands of the London clubs. "What nobody in England has really understood," said bass player Denman, "is that it's a live thing and not a style thing. We have never been influenced by what's going on. Before we recorded *Diamond Life* we'd been going around playing those songs for years. We still record a lot of our best stuff just how we perform it, live in the studio."

'Your Love Is King' was the standout track that established Sade's style – erotic and gentle, humorous and languid in the tradition of the best pop jazz. Mostly, though, it had a melodic line that just wouldn't quit. Where her bigger hit 'Smooth Operator' seemed bound up in the ambitions of the '80s, 'Your Love Is King' is as inviting as ever.

"We were picked up on because we were different from anything else that was going on at that time," said the singer. "I am much more myself and less committed to promoting an image than, say, Morrissey or Bruce Springsteen or Mick Jagger."

My Ever Changing Moods The Style Council

(Paul Weller) ✳ Polydor ✳ 1984 ✳ Appears on: *Cafe Bleu*

Paul Weller's changing moods played a significant part in changing a nation. In 1977 the Jam arrived as the third part of the punk triumvirate. They represented youth (Weller was only seventeen) and Englishness – a tradition going back to the Who and the Kinks. While others conquered America, the Jam had a three-year lock on the UK singles' charts and Weller became a national hero. So, when he broke up the Jam in 1982 for a new direction in music, he took a large section of Britain on the journey.

The other half of the Style Council was organist Mick Talbot; a soul-jazz feel replaced the Motown rave-ups of the Jam. 'My Ever Changing Moods' is a good example of the Style Council's debt to Curtis Mayfield with its discreet but intoxicating groove.

Weller hung up his Rickenbacker guitar in favour of Talbot's keyboards. This was indicative of a shift away from rock music and into the more sophisticated realm of club music. In Britain pop music is an important medium to express changes in the culture. The Style Council did exactly that. The sweaty authenticity of punk rock was junked in favour of a middle-class aspirational lifestyle where fashion and design and modernism existed in a disciplined, engaged and thoughtful lifestyle. Punk symbolised catharsis and abandon. The Style Council stood for improvement and change and reason and control. Punks wore rags held together by safety pins; the Style Council were casual but neat with jumpers tied around their shoulders in case the weather should become inclement. This shift of values has been a part of British popular culture ever since. 'My Ever Changing Moods' is a manifesto for a lifestyle unencumbered by ideology. And it has a nice tune.

Pride (In the Name of Love) U2

(U2) ✳ Island ✳ 1984 ✳ Appears on: *The Unforgettable Fire*

The sessions for U2's *Unforgettable Fire* were as fraught as any for the group. It was here that producers Daniel Lanois and Brian Eno helped U2 to find their mature voice. The textures between bass and guitar are more complex and Lanois' ambient atmospheres start to creep in. But that aside, it's here that U2 really start to swing. The group still had those ringing guitar tunes over a throbbing beat but they were starting to stretch. 'Pride' was inspired by the life and work of Martin Luther King, who combined political activism with his Christian beliefs in a way that the Irish could understand. According to the Edge, "Because of the situation in our country, non-violent struggle was such an inspiring concept."

"I originally wrote 'Pride' about Ronald Reagan and the ambivalent attitude in America," Bono told the *NME*. "It was originally meant as the sort of pride that won't back down, that wants to build nuclear arsenals. But that wasn't working. I remember a wise old man who said to me, don't try to fight darkness with light, just make the light shine brighter. I was giving Reagan too much importance, then I thought Martin Luther King, there's a man. We build the positive rather than fighting with the finger."

The track was U2's first Top 40 hit in the US and has been one of their most enduring songs.

Close to Me The Cure

(Robert Smith) ❋ Fiction ❋ 1985 ❋ Appears on: *Head on the Door*

Robert Smith had been through the wringer a couple of times by the mid-'80s. His group the Cure started out as moody existentialist art rockers who were immediately successful, despite their limited musical talents. Smith struggled with his success through career defeating albums and years of drug and alcohol abuse. However, the pop songs kept creeping out. In an attempt to demystify the Cure he had penned 'Let's Go to Bed' and inexplicably the track was a hit in the US.

In early 1985, Smith resolved to get happy. In two weeks he wrote a new album, *Head on the Door*. It was recorded with an unashamed delight for hooks and catchy melodies. Smith and the group's video director Tim Pope cut some of the group's most whimsical film clips.

"I think the Cure really started again at this point," said Smith. "It felt like being in the Beatles – and I wanted to make substantial 'Strawberry Fields'-style pop music. I wanted everything to be really catchy.

"We're in a very strange position in that we're able to play really crass pop songs and yet people still accept that I can sing about issues with far greater emotional depth and take it seriously."

Money for Nothing Dire Straits

(Mark Knopfler) ❋ Vertigo ❋ 1985 ❋ Appears on: *Brothers in Arms*

The '80s are remembered as a time of excess and extreme behaviour, but a look at the pop charts tells a different story. No-one exemplified the beige-ness of the decade more than Dire Straits. Mark Knopfler's endless instrumental passages had the patina of jazz and rock improvisation but were cold and detached; bourgeois muzak to relax with after a day on the money markets. Finally, on the fifth album, they broke a smile, cut back on the solos and made one of the blockbuster albums of all time.

'Walk of Life' was a delightful, jaunty single with a touch of rockabilly. Then came the knockout punch – 'Money for Nothing' – which satirised MTV and rock stardom while getting high rotation MTV exposure and making Mark Knopfler a rock star. Of course, there was irony here (finally). No-one could imagine Knopfler – the man who made a fashion statement of headbands – getting chicks. MTV notwithstanding.

Would I Lie to You? Eurythmics

(Annie Lennox/Dave Stewart) ❊ RCA ❊ 1985 ❊ Appears on: *Be Yourself Tonight*

Having invented electro pop, Eurythmics guitarist/producer Dave Stewart then developed a number of other production styles, the most powerful of which was his soul period.

In the mid-'80s he applied the clean lines and discreet sound of electronic music to the beat and feel of classic soul. As he said in response to a review in the British music press, "That was one thing I couldn't understand in the review of the single in the *Melody Maker*. The guy was saying 'Stewart who fancies himself as the svengali producer' and all this, and he said it was like a kind of watery sound, where to me 'Would I Lie' is the most powerful, up, intense Stax sound of anything I've heard on the radio lately. When I watched *Top of the Pops* it all seemed like watery kind of discoey ... the whole thing was ploddy-ploop, y'know? And then suddenly our single comes on the radio and it's ..."

Everything is built around the massive drum sound that pushes right up against the beat. It's a tsunami of energy coloured by Lennox's impassioned vocals and Stewart's bluesy guitar lines.

"I was always looking for a good relationship, and you can see it in the songs, all this unrequited love," said Lennox. "I was never in one spot, so my emotions were in turmoil. I never really enjoyed it – I should have settled down. Eurythmics was the mainstay of my existence and yet it was hollow. The irony was that though I was lonely, miserable and unsatisfied, it's a fantastic source for songs. The more hurt I'd get, the more intense the songs. 'Would I Lie to You?' and 'Thorn in My Side' I'm afraid are honed from the same tree. It wouldn't take much of an IQ to figure out they came out of the break-up with my first husband."

Throw Your Arms Around Me Hunters & Collectors

(Hunters & Collectors) ❊ Mushroom ❊ 1985 ❊ Appears on: *Human Frailty*

Recorded live to a two-track machine, 'Throw Your Arms Around Me' became an anthem. A slight modal song, in its sparse lyric and melody is an ocean of romantic feeling. The song has been frequently covered, but never well. The Hunters recorded it four times, but never as well as the first. It's a song that has never been a hit single but is one of the most popular Australian ballads.

"When I came up with 'Throw Your Arms Around Me' the band and myself were pretty much entrenched in a different style of music," said lyricist Mark Seymour. "It was funk-orientated, heavy, very European sounding. And it wasn't driven by personal feelings. Whereas that song was very much my baby, I thought. I was writing about direct experience and I wanted to distil a very simple pure emotion.

"I was trying to make the song convey this idea of the inevitability of events: that when two people meet and they're passionate about each other, then things happen and there's nothing either of them can do to stop. There is an inevitability about love that fascinated me. I wanted to capture that idea that there was something happening that I couldn't stop, by setting the language in the future or the immediate future, like the next day or the next hour or the next minute.

"I wanted to capture that mood of being in a state of transition – like you've got your own abode in one part of the town and then she's at another end of the town and you have to keep travelling back and forth. And even though all the things around you are completely familiar your lifestyle has been thrown into upheaval and you're acutely aware of everything around you because of the fact that you're so deeply in love with this person.

"I keep getting asked to do it at weddings, like three or four times a year and sometimes I acquiesce and do it but most of the time I say no."

Just Like Honey The Jesus and Mary Chain

(William Reid/Jim Reid) ❈ Blanco y Negro ❈ 1985 ❈ Appears on: *Psychocandy*

'Just Like Honey' starts off with Phil Spector's drum phrase from 'Be My Baby' immersed in even more echo than the original and then followed by a guitar riff that is mostly echo and feedback in a majestic wall of '80s sound. The Reid brothers, who are the Jesus and Mary Chain, knew who they were quoting. This was a meeting of British punk rock attitude with classic rock.

"With *Psychocandy*, we never arrived drunk in the studio and went wild with guitars," said William Reid. "We sat for months making sure. We had white noise sampled on an AMS machine, punching it in at certain places. It wasn't as spontaneous as everybody would like it to be. A lot of people seem to think you turned up, you were on speed, you fucked around with guitars and that record magically happened. It's magic and it did happen, but not the way people wanted it to. It took time and a lot of effort."

The record inspired hundreds of imitators and prefigured the shoe-gazer fad that took over British rock for a couple of years in the '80s. 'Just Like Honey' is a record of terrible beauty. It's dark and obsessive but also strangely awe-inspiring. Unlike so many post-punks, the Jesus and Mary Chain weren't deconstructing rock but, rather, assembling it again from its decayed parts. The song is viscerally exciting and emotionally moving in a way that so few rock tracks from that period are.

Running Up That Hill (A Deal With God) Kate Bush

(Kate Bush) ✳ EMI ✳ 1985 ✳ Appears on: *Hounds of Love*

This duet between Peter Gabriel and Kate Bush was initially titled 'Deal with God'. "For me, that is the title," said Bush, "but I was told that if I insisted the radio stations in at least ten countries would refuse to play it because it had 'God' in the title – Spain, Italy, America, lots of them. I thought it was ridiculous. Still, especially after *The Dreaming*, I decided I couldn't be bloody-minded. You have to weigh up the priorities. Not creatively compromise, but not be so obsessive that ... I had to give the album a chance."

This song and its album represented a more mature phase for the idiosyncratic British singer/songwriter. She had steadfastly avoided getting her private life into the tabloids; however, her music was clearly personal and the specifics changed only slightly. Whether this song was part of an affair with Peter Gabriel or what the specifics of her marital difficulties were is not spelt out, but *Hounds of Love* is an album about coming to terms with the onset of mid-life. Much of the artifice of Bush's early hits was gone and what remained was infinitely more interesting.

He's on the Beach Kirsty MacColl

(Kirsty MacColl/Gavin Povey) ✳ Polydor ✳ 1985 ✳ Appears on: *Galore*

It's extraordinary that an artist of MacColl's abilities slipped through the cracks, relatively unknown at the time of her accidental death in 2000. The daughter of folk singer and songwriter Ewan MacColl and the wife of producer Steve Lillywhite, Kirsty MacColl was a songwriter with unique gifts and a singer with a voice that was by turns heartbreaking and uplifting.

MacColl led, by all accounts, a very full life. Much of it happy and some of it depressed. The spectre of her father who left the family before she was born cast an unfortunate shadow.

"It's misleading to say I had no contact with him or I didn't love him," MacColl said. "I didn't grow up in the same household but people assume that because my dad was into music and I've got two half-brothers who are performers that it was like the Waltons, all sitting around playing acoustics. It wasn't like that at all. I grew up with my mum. I felt really excluded from that lifestyle.

"Children are happy if their parents are happy. They shouldn't have to feel responsible for the cock-ups of grown-ups. I felt guilty about a lot of things that were nothing to do with me. Loving is not saying, 'I love you' to someone, it's giving them what they need. I'm not sure what I needed but I don't think I got it.

"I don't want to make my mum unhappy. She wanted it all to be all right. She didn't turn against my father, she loved him and she never loved anyone else. I wish I'd been closer to him, but he was a sad man and it made him close up. Childhood was just something I had to get over in order to get on with my life."

MacColl started in pop music when still a teenager. Her first song 'They Don't Know' was a minor hit for her and later a smash hit for Tracey Ullman. Her first real action came in 1981 at age nineteen with 'There's a Guy Works Down the Chip Shop Swears He's Elvis', which was both funny and an accurate portrait of male narcissism. MacColl's next hit was a version of Billy Bragg's 'A New England', that she made tuneful and meaningful in ways that Bragg never quite could.

Her follow-up to the Billy Bragg hit was 'He's on the Beach'. Like 'Elvis' this was a carefully rendered character study of a person who had escaped the dreariness of England for a free life. MacColl imbued the song with a wonderful sense of promise and sunshine and a taste of victory while on the same tune capturing the other character's feeling of loneliness and entrapment.

"If you live in England you do get depressed," she said in an interview some time after the release of 'He's on the Beach'. "You are surrounded by apathy all the time. It's dark half the winter. It has that effect on me. I feel rooted here but I spend a lot of time travelling and that's quite a relief. I can't imagine not going away from time to time, just to get things in perspective. There's something about England ... we just [exasperated sigh] ... I think you need to go abroad to realise how insignificant we are."

'He's on the Beach' is a perfect piece of pop that sounds like Beach Boys records and blue skies and the endless expanse of new possibilities.

West End Girls Pet Shop Boys

(Chris Lowe/Neil Tennant) ❋ Parlophone ❋ 1985 ❋ Appears on: *Please*

A pop journalist (Neil Tennant) and a synthesiser geek (Chris Lowe) were an unlikely pair. Not particularly photogenic, quite camp and possessed of a wry wit to compensate for dry vocals, the Pet Shop Boys nonetheless had a massive impact on the music scene in the '80s. They helped to make club music accessible for the mainstream white audience and they were so odd that they invited the suburban straight audience to check out hip-hop and dance music, which was confined to gay clubs outside the US.

"Slightly to the left of Stock, Aitken and Waterman," quipped Tennant shortly after their second album had sold over a million copies, surpassing the first. "And then we often get accused, particularly in Europe, of being a yuppie group, and that our LPs are bought on CD for people to listen to on their car stereos. To be honest, it's true to an extent. And when we did record signings in America, in Dallas a whole family came to see us: the mother, her daughter and the grandmother were all Pet Shop Boys fans. We do get a lot of letters from mothers. Mothers like me! And also I get the fans that write poetry: I have a slight David Sylvian crossover audience, whereas Chris gets the sex audience, the ones who write obscene letters! It's quite thrilling, actually!"

Their first single 'West End Girls' sold a million right out of the box. The track is sexy and dangerous. Lowe laid down a widescreen background for Tennant's story about class and seduction and the meeting of money and violence. 'West End Girls' has a haunting quality – recreating the late night streets, the possibility of getting into something one shouldn't. Tennant said that he was inspired by Grandmaster Flash's 'The Message' and transferred it to London. Which may be true but he has touched the subconscious, the pleasure zone. While it may be creepy, courtesy of Chris Lowe we have white suburban Englishmen laying out hip-hop beats and hypnotic melody lines.

As they often pointed out, the pair were not pin-ups. They made no pretence to be straight. Neither of these things were in the end obstacles that a great pop song couldn't overcome.

Dirty Old Town The Pogues

(Ewan MacColl) ❋ Stiff ❋ 1985 ❋ Appears on: *Rum, Sodomy, and the Lash*

It's unlikely that Ewan MacColl would have approved of the Pogues' version of 'Dirty Old Town'. MacColl saw himself as a socialist revolutionary, using folk music to celebrate the working classes, and as a medium for information and encouragement in the struggle against capitalism. When not penning songs or reviving old folk songs, MacColl wrote and acted in plays for the glories of the workers. An awkward scene change in 1949's *Landscape with Chimneys* called for a song and 'Dirty Old Town' was born.

'Dirty Old Town' is a waltz set allegedly in the northern industrial town Salford, Lancashire, where MacColl was born. It's a love–hate story – the sentimental memories of a first kiss by the factory wall and the dreams by the old canal lead into a reverie about the industrial landscape and finally the vow to destroy the poverty and despair of the place.

The Pogues' version floats on the ambiguous affection for the past and it's more maudlin than versions by Rod Stewart, Richard Thompson or Townes Van Zandt. Produced by Elvis Costello, it's one of their finest and roughest moments.

Addicted to Love Robert Palmer

(Robert Palmer) ❉ Island ❉ 1985 ❉ Appears on: *Riptide*

After years exploring funk, calypso, reggae, soul and electronica, Robert Palmer suddenly became a star. The Power Station, a "super group" helmed by Chic's Bernard Edwards and featuring Palmer as well as Tony Thompson and Duran Duran's Andy Taylor, was suddenly a pop phenomenon. The slightly disco feel and hard rock crunch, pumped up by Edwards' production, was crass but diverting pop.

Palmer brought it home alone with 'Addicted to Love'. The song is funky and bluesy but very modern in its production – massive gated drums and a thunderous, if simple, hook line.

"It's not like I was looking for hits," said Palmer. "I don't know why one takes off, and the other doesn't. Maybe it's the weather.

"Even though you get famous for one peak or kind of thing, it doesn't delineate everything you've done."

'Addicted to Love' was accompanied by an incredible video clip. There was Palmer, always comfortable in a suit, fronting an all girl band in little black dresses and classic cocktail styling. The clip may have been a self-parody but its images were so arresting that it has become one of the most famous video clips ever made.

"I think it was a package rolled into one that had to do with the timing, the sounds ... everything fell into place. It struck a fashion note in all directions. And I don't think any one aspect was more important than the other," Palmer recalled. "The director said, 'You stand there and mime'. I know it's become an icon but it's nothing to do with me. I don't regret it. It had an extremely fun and humorous tongue-in-cheek elegant humour about it. And as the French say, 'What is the use of audacity without grace?'"

Everybody Wants to Rule the World Tears For Fears

(Chris Hughes/Roland Orzabal/Ian Stanley) ❋ Mercury ❋ 1985 ❋
Appears on: *Songs from the Big Chair*

The English have perfected the irritating anthem that purports to be good for you. They write these saccharine hooks that are so tightly on the money and then they wrap them in layers of serious and sensitive male vocals. The lyric is pretty much fatuous nonsense but the riff is a killer. The companion piece to this track on the album is a football terrace anthem called 'Shout', disguised as a tune about primal scream therapy. 'Rule the World' could be a nice tune with which to advertise chardonnay.

After some success, 'Rule the World' put Tears For Fears over the top and number one on the American charts.

Tears For Fears were like Wham! without the wham part. Roland Orzabal who writes the material for Curt Smith to sing is perpetually whingeing about something. Often the subject of complaint was not readily discernible and perhaps irrelevant – simply a general sense of ill ease. Without wishing to be flippant, it's hard to understand what the problem is in as much as Orzabal is big on platitudes but short on specifics. He grew up on a council estate in Bath, a provincial English city where he was picked on at school and his dad founded the Portsmouth Philosophical Society. From there things were relatively simple – a deal with Mercury based on a demo of two songs – 'Suffer the Children' and 'Pale Shelter'. You could tell right there that they weren't gonna be a lot of fun. Half a decade later and they sold nine million albums. Largely thanks to this single. No wonder then it took three years to feel bad enough to make a follow-up.

Time Tom Waits

(Tom Waits) ❋ Island ❋ 1985 ❋ Appears on: *Rain Dogs*

Tom Waits said he wrote the *Rain Dogs* album "thinking of the guy going back to Philadelphia from Manhattan on the Metroliner with the *New York*

Times, looking out the window in New York as he pulls out of the station, imagining all the terrible things he doesn't have to be a part of."

This is a deeply melancholy album. Waits' jazz blues muse is orchestrated by Marc Ribot's tense, staccato guitar, which squeaks and squawks the most precise and elliptical lines against the funereal march bass of Larry Taylor and Waits' eccentric percussion – bits of drums and glass and metal.

All that cacophony is boiled down to just Waits on guitar, Taylor on double bass and William Shimmel on accordion for the drunken waltz at the heart of the album. 'Time' is that perfect moment between waking and sleep, between life and death – a still point where time itself stops and everything that you can see is simultaneously uplifting and sad and going neither up nor down: you're suspended out of time. "And the things you can't remember/ Tell the things you can't forget that/History puts a saint in every dream," Waits sings.

The LP's title refers to the condition of dogs after a rainstorm when all their markings have been washed away: "They go to sleep thinking the world is one way and they wake up and somebody moved the furniture." As he sings the refrain, "It's time, time, time/That you love" you have the sense of drifting off into the unknown.

Caught Up in the Rapture   Anita Baker

(Glenn Garry/Dianne Quander) ※ Elektra ※ 1986 ※ Appears on: *Rapture*

The queen of quiet storm, Anita Baker's second album drew comparisons with jazz greats Sarah Vaughan and Ella Fitzgerald although there was a strong strain of R&B and soul in her tracks and a strong groove as befits a Detroit girl. Baker had made one acclaimed album, *The Songstress*, before she signed with Elektra and cut an album that influenced the shape of R&B in the mid-'80s.

"I didn't know I had that in me," she said later. "I wanted a smooth product with energy and heart, but I surprised myself. There's passion there. I knew I could pop a note, but the nuances I think are what's important."

Baker executive-produced the album, choosing old friend Michael J Powell as producer for most of it. She fought a difficult legal battle to get out of her previous contract because she wanted creative freedom and she wasn't going to give it up. Elektra, she said, "left me the hell alone. I knew what I wanted to sing, and I knew what kind of production I wanted, which was the minimalist approach."

As the title suggests, *Rapture* is an album of sensual joy and spiritual peace. The combination of jazz, gospel, soul and R&B flavours was unique. It was music for adults as well as the pop charts.

The key track is the intense and intimate 'Caught Up in the Rapture'. Part of the charm of the record was that it was made without any expectations of major success and its unadorned romanticism made the grooves that much more sensual. From a virtual unknown, *Rapture* made Baker an instant superstar, no-one being more surprised than the singer herself. "I didn't think anybody was gonna hear it," she said.

Fight for Your Right   Beastie Boys

(Beastie Boys/Rick Rubin) ❋ Def Jam ❋ 1986 ❋ Appears on: *Licensed to III*

"As for us, when we were thirteen and fourteen and went to clubs and heard the DJ mix Big Youth and Treacherous Three with James White or Delta 5, it wasn't, 'Hey, now we're finding out about what people from another culture are about.' It was just great music," said Beastie Boy Mike D. "All the kids at my school were into Led Zeppelin and the Eagles and that was what I defined myself against. So it was more a case of cool music versus uncool music."

In fact Mike Diamond, Ad-Rock and MCA put the cool and uncool music together, aided by producer Rick Rubin, and the result changed music.

The Beastie Boys were just three kids from rich New York families who liked black culture. When they cut 'Fight for Your Right' they had little understanding of rap or black culture. They just liked the idea. Rick Rubin who had produced most of the old school rap on the New York Def Jam label was one of the few producers who understood metal crunching guitars and drums – especially John Bonham's drum sound from *Led Zeppelin IV* – and he also understood the rhythms of rap rhyme. Plus they were funny. What started as a lark turned into a revolution in sound.

Greetings to the New Brunette   Billy Bragg

(Billy Bragg) ❋ Go! Discs ❋ 1986 ❋ Appears on: *Talking with the Taxman about Poetry*

Billy Bragg was a middle-class boy writing about the working classes with a touch of BBC affectation – but beneath it all he had a fundamental belief that really the yobbos are missing the point. The characters in 'Greetings to the

New Brunette' are well drawn (if a little brutally) in the manner of Ray Davies, although Davies I think isn't overly harsh in his criticism. Bragg's enduring political statement would be his assertion of Englishness, the common or garden lifestyle that exists outside of global capitalism. "I'm not an angst depresso person, I try to be positive," he said. "But this is Britain and I'm afraid it isn't all 'Karma Chameleon' and happy happy. I don't think people need reality slammed down their throats but it doesn't hurt to remind people who, for whatever reasons, are not aware we're living in a country where we're not looking after everybody. We all say our priority is the welfare state but it doesn't even work anymore and the government is trying to pull it apart."

Bragg's mission, as was Woody Guthrie's, was to keep the forgotten and the dispossessed in the culture and the landscape. He does that with 'New Brunette' and he's funny as well: "How can you lie there and think of England/ When you don't even know who's in the team" and "Your sexual politics have left me all of a muddle/We are joined in the ideological cuddle," which is British college humour.

With some help from Smiths' guitarist Johnny Marr and singer Kirsty MacColl, 'New Brunette' was a new level of sophistication for Billy Bragg as a writer and the song is still strangely affecting.

Levi Stubbs' Tears   Billy Bragg

(Billy Bragg) ❋ Go! Discs ❋ 1986 ❋ Appears on: *Talking with the Taxman about Poetry*

The Levi Stubbs of the title is the singer in the Four Tops. This oddly affecting song tells the story of a working-class woman who marries too young to the wrong man and finds herself desperate, alone and miserable with only the sound of Motown to comfort her.

"When the world falls apart some things stay in place/Levi Stubbs' tears run down his face." Bragg sings the song accompanied only by his electric guitar and that too adds to the oddness. It's like something very crucial is missing (beyond tunefulness), Bragg just has the emotion of the song. "Yes, I listen to tapes and I'm sure I'm singing flat on all the songs," he said. "I want to sing like I talk so I'm never going to be a great singer. I don't think I have to sing in tune all the time for the lyrics to come across. It would be nice but it becomes behind a few other priorities. It's like what you wear onstage, what does it matter?"

Bragg made his name as a radical left-wing songwriter, a pamphleteer, so 'Levi Stubbs' Tears', which drips with sentimentality, sounds out of place alongside the workers' marching anthems. Its context on this album raises questions about how art, especially escapist art, functions and the song is decidedly and correctly ambiguous.

On the face of it, 'Levi Stubbs' Tears' should be a forgotten novelty but it remains a powerful and disturbing song.

Don't Dream It's Over Crowded House

(Neil Finn) ✻ Capitol ✻ 1986 ✻ Appears on: *Crowded House*

"We didn't know when we finished the first album that 'Don't Dream It's Over' was going to be a big hit at all," Neil Finn admitted. The track, accompanied by a magnificent video by director Alex Proyas and non-stop touring by Crowded House, eventually topped the US charts and was the cornerstone of their brilliant career.

The medium-tempo ethereal ballad owed a small debt to the Beatles' 'Across the Universe' and had a similar dreamlike quality. "I'm never conscious when I'm writing of any kind of intellectual requirement for the song," said Finn. "It's a case of being able to drift off and dream away in the right manner, and then falling upon something that seems to bring an emotion out within you. At that point you try and get as much of that feeling down on paper as you can and resist the urge to go off and make a cup of tea as a reward. 'Don't Dream It's Over' I wrote in one go on my brother's piano in his house in Melbourne. There were people around visiting at the time and I shut myself away in a room and that was the reason I wrote 'They come, they come to build a wall between us.'"

Recording the first album in Los Angeles was a difficult process. At one point producer Mitchell Froom brought in session supremos Jerry Scheff and Jim Keltner to replace House members Nick Seymour and Paul Hester. The next day they recorded 'Don't Dream' and the new trio clicked. "It had a particularly sad groove to it," said Finn. "I think because Paul and Nick had faced their own mortality."

The song brought a new beginning to the group, away from straight guitar pop and into a more sophisticated territory. "Mitchell was very influential on certain things about that first record and the feel in particular," said Finn. "Having come from a pretty white anglophile pop band with Split Enz, Mitchell played these very out of the way keyboards that just suspended the chords in a very dreamy and appealing way and that again was different."

The song was later covered by Paul Young and that version kicked off the House's career in Britain, and has been covered numerous times since.

Like most songwriters, Neil Finn remains uncertain why this particular song became a classic. "It has a certain universalness about it," he offered. "There's a hopeful, positive sentiment to it, but it's turned into melancholy and that's real life too. And I think in America if you put the word 'freedom' in the first line it really helps. Beyond that I have no idea, the way the chords and the melody work together is always a deep mystery and it just seems to work."

Say Goodbye   Hunters & Collectors

(Hunters & Collectors) ✳ Mushroom ✳ 1986 ✳ Appears on: *Human Frailty*

Perhaps the most direct song about the sexual revolution, 'Say Goodbye' is powered by the magnificent rumble of John Archer's bass guitar and Mark Seymour's refrain: "You don't make me feel like I'm a woman anymore!"

"People have run out of things to say about the power struggle between men and women," Seymour told me in 1986. "I wanted to write a lyric that expressed having gone through this whole process of negotiation, organising the relationship so it was all running smoothly, and suddenly one day the man looks up from his newspaper and realises he hasn't been giving her what she needs and she's pissed off about it. The most basic, fundamental thing you've forgotten about because you've been setting up your domestic environment."

The song became an instant classic; especially as a climax in the Hunters incendiary live performances. The group by this stage was just coming into its own, having flung off the pretensions of their early years in search of a sound that reflected their largely male Australian audiences. Although they set their sights on talking to the common punter, the Hunters were too eclectic a bunch to ever really cut straight rock songs, and that tension between ambition and their musical limitations is what made them exceptional. That and the notion that you could write a pub rock song with a feminist perspective.

"The whole song is a mixture of images," said Seymour. "One is a conversation I heard through a wall and another is having my girlfriend jump on top of me and grind her finger into my breastbone. It's pretty funny. It's ironic. It's even more ironic when you get a thousand blokes screaming it at the top of their voices."

Nasty Janet Jackson

(James Harris/Janet Jackson/Terry Lewis) ✳ A&M ✳ 1986 ✳ Appears on: *Control*

Unlike other members of her famous family, Janet Jackson got funkier as she matured. 'Nasty' was a defiant statement from a woman who was no longer going to be a wallflower making wallpaper music.

Jackson enlisted the team of Jimmy Jam and Terry Lewis to work up their Minneapolis funk as the basis for her personal makeover. Jackson was leaving her husband and the domination of her notoriously patriarchal father and the comfort zone of the Jacksons. She also had to compete for attention with her brother, who at the time had the biggest selling albums in history.

Jam and Lewis spent a week talking with Jackson about the issues she wanted to address in her songs and on the basis of those conversations worked up 'Nasty' and the other tracks on the *Control* album – cutting the entire disc in three weeks. Not only did 'Nasty' give a new view of Janet, its polished sheen over a hard-edged beat told the emotional story and reinforced her stand as a woman taking charge. It was a style that was quickly adopted by other female vocalists. More than any other album, *Control* put Jam and Lewis on the map as producers du jour.

"We knew it would be a successful black album," Jimmy Jam said. "We tried to make the hardest, funkiest black album – almost a male singer's album. The edginess that's evident in the music on *Control* is her; that's our interpretation of Janet.

"Before *Control* it wasn't acceptable to have hard-edged black music on the radio. Now, it's the norm."

Qhwayilahle (Leave Him Alone) Moses McHunu

(Moses McHunu) ✳ Shanachie ✳ 1986 ✳
Appears on: *The Indestructible Beat of Soweto*

In 1986 everything was about Africa. If it wasn't the famine up top it was apartheid in the south. Interestingly, the most potent messages about the fate of Africa came through music. Partly it was Peter Gabriel, but mostly it was the music that spoke for itself and there is no better indication of the power of the human spirit than the sound of "township jive".

Soweto was the largest "township" outside Johannesburg where the black workers lived in dormitory suburbs. The existence of Soweto itself was a monument to oppression that was compounded by chronic poverty.

Yet the music which came from there, known as mbaqanga or "township jive", was glorious in its chiming guitars and flavours of jazz and reggae and African folk styles. This is music that is full of celebration, more so even than reggae or blues. It's music for dancing.

The Indestructible Beat anthology album put a whole new range of sounds into the western vocabulary. Its most significant influence was felt the following year when Paul Simon recorded a couple of tracks with South African musicians led by Ray Phiri. This album, however, contains the full spirit of the music and artists like Ladysmith Black Mambazo, Mahlathini, and Moses McHunu in full flight.

According to Trevor Herman, who assembled this album, "In most parts of Africa, music is more than entertainment – it's part of life. Everything is celebrated in song, in the rhythm of living."

Leaps and Bounds Paul Kelly

(Paul Kelly/Chris Langman) ✳ Mushroom ✳ 1986 ✳ Appears on: *Gossip*

The grand themes of Paul Kelly's work are all here – Melbourne, football, transcendence and memory. Paul Kelly went through a transformation in the mid-'80s. He was a washed up singer/songwriter with two brilliant albums that no-one cared about. Many parts of his life were a mess.

Things really started to turn when he formed the Coloured Girls – Michael Barclay (drums), John Schofield (bass), Peter Bull (keyboards) and Steve Connolly (guitar). This was a versatile outfit that turned its mind to country, rock and reggae with equal alacrity. Then, with the *Gossip* album, a sprawling two dozen tunes, Kelly found his feet. Much credit goes to guitarist, the late Steve Connolly, whose apeggiated lines lifted Kelly's tunes two feet off the ground. This track had been written six years previously with his band the Dots, assisted by guitarist Chris Langman (who became a filmmaker).

'Leaps and Bounds' is a small moment – a remembrance of an autumn day in May that sends the singer's heart soaring. Paul Kelly is a detail man – the temperature, the location, the foliage – and through the particulars he captures the invisible, the intangible. The last verse here is about acceptance and the strength to start over.

"*Gossip*," said Kelly at the time, "is like that. It deals with really trivial things and also life and death issues, gossip reduces it all."

That being said, the Coloured Girls, and especially Connolly, built it all up again.

Graceland Paul Simon

(Paul Simon) ✳ Warner Bros. ✳ 1986 ✳ Appears on: *Graceland*

"After everything was finished, I had no title for the album. In the chorus where it says 'Graceland', I fought for a long time to get rid of it. I didn't like it," said Paul Simon. "I thought it was distracting. I figured people would think I'm writing about Elvis Presley, and this is a South African record and I'm now writing a song about Mississippi and Graceland ...

"I took a long time before it settled and I got comfortable with it and said, 'Oh that's fine. You're not writing about Elvis Presley and it doesn't matter if they think you are. Those that get it will know that you're not, and those that don't get it won't care, they'll be just as happy that you're writing about Elvis Presley. It's not going to do any harm and in fact, it's kind of fun in a way.'"

The title track of *Graceland* tells the story of three journeys. Ostensibly Simon is recalling a trip to Memphis, Tennessee, that he took with his son Harper after the break-up of his marriage. The township jive of his African band and Simon's melodic precision melding together is another journey whereby the New York superstar threw off his status and went to Africa to learn about music. That was an act of grace that led to Simon's redemption and his resurrection as an artist after a decade in the doldrums.

"Losing love is like a window in your heart," he sings. In opening the window, Simon found humility and grace.

The sanctity, too, is in the music, and there lies the third journey – from Africa to Memphis.

The *Graceland* album was surrounded by idiot politicians and activists charging that Simon had endorsed apartheid by using South African musicians. As Simon said, the project was akin to going to Nazi Germany and playing for the Jews. The message of this song is in the higher, redemptive power of music: that it can overcome the feeble hearts of men. "The thing about it is, you don't even know if you're right," he said. "I tried for months to try to dislodge the idea that I was writing a song about Graceland. I mean, really, I just spent months and months thinking, 'When is this going to go away?' And I ended up calling the album that. So I don't think that I know either. I don't really know."

Forgetting Philip Glass

(Laurie Anderson/Philip Glass) ❋ CBS ❋ 1986 ❋ Appears on: *Songs from Liquid Days*

High art meets pop. Phillip Glass broke down the distinction between minimal art music and pop songs with his album *Songs from Liquid Days*. He invited singer/songwriters Paul Simon, David Byrne, Suzanne Vega and Laurie Anderson to submit lyrics, to which Glass put his own music and then recorded using both pop singers and his own Ensemble and the Kronos Quartet. The result is intriguing and often haunting.

"I began by asking David Byrne to write words that I could then set to music," Glass wrote. "We had worked together once before, and I found it such an easy and natural collaboration that I thought of extending the process with an entire record of songs.

"The words come first. From these I fashioned a set of six songs which, together, form a cycle of themes ranging from reflections on nature to classic romantic settings."

The best of them is Laurie Anderson's 'Forgetting', which closes the record. The song starts with the image of a man waking from a dream of old lovers. Once awake he thinks of the qualities that go to making up a righteous man. It's an abstract piece that becomes more so as Linda Ronstadt and the Roches move from singing words to just singing the notes. It's a deeply haunting and beautiful song.

"Songs are perhaps our most basic musical expression," wrote Glass. "Though I have worked widely in the fields of opera and music theatre, I had not until this last year worked with the song form as such. Writing the song cycle *Songs from Liquid Days* became for me truly a voyage of discovery."

Wide Open Road The Triffids

(David McComb) ❋ White Hot ❋ 1986 ❋ Appears on: *Born Sandy Devotional*

The Triffids were already old hands by the time they cut *Born Sandy Devotional* in London in 1985. The group had begun as teenagers in Perth, high on New York punk rock and Perth's own Victims. Principal songwriter David McComb was kind of literary with a knack for writing sublime pop tunes but he also liked dirty rock & roll. McComb was a fervent admirer of Nick Cave; his modesty wouldn't permit him the realisation that he ploughed the same field as Cave but with far greater gifts.

Perhaps coming from Perth it's not surprising that distance and deserts,

THE EIGHTIES

385

both physical and emotional, played a big part in McComb's writing. Their first album, *Treeless Plain*, is a magnificent, muscular piece of work that pounds out simple, powerful rock songs – one of the best indie rock albums of its day. *Born Sandy Devotional* is a leap ahead of that album.

The Triffids left Australia behind for a life on the breadline in London squats. This album reeks of that sense of distance.

"How much longer will we be leaving friends behind in Australia?" McComb said to me once. "There's such a polarity in my personal and professional lives. It all gets very Faustian."

Nowhere is this more apparent than in the song 'Tender is the Night', which tells the story of a man who is emotionally torn apart to his core by ambition, and which also touches on what is lost when you travel across the planet. It's a chilling waltz.

The album is full of places. The grit of the Nullarbor desert sand gets in your eyes and you can almost taste the Indian Ocean.

These songs exist in their little hermetically sealed world. McComb's fables are wrapped in the heavenly melodic support of Graham Lee (pedal Steel), Rob McComb (violin) and, especially, the delicate bass lines of Martyn Casey.

The axel of the album is 'Wide Open Road'. It's an angry song that finds the cost of freedom is aloneness:

After some months the Triffids established themselves in London and made the cover of the *NME*. There were great expectations for this album. Young producer Gil Norton, who shortly afterwards recorded the Pixies, brought a lush sound to the group without losing their idiosyncratic dynamic. The sessions were jeopardised when the money ran out and the album was finished by maxing out a credit card. You can feel the urgency – lack of cash meets vaulting ambition.

As critic Clinton Walker said, "The Triffids brought a new bent – a dry indigenous light and air – to rock & roll."

Sweet Child o' Mine Guns N' Roses

(Guns N' Roses) ❈ Geffen ❈ 1987 ❈ Appears on: *Appetite for Destruction*

"Metal stems from sexual frustration," said Guns N' Roses guitarist Slash. "We come from an amazing background of repression, stifled childhoods ..."

Although they crawled out of the gutter, and perhaps because of that, Guns N' Roses had no interest in staying there. They were an outlaw group who grabbed for the gold with both hands. Their opportunity came with their second album, *Appetite for Destruction*. It was at a time when rock, especially hard rock, had become a parody of itself: a blow-dried big hair joke. A damp squib. Then out of the Los Angeles metal scene came Guns – junkies with a killer guitar player in Slash and a singer who wore his damaged psyche on his heavily tattooed arms. Guns N' Roses were the main event of the turn of the decade. Singer Axl Rose was totally plugged into the Zeitgeist – the '80s obsessions with self-psychobabble and money.

Although they looked and originally sounded like the love child of the Rolling Stones and the New York Dolls, Axl Rose's inspirations were closer to Queen and Elton John.

"I thought about trying to sell more records than Boston's first album," said Rose. "I always thought that and never let up. Everything was directed at trying to achieve the sales without sacrificing the credibility of our music. We worked real hard to sell this many records. Maybe *Appetite* will be the only good album we make, but it wasn't just a fluke."

Appetite for Destruction covered all the usual sociopathic bases, but the real classic was their epic 'Sweet Child o' Mine'. The delicate melancholy ballad written by Rose about an ex-girlfriend is his best vocal. It's perfectly in counterpoint to Slash's extensive, eloquent guitar melody. Spikey. Tough. Sad but brilliantly played. According to Rose, "My favourite part of the song is Slash's slow solo; it's the heaviest part for me."

"Most of the songs on *Appetite* are first, second, or third takes," said drummer Steven Adler. "'Sweet Child o' Mine' we only played once. I think that's why the record did so well – it was real."

Need You Tonight INXS

(Andrew Farriss/Michael Hutchence) ❋ Atlantic ❋ 1987 ❋ Appears on: *Kick*

Slinky, sparse and funky, 'Need You Tonight' was pretty much as sexy and funky as any white rock group has ever been. On their sixth album, INXS were forging a new direction. Producer Chris Thomas proved to be a hard taskmaster, forcing re-writes and re-takes but also allowing the group to stretch out.

The opening single on *Kick*, 'Need You Tonight' is not much in the lyrics. Michael Hutchence's delivery, however, says it all: he sings in a kittenish whisper, gently drawing back his breath, and makes his not-so-subtle declaration of intent. He sings this song with the inexorable lust of a tiger out hunting in the night – there's a carefully measured dance going on here. Restraint is everything, as though Hutchence knows that the prey will eventually come to him.

The vocals are aided by the crack rhythm section that is all about space. INXS in those days were like Curtis Mayfield-meets-AC/DC. Garry Beers' bass pads in between guitar and drums, dancing up the melody and mimicking the steady intent from the vocals.

The song was aided by a groundbreaking video by Richard Lowenstein and Lynne-Marie Milburn, but ultimately this was Michael Hutchence's moment. "I hate," he told me at the time, "more than anything else, sexless music."

Pump Up the Volume M/A/R/R/S

(Martyn Young/Steve Young) ❊ 4th & Broadway ❊ 1987 ❊
Appears on: *Pump Up the Volume*

"This is a journey into sound" – that sample was indeed a journey into a whole new way of making records out of samples. Certainly tracks had been made with samples before 1987, but 'Pump Up the Volume' was the Rosetta Stone of the form with its bits of hip-hop, soul and rock and found sounds.

M/A/R/R/S was put together by Ivo Watts Russell, the proprietor of 4AD records, using members of Colourbox and AR Kane, mixer CJ Mackintosh and London DJ Dave Dorrell. The samples came from hip-hop artists Eric B & Rakim (the line "Pump up the volume" and various other samples and bass lines), Public Enemy, Fab Five Freddy, Trouble Funk, the films *Wattstax* and *Mars Needs Women*, the sound effects demonstration record *Journey into Stereo Sound*, and various other sources. Most troublesome was the sample from Stock, Aitken and Waterman's 'Roadblock' on the 12 inch mix. Stock et al sued and effectively ended the M/A/R/R/S project, but not before the stable door was opened.

Beds are Burning Midnight Oil

(Garrett/Hirst/Moginie) ❊ Sony ❊ 1987 ❊ Appears on: *Diesel & Dust*

The rhythm of this track mimics a 4WD going flat-chat across the Western Desert with the corrugations syncopating the steady beat. Rising up out of bass is a massive horizon of guitars with a wide blue 360-degree vista and the acoustic guitar maintains time in a timeless landscape. 'Beds are Burning' would be remarkable even without a lyric that said everything that needs to be said about Aboriginal land rights.

In 1986 Midnight Oil toured the Aboriginal settlements of the Top End. In awe of the landscape and the people, Midnight Oil were equally horrified by the conditions that most of the Aboriginals suffered – chronic poverty, petrol-sniffing, inadequate medical care. The result was an album of songs, most of them touching on the desert experience.

"Musically I know it affected Rob and Jim and Martin in the way in which we started to put together the *Diesel* record," said singer Peter Garrett. "It became more rhythmic; it had more of an acoustic end to it. It also affected us because it made us understand that these people had been living in this place since time immemorial. They'd been telling their stories here for tens of thousands of years and they knew the land incredibly well and they could tell you a lot about it, they had a great knowledge. It gave us a sense that for these people it wasn't even an issue between competing rights and competing societies; it was actually an issue about their own profound being. Everything that they were was here because this was their home as well, and it really opened our eyes up to that."

The single 'Beds' was released six months before the 1988 Bicentennial – an event that highlighted the dispossession of Aboriginals by the Europeans. The congruence of the two events was not lost on Midnight Oil. The group had vowed to avoid being seen to support the Bicentennial celebrations and spent most of 1988 overseas where their extremely parochial song was an international hit.

Few protest songs have been so succinct and challenging and clear all at once and it remains one of the most powerful tracks ever to come out of Australia.

Fairytale of New York The Pogues

(Shane MacGowan/Jem Finer) ❋ Island ❋ 1987 ❋
Appears on: *If I Should Fall from Grace with God*

Drunken sentimentality came easily to singer Shane MacGowan, so perhaps it's not surprising that one of the Pogues' best known songs is a Christmas tune about being drunk and dreaming of Christmas in Manhattan.

The Irish acoustic band with a reckless and ribald approach to pop music was a delightful anomaly in the over-produced '80s. They built their reputation on white-knuckle breakdowns of folk tunes but their best work was the ballads. Their 1987 album *If I Should Fall from Grace with God* was recorded by producer Steve Lillywhite and sees the group sounding better than previously. Lillywhite also encouraged his wife Kirsty MacColl to duet with MacGowan on this track and her voice brings a bittersweet tang to MacGowan's tobacco rasp.

The title for this song comes from JP Donleavy's novel *A Fairytale of New York* but the subject matter has little in common. MacGowan mixes the caricatures of New York cops with name checks of traditional Irish songs in that Irish/American tradition. Were it not for the playing of the Pogues and their guest, the song would have been a parody of itself. 'Fairytale', like all good fairytales, is in the telling.

Sign o' the Times Prince

(Prince) ❊ Paisley Park ❊ 1987 ❊ Appears on: *Sign o' the Times*

By 1987, Prince was the gold standard by which almost every other artist was measured. His drive to keep pumping out new and provocative material, his changes of direction, of style, sound and groove set a cracking pace that few were able to match. In the '80s, marketing had overtaken the creative departments and careers were scheduled in the record label's financial forecasts. Artists were encouraged to be true to their branding. Prince, however, released records as he pleased and in whatever form he chose.

Sign o' the Times was originally intended to be a three-album set with a jazz tip but Warner Bros. baulked and it was cut down to a double. This was the first step in Prince's argument that Warner Bros. was stifling his creativity and that he was enslaved to the label.

In the end Prince wrote, recorded and performed almost the entire album and he took it off from his flower power period into a deeper soul-funk direction.

While still focused on being busy in the bedroom, *Sign o' the Times* also deals with wider social issues such as AIDS, gangs and racism.

The album was conceived and executed swiftly, marking the transition from the end of the *Revolution* period and the end of his relationship with Susannah Melvoin. The song 'If I Was Your Girlfriend' was, according to engineer Susan Rogers, a plea for Melvoin to have him back. Other people in Prince's circle identified 'Forever in My Life' as about her.

The icing on the cake was the title track – minimalist Curtis Mayfield's soul backing over a very direct lyric about AIDS and drugs. The song was written, recorded and mixed in a single day.

Saxophonist Eric Leeds said of the album, "There was a refreshing feeling about making his own music unencumbered again."

It's the End of the World as We Know It (and I Feel Fine) R.E.M.

(Michael Stipe/Peter Buck/Mike Mills/Bill Berry) ✳ IRS ✳ 1987 ✳ Appears on: *Document*

"These songs are like taking a picture of your bedroom," said guitarist Peter Buck of middle period R.E.M. "It may not make much sense to anyone else, but to you it's all the things in your life. We're certainly not setting out to be deliberately obscure, but you have to short-circuit the whole idea that literal language is what things are, because literal language is just codes for what happens. Without wanting to sound too arty about it, to bypass actions and go straight to the results is what we're trying to do, to make people feel moved by something without them even being sure of what we're writing about."

'It's the End of the World as We Know It (and I Feel Fine)' was one of the first R.E.M. songs to make sense or at least be decipherable. The group attacks the song at a breakneck pace as Michael Stipe sings out a litany of catastrophe and heroes, incidents and puns.

'It's the End of the World as We Know It (and I Feel Fine)' is an update of 'Too Much Monkey Business' and 'Subterranean Homesick Blues'. With the name checks for lost hipsters Lenny Bruce and Lester Bangs, 'End of the World' became a blueprint for alternative culture in the late '80s.

"We don't clarify things," said Buck. "When we first started, Michael and I used to say how much we hated most rock & roll lyrics. We had this idea that what we'd do is take clichés, sayings, lines from old songs, phrases you hear all the time, and skew them and twist them and meld them together so that you'd be getting these things that have always been evocative, but that were skewed just enough to throw you off and make you think in a different way. It seemed like a really pretentious thing to do, but that concept does work its way in."

They Dance Alone Sting

(Sting) ✳ A&M ✳ 1987 ✳ Appears on: ... *Nothing Like the Sun*

Even when he was pretending to be a punk rocker with the Police, Sting always seemed like he was slumming. In fact the Police were way too literate for a genuine rock band, with their quirky rhythms and sophisticated chord shadings. Once he embarked on a solo career, all trappings fell away and out came the jazzers.

This second album is Sting's most coherent and interesting statement. Like his contemporaries Peter Gabriel and David Byrne, Sting turned to ethnic rhythms – reggae, Latin, Brazilian, jazz. Lyrically it was as free-ranging, with topics as diverse as the "disappeared" in Chile and the legendary dilettante author Quentin Crisp. The former track, 'They Dance Alone', was one of the highpoints of Sting's career.

The album was written in 1987 during a five-month stay in New York. "I had this kind of monkish life," he said. "I lived on my own. I cooked my own food. I went to the gym every day. I took piano lessons. The phone was off the hook. I worked usually from twelve midday to very late at night."

The double album features Mark Knopfler, Ruben Blades and Eric Clapton as well as Branford Marsalis, who was so influential to Sting's jazz period.

"I don't give a fuck about rock music," Sting declared in 1987. Unfortunately he was never going to escape its pull, but this champing at the bit was a worthy attempt.

With or Without You U2

(U2) ❋ Island ❋ 1987 ❋ Appears on: *The Joshua Tree*

U2 started out as teenagers full of vigour and spit and attitude. By 1987 they had learnt the power of understatement and on 'With or Without You' they hit on the perfect balance.

It can be read as a song about either marital romance or spiritual need but singer Bono made it clear where the song came from. He told Timothy White when quizzed about it, "I've said it before, but to me there's nothing more radical, there's nothing more revolutionary than two people loving each other. One, 'cause it's so uncommon these days, and two, 'cause it's so difficult to do."

U2 were aware of their status as the band who were about to become superstars and the cost weighed heavily on Bono's head in the years leading up to and just beyond *The Joshua Tree*.

"In 'With or Without You' when it says 'and you give yourself away and you give yourself away' – everybody else in the group knows what that means," he told Niall Stokes. "It's about how I feel in U2 at times – exposed. I know the group think I'm exposed and the group feel that I give myself away. And funny enough, Lou Reed said to me, 'What you've got is a real gift: don't give it away because people might not place upon it the right value.' And I think that if I do any damage to the group, it's that I'm too open. Because there's a cost to my personal life and a cost to the group as well."

I Don't Want to Talk About It Everything But The Girl

(Danny Whitten) ❋ Blanco y Negro/Sire ❋ 1988 ❋ Appears on: *Idlewild*

Tracey Thorn and Ben Watt have had an odd career, negotiating the demands of the marketplace with their wandering muse. They started out as a folk duo playing in colleges, went rock for awhile and moved into a laid-back jazz tip like a literate Sade. Thorn has a intimate, plaintive voice and Ben Watt plays delicate, sophisticated melodies. Their admirers include Bono and Prince. They're not quite folk and not quite rock but with a bit of both and some jazz thrown in there as well. The songs have ranged from generalised romance to strict politics and the documenting of the dissolution of their own romantic relationship.

On *Idlewild* they absorb the lessons of the past and move on. While their own songs are intriguing and warrant close attention, their remake of Danny Whitten's ballad is breathtaking. Originally written for his band Crazy Horse's debut LP, Rod Stewart also did a great version of the song. But Everything But The Girl strips this song right back to its elements. Thorn's vocal is dry and exhausted but the purity of her tone and phrasing give the track an emotional nett. Watt's jazz-tinged backing is similarly minimal. But it's the spaces and the pieces left out that really anchor the emotional message.

I Should Be So Lucky Kylie Minogue

(Matt Aitken/Pete Waterman) ❋ Mushroom ❋ 1988 ❋ Appears on: *Kylie*

"Kylie came to us via the BBC," recalls Mike Stock, the producing partner in the team Stock, Aitken and Waterman. "I remember the conversation: 'This girl is going to be big. We're going to run 'Neighbours' every evening at 5:30', or whatever the time was. So David Howells, our business affairs man, agreed with Pete Waterman that she should come into the studio in London. But nobody told me. As I'm the person that wrote the songs and made the records I was a bit in the dark on the day she turned up, having been sitting in her hotel for ten days waiting for me to call and me blissfully unaware that she was even in England.

"Anyway, finally I say hello to Kylie and I have to do a very quick analysis of what I'm dealing with here. I find out she's nineteen. I find out she's in this soap. She's very successful in her country, she's doing this, she's doing that and she sings and she's gorgeous looking and ... so I thought well she must have something wrong and I thought that maybe she wasn't going to be lucky in love.

"That started off the process of thinking about what we'll write with her. I told her to go and sit and have a coffee while Matt Aitken and I sat in the studio to toss the idea around, and 'I Should Be So Lucky' was the result.

"The bass on 'I Should Be So Lucky' is the same bass rhythm as in the verse of Madonna's 'Into the Groove'. It's pounding the eight rhythm against a four bass drum on the bass but there's a kick, it adds syncopation into it and that was inspired by Madonna's 'Into the Groove'. I thought that gave it a bit of a kick. Didn't make it sound too bland and in terms of the brashness of the instruments that sit on top of that, the drums are just giving us a straight four underneath so your syncopation plays off your straight four. Her voice cuts so you have to support it with some weight underneath and the high hat doesn't interfere in its frequencies with the vocals so you can hear every word she's saying. Somebody told me that we said, 'I should be so lucky' eighty-five times. Whatever. There was just enough repetition to fill the three minutes and not be too boring. It's simple songs sung in an honest way really.

"We wrote the song in about forty minutes and it took less to sing it because she's extremely quick. But you can't ignore the years of experience that went before that. You had to get to the point where you could do that and I drew on all my experience. I felt that I had to pull something out of the bag very quickly because she was going to get back on a plane and go home. Her ear is very tuned in so I sang her the tune and she sang it back to me, and at that point I put the tapes aside and went on to other things. That particular day I had Bananarama in the morning, she was in at lunchtime until mid-afternoon and then by the time I got rid of her Rick Astley came in. I was doing lots of different artists: working on their songs, finishing tracks off. I put the tape aside and it was only later on in the year that somebody dug the tape up and said, 'this is quite good'."

The rest is history.

There She Goes The Las

(Lee Mavers) ✳ Go! Discs ✳ 1988 ✳ Appears on: *The Las*

This was the blueprint for '90s Brit pop, the template from which the Gallagher Brothers fashioned their tabloid fame. The Las were from Liverpool and played beautiful guitar melodies, hence inviting irrelevant comparisons with the Beatles. The Las were a live band with a solid repertoire at the centre of which was this pop diamond, a perfectly formed gem with an '80s edge.

Lee Mavers, who played guitar, sang and wrote the group's material, was steadfast in his pursuit of pop essence. Having toiled for some years to get the group off the ground, they made one album and were not heard from again.

When asked to describe the difference between the Las' sound and their contemporaries', he simply replied, "Ours is soul, theirs is fashion. The Las are the only ones who are making music; the others are just manners and things. Keep music alive, you know. Other music is nothing but sampled beats so everything feels and sounds the same."

Mavers was unhappy with the sound of the group's first album and made no bones about telling the public. Producer Steve Lillywhite had given the group's sound a modern treatment while hanging onto the integrity of their '60s style. But perhaps it wasn't authentic enough for Mavers.

"Can't you hear the church bells?" he said when queried about the group's jangling guitar sound. "That's what that sound means to me. I grew up listening to that sound and it fascinates me and never fails to move me. It has fuck all to do with the Byrds or any of this indie shit."

Tower of Song Leonard Cohen

(Leonard Cohen) ✳ Columbia ✳ 1988 ✳ Appears on: *I'm Your Man*

Emerging from four years of silence, Leonard Cohen's *I'm Your Man* album was full of dry humour at his own expense, lustful songs about women and a new keyboard-based sound that was part chanson and part Kraftwerk. The gem of that album was the immensely witty 'Tower of Song', which placed the singer in the delightful imprisonment of his muse.

"This is my story," he told an audience at the time. "It's a dismal story. It's a shabby story. It's a funny story. But it's my story."

Increasingly Cohen devoted himself to the service of his life as a whisky-drinking Zen monk and related his writing to his religious practice and vice versa.

"If you're going to think of yourself in this game, or in this tradition, and you start getting a swelled head about it, then you've really got to think about who you're talking about," he said in 1994. "You're not just talking about Randy Newman, who's fine, or Bob Dylan, who's sublime, you're talking about King David, Homer, Dante, Milton, Wordsworth, you're talking about the embodiment of our highest possibility.

"So I don't think it's particularly modest or virtuous to think of oneself as a minor poet. I really do feel the enormous luck I've had in being able to make a living, and to never have had to have written one word that I didn't want to write.

"But I don't fool myself, I know the game I'm in. When I wrote about Hank Williams 'A hundred floors above me in the tower of song', it's not some kind of inverse modesty. I know where Hank Williams stands in the history of popular song. 'Your Cheatin' Heart', songs like that, are sublime, in his own tradition, and I feel myself a very minor writer. I've taken a certain territory, and I've tried to maintain it and administrate it with the very best of my capacities. And I will continue to administrate this tiny territory until I'm too weak to do it. But I understand where this territory is."

Passionate Kisses Lucinda Williams

(Lucinda Williams) ❋ Rough Trade ❋ 1988 ❋ Appears on: Passionate Kisses

"My vocal style is kind of a culmination of the old country style and the old blues style coming together," said Lucinda Williams in an interview with Barney Hoskyns. "I was influenced by singers like Hank Williams and Loretta Lynn from an early age, and then later by a lot of the Delta country blues singers like Robert Johnson and Skip James. Just that real haunting kind of rougher edged style." She may as well have been talking about her songwriting as well. Williams confidently walked the road between country and blues.

The daughter of an English professor and poet, Miller Williams, Lucinda has a spare use of words. "He's been my mentor," she said. "Instead of going to college and taking creative writing, I learned by writing, by trial and error, and by showing [my father] what I was working on and listening to his criticism." Miller was a Hank Williams fan and Lucinda's mother liked Joan Baez. But for young Lucinda the whole thing came together when she heard Bob Dylan's Highway 61.

"That was it for me," she said. "I had somehow found the combination, the link of heavy, intense, brave lyrics – he'd obviously listened to a lot of blues – great melodies, and a voice that wasn't perfect."

Two of Williams' albums in the early '80s were promising, and then she came out with 'Passionate Kisses' and the album of the same name in 1988. Unusually for an American country singer, it was on Rough Trade, an independent English label.

'Passionate Kisses' is a post-feminist lyric, a reasonable demand for a woman to have it all – a full house, a rock & roll band and passionate kisses. The song is brimful of joyous energy. While the delivery may sound flippant, you get the feeling that there is a serious message underneath.

Mary Chapin Carpenter picked up on it and had a major hit and a Grammy with it in 1994.

Touch Me I'm Sick Mudhoney

(Mudhoney) ❋ Sub Pop ❋ 1988 ❋ Appears on: *Superfuzz Bigmuff Plus Early Single*

Mudhoney were just geeks playing obnoxious music in the late '80s. The group – guitarists Mark Arm and Steve Turner, bass player Matt Lukin and drummer Dan Peters – coagulated from seminal outfits like Green River and the Melvins who inhabited the Pacific Northwest around Seattle. Possessed of a fuzzbox and a crate of punk rock LPs, Mudhoney intended to have a good time. The first offering was 'Touch Me I'm Sick', which was funny, forceful, a little self-loathing and sometimes scary but mostly noisy.

The song was recorded quickly and two friends offered to start a label to release it as a 7-inch backed with 'Sweet Young Thing Ain't Sweet No More'. So began Sub Pop records and around Sub Pop in Seattle grew a music scene that was known as grunge. From here came Pearl Jam and Nirvana and Soundgarden and then a million groups in shorts and flannel shirts around the world. Few records that came after this founding release were as much fun.

"It's kind of surprising it took off as fast as it did," said drummer Dan Peters. "We didn't start off all that serious about it."

Black Steel in the Hour of Chaos Public Enemy

(Public Enemy) ❋ Def Jam ❋ 1988 ❋
Appears on: *It Takes a Nation of Millions to Hold Us Back*

Public Enemy's 1988 album, *It Takes a Nation of Millions to Hold Us Back*, was one of the most powerful albums ever made and they expressed the issue of race in the US as concisely and clearly as it had ever been stated. Chuck D drew on the tradition of African-American poets and intellectuals – the Last Poets, Rap Brown, Eldridge Cleaver, the nation of Islam, Gil Scott-Heron and others – and he opened a new chapter in that tradition. 'Black Steel in the Hour of Chaos' is one of his most acutely argued early songs.

As powerful a rapper as Chuck D clearly is, Public Enemy's real weapon is the Bomb Squad, their production team who mixed samples with sound effects to create a sound-scape like an aural battleground.

"The first thing we would do is the beat, the skeleton of the track," explained Hank Shocklee, head of the Bomb Squad. "The beat would actually have bits and pieces of samples already in it, but it would only be rhythm sections. Chuck would start writing and trying different ideas to see what worked. Once he got an idea, we would look at it and see where the track was going. Then we would just start adding on whatever it needed, depending on the lyrics. I kind of architect the whole idea. The sound has a look to me, and Public Enemy was all about having a sound that had its own distinct vision. We didn't want to use anything we considered traditional R&B stuff – bass lines and melodies and chord structures and things of that nature.

"Back in the day, things was different. The copyright laws didn't really extend into sampling until the hip-hop artists started getting sued. As a matter of fact, copyright didn't start catching up with us until *Fear of a Black Planet*."

In the late '80s when 'Black Steel in the Hour of Chaos' was made there was no regulation of sampling. Hence the entire record is made up of bits and pieces of other discs. Public Enemy was not the first to use samples to make songs. They were the first to do it with such violence though. The record's success meant, ironically, few more records could be constructed in this way – although Tricky used 'Black Steel' as a basis of a track of his own on *Maxinquaye*.

"The first thing that was starting to happen by the late '80s was that the people were doing buyouts," said Shocklee. "You could have a buyout – meaning you could purchase the rights to sample a sound – for around $1500. Then it started creeping up to $3000, $3500, $5000, $7500. Then they threw in this thing called rollover rates. If your rollover rate is every 100,000 units, then for every 100,000 units you sell, you have to pay an additional $7500. A record that sells two million copies would kick that cost up twenty times. Now you're looking at one song costing you more than half of what you would make on your album. It would be impossible to do *It Takes a Nation of Millions to Hold Us Back* now."

Teenage Riot Sonic Youth

(Sonic Youth) ✳ Blast First/Enigma ✳ 1988 ✳ Appears on: *Daydream Nation*

Sonic Youth were the godparents of alternative rock. They started out in the No Wave New York scene of the early '80s playing art music with guitars. Guitarists Thurston Moore and Lee Ranaldo were members of Glenn Branca's guitar orchestra. By the time they began recording as Sonic Youth in 1982 their path was clear – they were deconstructing rock & roll and creating noise soundscapes while simultaneously loving classic rock & roll.

"We've always been called art-rock, in the most derogatory way, meaning dilettante, which was one reason we always toured, to show we were a real band," said bassist Kim Gordon. "That always guided us, trying to put weird music in a rock context, but I don't think we care any more, especially since we can see where the whole alternative scene is going, into the mainstream, which is really uninteresting. For us, it's more of a lifestyle thing, like a jazz or blues musician."

In 1988 Sonic Youth cut the double album *Daydream Nation*. On 'Teenage Riot' the massed guitars of Moore and Renaldo are yoked into a soundscape that bristles with hooks. The seven-minute epic was inspired as a tribute to Dinosaur Jr's J Mascis. The group stated on its website that the song had a working title of 'Rock & Roll for President', supposedly written about a fantasy world where J Mascis is president. Suddenly, though, the immense power of the underground sounded palpable. There was a sense that there was a new mood about to break. It was one of the true landmark songs of its era.

"We're the young white hope, or something, for young white urban/ suburban/rural middle-class disaffected youth. Which is kind of funny," said Moore at the time. "They're promoting us as such. Like, for the entire fringe element of America, here's your band?"

She Set Fire to the House Stephen Cummings

(Stephen Cummings/Andrew Pendelbury) ✳ Liberation ✳ 1988 ✳ Appears on: *Close Ups*

Stephen Cummings is a very astute observer of the "murders that aren't murders" that we commit every day. This is a break-up song that is both simple in its small detail, and devastating. Cummings uses enough detail in the relationship between Monica and the narrator so that you know it's drawn from life, and it's general enough that you can write yourself into the scene. We've all been there – passionate romance – she's beautiful, he's passive-aggressive – she puts up with it for seven years and finally leaves with a can of kerosene and a match made in hell.

'She Set Fire to the House', like a romance, starts well, but Cummings and Shane O'Mara build the tune with layers of guitar. O'Mara is one of the best producers of acoustic-based music this side of Daniel Lanois, and Cummings is his ideal foil. The song that had started out so definite and realistic becomes expressionistic and a little deranged by the end. The rhythm of the lyrics takes over and the narrator is lost in a pyre of regret and exhilaration at the prospect of freedom.

Copperhead Road Steve Earle

(Steve Earle) ❋ MCA ❋ 1988 ❋ Appears on: *Copperhead Road*

In 1986, Steve Earle was the poster boy for the new Nashville. He'd paid his dues for twelve years since he first arrived as a folk singer. The capital of country music was hoping that it wouldn't be too different from the old Nashville, with handsome young guys in cowboy hats singin' about lost love and the like. Pretty soon though Steve Earle wasn't so welcome. He had a string of bad marriages and a raging and very public drug habit.

By 1987–88, when he made his third album, *Copperhead Road*, Steve Earle was out of control. The album he made with its mixed-up confusion he dubbed "heavy-metal bluegrass," and he welcomed the rock audience, 'cause Nashville wasn't too keen. Earle had crossed the line from favourite son to prodigal son.

The album deals with the screwed-up world as Earle sees America, and his own life. The title track however is based on a real incident, going to a baseball game with a friend who was a Vietnam Vet.

"I asked him if he thought the fireworks were going to bother him, 'cause if they were, we'd leave," Earle said. "But he said this was something he really needed to get through. And he tried his best, bless his heart, but after about thirty seconds, he stuck his head down between his knees.

"It wasn't the sound that got to him; it was the light. He was on one of those river patrol boats in the war, and they used to keep the rivers lit up at night with parachute flares. Explosions didn't bother him at all. He said they used to welcome the explosions; it was the quiet that drove everybody nuts, going up those rivers under those lights waiting for something to happen.

"So that's how I started to write 'Copperhead Road'. It's part of what's going on in the whole country: people who were in Vietnam have suddenly started talking about it. It's time; it's the only way a lot of those men are ever going to get well. That's why I wrote 'Copperhead Road'."

Earle's character in the song is an American stereotype – the country boy whose granddaddy made moonshine and who now grows marijuana. He nurses the scars of Vietnam and chooses to live outside the law.

This record is part of an outlaw tradition going back to Johnny Cash and Waylon Jennings and beyond, and forward into rock & roll. "I don't see that much difference, attitude-wise, between real rock & roll and real country," he said at the time. "It's really about your life and the way you live – which isn't about living up to the stereotypes and having to be fucked up. It's a matter of how committed you are to what you're doing. I'm a rock act because I'm being played on rock radio right now."

Copperhead Road was recorded in Memphis, some 320 kilometres from Nashville. "With 'Copperhead' some big steps were made socially," he said. "Some envelopes we'd been pushing at all along finally broke."

Wild Thing Tone Loc

(Matt Dike/Michael Ross/Anthony Smith/Marvin Young) ❊ Delicious Vinyl ❊ 1988 ❊
Appears on: *Loc-Ed After Dark*

One of the most delightful tracks from rap's first golden era, 'Wild Thing' gave the world a new phrase for love making. The song was funny and Loc's steel-wool vocal was, well, sexy. And the beats were just perfect.

Written by Loc, the Delicious Vinyl team and Young MC, 'Wild Thing' also launched producers the Dust Brothers and their witty use of beats and samples. 'Wild Thing' kicks courtesy of a sample from Van Halen's 'Jamie's Crying'. There was a great video that parodied 'Addicted to Love' and was shot for $350. Mostly though, it's the charm of Tone (Anthony Smith) Loc.

"When Matt and Mike started the label," said Loc, "they were really bored with East Coast rappers, they were looking for a West Coast rapper with a certain kind of voice or style. They spoke to me on the phone, fell in love with my voice and knew they had to make some kind of record with me.

"About nine years ago I had a stripped throat, you know when your throat kills you, it hurts to talk, you can't swallow. To soothe the soreness I drank some hot tea with brandy in it, and it scorched the shit out of my throat, it's been like that ever since."

They Took the Children Away   Archie Roach

(Archie Roach) ✳ Aurora ✳ 1989 ✳ Appears on: *Charcoal Lane*

Few songs have so clearly, concisely and emotionally covered the issue of the Stolen Generation as this. Archie Roach himself was stolen from his parents as a child and he lived in the halfway hell of many Aboriginals. Roach did it tough, at one point hitting bottom with the bottle. His salvation came through writing poetry and music and also through his relationship with fellow singer and songwriter Ruby Hunter.

"I wrote for myself and friends and family," he said. "Writing for me, at first, was cathartic. I was happy working during the day and singing when I felt like it, but I wouldn't change anything. I love this work."

Roach's song is emotive without sentimentality. His delivery is spare and considered but the song packs a terrific punch. Part of its success is that Roach expresses the universality of this matter within the specifics of the case.

"You start to get away from this tag of Aboriginal singer/songwriter," he said. "What does it mean? Does it mean I just write songs dealing with Aboriginal people? Of course not. Does Paul Kelly just write music on Irish/Italian themes? Music transcends barriers. I feel obliged, when things are going wrong, to get up, maybe not so much on behalf of my people but on behalf of every decent, intelligent, caring person in Australia."

Hey Ladies   Beastie Boys

(Beastie Boys/The Dust Brothers) ✳ Capitol ✳ 1989 ✳ Appears on: *Paul's Boutique*

"Most people viewed *Paul's Boutique* as a total commercial failure," Mike D told *iD* magazine, "but it was necessary to get us to where we are now." Mike Diamond is talking from the perspective of the Beastie Boys being the hippest white group on the planet in the '90s. Their debut, *Licensed to Ill* was a teenage dream – crunching rap music with heavy metal and mocking anything that moved. Three years later they showed, with *Paul's Boutique*, that white, middle-class kids could understand rap music.

'Hey Ladies' has that Beastie Boys irreverence and the video is loaded with '70s iconography. It's like a dream set in a second-hand store. But so is the music. Of course many of the group's fans couldn't understand the dense mix of sounds without the crunch. On the first record the Beastie Boys were obnoxious kids fighting for the right to party. On 'Hey Ladies' they're still sort of obnoxious, but also very, very smart with the samples.

But the Beastie Boys were ahead of the curve here. In partnership with the Dust Brothers, the New York trio constructed an album of samples from all over the place but with a unique sensibility. *Paul's Boutique* didn't have any hits and it didn't sell, but it demonstrated that the Beastie Boys had a talent beyond being obnoxious.

Like a Prayer Madonna

(Patrick Leonard/Madonna) ✳ Sire ✳ 1989 ✳ Appears on: *Like a Prayer*

Madonna took the manipulation of media and PR to a new level in the '80s and right into the '90s. Her shows were outrageous. If there was a holy cow she ran into it. It came to a head with 'Like a Prayer'. Having accepted a massive sponsorship deal from Pepsi, Madonna then released her first Pepsi-sponsored video and caused a massive storm. The song had its spiritual overtones. The video took scandal to a new level with Madonna not only eroticising Christ but a black Christ at that. Pepsi immediately cancelled their sponsorship. Madonna had found the limits and the reality of corporate sponsorship of the arts.

The religious overtones of 'Like a Prayer' were apparently not motivated especially by a desire to cause controversy.

"Spirituality is still really important to me," Madonna told *The Face*. "But I don't feel so inspired to write songs about it. I mean, I go to church: I go to Church of England, I go to Catholic churches, I go to synagogues, I partake in all religions. In my bones, I'm Catholic, because that's how I was raised, but I am just as intrigued by Judaism as I am by Catholicism."

'Like a Prayer' is a beautifully crafted devotional song in the guise of perfect pop. God is in the drum machine.

Buffalo Stance Neneh Cherry

(Booga Bear/Neneh Cherry/Jamie J Morgan/Phillip Ramacon) ✳ Circa/Virgin ✳ 1989 ✳ Appears on: *Raw Like Sushi*

Neneh Cherry is as eclectic as her heritage – her mother is Swedish, her father is West African and her stepfather is the great jazz trumpeter Don Cherry. Neneh started her music career as a teenager with the jazz/post-punk combo Rip Rig and Panic and then in the late '80s dropped one of the great club hits of the era.

'Buffalo Stance' is an eclectic track referencing Malcolm McLaren, the Wild Bunch and Bomb the Bass. It is one of the masterpieces of the late '80s club era.

The lyric is directed specifically at a gigolo attempting to corrupt young women, but it is more generally applicable to the macho sensibility. This is an empowerment anthem that seduces with its grooves and melodic hooks. Cherry's rap is right on the money – conscious, tuneful and masterfully syncopated with the music.

Production on the track is by Tim Simenon (aka Bomb the Bass) but the sound is strongly influenced by the Bristol style of the Wild Bunch and Massive Attack, with whom Cherry and her husband Cameron 'Booga Bear' McVey often recorded. There are touches of reggae and dub in this dense hip-hop mix.

"It really encompassed a vibe that was around at that time," said Cherry of 'Buffalo Stance'. "The whole club thing had started to happen, like hip-hop – still more underground than, say, now. But it was definitely something that people could identify with. And 'Buffalo Stance' was like a song that bridged over that, while at the same time it was a pop record. It also shed a lot of stereotypes that people were bored with – it seemed to make them happy or relieved."

Fuck tha Police NWA

(Ice Cube/MC Ren) ✳ Priority ✳ 1989 ✳ Appears on: *Straight Outta Compton*

Niggaz With Attitude (NWA) were the most important rap group on the US West Coast. Where Public Enemy had pioneered political hip-hop on the East Coast and saw their work as part of a struggle for emancipation, NWA on their second album, *Straight Outta Compton*, were more anarchic. This was ghetto life of bangin – sex and drugs and fighting cops.

NWA was the home of some heavyweight talent, not least of which was Eazy-E (Eric Wright), Dr Dre (Andre Young) and Ice Cube (O'Shea Jackson). Eazy was more your traditional rap producer big on the blackface style of rap. Ice Cube and MC Ren, however, upped the ante in glamorising ghetto life. In their view, rap music was the story of the streets but it needed to be told in full Panavision. It was exciting – the idea of running with guns and women.

Straight Outta Compton was the real beginning of gangsta rap. Where Ice T had recorded his life on the street, NWA made it seem heroic. The crucial tracks on this album are Ice Cube's 'Express Yourself' and its following joint: 'Fuck tha Police'. This latter track drew the line. It justified outlaw behaviour and drew a line around the Compton ghetto defining who was in and who out; it was, at base, a call to anarchy. It was uncompromising. The strength of the hip-hop on the track, its muscularity and its undeniable invention made the record an underground hit. It couldn't be a mainstream hit because the FBI and law enforcement agencies the world over tried hard to suppress the violently anti-police message.

This was virtually the end of NWA though. Ice Cube went solo and became a big star. Dr Dre became the most important single producer in hip-hop. They left a legacy in NWA that would last for ten or more years.

Debaser Pixies

(Black Francis) ❋ 4AD ❋ 1989 ❋ Appears on: *Doolittle*

"The closest I get to a manifesto is that I like the Surrealists. I agree with their idea that reason is overrated," said Black Francis. "Rock & roll has been a pose from the beginning. There are those who still hail rock as being a force for radicalism, but it's not any more, it's a force on the stock market. The Pixies are just a tiny hiccup in a huge industry. Our records are in the racks next to all the others. It's only our content that isn't quite as stale or stiff as the other groups. You don't have to hike into the desert to see us. We're a part of mass culture."

The Pixies were, in the end, more than just a hiccup. Black Francis' quirky, surreal songs with their stop/start tempos and quiet/loud arrangements were the prototype for the alternative rock revolution of the '90s – especially the work of Kurt Cobain. The Nirvana leader wrote 'Smells Like Teen Spirit' in what he thought was the style of the Pixies.

'Debaser' is a classic hook-laden track from the Pixies' breakthrough album. The song is about the joys of watching the Luis Buñuel film *Un Chien Andalou*, a surrealist classic, and is the most perfect 'stream of unconsciousness' ever made.

Monkey Gone to Heaven Pixies

(Black Francis) ❊ 4AD ❊ 1989 ❊ Appears on: *Doolittle*

Black Francis started the Pixies in 1986 with more enthusiasm than know-how and aimed for a sound somewhere between Hüsker Dü and Peter, Paul and Mary. That's just about what he got.

When all is said and done, however, it was the songs by Black Francis (who later changed his stage name to Frank Black), and especially his unique imagery, that made the Pixies the seminal alternative rock band. Bass player Kim Deal would go on to lead the Breeders, one of the best alternative bands of the '90s, while the flatish drumming of David Lovering and the bristling guitars of Joey Santiago played their part in establishing the alternative rock blueprint. "We tend to get along just fine," said the singer. "We're all sort of pleasantly mismatched. And it's kind of nice."

'Monkey Gone to Heaven' is one of the Pixies' best songs, with the group providing a backing as quirky as the lyrics and somehow piling in the hooks to a song that sounds like it will fall apart at any moment. Meanwhile Black Francis ponders the animalism of mankind and our simian nature – though not quite so specifically of course. "We're not trying to be wacky or kitsch like the Cramps or the B-52's," said Black Francis. "I'm trying to romanticise sci-fi and treat it like it's reality at the same time. It's not a pastiche."

Back to Life Soul II Soul

(Paul Hooper/Simon 'The Funky Ginger' Law/Beresford Romeo/Caron Wheeler) ❊ Virgin ❊ 1989 ❊ Appears on: *Club Classics, Vol. 1*

Throughout the '80s the warehouse party scene in Britain was where the true underground music was being made. Much of it came from the sound system DJs – a Jamaican tradition of DJs who set up their own mobile discotheques for parties. That tradition was co-opted into warehouse parties and a new type of music began to develop – heavy on the reggae and dub but with soul music, rare groove and R&B in the mix.

The most popular of these outfit was the Soul II Soul sound system, run by Beresford Romeo aka Jazzie B and childhood friend Philip 'Daddae' Harvey. Jazzie's family had operated sound systems so there was already a record collection of reggae discs. To this they added some hip-hop. "It's a love train, a family," Jazzie told *The Observer*'s Cynthia Rose. "Many an early occasion we would put up the money to play. Then came hip-hop, warehouse parties and the pirate radio explosion. Those things changed British music and helped shape Soul II Soul."

The collective grew to incorporate singers Caron Wheeler, Rose Windross and Do'reen Waddell to augment the dance floor beats.

Soul II Soul moved into recording and enlisted Bristol producer Paul Nellee Hooper who understood the bass-heavy grooves and sweet melodies they wanted.

'Back to Life' featuring Caron Wheeler was the sound of the summer of 1989. It blasted from radios and in every club on the planet that year, a unique, sublime blend of Jamaica, Africa and Europe.

"When you nurture a sound and build the system yourself, like Soul II Soul, you know your speakers very well," said Jazzie. "But then you need to know your studio monitors and every separate stage of record production. And, more important than all of this, is giving it that emotion."

Bust a Move Young MC

(Matt Dike/Michael Ross/Marvin Young) ✳ Delicious Vinyl ✳ 1989 ✳
Appears on: *Stone Cold Rhymin'*

Young MC (aka Marvin Young) was a promising hip-hop writer/performer who became known for this humorous, sexy invitation to shake one's booty. One of the great dance singles of the '80s, it may not have been heavy but it did spread the hip-hop gospel onto the pop charts.

Young was of Jamaican descent and had an eye on a straight career in business when he got sidetracked into performing and writing. "I listen to really deep, intense dancehall reggae, and I must admit that I get a lot of my style from it, 'cause I like it. I was actually rapping very early, before I listened to reggae, but when I heard how fast and clear the toasters were toasting, I knew I had to emulate them, and start writing my lyrics that way."

Quincy Jones signed on to produce Young MC's debut album, which was a massive hit. Unfortunately his subsequent work failed to live up to the promise of the first light-hearted and funky joint.

"I'm starting a production company and a publishing company, and hopefully later a record company. My knowledge of data processing helps me with all the complicated instruments and studio equipment, and my knowledge of economics will help with the accounting," he said. But it didn't help his rhythm thing at all. It doesn't matter, 'Bust a Move' is still perfect.

The Nineties

GEN X AND ITS DISCONTENTS

1979
The Smashing Pumpkins

The Ship Song
Nick Cave & The Bad Seeds

Fuck and Run
Liz Phair

It's a Shame About Ray
The Lemonheads

Buy Me a Pony
Spiderbait

Dirty Jeans
Magic Dirt

Freak
silverchair

Drugs
Ammonia

Monsters
Something for Kate

100%
Sonic Youth

Cannonball
The Breeders

Common People
Pulp

Where It's At
Beck

Unfinished Sympathy
Massive Attack

Buffalo Stance
Neneh Cherry

Born Slippy
Underworld

Bitter Sweet Symphony
The Verve

Mr. Jones
Counting Crows

Thou Shalt Not Steal
Kev Carmody

Dropout
Urge Overkill

Jewels and Bullets
You Am I

Cut Your Hair
Pavement

Glycerine
Bush

Dyslexic Heart
Paul Westerberg

Don't Want to Be Grant McLennan
Smudge

Two Princes
Spin Doctors

Criminal
Fiona Apple

Damn, I Wish I Was Your Lover
Sophie B. Hawkins

Buddy Holly
Weezer

Stay (I Missed You)
Lisa Loeb & Nine Stories

Groove Is in the Heart Deee-Lite

(Deee-Lite) ✳ Elektra ✳ 1990 ✳ Appears on: *Groove Is in the Heart*

The ultimate New York club outfit of 1990, Deee-Lite was multi-racial and multi-gendered. Lady Muss Keir made an impressive and charismatic vocalist while DJ Dmitry and DJ Towa Towa just looked cool. Deee-Lite was playing all styles – hip-hop, pop, jazz and funk. But they did it with incredible verve. Their finest moment was 'Groove Is in the Heart', which featured Bootsy Collins on bass and the saxophone of Maceo Parker.

'Groove' is one of the best hooks of the decade – light and bouncy but irresistible as well. If nothing else, they had good taste, sampling the likes of Herbie Hancock. Hancock said, "Deee-Lite, that's the group. I was told that somebody had sampled something from the *Blow-Up* soundtrack that I had done. I had never heard it. And then one day, my daughter and I were getting in my car and the radio was on and she said, 'Dad, that's that song.' She pointed it out because I didn't even remember the song. I had to go and get the record to remember what the thing was."

Everything I've Got Belongs to You Ed Kuepper

(Ed Kuepper) ✳ Hot ✳ 1990 ✳ Appears on: *Today Wonder*

This song was recorded in two days with just Ed Kuepper playing guitar and Mark Dawson playing drums and cardboard box. After the incendiary years of the Saints – which were a roller coaster from hard rock through R&B to jazz – and then his years with the jazzy rock of the Laughing Clowns, Kuepper had begun to simplify his work.

The most striking thing about Kuepper at this time is his openness. He had been a master of the poetic dissemble through a dozen records. Whether it was midlife crisis or something else, Kuepper is sufficiently liberated to pen songs that are as simple and direct as his instrumentation.

"I think where I made the first tentative step was with *Today Wonder*," Kuepper told *Juice* magazine. "That's where I first thought: 'I can do this ...' I get self-conscious about being on stage and singing and I get self-conscious about writing personal lyrics."

Taking the title from a jazz standard, Kuepper puts on his best Mel Torme voice. There are the classic lines, "Time has proved I'm churlish and I'm rude/ And I find a real contentment in bad moods." It's a complex self-portrait from a guarded man and it's also a beautifully rendered portrait of a marriage. Plus he deserves extra credit for getting the word "churlish" into a song.

Unfinished Sympathy Massive Attack

(Robert '3D' del Naja/Grantley 'Daddy G' Marshall/Shara Nelson/J Sharp/Andrew 'Mushroom' Vowles) ✳ Virgin ✳ 1990 ✳ Appears on: *Blue Lines*

The Wild Bunch were a group of DJs in Bristol, a provincial British town. Gradually the members of the Bunch and their friends seeped into recording and have been some of the most potent figures in British music since 1990: producer Nellee Hooper, Tricky, Goldie, Portishead, Neneh Cherry and the three DJs behind Massive Attack – Andrew 'Mushroom' Vowles, Grant 'Daddy G' Marshall and Robert '3D' del Naja.

"When we were the Wild Bunch," said Daddy G, "we got our reputation as a sound system from the fact that we played all kinds of music – punk, funk, reggae. For us to try and make an album that's all one sound just wouldn't be natural."

Instead *Blue Lines* is a sublime melding of soul, R&B, rare groove, hip-hop, reggae and dub.

The music was made organically with the players improvising with samples and grooves in the studio, gradually assembling the tracks. The songs have the ambience and the energy of a group of people who know that they're on the verge of making something entirely new. Indeed the sound of *Blue Lines* has spawned thousands of imitators.

Much of it is due to the phenomenally soulful voice of Shara Nelson. But the songs are also mesmerising. 'Unfinished Sympathy' has an incredible groove that just grabs you along like the Nile in flood – big and deep and wide. It's a song that resonates through your consciousness; it taps into the eternal where only the best music can go.

'Unfinished Sympathy' began as a jam with just Nelson and a drum machine and a keyboard and it gradually built up the groove with strings and layers of keyboards.

"Right from the start, we never made music in line with the tempos that were required in clubs," said Daddy G. "It's made for after clubs, when you want to chill out, learn how to breathe again."

Blue Sky Mine Midnight Oil

(Midnight Oil) ❋ Sony ❋ 1990 ❋ Appears on: *Blue Sky Mining*

Having refashioned their sound on the *Diesel and Dust* album, Midnight Oil's next project was more forceful.

The opening track on the album begins with a harmonica riff from singer Peter Garrett that signals the fact that the group is back on the barricades.

The target this time are the corporate giants who continued to mine asbestos even after they knew that they were sending the workers to certain, protracted and painful death from mesothelioma. Not only that – once the death toll started to mount, the mining and sugar cane companies adopted delaying tactics through the courts so that the workers died and their compensation claims expired with them. It remains one of the great acts of capitalist bastardry of the 20th century. 'Blue Sky Mine' pulls no punches in bringing the matter to the fore. The fact that the story is set against a backing track that is full of as much melody as righteous indignation only ensured that the song would be a hit.

From Little Things Big Things Grow
Paul Kelly & the Messengers

(Paul Kelly/Kev Carmody) ❋ Mushroom ❋ 1990 ❋ Appears on: *Comedy*

In the '60s the Gurindji people on Wave Hill Station in the Northern Territory made a claim to the land on the grounds that it was sacred to them. The land was owned by Vestey's, a British corporation, then one of the largest landholders in Australia. Vincent Lingiarri led the Gurindji protest for eight long years, quietly demanding justice and refusing to be bought off.

The matter was eventually settled in favour of the Gurindji. In 1975, the prime minister Gough Whitlam flew to Wave Hill to formally acknowledge the handover. At the suggestion of his adviser Nugget Coombes, Whitlam bent down and picked up a handful of dirt that he ran through his fingers into the hands of Lingiarri.

The Wave Hill dispute was a significant step towards acknowledging the rights of Aboriginal people in Australia.

Carmody and Kelly tell the story of Vincent Lingiarri with careful detail and a strong sense of character. They are as understated in their language as Lingiarri was with his.

Merry Go Round The Replacements

(Paul Westerberg) ❋ Sire ❋ 1990 ❋ Appears on: *All Shook Down*

The Replacements were known as a hard-drinking band. That was part of their shambolic charm. Then Paul Westerberg, the singer, songwriter and guitarist, resolved to get himself sober and move on from the group. For contractual and personal reasons, however, *All Shook Down*, which is effectively a Westerberg solo album, became the Replacements' swan song.

It had been a long decade for Westerberg. The group was lauded around the globe as one of the great rock & roll bands of all time. Success, however, eluded them. By 1990 Westerberg was tired and burnt out. His personal life was in upheaval. He was tired of the responsibility of leading a band. He was also moving away from the Replacements sound in search of something more personal and intimate.

'Merry Go Round' was Westerberg's farewell to the past. A song that celebrates the abandon, the wildness of life. "Yeah, 'Merry Go Round' is really 'Achin' To Be' in a different key," he said. "It's the kind of character I tend to be interested in. The winners in life don't attract me.

"I've never been able to get a handle on that, I've tried to write 'em [songs about winners], but they always ring false. It's like someone else's words coming out my mouth, just a slogan to pat yourself on the back and kid yourself that it's all gonna be all right. 'We're gonna make it.' That emotion has never been strong with me. I've always been kinda defeatist! A lot of it does come from drink. I didn't stop drinking in the hope that now I'd have a positive outlook on life. But at least maybe I'll be able to see some glimmers of the other side of life."

The *All Shook Down* sessions were still ragged – emotionally raw – but musically more sophisticated. This is one of those songs where the artist is standing naked, for better or worse. As it happens, this was one of Westerberg's best moments.

"I sound very tired and weak on it, and I was," he said. "I was not healthy, not caring much. I sort of erased all the real angst, the pissed-off and the humour and took only the elements that were a little deranged, a little sad and a little pathetic and put them together. I was pretty fucking desperate there, and it shows.

"I'm glad we captured it."

Nothing Compares 2 U Sinéad O'Connor

(Prince) ✻ Ensign/Chrysalis ✻ 1990 ✻ Appears on: *I Do Not Want What I Haven't Got*

The Irish singer's first album, *The Lion and the Cobra*, was a cross between Celtic harmonies and post-punk folk rock. O'Connor had a difficult childhood – her alcoholic mother sexually abused her – and much of her work as a musician and her sometime erratic public statements can largely be attributed to this upbringing.

Perhaps as a result of that past, O'Connor is a powerful artist, not so much for her singing voice or for her lyrics, but her entire personality that she brings to a song.

Her second album featured a cover of a forgotten song that Prince had written for The Family, one of his protégé groups. O'Connor, in her version, strips the song back even further than Prince might have. She takes off the adornment and she inhabits the shell. This is a song of obsessive love and O'Connor finds its centre. She tries to do nothing but slowly lead herself through the modal arrangement. Mostly, though, it's just O'Connor. She holds her singing back as though there's a huge body of emotion behind her voice and she's just keeping it in check.

'Nothing Compares 2U' opened the way for the rest of the *I Do Not Want What I Haven't Got* album and even more candid songs about O'Connor's life.

"They said it was a piece of shit, like reading someone's diary," she said at the time when asked about her album. "They said it wouldn't sell and it would end up in the warehouse like, and I quote, 'Terence Trent D'Arby's second album.' I came up against that a lot. U2's the Edge said that the songs were too personal, but a guy who can't even call himself by his own name is obviously uncomfortable with his emotions."

Kool Thing Sonic Youth

(Kim Gordon/Thurston Moore/Lee Ranaldo/Steve Shelley) ✻ DGC ✻ 1990 ✻ Appears on: *Goo*

Sonic Youth opted to leave their downtown loft and suck on the corporate teat for the album *Goo*. That means that they wrote some songs with standard verse and chorus arrangements that come in at around four minutes. However that doesn't mean they would be any less radical.

'Kool Thing', for instance, gets right into the middle of the culture wars. Using satire as a weapon, Kim Gordon takes on the MTV world and the sexual politics involved in the images that come through popular culture. She also takes aim at the sexual politics of most militant male rap, posing the question "Fear of a female planet?" Or even better, the line "Something I gotta ask ya. I just wanna know, what are you gonna do for me? I mean, are you gonna liberate us girls from male white corporate oppression?" When LL Cool J was unavailable to spar with Gordon, Public Enemy's Chuck D stepped into the breach.

The polemics of the song would be meaningless without the support of a great, kicking groove from Sonic Youth. The Youth at their best sound like the Rolling Stones meets Marc Bolan and the Velvet Underground.

'Kool Thing' is one of the most potent feminist statements of '90s music and it lives up to its title.

Excursion A Tribe Called Quest

(Jonathan Davis) ❋ xJive ❋ 1991 ❋ Appears on: *The Low End Theory*

Yet another outfit from the Native Tongues Posse alongside De La Soul and the Jungle Brothers, A Tribe Called Quest were into conscious hip-hop that combines sharp rapping with jazz and bass-heavy grooves. 'Excursion' opens the rap quartet's second album – one that is widely considered to be a milestone in rap music. *The Low End Theory* carries the Afrocentrism of the Tribe one step further with the engagement of master bass player Ron Carter, one of Miles Davis' great sidemen.

Q-Tip kicks off *The Low End Theory* with the 'Excursion' manifesto:

> Back in the days when I was a teenager
> Before I had status and before I had a pager
> You could find the Abstract listening to hip-hop
> My pops used to say, it reminded him of bebop
> I said, well daddy don't you know that things go in cycles
> The way that Bobby Brown is just ampin like Michael

The rhymes and beats here are perfectly in sync, bouncing around and making a point without preaching. Q-Tip and Phife Dawg swap rhymes effortlessly. They roll with the beat rather than attack it and they allow their words to sit with groove rather than fight it. So while their message is by no means weak, their style is less macho and confronting than the gangstas.

Blind Willie McTell Bob Dylan

(Bob Dylan) ✳ Columbia ✳ 1991 ✳

Appears on: *The Bootleg Series Vol. 1–3 (Rare & Unreleased) 1961–1991*

Blind Willie McTell was born in 1901. Like many blind black men of the time, unable to perform manual labour, he became an entertainer and later a preacher. McTell's compositions were amongst the most popular folk blues of the time, including classics 'Statesboro Blues' and 'Delia'. He died in 1959 at the height of the folk renaissance, just as his music was reaching a white college audience. One college student at the University of Minnesota picked up on McTell's songs and sang some of them in 1960 in coffeehouses. Later in life, when he was the greatest songwriter of his generation, he would return to Willie McTell's 'Broke Down Engine' for one of his albums.

'Blind Willie McTell', regarded as one of the finest of Bob Dylan's recordings, was cut for the *Infidels* album in 1983 and lay unnoticed even by Dylanologists for eight years until uncovered for *The Bootleg Series Volumes 1–3*.

The tune is based on the traditional 'St James Infirmary'. Dylan refers in the song to "... staring out the window/of the old St James Hotel" and from that window he looks across the world and sees only "power and greed and corruptible seed". 'Blind Willie McTell' comes at the end of Dylan's preaching period. No longer writing evangelical songs, he returns to writing apocalyptic ones. He sees the corruption of the modern world and hears in Blind Willie's music the sound of history – which is more of the same.

I Can't Make You Love Me Bonnie Raitt

(Mike Reid/Allen Shamblin) ✳ Capitol ✳ 1991 ✳ Appears on: *Luck of the Draw*

At home in Nashville one day, former football star Mike Reid read a story in the morning paper. A local man had been arrested for getting drunk and shooting his girlfriend's car. When asked what he had learnt from his experience he replied, "I learned, your Honour, that you can't make a woman love you if she don't". The irrefutable wisdom of that and the poetic way in which it was revealed stayed with the songwriter when his partner Allen Shambin arrived for a writing session.

The song was tried a number of ways before Reid stripped it right back to the melody and lyric and let the pathos out. The pair decided that the song belonged to either Bonnie Raitt or Linda Ronstadt. The former was looking for tracks for her post-comeback album. Raitt started recording in the early '70s as a hardcore blues singer who drifted into rock before her life and career hit the skids of alcoholism. Then, in one of the most startling resurrections in 1989, her *Nick of Time* album turned her into a superstar. A rollercoaster life such as this allowed Raitt to inhabit a song as deep as 'I Can't Make You Love Me'.

"I was astounded the first time I heard it," said the singer. "And I knew I had to record it. I'm a big fan of Mike's voice, and the two of them together wrote probably one off the most exquisite songs I've ever heard. I think it stands among the best songs ever written."

That's a sentiment that's widely shared. Both Prince and George Michael have recorded the song. Carole King recently told *MOJO* magazine, "It's torn from the depths of feeling, from that really horrible place where your love is unrequited".

Weather With You   Crowded House

(Tim Finn/Neil Finn) ❋ Capitol ❋ 1991 ❋ Appears on: *Woodface*

The brothers Finn write sweet songs that generally disguise enormous turmoil. Both Neil and Tim Finn have demons lurking not far beneath the surface. In 1990, Neil had experienced success in America with Crowded House's debut album but the second one had failed to fire. He'd also had chronic writer's block and he turned to his brother Tim to help with inspiration. The result was a magnificent pop album. *Woodface* was a series of dark and deeply personal songs like 'Weather With You'.

"I had the opening chords E minor 7th to A7, to A9th," Tim recalled. "I had that as a strum going on the guitar and I had, [lyric] 'Walking round the room singing 'Stormy Weather''. That's all I had and I played that to Neil.

"He liked it; he came back with 'At 57 Mount Pleasant Street'. We had this place and we had this feeling of some guy walking around singing 'Stormy Weather' so things weren't that great. We had a mood and then Neil came up with, 'Things ain't cookin' in my kitchen', and that sounded like it could've almost been a chorus for a while. For a day or so that was what we had and then I'd remembered this other part, which I wrote backstage when I was doing a TV show in Portugal.

"I'd never been to Portugal before, never been since, but I loved it and I was feeling very buoyant and they made me feel like a star. I was feeling pretty wacky and pretty loved and I started singing, so I had that and then after a day or so I suddenly realised that 'always take the weather with you' would fit perfectly as a chorus. So I played it to Neil and he agreed and it all came together. You've got the verse part, and then the middle part, then the chorus. But the guitar figure is extremely hooky and it's one of the most memorable parts of the song obviously. That was Neil just jamming over those first two chords, the E minor and the A."

Enter Sandman Metallica

(Kirk Hammett/James Hetfield/Lars Ulrich) ✳ Elektra ✳ 1991 ✳ Appears on: *Metallica*

The album's first track and the first hit single, 'Enter Sandman', was the key to Metallica's new direction – more personal, more simple and more radio friendly. The song was an instant smash that put the record in the charts at number one and eventually sold eight million copies.

"We went into the studio with the intent of making a real lively record that bounces off the walls," said Ulrich. "It should have gone quicker, in theory, than trying to get everything note perfect like we have before. But as usual with Metallica, all those theories and normalities go straight out the window." In fact, Ulrich confessed, "it took us twice as long to make a record that is twice as loose."

"We wanted to create a different record and offer something new to our audience," said Hammett. "I hate it when bands stop taking chances. A lot of bands put out the same record three or four times, and we didn't want to fall into that rut." Metallica turned the rut into the Grand Canyon.

"There are fewer key changes," guitarist Kirk Hammett said. "There aren't many flatted fourth progressions, or anything like that just straight-ahead major and minor keys. The most complex song is probably 'Anywhere I Roam', which suggests a Phrygian dominant scale."

Nothing Else Matters Metallica

(James Hetfield/Lars Ulrich) ✳ Elektra ✳ 1991 ✳ Appears on: *Metallica*

"We're just as pissed, but we're using the anger and hatred in a different way," said guitarist James Hetfield when discussing the remarkable about-face that was their fifth album, *Metallica*. "We're not battling it so much, we're more or less laughing at it. There's things every day that piss me off, but they don't affect me as much in the music. There's better things to think about than some old son of a bitch cutting me off in my car or some shit on the news. All that political stuff is shit that you can't change, which is not gonna matter in the long run anyway. I think instead of anger, boredom has become more of the theme in the last few albums. Life is about avoiding boredom, really. You gotta seize the day.

"It was never put on, so you can't just take it off. Life is much easier for us now than it was ten years ago, but god damn, there are still things in my past that really still piss me off. It's too personal to talk about, but I don't think those initial feelings will ever go away."

After the fast and furious and political stance of their first four albums, Metallica enlisted pop metal producer Bob Rock to spend a year making their fifth, complete with power ballads, orchestral arrangements and lush videos. Just weeks before the grunge revolution would overtake the young and the disaffected, Metallica moved themselves to the next level.

The most notable change was a departure from the quirky time changes and labyrinthine arrangements of the previous LP (... *And Justice For All*). The political bent that guided *Justice* was dumped for a more personal style based on Hetfield's bitter and perverse internal monologue. 'Nothing Else Matters' was a huge power ballad with lush orchestration.

When You Sleep My Bloody Valentine

(Kevin Shields) ❋ Creation ❋ 1991 ❋ Appears on: *Loveless*

Kevin Shields, for all intents and purposes, is My Bloody Valentine, and is as difficult and conflicted as his music. Shields was born in New York but grew up in Dublin before moving to the UK where he became a demi-god. The British love their rock stars half-mad. This is partly why Shields and My Bloody Valentine are regarded with such reverence in the UK. With only two albums and a handful of other songs to their credit, My Bloody Valentine are said to have saved British rock, first in the late '80s by inventing the shoe-gazer sound and then in 1991 with the *Loveless* album, which put British rock back on its feet.

My Bloody Valentine doesn't deal in songs so much as soundscapes, huge shards of guitar noise from which melody appears. Shields piles up the guitars in magnificent, flowing arrangements.

Loveless is the soundtrack to a mind in glorious meltdown.

After the success of *Is It Anything* in 1988, Shields retreated to his house and became almost a recluse for much of the three years it took to finish *Loveless*.

"I'm crazy, but I'm not mentally ill. There's a difference. I was pretty crazy, for sure," he said, "and it was a very manic, overdrive kind of state, but it never got out of control. I can look after myself better than most people; I'm self-contained. I just didn't do what I didn't want to do. And I got away with it. When you keep on getting away with it year after year, you think you can just live like that. And you can. I wouldn't work. I wouldn't get up till late afternoon. I watched a lot of shit films."

It was worth it. Shields had a singular vision for his guitar rock & roll, which was somewhere between Paul McCartney and Sonic Youth. The voices too – Shields and girlfriend Bilinda Butcher – were all worked into the densely mixed texture of a volatile emotional landscape. It was a record of breathtaking courage.

"I've never been normal and I never will be," said Shields. "The world will change before I will."

Lithium Nirvana

(Kurt Cobain) ✳ DGC ✳ 1991 ✳ Appears on: *Nevermind*

Kurt Cobain was the leader not of the alternative nation but of the Ritalin Generation. The singer had a troubled childhood, growing up poor in a fractured family. "It was when I was seven," he told Jon Savage. "I had a really good childhood and then all of a sudden my whole world changed, I remember feeling ashamed. I became antisocial and I started to understand the reality of my surroundings, which didn't have a lot to offer. It's such a small town that I couldn't find any friends who were compatible. I like to do artistic things; I like to listen to music. I could never find any friends like that.

"I felt so different and so crazy that people just left me alone. They were afraid. I always felt that they would vote me 'Most Likely to Kill Everyone' at a high school dance. I could definitely see how a person's mental state could deteriorate to the point where they could do that. I've got to the point where I've fantasised about it, but I'd have always opted for killing myself first."

Cobain's family suffered through the great changes that happened in society in the '60s and '70s with prescription drugs and blurred notions of family. These kids were the victims of massive social change. Cobain clearly went through the eye of that storm medicated with Ritalin and other drugs, both from the pharmacy and the street corner. He was a junkie primed to happen.

'Lithium' reflects the intense emotional confusion that was Cobain's short life. The phrases "I love you," "I miss you," "I killed you" are contrasted with the cry "I'm not gonna crack!" On this track you can hear Cobain holding it all inside and, in hindsight, that last cry was actually bravado.

Smells Like Teen Spirit Nirvana

(Kurt Cobain/Dave Grohl/Krist Novoselic) ❊ DGC ❊ 1991 ❊ Appears on: *Nevermind*

The crowd at the OK Hotel in Seattle on the night of 17 April 1991 heard history being made. It was the public debut of 'Smells Like Teen Spirit', a new song that the group Nirvana had worked up in preparation for the major label recording sessions that summer. Cobain introduced the band by proclaiming, "Hello, we're major label corporate rock sell-outs." Although the lyric and the arrangement would change, 'Teen Spirit' was a song that sounded like a hit.

That January, Nirvana, a promising punk rock band from Olympia, Washington, via Seattle had moved from the local independent label Sub Pop to DGC, a subsidiary of Geffen Records. They had a solid first album out in the underground scene with its hardcore and Black Sabbath riffs. Nirvana and Geffen decided on Butch Vig to produce and sent him some indecipherable demo tapes. Rehearsals began in May at Sound City Studios in Van Nuys, California. In the '70s and the '80s it had been home to Tom Petty, the Jacksons, Rick Springfield and Fleetwood Mac. The group liked the room's "live" sound and the ancient equipment. The album was cut there in June on a budget of $130,000.

Teen Spirit was a cheap fragrance for teenage kids. Fellow punk rocker Kathleen Hanna of Bikini Kill graffitied the phrase "Kurt smells like Teen Spirit" on Cobain's bedroom wall after a party one night and the phrase stuck. Cobain turned it into an attack on consumerist society. He was also venting his own self-loathing. Signing to Geffen was, he believed, selling out his indie-rock principles.

"The songs were basically in really good shape, but I did do more arranging with them," said Vig. "'Teen Spirit' was longer and the little ad-libs after the chorus were actually at the end of the song. I suggested putting those in at the end of each chorus as a bridge into the next verse. And I remember Kurt sitting down with the acoustic and he had a couple of variations of the melody and the verse he was singing and we picked the one that was best. But most of the songs were fairly finished. I don't know whether they played them live a lot, but I know that they did practise a lot. It wasn't like, 'What are you playing here?' They knew. Chris had figured out his bass lines, and the drum patterns for the most part were worked out, and Kurt had a pretty good idea of what he wanted to do. But he had a couple lines in some songs that he was still working on. I was so into the song I had them play it as much as possible! The song was amazing."

For the most part, Vig says the sessions were fairly relaxed. "The band was really loose. They were going out all night and partying. I think that they had a certain sense of 'We can do whatever we want.' Typically, I would go in before them, like around noon or one, and they would get in mid-afternoon, 3 or 4 o'clock and we'd work until 11 o'clock or midnight. And they'd leave and I'd usually work a little longer."

"Kurt had the chorus of the song – that four-chord riff and the vocal melody," said Novoselic. "We jammed on that riff, broke it down into a groove, and that turned out to be the verse of the song. There's that little bridge. And that's the song. The recording was just as brisk. Nirvana cut the basic track for 'Teen Spirit' live in three takes; the second was the keeper."

'Teen Spirit' is a strange combination of garage rock and the big chording of FM rock bands like Boston. Cobain claimed that his inspiration was the Pixies, who pioneered the loud/soft dynamic.

"He squashed his pop sensibility," said Vig. "He had that dichotomy of punk rage and alienation but also this vulnerable pop sensibility. In 'Teen Spirit', a lot of that vulnerability is in his singing, in the tone of his voice."

The song recorded, Andy Wallace mixed it into an epic.

'Teen Spirit' was accompanied by a video directed by Samuel Bayer. The group here played in a basketball court from hell with a pack of screaming fans and a line of cheerleaders played by strippers recruited at the last minute. Dressed in their usual thrift shop clothes and flannelette shirts, Nirvana suddenly put the working-class underground onto MTV. It was clear that a whole subculture existed that was just full of energy in a way that hadn't been seen in rock & roll for decades.

'Smells Like Teen Spirit' was released on 10 September 1991. By the end of the year Nirvana was the hottest band in the world. The grunge revolution had started.

"The song was a call to consciousness," Novoselic said. "There was this conservative government. Culture was stagnant. The song was this sledge-hammer that came along and bonged it all."

Alive Pearl Jam

(Stone Gossard/Eddie Vedder) ❋ Epic ❋ 1991 ❋ Appears on: *Ten*

"It's about incest; and it's about murder; and you know all those good things," said Pearl Jam singer Eddie Vedder. "And if you can picture it in your mind, the third song takes place in a jail cell. So this is our own little mini-opera here."

The first part of the mini-opera is 'Alive', the first song on Pearl Jam's debut album, *Ten*.

Vedder explained the lyrics to filmmaker Cameron Crowe. "Everybody writes about it like it's a life-affirmation thing – I'm really glad about that. It's a great interpretation. But 'Alive' is … it's torture. Which is why it's fucked up for me. Why I should probably learn how to sing another way. It would be easier. It's … it's too much.

"The story of the song is that a mother is with a father and the father dies. It's an intense thing because the son looks just like the father. The son grows up to be the father, the person that she lost. His father's dead, and now this confusion, his mother, his love, how does he love her, how does she love him? In fact, the mother, even though she marries somebody else, there's no-one she's ever loved more than the father. You know how it is, first loves and stuff. And the guy dies. How could you ever get him back? But the son. He looks exactly like him. It's uncanny. So she wants him. The son is oblivious to it all. He doesn't know what the fuck is going on. He's still dealing, he's still growing up. He's still dealing with love, he's still dealing with the death of his father. All he knows is 'I'm still alive' – those three words, that's totally out of burden.

"Now the second verse is 'Oh she walks slowly into a young man's room … I can remember to this very day … the look … the look.' And I don't say anything else. And because I'm saying, 'The look, the look' everyone thinks it goes with 'on her face'. It's not on her face. The look is between her legs. Where do you go with that? That's where you came from.

"But I'm still alive. I'm the lover that's still alive. And the whole conversation about 'You're still alive, she said. And his doubts: 'Do I deserve to be? Is that the question?' Because he's fucked up forever! So now he doesn't know how to deal with it. So what does he do, he goes out killing people – that was [the song] 'Once'. He becomes a serial killer. And 'Footsteps', the final song of the trilogy, that's when he gets executed. That's what happens. The Green River killer … and in San Diego, there was another prostitute killer down there. Somehow I related to that. I think that happens more than we know. It's a modern way of dealing with a bad life.

"I'm just glad I became a songwriter."

Vedder had a serious Who habit, which may explain his desire to write rock operas. In any case it's sufficiently impenetrable for most Pearl Jam fans that simply adopted the song as an anthem.

The music for the song comes from 'Dollar Short', a tune that guitarist Stone Gossard had worked up some months earlier and was one of the songs he played to prospective band members. "I knew we had a band," guitarist Mike McCready said, "when we started playing that song 'Dollar Short'."

The tape with 'Dollar Short' and some other tracks was posted to Eddie Vedder to add lyrics and as a result, Vedder came to Seattle and joined Pearl Jam. The first song they played together was 'Alive'.

On 11 March 1991 Pearl Jam embarked on a month in the studio where they cut *Ten*, which was released the following September. It took five months to make the charts but once there, Pearl Jam went on to dominate the rock scene for the next three years.

Loaded Primal Scream

(Bobby Gillespie/Andrew Innes/Robert Young) ❋ Creation ❋ 1991 ❋
Appears on: *Screamadelica*

Primal Scream spanned so many moments in British rock. Bobby Gillespie got his start in the pop scene as the drummer of the Jesus & Mary Chain. Gillespie's friendship with Creation Records supremo Alan McGhee placed him in the midst of the Manchester scene. In 1986 Primal Scream's debut was a return to the eternal rock values. All these elements and the club and rave culture of the late '80s came together on Primal Scream's classic album *Screamadelica*. This was rock music with a new flavour.

'Loaded' is based on Andy Weatherall's remix of Primal Scream's 1989 track 'I'm Losing More than I'll Ever Have', updating the rock & roll song with the ambience of acid and club land. Most of all, 'Loaded' accentuates a groove. Described by one critic as "a bizarre cross between the Rolling Stones' 'Sympathy for the Devil' and Soul II Soul".

"All the great white rock of the past has been influenced by black music, but post-punk music lost touch with that influence," Gillespie said. "'Loaded' taught us about rhythm and space. We've always been good at harmony, but learning how to use a sampler gave us a new palette of colours. The sampler opens up a whole new world of psychedelic possibilities."

The *Screamadelica* album is full of humour and sensuality. It's joyful in the way that so much rock of the '90s wasn't and it bridged the gap between rock and dance music.

'Loaded' pretty much explains itself in the title. Gillespie was allegedly taking drugs for England. The chemicals brought a spiritual or at least spacey aspect to *Screamadelica*.

"When I was younger, I really thought that by 1991 we'd all be living in outer space and wearing cool silver space suits," he said. "I thought that automation would have taken over all manual labour so that people could be free to express themselves. All those moon shots in the late '60s and early '70s, I think they affected me and lot of my generation. I was really bummed out when I found out that NASA have wound down the whole space program. See, I have this romantic image of the early explorers like Vasco Da Gama or Columbus, who were going into the beyond despite the fear that the world was flat and they'd disappear into oblivion. I think there should be a space program for spiritual reasons, as a leap into the unknown.

"I keep thinking about all these astronauts. Surely they must have been drastically altered by going up there? What did they think about while looking down at the world? I'm sure they must discover a lot about themselves, during the training and while they were in space looking at the Earth. I'd still love to go up there. But I've got to get an album out! But one of the ideas behind 'Higher than the Sun' is this really crazy thought I had that, because the prospect of people going into outer space has disappeared, we've got to explore inner space."

Nighttrain   Public Enemy

(Chuck D/Cerwin Depper/Gary G-Wiz/JBL/Stuart Robertz) ❋ Def Jam ❋ 1991 ❋

Appears on: *Apocalypse 91 ... The Enemy Strikes Black*

Chuck D, Public Enemy's mouth-in-chief, described rap music as the black CNN. Their music certainly sounded like it was coming from the front with its aural gunfire and bomb bursts.

Most of Chuck D's vitriol was directed at the white Establishment, but he was not above sending a message to the ghetto. 'Nighttrain' on *Apocalypse 91* is a terrifying missive about the drug epidemic affecting black America. In this context he describes drug dealers as agents of white capitalism.

"Of course," he said, "they're victims too, but they're conscious. They know what they're doing. And when they're doing the wrong thing, they've got to suffer severe penalties. No more time for the psychoanalytical approach. We can't feel sorry, we can't even get emotional. It's damn near prophesied that the motherfuckers will be slain outright, by the doers of good over the doers of evil.

"What's going to happen is the same thing that developed in South Africa, where the only way to develop unity and organisation is to eliminate the agents. In South Africa, they put 'rubber neckties' on them. Here in America, you're soon gonna see brothers who want to get paid saying to themselves: 'Why bother to sell drugs, why don't I just stick up and kill drug dealers?' You already got groups coming up who say, 'We love to rob the dope man.' We're gonna see an apocalyptic situation with the rise of black vigilantism."

'Nighttrain' is a scarifying ride with sounds from the Bomb Squad that match the ferocity of the great free jazz players. The extremity of Public Enemy's position is somewhat undercut by the drug use of one of its own – Flavor Flav – and by the outrageousness of Chuck D's solution. But it is one hell of a piece of rap music.

Under the Bridge The Red Hot Chili Peppers

(Flea/John Frusciante/Anthony Kiedis/Chad Smith) ✳ Warner Bros. ✳ 1991 ✳
Appears on: BloodSugarSexMagik

During the '80s California's funk rockers were more likely to wind up dead in the bath than to have a number one record. The group was legendary for its drug use – especially singer Anthony Kiedis – and they had already lost one guitarist to an overdose. For BloodSugarSexMagik the Chili Peppers enlisted producer Rick Rubin, who had a feel for both hard rock and funk. Then they holed up in a large house in Los Angeles and remade themselves.

BloodSugarSexMagik is one of the strongest albums of the '90s. Mostly it comes down to the strength of the songs – the pounding funky rock of 'Give It Away' and the heartbreaking melodies of 'Under the Bridge'. "The album title is an eloquent but abstract description of how we feel," said Kiedis. "We live in a world packed with desensitising forces, that strip the world of magic. And music can help restore a sense of magic. The world is full of negativity, but we fight back with positivity. We're inspired by oceans, forests, animals, Marx Brothers films. We can't help but project uplifting vibrations, because we love each other so much and get off on playing together."

'Under the Bridge' is a love song to Los Angeles, where Kiedis and bass player Flea grew up on the streets. The bridge in question was a shelter for the homeless and a place to score. For Kiedis' dysfunctional family life, the city was more a home to him than any house could be.

Guitarist John Frusciante, whose spidery guitar lines are elegant, shimmering and slightly tart – bittersweet, in fact – evocatively renders Kiedis' heartfelt tribute to Los Angeles.

"You know what LA is to me?" said Flea. "It's that bird that goes, ooooh-ah-oooh, ooh-ooh. The soul of this city is a huge part of who we are and I think the soul of this city is an old and beautiful thing."

Losing My Religion R.E.M.

(Michael Stipe/Mike Mills/Peter Buck/Bill Berry) ❄ Warner Bros. ❄ 1991 ❄
Appears on: *Out of Time*

This was the song that would make R.E.M. household names in 1991. Stipe's beautiful, yearning voice sings about indecision and regret and fear in an abstract lyric that sits atop their most beguiling tune. The melody was written by Peter Buck in 1990, shortly after he bought his first mandolin – an instrument he barely uses other than for this song.

The group thought that the song would keep them out of the charts and maintain their cult status. "There's no chorus, there's no guitar, it's five minutes long, it's a fucking mandolin song. What kind of a pop song is that?" asked Stipe.

"Musically it's very straightforward," said bass player Mike Mills. "There's something satisfying about that song, in the sense of the way the sound of the mandolin combines with the chords, the appealing, evocative nature of the lyrics – and a fabulous video. And you put that together and it's kind of a fluke, but thank goodness. I'm not even sure if that song could be a single now but it came out in the right time at the right place."

One U2

(Bono/Adam Clayton/The Edge/Larry Mullen Jr) ❄ Island ❄ 1991 ❄
Appears on: *Achtung Baby*

'One' is one of the best pop songs of the '90s. Its surly momentum owes more to German industrial music than to rock. There's a darkness to the song – it's not about harmony, but acknowledging differences and the fact that we are stuck with each other. Like the best U2 songs, it's a record that is both intensely personal and universal as well.

Over the twelve months that U2 spent working on *Achtung Baby* there was slow progress made through the compiling of ideas. Both singer Bono and guitarist the Edge were trawling through fragments of work and 'One' came about from the melding of ideas. The Edge's marriage was finishing and that inspired the beginning of it. According to Bono, "There were a couple of things going on, and as usual I meant to resolve them, but the best U2 songs seem to occupy this place of contradictions. I had a lot of things going on in my head at the time, about forgiveness, about father and son angst. I was trying to write a story song I think, and I'm just not good at that. The lyrics came really quickly. The humbling bit about songwriting is that anything above good usually feels like an accident. A lot of U2 songs are first drafts."

The group was recording at Hansa Studios in Berlin, where Bowie and Iggy Pop had made their Kraut-rock albums.

"It wasn't going well," the Edge told Q magazine. "Adam and Larry's rather jaundiced view of Bono's and my songwriting ability was becoming more and more evident as our various experiments went nowhere. We were listening to a lot of industrial music, and the sounds we were making were quite intense.

"In the midst of all this I go off into another room to put together some ideas for 'The Fly'. I came back with two, neither of which worked where they were meant to, but on Daniel Lanois' suggestion we put them together and Bono was really taken with it. So we all went out into the big recording room – a huge, eerie ballroom full of ghosts of the war – and everything fell into place. Bono's melodies and phrases were following, and by the end of the day we basically had everything, the whole form of the song.

"Everyone recognized it was a crucial moment in the development of what became *Achtung Baby* – ironically it went in a totally different direction from everything we'd been working on. But everyone recognized it was a special piece. It was like we'd caught a glimpse of what the song could be. Then it was about capturing its essence, but also trying to keep our hands off it. Those songs that seem to arrive perfectly formed – you don't want to mess with them too much.

"The lyric was the first in a new, more intimate style. It's two ideas, essentially. On one level it's a bitter, twisted, vitriolic conversation between two people who've been through some nasty, heavy stuff: 'We hurt each other/Then we do it again.' But on another level there's the idea that 'we get to carry each other.' 'Get to' is the key. The original lyric was 'we have to carry each other' and it was never quite right – it was too fuckin' obvious and platitudinous. But 'get to'? – it's like our privilege to carry one another. It puts everything in a different perspective, introduces that idea of grace.

"Still, it blows me away when it's played at weddings. I wouldn't have played it at any wedding of mine. But I suppose it's because, despite all the other stuff in there, the power of 'we get to carry each other' overwhelms everything. And the honesty of it helps – the bare-knuckle telling-it-like-it-is-ness."

Zoo Station U2

(U2) ❋ Island ❋ 1991 ❋ Appears on: *Achtung Baby*

In November 1989 in a Sydney pub, Bono Vox, the most potent rock star of that decade, declared, "The '80s was just a rehearsal. I mean that." Two years later U2 fulfilled their promise with a radical reinvention of everything they stood for and sounded like with the album *Achtung Baby*.

Co-producer Brian Eno wrote of the year-long sessions that went into making the record, "Buzz words on this record were trashy, throwaway, dark, sexy and industrial (all good) and earnest, polite, sweet, righteous, rockist and linear (all bad). It was good if a song took you on a journey or made you think your hi-fi was broken, bad if it reminded you of recording studios or U2. Sly Stone, T. Rex, Scott Walker, My Bloody Valentine, KMFDM, the Young Gods, Alan Vega, Al Green and Insekt were all in favour. And Berlin itself, where much of the recording was done, became a conceptual background for the record ...

"U2's state of mind was similar to that before *The Unforgettable Fire*: ready for something bigger, rebelling against its own stereotypes ... you might be forgiven for thinking that the band knew just what they wanted before they went in, but I don't think that's true."

Beginning in January 1989 with the team of co-producer Daniel Lanois and engineer Flood, with Eno overseeing, U2 turned itself on its head, absorbing the energy of the still nascent hardcore and grunge scene with European techno and dance. While the Edge searched out the angular and the extreme, Larry Mullins and Adam Clayton kept the big picture in sight.

The furious industrial noise of 'Zoo Station' opened the record like a futuristic poem to the new, chaotic and free Europe. The record was also more highly sexed than their anthemic '80s albums. As Bono said, "Rhythm. That is the sex of music ... That's what was missing in the puzzle for U2."

In changing direction so radically with *Achtung Baby*, U2 avoided becoming parodies of themselves and being swept aside by the grunge and techno revolutions. *Achtung Baby* prefigured the even more experimental direction they pursued for the next ten years. They may have lost their old fans but they maintained the rage.

Nuthin' but a 'G' Thang Dr Dre

(Dr Dre) ❋ Death Row ❋ 1992 ❋ Appears on: *The Chronic*

Coming out of the powerful NWA, Dre developed a sound that was so funky and fat that he quickly became one of the most inventive and powerful of rap producers. Part of his appeal came from his old school knowledge – he cleverly used Parliament/Funkadelic grooves, some funk guitar as well as the mega bass sound, and a clipped rhythm style.

'Nuthin' but a 'G' Thang' is a West Coast rap classic. As the title suggests, this is a song about gangsta life. However, while NWA were nominally political, 'G Thang' reduces life to chasing pussy. The song, on which Snoop Dogg does most of the rapping, is a piece of misogynistic nonsense.

It's a discussion of the possibilities of scoring some ass. The level of discourse is completely offensive to women and reads like the patter between two adolescent boys. Which is perhaps why gangsta rap essentially appealed to teenage males.

My Drug Buddy The Lemonheads

(Evan Dando) ❋ Atlantic ❋ 1992 ❋ Appears on: *It's a Shame About Ray*

Well, the title is self-explanatory. It's a story of a couple of slackers who spend their days scoring drugs and then doing it again. Not the most interesting of stories but Dando makes the scenario something more profound than just the routine of addiction. The melody here is wistful and dreamy. He creates a relationship between the two characters that is more than just getting out of it. Part of it is the matter-of-fact tone with which he delivers the song. Without either moral judgement or a description of the excitement of getting high, Dando here is describing a bond between two people. Maybe it's romance, maybe it's friendship. There's a dreamy quality that really makes it irrelevant. The melody on the song is just sublime.

"*Ray* is all about this girl from the Hummingbirds, Alannah, who suggested that the Lemonheads should come out to Australia," said Dando, describing the classic *Shame about Ray* album. "I'm proud of that record! It's glowy, bright and shiny."

Aneurysm Nirvana

(Kurt Cobain/Dave Grohl/Krist Novoselic) ❈ DGC ❈ 1992 ❈ Appears on: *Hormoaning*

According to Nirvana this was "a recent attempt at getting back to our New Wave roots". 'Aneurysm' definitely rocks. It's more of a pop song than almost everything else on the *Nevermind* album. 'Aneurysm' has a gigantic, crunching two-chord chorus and a massive descending riff that is just perfect for arenas and blows the walls out of the small theatres in which Nirvana mostly played.

The rush of the tune and the lyrics suggest that the inspiration for the song was Kurt's affection for heroin. The drug was readily available in his teens and indeed it swept through the Seattle music scene like a plague. Cobain had been a long-term junkie. He claimed the heroin was mostly for the analgesic benefits it gave him as relief from his chronic stomach pain.

"I'd taken heroin for a year-and-a-half," Cobain told Jon Savage, "but the addiction didn't get in the way until the band stopped touring about a year and a half ago. But now things have got better. Ever since I've been married and had a child, within the last year, my whole mental and physical state has improved almost one hundred per cent. I'm really excited about touring again. I'm totally optimistic: I haven't felt this optimistic since my parents got divorced, you know."

Like most junkies, Cobain was not being honest about his drug use, which was chronic. It had been bad before the group started and it just got worse as Cobain's responsibilities increased. A year after this track was released, Cobain's drug habits had torn the band asunder and made recording nigh impossible.

But on 'Aneurysm' he's full of life. Everything is possible and nothing matters except riding this firestorm of a track.

Rid of Me PJ Harvey

(PJ Harvey) ❈ Island ❈ 1992 ❈ Appears on: *Rid of Me*

"There's nothing wrong with provocative art. I hope to do something that shocks even myself," PJ Harvey told Phil Sutcliffe from the *Melody Maker* prior to the release of her second album. "In fact, I've done it. It's a song called 'Rid of Me'."

Having come from the west country wilds of Dorset only a year or so earlier, PJ Harvey burst onto the British music scene with a fierce and confronting take on the relations between men and women.

Harvey's music was spare and dry and uncompromising, to match her lyrics. For her second album, *Rid of Me*, she enlisted the production support of hardcore guru Steve Albini, who made her sound even more brittle.

This title track with its masochistic refrain is blanching in its candour – the sublimation of everything including sex just to keep a wayward lover. Harvey said that, at the time, she was listing to Chess blues artists Howlin' Wolf and Willie Dixon and was impressed by their raw sexuality and dispassion.

"What I listen to mostly now is Howlin' Wolf and every single song is about sex," she said. "Well, I think that is the most invigorating, exciting and extreme subject I can write about.

"Love? Mm. Sex and love, they don't always go together, do they? I like the darker shades, like in 'Wang Dang Doodle'. I admire Willie Dixon's lyrics so much. There's a party going on in that song, but what kind of party? All the people he describes: Butcher-Knife-Totin' Annie, Razor-Totin' Jim, Fast-Talkin' Fanny. Then there's that line, 'Now when fish scent fills the air/There'll be snuff juice everywhere'. Fish scent must be female genitalia, 'my little oyster' and all that, but 'snuff juice'? I'm not sure."

The sound she aimed for on the album is a mixture of that spare, dark Chess sound and the size and heft of Led Zeppelin. And she and Albini did achieve something of that.

"If I play *Rid of Me* at home I get to the end of the first side and I can't breathe. Can't handle it. I'm taking it apart all the time. Analysing. I certainly wouldn't put it on for an enjoyable evening. It's uncomfortable."

That's not a bad thing.

Creep Radiohead

(Thom Yorke) ✳ Parlophone ✳ 1992 ✳ Appears on: *Pablo Honey*

"It's an on and off song," said Radiohead's vocalist Thom Yorke describing 'Creep'. "It's all about being drunk and following people around." The ironic self-loathing of the lyrics made 'Creep' a perfect gimmick song just as everything was going Generation X and grunge. Although Yorke acknowledged the humour in his unlikely hit, there was a truth at the heart of the tune. "Certain people self-destruct," he told *Juice* magazine. "Emotionally, it's a way of absorbing things that really hurt. What happens is that your lifestyle becomes twisted. Self-destruction is something I have to live with within myself. It comes and goes involuntarily, and I'm shocked to say it still does as well."

Radiohead were an unlikely act to rise to the top in a sea of alternative rock. Yorke's poetic lyrics were set against the elegiac playing of guitarists Jonny Greenwood and Ed O'Brien and the whole owed more to XTC and R.E.M. than grunge rock.

"I'm anti-rock & roll in the sense of long hair and blow jobs. Rock & roll to people back in the '60s was an attitude," Yorke said. "Rock & roll now is just the relics of that and it doesn't actually represent people, it's just something that they turn to as if it's still there, when it's not. They should be looking elsewhere.

"The only way that people seem to consume these things now is through pure hysteria. It's either hysteria or nostalgia. It's never their own genuine feelings. It's always something they're trying to borrow from other people all the time."

Radiohead transcended their gimmicky reputation and within a couple of years had become the saviours of rock & roll themselves.

Killing in the Name Rage Against the Machine

(Rage Against the Machine) ❋ Epic ❋ 1992 ❋ Appears on: *Rage Against the Machine*

Wow, these guys were angry. The cover of the eponymous first album pictured a Buddhist monk on fire, but Rage didn't go in for that kind of passive aggression. Guitarist and Harvard graduate Tom Morello and singer Zack De La Rocha were both second-generation militant leftists who saw Rage as a vehicle for insurgency as well as entertainment. Morello, drummer Brad Wilk, bass player Tim Commerford and De La Rocha were familiar with rap, hip-hop and heavy rock and fused the styles with the solder of righteous indignation. But they could also play. Morello, especially, found a new language for the electric guitar – capricious and vengeful and just plain gobsmacking in his virtuosity.

"Throughout the course of my guitar playing in a lot of the bands I've been in," he said, "much of it was a search for my voice on the instrument to find a unique way to express the anxiety of suburbia through six strings and a piece of wood. I began to really find that in Rage Against the Machine."

'Killing in the Name' was the centrepiece of the debut album and a rallying call for millions of angry young men and women with its chorus of, "Fuck you, I won't do what you tell me!"

Rage Against the Machine only made two proper albums in six years, in most part due to internal conflicts. After them, however, came the deluge of rap rockers such as Linkin Park, Limp Bizkit and Korn. None of them had the depth or the wit of Rage Against the Machine although there is now a tradition of political hardcore in groups such as System of a Down that is Rage's legacy. Neither hip-hop nor hardcore nor heavy metal, Rage Against the Machine were completely uncompromising in their politics and their music.

Everybody Hurts R.E.M.

(Michael Stipe/Peter Buck/Bill Berry/Mike Mills) ❄ Warner Bros. ❄ 1992 ❄
Appears on: *Automatic for the People*

You'd think they'd be happy. R.E.M. were kings of the world in 1992 after the commercial breakthrough of the *Out of Time* album. Their next record, though, was sorrowful and brooding. The album took a relatively long time to record, cut in studios in three cities. The songs were superficially simple but were made up of complex layers of atmospherics and subtle touches.

"The stuff we were turning out was pretty dark," guitarist Peter Buck told John O'Donnell. "It wasn't as if we gave him a bunch of pop songs and he wrote down these lyrics. And overall I think the record is pretty positive, but there are certain songs about death. It's kind of inward looking more than anything.

"Sometimes you've got to let the music direct you and this time it just felt that everything we wrote that was really quality, musically and lyrically, tended to be more reflective and slower."

'Everybody Hurts' is a painful ballad with a straightforward melody line – courtesy of drummer Bill Berry – and an almost prosaic lyric from Stipe that is sung with heartbreaking directness. "The subject of 'Everybody Hurts' is exactly what it sounds like," said Mills. The song became the group's biggest hit, as was the album *Automatic for the People*.

"I bought this awful $20 Univox drum machine," said Buck. "But it made sense, because the song had a metronome-ish feel. Mike and I cut it live with this dumb drum machine which is just as wooden as you can get. We wanted to get this flow around that: human and non-human at the same time."

Big Time Sensuality Björk

(Björk/Nellee Hooper) ❊ Elektra ❊ 1993 ❊ Appears on: *Debut*

"A lot of my songs – including 'Big Time Sensuality' – are about my friends, not my lovers," said Björk to *Record Collector* magazine. "It's not erotic or sensual even if it may sound like that. As you know, you create pretty deep, full-on love relationships with friends. A lot of it is also about myself. I can be a coward a lot of the time and there comes a moment when I write a song when I get quite brave. It's a lot about me dealing with myself rather than attacking other people. Would I like to know the future? No. There's a side to me that likes to plan a little bit ahead and there's a side that just needs to be free. I've got problems with booking airline tickets – I always change them. Sometimes I wonder if it's just for me to feel free. To kind of not be nailed in is really important to me."

It was a time of courage for the Icelandic singer: after arriving on the world stage five years earlier with the Sugarcubes, Björk set out on her own. She had initially been a solo artist, cutting her first album at the age of eleven. This time she opted to work with Soul II Soul svengali Nellee Hooper and together they crafted a pop record unlike any heard before.

Brassy with jazz and R&B flavours inside an avant-rock framework, *Debut* is haunting and beguiling.

"In my head there were all these little ideas that had to be completed, or I would go mad," said the singer. "I was always very happy singing with the Sugarcubes, being a housewife in Iceland and making film music. But slowly I began to feel that I had to do this thing, get my songs out, otherwise I would feel guilty for the rest of my life. And to do this properly, I had to move to London. It's very precious to me, this album. It may be the only album I ever make, so I wanted to do it right.

"I met this guy in LA and fell in love with him, and he turned out to be Nellee's best friend. So when he brought me back to London, he introduced us. I would probably never have thought of Nellee, because what he has done in the past has been too sophisticated, too tasteful compared to what I was thinking. I was bored to death with current pop music. But when I got to know Nellee, I felt that he was the person who could do the whole thing with me, so I ended up dropping everybody else. I'll work with them later, but it became a bit of a Björk/Nellee affair. I start the songs, and he finishes them."

Mr Jones Counting Crows

(David Bryson/Adam Duritz) ✳ Geffen ✳ 1993 ✳
Appears on: *August and Everything After*

Counting Crows always did have high-profile fans. No less than the Band's Robbie Robertson encouraged his daughter to see their show with the advice: "They're a really good band, a little derivative perhaps, but worth seeing".

Duritz is a songwriter who sees himself very clearly in the American tradition of Robertson and the Band, Tom Petty and Bob Dylan. His breakthrough song, in fact, takes its title from Bob Dylan's hapless reporter in 'Ballad of a Thin Man'.

"I really wanted to be a rock star – since I was five years old doing 'Can't Buy Me Love' in front of the mirror with a tennis racquet," Duritz confessed. "But I also thought that it was a really crazy thing to want, that there was a disaster in there that I wasn't seeing clearly. That's what 'Mr Jones' is actually about – a rather sad but tongue-in-cheek song about daydreaming of being famous. Now it's happened, the tongue-in-cheek part's gone and all that's left is bitterness."

The Counting Crows debut album sold about five million copies worldwide, in part due to 'Mr Jones'. It was a time when angst was very popular and Duritz was angsty but knew how to give his pain the sweetest possible context.

"People say to me it should be fun, but I don't agree," Duritz told *MOJO*. "I don't care about fun. Not in music. It's not fun. I don't enjoy it. I feel it though. It moves me deeply; I have a deep satisfaction. But fun? Fuck fun. Go have fun somewhere else. I do it so I can be who I am in my life. But fun? Go have fun later. But right now, I want your soul and I want it on tape …"

Are You Gonna Go My Way? Lenny Kravitz

(Lenny Kravitz/Craig Ross) ✳ Virgin ✳ 1993 ✳ Appears on: *Are You Gonna Go My Way?*

"The people I gravitate to are the older ones – Jagger and Bowie, whoever," Lenny Kravitz told Mat Snow shortly after the release of *Are You Gonna Go My Way?* "I was raised on good music," he continued, "and I haven't met a lot of musicians from this time period that inspire me. I listen out for good new music, but the recording fucks me off right from the beginning. People accuse me of being Mr Romantic for the old stuff – I'm sorry, but I hear better melodies, better musicianship, better music. Maybe I'm just stuck, but I think the whole thing was better. I'm a snob."

Unashamedly retro in its sound and approach 'Are You Gonna Go My Way?' was a song completely out of time. It had huge drum patterns like souped up soul music and layers of guitars pulsing forward.

Kravitz could get away with it because he exudes pure sex appeal and the song had an immense sense of humour about it. The early '90s were caught up in the style wars – Generation X, grunge and club culture – whereas Kravitz was having none of it. Going his way meant letting the freak flag fly and having a great time. Who can argue with that?

Fuck and Run   Liz Phair

(Liz Phair) ❋ Matador ❋ 1993 ❋ Appears on: *Exile in Guyville*

"They're totally how I talk, I have a potty mouth," said Liz Phair. "I know what I'm doing when I use the word fuck, but I think it's termed explicit because I'm a girl. The thrill of it is like, your little sister could be up there having these thoughts and you wouldn't know it. That's the titillation. It makes you look around at all the good girls and wonder what's going on in their heads." That was exactly the attraction of Liz Phair – she told the world what was really going on inside some women's heads.

She emerged in the wake of grunge as a straight-talking woman with a great feel for bare rock & roll. Her early tapes led to a recording deal and the sessions that resulted in her stone classic album *Exile in Guyville*.

Guyville was a song-to-song answer to the Stones' 1972 *Exile on Main Street*. "I started listening to *Exile on Main Street* over and over again and hearing what was underneath it," she said. "I kept thinking, I've got answers to this! But it wasn't like, 'You say this, I say that.' Sometimes it was like, 'I see it your way', or 'It's this way in my girly world'. I gave myself room, whether I was contradicting what they said, relearning it or using a parallel symbol. It was like answering a letter."

That would make 'Fuck and Run' the response to Keith Richard's 'Happy'. It's about a girl who's not happy. It's a clear and rather emotional response to a one-night stand. It captures the ambivalence and the emotional awkwardness that is stirred by random passion and the niggling longing for a love that will last.

"Liz is often imaged as a slut because she sings about blow jobs and sings the word fuck," said producer Brad Wood. "It's like they miss the whole point."

Fade into You Mazzy Star

(David Roback/Hope Sandoval) ✳ 4AD ✳ 1993 ✳

Appears on: *So Tonight that I Might See*

It was said of Mazzy Star guitarist/songwriter David Roback that he had three tempos – slow, slower and slowest. His somnolent psychedelic atmospheres were a comfortable environment for the waifish whisperings of singer Hope Sandoval. One writer described their creative relationship as, "She's moody and he's withdrawn". There is something of a narcotic magic to their occasional recordings. They're a little bit country and a little bit Velvet Underground but their songs are enduring in the sense that they are spectral in substance but they haunt the imagination long after the record has finished spinning. Roback had been around the Los Angeles alternative rock scene since the early '80s. Even then he was playing moody, slow country music. Sandoval had been a fan of his group the Rain Parade and they eventually began an affair – since ended – and a writing partnership. Mazzy Star are steadfast in their introverted dreamscapes, each song being an exquisite small world of gently sliding guitar notes as perfectly expressed on their most well-known song.

"I don't often hear how people interpret our music," said Roback. "But it wouldn't really surprise me if people interpreted it in a very personal way, because I think that that's the way that people react to music. If you took a well-known song and asked ten people to write down what the lyrics are, you'd find surprisingly different interpretations of what the lyrics are because people hear what's in their own imagination."

All Apologies Nirvana

(Kurt Cobain) ✳ DGC ✳ 1993 ✳ Appears on: *In Utero*

The last song on the last studio album from Kurt Cobain is a song of regret and "apology". As usual he seems lost in a fog of other people's expectations and his own low self-esteem.

He was sorry to his fans that he had abandoned them by being successful, he was sorry to his family, but mostly he was sorry for himself.

In Utero was the follow-up to *Nevermind*. Naturally Nirvana rejected the pop sound of that breakthrough album and went for the most hardcore producer they could find – the notoriously hardline Steve Albini.

"The main reason we recorded the new album *In Utero* with Steve Albini is he is able to get a sound that sounds like the band is in a room no bigger than the one we're in now," said Cobain. "*In Utero* doesn't sound like it was recorded in a hall, or that it's trying to sound larger than life. It's very in-your-face and real."

Like most of Cobain's lyrics, 'All Apologies' is based around a number of images that are strung together with a solid emotional through line in the melody. "For the most part, I write songs from pieces of poetry thrown together," he told Jon Savage. "When I write poetry it's not usually thematic at all. I have plenty of notebooks, and when it comes to a time to write lyrics, I just steal from my poems. Sometimes, I finish the lyrics months before we go into the studio, but for the most part, ninety per cent of them are done at the last minute."

'All Apologies' is right up close and perfectly in the minute.

Heart Shaped Box Nirvana

(Kurt Cobain) ✳ DGC ✳ 1993 ✳ Appears on: *In Utero*

Courtney Love gave her husband a heart-shaped box. Then followed a tempestuous romance of drugs and fame and power and children all conducted under the perpetual gaze of the tabloid media.

Cobain was a star and Courtney wanted to be. There's no doubt that he loved her and that she gave him something he needed. But it's also clear that he regarded the volatile relationship as a co-dependency. After police were called to his house following a particularly loud argument, Cobain was accused of choking his wife, something both parties denied.

"Sure. Courtney and I fight. We argue a lot," he told Jon Savage. "But I've never choked my wife. It's an awful fucking thing to be printed, to be thought of you. You know, we haven't had any problems, any bad reports, any negative articles written about us in a long time. We thought we were finally over it – that our curse had worn itself out". When Savage suggested that "people have perceived you as a threat," Cobain replied, "I think Courtney is more of a threat than I am".

As usual, Cobain hedges his bets. Perhaps he never really knew himself. The arrival of his daughter Frances Bean complicated matters further. There's a feeling of entrapment in 'Heart Shaped Box'. Kurt Cobain was indeed trapped at the time by his addiction, his fame, his desire for fame and his marriage. It's surprising that he made such a pretty song out of it all.

Disarm The Smashing Pumpkins

(Billy Corgan) ❋ Virgin ❋ 1993 ❋ Appears on: *Siamese Dream*

Chicago's Smashing Pumpkins released a single on Seattle's Sub Pop label and issued their first album, *Gish*, on the same day as Nirvana's *Nevermind*. Consequently they were lumped in with the grunge sound of the early '90s, despite the fact that musically they were worlds apart. If *Gish* was raw, though, the second album, *Siamese Dream*, demonstrated that head Pumpkin Billy Corgan had a unique sense of arrangement and a revolutionary vision for rock & roll songs.

"The whole idea behind the band is not at all to go backwards," said Corgan. "It's all about going forwards. But there are intangible elements to rock & roll that you cannot get around. Loudness. Powerful grooves. And you look at any music – an industrial band uses a drum machine, but they're doing the exact same things. They still have loudness and they're still playing with heavy rhythms.

"Here's the thing: if you grew up in America, whether you like it or not you heard Aerosmith, you heard Black Sabbath, you heard Led Zeppelin. It's just part of the culture. Even our manager had a hard time understanding why we played loud, hard music. Because he just didn't understand it. He said, 'You play such beautiful music, why are you playing this ugly rock music?' But it's part of what we are."

'Disarm' from *Siamese Dream* has the heavy atmosphere of a Black Sabbath song but presented with an angular guitar figure and Corgan's pleading vocal. Even though the song was lighter than much of their rock fare it was equally disturbing.

Berlin Chair You Am I

(Tim Rogers) ❋ RooART ❋ 1993 ❋ Appears on: *Sound As Ever*

The Berlin Chair is a sculpture in Canberra that singer/songwriter Tim Rogers thought symbolised his relationship with his girlfriend Tracey Forrester. She provided the strength Rogers needed to stay upright. As he told Craig Mathieson in *Juice* magazine, "I was feeling that at the time with Trace that I had a typical male ego that couldn't be honest or express the way I felt. It's like, 'I should support you, but I'm not going to be that supporting. I'm this cold but frail thing.'"

Rogers' lyric wears his heart and his insecurities strongly on his sleeve. It's hard not to be charmed by the song, however. You Am I make the most of it with their explosive mod sound. Recorded in America with Sonic Youth's Lee Ranaldo producing, the group sidestepped being caught up in grunge whilst having sufficient attitude and taste to stay current with the early '90s hit parade. The track just bursts out of the radio. The song was their biggest hit as a single and propelled the album to number one on release.

"But y'know, making records and travelling is the greatest thing," said Rogers. "We had some big laughs, discovered Maker's Mark Bourbon, cheap Milwaukee beer, and I got to say I never, never thought 'Berlin Chair' was ever going to be a single!"

Bonde Ali Farka Toure with Ry Cooder

(Ali Farka Toure) ❄ Hannibal ❄ 1994 ❄ Appears on: *Talking Timbuktu*

Most of Mali is the Sahara Desert. Timbuktu was a once great trading city and is now a shadow of its former self. Mali is one of the poorest countries in Western Africa and blighted by poverty and AIDS. The music of Mali is rich with French, Arab, Moorish and African influences. Into this mix comes the particular talent of Ali Farka Toure.

He began playing the guitar in 1956 at age seven and developed a style of his own that sounds, to western ears, not too far removed from the rural blues of Lightnin' Hopkins and John Lee Hooker. Essentially his tunes set up a drone and a groove that he embellishes on the guitar or with other instruments.

American guitarist Ry Cooder made the trip to Timbuktu with bassist John Patitucci, drummer Jim Keltner and blues guitarist Gatemouth Brown to play with Toure, who brought along his cousin Hamma Sankare on calabash and his brother Oumar Toure on congas. Over the course of the album *Talking Timbuktu*, Toure sings in a number of languages (none of them English) with a warm, expressive style and lets the groove do the talking. Absolutely sublime music that transcends time and space and nationality.

Loser Beck

(Beck/Karl Stephenson) ❄ Bongload ❄ 1994 ❄ Appears on: *Mellow Gold*

The other slacker anthem, 'Loser' was more humorous than Nirvana's 'Smells like Teen Spirit'. Beck Hansen had twenty-something world-weariness, a disdain for slickness, a homemade, lo-fi sound and the general fuck-you attitude – but it was also kind of funny. It was an instant anthem for Generation X. There was a hip-hop groove and bashed-up acoustic guitar line and the whole thing sounded like it had come out of a trash can and been dusted off.

"The first time I heard it on KCRW, they said it was a slacker anthem, but it was a completely silly song, just a takeoff on rap," said Beck. "It was very braggadocios [sic], like you hear in rap songs, but it was so not the mack. It was the opposite of mack.

"It's pretty jarring to be thrown in the air in plain view and be scrutinized and sized up and chopped up and sewn back together. You just have to have a sense of humour about it. You know, somebody saying you're great. Somebody saying you should be exterminated. I saw a lot of negative stuff out there."

Beck and his friend Karl Stephenson recorded 'Loser' in January 1992 on a home eight-track recorder. The following year it came out on the indie label Bongload and came to the attention of Geffen records. Beck was signed and the single was released followed by the cathartic *Mellow Gold* album, which had a similarly psychedelic hillbilly sound.

"It's a tribute in a way to those Greatest Hits packaged records of the '70s, the 'freedom rock' records," said Beck of his sound. "The easy-goin' rockin' order-it-over-the-mail C.O.D. for $19.95, or $6.66 C.O.D. – 'Care of the Devil'. It's sort of taking those songs, peeling the surface off and checking out the mixture of sausage and fibreglass."

'Loser' made Beck a star overnight. "I was the überslacker, which was always kind of ridiculous to me. I don't even know what slacker means," he said. "I wore clothes from thrift stores because I was poor."

That made his next step harder than the first. "Truly cool people aren't afraid of making an ass of themselves, not at the expense of others at least," Beck told *Dazed and Confused*. "The same thing applies with irony. It's a good device, a humorous device, and in such a straight, unimaginative time it's sometimes the only way to get some oxygen, y'know, but it can be over-indulged. It can be another mask, it's very easy to latch onto that, it's much harder to break through the stifling normalcy that's around. But y'know, there's a real American spirit still alive, where people really communicate, that's a real old school thing. But a lot of the time all people can do is look at a screen …

"The nihilism of the whole grunge thing in America was just a purge. A purging of the materialism and elitism that was the '80s. But ultimately there's a place to go after that. Trouble is, people have got stuck in that. A lot of people are still there, y'know? It's very easy for people to uprise and rebel against something, but it's harder once you've done that to come up with something better. To get a functioning state of things back …"

Girls & Boys Blur

(Damon Albarn/Graham Coxon/Alex James/Dave Rowntree) ✳ Food ✳ 1994 ✳
Appears on: *Parklife*

Singer Damon Albarn was inspired to write Blur's real breakthrough single while on holiday in the Mediterranean. "It's about those sorts of holidays," he told the *NME*. "I went on holiday with Justine last summer to Magaluf and the place was just equally divided between cafés serving up full English breakfasts and really tacky Essex nightclubs. There's a very strong sexuality about it. I just love the whole idea of it, to be honest. I love herds. All these blokes and all these girls meeting at the watering hole and then just … copulating. There's no morality involved, I'm not saying it should or shouldn't happen. My mind's just getting more dirty. I can't help it.

"The Pet Shop Boys have agreed to do a mix of it for us, and that should be brilliant. What I'm hoping for is that they can come up with a version that becomes the big summer hit in all those nightclubs in Spain and Majorca. That's exactly what we want. I'd love those people to be into Blur …"

The *Parklife* album from which 'Girls & Boys' came has a very Kinks-y view of modern Britain where after Margaret Thatcher's innovations brought middle-class prosperity to middle Britain so much of the national character became simply consumerist and bland.

'Girls & Boys' is cheeky and trashy and vaguely sexual in the way that David Bowie once was. It also has a Benny Hill/seaside postcard feel to the jaunty chorus: "Looking for girls who are boys/Who like boys to be girls/Who do boys like they're girls/Who do girls like they're boys/Always should be someone you really love".

"For me the album is like a loosely linked concept involving all these different stories. It's the travels of the mystical lager-eater, seeing what's going on in the world and commenting on it," said Albarn. "Everyone goes on about the idea of the sensitive artist, but for me that's all bollocks. I can't stand the idea of being a sad, lonely bedsit poet. I'd much rather be perceived as loud and arrogant, because all our sensitivity's in our records."

Doll Parts Hole

(Hole) ✳ DGC ✳ 1994 ✳ Appears on: *Live Through This*

"I wrote this in Boston," Courtney Love told the TV show *Rage*. "I wrote this song in Joyce Linehan's apartment. I was really impressed. She was a lower level music executive and she had lots of matching Body Shop shampoo and I'd never seen that before. And I thought one day I'll have enough money and all my cosmetics are gonna match. I also thought that the guy I was going out with – who I later married ... and that wasn't the transvestite in Las Vegas the other time ... I thought that he didn't like me and that he liked this total poser idiot girl, so I wrote this song about him and it's called 'Doll Parts'."

Courtney Love will be forever bound to the memory of her husband Kurt Cobain. Their love affair was as epic as his short life was tragic. He was the singer and songwriter of the disaffected youth of the '90s. Courtney Love tried on his role and made herself a feminist warrior. However, where Cobain had a natural gift for rock & roll, Love had merely the determination to be a rock & roll star. To watch her struggle with her career as a musician was to see a struggle of pure will. Then, of course, Cobain committed suicide on the eve of the Hole's album release, leaving a note wishing Love all the best with album sales. (The saddest part of Cobain's saga is his obsession with the mythology of rock.)

'Doll Parts' could be Courtney's anthem, but then it is a song that perfectly expresses the fears that are common to so many women. Love turns those fears into a revenge story: "I want to be the girl with the most cake/I love him so much it just turns to hate/I fake it so real, I am beyond fake/And someday, you will ache like I ache." It's a powerful lyric, perhaps more so as she did get the most cake.

The backing by Hole is the group at its pop best, with textured production from Paul Kolderie that smooths Hole's rough edges without losing their raw power.

Last Goodbye Jeff Buckley

(Jeff Buckley) ✳ Columbia ✳ 1994 ✳ Appears on: *Grace*

Ethereal, intangible, otherworldly – these are the kinds of words brought to mind by Jeff Buckley's short career. Buckley seemed fragile – abandoned by his rock star father, he was a songwriter with a tremulous voice, a beautiful face and a clear picture of the dark side of life.

Buckley was also out of sync with the times. His songs didn't fit with alternative rock, which was the prevailing style of 1994. Buckley's music was literate – understanding jazz and blues and ethnic styles as well as rock.

'Last Goodbye' was as close to a conventional pop song as Buckley would write. In it he absorbs influences from Pakistan to Memphis and turns them into something resembling rock music.

The sessions for *Grace* where 'Last Goodbye' was cut took place at Bearsville, outside New York, with producer Andy Wallace, who had mixed Nirvana's *Nevermind* and was therefore hot.

Buckley had made a name for himself as a singer/songwriter playing small clubs in New York and it was expected that the debut album would reflect that. However, over the five weeks spent at Bearsville, the chemistry in the group – guitarist Michael Tighe, bass player Mike Grondahl and drummer Matt Johnson – brought these songs to new and better lives.

"'Last Goodbye' means a lot to me because at the time that I wrote it, a long time ago, I was around an environment that thought that [my songs] were completely loser songs," Buckley told me in 1996. "I put them on the album to prove at least to the songs that they weren't losers. They were worth recording. Sort of like finding kids that have been told all their lives that they're pieces of shit, and finally you have to go around proving to them, by putting them in a completely other setting, that no, they are worth knowing and loving."

'Last Goodbye' covers that sense of loss that stalks so much of Buckley's work. So many of his inspirations – Edith Piaf, Miles Davis, Judy Garland and Nina Simone – were artists who had trouble living. Buckley's music is haunted by them. The muscular guitar and bass riffs that drive this song play off against the raga-like second guitar and the spectral atmosphere of the tune.

"Some people are just born into bodies, born into lifespans that just don't fit anywhere else and they have very little to hang onto to validate and also it's a very lonely thing to notice a certain sense of life and be able to relate that to anyone," he told me. "It's probably the onset of madness, or it must seem so to the person who sees the world in a certain way. Maybe they see spirits everywhere or maybe they divine information from certain happenings and certain peoples that are invisible to most of us, and as a result people deem those experiences not valid and not important, and crazy too, and that can damage a person ... There's a lot of strength to the self-destructive soul."

Sleeps with Angels Neil Young & Crazy Horse

(Neil Young) ✳ Reprise ✳ 1994 ✳ Appears on: *Sleeps with Angels*

Many people were shocked by the 1994 suicide of Nirvana singer Kurt Cobain, but only Neil Young was quoted in his suicide note. Although they had never met, there was a mutual admiration. "I really could hear his music," said Young. "There's not that many absolutely real performers. In that sense, he was a gem. He was bothered by the fact that he would end up following schedules, have to go on when he didn't feel like it, and be faking, and that would be very hard for him because of his commitment."

The *Sleeps with Angels* LP was hastily assembled following Cobain's death. Young corralled Crazy Horse up at his ranch and together they made the best album they'd done since *On the Beach* twenty years earlier. On the title track Young marshals the awesome power of Crazy Horse in full cry and then subsumes it in murky production, buries it in a fog of sound so that it's full of ethereal menace.

Although the album is one of Young's masterpieces, he refused to promote the record or discuss it, in deference to Cobain's memory.

As he said to Nick Kent in *MOJO*: "*Sleeps with Angels* has a lot of overtones to it, from different situations that were described in it. A lot of sad scenes. I've never really spoken about why I made that album. I don't want to start now."

He doesn't have to; the title track says it all.

Live Forever Oasis

(Noel Gallagher) ❋ Creation ❋ 1994 ❋ Appears on: *Definitely Maybe*

Oasis charged out of Manchester full of attitude. They harked back to the glory days of the empire when the Englishness of the Faces and the Kinks was forgiven because they represented the true spirit of the English. Oasis were the prophets of Cool Britannia – proud to be English and not terribly educated. The Gallagher brothers were naturals – they loved being in the tabloids, Noel could write a classic song just like ringing a bell and Liam could sing with wounded passion. 'Live Forever' was their anthem, a manifesto of the promise of good times.

"If you're on the dole and writing songs, you're not going to write about how crap your life is, 'cause you already live that life. You want to write about how great life could be if you were a rock & roll star," said Noel. "Damon Albarn [Blur] and Brett Anderson [Suede] write songs about going to the dogs and being pantomime horses, which is all very well but it doesn't mean fuck-all to me, it means nothing to 99% of the population, it's too self-centred, too me-me-me. It's why those bands never make it in America, 'cause it's just not universal enough.

"I'm not mithered about this or that, or being a sex symbol or the voice of a generation. All I'm arse about is getting down alongside Ray Davies,

Morrissey and Marr, Jagger and Richards, Lennon and McCartney, Pete Townshend, Paul Weller and Burt Bacharach."

Cut Your Hair Pavement

(Stephen Malkmus) ❋ Matador ❋ 1994 ❋ Appears on: *Crooked Rain Crooked Rain*

No genre in popular music had been so self-aware as indie rock. A side effect of mass media and post-modernism in the early '90s was the notion that each and every one owed their personality to marketing departments. The grunge revolution was not only televised but it was in re-runs and on talk shows rather than MTV. Pavement, the brainchild of Stephen Malkmus, fitted perfectly into the lo-fi movement – he cited influences as Black Sabbath and Rush – while having ambivalence to it.

The second Pavement album, *Crooked Rain Crooked Rain*, was their first masterpiece – flawless slacker rock music and witty, pertinent lyrics. Malkmus proved to be a gifted songwriter; playful and acute. 'Cut Your Hair' was an ode to grunge rock – the importance of style and appearance, the flood of groups who were largely interchangeable but all right-on:

Bands start up each and every day
I saw another one just the other day/A special new band
I remember lying/I don't remember a line
I don't remember a word/But I don't care, I care, I really don't care
Did you see the drummer's hair?

Malkmus was sufficiently confident of Pavement's abilities to satirise the scene. But what do you expect from Generation X?

Glory Box Portishead

(Geoff Barrow/Henry Brooks/Beth Gibbons/Lalo Schifrin/Otis Turner/Adrian Utley) ❋ Go! Discs ❋ 1994 ❋ Appears on: *Dummy*

Seeping out of Bristol in the early '90s, Portishead turned trip hop into something. Geoff Barrow, a hip-hop producer, met singer Beth Gibbons at the dole office and began collaborating. The album *Dummy* was dark, mysterious, cinematic and enigmatic. The elegantly doomed break-beats were strangely popular, giving Portishead an instant mainstream audience.

Completed with guitarist Adrian Utley, *Dummy* was also a mixture of tenderness and dissonance, of torch songs and break-beats. There are starkly beautiful lines from the guitar and elegant moods from Barrow over gently pulsing beats, and then the deflowered, painfully dignified voice of Gibbons, which occasionally lets forth with rage. The overriding mood is dark and contemplative. "I can't stand the light stuff," said Barrow. "I'm not into it. All the hip-hop I liked was very, very dark hip-hop. And when I was sampling, I was always looking for something that had a strange emotional content to it, something that sparks some kind of emotion or theme or atmosphere. That's always my problem when we're working. I always think it's not enough. It's not dark enough. It's not emotionally hooked enough. But if I can get some emotion musically before Beth begins to write and sing over the tracks then there's something for her to hook into. A thread she can follow. We're looking for something that is quite emotionally powerful. And I don't want to take anyone down when they listen to our music, but I just don't think there's an awful lot of music out there that does it to people. And people can handle emotion."

Waterfalls TLC

(Marqueze Etheridge/Lisa 'Left Eye' Lopes/Organized Noize) ❄ La Face ❄ 1994 ❄ Appears on: *Crazy Sexy Cool*

In their short and volatile career, TLC made some of the best R&B of the '90s. Starting out pretty rough with raps and attitude, by the time they made *Crazy Sexy Cool* they had incorporated Prince's erotic moves, LA Reid and Babyface's no-nonsense new jack production, and their own street smarts. They made the tabloids with fights with lovers and hard partying. In the meantime they sold a lot of records.

"What I really loved about TLC when I first met them was that they had a definite opinion of what kind of group they wanted to be," said LA Reid. "TLC won't sing songs that don't represent their points of view – I don't care who wrote it or how big a hit it could be."

The group started as part of Organized Noize in Atlanta where the hip-hop scene thrived around writer/producers such as Dallas Austin (Boyz II Men) and Rico Wade, who co-wrote 'Waterfalls'.

Lisa 'Left Eye' Lopes tended to supply the attitude while Tionne Watkins and Rozonda Thomas brought the vocals, which were both sexy and inviting while also being strong and conscious. TLC might go out with you but they weren't going to leave the attitude behind. TLC were emancipated women and modern women responded.

'Waterfalls' was TLC at their most Princely and seductive.

"See, we came pretty much as is," said Watkins. "We knew how we were going to sing, dress and everything. All you had to do was the paperwork."

You Oughta Know Alanis Morissette

(Glen Ballard/Alanis Morissette) ✳ Maverick ✳ 1995 ✳ Appears on: *Jagged Little Pill*

Alanis Morissette was like a fantasy – the teen singer disappears and then comes back looking beautiful and talking dirty. The Canadian teen queen emancipated herself by moving to Los Angeles at age nineteen, found a producer in Glen Ballard and then let it all out on the album *Jagged Little Pill*. Then there was the single 'You Oughta Know' with its hook lines, "Are you thinking of me when you fuck her?" and "Would she go down on you in a theatre?"

"'You Oughta Know' was written from a desperate, dark almost pathetically sad place within my subconscious," she said.

Alanis was a person in the right place at the right time with the right record. The anger that filled the airwaves with grunge was mostly male. Morissette tapped into a female energy with its own issues. It was a time when candour was the coin of the realm.

"This record came from a place in me I had to release," she told Mat Snow at the time. "A lot of the anger comes from the fact that I didn't face it, out of fear, the whole Pollyanna approach I had when I was younger. I denied myself any revelling in my darker side. But as soon as I started writing, I came to terms with it."

Ballard was a professional songwriter/producer, mostly for middle-of-the-road acts, when he met Morissette in 1994. Rather than turn her pop, Ballard encouraged her instincts and helped to arrange them on record. No matter where they went.

"A few lines in 'You Oughta Know' had me thinking, 'God, this is exactly how I feel, but I don't want to hurt anybody.' For years I had been a little guarded, but that was horribly unfulfilling," the singer recalled. "Glen said to me, 'Just remember how bad you felt when you did censor yourself. You have to do this.'

"So, 'Are you thinking of me when you fuck her?' was one hundred per cent honest. For me to take that back would be telling a half-truth and I didn't want to do that ever again. It took me about a day to get over it, to let go of the fear of how it was going to be responded to."

Better Get a Lawyer The Cruel Sea

(James Cruickshank/Jim Elliott/Ken Gormly/Stephen Perkins/Danny Rumour/Wayne) ❋ Red Eye ❋ 1995 ❋ Appears on: *Three Legged Dog*

It was the combination of soulful and sinful that crossed the Cruel Sea from the alternative market to the mainstream. For this album they chose to heap on the voodoo. *Three Legged Dog* reversed the platinum formula of past releases, which is just as well. The Cruel Sea was in danger of becoming muzak for the politically correct.

The Cruel Sea swings. Jim Elliott is a drummer of exceptional versatility. With the bass of Ken Gormly to anchor the rhythms and provide nicely sprung melodies, the Cruel Sea packs a funk. The guitars of James Cruickshank and Danny Rumour are very erudite. They continue on this album to play with different forms of roots music, from the Caribbean to the African coast. Unlike previous albums, however, they are drawing more on blues and R&B.

The combo started as an instrumental outfit augmented by occasional vocals by Tex Perkins who was, it appeared, on loan from the Beasts of Bourbon. If the Cruel Sea was ironic and wistful, the Beasts was a roaring, blues-wailing monster and it was common for pundits to wonder whether Perkins could reconcile these two sides of his muse. Perkins' worldview is generally confrontational. Tales like 'Better Get a Lawyer', 'Too Fast for Me' or 'Brain Wash' are told from a point of view of action first, regrets later. His romances are part passion and mostly confusion. They are rarely happy affairs, sometimes comic and often just hard. The quizzical funk of most of this album gives an appropriate ambiguity to Tex's tall stories.

Where the previous Cruel Sea albums have covered psychedelic surf music and afro-reggae pub rock, this album sticks close to the "down home". 'This Is What It Is' features an organ riff that could have come straight off Booker T. That's about all that's straight. If there are influences or echoes in these tracks there is more than a touch of Captain Beefheart, some bone-crackling riffs that recall the team of Taylor and Richards keeping the riffs dirty and the slide guitar slippery. But these are just like spectres in the crypt. Ultimately, and as on their previous turf, the Cruel Sea has created a roiling storm all their own. This record shines like vinyl: black and sexy.

(What's the Story) Morning Glory? Oasis

(Noel Gallagher) ✳ Epic ✳ 1995 ✳ Appears on: *(What's The Story) Morning Glory?*

The title track of Oasis' second album is a state-of-the-nation message. Oasis came flying out of the New Britain. Specifically the New North. For decades poverty and indifference of the south had cowed the industrial north of England. Northern culture had just gotten stronger, especially in music and football. As Britain crawled its way back to the first world there was resurgence in national pride and a confident pop culture. Oasis' big guitar sound announced that attitude.

'(What's the Story) Morning Glory?' is a masterpiece of production. It opens with the sound of choppers as if we're back in *Apocalypse Now!* The adrenaline is pumped further by the guitar squalls and then Noel Gallagher crashes in with a massive wall of guitar noise (and later, with a chorus riff that sounds almost identical to the one in R.E.M.'s 'The One I Love'). Then Liam Gallagher chimes in with his song about modern life and being chained to the razor and the spoon.

"I put drug references in Oasis' songs because I take them and I write about what I know," said Noel Gallagher. "Me and my mates have been doing drugs since we were fourteen and, personally, I can't help it.

"The number of times I've sat round this flat off my tits and sorted out what's wrong with everything in the world and the next morning I can't remember a thing. It gets so that you can only operate when you're out of it – while you're chained to the drugs, sure, your life is a bowl of cherries. But it's exactly that, you're chained to it. And I do know a lot of people will take that lyric in 'Morning Glory' straight, which is a shame."

'Morning Glory' is, however, one of the best pieces of rock & roll music recorded in the '90s. If you want to know what it was like to be up for it in 1996, this is it.

Wonderwall Oasis

(Noel Gallagher) ✳ Epic ✳ 1995 ✳ Appears on: *(What's the Story) Morning Glory?*

Noel Gallagher, not known for wearing his heart on his sleeve, wrote this song for his then girlfriend Meg Matthews. There are the obvious Beatle references – *Wonderwall* was a film for which George Harrison wrote the music. Mostly though, Gallagher nailed the chord progression and crafted a ballad that had instant classic written all over it. Just as it seemed rock & roll had used up its vocabulary, Oasis came up with the song.

Gallagher felt sufficiently strongly about the melody to want to sing it himself, but brother Liam insisted on taking the lead vocal.

"But I don't need no pat on the back," said Liam. "I know how good I am and how shit everyone else is, I just get in there and do it. Noel writes his words down, does me a guide vocal. I have a read, have a little sing in my head and that's it, I'm done. I had a bad throat halfway through recording the album, and when it came time to do 'Wonderwall' our kid was wanting to do the vocal, saying, 'You can't even speak.' But I did it, and it worked straight off. Big time. It didn't matter to me that Noel had written that song as a personal love song about his girlfriend Meg. It doesn't matter if it's about President Clinton or whatever, because if a song needs to be sung about that kind of feeling then I'm the man to do it.

"When I sing a song like 'Wonderwall', I'm not thinking about one person. Not ever. I just think about love in general. Love's just mood isn't it? It's a solid, positive thing, it's about everything."

Common People Pulp

(Nick Banks/Jarvis Cocker/Patrick Doyle/Steve Mackey/Russell Senior) ✳ Island ✳ 1995 ✳ Appears on: *Different Class*

At the height of Brit pop in the mid-'90s when Oasis were tipped to take over the world and Blur were to redefine Englishness for the new millennium, Pulp came out with a classic British pop tune that was a state of the nation. Essentially, as singer/lyricist Jarvis Cocker observes on this track, Britain is now and ever will be a land of small people living small lives.

The pop rock band Pulp came out of the impoverished and provincial city Sheffield in the early '90s. Early on it became clear that Cocker had all the makings of Ray Davies when it came to observing his fellow English. This was not a band given to grand statements but rather to acute, witty sketches accompanied by delightful, naïve tunes.

'Common People' is ostensibly about young rich girls wanting to slum it with proletarian chic. Jarvis certainly makes fun of both sides of that bargain, but there is a dark and angry strain of class contempt in his lyric, the acknowledgment that art students can slum it with the working class but they always have an escape. This was not a popular view in the gung-ho new Britain.

"'Common People' was written in about June of '94 and the first time we played it, it became clear to me it was a significant song," Cocker told *Q* in

1996. "It seemed to be in the air, that kind of patronising social voyeurism, slumming it, the idea that there's a glamour about low-rent, low-life. I felt that of [Blur's album] *Parklife*, for example, or [Oliver Stone's film] *Natural Born Killers* – there is that noble savage notion. But if you walk round a council estate, there's plenty of savagery and not much nobility going on. In Sheffield, if you say someone's common, then you're saying they're vulgar, coarse, rough-arsed. The kind of person who has corned-beef legs from being too close to the gas fire. So that's what attracted me to calling it 'Common People', the double meaning, 'Oh, you're common as muck' and then Emerson, Lake & Palmer's 'Fanfare for the Common Man'."

Fake Plastic Trees Radiohead

(Colin Greenwood/Jonny Greenwood/Ed O'Brien/Phil Selway/Thom Yorke) ❊
Capitol ❊ 1995 ❊ Appears on: *The Bends*

Radiohead supremo Thom Yorke has said that 'Fake Plastic Trees' was the first song of which he was not embarrassed. The first single, 'Creep', from their debut album was a kind of grunge novelty hit which nonetheless shot Radiohead to success, selling a million copies of the LP *Pablo Honey*. A second album, *The Bends*, appeared to be titled in response to their new circumstances. The bends is a life-threatening condition suffered by divers who surface too quickly.

Radiohead are generally miserabilists and 'Fake Plastic Trees' appears to be a whinge about the superficiality of the modern world. The lyrics are possibly the least interesting aspect of the song. "When we did demos, words would be made up on the spot," said Yorke. "You throw it away or it sticks because it sounds amazing and you find the significance in it when you read it afterwards."

The real guts of it are in the atmosphere created by the band, and Jonny Greenwood's guitars and electronics in particular. This dense wall of musical texture is an environment that well suits Yorke's voice. There's a general malaise in the air but a beautiful one – a technicolour melancholy that is so rich the group became popular despite itself. This is not a pop song but it has the majesty of the best pop.

"I'm not sure what we all thought would happen when we started doing this," said Yorke. "But definitely not what actually happened. It's been a very strange experience."

Crush With Eyeliner R.E.M.

(Michael Stipe/Bill Berry/Mike Mills/Peter Buck) ❊ Warner Bros. ❊ 1995 ❊
Appears on: *Monster*

After hitting the mainstream charts in a big way with cheesy pop tunes and then the lush ballads 'Drive' and 'Everybody Hurts', R.E.M. wanted to make a tough rock & roll record that they could take on tour. The sessions for the album became overshadowed by Kurt Cobain's suicide and his wife Courtney Love's public meltdown. Stipe was a close friend of both the Cobains and so every track on this album appeared to have something to do with the doomed couple.

Is 'Crush With Eyeliner' about Courtney Love? Who knows? It is a great rock & roll song though.

According to Stipe, "'Crush With Eyeliner' is completely, to me, a paean to the New York Dolls, with reference to 'Frankenstein', which of course is one of their songs, and a lot of this album is referring back to Iggy and the Stooges and Patti Smith and Television, and stuff like that. I went back and listened to *Marquee Moon* while we were making this record, and to this day I have no idea what those songs are about, but I can sing each one from beginning to end. There are unbelievable analogies and images: 'The Cadillac pulled out of the graveyard' and 'Dressing up like cops'. So cool, all that stuff."

The song came out of a distorted tremolo guitar riff from Peter Buck. "They knew it had to sound sonically very different," producer Scott Litt told writer Michael Goldberg. "The pulsing guitars and pulsing bass would usually start with that effect. They'd find a tremolo effect box and plug it in and say, 'Wow, this is a neat sound.' They'd build stuff from that. And that really goes with Michael's philosophy of having a little bit of a sound-scape from which to work, and some space. And tremolo pulses give you that space."

The glam-meets-grunge sense of the song was aided by the guest appearance by Sonic Youth's Thurston Moore.

"Michael had always heard Thurston doing that part, 'I'm the real thing', in the way that only Thurston can do it. Michael wanted to work with those guys. He really admires them. Thurston is a friend. He was out in LA for maybe some MTV thing and came by and did that part in like twenty minutes. Just came to the studio and sang it."

The beauty of 'Crush With Eyeliner' is the glam rock groove over the grunge sounds – the distorted guitar and the loping bass and Stipe's lyrics. Mostly, after all those serious ballads, it sounds like R.E.M. being a rock & roll band. As Litt said, "They wanted to turn up and play loud and add some guitars. So there was a concept there."

Bullet with Butterfly Wings The Smashing Pumpkins

(Billy Corgan) ❋ Virgin ❋ 1995 ❋ Appears on: *Mellon Collie and the Infinite Sadness*

The most ambitious record of the alternative rock era, at least in scope, *Mellon Collie and the Infinite Sadness* placed Billy Corgan's intimate pain on a large stage, inviting influences from progressive rockers such as Queen and early Elton John.

'Bullet with Butterfly Wings' is vicious in its majestic attack. It's a song where Corgan opens up and the pain just screams out. Corgan is lashing out at the world at large and internally at himself. This is a song about a struggle to overcome self-hatred. Corgan, though, transcends himself with the track and makes one of the most complex pieces of music of the era.

"You're talking about a bunch of people who can't understand why they feel so empty and jaded and apathetic," said Corgan shortly before the release of the *Mellon Collie* album. "I mean, people who feel hateful. People used to take their hate out on black people and minorities. In some parts of Europe, they're starting to do that again. But in America, I don't feel that our generation feels those feelings. They're not taking them out on anybody. They're taking it out on themselves. They don't even know why they feel this hatred, why they feel such apathy. I don't know if this will make any sense to you, but to play a concert and to stand before your generation and the one that's about to follow us, ages fourteen through twenty-eight, and just see how jaded people are. A good song, a smiling face, a true feeling, doesn't do it. People want to see things smashed to bits. They want to see you rip your heart out. Then you start to wonder, you start to question what is this. It's not a feeling. It's a lack of it.

"And I do really identify with that. It's built into our psyche to feel this. Even if you didn't come from a broken home, you grew up around people who did. Call it what you will, Generation X or whatever. We're it."

Corgan was abandoned by his mother and then shortly afterwards by his father and left to be raised by his stepmother. The emotional scarring was deep and informed everything that Corgan did as a composer. He chose to channel the anger into the music.

"The classic story is that after eighteen months on the road behind *Siamese Dream*, we came off [concert tour] Lollapalooza and three days later I started writing *Mellon Collie*," he said. "There is no break for me. I'm twenty-nine years old, and every year that goes by I lose some of that chip-on-the-shoulder energy of youth."

Born Slippy Underworld

(Darren Emerson/Karl Hyde/Rick Smith) ❋ Junior Boys Own ❋ 1995 ❋
Appears on: *Trainspotting*

The hook line "lager, lager, lager" ensured that Underworld's breakthrough techno hit would reach beyond clubland to the furthest regions of the suburbs and the heights of the football terraces. The song's appearance in Danny Boyle's film *Trainspotting* put it right over the edge – an overdose of drugs and adrenalin. The song is a relentless, intoxicating electronic track of keyboards and drum machine driven by a rhythmic vocal chant. *Trainspotting* was a key moment in the '90s; an underground film full of moral complexity and great music. It had a definite '90s atmosphere; the '80s were like ancient history, and Underworld had gone through that same transformation. They were an '80s pop rock band with one small hit ('Underneath the Radar'). Then singer Karl Hyde and his long-time collaborator Rick Smith enlisted DJ Darren Emerson and refashioned their sound.

'Born Slippy', which takes its name from a greyhound, was a song that Hyde wrote about his personal battle with alcoholism. "It was all about the horrors I'd experienced whilst being over-medicated on alcohol for a lot of years," he explained. "And I kind of thought if I just write out this autobiographical piece that's horrific, you know, people will go 'Oh, my God, Jesus, what's that about? That's horrible, what's that about?' And I'd be able to say 'That's about me, how's about a bit of help?' But we came out and explained it and then Danny did what he did with the film, and I think that the whole balance was redressed and it's fine if people want to use it as a drinking anthem, I really don't have any problem with that now."

Where It's At Beck

(Beck Hansen/John King/Michael Simpson) ❋ DGC ❋ 1996 ❋ Appears on: *Odelay*

Beck Hansen's mother was a former acolyte at Andy Warhol's Factory, his grandfather was an avant-garde artist and his father a bohemian musician. Beck grew up poor and white in black and Hispanic neighbourhoods. He was a true child of alternative culture. It's impossible to speculate on how his background – the nature and/or nurture of it – created his artistic vision, but we can say that Beck understood the fundamentals of folk art in the most profound ways and reinterpreted those folk arts in an entirely fascinating series of records. By the time he released the *Odelay* album he was light years ahead of the pack. That album's lead single, 'Where It's At', was indeed where it was at.

The first thing is the blues. Beck cites Woody Guthrie and Mississippi John Hurt as primary influences. "It was just a guitar, and I liked the sound of it," he said. "It was really simple, the antithesis of the '80s. Once I discovered this traditional folk music, country music, Delta blues, I had a whole world to get lost in."

Beck understood the connection between Mississippi John Hurt and hip-hop. He recognised the hip-hop groove that was implied in the Delta blues and having identified the groove, he made it explicit.

"The interchange between black and white music doesn't seem to have continued," he told *Dazed and Confused* back in 1996. "It has in hip-hop, and in the dance world, but as for alternative bands there doesn't seem much of an understanding left. I recognize that things are headed in a certain direction: I just hope to attempt to preserve some things that are lost, some of the old sensibilities. Like the way we looked at the world before machines ran our lives ...

"I walk a fine line because I don't want to surrender to the '90s, I just feel that a lot of the '90s is incredibly fad-based and already dated, even like this new U2 thing. I look at a lot of the alternative bands and it's already so played out, it's already been done over and over. The silver pants and that sexy-but-not-sexy attitude. That sort of phoney ambivalence. It's the whole attitude of angst and cynicism."

As an artist working in pop culture, Beck trawled through the recent pop past, the discards of yesterday's fashions, and he refashioned them into something new. The arrival of the sampler was a key tool. On *Odelay* he had the assistance of the Dust Brothers (John King and Michael Simpson), who had been so pivotal to the Beastie Boys' *Paul's Boutique*.

'Where It's At' was a homage to hip-hop constructed mostly out of acoustic moods and sounds. The refrain "two turntables and a microphone" recalled the punk simplicity of the seminal Bronx parties where hip-hop started in the '70s. The samples of found sounds were playful; the rock & roll flavours brought it together.

"I draw on the past because there's so many things there that were really great, that we undervalue and scoff at," he said. "We're so led by this idea of laughing at the past. We're driven by this consumer need to have the newest thing all the time, so we tend to dispose of what was good. But at the same time I'm against that one-dimensional nostalgia, just doing a retro thing. I think it negates the past, it just makes it one-dimensional. I try to be subtle."

Song 2 Blur

(Damon Albarn/Graham Coxon/Alex James/Dave Rowntree) ❋ Food/Virgin ❋ 1996 ❋
Appears on: *Blur*

Blur are a British band in the tradition of the Kinks and the Jam, which means that their best work passeth the understanding of Americans. With a view to crossing the great water, Blur's self-titled album embraced rock and grunge. Albarn told me at the time that the group's new sound was due to his friendship with Pavement's Steve Malkmus and that may be a part of the story. In any case, the coy humour was dropped for something louder and subtler.

"Our choice of singles has been spectacularly inept for the American market, really," said Albarn at the time. "With 'Song 2', we've released something that is at least tangible. Whether it'll do business, I don't know. But it's the first thing I think we've done since 'Boys and Girls' that is tangible. It feels right in America."

'Song 2' is a parody of Nirvana. The lyric mocks the self-loathing of Kurt Cobain while the music is a better produced and louder version of the soft/loud arrangements that Nirvana based their work on. In essence the big guitar riff is matched with Albarn's "Woo hoo!" shout as if he melded Homer Simpson and Kurt into one.

Albarn claimed that the whole album was a portrait of the band. "The songs are entirely about a band, about being in a band, about this band," he said to Erik Himmelsbach. "It's been really interesting to start thinking like that when I'm writing a song. I've always found songs to be magic things, and that by playing them they can somehow become guardians of your future in the sense that you can sing about things and make them come true.

"So once you start singing about yourself, it's a precarious thing. Because if you're honest about how you feel, you can sing really quite dark things, which are then a source of somehow obsessive stories of possibilities of your own demise."

'Song 2' was hardly their demise, even if it didn't break them in America. In fact it has become even more ubiquitous than 'Teen Spirit'. In the US the National Hockey League used the song. It is heard in ads for Paul Verohoven's *Starship Troopers* and has appeared on many soundtracks and, most memorably, as a car commercial around the world.

Setting Sun The Chemical Brothers

(Noel Gallagher/Tom Rowlands/Ed Simons) ❋ Heavenly ❋ 1996 ❋

Appears on: *Dig Your Own Hole*

The Chemical Brothers described their second album, *Dig Your Own Hole*, as "the best breaks they've ever broken. A bloody good soundtrack for people living today." The Chemical Brothers (Tom Rowlands and Ed Simons) were the most fashionable DJs in Britain and Noel Gallagher was the biggest rock star when they put rock and big beat together on this single. The Chemical Brothers had a spot at the ultra-hip Heavenly Social – a club night in London. The pair looked the part – like Chaucer-reading nerds with turntables. They were photogenic and visible and they toured, and thus they were important in making DJs a significant part of the music landscape as artists. On 'Setting Sun' Oasis' Noel Gallagher added his vocal and guitar to the mix of white noise paranoia and artillery-like break beats.

"We had this idea to do something like that for quite a while," said Rowlands, "the past couple of years or whatever. It was good that we managed to get Noel – he offered to do something with us back in '95 when we saw him at this festival. He was saying 'On the next album you should get me in'. That was kinda nice really, it was just cool that he was up for doing it and he liked the track. It was a painless procedure."

The Chemical Brothers were always eclectic both in their DJ sets and on record. From straight-ahead techno to rock party chemical beats to 'Setting Sun', to low looping weird tracks with Beth Orton singing on them. Where many techno/dance artists were regarded as faceless, the Chemical Brothers exuded personality.

"We've always based what we do on a wide appreciation of music, and we aren't frightened to show it," said Rowlands. "Dance music is made to play in clubs, even if it's nosebleed techno, it's still for a certain section of the population to enjoy this music … There's not a lot of intellectualising that has to go on if you dance a lot. Dance is the pivotal thing."

Building Steam with a Grain of Salt DJ Shadow

(Jeremy Storch/DJ Shadow) ❋ Mo' Wax ❋ 1996 ❋ Appears on: *Endtroducing …*

Josh Davis (aka DJ Shadow) elevated record collecting to an art form. His collage songs made entirely of samples from obscure and not-so-obscure vinyl stretched the boundaries of music in the '90s.

His first album, *Endtroducing ...*, is one of the seminal records of the century. The powerful 'Building Steam with a Grain of Salt' is built from a sample from a 1970 song by Jeremy Storch titled 'I Feel a New Shadow'.

"I called [the album] *Endtroducing* because to me it's an introduction," he said. "On the other hand, this is a sound I've been developing for four years, and I don't intend to be doing this next year or the year after. In a lot of ways it represents not just the nine months of work that it took to make it, but like what we are up to now. So the next album is going to be a lot different, 'cause I will be inspired by different things. And so the album is an end to that sound."

He told *Salon* magazine, "What I've noticed more and more is that what I do appeals mostly to people who are older and have been listening to hip-hop. All the people that I respect and that I credit for giving me my inspiration – because everything I do is based on something else – those people understand what I do and are not threatened by it."

Fu-gee-la The Fugees

(Lauryn Hill/Natalie Jean/Teena Marie/Allen McGrier/S Michel/Salaam Remi) ❋
Ruffhouse ❋ 1996 ❋ Appears on: *The Score*

Refugee Camp, which became the Fugees, brought a whole new style to hip-hop in the mid-'90s. Prakazrel Michel ('Pras') and his cousin Wyclef Jean ('Clef') were of Haitian descent, which may have added some exotica to an already diverse mix of sounds and styles – reggae, soul, R&B, rap and jazz all found their place on the Fugees' second album, *The Score*. And let's not forget Lauryn Hill, one of the great voices of her time.

The Score reinvented black American pop music. It featured a couple of interesting covers, including Roberta Flack's 'Killing Me Softly with His Song' and Bob Marley's 'No Woman, No Cry', which were reinterpreted with a hip-hop frame of mind. 'Fu-gee-la' was their statement of purpose, though. It was a song of strength and struggle but freed of the violent hype of so much revolutionary rap music. The reggae beats and the eloquent bass rumbles powered the song as the three MCs stood their ground.

With this manifesto the Fugees sold more than seventeen million albums of literate, intelligent and non-violent hip-hop.

Firestarter The Prodigy

(Kim Deal/Anne Dudley/Keith Flint/Trevor Horn/Liam Howlett/Johnathon J Jeczalik/
Gary Langan/Paul Morley) ❋ Mute ❋ 1996 ❋ Appears on: *The Fat of the Land*

Somewhere in the mid-'90s the next big thing was going to be called electronica. Rock was dead again, caught in its own morbidity following the grunge years. As interest in rock declined, thousands of young people were putting on raves – immense parties with large sound systems, often in the country. A platoon of DJs and a seamless fabric of repetitive beats to accompany ecstasy trips. Songs were no use. The beat was everything. The buzzards of music industry descended on rave culture and within a few years it was, of course, gone. Given the heat it generated, rave music produced few artists of any substance. One of the half-dozen was the Prodigy.

Liam Howlett is the brain behind the Prodigy. His singular gift is to use electronic music to express emotion – in his case a passionate misanthropy. Howlett had a chip on his shoulder and he made angry techno. He used hip-hop and rock sounds. It wasn't just about the beat any more. The rest of the Prodigy was dancer/vocalists Keith Flint, Leeroy Thornhill and Maxim Reality. The former's spiky hair and copious facial piercings made him look genuinely menacing.

The Fat of the Land was one of the high points of electronica (the Chemical Brothers had the other) and its signature tune was 'Firestarter', which featured Flint on vocals. The song had the relentless, mind-numbing techno beat, amped up a notch. With Flint's vocals it also moved further towards rock and it was nasty. The music track was built around the rocking Breeders' song 'SOS' and the Art of Noise's dark electronic mood, 'Moments in Love'.

Howlett told Ben Thompson in his book *Seven Years of Plenty*, "He [Flint] expresses himself onstage dancing, but I guess he felt like he'd done as much as he could do in that area, and he just needed something else to let himself go with. When he first said he wanted to have a go at doing some vocals, I didn't realise how serious he was, but then he came round to my house and we both sat down and wrote the lyrics. Basically, they're just a description of Keith: what happens with him onstage, the way he is – his headstrong personality. That record sums him up.

"We didn't go out to write a song you could play on the piano. The records I've always liked are the ones you can't sing along to."

Into My Arms Nick Cave & the Bad Seeds

(Nick Cave) ❋ Mute ❋ 1997 ❋ Appears on: *The Boatman's Call*

Perhaps it was encroaching middle age. Perhaps it was the end of his relationships with Vivien Carneiro and PJ Harvey. Perhaps it was just luck, but on *The Boatman's Call* Cave brings together his two great themes of love and God. The album opens with 'Into My Arms' – the only love song couched in a theological discussion about the nature of the Creator.

"This is my most personal album to date," he said at the time. "I kind of write what I'm given in a way, and I just felt at particular times, this year, very excited about writing about things that had happened to me, and that's simply the nature of doing what I do.

"I think that I've just been much more able to understand a lot of things that have gone on in my life whereas before I was more concerned with fictional writing, and it was far more exciting for me to write about other things that were outside of myself.

"To me this is the record I've always wanted to make. The record that took a reasonable amount of courage to actually do."

While writing this album Cave was completing his *Murder Ballads* album – a record of narratives about homicide. That siphoned off one strand of Cave's material and possibly as a result *The Boatman's Call* got an increase in the love songs.

Cave separated from Carneiro, the mother of his son and the longest nurturing relationship in his life thus far. He also had a passionate, intense relationship with songwriter Polly Harvey and possibly also with Tori Amos.

While his personal life may have been busy, Cave's career took off. The decade and half of work he had done had paid off and by 1996 he had a sizeable international following – so much so that Kylie Minogue agreed to a duet on one of the murder ballads and sent that record to the top of the charts.

'Into My Arms' is a vulnerable song. Cave is not only being candid about his feelings but matches the lyric with a tune worthy of their poetic qualities.

"So I didn't set out to write a personal record as such," he said. "I just found myself writing things in that way, and with quite a few of those it was significant for me at the time to articulate the events that had happened.

"I think there's some very bracing and sobering lessons that can be learnt from love. It doesn't really go the way it's supposed to go, or the way I've always believed that should be, which is the way we're constantly fed about the idea of love and particularly about committed relationships like marriage.

That love, in terms of relationships, actually has little to do with things at all. It's about a commitment to a greater thing and that is the relationship and the relationship being the commitment of two people."

The Outdoor Type Smudge

(Tom Morgan) ❋ Half a Cow ❋ 1997 ❋ Appears on: *Mo' Poontang*

This song, made famous by Evan Dando and the Lemonheads, was originally intended for songwriter Tom Morgan's trio, Smudge. Possibly the slackest band in the history of rock, Smudge had a certain magic. There is, in the unfinished quality of their records, room for the divine to shine. Smudge and the songs of Tom Morgan are one of Australia's best-kept secrets. For ten years Morgan has been popping out gems that are literate and funny and true – but also rarely heard.

'The Outdoor Type' was written by Morgan, who is decidedly the indoor type. On the one hand it's a funny story with nice asides about the virtues of first-run TV versus mountain biking. The song works, though, like the best of Cole Porter and the great Tin Pan Alley songsmiths, by having an emotional truth just under the surface. Here there is the eternal dilemma of honesty in a relationship, drawn neatly and with considerable wit.

I Still Carry You Around Steve Earle

(Steve Earle) ❋ Warner Bros. ❋ 1997 ❋ Appears on: *El Corazón*

Steve Earle took the bad boy image a little too far. A heroin addiction that lasted more than twenty years and five marriages followed by a crack habit finally landed the Texan singer/songwriter in jail. Prior to his sentence he had been in a revolving door of arrests and court appearances that was crippling his career and, between the lawyer and the drug dealers, sucking away his time and creativity.

Suddenly, in 1995, after the jail sentence looked too real, Earle quit drugs. He returned to performing and writing; first solo then with various outfits.

El Corazón (the heart) was his third post-rehab album. It crossed the entire spectrum of Earle's work. "Well, you understand where my writer's block came from," he said. "From about $750–$800 a day's worth of writer's block. My drug habit reached a point where there wasn't any time or energy to do anything else. So now that I don't have to find hundreds of dollars worth of drugs just to get up in the morning, it's amazing – I feel like I have all the time and energy in the world. I write something every day. The only thing that scares writers worse than ex-wives is a blank piece of paper.

"With *El Corazón* I finally managed to write an entire album without the devil in one song. I'm proud of that. I just wanted to see if I could do it."

Earle re-embraced country music styles, especially bluegrass. For one song he teams up with Del McCoury, a bluegrass bandleader well into his seventies at the time. As he wrote in his notes for the album, "I wrote this song specifically to have something to play with the Del McCoury Band. They are just the best bluegrass outfit in the business right now. Del is the best tenor, Ronnie is the best mandolin player, and Rob plays banjo like no-one else.

"Bluegrass is the original alternative country music. After I retire, I'm gonna buy a bus and play bluegrass festivals."

Bitter Sweet Symphony The Verve

(Richard Ashcroft/Mick Jagger/Keith Richards) ❋ Hut ❋ 1997 ❋
Appears on: *Urban Hymns*

"When you live in a place like Wigan, your senses aren't exactly bombarded with stimuli," said Richard Ashcroft, lead singer of the Verve, on the occasion of the release of the group's first album, *A Storm in Heaven*. "So, when you make music, you don't want to reflect your environment, you want to create something bigger than what you see around you. That's what we want our music to do – transport the audience beyond the everyday. I've had enough of Billy Bragg and that brand of social-realist pop. I've got enough shit going on in my life; I don't want to be reminded of how dismal everything is. I want to be elevated, not dragged down."

Ashcroft was one of the last true romantics of British rock. The Verve was about big soundscapes and often dark lyric themes. Ashcroft, however, had the skeletal demeanour and sunken cheeks to pull it off. Despite a loyal following – which included Noel Gallagher of Oasis, who wrote a song about Ashcroft – the Verve seemed unlikely to see out the decade. Ashcroft and guitarist Nick McCabe fought vigorously and Ashcroft had a reputation as a heavy drug consumer.

Things were not looking up until Ashcroft brought the song 'Bitter Sweet Symphony' along to the sessions for the group's third album, *Urban Hymns*.

Here was an urban hymn. It had the majestic sweep of a conversation with the eternal and almighty. It was lush and lonely and troubled and elegant, expressing some of Ashcroft's alienation.

"All I can think of is that music gives you an excuse to go on stage and be something else, do something else and get something out," Ashcroft told Sascha Stojanovic. "I think we are all a million different people every day. I think we all play games with each other, mind games to protect ourselves. When I write lyrics I mean it. I've got nothing to hide from."

The track as produced by Youth is a magnificent epic with grand string arrangements and the group's impassioned backing of Ashcroft's soulful vocal. The song recalled the '60s British pop in that it criticised the wage slavery and at the same time recognised the redeeming power of music. Certainly it worked and 'Bitter Sweet Symphony' was a massive global hit. Unfortunately, Ashcroft lost all the publishing royalties on the song in a dispute over an uncleared sample.

It Could Have Been a Brilliant Career
Belle & Sebastian

(Stuart Murdoch) ❊ Matador ❊ 1998 ❊ Appears on: *The Boy with the Arab Strap*

Belle & Sebastian was the band that Britain had to have. The Scottish combo, which took its name from a kids TV show, started with just two – Stuart Murdoch and Stuart David. They put themselves in that English tradition going back to Nick Drake and Ray Davies and Morrissey – all bedsits and wet weekends and weak tea leavened with sarcasm and irony. Belle & Sebastian weren't afraid to build delicate melodic arrangements, but they also weren't afraid to be playful with them either. While there is a sense of melancholy through their work, there's little of Nick Drake's self pity.

Belle & Sebastian's version of kitchen sink folk rock arrived just as Brit-pop priapism had reached its peak. Their first LP was a critical triumph, though, most of the public never heard it. A second LP was better realised. By this third album, Belle & Sebastian were finding their feet.

'It Could Have Been a Brilliant Career' opens *The Boy with the Arab Strap* with Belle & Sebastian's beautiful sense of melody and Murdoch's wry take on the possibilities of youth.

"What really excites me is bands prepared to borrow from absolutely everything but come up with something their own," said bass player Stuart David. "And we're becoming a wee bit more willing to do that."

... Baby One More Time Britney Spears

(Max Martin) ❋ Jive ❋ 1998 ❋ Appears on: ... *Baby One More Time*

Britney Spears was the turn-of-the-century ingénue. Her story was loaded with contradictions. Here she was a fresh-faced teen from the Mickey Mouse show who acted like a porn star and claimed, against commonsense, that her virtue was still intact. Britney Spears was the embodiment of the decline of America in as much as she sold highly sexualised chastity and Baptist Christianity in the one, bare-midriff package.

Spears' '... Baby One More Time' was a massive global hit for the sixteen-year-old. Swedish hit maker Max Martin who had also given careers to the Backstreet Boys wrote the song. It was controversial to start off with. The hook line "Hit me baby, one more time," has sadomasochistic overtones and an odd acceptance of domestic violence. "It doesn't mean physically hit me," said Spears in a vain attempt at rationalisation. "It means just give me a sign basically. I think it's kind of funny that people would actually think that's what it meant." This begs the question of whether a sheltered Baptist child star understands the implications of her lyrics. However, in the same *Rolling Stone* interview she does go on to discuss the marketing trajectory of her sexuality.

"It was a sexual song. This may be a little old for me. Because of my image thing. I don't want to go over the top. If I come out being Miss Prima Donna, that wouldn't be smart. I want a place to grow," said Spears.

All of this is only an issue because '... Baby One More Time' is a fantastic piece of pop. The beat, a loping R&B groove bounces around Spears' vocal giving her just enough lift and never losing sight of the dance floor.

"Pop music is popular music," said the Lolita diva. "I'm just bringing pop music to a different level. It's always going to be pop music. That's what I love to do. I love to dance, and pop music incorporates that. I'm just bringing it to the next level."

The Rockafeller Skank Fatboy Slim

(John Barry/Fatboy Slim/Winford Terry) ❋ Skint ❋ 1998 ❋
Appears on: *You've Come a Long Way, Baby*

This track was the beginning of the end of club culture. Fatboy Slim's 'The Rockafeller Skank' was a monster that went beyond its genre (big beat). Recorded at home, 'The Rockafeller Skank' has a touch of the novelty record about it. It is kind of funny but mostly it has a huge fat vocal hook in the sample "Check it out now, the funk soul brother". It has big dirty guitar lines in its eclectic selection of samples from the John Barry Seven's score for the movie *Beat Girl* and the Just Brothers' *Sliced Tomatoes*. The record sold five million copies and at that point, dance culture, which required an alternative self-image, was blown wide open. It's still a great track and the break beats are still compelling. Most of all, Norman Cook (aka Fatboy Slim) mixes the track like he's DJing at a great party and having a wonderful time doing it. "I think what separates me from other DJs is the vaudeville element of it," he said.

To Zion   Lauryn Hill

(Lauryn Hill) ❊ Ruffhouse ❊ 1998 ❊ Appears on: *The Miseducation of Lauryn Hill*

The Fugees singer didn't take long to break out on her own with *The Miseducation of Lauryn Hill*. "I think the piece as a whole communicates my personality; it is the culmination of my experiences, the sum total of what I had gone through at a certain point in my life," she said to the *Times*.

One of the key factors in cutting her first solo album was the birth of her child Zion David to boyfriend Rohan Marley – son of the late reggae legend. Her pregnancy effectively put a hold on the Fugees and she clearly felt some pressure to make compromises about competing loyalties. It's most clearly spelt out in the song 'To Zion'.

"That song," she said, "is about the revelation that my son was to me. I had always made decisions for other people, making everybody else happy, and once I had him that was really the first decision that was unpopular for me. It was one that was based on my happiness and not what other people wanted for me or for themselves. And it was the best decision that I could have ever made, because I'm the happiest and healthiest that I have ever been. It also revealed to me which relationships were right, which ones were sincere, and which ones were based on exploiting and hurting me. It was a godsend all the way round – 360 degrees of that whole situation were nothing but a blessing. And I'm so happy that I made the choice that I did."

Hill enlisted the help of Carlos Santana for the guitar part.

"That totally came from my parents' record collection," she said. "I remember finding *Abraxas* in the basement, and looking at the cover going, 'Wow! This is real. What's this?' It had all this stuff going on, all this beautiful artwork on the cover. And then I remember putting on the record and wanting to cry. I put on this one song, 'Samba Pa Ti', and it just gave me chills. I used to write my first songs to other people's music, and this particular album had this beautiful, soulful guitar, and it was instrumental, so I was in heaven.

'To Zion' is a song about a future, specifically the future of her son, but it also spelt out Lauryn Hill's future as a major hip-hop writer.

Opus 40 Mercury Rev

(Jonathan Donahue/Mercury Rev) ❋ V2 ❋ 1998 ❋ Appears on: *Deserter's Songs*

Mercury Rev is one of those few groups who can overcome their own hype. The Rev – Jonathan Donahue and Sean 'Grasshopper' Mackiowiak – came in on the same dispassionate slacker horse as Dinosaur Jnr. Based in upstate New York, however, they gradually became less slacker and with that commitment came some of the most passionate American music of recent years. Their breakthrough was *Deserter's Songs* and the key track 'Opus 40'. Donahue has a vaporous singing style that blows around the melody. On *Deserter's Songs* they teamed up with a couple of locals – drummer Levon Helm and organist Garth Hudson of the Band. Not only does their presence put Mercury Rev into a definite tradition, but it also gives the record an earthy grounding. Donahue in particular has a great ear for texture and for experiment but the end result on 'Opus 40' is the synthesis of the avant-garde and roots music. The music, too, matches the lyric, which dives into existential pain. "*Deserter's Songs* is more internalised," Donahue told *MOJO*'s Andy Gill. "I think the lyrics are a lot deeper embedded emotionally. The record has to do with feeling deserted and at the same time deserting someone. It's like love: sometimes you're leaving and sometimes she's leaving – it's never easy to quite say which."

E-Bow the Letter R.E.M.

(Michael Stipe/Bill Berry/Mike Mills/Peter Buck) ❋ Warner Bros. ❋ 1998 ❋ Appears on: *New Adventures in Hi-Fi*

"I think it's one of the best things I've ever written," is Michael Stipe's summation of the song. "I feel it plumbs something inside of me that I wish I could ... I wanted this record to have heart. And that song maybe comes as close as anything on the record to being really real."

The E-Bow is an electromagnetic device that, when held over the strings of an electric guitar, creates a sustained note.

"I've had one for a while now and I've used it on a couple of things just as background," said Buck. "It's really nice ... If you're looking for a cello-type sound, you can get a really nice sustain out of it. And it's really nice for background stuff. When I first wrote the thing and we demoed it, I just did that as an overdub. And it was really cool. It was totally chaotic and noisy. And the demo is really pretty amazing. It's totally fucked up and out of time because we'd only really played it once but it sounds really neat. I always kind of thought, well E-Bow, I'll keep using it on that song."

The track for the song had been around for two years and was recorded for the sessions of the *Monster* album but was put on ice. Then Stipe came up with an appropriate lyric.

"Michael basically had a rough draft of a letter," Buck recalled. "It was kind of stream of consciousness communication. Instead of sending the letter, he started singing it to the song and it fit in perfectly. It just had the rhythm. And it was like some words he had and he actually just did them in one pass in sound check one day and it sounded great."

Patti Smith was invited to duet with Stipe on the song. The singer credits Smith's *Horses* as one of the defining moments of his life, "I bought it the day it came out," he said. "I went home and listened to it all night on headphones. I didn't take them off till the morning, when I had to go to school. It was one of the single most cathartic moments of my life. It just felt right. It felt like: this is music, this is what I'm going to do." He laughs. "I was really naïve; I mean, I was fifteen. I was simple-headed, but it was a defining moment for me. Remember the whole punk aesthetic was that anybody could do it. You didn't have to be special or talented. Or beautiful or rich or whatever. I just decided that I knew I'd be a singer. That was that."

Smith had only recently returned to the public eye following the death of her husband Fred Sonic Smith. Her presence on this song is haunting. "You've got this one monochromatic musical element going through the verses and the chorus seemed to be somehow really different in texture," Buck told Michael Goldberg of Addicted to Noise. "We're friends with Patti. He brought it up and we just went, 'Yeah. Let's see if Patti would want to sing it.' I was thrilled with the idea that she would even consider it. She came in and it worked out perfectly. It was moving to see someone whom I've admired for so long come in and sing a song that I wrote."

Stipe's typically allusive lyric is built around the mantra, "aluminium tastes like fear".

"Have you ever really been afraid? You get a taste in your mouth – it tastes like chewing on aluminium foil," said Stipe. "Adrenaline tastes like aluminium, and when you're really afraid, you taste it in your mouth. It's when the creature part of us completely takes over human, rational everything. Your eyes dilate. Your nuts creep up inside you. You start breathing through your mouth. Your mouth tastes like aluminium. That's what fear tastes like."

The image is Stipe at his best – particular detail with a truth that makes an emotional connection unattached to any literal meaning.

"And there was a time in the mid-'80s when I was not in a good head. I was just stretched too tight. I wasn't sure if I wanted to be in a band or anything. And if someone slammed a door or if a car blew a horn, or someone came up behind me and touched me on the shoulder, it would alarm me, and I would taste it. I can kind of taste it now, but it's coffee and bad dental work. It's not fear.

"You get it when you drink mineral water in Mexico. All the *agua mineral* in Mexico tastes like fear. It's because they recycle the bottles and put the caps on."

My Name Is Eminem

(Dr Dre/Eminem) ✳ Interscope ✳ 1999 ✳ Appears on: *The Slim Shady LP*

Marshall Mathers has an identity crisis. First up there's Marshall Mathers, then there's his homicidal, misogynistic alter ego, Slim Shady, and finally there's Eminem – the white rap superstar. His breakthrough single, 'My Name Is', as its title suggests, is a meditation on identity. To that end, Eminem relates the trash existence that is the lot of the America underclass and then he lights a fuse on the garbage heap introducing the contentious subject of race and sex.

Part of Eminem's success is due to the hip-hop smarts of producer Dr Dre who helped Eminem cut 'My Name Is' in about an hour. The connection with Dre also allowed Eminem to get past the "can a white boy rap" issue.

"My whole market, my whole steez, is through the underground; if those hip-hop heads love it, I'll rise above," he told *Spin* shortly after 'My Name Is' topped the charts. "It's like, you hardly ever hear a Wu-Tang song on the radio, but they rose from the underground on word of mouth.

"In the beginning, the majority of my shows were for all-black crowds, and people would always say, 'You're dope for a white boy', and I'd take it as a compliment. Then, as I got older, I started to think, nobody asks to be born, nobody has a choice of what colour they'll be, or whether they'll be fat, skinny, anything. I had to work up to a certain level before people would even look past my colour; a lot of motherfuckers would just sit with their arms folded and be like, 'All right, what is this?' But as time went on, I started to get respect. The best thing a motherfucker ever said about me was after an open mic in Detroit about five years ago. He was like, 'I don't give a fuck if he's green, I don't give a fuck if he's orange, this motherfucker is dope!' Nobody has the right to tell me what kind of music to listen to or how to dress or how to act or how to talk; if people want to make jokes, well fuck 'em. I lived this shit, you know what I'm sayin'? And if you hear an Eminem record, you're gonna know the minute that it comes on that this ain't no fluke."

"If he remains the same person that walked into the studio with me that first day, he will be fucking larger than Michael Jackson," said Dre. "There are a lot of ifs and buts, but my man, he's dope and very humble."

Why Does My Heart Feel So Bad? Moby

(Moby) ※ V2 ※ 1999 ※ Appears on: *Play*

Moby had been there at the start of the dance music movement back in the mid-'80s, before it was fashionable. That credibility allowed him to bring home an album like *Play* that put techno at every dinner party in the bourgeois world. Having done techno and experimental electronica and hard rock, Moby (aka Richard Hall) made an album around the idea of mixing Negro spirituals and field recordings as the vocals over an electronic tune.

"I'm a white guy who doesn't really understand African-American culture," he said. "But if you look at contemporary black music, they borrow heavily from soul, disco, jazz, R&B, and funk, but they don't borrow from the blues tradition. The only conclusion I can come to is that the blues and traditional Negro spirituals, music from the fields, is poverty music. Hip-hop is about money, cash, respect. So maybe the blues represent a part of the tradition they're not comfortable with any more. I love contemporary black music but I also love Negro spirituals. I see it as part of a great continuum that the African-American community doesn't seem to reflect."

Moby was no doubt excited by *Sound of the South* some forty years after Alan Lomax lugged his Nagra tape recorder through the cotton fields. But it wasn't the ethnomusicologist in Moby that assembled 'Why Does My Heart Feel So Bad?'. He recognised the deep and vigorous sound of the spiritual singers and how that would contrast to the thin, blanched electronica.

"I was responding to the music genuinely with a love of the source material," he said. "I didn't hear it and think to myself that I could use it and make a lot of money off of it. I just thought, what wonderful performances."

21 c.

WHEN HIP HOP DROVE THE BIG CARS

Get Ur Freak On
Missy Elliott

99 Problems
Jay Z

Jesus Walks
Kanye West

Lose Yourself
Eminem

Heard It All
Illy

In Da Club
50 Cent

Stan
Eminem

Drop It Like It's Hot
Snoop Dogg ft. Pharrell Williams

My Humps
Black Eyed Peas

Shakey Dog
Ghostface Killah

Hey Ya
OutKast

One Mic
Nas

Kick, Push
Lupe Fiasco

B.O.B.
OutKast

Gold Digger
Kanye West ft. Jamie Foxx

Fancy
Iggy Azalea

The Motto
Drake ft. Lil Wayne

Pyramids
Frank Ocean

I Love It
Hilltop Hoods feat. Sia

Bullet and a Target
Bliss n Eso

**I Was Only Nineteen
(A Walk in the Light Green)**
The Herd feat. John Schumann

Get Lucky
Daft Punk feat. Pharrell Williams

Drunk in Love
Beyoncé feat. Jay Z

Clint Eastwood
Gorillaz

New York State of Mind
Jay Z and Alicia Keys

Cry Me a River
Justin Timberlake

Hollaback Girl
Gwen Stefani

California Gurls
Katy Perry feat. Snoop Dogg

Dance Wiv Me
Dizzee Rascal
feat. Calvin Harris & Chrome

Maneater
Nelly Furtado

Things Have Changed   Bob Dylan

(Bob Dylan) ✳ Columbia ✳ 2000 ✳ Appears on: *Wonder Boys OST*

"A song that doesn't pussyfoot around or turn a blind eye to human nature" is how Bob Dylan described 'Things Have Changed' as he collected the Academy Award for Best Song in 2001. The song was written for Curtis Hanson's 2000 film *Wonder Boys* about a college professor and author (Michael Douglas) who is falling apart with a midlife crisis while keeping company with Robert Downey Jr. and Tobey Maguire. Hanson got the script to Dylan and pressured the singer/songwriter to come up with a theme song.

Dylan's career had recently taken a resurgence with the *Time Out of Mind* album. He was reconnecting on record with the eternal issues; death and a purposeful life. *Time Out of Mind* was a hugely important record because no rock & roll performer had reinvented themselves after the age of 50. No-one had showed that rock & roll music could mature like this.

If *Time Out of Mind* was a triumph, it was not a pleasant experience for Dylan and he fell back once again with his band. They had been together for a significant time and by 2000 were a well-oiled, tight, dark folk blues group with a unique sound. Dylan hadn't had a group like this since The Band in 1966. When the challenge of writing this movie theme song came up Dylan went into the studio with his road ensemble and produced the track himself.

I've been walking forty miles of bad road
If the Bible is right, the world will explode
I've been trying to get as far away from myself as I can

Some things are too hot to touch
The human mind can only stand so much
You can't win with a losing hand

This is just a beautiful meditation on life, both witty and accurate. A man, not alone, who has fought all the battles and put up with the bullshit finally finds acceptance. It's a song about age but it's also a lyric about modern times such as they are.

"I just come down the line too far to make any superfluous song," Dylan said in an interview with *Rolling Stone* around the release of *Wonder Boys*. "I mean, I'm sure I've made enough of them, or that I've got enough superfluous lines in a lot of songs. But I've kind of passed that point. I have to impress myself first, and unless I'm speaking in a certain language to my own self, I don't feel anything less than that will do for the public, really."

Since I Left You The Avalanches

(Robbie Chater/Tony Diblasi/Edward Drennen/Gordon McQuilten/Jeanne Salo/Darren Seltmann/Jimmy Webb) ❋ Modular, XL, Elektra ❋ 2001 ❋ Appears on: *Since I Left You*

Darren Seltmann and Robbie Chater are the core of the Avalanches. Their friendship was cemented in crate digging and assembling songs with bits of music sampled from lost and discarded LPs. The Avalanches were not alone in this enterprise but they did have a particular quirkiness. Songs like the initial single 'Frontier Psychiatrist' were just mad.

According to Seltmann, "Robbie went to university as soon as he got out of high school and did a media arts degree that was based on film soundtracks and things like that. He ended up hijacking the soundtrack part because everybody wanted to make films and nobody cared about the soundtracks, so we were given free rein in the studio. They'd close doors at nine at night and reopen at nine in the morning — all the other hours we could have. That was sort of the blueprint for the way we worked from there — we've really closed everything off and become very isolated. It's something that we love too much to give up."

Living pretty much in their own world, they were surprised at the interest in their tracks and doing it all mostly for themselves they didn't bother with the legalities of clearing the samples for sale. "People think you buy a sampler and away you go, you turn into DJ Shadow or something," Seltmann told *Sound On Sound* magazine. "It's really a game of patience. In the beginning it was literally 'OK, I've got 10 sounds. Two are in tune.' Creating chord changes can take a week — to make the chord change that you need without plugging in an organ. There is a bizarre satisfaction to be got out of that, and maybe that's a more intense satisfaction than actually playing it yourself."

'Since I Left You' is one of the most haunting love songs of its era; psychedelic and soulful, melancholy and bittersweet. The song became an international hit in dance music circles. *The Guardian* called it one of the songs of the century. Success brought lawyers and the negotiations to clear the samples took almost as much time as making the record.

Seltmann estimates that there were upwards of 3500 samples in the album *Since I Left You*. "We were really unorganised and were just sampling on the fly as tracks progressed," Chater added. "We had no idea the record would get such a wide-scale release so we saw no need to keep track of what we were using — we were definitely guilty of harbouring a 'No-one's going to listen to it anyway' sort of attitude. Plus that was in our days of getting kinda, um, lubricated so who the fuck knows. It's all kinda fuzzy!"

Seltmann rued, "I remember when we started clearing the album, the first sample we tried to clear was the first sample we heard, which was from Rodgers & Hammerstein — a beautiful introduction — and it was rejected and we thought 'The record's never coming out!' But from then on, it seemed to have a really charmed life. That was pretty much the only hiccup."

The Seed (2.0) The Roots featuring Cody ChesnuTT

(Cody ChesnuTT/Black Thought) ✳ MCA ✳ 2003 ✳ Appears on: *Phrenology*

Ahmir 'Questlove' Thompson and Tariq 'Black Thought' Trotter were friends since high school and formed the Roots in the early 1990s as a mostly jazz-inflected band in Philadelphia. The Roots in the early days eschewed samples in favour of playing all the instruments themselves. Their hip hop- and jazz-inspired music underpinned an attitude that harked back to the black renaissance in the 1970s. For some the Roots were too purist and too righteous. But those people never heard the band in full swing. According to one writer, "Padded with onstage jamming, their live shows lasted for weeks."

Surprisingly, in 1999 'You Got Me', their collaboration with Erykah Badu, was a major hit and the Roots drifted toward the mainstream. That process accelerated when Jay Z had them back him for his *Unplugged* project and some live dates. Success messed with the Roots' heads. "We probably made four records in that mindset, and that definitely started with *Phrenology*," said Questlove. "I thought, 'We had our peak, and rap groups don't last more than six records. We'll probably get dropped.' At some point, we were just thinking of it like a suicide mission, so we did everything with reckless abandon."

Phrenology is a very eclectic mix of psychedelics, hip hop, rock and pop that somehow just works. If you're in an eclectic state of mind you could do worse than call Cody ChesnuTT. This neo-soul and hip hop guitarist had been scuffling around with a band in the 1990s and things were not working out so he retreated to his bedroom where he wrote and recorded all of the double album *The Headphone Masterpiece* on a 4-track machine. One of the tracks from that LP interested the Roots, hence 'The Seed (2.0)'.

The authoritative snap of Questlove's drums propels this track along a path that is neither quite hip hop nor rock. ChesnuTT's sweet vocals complement Trotter's rougher edge. It just doesn't sound like anything else.

99 Problems Jay Z

(Jay Z/Norman Landsberg/Felix Pappalardi) ☀ Roc-A-Fella / Def Jam ☀ 2004 ☀
Appears on: *The Black Album*

Sometimes a lyric is apposite that it enters the world and becomes common usage, part of the vocabulary of the time. The hook from this song – "If you're having girl problems I feel bad for you son / I've got 99 problems but a bitch ain't one" – is just such a line. Jay Z's tale of running drugs and the underclass life from which he came sums up our era. It's beyond masterful.

The line came from rapper Brother Marquis of 2 Live Crew having a conversation with Ice-T who loved the line and used it in his song called '99 Problems' back in 1993. Chris Rock brought Ice-T's song (which is just vile misogyny) to producer Rick Rubin who suggested it to Jay Z.

Jay Z is the perfect embodiment of the American Dream. He is a black Jay Gatsby in flesh and blood. Shawn Carter grew up in the Marcy Houses housing project in New York's Brooklyn and began dealing drugs while still a teenager. With his natural ability with words and rapping he hustled himself out of poverty and progressively through executive positions in Def Jam Records via all the usual corporate enterprises – clothing and consumables and then into management, of music and sports artists and the like. Jay Z is, in business terms, the most successful artist of all time.

In the first verse of '99 Problems' the lyrics relate to Jay Z being criticised in the press and exploited by the media. The crux of this song, though, is the second verse which tells the story of a police stop and search, based on Jay Z's own experience in 1994. He describes being pulled over by highway patrol – a sweep for weapons and drugs – but Jay Z refuses to allow a search without a warrant. The highway patrol calls for sniffer dogs but Jay Z moves off before they arrive. As he is driving away he passes the dog car, hence the line "but a bitch ain't one." This is a classic American standoff where both parties are in the wrong – the policeman for racially profiling the driver and the driver for trafficking drugs.

Jay Z explains, not too convincingly, that his use of the word 'bitch' was not anti-women. "That was the writer in me being provocative, because that's what rap music should be at times," he told PBS. "That was really directed to all of the people who hear buzz words in rap music – they hear 'bitch' or 'ho' or something and immediately dismiss everything else that takes place. And everything has to be put in context. And when you put it in context, you realize that I wasn't calling any female, besides a female dog, a 'bitch' on this song."

The production is classic Rick Rubin with monstrous drum beats, notably sampling 'Long Red' by '60s hard rockers Mountain and 'The Big Beat' by Billy Squier. Almost as impressive as the production is the film clip by Mark Romanek which trails through the madness and the despair of the Marcy projects with an unstinting eye. '99 Problems' proved that although Jay Z was now hanging out with the 1% he understood the 99.

Mr Brightside The Killers

(Brandon Flowers/Dave Keuning) ❋ Island ❋ 2004 ❋ Appears on: *Hot Fuss*

Singer Brandon Flowers was trying to get a rock & roll thing happening in his home town of Las Vegas with his guitarist pal Dave Keuning. They were heading in a garage rock direction, writing a few things, until they heard the Strokes' *Is This It* album. At that point they threw out everything they had except for one song – 'Mr Brightside'. Wise decision to keep it, 'Brightside' launched the band and became enough of an album that they eclipsed the Strokes.

The song was mostly written by Keuning, but the lyrics are about Flowers, after he discovered his girlfriend cheating. "I was asleep and I knew something was wrong," he said. "I have these instincts. I went to the Crown and Anchor and my girlfriend was there with another guy." Flowers then added his own take to the guitarist's lyrics. "I remember being in the studio, recording the demo but still writing the lyrics," the singer told *NME* in 2013. "I was procrastinating, and that's why the second verse is the same as the first one, but it just stuck. What strikes me about it is how powerful that song still is, and the second verse is still as powerful as the first one, every night. There's just something about it. It's a moment.

"All the emotions in the song are real. When I was writing the lyrics, my wounds from it were still fresh. I am Mr Brightside! But I think that's the reason the song has persisted – because it's real. People pick up on those things. And that goes all the way down to the production; we recorded it in a couple of hours, but it just sounds right, you know?" The demo did the rounds and eventually led to the Killers signing with Island Records. They were the perfect band to finish off the back-to-rock fashion that swept the music business at the turn of the century, with the elements of a strong guitar attack and some intelligent lyrics, with Flowers a perfect front man. As one critic said of the single, but could be said of the band: filled with "ambition, sex and noise".

Rebellion (Lies) Arcade Fire

(Arcade Fire) ✳ Rough Trade / Merge ✳ 2005 ✳ Appears on: *Funeral*

Win Butler is the leader – vocalist, songwriter and visionary – of Canada's Arcade Fire. Few would have imagined that this diverse collection of musicians playing mostly old-time acoustic instruments and singing sometimes in a foreign language (French) would come to dominate early 21st century music. Certainly Win Butler held those aspirations but kept them pretty much to himself. An eponymous EP got people talking and in 2004 a local music website commissioned an email interview with Butler while he was working on the Arcade Fire's debut LP *Funeral*. One of Win's responses was particularly revealing: "In fact even as I am writing this Régine and I just wrote a song called 'Rebellion' that I'll bet 50 dollars will be on the record. The other guys haven't even heard it yet."

Régine is Régine Chassagne, Butler's multi-instrumentalist, French-speaking muse and wife of Haitian descent. They met in Montreal and became the core of Arcade Fire, joined on *Funeral* by Richard Reed Parry, Tim Kingsbury, Howard Bilerman and Win's brother William. A cast of pals made up more noise. The band members all play numerous instruments and roles under Win Butler's dictatorial eye. The group's modus operandi – collective, acoustic, obscure, homemade, retro – marked them as an 'alternative' rock band. While that was part of the story, there is an epic pop quality to Butler's vision that is first unleashed on *Funeral*'s penultimate track. The album is called *Funeral* because many of their family and friends had recently died. Themes of family and childhood run deep through the LP. Chassagne has a delicate song, 'Haiti', about the country her parents fled before she was born. A drumbeat segues the ballad into a call to 'Rebellion' and a call to arms.

'Rebellion (Lies)' is ostensibly a lullaby but the song sounds to me like fighting sleep or really embracing the adventure underneath the covers: "People say that your dreams are the only things that save ya / Come on baby in our dreams, we can live our misbehavior". In any case, the core of the song is the relentless beat on the kick drum set against an equally insistent piano figure. The drum pattern has a marching quality to it and you can see the 6'6" Butler leading his motley crew against the enemy. It's this anthemic beat that became Arcade Fire's signature.

This same quality made the group a bridge between alternative rockers such as Radiohead and classic rock from Bruce Springsteen and U2. The first concert that Butler ever saw was the U2 *PopMart* tour in 1997 while in later years U2 took to using Arcade Fire in their intro music. Coldplay's Chris

Martin said, "When we heard *Funeral*, we were all prepared to get day jobs. But instead of giving up, we just tried harder."

"I discovered the Arcade Fire a year ago," David Bowie declared recently. "Coldplay's Chris Martin has been saying he's discovered them first. But I did. So there," quipped Bowie. "There's a certain uninhibited passion in the Arcade Fire's huge, dense recording sound. They meld everything from early Motown, French chanson and Talking Heads through to the Cure in a kaleidoscopic, dizzy sort of rush. I bought a huge stack of the CDs last September and gave them to all my friends."

I Bet You Look Good on the Dancefloor
Arctic Monkeys

(Alex Turner) ❈ Gentlemen of the Road / Domino / EMI ❈ 2005 ❈
Appears on: *Whatever People Say I Am, That's What I'm Not*

Arctic Monkeys were here to prove that British rock was not dead. They were in so many respects the heirs to a long British tradition of working-class lads, no-hopers and out-of-workers getting together and bashing out gritty songs of life up north. It's a tradition that started with the Animals and continued on through Mott the Hoople and Slade to the Buzzcocks, Pulp and Oasis. Or indeed fellow northerners Duran Duran who are referenced twice in 'You Look Good on the Dancefloor'.

Arctic Monkeys formed in Sheffield and it was here that they recorded and gave away their first demos. Such was the passion of their fans that they started a MySpace page for the Monkeys and ran one of the earliest viral campaigns. Arctic Monkeys were hot before they even made London. They did sign with the independent Domino label, with whose help their first proper single 'I Bet You Look Good on the Dancefloor' entered the UK Charts at #1 as did the album *Whatever People Say I Am*.

Previous northern heroes Oasis had made their name from being egomaniacs and very funny at that. Arctic Monkeys had attitude and a great drum part. And they worked fast. Alex Turner told *NME*, for the album, "We recorded ten songs in a week but everything was recorded at 300 miles an hour ... It was a bit too live."

"Early on I was kind of embarrassed about that word [songwriter], it made me think of when we were in school, when bands were pretty shit before the Strokes and all that," Turner told *Spin*. "The 'songwriting thing' just sounded a bit boring. I didn't know about Leonard Cohen or Scott Walker or people

I've since absorbed. When we made that first record, there was so much shit I hadn't heard. And that's fine, that's what that record had in spades, you know: naiveté. You're never going to get that back ... You can't go experimenting with the colours from different rainbows if you haven't got that base there in the first place to support it all."

Turner has over the years proven to be the equal of his English forebears, even referencing another prolific wordsmith, Shakespeare:

Oh, there ain't no love, no Montagues or Capulets /
Are just banging tunes and DJ sets and ... /
Dirty dance floors, and dreams of naughtiness!

That's certainly the spirit of the Bard.

Best of You Foo Fighters

(Foo Fighters) ❋ RCA ❋ 2005 ❋ Appears on: *In Your Honor*

Dave Grohl started the Foo Fighters very soon after Kurt Cobain put an end to the band Nirvana. Foo Fighters came bursting out of the block with a stripped back, righteous but decidedly fun rock & roll attitude. After those years of heroin and despair and superstardom in Nirvana you can't blame Grohl for keeping the passion high and the emotions much lighter. So it has continued.

The Foo Fighters are one of the most ferocious live bands in the world. Few groups could power a stadium with just guitars, bass and drums like the Foo Fighters. They are conscious and they are concerned but they don't spend a lot of time on the dark side where Cobain and the other grunge rockers played.

Ten years on from Cobain's death and the first Foo Fighters' LP, the band had become one of the biggest live drawcards in the world. Grohl had moved from behind the drum kit to a place like Bruce Springsteen as a straight-talking part of the national conscience. He was a strong supporter of John Kerry's bid as the Democratic nominee in the 2004 Presidential election and it was that experience that inspired 'Best of You'.

"'Best of You' was one of the first songs we wrote for the album, one of the only songs on the record that made it from the original sessions," Grohl explained to *CD:UK*. "It was inspired by seeing people stand up in the face of struggle. It's meant to make you feel empowered."

Being one of the first songs written for the record, the band experimented with it quite extensively and by the time they were cutting tracks the singer was over it. The band's manager, however, persuaded them to give it a spin and it became the Foos' highest charting single. And it was covered by Prince. Grohl has changed his tune about 'Best of You' but then, as he said of the song, "It's about breaking away from the things that confine you."

Hollaback Girl Gwen Stefani

(Pharrell Williams/Gwen Stefani/Chad Hugo) ✳ Interscope ✳ 2005 ✳
Appears on: *Love. Angel. Music. Baby.*

Gwen Stefani was a major star as the singer of '90s ska punks No Doubt but when she went solo she freaked out. Her first solo album *Love. Angel. Music. Baby* was a cathartic experience which she detailed on 'What You Waiting For?', the first single. Overcoming writer's block, working with new producers, and having a family was all a bit much.

Amongst the horde of producers, Stefani hooked up with the Neptunes (Pharrell Williams and Chad Hugo). After little initial success and an agreed hiatus they got back together for another crack and quickly knocked out two songs. Stefani packed up to leave, believing that she now had an album and Pharrell called her back to the studio. Reluctantly she sat through a playback of one of his own tracks and was so inspired she got out the pen and they worked up 'Hollaback Girl'.

A hollaback girl is a woman who responds verbally to insults or catcalls. The correct response would be to come back and duke it out or perhaps rise above it. In Gwen Stefani's case the dissing came from grunge godmother Courtney Love who said to *Seventeen* magazine, "Being famous is just like being in high school. But, I'm not interested in being the cheerleader. I'm not interested in being Gwen Stefani. She's the cheerleader, and I'm out in the smoker shed." Stefani replied, "Someone one time called me a cheerleader, negatively, and I've never been a cheerleader. So I was like 'Ok, fuck you, you want me to be a cheerleader? Well I'll be one then. And I'll rule the whole world. Just you watch me.'"

'Hollaback Girl' is a magnificent jam from the Neptunes, brilliantly percussive with handclaps and the jagged beats of a cheer squad. This was the first digital single to sell one million copies. Stefani also led the way for the next generation of white girls – Iggy Azalea, Ke$ha – dipping their toes in hip hop.

"I did the whole record," Stefani told *Rolling Stone* about the late inclusion of 'Hollaback Girl'. "But I knew I didn't have my attitude song – my 'this is my history, fuck you because you can't erase it' song. I knew I wanted a song like that."

Gold Digger Kanye West featuring Jamie Foxx

(Kanye West/Ray Charles/Renald Richard) ✻ Roc-A-Fella, Def Jam ✻ 2005 ✻
Appears on: *Late Registration*

"There are colours and ideas that make [*Late Registration*] different from average hip-hop, but Kanye is already different from the average hip-hop guy," according to co-producer Jon Brion. "He's got this sense of pop record-making which is really solid, and he likes tracks with a lot of things going on in them — which is not necessarily common for hip-hop. He was already barking up that tree." Choosing Jon Brion as your co-producer was another uncommon call.

Kanye West arrived as the new visionary hip hop artist with his first LP *The College Dropout* after some years as a successful producer. A lot was a riding on *Late Registration*, his second album. Instead of reaching for a superstar hip hop or rap producer, West called up Brion, the ultra-white composer of art movie scores (*Eternal Sunshine of the Spotless Mind, Punch Drunk Love, I Heart Huckabees*) and the sometime producer of Fiona Apple and Aimee Mann. West was an Apple fan and then after watching *Eternal Sunshine* he knew that Brion was his next producer.

West does bring freshness to 21C hip hop. He casts his eye back too, using a riff from Ray Charles' 'I Gotta Woman' on 'Gold Digger'. Who better to cover Brother Ray than Jamie Foxx, who won an Academy Award playing Ray. Where Charles' 'I Gotta Woman' is about a man whose girlfriend will do anything for him, 'Gold Digger' is the reverse. Foxx changes the lyrics from "She gives me money when I'm in need" to "She TAKES my money when I'm in need."

'Gold Digger' is a comical take on the battle of the sexes and the suggestion that women are looking for a candy man while black men are looking for white women. West originally wrote the song for a woman, rapper Shawnna, which explains the frequent switching of the singer's gender. It was left off her 2004 album. Other lyrics were left over from another production with Murphy Lee. What holds it together is the freewheeling spirit that West brings to his rapping and the dead-on swing in the rhythm track.

'Gold Digger' was one of the first jams West and Brion worked on. "It was completely apparent that he was open to investigating new ideas," Brion told MTV. "I was playing something on a track and he was completely psyched, and then he left after a few hours and said, 'I'll see you tomorrow.' On your sophomore record, that's the ultimate time to not fuck with the formula, right? And he gets me — a guy who has never made a hip-hop record in his life — and gives me half the reins? That is not an egomaniac.

"He has vision, and when the guy makes quick, intuitive decisions, he just has it. I'd watch him take a rough track that I had worked on and completely stand it on its head in 10 minutes — and it's just better. It was mind-boggling."

Rehab Amy Winehouse

(Amy Winehouse) ✳ Island ✳ 2006 ✳ Appears on: Back to Black

There are so many emotions that come forth when this song spins. First up there is the joy of hearing the snap and the swing of the Dap-Kings hitting that '60s groove, the sassy sashaying of Amy Winehouse's vocals, and of course the play on words in the title which links love with the drug. But behind it all is the fact that drugs and liquor played such a large part in the sadness of her too short life. That is, right there, the definition of great soul music.

Winehouse was already an upcoming diva by the time she made her second album Back to Black. She was well versed in soul and funk music and '60s girl-group pop. So Winehouse had the vision but like many divas she also had her demons. A poor self-image and other issues left her vulnerable to relationships with the wrong sort of men, which led to escape through drink and drugs and the raw material for more songs.

For Back to Black she used her original producer Salaam Remi but also hooked up with American DJ/producer Mark Ronson. It was kind of the perfect partnership. Ronson brought the Dap-Kings to the party, the New York ensemble the best keepers of the '60s flame. The theme of the record was the struggles of a good girl trying not to be bad and to find true love. 'Rehab' was the centrepiece. Ronson told the BBC, "I was walking down the street with Amy. We were in New York and we'd been working together for about a week and we were walking to some store. She wanted to buy a present for her boyfriend and she was telling me about a specific time in her life that was ... I feel bad, like, talking about a friend like this, but I think I've told this story enough times ... but she hit, like, a certain low and her dad came over to try and talk some sense into her. And she was like, 'He tried to make me go to rehab and I was like, 'Pfft, no no no.' And the first thing I was like, 'ding ding ding ding ding.' Like, I mean I'm supposed to be like, 'How was that for you?' and all I'm like is, 'We've got to go back to the studio.'" That idea for the song had been in Winehouse's notebooks for some years until Ronson convinced her to change it from a blues into a Motownish number. Everyone is on their best behaviour on this track – Ronson keeps it tight and the band put in jazz colours and blues in a honey-smooth blend while Amy sings and smiles through the pain of the song.

As it happened, Winehouse did go to rehab, but it didn't in the end save her. In an interview she gave after the release of her first album, before everything went mental with the drugs and the husband she said, "Ten years from now I'll be 30, so I'll maybe have one baby. I'll have out my second album ... and my real honest music will be saved up for the big albums. I'd like to be remembered as someone who wasn't satisfied with just one level of musicianship ... as someone who was a pioneer. I've got all this time to make that happen, that's what's so exciting. I've got years to do music."

LDN   Lily Allen

(Lily Allen/Iyiola Babalola/Darren Lewis/Tommy McCook) ✻ Regal ✻ 2006 ✻
Appears on: *Alright, Still*

One of the few pop singles inspired by Wordsworth's poem 'Composed upon Westminster Bridge, September 3, 1802' (although Van Morrison has a bit of Wordsworth going on), Lily Allen's portrait of London in fact is up there with Ray Davies' best songs. Her lilting slightly ska jaunt through the tune belies the complex ideas in the lyrics. She explained to Daniel Rachel, "I was thinking, I want to write about London, and looking at that poem and thinking, 'That's what he thought, what do I think?' I was looking at his viewpoint; how he told what he felt at that particular moment."

Lily Allen is the daughter of a well-known British actor and the god-daughter of Joe Strummer so the slightly Cockney style is perhaps a little faux. Nevertheless, Allen has put herself into a long tradition of English and especially London writers who glorify the mundane, who find inspiration in the smallest details. This company would include Glenn Tillbrook and Chris Difford from Squeeze, Nick Lowe, Davies, McCartney, Ian Dury and others. "I'm not writing all of these songs as if they were from my perspective, and those are the things I'm experiencing," she told *Pitchfork*. "But at the same time, my mother came to London when she was 17 years old with one daughter and a suitcase and nothing else – no money, no education. She was a punk. And, we didn't have any money for the first 10 years of my life. We lived in what you call the projects, and we ate beans on toast. My mum came from that background, but she just worked really hard to feed us and keep a roof over our head, and that probably keeps my eyes open."

Allen signed to Regal but rather than wait for the label to get around to looking after and promoting her, Allen began to post her demos direct to MySpace where she quickly developed a devoted audience. One of those demos was 'LDN' and the record company did have to take notice. A small run of singles including 'LDN' were pressed and quickly sold out. Allen was developing a reputation. However, the release of 'LDN' as a limited edition 7-inch single caused a real buzz and gave Allen the media exposure she needed. Once in front of camera she was relentlessly provocative.

The sound on this track is a light ska on a bed sampled from 'Reggae Merengue' by Tommy McCook and the Supersonics. On top of this is a playful tune with a live band.

"My mum is a film producer and my dad is an actor... They think it must be really easy – 'she was really rich' – and that's not true. My dad left home when I was four. I didn't speak to him really until I was 15. So, I feel that I can talk about things with some conviction because I have experienced them to some extent. But it doesn't mean that I'm saying, 'This is my life.' I don't live in a council flat, but I live in London, which is an incredibly cosmopolitan city. I see a variety of people and things just riding through it."

Paper Planes M.I.A.

(Mathangi Arulpragasam/Wesley Pentz/Topper Headon/Mick Jones/Paul Simonon/ Joe Strummer) ❋ XL/Interscope ❋ 2007 ❋ Appears on: *Kala*

Maya Arulpragasam, who performs under the name M.I.A., is one of the few music stars who can claim a father who is a genuine revolutionary. Maya was born in 1975, in the middle of the decades-long bloody civil war between the Tamil minority and the Sinhala majority in Sri Lanka. Maya left Sri Lanka when she was eight and her father stayed behind to push the Tamil cause. Maya attended art school in London and gradually transitioned from a visual artist into a rapper and musician. A part of the strength of her work is an ability to channel anger – at her father, at politics – into her music.

'Paper Planes' is a song built on a sample of the Clash classic 'Straight to Hell' created by Maya's producer Diplo. The paper planes of the title are visas, which were top of Maya's mind at the time. She was refused an American work visa and was placed for a time on a Homeland Security watchlist, probably as a result of her father's activism. Much of the song is sung from the point of view of someone who manufactures visas for illegals and immigrants. The song also features a dramatic sequence of gunshots and cash registers. Here the meaning is that immigrants like her grow up in places where one hears gunfire and the cash registers reference some people's belief that immigrants are only coming for your money.

"I was having this stupid visa problem," she said, "and I didn't know what it was, aside from them thinking that I might to fly a plane into the Trade Center – which is the only reason that they would put me through this. I actually recorded that in Brooklyn, in Bed-Stuy. I was thinking about living there, waking up every morning – it's such an African neighbourhood. I was going to get patties at my local and just thinking that really the worst thing that anyone can say [to someone these days] is some s--t like: 'What I wanna do is come and get your money.' People don't really feel like immigrants or refugees contribute to culture in any way. That they're just leeches that suck from whatever. So in the song I say 'All I wanna do is [sound of gun shooting and reloading, cash register opening] and take your money.' I did it in sound effects. It's up to you how you want to interpret. America is so obsessed with money, I'm sure they'll get it."

But according to producer Diplo, "Mostly, Maya was making fun of American rapper culture. 'Paper Planes' was making fun of being what American kids are into, of being 'gangsta.'" The Clash sample is a very powerful bed and it comes with baggage – it's a song about internationally displaced persons and their difficulty in finding a haven. For some reason when the song was played on MTV or other American network shows, the gunshots were altered. The song was also featured in the pot-heist film *Pineapple Express* and the producers asked her to take out drug references. Maya refused. It went in the film and the film greatly increased the spread of the song until it became a major hit record.

Droving Woman Paul Kelly, Missy Higgins, Glenn Richards

(Kev Carmody) ❊ EMI ❊ 2007 ❊ Appears on: *Cannot Buy My Soul*

Paul Kelly decided that it was time to make a tribute album for his friend and colleague Kev Carmody. The pair had written some classics together such as 'From Little Things Big Things Grow' and Paul had long been a fan of Carmody's eclectic songwriting.

In the event, Paul got a who's who of Australian songwriting to the party including Bernard Fanning, Tex Perkins, the Waifs, the Herd, the Drones, Steve Kilbey, Clare Bowditch, Dan Sultan, Archie Roach, the Pigram Brothers, Dan Kelly, Sara Storer and the Last Kinection.

There was always going to be one big hurdle. "I knew we had to do 'Droving Woman' but it's a 9-minute song and there's 21 verses," Kelly told me with a laugh. The answer was to get three singers to take turns.

Kev Carmody has lived many lifetimes – he's been a bouncer, an Aboriginal activist, an intellectual and scholar, a folk singer and he's worked the land. 'Droving Woman' comes from that period of his life where he was an itinerant bushie and stockman. It's the story told from a wife's point of view of a life spent droving cattle through Queensland, forever on the move. This is a bush ballad with depth and detail of the night skies, of the weather and the terrain and the hardship. Through it all though shines a majestic sense of pride and strength and love.

The drama in the song comes after the children have been raised, after the couple have almost become one with their landscape and then the husband is thrown from his horse and lies dying in his wife's arms, too far from medical help for anything to be done. She stoically carries on, too old to move to the city, too much part of the country. In these 21 short verses, Carmody tells us so much about a long gone lifestyle, about the characters of these people, of the privations of rural life. He is unsparing in his eye, not romanticising it but not running from the beauty and the pathos in his words.

Kelly was right in his pick of colleagues. Glenn Richards has a keening tenor voice that squeezes out emotion. He sounds like the cold of the winter nights described in the words. Missy Higgins is more emotive, more passionate and then Paul brings it home. This is a bush ballad but one that sounds completely modern. The melody line and the flat declamatory style of most of the song give it a very modern realness and add to the drama. It is nine minutes you'll never forget.

Gone Gone Gone (Done Moved On)
Robert Plant and Alison Krauss

(Don Everly/Phil Everly) ❊ Rounder / Zoe ❊ 2007 ❊ Appears on: *Raising Sand*

Like many stars of the 1950s, the Everly Brothers had a hit-and-miss time on the charts that decade. Perhaps it was arrival of the Beatles with a sound that clearly owed a substantial debt to the brothers' rockabilly and country music that catapulted them back onto the charts in 1964. They returned at the height of Beatlemania with 'Gone Gone Gone (Done Moved On)'. The original track featured a jungle beat pounding out of the toms over a massively echoed piano. It was strangely modern even for 1964.

Some four decades on T-Bone Burnett suggested the track to one of the most unlikely pairs in contemporary music: Robert Plant, the leonine sex god of Led Zeppelin, the hardest rocking band of all time; and Alison Krauss, the Appalachian-born queen of modern bluegrass. They were to duet over a Leadbelly song for a tribute record but they hit it off and went into the studio with the master of modern roots music Burnett. The result is an extraordinary mixture of old and new, welded seamlessly. Burnett brings his bag of tricks and guitarist Marc Ribot takes guitars to places never dreamed of. 'Gone Gone Gone' fits perfectly within those textures. That song appeared alongside material by the greatest American songwriters – Gene Clark, Townes Van Zandt, Allen Toussaint, Mel Tillis and Tom Waits.

Producer Burnett told the *New York Times*, "Robert and Alison, they're two very mystical voices, and the blend of them is mystical. They both sound like they're singing from some other time. Alison sounds like she just stepped out of the Black Forest, and Robert sounds like Ozymandias the Egyptian pharaoh."

The challenge was to create an album using existing songs but not make the record sound nostalgic. "Robert said send five, six songs over, and I played him a couple," according to Burnett. "He said, 'that's a nice little ditty, but Alison wants to do something dark.' And that was the starting point. I think this album is looking into the skull of the present. It represents all of the danger and the darkness and the outsiderness and the bleakness that seemed appropriate to this time."

"I was quite nervous about the idea of finding out just how much of a one-trick pony I am," said Plant. "Robert and I did it to have fun and see what would happen," Krauss said at the time. "But to start with it was very scary because both of us were out of our comfort zones. We were away from our usual environments so we just had to go with what we felt – it made for a very exciting recording process, though. I vividly remember calling him before we started *Raising Sand* and saying, 'I'm worried', and he said, 'That's good, because I am too.'"

Skinny Love Bon Iver

(Justin Vernon) ❋ 4AD / Jagjaguwar ❋ 2008 ❋ Appears on: *For Emma, Forever Ago*

"Yeah, I went up to the cabin in the woods and I made a record. It's sort of odd to look back and see it as magical, because it felt like a lonely few months at the cabin, where I plugged in the laptop and fucked around," is how Justin Vernon describes the making of his classic album, *For Emma, Forever Ago.*

It all started with Emma, the girl in the title, who ended her relationship with Justin Vernon who was then on the periphery of the indie rock scene in North Carolina. Heartbreak, a dose of pneumonia and then hepatitis and mononucleosis sent Vernon off to the family's cabin in the wilds of Wisconsin in winter. No wonder the album is a downer. It was here that he composed and mostly recorded the album, thinking the songs were just demos. Some pals back in Raleigh NC convinced him that he had a complete record on his hands. When not making the record he watched re-runs of *Northern Exposure* where he picked up the name Bon Iver (a mangling of the French phrase for 'good winter'). As for using a band name, Vernon says "When I made *For Emma*, I knew that I couldn't name it [after] me, because it felt like something different, almost like I had set up some fake land or something. It was something outside, and something over there."

Perhaps because the emotions were so raw, perhaps because the illness made feelings more acute ... for whatever reason *For Emma* is a very intimate and intense album. The song 'Skinny Love' stands out largely because it sounds less like an alternative rock song than an R&B classic. Vernon's falsetto and his lilting phrasing recall legends like Marvin Gaye. "For the most part," he told the *AV Club*, "I've been influenced by black singers and singers I couldn't sound like. Whenever I tried to do a dark note or a bent note, I would just sound like Hootie and the Blowfish. [Laughs.] I was really insecure about it, so I just ended up writing rock & roll songs where I didn't have to do that. But I feel so much more comfortable being able to access painful melodies. I feel freer singing the high stuff.

"I've always been into the Springsteen thing, writing pretty literally and trying to tell stories. With these songs, I was creating sounds first. I would create a space for the vocals, then transcribe vocal sounds and listen to what it sounded like. I would get lyric ideas from the sound of the voice. And I was actually able to pull out more meaningful stuff, personally speaking, because of that. I would surprise myself by what I was singing about, just all these weird, subconscious melodies and sounds. I had no proper idea of what I should be doing. It was a great release, actually, to break up with my band and not have that support system anymore. I was alone, I had no rules, I had no band, I had no sound I sounded like, and I had no one to answer to. I just felt a little freer. I went back to those days as a 14-year-old, working on an 8-track."

'Skinny Love' is haunting in the way that the best lost love songs are: the winter, the cabin, the tears. This is the beginning of a new genre – folk-soul.

I Kissed a Girl Katy Perry

(Katy Perry/Lukasz Gottwald/Max Martin/Cathy Dennis) ✳ Capitol ✳ 2008 ✳
Appears on: *One of the Boys*

A perfect 21st century pop moment – Katy Perry, the American daughter of born-again Christian pastors, sings a delightful song about having a lesbian moment. So much of the public debate over the past decades has been about same sex relationships: marriage, adoption, equal rights, don't ask/don't tell. Pop music has a refreshing ability to take these debates out of the poisonous arenas of social media and the press and just cast a new light on things.

"I was really excited to put that out because it was such a fun song that could be both silly and mean something to someone," she said. "It was a subject matter that was on the tip of everyone's tongue at that moment, so it was kind of like a snapshot of things that were happening in 2008."

The song is essentially a new wave-lite jaunt through a mildly flirtatious party. Although Perry has always denied it, the title is exactly the same as Jill Sobule's 1995 folk/punk song about a woman discovering the complexities of her sexuality. Katy Perry's protagonist, however, is exploring the novelty of the experience and of breaking down barriers.

Unlike Sobule, Perry co-wrote the song with some of the most high-powered songwriters of the era: Max Martin ('Oops... I Did It Again', 'Baby One More Time', 'I Want It That Way') and Cathy Dennis ('Can't Get You Out Of My Head', 'Toxic', 'About You Now') and the track was co-written and produced by Dr Luke (Lukasz Gottwald) who was then the magic man with chart hits.

There is no doubt that, heavy hitters notwithstanding, Capitol records was nervous about the track and the response from radio stations and the public, especially in the very religious south. Interestingly the first American radio station to pick up the song was in Nashville. From there it spread all the way to the top of the charts around the world. Perry remained oblique when pressed about her experiences in this area. She told the *Observer*, "I'm talking about the way girls are really touchy-feely and sisterly. Especially when we're growing up ... I wish I had kissed that girl I had the girl-crush on when I was growing up. I would have been much more prepared for my dating life, I think."

Katy Perry by this stage in her career had suffered a lot of setbacks. Her first record of Christian music had died. She had been dropped by Columbia records. Her album with producers the Matrix had been shelved. She was in need of something to kick start her career and really had nothing to lose.

In any case, the finer details of the lyrics are not especially important. What people heard was 'I kissed a girl and I liked it!' and pumping that over the airwaves was certainly a positive step. Look what's happened since!

Time to Pretend MGMT

(Ben Goldwasser/Andrew VanWyngarden) ⁂ Columbia ⁂ 2008 ⁂

Appears on: *Oracular Spectacular*

According to Andrew VanWyngarden, "We wrote 'Time to Pretend' our senior year of college, and the music was inspired by a praying mantis we had in our house. She laid eggs ... and we laid the egg case on this kinda model pirate ship on the mantelpiece, and the eggs hatched and all these baby praying mantises were climbing up the rigging of the ship, and it was pretty crazy ... uhm so the music was inspired by our praying mantis that liked to dance to the Clash and the lyrics are just about us imagining living the fantasy rock star life."

According to Ben Goldwasser, 'Time to Pretend' "refers to this fantasy, this joke of us being sell-out rock stars. It's not like we ever set out to have that lifestyle – we didn't really want that, but it's definitely different now we're playing big festival shows and touring all the time. Some of it is true. It's pretty weird. I don't think the fame is really the ultimate part of the fantasy. We wanted to get to the point where we could do really ridiculous things. We want to have some really crazy stage production." They achieved that.

Ben Goldwasser and Andrew VanWyngarden met at college in 2002. Goldwasser played keys and VanWyngarden was a drummer. They recorded 'Time to Pretend' while playing with computers and this early stage of the group was known for a 45-minute 'instrumental demolition of the Ghostbusters theme'. They went separate ways until Columbia Records fell in love with 'Time to Pretend' and offered them a record deal.

The preferred list of producers submitted to Columbia included "anyone but Sheryl Crow" and Barack Obama. They settled with Dave Fridmann, best known for his work with the similarly psychedelic Flaming Lips. MGMT have a stronger version of modern psych rock; the bottom end is close to electronic dance music but over the top the guitars and keyboards are often startlingly and generally delightful.

MGMT sound like everything mostly happened randomly, especially their good fortune, and they just don't care. It's a refreshing attitude in a music culture that is so bogged down in its own self-importance. MGMT have that prankster attitude that is supposed to go with getting high and having fun. But they are clearly dedicated enough to turn out genuinely provocative music. "We're serious, not serious," VanWyngarden told *The Guardian*. "We want to make music that a 20-year-old kid could interpret as a call for revolution, but not blatant revolution. We want to inspire people to be subversive, and scare the squares."

Empire State of Mind   Jay Z featuring Alicia Keys

(Angela Hunte/Alicia Keys/Alexander Shuckburgh/Bert Keyes/
Jane't "Jnay" Sewell-Ulepic/Shawn Carter/Sylvia Robinson) ✳ Roc Nation / Atlantic ✳
2009 ✳ Appears on: *The Blueprint 3*

All kinds of magic can happen on the streets of the Big Apple. There were already a number of classic songs about the city that never sleeps; Frank Sinatra and Billy Joel immediately spring to mind. It was perhaps for this reason that when Angela Hunte, along with writing partner Jane't Sewell-Ulepic submitted 'Empire State of Mind' to Jay Z's label Roc Nation they got knocked back. She was a native New Yorker growing up at 560 State Street, the same address as Jay Z had back in the day.

The two girls had been in the UK and life in London reminded them of much they missed about New York, for all its challenges and frustrations. 'Empire State of Mind' came easily but once it was knocked back from Roc Nation they moved on. A few months later, Jon 'Big Jon' Platt from EMI heard the track at a barbeque and thought it would be perfect for Jay Z. The song didn't get through the front door but round the side; the superstar heard the song and immediately fell in love with it.

Jay Z adjusted the song from a soul ballad to incorporate his rap. He kept the female chorus and invited Alicia Keys to sing the hell out of it. "There was a first phone call, and Jay hit me up like, 'I feel like I have this record that's going to be the anthem of New York,'" she said. One of the hooks in the song is from 'Love on a Two-Way Street' by the Moments and Keys' piano skills blended with the sample.

"I've admired Jay Z for a long time," Keys said. "He reached out to me, said, 'I have this big New York record. I feel it's right for us to do it together. It has this big Frank Sinatra, take-it-there feeling. I feel like you could really do something with it.'"

Jay Z made 'Empire' into a travelogue, sweeping through the mean streets where he grew up, dealing drugs to the high life, hanging with Anna Wintour and the *Vogue* crowd. This is an epic song that looks into the nooks and crannies of New York in ways that other writers haven't been able to do. The string arrangements and the huge walls of keyboards give an appropriate scale to the song and they're matched by Alicia Keys' vocal gymnastics. This song is as big as New York.

"I'll never forget when Jay and I were finishing the song, and he said, 'Do you think it's too New York?' and I said, 'Kind of, but what else is it going to be?'" she told *The Guardian*. "But it's not about New York, it's about coming from nowhere and being successful. Anyone can relate to it."

Little Lion Man Mumford & Sons

(Marcus Mumford/Ted Dwane/Winston Marshall/Ben Lovett) ✻
Gentlemen of the Road / Dew Process ✻ 2009 ✻ Appears on: *Sigh No More*

In the middle of a massive revolution in electronic music of all kids, Mumford & Sons burst forth in their waistcoats, toting guitars and banjos and kicking on a bass drum and just rode a new folk wave to the top of the pop charts. They looked like a London version of The Band and like the boys from Big Pink, they had absorbed an enormous dose of Americana which they refashioned in their own image. They joined a long line of neo-folk artists like the Pogues and the Waterboys.

Marcus Mumford's parents Eleanor and John are evangelical, charismatic Christians who lead the English congregation of the Vineyard. This was a church which grew up in California in the late '70s and was partly responsible for Bob Dylan's conversion to Christianity. T-Bone Burnett, the record producer and singer/songwriter was for a time also associated with the church. In any case, Mumford attended prestigious private schools and it was here he met Rob Lovett and they played music together. Mumford read classics at Edinburgh University. Munford gradually accumulated the band with finds Winston Marshall and Ted Dwane while he was also backing folksinger Laura Marling. There was quite a fertile folk/American scene happening in London at the time. Apparently the Mumfords mostly bonded over the *O Brother! Where Art Thou?* soundtrack of bluegrass and blues that was produced by T-Bone Burnett.

The Mumford band all come from well-to-do English families and there is a sense of ease and entitlement that perhaps wasn't with The Band who had a raw bar-room feel. What they do have is a tightness in their arrangements and performances that compensates for the lack of shit on their shoes (as the

Rolling Stones would have it). According to producer Markus Dravs, "The secret is a supertight performance. The tighter something is, the louder it can be. The secret to that is just rehearse, then go fucking rehearse once more."

'Little Lion Man' was one of Mumford's first songs and he claims this tale of fear and self-loathing is largely autobiographical. He has never elaborated on that but it appears his year at the University of Edinburgh encouraged him to start writing songs. "I guess I experienced failure in my small, undramatic way," he told *Rolling Stone*. "I had my heart broken. I failed to get into the colleges I'd wanted to, which was what I'd pinned all my hopes to, really. I had no idea what I wanted to do. I'd left home and kind of left behind the values that I grew up with and I didn't really have anything to fall back on. I wasn't very cool. I wasn't very popular. I don't know what my purpose was that year at university. I kind of knew what my purpose was before, and then I didn't know." The key though is in the chorus where he sings, with appropriate gusto, "It's not your fault but mine … I really fucked it up this time." Hardly.

We Won't Run Sarah Blasko

(Sarah Blasko) ✳ Dew Process ✳ 2009 ✳ Appears on: *As Day Follows Night*

For Sarah Blasko every album is an adventure. For this one she hopped on a plane and travelled around the world to a man she barely knew. "I'd gone from the hottest day you can possibly imagine in Sydney and now it was minus 10," she recalled. "It was snowing and I was on my own … every now and then they were joking in Swedish and I was standing there like a loser and I just thought, what the hell…! It's really hard to get over there and really trust somebody who's got all their buddies around them – you're just a little bit scared that you're not going to be heard. It's just a natural instinct to be confronted by that. I get Björn more now, but at that time, it's really hard to put your faith in somebody when you've spent a good year of your life working hard on your songs, and to put your trust in a complete stranger to understand them the correct way. So I really had to let go a bit."

The Björn to whom she refers is Björn Yttling from alt pop group Peter, Bjorn and John. This was Blasko's third album and the first which she made solo. She had been in a relationship with Robert Cranny who had written and co-produced her two acclaimed albums, *What the Sea Wants, the Sea Will Have* and *The Overture & the Underscore*. The material was quite close to the surface emotionally. Perhaps for that reason she went for completely acoustic backing tracks – strings, acoustic bass, acoustic guitar and piano dominate – and the result is definitely intimate. She told *The Vine*, "I was listening to modern stuff that was a bit bluesy, like M Ward, but I guess we were listening to a lot of old stuff when we were recording like Nina Simone, Alice Coltrane, Billie Holiday, all kinds of things really."

"I was having a really, really hard time," she told *Rolling Stone*. "I don't even feel like I need to say it because if you hear the record, you know when somebody's gone to hell and back. You just can feel it. I don't know if I bring it upon myself but I feel like in the last ten years, I've had a lot of full on things to deal with.

"Writing this album brought a lot of beauty and happiness to my life to be. I don't think I've even found it so cathartic. It really pulled me out of my life and into – without sounding kinda hippy – a magical world, a spiritual thing."

Blasko had learned to sing in church – mostly Pentecostal and charismatic Churches. That certainly gave a soulful edge to her songs but there was also something brisk and occasionally uncomfortable about them; as though she was revealing inconvenient truths. 'We Won't Run' is one of her less demanding tunes; it's sweet and Moorish and has all the hallmarks of a classic.

I Gotta Feeling The Black Eyed Peas

(William Adams/Allan Pineda/Jaime Gomez/Stacy Ferguson/David Guetta/
Frédéric Riesterer) ✻ Interscope ✻ 2009 ✻ Appears on: *The E.N.D.*

Prior to starting work on the fifth Black Eyed Peas LP, main motivator Will.i.am came to Australia to play the part of John Wraith in the film *X-Men Origins: Wolverine*. While in Sydney he took in the clubs and was impressed by the electro music that was then banging down the doors, specifically the work of the Presets. As he put it, "The energy on the Presets' small little stage was crazy energy. That song 'My People' – that is wild. That's the reason why this record sounds the way it does – my three months in Australia." The track also sounds like Silverchair's 'Straight Lines' which was co-written with the Presets' Julian Hamilton.

According to uber record producer and executive Jimmy Iovine the melody for 'I Gotta Feeling' was inspired by 'I'll Go Crazy If I Don't Go Crazy Tonight' by U2 which was remixed by Will. The singer has told *Rolling Stone* that the lyrics came to him watching Barack Obama's inauguration. The year 2009 was the most intense point of the global financial crisis and Will.i.am thought that the world really needed to be cheered up. Whatever the specific triggers for 'I Gotta Feeling', the track and the LP it comes from suggest a switch away from the Peas' hip-hop roots towards electronic dance music. Who better to lead the way down that dark alley than David Guetta? It was just around that moment that the Parisian DJ was breaking out with his own music. The hard-style dance tracks he was doing were the basis for what is now called EDM and this hybrid of the Peas and Guetta took the DJ over the top. This was at the time the biggest selling download in history and the highest-selling non charity single of all time.

"Will, at the time, was embracing the electronic music from Europe," says Guetta. "Other artists have taken sounds from us and incorporated it a little bit. But what I respect a lot about him and the band is that he fully immersed himself in the culture. He called me, and he was like, 'Okay. I love that sound and I want to experiment with it a bit.' So I sent him some tracks, and he selected a few. Then, I went to Los Angeles and we worked together. When the song started coming together, I got a crazy feeling and I was screaming: 'this is huge, this is a monster, this is crazy.'

"Will came up with a hook of a hook! It has such a positive vibe. And I think a lot of success with the song is because of that really positive message, especially at the time when things are difficult for everybody ... Our music is the bridge between electronic culture from Europe and hip-hop culture from America. This is the music of the future. It's not electro. It's not hip-hop. It's electrohop."

According to Will.i.am in an interview with *Marie Claire*, "Mostly every song on the Black Eyed Peas record is painting a picture of our party life. It was a conscious decision to make this type of record. Times are really hard for a lot of people and you want to give them escape and you want to make them feel good about life."

Rolling in the Deep Adele

(Adele/Paul Epworth) ✳ XL ✳ 2010 ✳ Appears on: *21*

"It was my reaction to being told that my life was going to be boring and lonely and rubbish, and that I was a weak person if I didn't stay in a relationship. So I wrote that as a sort of fuck you," according to Adele Adkins.

Simply known as Adele, her first album, *19*, announced the arrival of a woman with an amazingly powerful voice and the courage to lay her emotions out. It was a compelling package and completely contrary to the highly sexed but vapid divas being churned out by the entertainment industry.

In any case, *19* brought Adele stardom but not necessarily happiness. Two years later she was struggling to find the songs and the producer for her next record and frankly her personal life had its ups and downs.

It all came together on a fateful day when she was supposed to meet Paul Epworth, the producer of Florence and the Machine and other indie giants. "I didn't know what to expect because he is known for being very indie and I'm known for being very pop so I wasn't sure if it would work well but it ended up being a match made in heaven."

Anyway, that morning the boyfriend made the comment about boring and lonely and Adele stormed out of the house. On arriving at the studio she was about to pen a ballad and see how that went. Epworth said under no circumstances. He encouraged her to get mad and get even. Which she did. They wrote 'Rolling in the Deep' in three hours. The title, she explained, was an "adaptation of a kind of slang in the UK called 'roll deep,' which means to have someone, always have someone that has your back, and you're never on your own, if you're ever in trouble you've always got someone who's going to come and help you fight it. And that's how I felt in the relationship that the record's about ... That's how I felt, you know, I thought that's what I was always going to have, and um, it ended up not being the case."

So far the single 'Rolling in the Deep' has sold 7,600,000 copies and the album has topped 30 million. They say that living well is the best revenge.

Big Jet Plane Angus & Julia Stone

(Angus Stone) ❋ EMI ❋ 2010 ❋ Appears on: *Down the Way*

The Stones siblings are Australia's most unlikely stars. Angus and Julia Stone were raised on Sydney's Northern Beaches and they grew up as hippies in that idyllic environment. But their sweet acoustic songs were just devoured by the Australian public and indeed audiences in Europe and America.

The Stones had been quietly moving along the alt folk scene around the world when a re-recording of one of Angus' songs literally took off. 'Big Jet Plane' was recorded for an album *Smoking Gun* he put out under the name Lady of the Sunshine in 2009.

"I didn't know what to do this one summer," he recalled to Triple J, "so I thought I'd hitchhike up to the Woodford Folk Festival. It was one of those Woodfords where it was melting hot. So on one of the first days I went down to the local waterhole ... I was swimming around, and met a girl there. I was a kid in love!" he laughs. "She had the daisy-chains, the light glowing off her, and you know … it was just one of those moments. We got together and spent the festival frolicking about, but then I had to go. I never saw her again."

That kind of post-Woodstock serendipity fills the track which, like most of the record, was produced by Angus and Julia. There's a calmness that belies the intensity in this track and that tension makes it work.

"You know, it's pretty cruisy, quite simple," he says. "We write songs, we play shows, and people like it. I don't really know why. But for me, when I hear honest writing I'm always drawn in. And I want to always try and be honest, in the way that I view things. I'm really excited when I'm sitting down and I'm in that world, there's nothing else quite like it. So maybe, listening to us, people can feel that."

Runaway Kanye West featuring Pusha T

(Kanye West/Terrence Thornton/Emile Haynie/Jeff Bhasker/
Mike Dean/John Roger Branch) ※ Roc-A-Fella, Def Jam ※ 2010 ※
Appears on: *My Beautiful Dark Twisted Fantasy*

Everybody saw Kanye West at the 2009 MTV Awards interrupt Taylor Swift's acceptance. It's become a defining pop culture moment of the decade. It may have been the straw that broke West's back and sent him retreating to Hawaii. But it was a big time for him and the result was the classic album *My Beautiful Dark Twisted Fantasy*. According to some of West's tweets 'Runaway' was written for Taylor Swift.

The English critic Andy Gill put his finger right on it when he wrote, "Kanye can certainly be an utter toerag at times, and it's clear that when, on the nine-minute 'Runaway', he proclaims a toast for the world's 'douchebags, assholes and scumbags', he's including himself among their number. He proceeds to confront his own failings – his rudeness, promiscuity, hedonism, egotism and liking for tacky, bling-tastic glamour – but does it over a backing track on which delicate piano and sensitive cello are assaulted by nasty, distorted guitar, bearing out his self-assessment that he's 'just young, rich and tasteless.'"

Kanye West, or 'Ye, has pushed hip hop in all kinds of new directions but his main innovation is his ability to just really open up about what's going on in his head and his heart. West didn't grow up in the projects, he grew up among the black intelligentsia of Chicago. That explains a lot about his innovations.

By the time he came to make his fifth album, West was perhaps America's greatest rap star. All of the decadent gifts available to a superstar were there for his pleasure. His prodigious ego was stroked beyond imaginings and, like so many in that position, he found the whole experience spiritually unsatisfying. Meanwhile his mother, who gave up a position as an academic to manage him, died.

'Runaway' is an epic version of Piaf's theme 'Je ne regrette rien'. With just cello and minimal piano, West lays it all out and then, to prove his tastelessness, adds a distorted guitar at the end. To confirm his egomania he made a 30-minute film about the whole thing which he explained to *New York*, "It's the story of a phoenix fallen to Earth ... I've been feeling the idea of the phoenix. It's been in my heart for a while. It's maybe parallel to my career. I threw a Molotov cocktail on my career last year, in a way, and I had to come back as a better person."

I guess if you're going to be remorseful and modest it's best to do it with an epic.

Somebody That I Used to Know   Gotye featuring Kimbra

(Wally de Backer) ✳ Eleven ✳ 2011 ✳ Appears on: *Making Mirrors*

There was a time in 2011 that you could not escape 'Somebody That I Used to Know'. If you weren't hearing the song itself you were hearing a parody of it or seeing a parody of the video like the one where a naked Darth Vader is painted by a naked George Lucas as they discuss how terrible the *Star Wars* films became ... such is the nature of a genuine smash hit. Gotye became the first Belgium-born act to top the Hot 100 since the Singing Nun spent four weeks at #1 with 'Dominique' in 1963.

Wally de Backer, aka Gotye, came to Australia from Belgium at the age of two and since his late teens had been involved in the vital alternative music scene in Melbourne. Mostly he was playing drums with trio the Basics, under his real name. In his spare time he made records as Gotye. *Making Mirrors* was his third album.

'Somebody', he confesses, was a composite tale of a number of his romantic failures. He told *Rolling Stone*, "There is an ex-girlfriend. It was five-six years ago. It wasn't a nasty breakup, but it was messy in the sense that we hurt each other more than we needed to because it wasn't a clean break. I guess it's closest to what the chorus is about. We both realised we had to move on and we haven't seen each other since."

The tune began with a sample of Luiz Bonfá's song 'Seville' from his 1967 album *Luiz Bonfá Plays Great Songs*. De Backer told *Sound on Sound* magazine that composition was quite long and laboured and it wasn't for some weeks until he hit upon the idea of the female part. "So the third session," he said, "was all about writing the female part and changing the perspective. The arrangement of 'Somebody' is reflective of me moving towards using sounds that provide me with inspiration for a texture or a platform for an idea, and then through sonic manipulation and coming up with original melodies and harmonic ideas to make it my own. I guess the balance of sounds taken from records and samples I created myself is perhaps 50–50." Finding the right duet voice was also a protracted process. De Backer always had Kimbra in mind but they tried out with two or three other, better known, voices before settling with her.

'Somebody' became one of the biggest selling songs of the century, in part because it crossed over from the alternative scene where de Backer started to the middle of the road. It was a universal story. As he told *American Songwriter* magazine: "I think it's the kind of slow build and drama that it has, the two-part story, and the multiple perspective aspect that has struck people. It's written openly enough that it expresses that confusion you can have after a broken relationship."

Video Games Lana Del Rey

(Lana Del Rey/Justin Parker) ❊ Stranger ❊ 2011 ❊ Appears on: *Born to Die*

No question, there was something decidedly creepy about Lana Del Rey when she went viral in 2011. She has an ethereal beauty and an overdose of poise which made her seem not so much statuesque as a statue or a mannequin. 'Video Games' was a controversial track straight up and then she appeared on *Saturday Night Live* looking almost lifeless and people started to talk. They questioned her origins and whether she was just a trustafarian. They questioned whether she had had plastic surgery. Was she for real? It turns out that she was. All of these questions go to the public conversation that rages these days about identity and feminism. Lana Del Rey embodied those questions and made everyone a little uncomfortable. The sweet haunting quality of 'Video Games' just made it all harder to ignore.

Lana Del Rey was born into privilege as Elizabeth Grant. An album recorded under that name was shelved and so she had a makeover and emerged with this Hollywood name and enigmatic persona. She was like a pop star dreamed of by David Lynch. How could a woman that beautiful be lonely? Or be sad? Why did she sing in those spooky low tones? What the hell was the point of the video games?

It turns out that the video game was *World of Warcraft* and she was describing an old relationship. "I was writing about this guy I'd been seeing and the way our relationship was at the time," she told *Spin*. "It was a time in my life when I had let go of my own personal career ambitions and just enjoyed being with him at home." In other interviews she has said that the man in the song is a composite of two or more boyfriends. It matters little; the point of the song is that image of the woman looking longingly at her man who is absorbed, lost totally in the screen world. She is adjacent to him but still lonely.

This is the deepest kind of sorrow and it's mirrored by the piano parts from Justin Parker. The minimalist instrumentation adds to the sad sentimentality. But it's quite unlike pop music which has come before.

Lonely Boy The Black Keys

(Dan Auerbach/Patrick Carney/Brian Burton) ✳ Nonesuch ✳ 2011 ✳
Appears on: *El Camino*

"This is the first record we've made where it's all rock & roll," drummer Patrick Carney claimed during sessions for the album *El Camino*. "It only took us 10 years to figure out how to make our records sound fucked up in the right way," guitarist Dan Auerbach added.

Childhood pals, the duo began making music together in 2001 and playing a kind of random '60s and '70s blues rock around the alternative circuit. There were a lot of duos coming through at the time like the White Stripes who had a similar line-up. But any kind of intelligent reversioning of the blues is bound to work sooner or later.

The car on the cover of *El Camino* put in thousands of miles as the pair pursued blues/rock nirvana. Their early releases stirred up interest but it wasn't until 2007 when they teamed up with Danger Mouse (Brian Burton) for the *Attack & Release* album that things started to come together. On *El Camino*, their seventh album, there's a magic seeping into the tracks. Dan Auerbach's guitar is channelling all kinds of ghosts – Billy Gibbons from ZZ Top, blues legends Hubert Sumlin and Muddy Waters and even some Robert Johnson. There's a touch of early Boz Scaggs and even Jack White.

Danger Mouse was back for *El Camino* and 'Lonely Boy.' According to the guitarist, the basis for the song was Johnny Burnett and the Rock & Roll Trio's 'Train Kept A' Rollin' which was also recorded by the Yardbirds. "It started with that riff and we just built it from the ground up and the vocals came at the end," he explained. "We wrote this record from scratch in the studio, which isn't the norm for us. We were listening to old rock & roll records, from the '50s, '60s, '70s, '80s. Music that was very simple and fun – drums, bass, guitars, organ and not a lot of bells and whistles on top."

Everything was done on the spot which gives the album an immediacy and "none of the songs," Auerbach confessed, "really have any meaning."

Man on Fire Edward Sharpe and the Magnetic Zeros

(Edward Sharpe & the Magnetic Zeros) ❋ Rough Trade/ Communion ❋ 2012 ❋ Appears on: *Here*

There is no Edward Sharpe. Alex Ebert created him supposedly after a wasted youth of drug addiction and electronica with his former band Ima Robot but Edward Sharpe is nothing like that. It's like the *Easy Rider* scene in the desert where Captain America and Billy come across a hippy commune. There's around a dozen Magnetic Zeros playing the usual ensemble of string, brass and percussion instruments and vocalising. The whole thing looks exactly like a hippie troupe – thrift shop or homemade clothes and film clips that involve a lot of wandering through dappled sunlight in the countryside. Ebert is generally accompanied by Jade Castrinos who often acts as a foil, singing verses back and forth with Ebert. Her open-faced joy and modesty comes across as a welcome contrast to Ebert's full-on persona. He's not short of ego. The counterculture image goes with the acoustic instruments and the campfire unison singing, but really the Magnetic Zeros sound completely modern. The lyrics are not naive or twee as some hippie throwbacks would be. In live shows Ebert often goes out into the audience, which is both warm and confronting. That's what their songs are like. They touch on some big issues.

"I try to give the music more of a campfire feel as opposed to a library atmosphere," he told *Spin*. "I like when you can hear people hanging out in the songs and doing a little shuffling. It creates a feeling of participation. I never really went to church growing up, but I would see wild church services in movies and be really taken with it. The celebratory aspect of that is a big part of what we're doing."

Ebert grew up in a privileged Los Angeles family and hit the skids pretty young. After pulling himself together he formed Edward Sharpe and the Magnetic Zeros in 2009 and released the debut album *Up from Below* which features the song 'Home' which you have heard in a number of ads even if you don't recall it.

The second LP *Here* is a more rounded effort. The band, according to Ebert, had a greater role in writing the album and, after two years on the road, were more confident. 'Man on Fire' has the best of the Zeros' sweet music with some of the demons that Ebert clearly still caries around. As he said at the time of the album's release, "Yes, in 'Man on Fire' I might sing that I want the whole world to dance with me, but it's over murder and pain and heartache and shame. All those qualities are in there. When I wrote that song I was really fucking pissed off. I was very upset with myself for not being more of a superhero. Because I think human potential is so much farther beyond what we expose of ourselves, you know? And I feel like I was just coming up short constantly because of social anxiety, which is such bullshit. So I wrote that song as a 'fuck you' to myself, to convince myself to really act and try to be free."

One Thing One Direction

(Carl Falk/Savan Kotecha/Rami Yacoub) ❋ Syco / Columbia ❋ 2012 ❋
Appears on: *Up All Night*

Pop music is an amazing, amazing phenomenon. As much as it seems like a science it is really a dark art. Millions are spent each year developing and launching careers that never take flight. Television talent contests are perpetually pushing forward one gormless suburbanite after another whom the judges will say are 'amazing', 'spectacular', a 'natural'. Tears will be shed. Air will be pumped, expectations raised and then hopes dashed. How many winners have there been of these talent shows? And how many have gone on to greater things? One Direction were, as the legend goes, not even winners. Simon Cowell, the black t-shirted Svengali of *The X-Factor* told these five boys, who individually would have failed, to form a group and become, overnight, a boy band. Of course they did. Even then they didn't win *The X-Factor*. They came third. But they were the only act who has ever been on that show in any of its thousands of territories who did in fact have the X-factor. Does anyone recall who came second that year?

Almost overnight, One Direction captured the hearts and the minds of tens of millions of teenage girls. There have been boy bands before but I think you have to go back to the Beatles to find an act which has had such mania – the American boy bands didn't translate to Europe and vice versa.

Is it the sex appeal? They are certainly good looking boys and they have some charm but it would be hard to say whether they were exceptionally good looking. Harry Styles has the most charm and wit. The others are essentially suburban boys.

Is it the songs? Again, it's hard to know whether these songs are particularly catchy. They are not by any means Lennon/McCartney- or even Motown-sophisticated or intriguing. Yet there is clearly something magical, alchemical going on here. It's undeniable though that One Direction make great pop records.

Carl Falk, Rami Yacoub and Savan Kotecha produced three songs on the band's debut album *Up All Night*: 'What Makes You Beautiful', 'One Thing' and 'I Wish'. They were all teenage dreams of love and romance – nothing too sexy really. Perhaps that is part of the attraction; when teenage years are so sexualised, when teenage boys have so much access to digital sex, maybe teenage girls just instinctively want to cool it a bit with a fantasy boy in a sweater.

It may also be the case that, like the Monkees half a century ago, sometimes prepacked pop music can offer something. As Stephen Cummings put it, "It's just some magic, there's still some fun/If you don't pay too much attention."

Feels Like We Only Go Backwards Tame Impala

(Kevin Parker) ✳ Modular ✳ 2012 ✳ Appears on: *Lonerism*

The title of this song could mistakenly be applied to the band Tame Impala in the sense that the Impala are drenched in psychedelica. A cursory listen to Tame Impala's second album *Lonerism* is not some '60s freak-out. It's way further out than anything made in the 1960s.

Kevin Parker, who writes Tame Impala's records and plays almost all of the instruments, has a completely unique vision. There are swirling effects and banging drums, floaty vocals, pop guitars, a soupçon of hip hop, some prog synthesiser and something else. If you mashed all the tracks on *Revolver* together you would have some idea of a Tame Impala track.

The 2010 debut LP *Innerspeaker* announced Tame Impala to the world and the pressure was on for Parker to step it up for 2010's follow-up. "[*Lonerism*] almost drove me insane. In fact, it pretty much did; it was two agonising years, one in Perth, one in Paris," he told *The Guardian*. "Without wanting to sound like I'm some fucking spiritual being, they come in flashes. I'd have the idea and do most of the song in about a night and spend the next two years listening to it over and over. I'd cycle through different drum sounds, different guitar sounds, and do a lot of pointless stuff. Not a lot changes, that's the fucking crucifying thing.

"If you don't have anyone to talk to at the time, it grows into a massive beast ricocheting inside your head. A bad thought can spiral and you can get so depressed you just think you're worthless. There were times recording this album that I thought, 'This the worst fucking thing I've ever heard in my life'. Conversely, sometimes I listen to it and think it's the best thing ever."

Parker said that he wanted *Lonerism* to be more personal and raw. 'Feels Like We Only Go Backwards' feels like he has put a part of himself on the line. The hip hop drum part underlies some spare and soulful keyboard parts and Parker's almost weeping falsetto. Unlike so many Impala tracks, the songwriter isn't just piling sounds on top of each other because he can. That leaves some space for the emotion to seep through.

'Feels Like We Only Go Backwards' was covered by Arctic Monkey Alex Turner in an acoustic radio session recently and in that almost naked format the song still shines through. Parker and Kendrick Lamar have also cut a duet version of the song. From one extreme to another.

"Melodically, *Lonerism* is definitely peppier, but not many of the songs have that verse-chorus-verse-chorus pop structure. I just forgot about that whole thing," Parker told *Mess + Noise*. "The production is meant to be a bit fucked-up and weird. I like the way those elements play off each other. Really cheesy pop melodies in this bed of craziness."

Avant Gardener Courtney Barnett

(Courtney Barnett) ❋ Milk! Records ❋ 2013 ❋ Appears on: *A Sea of Split Peas*

This is the first song about an anaphylactic panic attack in Melbourne while checking on the weeds. Despite, or perhaps because of, its subject matter, Barnett has had offers all around the world to come and play.

Barnett is very much an indie girl down to the workboots and the flannel shirt. Born and mostly raised by arty parents in Sydney and then Hobart, Barnett later gravitated to the fertile ground of the Melbourne alternative rock scene. It was her lyrics though that made her stand out, like Jonathan Richman. The songs are quirky takes on the suburban life of a young girl in the inner city, dealing with the search for share housing ('Depreston'), food or the aforementioned hospital visit after encountering the wrong plant. The classic line is "The paramedic thinks I'm clever cos I play guitar/I think she's clever cos she stops people dying."

"I was just trying to see the humour in it," she says of her near death experience. "I didn't think it was catchy and I didn't think other people would find funny what I thought was funny. It's funny that it worked." Barnett is a consistently brilliant lyricist whose tunes are serviceable and catchy but not very slick. Her presentation is thrashy and naive. "I didn't really sing until I was 19, just because it was so scary," she says. "It's such a personal kinda thing. When I finally found my own way of singing, I became a lot more comfortable and I didn't have to worry so much about what I was doing. I could let it fall out."

Of her earlier songwriting, Barnett said, "It was the first EP when I stopped trying to write something that I thought people would like. I was locked in my room, not doing shows and not caring what people would think if they heard them." Part of her appeal is her honesty. Open about her anxieties, and tentatively assessing her abilities as a songwriter now she said, "I wouldn't say confident ... That's not a word I would use."

Royals Lorde

(Ella Yelich-O'Connor/Joel Little) ✳ Lava, Republic, Virgin ✳ 2013 ✳

Appears on: *Pure Heroine*

Auckland, one of the most isolated cities in the world, was heard all around the world in 2013 as 16-year-old Ella Yelich-O'Connor released 'Royals' and was catapulted to international stardom. Over finger popping and a spare drum beat with layers of choral vocal, this song is about status envy in the world of consumer culture and the outsiders who are driving Cadillacs in their dreams.

"I'm really interested in the Ivy Leagues, the final clubs, all the really old-money families, the concept of old money," she told *Rolling Stone*. It's a fascination with elites that led to Ella's stage name Lorde. She sings with great conviction about the feckless youth on the outside of society – stealing food and the like. That's part of her art. She comes from a middle-class family; her father is an engineer and her mother is a highly regarded New Zealand poet.

Lorde has about her a swag; she is unimpressed by most things, a world weariness that belies her age or may just be precociousness. She is similarly cavalier about music. Her tastes are varied, namedropping A$AP Rocky and the Replacements in the same breath. Perhaps the freedom of not being pigeonholed emboldened her and co-writer/producer Joel Little on 'Royals' and the album *Pure Heroine*. It's hip hop but not as we usually know it.

Given her confession about a fascination with her betters, it's curious that the Royals in the hit song are not from the House of Windsor but the Kansas City Royals baseball team. Lorde had seen a photo in a 1976 *National Geographic* of a player signing balls with the team shirt on and she was captivated by the word Royals. From there she made creative leaps to the hip hop lifestyle and the social critique, such as it is, in the song. The process took half an hour, she claimed.

Ultimately 'Royals' is a song written and performed with grace that contrasts with the Kardashian age in which it floats.

Diane Young Vampire Weekend

(Ezra Koenig/Rostam Batmanglij) ❊ XL ❊ 2013 ❊

Appears on: *Modern Vampires of the City*

Vampire Weekend can be hard to pin down. The preppy quartet rose through the ranks of the rock revival like a slicker, richer version of the Strokes (if that was indeed possible). Where the Strokes were gloomy and faintly stoned, Vampire Weekend are bright eyed and bushy tailed and their sweaters are slung neatly around their shoulders. Anyone for tennis?

The band burst onto the alternative music scene in 2007 with a unique blend of post-punk rock with African flavours. Their high energy shows won them fans and a hectic schedule of touring and recording. It wasn't until 2011 that the group really caught its breath and began working on tracks for the third LP *Modern Vampires of the City* with some kind of critical distance.

The song 'Diane Young' started, according to Ezra Koenig, as a "punky saxophone" song with a rockabilly vibe to which he added words and a long back-and-forth process went on. The song was shelved for a while and then dragged out by producer Ariel Rechtshaid who was concerned that the LP was too dark in its themes. "We had been working on beautiful down-tempo songs," says the producer, "and I felt that the record was missing some high-energy stuff. I'd heard the demo of 'Diane Young' but they'd dismissed it as a boring rockabilly song, so I asked to have a go at it."

Which is strange because the song title 'Diane Young' is a play on the phrase "dying young". The subject of the song is a young woman who is out of control, raging through polite society and not leaving a pleasant trail.

The band's first album documented the high life of Manhattan's young, rich and beautiful. This third album according to Koenig is the final part of the trilogy, as the subjects of the songs move into adulthood and take a more sober view of the self-destructive party life. "There's a lot of stuff on [*Vampires of the City*] about getting older, searching for meaning, thinking about identity," he says. "The narrator's voice is critical: 'You're fucking around doing all this shit.' But then they have their own doubts: 'I live my life in self-defence. I love the past because I hate suspense.' And that felt very true of a certain type of person – which, sometimes, I think is me – who is ultimately a coward and maybe secretly envious of people who really don't give a fuck."

Shake It Off Taylor Swift

(Taylor Swift /Max Martin/Shellback) ❊ Big Machine ❊ 2014 ❊ Appears on: *1989*

Taylor Swift grew up in public. At 14 she was a songwriter in Nashville with a publishing deal and at 16 had topped the country charts twice. "I've had every part of my life dissected — my choices, my actions, my words, my body, my style, my music," she told *Rolling Stone* during a discussion of her song 'Shake It Off'. "When you live your life under that kind of scrutiny, you can either let it break you, or you can get really good at dodging punches. And when one lands, you know how to deal with it. And I guess the way that I deal with it is to shake it off."

For the past few years, Swift has regularly been a target for the tabloids. Her possible relationships with other stars such as Harry Styles of One Direction or guitarist John Mayer have been speculated about and she makes fun of the tabloids at the top of the song. But the track quickly becomes not just about her but about anybody who is victimised or harassed about their differences.

She also wanted to shake off the constriction of being just a country star. In moving towards pop, Swift naturally went to Swedish uber pop meisters Max Martin and Shellback. They had collaborated on her earlier hit 'We Are Never Ever Getting Back Together' but the *1989* album was going to be a new chapter completely. "I woke up every single day not wanting, but needing, to make a new style of music," she said of the two years between *Red* and *1989*. "In the process, my music changed. This album is a rebirth for me.

"I think the goal for the next album is to continue to change, and never change in the same way twice," she told *Rolling Stone* last year. "How do I write these figurative diary entries in ways that I've never written them before and to a sonic backdrop that I've never explored before? I'll bring in ideas and they'll take such a different turn than where I thought they were going to go, and that level of unexpected spontaneity is something that really thrills me in the process of making music. What if we did this? What if we made it weirder? What if we took it darker? I love people who have endless strange and exciting ideas about where music can go."

Taylor used dance as a metaphor for 'Shake It Off' setting up a number of sequences where she was surrounded by professionals and she bumbled her way through. "All I think about are metaphors and cats," Taylor said on an online discussion around the release of 'Shake It Off'. "And life can be greatly reflected in your willingness to dance."

Song Index

Artist Index

10CC 236
13th Floor Elevators, The 50
1910 Fruitgum Company 92

ABBA 223, 271
AC/DC 237, 317
Adele 494
Aerosmith 237
Alexander, Arthur 10
Allen, Lily 482
Allman Brothers Band, The 168, 212
Anderson, Laurie 333
Animals, The 24
Arcade Fire 476
Arctic Monkeys 477
Avalanches, The 472
Average White Band, The 225

Bacharach, Burt see Franklin, Aretha;
Pitney, Gene and Warwick, Dionne
Badfinger 145
Baker, Anita 376
Band, The 95, 96, 97, 98, 119
Barnett, Courtney 503
Barry, Jeff see Crystals, The; James, Tommy
& the Shondells and Turner, Ike & Tina
Barry, John see Fatboy Slim and John Barry
Orchestra
Beach Boys, The 169
Beastie Boys 377, 401
Beatles, The 11, 12, 18, 19, 20, 24, 38,
51, 52, 53, 69, 70, 72, 73, 99, 100,
121, 122, 145, 146, 147
Beck 439, 454
Bee Gees, The 53, 74, 238, 271
Belle & Sebastian 463
Berry, Bill see R.E.M.
Big Brother & the Holding Company 101
Big Star 192
Birthday Party, The 327
Björk 433
Black Eyed Peas, The 493
Black Keys, The 499
Black Sabbath 170
Blasko, Sarah 492
Blind Faith 123
Blondie 317
Blur 441, 456
Bobby Fuller Four, The 39
Bon Iver 486
Booker T & the MGs 124
Bono see U2

Bowie, David 126, 195, 244, 274, 291;
see also Mott the Hoople
Boys Next Door, The 318
Bragg, Billy 377, 378
Brown, James 43
Browne, Jackson 227
Buck, Peter see R.E.M.
Buckley, Jeff 442
Buckley, Tim 188
Burning Spear 244
Bush, Kate 295, 371
Buzzcocks, The 301
Byrne, David see Talking Heads

Campbell, Glen 105
Carpenters, The 172
Carr, James 80
Cash, Johnny 30, 155; see also Cooder, Ry
Cave, Nick (& the Bad Seeds) 460; see
also Birthday Party, The
Cheap Trick 288
Chemical Brothers, The 457
Cherry, Neneh 402
ChestnuTT, Cody see Roots featuring Cody
ChesnuTT, The
Chic 288, 301
Clapton, Eric see Blind Faith; Cream and
Derek & the Dominos
Clayton, Adam see U2
Clash, The 272, 302
Cliff, Jimmy 200
Cline, Patsy 9
Cobain, Kurt see Nirvana
Cohen, Leonard 83, 230, 394
Cold Chisel 289
Collins, Judy 108
Coltrane, John 2, 29
Cooder, Ry 208; see also Toure, Ali Farka
Cooke, Sam 18
Cooper, Alice 166, 167
Corea, Chick & Return to Forever 194
Costello, Elvis (& the Attractions) 319;
see also Imposter, The
Cougar Mellencamp, John 351
Counting Crows 434
Cream 76, 102
Creedence Clearwater Revival 125, 147
Crosby, David 174; see also Crosby, Stills,
Nash & Young
Crosby, Stills, Nash & Young 173
Crowded House 379, 415
Cruel Sea, The 448
Crystals, The 20
Culture 257